一二三四五六七八九十

XĪNHUÁ XIĔZÌ ZÌDIĂN

新华写字字典

商务印书馆辞书研究中心编写

商务印书馆

2010年·北京

此扉页用含有商务印书馆注册商标 的水印防伪纸印制，有这种扉页的《新华写字字典》是正版图书。请注意识别。

国家推广普通话,
推行规范汉字。

——《中华人民共和国国家
通用语言文字法》

策　　划　　江　远　　周洪波

主　　编　　费锦昌

编　　者　　费锦昌　　李青梅

版面设计　　毛尧泉

封面设计　　孙元明

宝	宝	宝	室
报	报	报	报
备	备	备	备
笔	笔	笔	笔
边	边	边	边
变	变	变	变
标	标	标	标

规范汉字毛笔书法作品

天地玄黄　宇宙洪荒

天地玄黄　宇宙洪荒

天地玄黄　宇宙洪荒

天地玄黄　宇宙洪荒

德建名立　形端表正

德建名立　形端表正

德建名立　形端表正

德建名立　形端表正

德建名立　形端表正

出 版 说 明

我馆出版的《新华字典》是一部早有定评、影响很大的语文工具书。但限于篇幅，它不可能把日常语言文字方面的问题——交代得十分周详。随着全社会对提高语文素养的要求越来越高，我们产生了围绕着《新华字典》编写出版系列语文工具书的想法。

这些工具书都以《新华字典》为基础，在语言文字的某一方面进一步开拓扩展，加深加宽，作为《新华字典》的补充。已确定的第一批书目有《新华写字字典》《新华正音词典》《新华拼写词典》等。

编写新华系列字词典是一种尝试。限于学力和经验，工作中会有粗疏和不当的地方，敬请方家和广大读者指正。

商务印书馆辞书研究中心

目　　录

凡　例

1. 这本字典通过分析、描述现代汉字规范字形，讲述有关书写汉字的基本知识，指导读者正确、端正地书写汉字。目的是帮助写字教学，提高全民族书写汉字的水平，促进社会用字规范化、标准化。

2. 这本字典的读者对象以小学、中学、师范院校、业余学校的师生，以及公务员和文秘人员为主，兼顾编辑、记者、校对、学习汉语汉字的非汉族学生和外国留学生、书法爱好者和其他语文爱好者。

3. 这本字典收录国家语言文字工作委员会和国家教育委员会联合发布的《现代汉语常用字表》中的2500个常用字。这2500个汉字的字形都跟《现代汉语通用字表》所定规范字形相符。结合2500个字头简明讲述现代汉字笔画、笔形、笔顺、部件和整字结构的规范书写知识。

4. 2500个字头按照读音的汉语拼音字母顺序排列先后。读音相同的，按笔画数由少到多排列。笔画数也相同的，按起笔的笔画形状横(一)、竖(丨)、撇(丿)、点(丶)、折(乛)的次序排列。起笔笔形相同的再按第二笔的笔形，依此类推。

5. 为便于读者辨析，2500个字头都用大号楷体排印。有繁体字形的，用( )标在字头的右上方。有多个繁体字形的，分别用 *、**、*** 号把相关的繁体字形和右侧的例词对应标出。如：

　摆 (擺 * 襬) bǎi 摆设、摆事实、摆阔、钟摆、*(衣裙的)下摆

表明只在"(衣裙的)下摆"这一例词中，繁简转换时才用"衤"旁的繁体字。

系（＊係＊＊繫）xì 派系、中文系、＊关系、＊＊系念／jì＊＊系领带

表明在繁简转换时，例词"派系、中文系"仍用"系"，"关系"用"係"，"系念""系领带"用"繫"。

6. 字头右侧共有七项内容：

(1) 注音。全部字头都按《汉语拼音方案》的规定，用汉语拼音字母照普通话读音注音。有不同读音的字，一律按《普通话异读词审音表》审订的读音注音。多音字，根据这本字典的性质，只选列常用读音，分别标注在相关例词前面，并用／隔开。

(2) 例词。所举例词大致反映了这个字头的主要字义和基本用法。多音字例词按不同字音分列，中间用／隔开。

(3) 字头的笔画数，按照《现代汉语通用字表》规定的笔画数用 ╲ 标出；部首，按照《汉字统一部首表(草案)修订稿》用 ▨ 标出；结构，按照规范字形用 ▣ 标出。

(4) 构件组合图。用线条对每个字头的构件组合方式作了形象直观的图解。

(5) 提示。凡应该提醒读者注意的字形，都对该字的特点、难点作了客观、细致的描述。考虑到这些规范内容都是从印刷字体移用来的，描述时尽量避免使用"不要……"一类的命令语气。提示前一律加 ⌒。同页内两个或多个字头提示内容相同的，统一标在该页眉端的汉语拼音旁。

(6) 笔顺。为了方便阅读，仿照描红形式，逐笔标出笔顺。

(7) 知识窗。简明扼要地介绍有关的汉字知识和书写知识(包括170个汉字的字源)。为了增加可读性和趣味性，还精选了53则跟书写汉字有关的趣事逸闻和45条能反映字形结构的字谜。"知识窗"散见于各字头下。为了表明编者的安排意图和方便读者查阅，在书前编有"知识窗索引"。

规范写字 8 问 （代前言）

1 写字为什么一定要合乎规范？

从2001年1月1日即新世纪第一天起开始施行的《中华人民共和国国家通用语言文字法》规定："国家推广普通话，推行规范汉字。"有人可能不理解：为什么要用国家法律的形式来推行规范汉字呢？回答得简单一些，就是因为有三个需要：社会发展的需要、书面交际日益频繁的需要、信息社会要求大量地快速地传递和处理语言文字信息的需要。

写字的主要目的是为了传递信息。从人类组合成社会以后，为了协调人与人之间在生产和生活中的配合关系，人们要用语言来表达和传达信息。开始只有口头语言，后来发明了文字，就又有了书面语言。今天某甲给某乙写一张字条；明天某乙回某甲一封短信；后天某丙又给某甲和某乙发一份通知……像这样的书面交际，在人类社会有文字存在的每一个角落、每一个时刻都频繁地进行着。正因为有了这样的书面交际，人们才能够克服空间和时间的阻隔，使社会生活顺畅地运转了好几千年……

既然写字的主要目的是为了交际，这就有一个让交际的对方认清、看懂的问题。如果字写错了，或者写成另外一个字了，对方当然就读不懂或不容易读懂，无法顺利地准确地了解你的意思。字虽然写对了，但笔飞墨舞，字迹潦草，对方费了半天劲也看不清楚是个什么字，还是无法知道你书写的内容。即使最后连猜带蒙地把大致意思搞明白了，但这样的交际活动太累了，效率太低了，而且很容易误事。由于这样的事情历朝历代经常发生，老百姓曾经收集和传布过不少故事来教训他们的后代：

古时候有个外出经商的年轻人，托人捎信让老爸老妈送伞，而信上误写成"送命"，让老爸老妈灵魂出窍；

县官请客，写字条让衙役买猪舌，"舌"字上下两部分离得太远，又是竖写，让衙役看成"买猪千口"，以至县衙变成猪圈；

"文革"期间，个别插队青年把"跟老大娘住一个炕"写成"跟老大狼住一个坑"，让全家心惊肉跳；

前几年，社会开始重视商品包装。乌鲁木齐一家工厂让日本印制包装袋，误把"乌鲁木齐"印成"鸟鲁木齐"，误事不算，还白白损失了大量钱财；

前些日子，北京街头居然挂出一幅大字标语，把"见义勇为"写成了"建议勇为"。于是，政府的庄严号召降格为可做可不做的提议，"义勇"也成了盲目的匹夫之"勇"……

出现这些现象，有的是因为文化水平太低，有的是因为写字态度不端正。对于写字不认真不规范、让人连蒙带猜的现象，可以套用鲁迅先生在《门外文谈》中的一句话来批评：无端的空耗别人的时间，其实是无异于谋财害命的。

人类进入信息时代，整个社会的节奏加快了，对信息传递准确、高速的要求更加迫切了。在书面信息传递还是大量依靠纸笔的中国，用国家法律的形式来要求公民确立规范写字、用字的意识，实在是当务之急。

② "规范汉字"具体指什么样的字？

说到"规范汉字"，不同时代、不同地区会有不同的标准和要求。在当今中国内地，规范汉字应该包括两大部分：

第一部分是经过整理、简化的汉字，它们由国务院或国家有关主管部门以字表等形式正式发布。具体有：

1. 1986 年重新发表的《简化字总表》收录的简化字。它告诉你，比如"場"字已经简化，规范的简化字形是"场"，而有些人平时写惯的"坊"是不规范的简化字；

2. 1955 年文化部和中国文字改革委员会联合发布的《第一批异体字整理表》中的选用字。它在同一个字的众多异体中选定一个规范字形，并淘汰了其他异体。比如"金杯"不能写成"金盃"，因为"盃"这个字形已在被淘汰之列；

3. 1988 年国家语言文字工作委员会和新闻出版署联合发布的《现代汉语通用字表》所收 7 000 字的笔画数、笔画形状和字形结构等。比如"鬼"是 9 画而不是 10 画，第六画直接从"白"中撇下。"餐"右上的"又"和下部的"良"，它们的末笔捺都要改为点。"感"是上下结构，上部"咸"的第二画撇不包孕下部的"心"；

4. 1955 年至 1964 年国务院分九次公布的用来更改地名中生僻字的地名用字。比如以前的广西"鬱林县"后来改为"玉林县"，四川的"酆都县"后来改为"丰都县"；

5. 1977 年中国文字改革委员会和国家标准计量局联合发布的《部分计量单位名称统一用字表》中规定的计量单位用字。比如：淘汰"瓩"改用"千瓦"，淘汰"浬"改用"海里"；

6. 1997 年国家语言文字工作委员会标准化工作委员会编的《现代汉语通用字笔顺规范》显示的笔顺。比如"敝"的笔顺是 丶 丷 亠 宀 疒 冎 冎 冎 敝 敝 敝。

第二大部分是历代沿用的传承字。这些字，除了其字形跟《印刷通用汉字字形表》规定的新字形有或多或少不一致、需要把旧字形改为新字形的以外，大多是新中国成立后未经简化整理也不需要简化整理的汉字，如"人、土、大、小、王、田、心"等。

③ 目前社会用字不规范的主要表现有哪些？

目前在中国内地社会用字不规范的表现，主要有四个方面：

一是写错别字，如把"烧、浇、绕、娆"等字的右上部分写成"戈"或"弋"，把"启事"写成"启示"等；

二是写不规范的简化字，如把"市场"写成"市坊"，把"餐厅"写成"歺厅"，把"烧饼"写成"烧并"等；

三是使用已被淘汰的异体字，如把"群众"写成"羣众"，把"奖杯"写成"奖盃"等；

四是滥用繁体字，如把"美容美发厅"写成"美容美髮廳"，把"宾馆"写成"賓館"等。

4 印刷体与手写体有哪些主要差别？

印刷体指汉字在书籍、报纸、杂志等印刷品上出现的字体形式，它是为读者阅读服务的，说得文雅一点，就是为了"目治"，所以，它的笔画、结体都以让读者感到醒目舒适、节省视力为第一要义。举印刷体中用得最多的宋体为例，它横细竖粗、结体端庄、疏密适当、字迹清晰。读者长时间阅读宋体，不容易疲劳。所以书籍报刊的正文一般都用宋体刊印。

手写体日常的主要功能也是供人阅读，人们对日常的手写体的要求也是清晰整齐，但手写体既会受到人手生理机能的制约，又应充分发挥人手生理机能的特长。同样是横平竖直的要求，手写体就不可能像印刷体那样板正，而会更富弹力，更易体现书写者的个性特点。

现在，有关主管部门提供的字形标准是印刷体的，那么，当我们写字的时候，应该怎样来运用这些印刷体的字形标准呢？我们理解，这些标准的规范作用主要在笔画数、笔画类型、笔顺和结体方式等方面，而不应该要求习字者一笔一画都刻板地仿照印刷体特别是印刷宋体的外在形式去书写。我们呼吁手写体的规范标准早日出台。

5 宋体与楷体有哪些主要差别?

同为印刷体的宋体与楷体，在字形上仍有较多的差别。

宋体是印刷品中用得最多的一种字体。由于它起源于宋朝精印本字体，所以称为"宋体"。又由于现今的宋体成形于中国明朝，故而日本称之为"明朝体"。为了使读者阅读时感到舒服、节省目力，宋体的笔画为横细竖粗，结体方正严谨。

楷体则是印刷体中跟日常手写体最为接近的一种字体。它的笔迹刚柔相济，结体自然流畅，便于初学文化的读者认读，因而多用来排印识字课本、儿童读物和通俗书刊。

宋体和楷体的具体差别，举例如下:

1. 宋体的撇（丿），楷体有的写成点（丶），如"小"的第二画:

小(宋体) ／ 小(楷体)

2. 宋体的竖（丨），楷体有的写成撇（丿），如"艹"的第三画:

艹(宋体) ／ 艹(楷体)

3. "雨字头"的框内，宋体是四短横，楷体是四点，如:

雪(宋体) ／ 雪(楷体)

4. "走之旁"（辶）的第二笔，宋体是横折（𠃌），楷体是横折折撇（㇋），如:

近(宋体) ／ 近(楷体)

5. 框内的横笔跟两边的竖笔，宋体是相接的关系，楷体有的是相离的关系，如:

月(宋体) ／ 月(楷体)

这本字典是供读者学写规范汉字时参考的，所以，字头都采用接近手写体的楷体，并在"提示"中说明楷体和宋体的某些差别。

6 硬笔字与毛笔字有哪些主要差别？

中国的书写工具大致经历了从硬笔到以软笔为主再到以硬笔为主的发展过程。最初用来书写的笔是简陋的木棍、竹片、骨片、刻刀等，它们是早期的硬笔。春秋战国时代，书写工具革新，开始出现成形的毛笔。从此，用竹管、兽毛制成的软笔成为书写汉字的主要工具。18世纪以后，铅笔、钢笔、圆珠笔等相继传入我国，并成为人们随身携带、日常应用的书写工具。

书写工具的变革给汉字字体的演变带来重大的影响。一般来说，用硬笔写出的字形峻峭挺拔，富有刚气；用毛笔写出的字形刚柔相济、富于变化，肥笔、瘦笔、枯笔……似断还连，给汉字字形注入了无限诗意。

当今，人们日常书写时以铅笔、圆珠笔为主。它们的弹性比钢笔还要差。如果缺少训练，写出的笔画很容易显得僵直，像一根根堆砌起来的火柴棍儿。但这不等于说，用硬笔写不出好字。只要思想重视、方法得当，再加上努力练习，用硬笔同样能写出既规范又漂亮的好字。如果在学习书写的阶段，适当地练练毛笔字，也会有助于写好硬笔字。只要胸中有笔画形态的变化规律和结体组合的匠心，即使用铅笔、圆珠笔、钢笔等硬笔工具，也能在落笔的力度上轻重得当，在运笔的方法上断连相配，在字形的结体上布局合理，写出合乎规范、个性鲜明的字形来。硬笔书法的优秀作品就是最好的例证。

7 写字为什么要讲究笔顺？

只要一个字由两个或两个以上的笔画构成，书写的时候就会有笔顺的问题。

在汉字学中，笔顺包括两方面的内容：一是笔画的走向或称为"笔势"，比如横笔是从左到右写的，竖笔是从上到下写的；二是书写笔画的先后次序或称为"笔序"，比如"山"由三笔组成，它们出现的次序是：丨山 山。笔势和笔序二者合起来统称为笔顺。

讲究笔顺的目的主要是为了书写时能够顺应手腕的生理机能和汉字的构形原理，使书写顺手、快速，使写出的字形平衡、稳定、匀称、凝聚。加快书写速度的关键有两个，一是增加运笔的连贯性，做到笔断意连；二是缩短前后两笔之间的"路程"。要做到这两点，一定要笔顺合理。每个汉字，不管有多少笔画，都要均衡地分布在一个个方方正正的框框里，而要把字写得方正平稳、布局合理，也要注意笔画的走向和顺序。比如"山"，为什么要先写中间一竖呢？目的是为全字的布局先确定一条基准线。

讲究笔顺还出于检索的需要。成千上万个汉字，为了便于查检，就要排一个次序。人们经常用到的查字法有部首法、音序法、笔画法等。由于汉字结构复杂，单用一种查字法往往不可能做到字字定位，于是常以一种方法为主，辅之以另一种方法。笔顺就是在查字法中被经常用到的一种辅助方法。如果不准确、熟练地掌握笔顺，就很难在众多笔画数相同的汉字中快速查到需要的字。

随着汉字用电脑处理的项目越来越多，笔顺在电脑的汉字编码中也成为一个重要的信息因素。

汉字书写的笔顺规则是人们长期书写实践的总结和归纳，是先有书写实践，而不是先有笔顺规则。一般来讲，约定俗成的规则往往是多元的，再加上汉字字形千变万化，手腕的生理机能又有较大的适应性，这就决定许多字的笔顺不可能是惟一的。可行的办法就是归纳出尽可能少的基本规则，以不变应万变(参看附录：《汉字笔顺规则表》)。另一个办法就是启动法规的权威性，由主管部门在几个可能性中规定一种。目前，中国内地日常用字的笔顺应该以国家语言文字工作委员会标准化委员会编的《现代汉语通用字笔顺规范》(语文出版社，1997年)为准。我们编写的这本小字典用逐笔显示的方式提供了2500个常用字的规范笔顺，基本反映了通用字规范笔顺的内容。

8 规范写字跟书法艺术是什么关系？

在咱们中国，由于汉字使用了几千年，无论是在文化人还是一般老百姓中间，都有一种很深很牢的"汉字情结"。写汉字，除了记录语言之外，还成为一种高尚的文化艺术活动，这就是"书法"。书法这种艺术，在非汉字的国家也有，但往往只限于把文字美术化，绝没有像中国的书法这样源远流长、奇峰叠起、群星璀璨、异彩纷呈，饱含着浓浓的文化内涵。所以，在中国谈写字，就不能不提到书法。

书写汉字的标准可以分为两个层次，一是规范、整齐，一是个性化、艺术化。前一个标准是对日常应用领域的要求，后一个标准是对书法艺术领域的要求。但二者也不是风马牛不相及的。

书写规范了，就可以保证日常书面交际的顺利进行，但就写字而言，仅仅达到了一个基本的、起码的要求。文字，特别是汉字，除了记录语言、传递信息以外，它本身还有使阅读者获得美感享受的功能。一篇字虽然写得正确，但形状太笨拙、布局不合理，也会使读者产生别扭、厌烦的心情。反之，除了正确以外，字字见功力，通篇显神韵，读者就会在接受信息的同时获得一种艺术享受。这应该是我们在学习书写时努力追求的另一个更高层次的目标。要达到这一目标，光用《现代汉语通用字表》《现代汉语通用字笔顺规范》作为标准就远远不够了。当然，这不应当成为对一般读者的普遍要求，也已经超出了这本字典编写的知识范围。正是出于这样的理解，这本字典定名为《新华写字字典》，而不是《新华书法字典》。但话还要说回来。尽管是两个不同的层次，却仍有相通的地方。简单地说就是，规范写字是步入书法艺术殿堂的基础，书法艺术是学会规范写字后某些有志者继续攀升的目标。我们不相信一个满纸错别字、通篇七扭八歪的书写者能够在书法艺术上会有很深的造诣；我们不敢也不必夸口或许诺，学会了规范写字就一定能够成为名声显赫的书法家。

对于大多数读者来说，只要求他们写字规范、整齐、有一定速度，以保证社会日常书面交际能够顺畅地进行，并促使全社会的文化素质得以逐步提高，所以，这本写字字典主要是为了满足日常应用领域书面交际的需要而编写的。我们当然希望中国多出一些可以跟古今书坛名家比美的书法家，但我们更切实地期盼大多数老百姓能够不断提高语文素养，把字写正确，写规范，写整齐。如果这本小字典能够为国家"推行规范汉字"略尽绵薄，那我们就心满意足了。

汉语拼音音节索引

（音节后面是例字。凡加括号的代表字本书缺收。右边的号码是字典正文的页码）

笔画查字表

说　明

1. 本表单字按汉字笔画数的次序排列。笔画数相同的字按起笔的笔形顺序（横、竖、撇、点、折）排列。起笔相同的字，按第二笔的笔形顺序排列。依此类推。

2. 横、竖、撇、点、折以外的笔形作以下规定：

(1) 提（ㄏ）作为横（一）。如："埋"的偏旁"土"是一丨一；"冷"的偏旁"冫"是、一。

(2) 捺（乀）作为点（、）。如："又"是㇇、。

(3) 竖钩（亅）作为竖（丨）。如："排"的偏旁"扌"是一丨一。

3. 单字右面的数码是本字典正文的页码。

1 画	
〔一〕	
一	269
〔乙〕	
乙	271
2 画	
〔一〕	
二	55
十	204
丁	48
厂	24
七	176
〔丨〕	
卜	17
〔丿〕	
八	3
人	190
入	193
儿	55
九	116
几	97
〔乙〕	
了	140
乃	162
刀	42
力	135
又	279
3 画	
〔一〕	
三	194
干	67

于	279
亏	128
士	205
土	231
工	73
才	18
下	246
寸	38
丈	293
大	39
与	280
万	234
〔丨〕	
上	198
小	251
口	125
山	196
巾	111
〔丿〕	
千	179
乞	178
川	33
亿	271
个	72
么	153
久	116
勺	199
丸	234
夕	242
凡	57
及	96
〔丶〕	
广	79
亡	235

门	154
义	272
之	298
〔一〕	
尸	203
已	271
弓	73
己	97
卫	237
子	309
也	268
女	166
飞	59
刃	191
习	244
叉	22
马	149
乡	249
4 画	
〔一〕	
丰	61
王	235
井	114
开	121
夫	63
天	226
元	283
无	240
云	285
专	307
扎	290
艺	272
木	160

五	241
支	298
厅	227
不	17
太	220
犬	188
区	186
历	136
友	278
尤	278
匹	172
车	26
巨	118
牙	262
屯	232
比	11
互	88
切	183
瓦	233
〔丨〕	
止	300
少	199
日	191
中	302
贝	9
内	163
水	213
冈	69
见	103
〔丿〕	
手	208
午	241
牛	165
毛	152

气	178
升	202
长	24
仁	190
什	204
片	172
仆	175
化	89
仇	31
币	11
仍	191
仅	112
斤	112
爪	293
反	57
介	111
父	65
从	37
今	112
凶	256
分	60
乏	56
公	73
仓	20
月	284
氏	206
勿	241
风	62
欠	181
丹	40
匀	285
乌	240
勾	74
凤	63

〔丶〕		未	237	旧	117	仪	270	汉	82
六	143	示	206	帅	212	白	4	宁	165
文	238	击	95	归	79	仔	309	穴	259
方	58	打	39	目	160	他	219	它	219
火	94	巧	183	旦	41	斥	30	讨	224
为	236	正	297	且	183	瓜	76	写	253
斗	50	扑	175	叮	48	乎	87	让	190
忆	272	扒	3	叶	269	丛	37	礼	135
计	98	功	73	甲	100	令	143	训	261
订	49	扔	191	申	200	用	277	必	11
户	88	去	187	号	82	甩	212	议	272
认	191	甘	68	电	46	印	274	讯	261
心	254	世	206	田	226	乐	133	记	98
〔一〕		古	75	由	278	句	118	永	276
尺	30	节	110	只	300	匆	36	〔一〕	
引	274	本	10	央	265	册	21	司	213
丑	32	术	211	史	205	犯	57	尼	163
巴	3	可	124	兄	256	外	233	民	157
孔	125	丙	15	叨	47	处	33	出	32
队	53	左	312	叫	108	冬	49	辽	140
办	6	厉	136	叨	223	鸟	165	奶	162
以	271	石	204	另	142	务	241	奴	166
允	285	右	279	叹	221	包	7	加	99
予	280	布	17	四	214	饥	95	召	294
劝	188	龙	144	〔丿〕		〔丶〕		皮	172
双	212	平	174	生	202	主	305	边	13
书	209	灭	157	失	203	市	206	孕	285
幻	90	轧	262	禾	83	立	136	发	56
		东	49	丘	185	闪	197	圣	202
5画		〔丨〕		付	65	兰	131	对	53
〔一〕		卡	179	仕	293	半	6	台	220
玉	281	北	9	代	39	汁	298	矛	152
刊	122	占	291	仙	246	汇	93	纠	116
末	159	业	269	们	154	头	229	母	160

幼	279	再	286	当	42	乓	169	肌	95
丝	214	协	252	早	287	休	256	朵	54
		西	242	吐	231	伍	241	杂	286
6 画		压	261	吓	246	伏	63	危	236
〔一〕		厌	264	虫	31	优	277	旬	260
式	206	在	286	曲	186	伐	56	旨	300
刑	255	百	4	团	231	延	263	负	65
动	50	有	278	同	228	件	103	各	72
扛	122	存	38	吊	47	任	191	名	158
寺	214	而	55	吃	29	伤	197	多	54
吉	96	页	269	因	273	价	100	争	296
扣	126	匠	106	吸	242	份	61	色	195
考	123	夸	127	吗	149	华	89	〔、〕	
托	232	夺	54	屿	280	仰	266	壮	308
老	133	灰	92	帆	56	仿	59	冲	30
圾	95	达	39	岁	218	伙	94	冰	14
巩	74	列	140	回	92	伪	237	庄	307
执	299	死	214	岂	178	自	310	庆	185
扩	129	成	28	则	288	血	260	亦	272
扫	195	夹	100	刚	69	向	250	刘	143
地	45	轨	79	网	235	似	215	齐	177
扬	266	邪	252	肉	192	后	86	交	106
场	24	划	89	〔丿〕		行	255	次	36
耳	55	迈	150	年	164	舟	303	衣	270
共	74	毕	11	朱	304	全	187	产	23
芒	151	至	301	先	246	会	93	决	120
亚	262	〔丨〕		丢	49	杀	195	充	30
芝	298	此	36	舌	199	合	83	妄	235
朽	257	贞	295	竹	305	兆	294	闭	11
朴	176	师	203	迁	179	企	178	问	239
机	95	尘	27	乔	182	众	303	闯	34
权	187	尖	101	伟	237	爷	268	羊	266
过	81	劣	140	传	33	伞	194	并	15
臣	26	光	78	乒	174	创	34	关	77

米	155	阶	109	扶	64	扭	165	励	136
灯	44	阴	274	抚	64	声	202	否	63
州	303	防	58	坛	221	把	3	还	90
汗	82	奸	101	技	98	报	8	歼	101
污	240	如	192	坏	90	却	188	来	130
江	105	妇	66	扰	190	劫	110	连	137
池	29	好	82	拒	118	芽	262	〔丨〕	
汤	222	她	219	找	293	花	88	步	18
忙	151	妈	149	批	171	芹	184	坚	101
兴	254	戏	244	扯	26	芬	60	旱	82
宇	280	羽	281	址	300	苍	20	盯	48
守	208	观	77	走	310	芳	58	呈	28
宅	290	欢	90	抄	25	严	263	时	204
字	310	买	150	坝	3	芦	145	吴	240
安	2	红	85	贡	74	劳	132	助	306
讲	106	纤	181	攻	73	克	124	县	247
军	121	约	284	赤	30	苏	216	里	135
许	258	级	96	折	294	杆	68	呆	39
论	147	纪	98	抓	307	杜	52	园	283
农	166	驰	29	扮	6	杠	69	旷	128
讽	63	巡	260	抢	182	材	18	围	236
设	199			孝	251	村	38	呀	261
访	59	**7 画**		均	121	杏	255	吨	53
〔一〕		〔一〕		抛	169	极	96	足	311
寻	260	寿	208	投	230	李	135	邮	278
那	161	弄	166	坟	61	杨	266	男	162
迅	261	麦	150	坑	125	求	186	困	129
尽	113	形	255	抗	122	更	72	吵	26
导	43	进	113	坊	58	束	211	串	34
异	272	戒	111	抖	50	豆	50	员	283
孙	218	吞	232	护	88	两	139	听	227
阵	296	远	284	壳	123	丽	136	吩	60
阳	266	违	236	志	301	医	270	吹	35
收	208	运	285	块	127	辰	27	鸣	240

吼	86	佛	63	况	128	牢	133	妙	157
吧	4	近	113	床	34	究	116	妖	267
别	14	彻	26	库	126	穷	185	妨	58
岗	69	役	272	疗	140	灾	286	努	166
帐	293	返	57	应	275	良	138	忍	191
财	18	余	279	冷	134	证	297	劲	113
〔丿〕		希	242	这	295	启	178	鸡	96
钉	48	坐	313	序	258	评	174	驱	186
针	295	谷	76	辛	254	补	17	纯	35
告	70	妥	232	弃	178	初	32	纱	196
我	239	含	81	冶	269	社	199	纲	69
乱	147	邻	141	忘	235	识	204	纳	162
利	136	岔	22	闲	246	诉	216	纵	310
秃	230	肝	68	间	101	诊	296	驳	16
秀	257	肚	52	闷	154	词	36	纷	61
私	214	肠	24	判	168	译	272	纸	300
每	153	龟	79	灶	288	〔一〕		纹	238
兵	15	免	156	灿	20	君	121	纺	59
估	75	狂	128	弟	45	灵	142	驴	146
体	225	犹	278	汪	235	即	97	纽	166
何	83	角	108	沙	196	层	22		
但	41	删	196	汽	179	尿	165	**8画**	
伸	200	条	226	沃	239	尾	237	〔一〕	
作	313	卵	147	泛	58	迟	29	奉	63
伯	16	岛	43	沟	74	局	118	玩	234
伶	141	迎	275	没	153	改	67	环	90
佣	276	饭	57	沈	201	张	292	武	241
低	44	饮	274	沉	27	忌	98	青	184
你	164	系	245	怀	89	际	98	责	289
住	306	〔丶〕		忧	277	陆	145	现	248
位	237	言	263	快	127	阿	1	表	14
伴	6	冻	50	完	234	陈	27	规	79
身	200	状	308	宋	215	阻	311	抹	159
皂	288	亩	160	宏	86	附	66	拢	144

拔	3	苗	157	态	220	固	76	使	205
拣	102	英	275	欧	167	忠	302	例	136
坦	221	范	58	垄	144	咐	66	版	5
担	41	直	299	妻	176	呼	87	侄	299
押	261	茄	183	轰	85	鸣	158	侦	295
抽	31	茎	114	顷	185	咏	277	侧	21
拐	77	茅	152	转	307	呢	164	凭	174
拖	232	林	141	斩	291	岸	2	侨	182
者	295	枝	298	轮	147	岩	263	佩	170
拍	167	杯	9	软	193	帖	227	货	94
顶	49	柜	79	到	43	罗	148	依	270
拆	23	析	243	〔丨〕		帜	301	的	46
拥	276	板	5	非	59	岭	142	迫	175
抵	45	松	215	叔	209	凯	121	质	301
拘	117	枪	181	肯	124	败	5	欣	254
势	206	构	75	齿	30	贩	58	征	296
抱	8	杰	110	些	252	购	75	往	235
垃	129	述	211	虎	88	图	230	爬	167
拉	130	枕	296	虏	145	〔丿〕		彼	11
拦	131	丧	195	肾	201	钓	47	径	115
幸	255	或	94	贤	247	制	301	所	218
拌	6	画	89	尚	198	知	298	舍	200
招	293	卧	240	旺	235	垂	35	金	112
坡	174	事	206	具	119	牧	161	命	158
披	171	刺	36	果	80	物	242	斧	65
拨	15	枣	288	味	238	乖	77	爸	4
择	289	雨	281	昆	129	刮	77	采	19
抬	220	卖	150	国	80	秆	68	受	208
其	177	矿	128	昌	24	和	83	乳	193
取	187	码	149	畅	25	季	98	贪	220
苦	126	厕	21	明	158	委	237	念	164
若	193	奔	10	易	273	佳	100	贫	173
茂	152	奇	177	昂	2	侍	206	肤	63
苹	174	奋	61	典	46	供	73	肺	60

肢	299	刻	124	性	256	居	117	奏	311
肿	302	育	281	怕	167	届	111	春	35
胀	293	闸	290	怜	137	刷	211	帮	6
朋	170	闹	163	怪	77	屈	186	珍	295
股	76	郑	297	学	260	弦	247	玻	16
肥	59	券	188	宝	8	承	28	毒	51
服	64	卷	120	宗	310	孟	155	型	255
胁	252	单	41	定	49	孤	75	挂	77
周	303	炒	26	宜	270	陕	197	封	62
昏	93	炊	35	审	201	降	106	持	29
鱼	279	炕	123	宙	304	限	248	项	250
兔	231	炎	263	官	77	妹	154	垮	127
狐	87	炉	145	空	125	姑	75	挎	127
忽	87	沫	159	帘	137	姐	111	城	28
狗	74	浅	181	实	204	姓	256	挠	163
备	9	法	56	试	207	始	205	政	297
饰	207	泄	253	郎	132	驾	100	赴	66
饱	8	河	83	诗	203	参	19	赵	294
饲	215	沾	291	肩	102	艰	102	挡	42
〔丶〕		泪	134	房	59	线	248	挺	228
变	13	油	278	诚	28	练	138	括	129
京	114	泊	16	衬	27	组	311	拴	212
享	249	沿	263	衫	197	细	245	拾	205
店	47	泡	169	视	207	驶	205	挑	226
夜	269	注	306	话	89	织	299	指	301
庙	157	泻	253	诞	41	终	302	垫	47
府	65	泳	277	询	260	驻	306	挣	298
底	45	泥	164	该	67	驼	232	挤	97
剂	99	沸	60	详	249	绍	199	拼	173
郊	106	波	15	〔一〕		经	114	挖	232
废	60	泼	175	建	103	贯	78	按	2
净	115	泽	289	肃	216			挥	92
盲	151	治	301	隶	136	**9画**		挪	167
放	59	怖	18	录	145	〔一〕		某	160

甚	201	厘	134	趴	167	拜	5	盾	53
革	71	厚	86	胃	238	看	122	待	40
荐	104	砌	179	贵	79	矩	118	律	146
巷	250	砍	122	界	111	怎	289	很	84
带	40	面	156	虹	86	牲	202	须	257
草	21	耐	162	虾	245	选	259	叙	258
茧	102	耍	212	蚁	271	适	207	剑	104
茶	22	牵	180	思	214	秒	157	逃	223
荒	91	残	20	蚂	149	香	249	食	205
茫	151	殃	265	虽	217	种	303	盆	170
荡	42	轻	184	品	173	秋	186	胆	41
荣	191	鸦	261	咽	262	科	123	胜	203
故	76	皆	109	骂	149	重	303	胞	7
胡	87	〔丨〕		哗	88	复	66	胖	169
南	162	背	9	咱	287	竿	68	脉	150
药	268	战	292	响	249	段	52	勉	156
标	14	点	46	哈	81	便	13	狭	245
枯	126	临	141	咬	268	俩	137	狮	203
柄	15	览	131	咳	124	贷	40	独	51
栋	50	竖	211	哪	161	顺	213	狡	108
相	249	省	202	炭	221	修	257	狱	281
查	22	削	250	峡	245	保	8	狠	84
柏	4	尝	24	罚	56	促	37	贸	152
柳	143	是	207	贱	104	侮	241	怨	284
柱	306	盼	168	贴	227	俭	102	急	97
柿	207	眨	290	骨	76	俗	216	饶	190
栏	131	哄	85	〔丿〕		俘	64	蚀	205
树	211	哑	262	钞	25	信	254	饺	108
要	268	显	247	钟	302	皇	91	饼	15
威	247	冒	152	钢	69	泉	187	〔丶〕	
威	236	映	276	钥	268	鬼	79	弯	233
歪	233	星	254	钩	74	侵	183	将	105
研	264	昨	312	卸	253	追	308	奖	106
砖	307	畏	238	缸	69	俊	121	哀	1

亭	227	洁	110	语	281	柔	192	起	178
亮	139	洪	86	扁	13	垒	133	盐	264
度	52	洒	194	袄	2	绑	6	捎	198
迹	99	浇	107	祖	311	绒	192	捏	165
庭	228	浊	308	神	201	结	110	埋	150
疮	34	洞	50	祝	306	绕	190	捉	308
疯	62	测	21	误	242	骄	107	捆	129
疫	273	洗	244	诱	279	绘	93	捐	120
疤	3	活	94	说	213	给	72	损	218
姿	309	派	168	诵	215	络	148	都	51
亲	183	洽	179	〔㇏〕		骆	148	哲	294
音	274	染	189	垦	125	绝	120	逝	207
帝	46	济	99	退	231	绞	108	捡	103
施	204	洋	266	既	99	统	229	换	90
闻	239	洲	303	屋	240			挽	234
阀	56	浑	94	昼	304	**10 画**		热	190
阁	71	浓	166	费	60	〔一〕		恐	125
差	23	津	112	陡	50	耕	72	壶	87
养	266	恒	85	眉	153	耗	83	挨	1
美	154	恢	92	孩	81	艳	264	耻	30
姜	105	恰	179	除	32	泰	220	耽	41
叛	168	恼	163	险	247	珠	304	恭	73
送	215	恨	85	院	284	班	5	莲	137
类	134	举	118	娃	233	素	216	莫	159
迷	155	觉	120	姥	133	蚕	20	荷	84
前	180	宣	259	姨	270	顽	234	获	95
首	208	室	207	姻	274	盏	291	晋	113
逆	164	宫	73	娇	107	匪	60	恶	55
总	310	宪	248	怒	166	捞	132	真	295
炼	138	突	230	架	101	栽	286	框	128
炸	290	穿	33	贺	84	捕	17	桂	80
炮	169	窃	183	盈	275	振	296	档	42
烂	131	客	124	勇	277	载	286	桐	228
剃	225	冠	78	怠	40	赶	68	株	304

桥	182	监	102	乘	28	舱	20	疼	224
桃	223	紧	112	敌	45	般	5	疲	172
格	71	党	42	秤	29	航	82	脊	98
校	251	晒	196	租	311	途	230	效	252
核	84	眠	156	秧	265	拿	161	离	134
样	267	晓	251	积	96	爹	48	唐	222
根	72	鸭	261	秩	302	爱	1	资	309
索	219	晃	91	称	27	颂	215	凉	139
哥	70	晌	197	秘	155	翁	239	站	292
速	217	晕	285	透	230	脆	38	剖	175
逗	51	蚊	239	笔	11	脂	299	竞	115
栗	137	哨	199	笑	251	胸	256	部	18
配	170	哭	126	笋	218	脍	70	旁	169
翅	30	恩	55	债	291	脏	287	旅	146
辱	193	唤	91	借	111	胶	107	畜	258
唇	35	啊	1	值	299	脑	163	阅	284
夏	246	唉	1	倚	271	狸	134	羞	257
础	33	罢	4	倾	184	狼	132	瓶	174
破	175	峰	62	倒	43	逢	62	拳	188
原	283	圆	283	倘	222	留	143	粉	61
套	224	贼	289	俱	119	皱	304	料	140
逐	305	贿	93	倡	25	饿	55	益	273
烈	141	〔丿〕		候	87	〔丶〕		兼	102
殊	209	钱	180	俯	65	恋	138	烤	123
顾	76	钳	180	倍	9	桨	106	烘	85
轿	109	钻	311	倦	120	浆	105	烦	57
较	109	铁	227	健	104	衰	212	烧	198
顿	54	铃	142	臭	32	高	70	烛	305
毙	12	铅	180	射	200	席	244	烟	263
致	301	缺	188	躬	74	准	308	递	46
〔丨〕		氧	266	息	243	座	313	涛	223
柴	23	特	224	徒	230	症	298	浙	295
桌	308	牺	243	徐	258	病	15	涝	133
虑	146	造	288	舰	104	疾	97	酒	117

涉	200	袖	257			菜	19	眼	264
消	251	袍	169	**11 画**		萄	224	悬	259
浩	83	被	10	〔一〕		菊	118	野	269
海	81	祥	249	球	186	萍	174	啦	130
涂	230	课	124	理	135	菠	16	晚	234
浴	281	谁	200	捧	171	营	275	啄	309
浮	64	调	227	堵	51	械	253	距	119
流	143	冤	282	描	157	梦	155	跃	285
润	193	谅	139	域	282	梢	198	略	147
浪	132	谈	221	掩	264	梅	153	蛇	199
浸	113	谊	273	捷	110	检	103	累	134
涨	292	〔丿〕		排	168	梳	209	唱	25
烫	223	剥	16	掉	47	梯	225	患	91
涌	277	悬	125	推	231	桶	229	唯	236
悟	242	展	292	堆	53	救	117	崖	262
悄	183	剧	119	掀	246	副	66	崭	292
悔	92	屑	253	授	209	票	173	崇	31
悦	284	弱	194	教	109	戚	176	圈	187
害	81	陵	142	掏	223	爽	213	〔丿〕	
宽	127	陶	224	掠	147	聋	144	铜	229
家	100	陷	248	培	170	袭	244	铲	23
宵	251	陪	170	接	109	盛	203	银	274
宴	265	娱	279	控	125	雪	260	甜	226
宾	14	娘	164	探	221	辅	65	梨	134
窄	291	通	228	据	119	辆	140	犁	135
容	192	能	163	掘	120	〔丨〕		移	270
宰	286	难	162	职	300	虚	258	笨	10
案	2	预	281	基	96	雀	188	笼	144
请	185	桑	195	著	306	堂	222	笛	45
朗	132	绢	120	勒	133	常	24	符	64
诸	304	绣	257	黄	91	匙	29	第	46
读	51	验	265	萌	154	晨	27	敏	158
扇	197	继	99	萝	148	睁	297	做	313
袜	233			菌	121	眯	155	袋	40

悠	277	〔丶〕		渔	280	隐	274	搜	216
偿	24	凑	37	淘	224	婚	93	煮	305
偶	167	减	103	液	269	婶	201	援	283
偷	229	毫	82	淡	41	颈	115	裁	19
您	165	麻	149	深	201	绩	99	搁	71
售	209	痒	267	婆	175	绪	258	搂	144
停	228	痕	84	梁	139	续	259	搅	108
偏	172	廊	132	渗	201	骑	177	握	240
假	100	康	122	情	185	绳	202	揉	192
得	44	庸	276	惜	243	维	237	斯	214
衔	247	鹿	145	惭	20	绵	156	期	177
盘	168	盗	43	悼	43	绸	31	欺	177
船	34	章	292	惧	119	绿	147	联	137
斜	252	竟	115	惕	225			散	194
盒	84	商	197	惊	114	**12 画**		惹	190
鸽	71	族	311	惨	20	〔一〕		葬	287
悉	243	旋	259	惯	78	琴	184	葛	71
欲	282	望	236	寇	126	斑	5	董	49
彩	19	率	212	寄	99	替	226	葡	176
领	142	着	309	宿	217	款	127	敬	115
脚	108	盖	67	窖	267	堪	122	葱	37
脖	16	粘	291	密	156	塔	219	落	149
脸	138	粗	37	谋	160	搭	39	朝	25
脱	232	粒	137	谎	92	越	285	辜	75
象	250	断	52	祸	95	趁	27	葵	128
够	75	剪	103	谜	155	趋	186	棒	7
猜	18	兽	209	〔一〕		超	25	棋	177
猪	305	清	184	逮	40	提	225	植	300
猎	141	添	226	敢	68	堤	45	森	195
猫	152	淋	141	屠	231	博	17	椅	271
猛	155	淹	263	弹	42	揭	109	椒	107
馋	248	渠	187	随	217	喜	244	棵	123
馆	78	渐	104	蛋	42	插	22	棍	80
		混	94	隆	144	揪	116	棉	156

棚	171	跌	48	税	213	然	189	慨	121
棕	310	跑	169	筐	128	馋	23	割	71
惠	93	遗	270	等	44	〔、〕		寒	81
惑	95	蛙	233	筑	307	装	307	富	66
逼	10	蛛	305	策	22	蛮	150	窝	38
厨	32	蜓	228	筛	196	就	117	窝	239
厦	196	喝	83	筒	229	痛	229	窗	34
硬	276	喂	238	答	39	童	229	遍	13
确	188	喘	34	筋	112	阔	129	裕	282
雁	265	喉	86	筝	297	善	197	裤	126
殖	300	幅	64	傲	2	羡	248	裙	189
裂	141	帽	152	傅	66	普	176	谢	253
雄	256	赌	51	牌	168	粪	61	谣	267
暂	287	赔	170	堡	8	尊	312	谦	180
雅	262	黑	84	集	97	道	43	〔一〕	
〔丨〕		〔丿〕		焦	107	曾	289	属	210
辈	10	铸	306	傍	7	焰	265	屡	146
悲	9	铺	176	储	33	港	69	强	181
紫	309	链	138	奥	3	湖	87	粥	303
辉	92	销	251	街	109	渣	290	疏	210
敞	25	锁	219	惩	29	湿	204	隔	72
赏	198	锄	32	御	282	温	238	隙	245
掌	292	锅	80	循	260	渴	124	絮	259
晴	185	锈	257	艇	228	滑	89	嫂	195
暑	210	锋	62	舒	210	湾	233	登	44
最	312	锐	193	番	56	渡	52	缎	53
量	139	短	52	释	208	游	278	缓	90
喷	170	智	302	禽	184	滋	309	骗	173
晶	114	毯	221	腊	130	溉	67	编	13
喇	130	鹅	54	脾	172	愤	61	缘	283
遇	282	剩	203	腔	181	慌	91		
喊	81	稍	198	鲁	145	惰	54	**13画**	
景	115	程	28	猾	89	愧	129	〔一〕	
践	104	稀	243	猴	86	愉	280	瑞	193

魂	94	酬	31	蜂	62	腿	231	〔一〕	
肆	215	感	68	嗓	195	触	33	群	189
摄	200	碍	1	置	302	解	111	殿	47
摸	158	碑	9	罪	312	〔、〕		辟	12
填	226	碎	218	罩	294	酱	106	障	293
搏	17	碰	171	〔丿〕		痰	221	嫌	247
塌	219	碗	234	错	39	廉	138	嫁	101
鼓	76	碌	146	锡	243	新	254	叠	48
摆	4	雷	133	锣	148	韵	286	缝	62
携	252	零	142	锤	35	意	273	缠	23
搬	5	雾	242	锦	112	粮	139		
摇	267	雹	7	键	105	数	211	**14 画**	
搞	70	输	210	锯	119	煎	102	〔一〕	
塘	222	〔丨〕		矮	1	塑	217	静	116
摊	220	督	51	辞	36	慈	36	碧	12
蒜	217	龄	142	稠	31	煤	153	璃	135
勤	184	鉴	104	愁	31	煌	91	墙	182
鹊	189	睛	114	筹	32	满	151	嘉	100
蓝	131	睡	213	签	180	漠	159	摧	38
墓	161	睬	19	简	103	源	283	截	110
幕	161	鄙	11	毁	92	滤	147	誓	208
蓬	171	愚	280	舅	117	滥	132	境	116
蓄	259	暖	167	鼠	210	滔	223	摘	290
蒙	154	盟	154	催	38	溪	243	摔	212
蒸	297	歇	252	傻	196	溜	143	撇	173
献	248	暗	2	像	250	滚	80	聚	119
禁	113	照	294	躲	54	滨	14	慕	161
楚	33	跨	127	微	236	粱	139	暮	161
想	250	跳	227	愈	282	滩	220	蔑	157
槐	90	跪	80	遥	268	慎	202	蔽	12
榆	280	路	146	腰	267	誉	282	模	158
楼	144	跟	72	腥	255	塞	194	榴	143
概	67	遣	181	腹	67	谨	113	榜	7
赖	130	蛾	54	腾	224	福	64	榨	290

知识窗索引

1. 知识窗分五类：言论、知识、字源、字谜、逸闻。
2. 言论、知识这两类按内容编排，字源、字谜和逸闻均按标题的汉语拼音字母顺序排列。
3. 标题后括号内的数字是字典正文的页码。

字源

字谜

逸闻

ā 阿姨、阿哥／ē 阿谀奉承

📝 7 画
🔲 阝部 左右

阿　阿阿阿
阿阿阿阿

ā 啊，太美了／á 啊，她说什么呢／ǎ 啊，这是怎么回事／à 啊，就这么办吧／a 景色多美啊

📝 10 画
🔲 口部 左右

啊　啊啊啊啊啊啊啊啊啊啊

āi 哀伤、哀求

☞ 中部是口，嵌在衣中。

📝 9 画
🔲 亠部 上下

哀　哀哀哀哀哀哀哀哀哀

说来上下本是衣，中间张口两分离；好像孝子哭先人，只见大口伴丧衣。　字谜

āi 挨近、挨门挨户／ái 挨饿、挨到抗战胜利

📝 10 画
🔲 扌部 左右

挨　挨挨挨挨挨挨挨挨挨

āi 唉声叹气、唉，请安静／ài 唉，这可不行／ài 唉，我就来

📝 10 画
🔲 口部 左右

唉　唉唉唉唉唉唉唉唉唉

ǎi 矮墙、比人矮三分

☞ 矢的末笔改点。禾的中间一竖不带钩。

📝 13 画
🔲 矢部 左右

矮　矮矮矮矮矮矮矮矮矮矮矮矮矮

（愛）

ài 疼爱、爱护、爱打扮

☞ 下部是友不是发。

📝 10 画
🔲 爪部 上下

爱　爱爱爱爱爱爱爱爱爱爱

（礙）

ài 碍事、妨碍

📝 13 画
🔲 石部 左右

碍　碍碍碍碍碍碍碍碍碍碍

安、按、案的女 3 画，第一画是 〈，不分为两笔。

ān 安全、安静、安装

1. install, fit, fix
2 where, what

古字形用女在屋下表示安定的意思。

𡩠（金文）𡨄（甲文）

✎ 6 画
☐ 宀 部
△ 上 下

安 安安安安安安

àn 河岸、岸边 *riverbank, shore, coast*

☞ 山 3 画，第二画是 ㄴ，不分为两笔。

✎ 8 画
☐ 山 部
△ 上 下

岸 岸岸岸岸岸岸岸岸

àn 按电铃、按压、按时 *press, push down control*

✎ 9 画
☐ 扌 部
△ 左 右

按 按按按按按按按按按

àn 肉案、档案、方案、破案 *case, record, file*

☞ 木的中间一竖不带钩。

✎ 10 画
☐ 木 部
△ 上 下

案 案案案案案案案案案案

àn 黑暗、暗号、暗笑 *dark dim dull murky*

✎ 13 画
☐ 日 部
△ 左 右

暗 暗暗暗暗暗暗暗暗暗暗暗暗暗

áng 昂头、昂贵、昂扬

hold (head) high soaring fearless. militant

☞ 下部是卬不是卯。

✎ 8 画
☐ 日 部
△ 上 下

昂 昂昂昂昂昂昂昂昂

（襖）ǎo 棉袄、皮袄 *a short chinese style jacket*

☞ 左部是 衤 不是 礻。右部是夭不是天。

✎ 9 画
☐ 衤 部
△ 左 右

袄 袄袄袄袄袄袄袄袄袄

ào 骄傲、傲然挺立 *proud, brave, defy*

☞ 中间部件6画，后两画是 𠃌、丿。右部是攵不是夂。

✎ 12 画
☐ 亻 部
△ 左 右

傲 傲傲傲傲傲傲傲傲傲傲傲傲

奥 ào 深奥、奥妙 *profound, dificult to understand*

☞ 上部上左右包围结构，下不封口：框内米的末笔改点。

✎ 12 画
部 大 上 下
独体

奥 奥 奥 奥 奥 奥 奥 奥 奥 奥 奥

八 bā 八个、七上八下 *eight*

✎ 2 画
部 八
独体

八 八

巴 bā 巴望、锅巴/bɑ 哑巴、尾巴 *hope earnestly*

✎ 4 画
部 一
独体

巴 巴 巴 巴

扒 bā 扒墙头、扒房/pá 扒手、扒草 *hold on to, dig up*

✎ 5 画
部 扌
左 右

扒 扒 扒 扒 扒

疤 bā 伤疤、疤痕 *scar*

☞ 上左包围结构。

✎ 9 画
部 疒
半包围

疤 疤 疤 疤 疤 疤 疤 疤 疤

拔 bá 拔草、选拔、拔火罐 *pull out, choose, select, raise*

☞ 右部是发不是友。

✎ 8 画
部 扌
左 右

拔 拔 拔 拔 拔 拔 拔 拔

朋友手上有粒痣，细看方知是根刺：想帮好友把刺取，先得认识这个字。

 字谜

把 bǎ 手把手、车把、把门、个把月/bà 刀把儿、花把儿 *hold, grasp, grip*

✎ 7 画
部 扌
左 右

把 把 把 把 把 把 把

（壩）**坝** bà 拦河坝、堤坝 *dam, dyke, embankment*

☞ 土的末笔改提。贝的第二画丁不带钩。

✎ 7 画
部 土
左 右

坝 坝 坝 坝 坝 坝 坝

徐中舒主编的《汉语大字典》，1990年出齐，收54678字。

霸上部的雨，第二画改点，第三画改横钩，里边楷体是四点，宋体是四横。

bà 爸爸

bàba - father

☞ 左上右包围结构。

✎ 8 画
部 父 部
囗 半包围

爸 爸爸爸爸爸爸爸爸爸

（罷） bà 罢工、罢免

stop, cease

☞ 上部是横"目"，不写成四。

✎ 10 画
部 罒 部
囗 上 下

罢 罢罢罢罢罢罢罢罢罢罢

bà 霸王、恶霸、霸占　☞ 廿4画，第二画竖、第四画横，不连成一笔。

✎ 21 画
部 雨 部
囗 上 下

霸 霸霸霸霸霸霸霸霸霸霸霸霸
霸霸霸霸霸霸霸霸霸

ba 好吧、再见吧

used at end of sentence to indicate suggestion

✎ 7 画
部 口 部
囗 左 右

吧 吧吧吧吧吧吧吧

bái 白色、白天、明白、白开水、白白浪费、白吃白喝

snow white, pure, truth

✎ 5 画
部 白 部
囗 独体

白 白白白白白

书之章法有大小，小如一字及数字，大如一行及数行、一幅及数幅，皆须有相避相形、相呼相应之妙。（写字要讲究章法，小到一个字、几个字，大到一行、几行、一幅、几幅，都要体现避让、递补、相互呼应的精妙。）——刘熙载《艺概》

bǎi 一百、百花齐放、千方百计

hundred

✎ 6 画
部 白 部
囗 独体

百 百百百百百百

bǎi 柏树／bó 柏林

cypress

☞ 木的中间一竖不带钩，末笔改点。

✎ 9 画
部 木 部
囗 左 右

柏 柏柏柏柏柏柏柏柏

（擺*襬） bǎi 摆设、摆事实、摆架子、摆手、钟摆、*（衣、裙的）下摆

put place, arrange

☞ 右上是横"目"，不写成四。

✎ 13 画
部 扌 部
囗 左 右

摆 摆摆摆摆摆摆摆摆摆摆摆摆

（敗）bài 败坏、败仗、打败、失败、衰败

be defeated lose, fail

☞ 贝的第二画 ㄱ 不带钩。右边是攵不是夂。

✎ 8 画　□ 贝 部　⊠ 左 右

 败败败败败败败败

bài 跪拜、拜年、拜访、崇拜

make a courtesy call

☞ 左部手的末笔改撇。右部四横一竖。

✎ 9 画　□ 手 部　⊠ 左 右

 拜拜拜拜拜拜拜拜拜

左旁手无钩，右边一丰收；堂前它下令，弟子都磕头。　字谜

bān 班级、晚班、上班、班车、一个班

class, team

☞ 左部王的末笔改提。

✎ 10 画　□ 王 部　⊠ 左 右

 班班班班班班班班班班

古字形像用刀把玉切分为二。班的古义是分赐。班 班（金文）

bān 百般关照、排山倒海般的声势

kind, way, like

✎ 10 画　□ 舟 部　⊠ 左 右

 般般般般般般般般般般

bān 黑斑、斑马、斑白

spot, speck, speckle

☞ 左部王的末笔改提。中部文的末笔改点。

✎ 12 画　□ 王 部　⊠ 左 右

 斑斑斑斑斑斑斑斑斑斑斑

bān 搬运、搬家、搬迁

take away, more, remove

✎ 13 画　□ 扌 部　⊠ 左 右

 搬搬搬搬搬搬
搬搬搬搬搬搬

1955年，《汉字简化方案修正草案》提交国务院汉字简化方案审订委员会审议。草案把"國"简化作口内一个王。有委员提出，现在是人民当家，不兴用"王"字。郭沫若解释：此乃张王李赵之王，非国王之王。后改定为从玉的"国"。

（*闆）bǎn 木板、板报、快板、死板、板脸、*老板

board, blank-hard, stiff, look serious

☞ 木的中间一竖不带钩，末笔改点。

✎ 8 画　□ 木 部　⊠ 左 右

 板板板板板板板板

bǎn 排版、修订版、头版、底版

printing plate, page of newspaper

☞ 片4画，末笔是 ㄱ。

✎ 8 画　□ 片 部　⊠ 左 右

版版版版版版版版

帮、绑的阝两画，第一画是丨，不分为两笔。

(辦) bàn 办理、办年货、创办、办工厂

handle, manage, attend to

✎ 4 画
部 力
⊠ 独 体 办　办 办 办 办

有些简化字形跟繁体字形不是一对一的关系。如简化字"钟"，跟它对应的繁体字有两个：一是意为一种乐器（"钟鸣鼎食"）、一种报时的响器（"晨钟"）的"鐘"，一是意为酒器（"旨酒万鍾"）、量器（"六斛四斗为一鍾"）、聚集专注（"鍾爱""鍾情"）的"鍾"。《简化字总表》第一表中"复""干""获""纤""苏""坛""团""系""脏""只"等11个简化字形跟繁体字形是一对二的关系，"蒙""台"等2个简化字形跟繁体字形是一对三的关系；第二表中"当""发""汇""尽""历""卤"等6个简化字形跟繁体字形是一对二的关系；第三表中"摆""弥""恶"等3个简化字形跟繁体字形也是一对二的关系。

bàn 一半、半夜、半成品、一星半点

half, semi

✎ 5 画
部 、
⊠ 独 体 半　半 半 半 半 半

bàn 扮演、扮相、假扮

✎ 7 画
扌 部
⊠ 左 右 扮　扮 扮 扮 扮 扮 扮 扮

bàn 同伴、伴侣、陪伴、伴唱

✎ 7 画
亻 部
⊠ 左 右 伴　伴 伴 伴 伴 伴 伴 伴

bàn 小葱拌豆腐、拌嘴

✎ 8 画
扌 部
⊠ 左 右 拌　拌 拌 拌 拌 拌 拌 拌 拌

bàn 花瓣、玻璃缸碎成几瓣　☞ 左部辛的末笔改撇。中部是瓜不是爪。

✎ 19 画
辛 部
⊠ 左 瓣　瓣 瓣 瓣 瓣 瓣 瓣 瓣 瓣 瓣 瓣 瓣　瓣 瓣 瓣 瓣 瓣 瓣 瓣

(幫) bāng 鞋帮、帮忙、匪帮

✎ 9 画
巾 部
⊠ 上 下 帮　帮 帮 帮 帮 帮 帮 帮 帮 帮

(綁) bǎng 绑人、捆绑

tie up, truss up

☞ 纟3画，上部不是幺。

✎ 9 画
纟 部
⊠ 左 右 绑　绑 绑 绑 绑 绑 绑 绑 绑

榜 băng 发榜、光荣榜 ☞ 木的中间一竖不带钩，末笔改点。　*a list of names posted, notice, proclamation*

✎ 14 画　🀫 木部　左右

榜榜榜榜榜榜榜榜榜
榜榜榜榜

膀 băng 肩膀、翅膀/pāng 膀肿/páng 膀胱

✎ 14 画　🀫 月部　左右

膀膀膀膀膀膀膀膀膀
膀膀膀膀

棒 bàng 木棒、棍棒、身体棒　*stick, club, strong, good excellent*
☞ 木的中间一竖不带钩，末笔改点。右下是卡不是丰。

✎ 12 画　🀫 木部　左右

棒棒棒棒棒棒棒棒棒棒棒棒

傍 bàng 依傍、傍晚　*draw near, be close to*

✎ 12 画　🀫 亻部　左右

傍傍傍傍傍傍傍傍傍傍

包 bāo 包饺子、邮包、书包、面包、包括、包工、包换、包饭、包围、一包书　*wrap, surround, encircle*
☞ 上右包围结构。　*2nd part "take home": 打包 dǎ bāo*

✎ 5 画　🀫 勹部　半包围

包包包包包

胞 bāo 同胞、胞妹、侨胞

✎ 9 画　🀫 月部　左右

胞胞胞胞胞胞胞胞胞

雹 báo 雹灾、冰雹、雹子
☞ 雨，第二画改点，第三画改横钩，里边楷体是四点，宋体是四横。

✎ 13 画　🀫 雨部　上下

雹雹雹雹雹雹雹雹雹雹雹雹雹

薄 báo 薄纸、地薄、酒薄/bó薄利多销、厚此薄彼、刻薄、淡薄/bò薄荷
☞ 艹3画，覆盖全字，第三画楷体是撇，宋体是横；甫的第三画改横折，去钩。

薄薄薄薄薄

✎ 16 画　🀫 艹部　上下

薄薄薄薄薄薄薄薄薄薄薄

(飽) bǎo 温饱、饱尝、饱满

☞ 饣，3画，第二画是横钩，不是点；第三画是竖提，不分为两笔。

✎ 8 画
部 饣
左 右

饱 饱饱饱饱饱饱饱饱

(寶) bǎo 珠宝、宝贵

treasure, precious

✎ 8 画
部 宀
上 下

宝 宝宝宝宝宝宝宝宝

古字形像屋内有贝（古钱币）、玉。有的还增加声旁缶。（金文）（甲文）

---

bǎo 保姆、保护、保暖、担保

protect, defend, safeguard

☞ 木的中间一竖不带钩。

✎ 9 画
部 亻
左 右

保 保保保保保保保保

---

bǎo 地堡 /bǔ (陕西) 瓦窑堡 /pù 十里堡

fort, fortress

☞ 木的中间一竖不带钩。

✎ 12 画
部 土
下

堡 堡堡堡堡堡堡堡堡堡堡

(報) bào 通报、晚报、电报、报答、报仇

announce, declare, reply RESPOND

☞ 右部是艮，4画，不是及。

✎ 7 画
部 扌
右

报 报报报报报报报

---

bào 抱不平、拥抱、一抱柴火、抱小鸡

hold or carry in one's arms, embrace, HUG cherish! adopt...

✎ 8 画
部 扌
左

抱 抱抱抱抱抱抱抱抱

---

sudden & violent, cruel, savage, hot-tempered

bào 暴露、暴风、暴徒、暴躁 ☞ 下部是氺，5画，不写成水。

✎ 15 画
部 日
上 下

暴 暴暴暴暴暴暴暴暴暴暴暴
暴暴暴暴

---

bào 爆炸、爆破、爆炒、爆冷门 ☞ 火的末笔改点。右下是氺，5画，不写成水。

✎ 19 画
部 火
左 右

爆 爆爆爆爆爆爆爆爆爆爆爆爆
爆爆爆爆爆爆爆

explode! quick fry, quick boil

bēi 玻璃杯、茶杯、奖杯　*cup or trophy cup*

☞ 木的中间一竖不带钩，末笔改点。

✎ 8 画　🗂 木部　⬜ 左右

杯 杯杯杯杯杯杯杯杯

bēi 悲伤、悲欢离合、慈悲　*sad, sorrowful*

☞ 非，中部是两竖，左右各三横。

✎ 12 画　🗂 非部　⬜ 上下

悲 悲悲悲悲悲悲悲悲悲悲悲

bēi 墓碑、纪念碑、碑刻　*an upright stone tablet*

☞ 卑的第六画从白中直接撇下，不分为两笔。

✎ 13 画　🗂 石部　⬜ 左右

碑 碑碑碑碑碑碑碑碑碑碑碑

bēi 路北、败北　*north*

✎ 5 画　🗂 匕部　⬜ 左右

北 北北北北北

古字形像两个相背的人形，应是相背的背的本字。
ʮ(金文) ʮ(甲文)

（贝）bèi 贝壳、贝雕、宝贝　*shellfish*

☞ 第二画丁不带钩。

✎ 4 画　🗂 贝部　⬜ 独体

贝 贝贝贝贝

（备）bèi 齐备、筹备、设备、备受关注　*be equipped w/ have, prepare get ready (provide, prepare against)*

☞ 左上右包围结构。上部是夂不是夂。

✎ 8 画　🗂 夂部　⬜ 半包围

备 备备备备备备备

bèi 脊背、违背、背井离乡、背诵、背静/bēi 背负、背债　*carry on one's back, bear, shoulder*

☞ 月的起笔改竖。

✎ 9 画　🗂 月部　⬜ 上下

背 背背背背背背背背

bèi 三的三倍是九、事半功倍、倍感亲切　*times, fold*

✎ 10 画　🗂 亻部　⬜ 左右

倍 倍倍倍倍倍倍倍倍倍

本、笨的木，中间一竖不带钩。

---

bèi 毛巾被、被动、森林被盗伐

　　☞ 左边是衤不是礻。

✎ 10 画
⊟ 衤 部
⊠ 左右

被 被被被被被被被被被被

（辈） bèi 鼠辈、长辈、我的一辈子

　　☞ 非，中部是两竖，左右各三横。车的第二画是乚，不分为两笔。

✎ 12 画
⊟ 非 部
⊠ 上下

辈 辈辈辈辈辈辈辈辈辈辈辈辈

---

go straight towards, head for

bēn 奔跑／bèn 投奔

　　☞ 左上右包围结构。

✎ 8 画
⊟ 大 部
⊠ 半包围

奔 奔奔奔奔奔奔奔

The root of a plant

běn 根本、本质、书本、成本 *foundation or basis for*

　　☞ 木下加一横，不写成上大下十。

✎ 5 画
⊟ 木 部
⊠ 独体

本 本本本本本

---

bèn 笨头笨脑、嘴笨、笨重

slow, stupid, thick-dumsy

✎ 11 画
⊟ 竹 部
⊠ 上下

笨 笨笨笨笨笨笨笨笨笨笨笨

---

bèng 蹦蹦跳跳　　☞ 左下止的末笔改提。山3画，第二画是乚，不分为两笔。

蹦 蹦蹦蹦蹦蹦蹦蹦蹦

✎ 18 画
⊟ 足 部
⊠ 左右

蹦蹦蹦蹦蹦蹦蹦蹦蹦

---

bī 逼近、逼迫、逼债 *force, compel, drive*

　　☞ 左下包围结构。辶3画，第二画楷体是㇋，宋体是ㄋ。

✎ 12 画
⊟ 辶 部
⊠ 半包围

逼 逼逼逼逼逼逼逼逼逼逼逼

---

bí 鼻子、鼻涕、门鼻儿　　☞ 下部是廾不是卄。

nose

鼻 鼻鼻鼻鼻鼻鼻鼻

✎ 14 画
⊟ 鼻 部
⊠ 上下

鼻 鼻鼻鼻鼻鼻鼻鼻

bǐ 比较、比例、比方
compare, emulate
✎ 4 画
部 比 部
四 左 右
比 比比比比

 bǐ 彼此、知己知彼
✎ 8 画
彳 部
四 左 右
彼 彼彼彼彼
彼彼彼彼

 （筆）bǐ 铅笔、笔顺、亲笔
pen, ballpoint pen
✎ 10 画
竹 部
四 上 下
笔 笔笔笔笔笔笔笔笔笔笔

 bǐ 卑鄙、鄙视、鄙人
☞ 阝两画，第一画是了，不分为两笔。
✎ 13 画
右阝 部
四 左 右
鄙 鄙鄙鄙鄙鄙鄙鄙鄙鄙鄙鄙鄙

 （幣）bì 钱币、纸币
money's currency, bank notes
☞ 起笔是撇，不是横。
✎ 4 画
巾 部
四 独体
币 币币币币

 bì 必须、骄兵必败
certainly, surely, have to...
☞ 第二画楷体是乀(卧钩)，宋体是乚(竖弯钩)。
✎ 5 画
丶 部
四 独体
必 必必必必必

 （畢）bì 毕业、毕生
finish, accomplish, conclude
✎ 6 画
比 部
四 上 下
毕 毕毕毕毕毕毕

 （閉）bì 关闭、闭气
shut, close, refuse – remain silent
☞ 左上右包围结构。起笔，嵌在第二笔丨和第三笔冂之间。
✎ 6 画
门 部
四 半包围
闭 闭闭闭闭闭闭

左右结构的字，如果两部分是相向的，如"叩、好"等，要注意组织好笔画，使全字出现内聚的视觉效果。如"好"，起笔由右上向下运笔，一开始就出现往右边顾盼的姿势；第三笔"横"不要太平，略微向上挑；第四笔先向右上仰，再向左下出锋；第五笔以弯钩的形态包住左边。这样，左右两部分的笔意都聚向字心。

人们在书写活动中创造了许多简化形体。《简化字总表》根据制定的原则，并没有全部收录。为了推进出版物上汉字形体的进一步规范化，凡是"自造"的简化字，属不规范的简化字，一律不准出现在出版物中。比如"餐厅"的"歺"(餐)、"展览"的"尸"(展)等。

辟、壁、避、臂的辟，左部上尸下口，不是启。

（斃）bì 枪毙、毙命

☞ 比，第二画是乚，不分为两笔。比的右边和死的右下是匕不是匕。

✎ 10　画
□ 比 部下
□ 上 下

毙 毙毙毙毙毙毙毙毙毙毙毙

（*闢）bì 复辟/pì *开辟、*精辟、*辟谣

✎ 13　画
□ 辛 部右
□ 左 右

辟 辟辟辟辟辟辟辟辟辟辟辟辟

bì 碧空、碧绿、金碧辉煌　☞ 左上王的末笔改提。

✎ 14　画
□ 石 部下
□ 上 下

碧 碧碧碧碧碧碧碧碧碧碧
碧碧碧碧

bì 隐蔽、遮蔽　☞ 艹3画，第三画楷体是撇，宋体是竖。左下的丨贯通上下，右下夂不是夂。

✎ 14　画
□ 艹 部下
□ 上 下

蔽 蔽蔽蔽蔽蔽蔽蔽
蔽蔽蔽蔽蔽蔽蔽

bì 弊病、作弊　☞ 左上的丨贯通上下。右上是攵不是夂。

✎ 14　画
□ 廾 部下
□ 上 下

弊 弊弊弊弊弊弊弊弊弊
弊弊弊弊

bì 墙壁、绝壁

✎ 16　画
□ 土 部下
□ 上 下

壁 壁壁壁壁壁壁壁壁壁壁壁
壁壁壁壁

bì 躲避、避免　☞ 左下包围结构。辶3画，第二画楷体是乛，宋体是𠃑。

✎ 16　画
□ 辶 部
□ 半包围

避 避避避避避避避避避避避
避避避避

bì 手臂、臂力/bei 胳臂　☞ 月的起笔改竖。

✎ 17　画
□ 月 部下
□ 上

臂 臂臂臂臂臂臂臂臂臂臂臂臂
臂臂臂臂臂

（邊） biān 海边、这边、边说边笑／bian 前边

☞ 左下包围结构。 ~Side, seaside border, limit~

✎ 5 画
辶 部
⊠ 半包围

边 边 边 边 边 边

（編） biān 编织、编号、编辑、编造

☞ 纟3 画，上部不是幺。 ~BAT~

✎ 12 画
纟 部
⊠ 左 右

编 编 编 编 编 编 编 编 编 编 编 编 编

~whip, lash~

biān 皮鞭、钢鞭、鞭炮 ☞ 廿4画，不要把第二画竖、第四画横连成一笔。

✎ 18 画
革 部
⊠ 左 右

鞭 鞭 鞭 鞭 鞭 鞭 鞭 鞭 鞭 鞭 鞭
鞭 鞭 鞭 鞭 鞭 鞭

biǎn 扁平、扁桃 ~FLAT~

☞ 上左包围结构。

✎ 9 画
户 部
⊠ 半包围

扁 扁 扁 扁 扁 扁 扁 扁 扁

（變） biàn 变化、变本加厉、政变

☞ 上边不是亦，中间是两竖。下部是又不是夂。

✎ 8 画
又 部
⊠ 上 下

变 变 变 变 变 变 变 变

biàn 方便、便饭、大便／pián 便宜、大腹便便

✎ 9 画
亻 部
⊠ 左 右

便 便 便 便 便 便 便 便

biàn 遍布、读了两遍

☞ 左下包围结构。

✎ 12 画
辶 部
⊠ 半包围

遍 遍 遍 遍 遍 遍 遍 遍 遍 遍 遍

~differentiate, distinguish, discriminate~

biàn 辨别、辨明 ☞ 左部辛的末笔改撇。中部是一点一撇。

✎ 16 画
辛 部
⊠ 左 右

辨 辨 辨 辨 辨 辨 辨 辨 辨 辨 辨
辨 辨 辨

(辯) biàn 辩论、争辩 *argue, dispute, debate* ☞ 中部讠两画，第二画是乚，不分为两笔或三笔。

辩辩辩辩辩辩辩辩辩辩辩
辩辩辩辩辩

✎ 16 画
⊟ 辛 部 右
⊠ 左

(辮) biàn 辫子、草帽辫儿 ☞ 中部纟3画，上部不是幺。

辫辫辫辫辫辫辫辫辫辫辫
辫辫辫辫辫

✎ 17 画
⊟ 辛 部 右
⊠ 左

(標) biāo 商标、标价、指标、夺标、治标不治本 *mark, sign, tag, label*
☞ 木的中间一竖不带钩，末笔改点。

标标标标标标标标标

✎ 9 画
⊟ 木 部 右
⊠ 左

(*錶) biǎo 表面、表现、表格、表妹、*手表

字义为计时器具时，表的繁体用錶，如手錶、懷錶、電子錶、夜光錶。计量器具仍用表，如電表、水表、儀表、體溫表。

表表表表表表表表

✎ 8 画
⊟ 一 部 下
⊠ 上

(*彆) bié 分别、区别、别人、别门/biè *别扭 *difference, distinction*

别别别别别别别

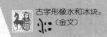

✎ 7 画
⊟ 刂 部 右
⊠ 左

(賓) bīn 贵宾、外宾 *guest, distinguished guest*

宾宾宾宾宾宾宾宾宾宾

✎ 10 画
⊟ 宀 部 下
⊠ 上

(濱) bīn 海滨、滨江路 *bank, brink, shore*

滨滨滨滨滨滨滨滨滨滨滨滨

✎ 13 画
⊟ 氵 部 右
⊠ 左

bīng 冰天雪地、冰手、冰糖 *ice, cool*

冰冰冰冰冰冰

古字形像水和冰块。
（金文）

✎ 6 画
⊟ 冫 部 右
⊠ 左

兵　bīng 士兵、兵器　*Soldier*

🖊 7　画
口 八　上　部下
兵 兵兵兵兵兵兵兵

丙　bīng 甲乙丙丁、丙等　*The third of the ten heavenly stems, third*

🖊 5　画
一 独　部体
丙 丙丙丙丙丙

柄　bīng 刀柄、话柄　*handle (of a knife) stem*
　☞ 木的中间一竖不带钩，末笔改点。

🖊 9　画
木 左　部右
柄 柄柄柄柄柄柄柄柄

（餅）bīng 烧饼、铁饼　*cake*
　☞ 饣3画，第二画是横钩，不是点；第三画是竖提，不分为两笔。

🖊 9　画
饣 左　部右
饼 饼饼饼饼饼饼饼饼

并　bīng 合并、并排、齐头并进、并且　*combine, merge, incorporate*

🖊 6　画
八 上　部下
并 并并并并并并

病　bīng 病人、弊病　*be taken ill　ailment*
　☞ 上左包围结构。

🖊 10　画
疒 半包围　部
病 病病病病病病病病病

（撥）bō 把表拨到8点、拨款、一拨人　*turn, move w/ finger, row boat poke.*
　☞ 右部是发不是友。

🖊 8　画
扌 左　部右
拨 拨拨拨拨拨拨拨

波　bō 波浪、波折、秋波
🖊 8　画
氵 左　部右
波 波波波波波波波波

古字形像双手拿着兵器。（金文）（甲文）

清朝乾隆皇帝以爱好书法著称。他的"三希堂"就是因为得到了晋王羲之《快雪时晴帖》、王献之《中秋帖》和王珣《伯远帖》三件稀世墨宝而命名。

用简单的音符替换复杂的音符是汉字简化的一种方法，如"攤"简化作"摊"（"雞"换成"又"），"優"简化作"优"（"憂"换成"尤"）。

bō 玻璃、玻璃纸 *(first part glass)*

☞ 王的末笔改提。

✎ 9 画
☐ 王 左 部右
凶

玻 玻玻玻玻玻玻玻玻玻

---

bō 生吞活剥、剥落、剥削／bāo 剥皮

☞ 左上是彐不是互。左下是氺，5画，不写成水。

✎ 10 画
☐ 刂 部右
凶

剥 剥剥剥剥剥剥剥剥剥剥

---

bō 菠菜、菠萝

☞ 艹3画，第三画楷体是撇，宋体是竖。艹覆盖波。

✎ 11 画
☐ 艹 上 部下
凶

菠 菠菠菠菠菠菠菠菠菠菠

---

bō 春播、广播 ☞ 右上7画：撇下米，不是采。

✎ 15 画
☐ 扌 部右
凶

播播播播播播播播播播播
播播播

(駁)

bō 伯父、李伯伯／bǎi 大伯子 *fathers older brother*

伯伯伯伯
伯伯伯

✎ 7 画
☐ 亻 左 部右
凶

(駁) *refute, contradict*

bó 反驳、斑驳、驳船

☞ 右上㐅的第二画改点。

✎ 7 画
☐ 马 部右
凶

驳 驳驳驳驳驳驳驳

汉字，少的只有一画，多的有几十画，但是都能用同一大小的框格去范围它。只要安排得当，笔画少的，不嫌空旷；笔画多的，不觉拥挤。前者如同一个人独自生活在宽敞的宅院中，伸手舒脚，俯仰自如，但仍须谨慎自律，不可越轨；后者酷似一个拥挤的部落，各人有各人的位置，各人有各人的分工，布局平稳，互让互补，繁密中不显出局促。

---

bó 停泊、飘泊／pō 湖泊、血泊

✎ 8 画
☐ 氵 部右
凶

泊 泊泊泊泊泊泊泊泊

---

bó 脖子、拐脖儿 *neck*

☞ 子3画，第一画𠃌、第二画亅，不连成一笔。

✎ 11 画
☐ 月 左 部右
凶

脖 脖脖脖脖脖脖脖脖脖脖

bó 广博、博览、赌博
☞ 左部是十，不是忄或扌。
◆ 12 画
◻ 十 部
◻ 左 右
博 博博博博博博博博博博博博

bó 搏斗、脉搏
☞ 左部是扌。
◆ 13 画
◻ 扌 部
◻ 左 右
搏 搏搏搏搏搏搏搏搏搏搏搏

笔画与笔画在左上角相接时，要分作两笔，如：厂、几、口、日。

膊 bó 赤膊
☞ 左部是月。
◆ 14 画
◻ 月 部
◻ 左 右
膊 膊膊膊膊膊膊膊膊膊膊膊膊膊膊

(*蔔) bǔ 卜卦、预卜／bo 萝卜
divination, foretell, predict
◆ 2 画
◻ 卜 部
◻ 独体
卜 卜卜

húluóbo - carrot

古字形像占卜时灼烤甲骨形成的裂纹。卜(金文) 卜(甲文)

(補) bǔ 修补、补充、于事无补
☞ 左部是衤不是礻。
◆ 7 画
◻ 衤 部
◻ 左 右
补 补补补补补补补

宋体是印刷中用得最多的一种字体。由于它起源于宋朝精刻本字体，故称为"宋体"。又由于现今的宋体成形于明朝，日本称之为"明朝体"。这种字体的特点是横细竖粗，结体端正，刚柔相济，疏密适中，给读者以醒目舒适的感觉。长时间阅读这种字体最省视力，所以，书籍报刊的正文一般都用宋体。如：新华写字字典。

bǔ 捕鱼、逮捕
◆ 10 画
◻ 扌 部
◻ 左 右
捕 捕捕捕捕捕捕捕捕捕捕

bù 不多不少、不明不白
☞ 中间一竖不带钩，末笔是点不是捺。
◆ 4 画
◻ 一 部
◻ 独体
不 不不不不

bù 麻布、分布、布置、宣布
cloth
(declare, pronounce, publish)
spread, disseminate
☞ 上左包围结构。
◆ 5 画
◻ 巾 部
◻ 半包围
布 布布布布布

bù 步行、步子、步骤、地步

☞ 下部少3画，不是少。

✎ 7 画
部 止上
四 上下

古字形用一前一后两只脚掌表示走路。
（金文） （甲文）

步 步步步步步步步步

bù 恐怖、可怖

✎ 8 画
忄 部
四 左右

怖 怖怖怖怖怖怖怖怖

bù 局部、部队、门市部、司令部

☞ 阝两画，第一画是了，不分为两笔。

✎ 10 画
右阝 部
四 右右

部 部部部部部部部部部部

cā 摩擦、擦桌子、擦粉 ☞ 察的中部是夕，6画，不是夕。

✎ 17 画
扌 部
四 左右

擦擦擦擦擦擦擦擦擦擦擦
擦擦擦擦擦

cāi 猜疑、猜谜语、猜想

☞ 月的起笔改竖。

✎ 11 画
犭 部
四 左右

猜 猜猜猜猜猜猜猜猜猜猜

(*纔) **cái** 口才、人才、*刚才

used before a verb to
indicate it has just happened!

✎ 3 画
一 部
四 独体

简体转为繁体时，字义是动作发生不久，繁体作
纔，如刚才、才回来；字义是能力、具有能力
的人，仍作才，如口才、才子。

才 才才才

cái 木材、材料、教材 material, timber

☞ 木的中间一竖不带钩，末笔改点。 teaching material

✎ 7 画
木 部
四 左右

材 材材材材材材材

(財) **cái** 财产、财富 wealth

☞ 贝的第二画丨不带钩。

✎ 7 画
贝 部
四 左右

财 财财财财财财财

cái 裁布、裁减、裁判

☞ 上右包围结构。左下衣的末笔改点。

✎ 12 画
□ 衣 部首
△ 半包围

裁 裁裁裁裁裁裁裁裁裁裁裁

---

cǎi 采花、采取、采集、兴高采烈

pick, pluck, gather

✎ 8 画
□ 爪 部首
△ 上 下

古字形像用手采摘树上的果或叶。
（金文）（甲文）

采 采采采采采采采采

---

cǎi 彩色、剪彩、喝彩、挂彩

☞ 朩的末笔改点。彡写在一条中轴线上。

colour, campaign, cheer, variety, splendor

✎ 11 画
□ 彡 部首
△ 左 右

彩 彩彩彩彩彩彩彩彩彩彩彩

---

cǎi 理睬、人家跟你说话，你怎么能睬也不睬

pay attention to, take notice

✎ 13 画
□ 目 部首
△ 左 右

睬 睬睬睬睬睬睬睬睬睬睬睬睬

---

cǎi 踩油门、踩高跷 *step on, tread, trample* ☞ 左上卜的末笔改提。

✎ 15 画
□ 足 部首
△ 左 右

踩 踩踩踩踩踩踩踩踩踩踩踩
踩踩踩

---

cài 白菜、酒菜 *vegetable, pickles*

☞ 艹3画，第三画楷体是撇，宋体是竖。

上菜 shang cai *to serve a dish*

✎ 11 画
□ 艹 部首
△ 上 下

菜 菜菜菜菜菜菜菜菜菜菜菜

（参）cān 参加／cēn 参差不齐／shēn 人参

☞ 彡写在一条中轴线上。

join, take part in

✎ 8 画
□ 厶 部首
△ 上 下

参 参参参参参参参参

---

cān 午餐、会餐 ☞ 又和良的末笔都改点。

food, meal

餐餐餐餐餐餐餐餐
餐餐餐餐餐餐餐餐

✎ 16 画
□ 食 部首
△ 上 下

规范简化字不作。

or start of napkin
餐 巾纟氏
cān jīn zhǐ

仓、苍、舱的仓，下部是巴，不是已、已或己，也不是匕。

(残) cán 残害、残暴、残余、残缺

☞ 戋5画，斜钩上是两横一撇，不是三横一撇。

✎ 9 画
戋 部首
⼜ 左 右 结构

 残残残残残残残残残

(蠶) cán 家蚕、蚕茧

☞ 左上右包围结构。上部是天不是夭。

 古字形像蚕。（甲文）

✎ 10 画
虫 部首
⼜ 半包围 结构

蚕蚕蚕蚕蚕蚕蚕蚕蚕蚕

(慚) cán 惭愧

☞ 车的第二画是乚，下部的横笔改提，笔顺改为先竖后提。

✎ 11 画
忄 部首
⼜ 左 右 结构

 惭惭惭惭惭惭惭惭惭惭惭

(慘) cǎn 惨无人道、惨败、悲惨

☞ 彡写在一条中轴线上。

✎ 11 画
忄 部首
⼜ 左 右 结构

 惨惨惨惨惨惨惨惨惨惨

(燦) càn 星光灿烂、黄灿灿的菜花

☞ 火的末笔改点。山的第二画是乚，不分为两笔。

✎ 7 画
火 部首
⼜ 左 右 结构

 灿灿灿灿灿灿灿

(倉) cāng 粮仓、仓库

stove house

☞ 左上右包围结构。

✎ 4 画
人 部首
⼜ 半包围 结构

仓 仓仓仓仓

写字讲究笔顺，可以提高书写的速度。书写就是不断落笔和提笔的过程。加快书写速度的关键有两个，一是增加运笔的连贯性，书写时做到笔断意连；二是缩短上下两笔之间的"路程"。要解决这两个关键问题，一定要做到笔顺合理。

(蒼) cāng 苍松、苍白

☞ 艹3画，第三画楷体是撇，宋体是竖。

✎ 7 画
艹 部首
⼜ 上 下 结构

苍苍苍苍苍苍苍苍

(艙) cāng 船舱、驾驶舱

☞ 舟的横笔改提，右端不出头。

✎ 10 画
舟 部首
⼜ 左 右 结构

 舱舱舱舱舱舱舱舱舱舱

藏 cáng 躲藏、藏粮/zàng 宝藏、藏药　☞ 艹3画，第三画楷体是撇，宋体是竖。

17 画　艹部　上下　藏

藏藏藏藏藏藏藏藏藏藏藏藏
藏藏藏藏藏

操 cāo 操刀、操作、操练、情操　☞ 木的中间一竖不带钩。

16 画　扌部　左右　操

操操操操操操操操操操操
操操操操

槽 cáo 水槽、牲口槽、河槽　☞ 木的中间一竖不带钩，末笔改点。

15 画　木部　左右　槽

槽槽槽槽槽槽槽槽槽槽槽
槽槽槽

grass; straw, careless, hasty, (Rough) draft

草 cáo 野草、稻草、草鸡、潦草、草稿
☞ 艹3画，第三画楷体是撇，宋体是竖。

first part of straw berry

9 画　艹部　上下　草

草草草草草草草草草

册 cè 手册、第一册　*volume*

5 画　丿部　独体　册

册册册册册

古字形像编串起来的竹木简。
用 (金文)　册 (甲文)

(厕) cè 厕所、公厕
☞ 上左包围结构。

8 画　厂部　半包围　厕

厕厕厕厕厕厕厕厕

(侧) cè 侧门、侧耳细听

8 画　亻部　左右　侧

侧侧侧侧侧侧侧侧

左右结构的字，如果左边笔画少、体形短，右边笔画多、体形长，写的时候，要使左右两部分的上面基本取平，以避免全字显得下坠，传统术语叫"上平"，如"喝、琛、煌"等。

(测) cè 测量、推测

9 画　氵部　左右　测

测测测测测测测测测

cè 计策、策划、策马扬鞭　☞ 下部是朿不是束。

策策策策策策策
策策策策策

📝 12 画
🏛 竹部
🀄 上下

(層) layer, stratum, story, floor

céng 云层、六层楼、层出不穷

☞ 上左包围结构。

层层层层层层层

📝 7 画
🏛 尸部
🀄 半包围

---

fork, cross

chā 钢叉、交叉 /chá 路口让车给叉死了 /chǎ 两腿叉开 /chà 劈叉

叉叉叉

📝 3 画
🏛 独体

---

chā 插花、安插

☞ 千不穿过臼的底部。

插插插插插插插插插插插

📝 12 画
🏛 扌部
🀄 左右

---

chá 茶水、喝茶、果茶、茶镜

☞ 艹3画，第三画楷体是撇，宋体是竖。下部是朩，不写成木。

茶茶茶茶茶茶茶茶茶

📝 9 画
🏛 艹部
🀄 上下

---

chá 抽查、调查、查资料 /zhā 姓

☞ 木的中间一竖不带钩。

查查查查查查查查查

📝 9 画
🏛 木部
🀄 上下

---

chá 察看、考察　☞ 中部是⺧，6画，不是⺕。

察察察察察察察察察察察
察察

📝 14 画
🏛 宀部
🀄 上下

---

chà 山岔、岔道、打岔、岔子

☞ 山，第二画是ㄥ，不分为两笔。

岔岔岔岔岔岔岔

📝 7 画
🏛 山部
🀄 上下

chà 质量差、差不多 /chā 差别、差错 /chāi 差遣、交差 /cī 参(cēn)差

☞ 上左包围结构。左上羊的末笔改撇。

✎ 9　画
□ 羊　部
◹ 半包围

差　差差差差差差差差差

chāi 拆墙、拆散

☞ 右部是斥不是斤。

✎ 8　画
□ 扌　部
◹ 左　右

拆　拆拆拆拆拆拆拆拆

chái 打柴、木柴

☞ 此，左部止的末笔改提，右部是匕。木的中间一竖不带钩。

✎ 10　画
□ 木　部
◹ 上　下

柴　柴柴柴柴柴柴柴柴柴柴

(饞) chán 嘴馋、眼馋

☞ 𠂇3画，第二画一，不是点；第三画乚，不分为两笔。

✎ 12　画
□ 饣　部
◹ 左　右

馋　馋馋馋馋馋馋馋馋馋馋馋馋

(纏) chán 缠毛线、纠缠　☞ 纟3画，上部不是幺。右部不是厘。

✎ 13　画
□ 纟　部
◹ 左　右

缠　缠缠缠缠缠缠缠
　　缠缠缠缠缠缠

字谜中有分拆字形的一半作为谜面的，可以称为"一半儿"字谜。如：半真半假（值）、半朋半友（有）、半部《春秋》（秦）、吃一半，拿一半（哈）、硬一半，软一半（砍）。

(産) chǎn 产妇、产木材、国产、物产

- to give birth, to produce

✎ 6　画
□ 亠　部
◹ 独　体

产　产产产产产产

(鏟) chǎn 铲子、铲土

☞ 钅5画，第二画是横，不是点；第五画乚，不分为两笔。

✎ 11　画
□ 钅　部
◹ 左　右

铲　铲铲铲铲铲铲铲铲铲铲铲

(顫) chàn 全身发颤 /zhàn 颤抖　☞ 左下旦的末笔改提。

✎ 19　画
□ 页　部
◹ 左　右

颤颤颤颤颤颤颤颤颤颤颤颤
颤颤颤颤颤颤颤

chāng 繁荣昌盛、科学昌明

prosperous, flourishing

✎ 8 画
日上 部日 下
四 昌昌昌昌昌昌昌昌

（長）

long, lengthy, strong point

cháng 长途汽车、长期、特长 /zhǎng 生长、长辈、首长

☞ 第三画ㄥ贯穿上下，不分为两笔。末笔捺上没有撇。

✎ 4 画
长独 部体
四 长长长长

古字形像人长着长发。 （金文）
（甲文）

（場）

site, spot, scene, field

cháng 场院 /chǎng 广场、开场、农场

☞ 土的末笔改提。右部第一画⃇（横折折折钩），不分为两笔。

✎ 6 画
土左 部土 右
四 场场场场场场

（腸）

cháng 胃肠、肠子 *intestines*

☞ 右部第一画⃇（横折折折钩），不分为两笔。

✎ 7 画
月左 部月 右
四 肠肠肠肠肠肠肠

现代汉字的基本笔画形状有六种：横（一）、竖（丨）、撇（丿）、点（丶）、捺（乀）、提（乁）。

（嘗）

cháng 品尝、尝试、备尝、未尝

taste, experience

✎ 9 画
小上 部小 下
四 尝尝尝尝尝尝尝尝尝

cháng 常识、常绿树、经常

ordinary, common normal

✎ 11 画
小上 部小 下
四 常常常常常常常常常常常

（償）

cháng 偿还、无偿、如愿以偿

偿偿偿偿偿偿

✎ 11 画
亻左 部亻 右
四 偿偿偿偿偿

现代汉字的笔画形状中以横和竖出现的次数最多，这就决定了现代汉字的方块形式和以直线为主很少弧线的特点。

（廠）

chǎng 工厂、厂家

factory, mill, plant

✎ 2 画
厂独 部厂 体
四 厂厂

chǎng 宽敞、敞亮、敞车、敞开、敞着口儿、敞胸露怀 *open, uncover, spacious, roomy, fluent, free*

☞ 右边是攵不是夂。

✎ 12 画
⊟ 攵 部
⊠ 左 右

敞 敞 敞 敞 敞 敞 敞 敞 敞 敞 敞 敞

(暢) chàng 畅销、畅通、欢畅、畅快、畅谈、畅所欲言 *smooth, proceed without hindrance, uninhibited, fluent FREE*

☞ 右边是昜不是易。昜的第一画𠃌（横折折折钩），不分为两笔。

✎ 8 画
⊟ 丨 部
⊠ 左 右

畅 畅 畅 畅 畅 畅 畅 畅

chàng 倡议、提倡 *initiate, advocate*

✎ 10 画
⊟ 亻 部
⊠ 左 右

倡 倡 倡 倡 倡
倡 倡 倡 倡 倡

chàng 唱歌、唱票、唱本 *sing, call, cry*

✎ 11 画
⊟ 口 部
⊠ 左 右

唱 唱 唱 唱 唱
唱 唱 唱 唱 唱 唱

chāo 抄写、抄袭、查抄、抄近道、抄起大棒 *copy, extranscribe*

✎ 7 画
⊟ 扌 部
⊠ 左 右

抄 抄 抄 抄 抄 抄 抄 抄

(鈔) chāo 钞票、现钞 *bank-note, paper money*

☞ 钅5画，第二画是横，不是点；第五画是乚，不分为两笔。

✎ 9 画
⊟ 钅 部
⊠ 左 右

钞 钞 钞 钞 钞 钞 钞 钞 钞

chāo 超过、超龄、超级 *exceed, surpass, overtake SUPER (market)*

☞ 左下包围结构。

✎ 12 画
⊟ 走 部
⊠ 半包围

超 超 超 超 超 超 超 超 超 超 超 超

朝 cháo 朝拜、朝代、坐南朝北 /zhāo 朝阳、今朝 *dynasty, court*

✎ 12 画
⊟ 龺 部
⊠ 左 右

朝 朝 朝 朝 朝 朝 朝 朝 朝 朝 朝

吵、炒的少，中间一竖不带钩；左侧楷体是点，宋体是撇。

cháo 潮水、寒潮、潮湿

✎ 15 画
氵部
左右

潮潮潮潮潮潮潮潮潮潮潮潮潮潮

---

cháo 吵闹、吵架／chāo 吵吵

✎ 7 画
口部
左右

口少口少口少口少口少口少口少

联撇的字，下撇的头要对着上撇的胸，如"形、须、彤"等。

---

cháo 炒菜、炒股票

fried (noodle)

☞ 火的末笔改点。

✎ 8 画
火部
左右

炒炒炒炒炒炒炒炒

（車）chē 汽车、车床／jū 车马炮

☞ 第二画是乚，不分为两笔。

✎ 4 画
车部
独体

车车车车

古字形像古代的车。
（金文）（甲文）

---

chě 拉扯、扯破、胡扯

✎ 7 画
扌部
左右

扯扯扯扯扯扯

（徹）chè 彻底、彻头彻尾

☞ 中部是七，末笔改乚（竖提）。

✎ 7 画
彳部
左右

彻彻彻彻彻彻彻

---

chè 撤职、撤退　☞ 月的起笔改竖。右边是攵不是夂。

✎ 15 画
扌部
左右

撤撤撤撤撤撤撤撤撤撤撤撤撤撤撤

宋代毕昇发明用泥活字印刷。后来有木活字、锡活字、铜活字、铅活字。现在，铅字时代也已经过去了，电脑激光排印技术使印刷实现"无铅化"。

---

chén 臣子、忠臣

☞ 上左下包围结构。末笔是乚，不分为两笔。

✎ 6 画
臣部
半包围

臣臣臣臣臣臣臣

(塵) chén 尘土、灰尘

☞ 小的起笔改竖，去钩。

✎ 6 画
▦ 小 部
△ 上 下

尘 尘尘尘尘尘尘

现代汉字中由一个部件构成的字，所占比例很小，多数汉字由两个或两个以上的部件构成。据统计，在7785个汉字中，由一个部件构成的字仅有323个，占4.149%；由两个部件构成的字有2650个，占34.040%；由三个部件构成的字最多，达3139个，占40.321%；其他是分别由四、五、六、七、八个部件构成的字。

chén 星辰、时辰

☞ 上左包围结构。

✎ 7 画
▦ 辰 部
△ 半包围

辰 辰辰辰辰辰辰辰

chén 沉底、低沉、沉着、沉思、沉重

✎ 7 画
▦ 氵 部
△ 左 右

沉 沉沉沉沉沉沉沉

(陳) chén 陈列、陈述、陈醋

☞ 阝两画，第一画是了，不分为两笔。右部东，第二画是乛，下边是小。

✎ 7 画
▦ 左 阝 部
△ 左 右

陈 陈陈陈陈陈陈陈

chén 早晨、清晨

✎ 11 画
▦ 日 部
△ 上 下

晨 晨晨晨晨晨晨晨晨晨晨

(襯) chèn 衬裤、鞋衬、衬托、陪衬

☞ 左部是衤不是礻。

✎ 8 画
▦ 衤 部
△ 左 右

衬 衬衬衬衬衬衬衬

chèn 趁早、趁便

☞ 左下包围结构。乡要写在一条中轴线上。

✎ 12 画
▦ 走 部
△ 半包围

趁 趁趁趁趁趁趁趁趁趁趁趁

(稱) chēng 称重量、称赞、称呼、名称/chèn 称职、对称

☞ 禾，中间一竖不带钩，末笔改点。尔，第二画是一(横钩)。

✎ 10 画
▦ 禾 部
△ 左 右

称 称称称称称称称称称

chēng　撑腰、撑船、撑门面、撑开、撑破

✎ 15　画
部　扌
左　右

撑撑撑撑撑撑撑撑撑撑撑撑撑

chéng　成功、成全、成品、成熟、成人、
成绩、形成、成天

✎ 6　画
戈　部
独　体

成成成成成成

小篆字形修长，线条匀称，给人以纯净简约的美感。小篆的形体具有很强的规范性。它的书体艺术的历史流变，以秦篆、唐篆和清篆为三大阶段，尤以清篆为篆书艺术的高峰。

chéng　面呈、呈现

✎ 7　画
口　部
上　下

呈呈呈呈呈呈呈

（誠）　chéng　诚恳、忠诚

☞ 讠两画，第二画是㇇，不分为两笔或三笔。

✎ 8　画
讠　部
左　右

诚诚诚诚诚诚诚诚

chéng　承载、承担、继承

☞ 对称结构。中部了上是三短横，不是两短横；左侧一画，是㇇；右侧两画，是丿和乀。

✎ 8　画
㇇　部
对　称

承承承承承承承承

chéng　城墙、城乡

☞ 土的末笔改提。

✎ 9　画
土　部
左

城城城城城城城城城

chéng　乘车、乘机、乘法　☞ 对称结构。禾的中间一竖不带钩。北的第三画是提，第四画是撇。

✎ 10　画
丿　部
对　称

乘乘乘乘乘乘乘乘

古字形像人爬在树顶上。
✢（金文）　✣（甲文）

chéng　章程、航程、启程、过程

☞ 禾，中间一竖不带钩，末笔改点。

✎ 12　画
禾　部
左　右

程程程程程程程程程程程程

(懲) chéng 惩罚、严惩

☞ 心的第二画楷体是乀(卧钩),宋体是乚(竖弯钩)。

✎ 12 画
▢ 心 部
△ 上 下

惩 惩惩惩惩惩惩惩惩惩惩惩

chèng 磅秤、过秤

☞ 禾,中间一竖不带钩,末笔改点。

✎ 10 画
▢ 禾 部
△ 左 右

秤 秤秤秤秤秤秤秤秤秤

chī 吃饭、吃苦、吃老本、吃透、口吃   *to eat*

☞ 右边是乞不是气。

✎ 6 画
▢ 口 部
△ 左 右

吃 吃吃吃吃吃吃

chí 水池、乐池

✎ 6 画
▢ 氵 部
△ 左 右

池 池池池池池池

王献之是王羲之的第七个儿子。七八岁的时候,有一天正在写字。王羲之从后面出其不意地抽王献之手中的笔,不料,王献之凝神敛志,握得很牢,没有被抽脱。王羲之惊叹说,这孩子的书法将来"当有大名"。

(馳) chí 奔驰、驰名中外

☞ 马3画,第一画𠃜、第二画𠃌,都不分为两笔。左上角开口。末笔改提。

✎ 6 画
▢ 马 部
△ 左 右

驰 驰驰驰驰驰驰

(遲) chí 迟缓、迟到   *late, tardy*

☞ 左下包围结构。尺的末笔改、。辶3画,第二画楷体是乀,宋体是㇋。

✎ 7 画
▢ 辶 部
△ 半包围

迟 迟迟迟迟迟迟迟

chí 持枪、主持、保持、僵持

☞ 右上是土不是士。

✎ 9 画
▢ 扌 部
△ 左 右

持 持持持持持持持持

chí 汤匙 /shi 钥匙

☞ 左下包围结构。右上是匕不是匕。

✎ 11 画
▢ 匕 部
△ 半包围

匙 匙匙匙匙匙匙匙匙匙匙

chǐ 木尺、尺寸 *a unit of length*

✎ 4 画
国 尸部
囚 独体

尺 | 尺 尺 尺 尺

（齒） chǐ 牙齿、齿轮
☞ 人的末笔改点。第七画是L，不分为两笔。

✎ 8 画
国 齿部
囚 上 下

齿 | 齿 齿 齿 齿 齿 齿 齿 齿

古字形像口中两排牙
齿。（甲文）

---

chǐ 羞耻、雪耻
☞ 耳的末笔改提。

✎ 10 画
国 耳部
囚 左 右

耻 | 耻 耻 耻 耻 耻 耻 耻 耻 耻

---

chì 充斥、排斥、斥责
shout, scold, denounce

✎ 5 画
国 斤部
囚 独体

斥 | 斥 斥 斥 斥 斥

上下结构的字，如果上
下两部分的偏旁部件
相同，应该力求两部分
的笔画形状有所变化。
一般是上半部的笔画
收缩，下半部的笔画伸
延，如"炎"的第四笔
捺收缩成点，而最后一
笔仍是伸延的捺，从而
收到下面托住上面的
效果。

---

chì 赤豆、赤胆、赤手空拳、赤膊

✎ 7 画
国 赤部
囚 上 下

赤 | 赤 赤 赤 赤 赤 赤 赤

---

chì 翅膀、展翅高飞
☞ 左下包围结构。

✎ 10 画
国 支部
囚 半包围

翅 | 翅 翅 翅 翅 翅 翅 翅 翅 翅

（*衝） chōng *要冲、*冲锋、冲茶／chòng *屋门冲南、*酒味太冲

✎ 6 画
国 氵部
囚 左 右

冲 | 冲 冲 冲 冲 冲 冲

黎锦熙主张制造"注
音铜模"。排字的时
候，拣一个铅字，该字
的注音符号就附在字旁一
起出来了。他说：这是一
件"很小很小的大事"。后
来在台湾得到实现，对台
湾普及国语大有帮助。

---

chōng 充满、充气、充当、冒充
ample, full, sufficient

✎ 6 画
国 亠部
囚 上 下

充 | 充 充 充 充 充 充

（蟲）chóng 昆虫、糊涂虫 *insect, worm*

- ✎ 6 画
- 虫部
- 独体

虫 虫虫虫虫虫虫

chóng 崇高、崇拜　☞ 山3画，第二画是L，不分为两笔。

- ✎ 11 画
- 山部
- 上下

崇 崇崇崇崇崇崇崇崇崇崇

右左结构的字，如果有一边的笔画少、结构单位小或窄，就应该让另一边。比如右边的结构小，它所占的空间就要相应地小，这样，笔画少的一边很紧凑，笔画多的一边也不局促，字的整体又显得主次分明、眉目清楚，传统术语叫"让左"，如"即、却、勤"等。反之，左边的应该让右边，传统术语叫"让右"，如"济、冯、侍"等。

chōu 抽出、抽调、抽穗、抽筋、抽烟、抽打

- ✎ 8 画
- 扌部
- 左右

抽 抽抽抽抽抽抽抽抽

chóu 报仇、仇敌／qiú 姓仇　*Hatred, animosity*

- ✎ 4 画
- 亻部
- 左右

仇 仇仇仇仇

（綢）chóu 丝绸、尼龙绸

☞ 纟3画，上部不是幺。

- ✎ 11 画
- 纟部
- 左右

绸 绸绸绸绸绸绸绸绸绸绸绸

chóu 酬金、稿酬、应酬

☞ 酉，框内有一短横。

- ✎ 13 画
- 酉部
- 左右

酬 酬酬酬酬酬酬酬酬酬酬酬酬酬

chóu 稠密、稠粥

☞ 禾，中间一竖不带钩，末笔改点。

- ✎ 13 画
- 禾部
- 左右

稠 稠稠稠稠稠稠稠稠稠稠稠

愁

chóu 忧愁、愁闷

☞ 禾的中间一竖不带钩，末笔改点。心的第二画楷体是乚(卧钩)，宋体是乚(竖弯钩)。

- ✎ 13 画
- 心部
- 上下

愁 愁愁愁愁愁愁愁愁愁愁愁愁

(籌) chóu 筹码、略胜一筹、筹办、筹划、筹款

✎ 13 画
部 竹 部
结 上下

筹 筹筹筹筹筹筹筹筹筹筹筹筹

~~tindi~~ UGLY, DISGRACEFUL

(*醜) chǒu *丑陋、*丑闻、*家丑、丑角、子丑寅卯

☞ 中部一横右端不出头。

✎ 4 画
部 乛 部
结 独体

丑 丑丑丑丑

---

smelly

chòu 臭气、臭名、臭棋、臭骂/xiù 无色无臭

☞ 下部是犬不是大。

✎ 10 画
部 自 部
结 上下

臭 臭臭臭臭臭臭臭臭臭臭

(*齣) to indicate completed action

chū 出席、出轨、出众、出事、*一出戏

☞ 凵两画，第一画是凵，不分为两笔。

1.(go or come out)

✎ 5 画
部 凵 部
结 独体

出 出出出出出

---

beginning,early

chū 初夏、年初、初衷、初稿、初犯、初等

☞ 左部是衤不是礻。

✎ 7 画
部 衤 部
结 左右

初 初初初初初初初

古字形像用刀裁剪
衣服，表示开始做
衣。 〔金文〕

---

chú 除根、除法、除外

☞ 阝两画，第一画是了，不分为两笔。

✎ 9 画
部 左阝部
结 左右

除 除除除除除除除除除

---

chú 厨房、帮厨

☞ 上左包围结构。左上是厂不是广。豆的末笔改提。

✎ 12 画
部 厂 部
结 半包围

厨 厨厨厨厨厨厨厨厨厨厨厨

(鋤) chú 铁锄、锄草、锄奸

☞ 钅5画，第二画是横，不是点；第五画是竖提，不分为两笔。且的末笔改提。

✎ 12 画
部 钅部
结 左右

锄 锄锄锄锄锄锄锄锄锄锄锄

（礎）chǔ 基础、础石、

☞ 出5画，第一、四画是乚，不分为两笔。

✎ 10 画
▢ 石 部
▢ 左 右

 础 础础础础础础础础础

（儲）chǔ 储蓄、储备

☞ 讠两画，第二乛，不分为两笔或三笔。

✎ 12 画
▢ 亻部
▢ 左 右

 储 储储储储储储储储储储储

---

chǔ 苦楚、清楚

☞ 上部两木，中间一竖不带钩，末笔都改点。下部第一画是一（横钩），不是横。

✎ 13 画
▢ 疋 部
▢ 上 下

 楚 楚楚楚楚楚楚楚楚楚楚楚楚

（處）chù 住处、坏处、办事处 /chǔ 设身处地、处理、处罚

place
dwelling place

☞ 左下包围结构。左下是夂不是夂。

✎ 5 画
▢ 夂 部
▢ 半包围

 处 处处处处处

（觸）chù 接触、触发

☞ 角，下部是用，框中不写成土。

✎ 13 画
▢ 角 部
▢ 左 右

 触 触触触触触触触触触触触

---

chuān 河川、川菜、米粮川

RIVER

✎ 3 画
▢ 丿 独
▢ 体

 川 川川川

古字形像河中流水。)ǀǀ（金文）)ǀ(（甲文）

---

chuān 穿衣、穿孔、穿针、贯穿、看穿

to wear

☞ 牙4画，第二画是乚，不分为两笔；左上开口。

✎ 9 画
▢ 穴 部
▢ 上 下

 穿 穿穿穿穿穿穿穿穿穿

（傳）
PASS, pass on, spread, transmit
chuán 遗传、传播、传唤、传热 /zhuàn 自传
express

☞ 专4画，第三画是乚，不分为两笔。

✎ 6 画
▢ 亻部
▢ 左 右

 传 传传传传传传

根据用坐标小格测定，汉字中没有真正死平死直的笔画。笔画中都有些弯曲，横画都有些斜上。这大约是人用右手执笔的原因。

chuán 乘船、渔船
☞ 舟的横笔改撇，右端不出头。右上不是几，第二画不带钩。
✎ 11 画
□ 舟 部
⊠ 左 右

船 船船船船船船船船船船船

chuǎn 气喘、哮喘、喘息 breath w/ difficulty
☞ 山3画，第二画是乚，不分为两笔。
✎ 12 画
□ 口 部
⊠ 左 右

喘 喘喘喘喘喘喘喘喘喘喘喘

chuàn 贯串、珠宝串儿、串通、串门儿、串种
string together, cluster
✎ 7 画
□ 丨 部
⊠ 独 体

串 串串串串串串串

（瘡）chuāng 冻疮 ☞ 上左包围结构。仓的下边是已，不是匕或巳。
✎ 9 画
□ 疒 部
⊠ 半包围

疮疮疮疮疮
疮疮疮疮

仿宋体是印刷体中比较常用的一种字体。它的特点是横笔和竖笔的粗细十分接近，且都纤细。仿宋体显得清秀、明晰，多用来排印文章中的引文、书籍的序跋、图版的说明、诗词的正文等。如：新华写字字典。

chuāng 窗户、纱窗
✎ 12 画
□ 穴 部
⊠ 上 下

窗窗窗窗窗窗
窗窗窗窗窗窗

chuáng 床铺、车床
☞ 上左包围结构。木的中间一竖不带钩。
✎ 7 画
□ 广 部
⊠ 半包围

床 床床床床床床床

（闖）chuǎng 横冲直闯、走南闯北、闯祸 rush, force one's way
☞ 左上右包围结构。马的第一画乛、第二画乚都不分为两笔；左上角开口。
✎ 6 画
□ 门 部
⊠ 半包围

闯 闯闯闯闯闯

（創）chuàng 创造、创举、创收/chuāng 创伤、重创 wound
☞ 仓的第二画改点；下部是已，不是匕或巳。
✎ 6 画
□ 刂 部
⊠ 左 右
创 创创创创创创创

chuī 吹拂、吹口哨、吹笛子、吹捧、告吹

✎ 7 画
口部
⼊ 左 右

吹吹吹吹
吹吹吹

chuī 炊烟、炊具

☞ 火的末笔改点。

✎ 8 画
火部
⼊ 左 右

炊炊炊炊炊炊炊炊

chuí 垂柳、垂涎、永垂不朽、垂死挣扎

✎ 8 画
丿部
⼊ 独 体

垂垂垂垂垂垂垂垂

(錘) chuí 秤锤、锤子、锤炼

☞ 钅5画，第二画是横，不是点；第五画是乚，不分为两笔。

✎ 13 画
钅部
⼊ 左 右

锤锤锤锤锤锤锤锤锤锤锤锤锤

chūn 春游、妙手回春　☞ 左上右包围结构。

✎ 9 画
日部
⼊ 半包围

春春春春
春春春春春

(純) chún 纯金、单纯、纯熟

☞ 纟3画，上部不是幺。

✎ 7 画
纟部
⼊ 左 右

纯纯纯纯纯纯纯

chún 嘴唇、唇膏

☞ 上左包围结构。

✎ 10 画
辰部
⼊ 半包围

唇唇唇唇唇唇唇唇唇

chǔn 蠢动、愚蠢

✎ 21 画
虫部
⼊ 上 下

春春春春春春春春春春春春
春春春蠢蠢蠢蠢蠢

慈、磁的兹，上部是⺍，不是艹。

（詞）　cí 词语、歌词

ɔ̄ 讠两画，第二画是乛，不分为两笔或三笔。

✎ 7　画
🀙 讠　部
囚 左　右

词 | 词词词词词词词

（辭）　cí 修辞、推辞、辞职、辞别

ɔ̄ 舌的起笔是撇不是横。

✎ 13　画
🀙 舌　部
囚 左　右

辞 | 辞辞辞辞辞辞辞辞辞辞辞辞辞

cí 慈悲、慈善

ɔ̄ 心的第二画楷体是乀(卧钩)，宋体是乚(竖弯钩)。

✎ 13　画
🀙 心　部
囚 上　下

慈 | 慈慈慈慈慈慈慈慈慈慈慈慈

cí 磁铁、磁石

✎ 14　画
🀙 石　部
囚 左　右

磁 | 磁磁磁磁磁磁磁
　　 磁磁磁磁磁磁磁

> 异体字指字音、字义都相同，仅仅字形不同的一组字。比如："杯""盂""桮"这三个字都读 bēi，它们的字义都是盛水和饮料的器皿或杯状的锦标，但字形不同："杯"从木、不声，左右结构；"盂"从皿、不声，上下结构；"桮"从木、否声，左右结构。这三个字互为异体字。现在以"杯"为规范字形。语文生活中对异体字的理解实际包括狭义和广义两类。狭义的异体字指用法完全相同的字(如"凳""櫈")，广义的异体字包含只有部分用法相同的字(如"采"除包含了"採"的用法外，还有别的用法)。

cí 此时此地、由此及彼、长此以往

ɔ̄ 止的末笔改提。右边是匕不是匕。

✎ 6　画
🀙 止　部
囚 左　右

此 | 此此此此此此

cì 次日、次品、次序

✎ 6　画
🀙 冫　部
囚 左　右

次 | 次次次次次次

cì 刺破、刺客、讽刺、鱼刺、刺鼻

ɔ̄ 左部不是束，中间一竖不带钩，末笔改点。

✎ 8　画
🀙 刂　部
囚 左　右

刺 | 刺刺刺刺刺刺刺刺

cōng 来去匆忙

ɔ̄ 上右包围结构。匆的中部有一点。

✎ 5　画
🀙 勹　部
囚 半包围

匆 | 匆匆匆匆匆

葱、聪的心，第二画楷体是乚(卧钩)，宋体是乚(竖弯钩)。

cōng 大葱、葱绿

☞ 艹 3画，第三画楷体是撇，宋体是竖。

✎ 12 画
▥ 艹 部
◲ 上 中 下

葱 葱葱葱葱葱葱葱葱葱葱葱葱

(聰) cōng 耳聪目明、聪明 ☞ 耳的末笔改提。

✎ 15 画
▥ 耳 部
◲ 左 右

聪聪聪聪聪聪聪聪聪聪
聪聪聪聪聪

(從) cóng 跟从、从犯、服从、从军、从古到今、从不盲从

☞ 左侧人的末笔改点。

✎ 4 画
▥ 人 部
◲ 左 右

从 从从从从

古字形像相随的两个人。
从(金文) 从(甲文)

(叢) cóng 野草丛生、花丛

☞ 左侧人的末笔改点。

✎ 5 画
▥ 部
◲ 上 下

丛 丛丛丛丛丛

còu 凑数、凑拢、凑巧

☞ 天的末笔改点。

✎ 11 画
▥ 冫部
◲ 左 右

凑 凑凑凑凑凑凑凑凑凑凑凑

cū 粗布、粗心、粗大、粗鲁

☞ 米，中间一竖不带钩，末笔改点。

✎ 11 画
▥ 米 部
◲ 左 右

粗 粗粗粗粗粗粗粗粗粗粗

cù 急促、促进

✎ 9 画
▥ 亻部
◲ 左 右

促 促促促促促促促促促

cù 米醋、老陈醋 ☞ 酉的框内有一短横。

✎ 15 画
▥ 酉 部
◲ 左 右

醋 醋醋醋醋醋醋醋醋醋醋醋醋
醋醋醋

催、摧右上的山 3 画，第二画是 ∟，不分为两笔；右下是隹，不是住。

（鼠）cuàn 东奔西窜、逃窜

✎ 12 画
部 穴部
结 上下

窜窜窜窜窜窜窜窜窜窜窜窜

cuī 催促、催眠

✎ 13 画
部 亻部 左右

催催催催催催催催催催催催催

cuī 摧毁、无坚不摧

✎ 14 画
部 扌部 左右

摧摧摧摧摧摧摧摧摧摧
摧摧摧摧

cuì 又薄又脆、脆弱、干脆

☞ 右下是㔾，不是巳、已或己。

✎ 10 画
部 月部 左右

脆脆脆脆脆脆脆脆脆脆

cuì 翠绿、翠竹　☞ 羽的第一、四画改㇖，去钩。卒中部的两人，末笔改点。

✎ 14 画
部 羽部 上下

翠翠翠翠翠翠翠翠翠翠
翠翠翠翠

cūn 农村、居民新村　☞ 木的中间一竖不带钩，末笔改点。

✎ 7 画
部 木部 左右

村村村村村村村

cún 存在、存款、寄存、存根、存心不良

☞ 上左包围结构。

✎ 6 画
部 子部 半包围

存存存存存存

cùn 尺寸、寸步难行

✎ 3 画
部 寸部 独体

寸 寸寸寸

数字诗：·一片一片又一片，两片三片四五片，六七八片九十片，飞入芦花都不见。（咏雪）·一去二三里，烟村四五家，亭台六七座，八九十枝花。（郊游）

古字形在手掌下画一短横，指明寸口的位置。彐（小篆）

(錯) cuò 错乱、错觉、错误、错不了、错开

☞ 钅5画，第二画是横，不是点；第五画是ㄴ，不分为两笔。

✎ 13 画
🔲 钅 部
🔲 左 右

 错错错错错错错错错错错错错

dā 搭放、搭车、搭桥、搭配

☞ 艹3画，第三画楷体是撇，宋体是竖。艹只覆盖右半。

✎ 12 画
🔲 扌 部
🔲 左 右

 搭搭搭搭搭搭搭搭搭搭搭搭

(達) dá 四通八达、到达、转达

☞ 左下包围结构。辶3画，第二画楷体是了，宋体是丁。

✎ 6 画
🔲 辶 部
🔲 半包围

 达达达达达达

dá 答题、报答 /**dā** 答应、答理

✎ 12 画
🔲 竹 部
🔲 上 下

 答答答答答答答答答答答答

dǎ 打敌人、鸡飞蛋打、打工、打扫、打南边来 /**dá** 一打毛巾

1st pt. "take home": 打包 dǎ bāo

✎ 5 画
🔲 扌 部
🔲 左 右

 打打打打打

dà 大风、大不相同、大名、大姨、大前天 /**dài** 大夫

BIG

✎ 3 画
🔲 大 部
🔲 独 体

 大大大

古字形像正面站立的人。大（金文）
↑（甲文）

dāi 呆头呆脑、发呆、呆板

☞ 木的中间一竖不带钩。

✎ 7 画
🔲 口 部
🔲 上 下

呆呆呆呆呆呆呆

dài 代替、朝代、传宗接代

☞ 右部是弋不是戈。

✎ 5 画
🔲 亻 部
🔲 左 右

代代代代代

左右结构的字，如果右边笔画少、体形短，左边笔画多、体形长，写的时候，要使左右两部分的下面基本取平，以避免全字显得不稳，传统术语叫"下平"如"歌、勒、就"等。

逮的辶 3画，第二画楷体是 ㇛(横折折撇)，宋体是 ㇆(横折)。

（帶）**dài** 磁带、带把伞、带队、连蹦带跳、寒带、车带

☞ 上部是一横三竖。第四画楷体是撇，宋体是竖。

✎ 9 画
囗 巾 部
囚 上 下

带 带带带带带带带带带

（貸）**dài** 贷款、高利贷、责无旁贷

☞ 上部是代不是化。贝的第二画㇆不带钩。

✎ 9 画
囗 贝 部
囚 上 下

贷 贷贷贷贷贷贷贷贷贷

dài 等待、待答不理、亏待、待客／dāi 待在姥姥家

☞ 左部是彳不是亻。右上是土不是士。

✎ 9 画
囗 彳 部
囚 左 右

待 待待待待待待待待待

dài 怠慢、怠工

☞ 心的第二画楷体是㇃(卧钩)，宋体是㇃(竖弯钩)。

✎ 9 画
囗 心 部
囚 上 下

怠 怠怠怠怠怠怠怠怠怠

dài 口袋、抽一袋烟

☞ 上部是代，不是伐或化。

✎ 11 画
囗 衣 部
囚 上 下

袋 袋袋袋袋袋袋袋袋袋袋袋

dài 逮捕／dǎi 逮坏人、逮耗子

☞ 左下包围结构。隶，上部是彐，横笔右端出头；下部是氺，5画，不写成水。

✎ 11 画
囗 辶 部
囚 半包围

逮 逮逮逮逮逮逮逮逮逮

dài 戴帽子、戴眼镜、爱戴　　☞ 上右包围结构。

✎ 17 画
囗 戈 部
囚 半包围

戴 戴戴戴戴戴戴戴戴戴戴戴戴
戴戴戴戴戴

dān 丹心、灵丹妙药

✎ 4 画
囗 丿 部
囚 独 体

丹 丹丹丹丹

笔画与笔画在右下角相接时，要分作两笔，如：由、自、口、田。

诞的延，右上是正4画，不是正5画；左下是廴两画，第一画乛，不分为两笔。

（擔）dān 担水、承担／dàn 货担、一担菜、勇挑重担

✎ 8 画　部 扌　左 右

担 担担担担担担担担

（單）dān 单独、单纯、菜单、单数／shàn 姓单／chán 单于(匈奴君主称号)

✎ 8 画　部 八 上 十 下

单 单单单单单单单

dān 耽搁、耽误

☞ 耳的末笔改提。

✎ 10 画　部 耳　左 右

耽 耽耽耽耽耽耽耽耽耽耽

（膽）dǎn 胆囊、胆量、球胆

✎ 9 画　部 月　左 右

胆 胆胆胆胆胆胆胆胆胆

dàn 通宵达旦、元旦、花旦

✎ 5 画　部 日 上 一 下

旦 旦旦旦旦旦

古字形像太阳升出地平线。

（金文）（甲文）

dàn 但是、但愿

✎ 7 画　部 亻　左 右

但 但但但但但但但

（誕）dàn 诞生、寿诞、怪诞

☞ 讠两画，第二画是乛，不分为两笔或三笔。

✎ 8 画　部 讠　左 右

诞 诞诞诞诞诞诞诞

dàn 淡水、淡蓝、冷淡、淡季、扯淡

☞ 右上的火，末笔改点。

✎ 11 画　部 氵　左 右

淡 淡淡淡淡淡淡淡淡淡淡淡

当、挡、档的彐，中间一横右端不出头。

（彈） dàn 泥弹、导弹/tán 弹簧、弹射、弹钢琴、弹棉花

☞ 弓3画，第三画是乛，不分为两笔。

✎ 11 画　囗 弓 画部　囗 左 右

弹 弹弹弹弹弹弹弹弹弹弹弹

dàn 鸵鸟蛋、山药蛋、笨蛋

☞ 第一画是横钩，不是横。

✎ 11 画　囗 疋 画部　囗 上 下

蛋 蛋蛋蛋蛋蛋蛋蛋蛋蛋蛋

（當 *噹） dāng 旗鼓相当、当家、当主人、当面、*当啷/dàng 适当、当晚

✎ 6 画　囗 小 画部　囗 上 下

当 当当当当当当

> 执笔讲究"指实掌虚"。"实"不等于用大力、死捏笔；"虚"只为表明无名指和小指不要抠到掌心处。如果后二指抠入掌心窝内，就妨碍了笔的灵活运动。

（擋） dǎng 阻挡、挡风、窗挡

✎ 9 画　囗 扌 画部　囗 左 右

挡挡挡挡挡
挡挡挡挡

（黨） dǎng 政党、党羽

☞ 上部是⺌不是⺍。

✎ 10 画　囗 小 画部　囗 上 下

党 党党党党党党党党党党

（蕩） dàng 荡涤、动荡、游荡、扫荡、芦苇荡

☞ 艹3画，覆盖全字，第三画楷体是撇，宋体是竖。右下是𭾱不是易。

✎ 9 画　囗 艹 画部　囗 上 下

荡 荡荡荡荡荡荡荡荡荡

（檔） dàng 存档、档案、档次

☞ 木，中间一竖不带钩，末笔改点。

✎ 10 画　囗 木 画部　囗 左 右

档 档档档档档档档档档档

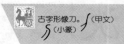

dāo 剃刀、冰刀

✎ 2 画　囗 刀 画部　囗 独 体

刀 刀刀

古字形像刀。〔甲文〕〔小篆〕

(導) dǎo 导游、开导、导热

☞ 上部是巳，不是已或己。

✎ 6 画
🗌 己 部
🗌 上 下

导 导 导 导 导 导

(島) dǎo 半岛、海岛

☞ 上右包围结构。第二画是⺄、第三画是乚，都不分为两笔。山 3 画，第二画乚，不分为两笔。

✎ 7 画
🗌 山 部
🗌 半包围

岛 岛 岛 岛 岛 岛 岛 岛

字谜
大鸟飞来把山抱，
山头遮去鸟儿脚；
此山原在水中立，
浪打潮涌不动摇。

---

dǎo 跌倒、倒闭、倒换、倒卖 /dào 倒流、倒退、倒水

☞ 至的末笔改提。 *fall, topple, collapse, change*

✎ 10 画
🗌 亻 部
🗌 左 右

倒 倒 倒 倒 倒 倒 倒 倒 倒 倒

---

dǎo 赴汤蹈火、舞蹈、循规蹈矩 ☞ 左下止的末笔改提。右部是舀不是臽。

✎ 17 画
🗌 足 部
🗌 左 右

蹈 蹈 蹈 蹈 蹈 蹈 蹈 蹈 蹈 蹈 蹈 蹈
蹈 蹈 蹈 蹈 蹈

---

dào 到达、到期、周到、收到、到朋友家坐坐

☞ 至的末笔改提。

✎ 8 画
🗌 至 部
🗌 左 右

到 到 到 到 到 到 到 到

---

dào 盗窃、金库被盗、强盗、盗贼

✎ 11 画
🗌 皿 部
🗌 上 下

盗 盗 盗 盗 盗 盗 盗 盗 盗 盗 盗

---

dào 追悼、哀悼、悼念、悼词

☞ 左部是忄，不是才。

✎ 11 画
🗌 忄 部
🗌 左 右

悼 悼 悼 悼 悼 悼 悼 悼 悼 悼 悼

---

dào 道路、道理、道德、道谢、能说会道、笔道儿

☞ 左下包围结构。辶 3 画，第二画楷体是乁，宋体是乀。

✎ 12 画
🗌 辶 部
🗌 半包围

道 道 道 道 道 道 道 道 道 道 道 道

dào 稻谷、早稻、双季稻　　禾，中间一竖不带钩，末笔改点。右部是舀不是舀。

15 画
禾 部
左 右　稻

稻稻稻稻稻稻稻稻稻稻
稻稻稻

dé 得胜、得体、得意 /děi 得交 300 元 /
de 拿得动、说得清

古字形用手持贝壳（古钱币）表
示有所得。

11 画
彳 部
左 右　得

得得得得得得得得得得得

dé 品德、同心同德、恩德　　心上有一横，横上是横"目"。心，第二画楷体是乚(卧
钩)，宋体是乚(竖弯钩)。

15 画
彳 部
左 右　德

德德德德德德德
德德德德德德德德

(燈) dēng 点灯、万家灯火
火的末笔改点。

6 画
火 部
左 右　灯

灯灯灯灯灯灯

科普作者
高士其，原名
"高仕锒"。后来，他
把名字简化为"士其"
并解释："去掉人
旁不做官，去掉
金旁不要钱。"

dēng 登山、登台、刊登、登记
左上右包围结构。上部是癶不是癶。

12 画
癶 部
半包围　登

登登登登登登登登登登登登

děng 等于、头等、等待、等到
寺的上部是土不是士。

12 画
竹 部
上 下　等

等等等等等等等等等等等等

dèng 凳子、板凳　　登的上部是癶不是癶。凳的下部是几，不是儿。

14 画
癶 部
上 下　凳

凳凳凳凳凳凳凳凳凳凳凳
凳凳

dī 低空、低温、低年级、低着头、地势低、低等动物
右部是氐不是氐。

7 画
亻 部
左 右　低

低低低低低低低

抵、底所含的部件是氐，不是氏。

dī 堤坝、河堤

☞ 土的末笔改提（丶）。

✎ 12 画
📖 土 部
⺇ 左 右

堤 堤堤堤堤堤堤堤堤堤堤堤堤

dī 滴水成冰、汗滴、滴眼药水　☞ 右部是商不是商，右下框内是古。

✎ 14 画
📖 氵 部
⺇ 左 右

滴 滴滴滴滴滴滴滴滴滴滴
滴滴滴

（敵）dí 敌人、敌国、寡不敌众、势均力敌

☞ 舌的起笔是撇不是横。右部是攵不是夂。

✎ 10 画
📖 舌 部
⺇ 左 右

敌 敌敌敌敌敌敌敌敌敌

dí 笛子、警笛　☞ 下部是由不是田。

✎ 11 画
📖 竹 部
⺇ 上 下

笛 笛笛笛笛笛笛
笛笛笛笛笛

书写汉字时下笔先后的顺序叫做笔顺。在汉字中，笔顺包括两方面的内容：一是笔画的走向，比如横是从左到右，竖是从上到下；二是笔画出现的先后次序，比如"山"由三笔构成，这三个笔画出现的先后次序为：竖（中间）、竖折、竖（右部）。笔势和笔序合起来称为笔顺。

dǐ 抵御、抵命、收支相抵、抵达

✎ 8 画
📖 扌 部
⺇ 左 右

抵 抵抵抵抵
抵抵抵抵

dǐ 河底、家底儿、底稿、月底

☞ 上左包围结构。

✎ 8 画
📖 广 部
⺇ 半包围

底 底底底底底底底底

dì 地球、拖地、内地、场地、境地、白地红字 /de 好好地学习

☞ 土的末笔改提。

✎ 6 画
📖 土 部
⺇ 左 右

地 地地地地地地

dì 兄弟、表弟

☞ 第五画是乚，不分为两笔。

✎ 7 画
📖 八 部
⺇ 上 下

弟 弟弟弟弟弟弟弟

小弟弟，真淘气，头戴小兔帽，身穿弓字衣，一条腿站立，一条腿翘起。

字谜

dì 目的 /**dí** 的确 /**de** 绿绿的水

✎ 8 画
⊞ 白 部 右

的 的的的的的的的的

dì 上帝、皇帝、帝国主义

✎ 9 画
⊞ 亠 上 部 下

帝 帝帝帝帝帝帝帝帝帝

古字形像花蒂，应是蒂的本字。（金文）（甲文）

（遞）**dì** 递交、递补

☞ 左下包围结构。辶3画，第二画楷体是ㄋ，宋体是ㄋ。

✎ 10 画
⊞ 辶 部 半包围

递 递递递递递递递递递

dì 第一、及第

✎ 11 画
⊞ 竹 上 部 下

第 第第第第第第第第第第

（顛）**diān** 塔颠、颠覆、颠簸　　☞ 真的框内是三横，不是两横。

✎ 16 画
⊞ 页 部 右

颠 颠颠颠颠颠颠颠颠颠颠颠
颠颠颠颠

笔画形状简称笔形。现代汉字的笔形可以分为基本笔形（有的称平笔笔形）和派生笔形（有的称折笔笔形）。

diǎn 字典、典范、庆典、典故、典押

✎ 8 画
⊞ 八 上 部 下

典 典典典典典典典典

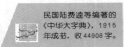

（點）**diǎn** 斑点、点钱、点头、点火、正点、起点、缺点、茶点

✎ 9 画
⊞ 灬 上 部 下

点 点点点点点点点点

（電）**diàn** 雷电、电灯、电死人、贺电

✎ 5 画
⊞ 丨 部 独体

电 电电电电电

民国陆费逵等编著的《中华大字典》，1915年成书，收44908字。

diàn 店主、旅店

☞ 上左包围结构。

✎ 8 画
□ 广 部
⊠ 半包围

店 店店店店店店店店

(墊) diàn 垫高、垫子、垫付

☞ 右上是丸不是九。

✎ 9 画
□ 土 部
⊠ 上 下

垫 垫垫垫垫垫垫垫垫垫

diàn 宫殿、殿后

☞ 右上不是几，末笔不带钩。不简化作屃。

✎ 13 画
□ 殳 部
⊠ 左 右

殿 殿殿殿殿殿殿殿殿殿殿殿殿殿

diāo 猫叼鱼、嘴叼烟

☞ 右边是刁不是刀。

✎ 5 画
□ 口 部
⊠ 左 右

叼 叼叼叼叼叼

diāo 大雕、雕刻、玉雕　☞ 右边是隹不是住。

✎ 16 画
□ 隹 部
⊠ 左 右

雕 雕雕雕雕雕雕雕雕
雕雕雕雕雕雕雕雕

> 汉字的古今字指汉字中记录同一个词所用的在时间上有先后差别的不同字形。如《汉书·司马相如传上》颜师古注："绔，古袴字。"古今字的"古"和"今"
>
>
>
> 是相对而言的。如前例"绔"是古字，"袴"是今字，后来"裤"字通行，"袴"也成了古字。所以（清）段玉裁说："古今无定时，周为古则汉为今，汉为古则晋、宋为今。随时异用者，谓之古今字。"

diào 吊唁、吊桥、吊装、吊销

✎ 6 画
□ 口 部
⊠ 上 下

吊 吊吊吊吊吊吊

(釣) diào 钓鱼、沽名钓誉

☞ ϧ 5画，第二画是横，不是点；第五画是乚，不分为两笔。右部是勺不是勾。

✎ 8 画
□ 钅 部
⊠ 左 右

钓 钓钓钓钓钓钓钓钓

diào 掉头、掉换、掉雨点、掉队、掉了字、忘掉

✎ 11 画
□ 扌 部
⊠ 左 右

掉 掉掉掉掉掉掉掉掉掉掉

diē 爹妈、亲爹

 左上右包围结构。多的两夕写在一条中轴线上。

10 画
父部
半包围

爹爹爹爹爹爹爹爹爹爹

diē 跌交、跌价

左下止的末笔改提。

12 画
足部
左右

跌跌跌跌跌跌跌
跌跌跌跌跌

diē 重叠、折叠　　上部三个又的末笔都改点。
中部是一不是宀。

13 画
又部
上下

叠叠叠叠叠叠
叠叠叠叠叠叠叠

> "叠"在原来的《简化字总表》(1964年)中被简化为"迭"。"叠"在日常的印刷物中被停止使用。1986年重新发表的《简化字总表》恢复了"叠"字的规范字身分,不再作为"迭"的繁体字。

diē 蝴蝶、蝶泳　　木的中间一竖不带钩。

15 画
虫部
左右

蝶蝶蝶蝶蝶蝶蝶
蝶蝶蝶蝶蝶蝶蝶蝶

dīng 甲乙丙丁、壮丁、园丁、人丁兴旺、妙三丁

2 画
一部
独体

丁丁

> 古字形像钉帽或钉子,是钉的本字。
> (金文) (甲文)

dīng 叮咬、叮嘱

5 画
口部
左右

叮叮叮叮叮

> 错别字是错字和别字的总称。虽然现行汉字中有这个字形,但本该写甲字的写成了乙字,这个乙字对于甲字来说就是别字,如把"包子"写成了"饱子",把"安装"写成了"按装"。对于"包子"的"包"来说,"饱"就是别字;对于"安装"的"安"来说,"按"就是别字。

dīng 盯人、盯住目标

7 画
目部
左右

盯盯盯盯盯盯盯

(釘) dīng 钉子、天天钉着孩子复习/dìng 钉马掌、钉扣子

 共5画,第二画是横,不是点;第五画是乚,不分为两笔。

7 画
钅部
左

钉钉钉钉钉钉钉

(頂) díng 山顶、顶好、顶着太阳、一个顶俩、顶撞、一顶帽子

🖉 8 画
📖 页部
△ 左右

顶 顶顶顶顶顶顶顶顶

(訂) díng 订正、制订、订货、装订

☞ 订 2画，第二画是乛，不分为两笔或三笔。

🖉 4 画
📖 讠部
△ 左右

订 订订订订

定 díng 安定、商定、定论、定做

🖉 8 画
📖 宀部
△ 上下

定 定定定定定定定定

丢 diū 丢失、丢掉

☞ 起笔是撇不是横。

🖉 6 画
📖 厶部
△ 上下

丢 丢丢丢丢丢丢

(東) dōng 东方、做东、房东

☞ 第二画是乚，不分为两笔。小的左侧，楷体是点，宋体是撇。

🖉 5 画
📖 一部
△ 独体

东 东东东东东

古字形像两端扎紧的布袋，后借作表示方向。
（金文）（甲文）

(*鼕) dōng 冬天、立冬、*鼓声冬冬

☞ 左上右包围结构。上部是夂不是夊。

🖉 5 画
📖 夂部
△ 半包围

冬 冬冬冬冬冬

董 dǒng 董事、董事会

🖉 12 画
📖 艹部
△ 上下

董 董董董董
董董董董董董董董

懂 dǒng 懂事、懂外语

🖉 15 画
📖 忄部
△ 左右

懂 懂懂懂懂懂懂懂
懂懂懂懂懂懂懂懂

冻、栋的东，第二画是乙，不分为两笔；右下小的左侧，楷体是点，宋体是撇。

(動) dòng 流动、改动、动心、闻风而动、动产

🖊 6 画
部 力 部右
四 左 右

动 动动动动动动

现代汉字中，**9画到12画的字比较多**，这是现代汉字字形既要便于区别，又要字形简易，兼顾"明"和"简"的结果。

(凍) dòng 天寒地冻、上冻、果冻

🖊 7 画
部 冫 部右
四 左 右

冻 冻冻冻冻冻冻冻

(棟) dòng 栋梁、三栋高楼

☞ 木的中间一竖不带钩，末笔改点。

🖊 9 画
部 木 部右
四 左 右

栋 栋栋栋栋栋栋栋栋栋

dòng 洞察、防空洞、漏洞

clear?
clearly?

🖊 9 画
部 氵 部右
四 左 右

洞 洞洞洞洞洞洞洞洞洞

(*鬥) dǒu 升载斗量、烟斗、斗室／dòu *斗争、*奋斗、*斗智

🖊 4 画
部 斗 部体
四 独 体

斗 斗斗斗斗

(1) 字音是dòu，字义是对打、争斗时，繁体为鬥。

(2) 斗(dǒu)的古字形像一种带把的舀取水酒的器具。𣁬（金文）𣁬（甲文）

dǒu 发抖、抖掉帽沿的雪、抖起精神、抖老底儿、外出打工的他抖起来了

🖊 7 画
部 扌 部右
四 左 右

抖 抖抖抖抖抖抖抖

dǒu 陡坡、楼梯太陡

☞ 阝两画，第一画是了，不分为两笔。

🖊 9 画
部 左阝 部右
四 左 右

陡 陡陡陡陡陡陡陡陡陡

🐟 **笔画与笔画在左下角相接时，有两种情况：全包围结构的字，分作两笔，如：回、田、囚、四；不是全包围结构的字，连为一笔，如：山、区、臣、函。**

dòu 黄豆、咖啡豆

🖊 7 画
部 豆 部下
四 上 下

豆 豆豆豆豆豆豆豆

dòu 逗留、逗乐、逗人喜欢、逗号

☞ 左下包围结构。辶3画，第二画楷体是了，宋体是了。

✎ 10 画
□ 辶 部
⊠ 半包围

逗 逗逗逗逗逗逗逗逗逗逗

dū 都市、建都 /dōu 都来植树、天都亮了

☞ 阝两画，第一画是了，不分为两笔。

✎ 10 画
□ 右阝部
⊠ 左 右

都 都都都都都都都都都都

dū 督察、督战

☞ 叔下的小，竖钩改竖，去钩；左侧楷体是点，宋体是撇。

✎ 13 画
□ 目 部
⊠ 上 下

督 督督督督督督督督督督督督督

dú 中毒、毒品、狠毒、毒死老鼠、流毒

☞ 母的第一画是乚，第二画是了，都不分为两笔。

✎ 9 画
□ 毋部
⊠ 上 下

毒 毒毒毒毒毒毒毒毒毒

(獨) dú 独身、独奏、独特

✎ 9 画
□ 犭部
⊠ 左 右

独 独独独独独独独独独

(讀) dú 读书、阅读、走读

☞ 讠两画，第二画是了，不分为两笔或三笔。右上是十，不是士。

✎ 10 画
□ 讠部
⊠ 左 右

读 读读读读读读读读读读

dǔ 堵塞、堵心、一堵墙

☞ 土的末笔改提。

✎ 11 画
□ 土部
⊠ 左 右

堵 堵堵堵堵堵堵堵堵堵堵

(賭) dǔ 赌钱、打赌

☞ 贝的第二画了不带钩。

✎ 12 画
□ 贝部
⊠ 左 右

赌 赌赌赌赌赌赌赌赌赌赌

dù 杜梨、杜绝

☞ 木的中间一竖不带钩，末笔改点。

✎ 7 画
木 部
左 右

杜 杜杜杜杜杜杜杜

同时用简单的意符和音符替换复杂的意符、音符，创造一个结构比较简易的新形声字，是汉字简化的一种方法。如"驚"简化作"惊"（意符"马"换成"忄"，音符"敬"换成"京"）。

dù 肚子、腿肚子／dǔ 牛肚

✎ 7 画
月 部
左 右

肚 肚肚肚肚
肚肚肚

dù 度量衡、制度、进度、态度、温度、度假／duó 揣度

☞ 上左包围结构。

✎ 9 画
广 部
半包围

度 度度度度度度度度度

dù 渡江、渡口、渡过难关

✎ 12 画
氵 部
左 右

渡 渡渡渡渡渡渡渡渡渡渡渡

端

duān 端坐、端庄、端枪瞄准、尖端、争端、诡计多端　☞ 立的末笔改提。山3

画，第二画乚，不分为两笔

✎ 14 画
立 部
左 右

端 端端端端端端端
端端端端端端端

短

duǎn 短裤、短暂、短缺、扬长避短、短见

☞ 矢的末笔改点。

✎ 12 画
矢 部
左 右

短 短短短短短短短短短短短

段

duàn 段落、工段、一段木头

☞ 左部是⻊不是阝；右上不是几，末笔不带钩，也不是⻈。

✎ 9 画
殳 部
右

段 段段段段段段段段段

（斷）　duàn 摔断、间断、诊断

☞ 米的末笔改点。米的左下是乚，不分为两笔。

✎ 11 画
斤 部
左 右

断 断断断断断断断断断断

缎、锻的右部不是段；右上不是几，末笔不带钩，也不是コ。

（緞）duàn 绸缎、缎被
🖊️ 纟3画，上部不是幺。
✏️ 12 画
🔲 纟 部
🏳️ 左 右

缎 缎缎缎缎缎缎缎缎缎缎缎

（鍛）duàn 锻造、锻炼 🖊️ 钅5画，第二画是横，不是点；第五画是竖提，不分为两笔。
✏️ 14 画
🔲 钅 部
🏳️ 左 右

锻 锻锻锻锻锻锻锻锻锻锻锻
锻锻

duī 堆积、垃圾堆、成堆
🖊️ 土的末笔改提。右边是隹不是住。
✏️ 11 画
🔲 土 部
🏳️ 左 右

堆 堆堆堆堆堆堆堆堆堆堆

（隊）duì 乐队、排队、队旗、一队人马
🖊️ 阝两画，第一画是了，不分为两笔。
✏️ 4 画
🔲 左阝 部
🏳️ 左 右

队 队队队队

(first part I'm sorry)

（對）duì 应对、对准、对流、对联、对脾气、核对、对错 🖊️ 又的末笔改点。
✏️ 5 画
🔲 又 部
🏳️ 左 右

对 对对对对对

有人误解"功夫"二字。以为时间久、数量多即叫做"功夫"。事实上"功夫"是"准确"的积累。熟练了，下笔即能准确，便是功夫的成效。譬如用枪打靶，每天盲目地放几百粒子弹，不如精心用意手眼俱准地打一枪……所以可说："功夫不是盲目地时间加数量的重复以达到熟练，而是准确的重复以达到熟练。"
——启功
《论书随笔》

（噸）dūn 1吨等于1000千克
✏️ 7 画
🔲 口 部
🏳️ 左 右

吨 吨吨吨吨吨吨吨

dūn 蹲下、半蹲 🖊️ 左下止的末笔改提。酋内有一短横。
✏️ 19 画
🔲 足 部
🏳️ 左 右

蹲 蹲蹲蹲蹲蹲蹲蹲蹲蹲蹲蹲
蹲蹲蹲蹲蹲蹲蹲

dùn 盾牌、银盾、矛盾
🖊️ 上左包围结构。
✏️ 9 画
🔲 厂 部
🏳️ 半包围

古字形像一块盾牌。🔲(金文) 🔲(甲文)

盾 盾盾盾盾盾盾盾盾盾

（頓） dùn 停顿、安顿、劳顿、一天三顿饭

☞ 屯的末笔改 l（竖提）。

✎ 10 画　□页部右　△左

 顿 顿 顿 顿 顿 顿 顿 顿 顿 顿

多 duō 凶多吉少、多疑、多余、多大

how

☞ 两夕写在一条中轴线上。

✎ 6 画　□夕部下　△上

 多 多 多 多 多 多

 古字形用两块肉表示多。
多（金文）多（甲文）

（奪） duó 夺眶而出、抢夺、争分夺秒、定夺

☞ 左上右包围结构。

✎ 6 画　□大部半包　△半包围

 夺 夺 夺 夺 夺 夺

电脑正在微
型化，传统的
砚台却在巨型化。
前几年报上说，河北
易县用终南山优等石料制
成巨型砚台，长 3 米，
宽 2.34 米，高 90 厘米，
重 5 吨。运到保定
市长期陈列于古
莲花池公园。

朵 duǒ 一朵红花、白云朵朵

✎ 6 画　□木部下　△上

 朵 朵 朵 朵 朵 朵

躲 duǒ 躲闪、躲藏

☞ 身的末笔上端不出头。

✎ 13 画　□身部右　△左

 躲 躲 躲 躲 躲 躲 躲 躲 躲 躲 躲 躲

惰 duò 懒惰、惰性

☞ 月的末笔改竖。

✎ 12 画　□忄部左　△左

 惰 惰 惰 惰 惰 惰 惰 惰 惰 惰 惰

（鵝） é 大白鹅、鹅卵石

☞ 鸟5画，第一画丿、第二画𠃌，不连成一笔；第四画𠃌，不分为两笔。

✎ 12 画　□鸟部右　△左右

 鹅 鹅 鹅 鹅 鹅 鹅 鹅 鹅 鹅 鹅 鹅

蛾 é 蛾子、飞蛾扑火

✎ 13 画　□虫部右　△左右

 蛾 蛾 蛾 蛾 蛾 蛾 蛾 蛾 蛾 蛾 蛾

(額) é 额头、匾额、超额　☞ 各的第三画捺改点。

✎ 15 画
📖 页 部
◫ 左 右

额额额额额额额额额额额
额额额

(恶* 噁) è 罪恶、凶恶、恶习 /wù 厌恶 /ě* 恶心
☞ 心的第二画楷体是乚(卧钩)，宋体是乚(竖弯钩)。

✎ 10 画
📖 心 部
◫ 上 下

恶恶恶恶恶恶恶恶恶恶

(餓) è 挨饿、饿他两天
☞ ✦ 3画，第二画是𠃌，不是点；第三画
是乚，不分为两笔。

✎ 10 画
📖 饣 部
◫ 左 右

饿饿饿饿饿饿饿饿饿

字谜

我把食物找，担心食太少；
有食不够吃，肚子咕咕叫。

ēn 恩怨、忘恩负义
☞ 因内大的末笔改点。心的第二画楷体是乚(卧钩)，宋体是乚(竖弯钩)。

✎ 10 画
📖 心 部
◫ 上 下

恩恩恩恩恩恩恩恩恩恩

(兒) ér 儿童、儿子、中华男儿、盖儿

✎ 2 画
📖 儿 部
◫ 独 体

儿儿

ér 少而精、挺身而出、从上而下、费力多而收效小

✎ 6 画
📖 而 部
◫ 独 体

而而而而而而

古字形像下垂的颊毛。

朲（金文）

ěr 耳朵、木耳、耳房

✎ 6 画
📖 耳 部
◫ 独 体

耳耳耳耳耳耳

汉字的正体字指汉字规范的字形。各个时期、各个地区所定的正体字形不完全相同。我国内地的正体字现在一般是跟异体字相对而言的，如"专"为正体字，"耑"为异体字；"桌"为正体字，"槕"为异体字，等等。

èr 三心二意、一心不可二用

✎ 2 画
📖 一 部
◫ 独 体

二二

发

(發*髮) fā 发射、发病、发起、发展、发面 /fà *理发

上左包围结构。第一画是𠃋(竖折)，不分为两笔。

5 画
又 部
半包围

发 发发发发发

字谜

像友不是友，模样记清楚：
左角向上拐，右角落彩球。

乏

fá 缺乏、人困马乏

4 画
丿 部
独 体

乏 乏乏乏乏

伐

fá 采伐、滥砍乱伐、讨伐，征伐

6 画
亻 部
左 右

伐 伐伐伐伐伐伐

古字形像戈刃架在人颈上。
（金文）（甲文）

罚

(罰) fá 罚款、赏罚分明

上部是横“目”，不写成四。讠两画，第二画⺀不分为两笔或三笔。右下是刂不是寸。

9 画
罒 部
上 下

罚 罚罚罚罚罚罚罚罚罚

阀

(閥) fá 军阀、安全阀

左上右包围结构。起笔丶嵌在第二笔丨和第三笔𠃌之间。

9 画
门 部
半包围

阀 阀阀阀阀阀阀阀阀阀

法

fǎ 守法、法则、办法、效法、法术

8 画
氵 部
左 右

法 法法法法
法法法法

汉字发展到隶书，已经谈不上古人造字的“精意”了。刘复（半农）诘问：“若说简笔字不合于六书，则太阳并不是方的（‘日’），狗并不是两条腿（‘犬’），试问楷书之合于六书者安在？”

帆

fān 扬帆、一帆风顺、帆船

6 画
巾 部
左 右

帆 帆帆帆帆帆帆

番

fān 番将、番茄、三番五次/pān 番禺(地名)

上部7画，丿下米，不是采。

12 画
釆 部
上 下

番 番番番番番番番番番番番番

fān 把碗打翻了、翻改、翻译、吵翻了、翻越

〒 左上7画，丿丨米，不是采；米的末笔改点。

✎ 18 画
⊟ 羽 部
⊠ 左 右

翻翻翻翻翻翻翻翻翻翻翻翻翻翻翻翻翻

fán 凡例、平凡、仙女下凡

✎ 3 画
⊟ 几 独体

凡 凡凡凡

古字形像船帆，应是帆的本字。

ꖓ（金文）　ꖓ（甲文）

(煩) fán 烦躁、烦人、烦劳

〒 火的末笔改点。

✎ 10 画
⊟ 火 部
⊠ 左 右

烦烦烦烦烦烦烦烦烦烦

字 谜

翻开一页是个火，再翻一页还是火；
页页是火真讨厌，让人越看越冒火。

fán 频繁、繁荣、繁殖、繁难

〒 下部小的左侧，楷体是点，宋体是撇。

✎ 17 画
⊟ 糸 部
⊠ 上 下

繁繁繁繁繁繁繁繁繁繁繁繁繁繁繁繁

fǎn 反扑、反作用、反对

〒 上左包围结构。

✎ 4 画
⊟ 厂 部
⊠ 半包围

反 反反反反

我在看颜鲁公的字时，仿佛对着巍峨的高峰，不知不觉地耸肩聚眉，全身的筋肉都紧张起来，模仿他的严肃。我在看赵孟頫的字时，仿佛对着临风荡漾的柳条，不知不觉地展颐摆腰，全身的筋肉都松懈起

fǎn 往返、返回

〒 左下包围结构。反的末笔改点。辶3画，第二画楷体是乛，宋体是𠃋。

✎ 7 画
⊟ 辶 部
⊠ 半包围

返返返返返返返返

来，模仿它的秀媚。从心理学看，这不是奇事，……这都是把墨涂的痕迹看作有生气有性格的东西，都是把字在心中所引起的意象移到字的本身上面去。——朱光潜《艺文杂谈》

fàn 侵犯、犯规、犯病、罪犯

〒 右边是㔾，不是巳、已或己。

✎ 5 画
⊟ 犭 部
⊠ 左 右

犯犯犯犯犯

(飯) fàn 米饭、饭前饭后、晚饭

〒 饣3画，第二画横钩，不是点；第三画竖提，不分为两笔。

✎ 7 画
⊟ 饣 部
⊠ 左 右

饭饭饭饭饭饭饭

fàn 泛舟、空泛、胃里泛酸水、泛滥、泛指

✎ 7画 氵部 ⊡左右 泛 泛泛泛泛泛泛泛泛

(*範) fàn *模范、*范围、*防范、姓范
廿3画，第三画楷体是撇，宋体是竖。右下是巳，不是巳、已或己。

✎ 8画 廿部 ⊡上下 范 范范范范范范范范

(贩) fàn 小贩、贩毒
贝的第二画丨不带钩。

✎ 8画 贝部 ⊡左右 贩 贩贩贩贩贩贩贩贩

fāng 正方、方言、西方、甲方乙方、千方百计、处方、立方、来日方长

✎ 4画 方部 ⊡独体 方 方方方方

fāng 街坊、牌坊/fáng 作坊、油坊
土的末笔改提。

✎ 7画 土部 ⊡左右 坊 坊坊坊坊坊坊坊

fāng 芳草、芳名
廿3画，第三画楷体是撇，宋体是竖。

✎ 7画 廿部 ⊡上下 芳 芳芳芳芳芳芳芳

fáng 堤防、预防、防御、国防
阝两画，第一画是乛，不分为两笔。

✎ 6画 左阝部 ⊡左右 防 防防防防防防

fáng 妨碍、不妨
女的横笔右端不出头。

✎ 7画 女部 ⊡左右 妨 妨妨妨妨妨妨妨

书面交际总有甲乙两方，一方发出信息，一方接收信息。交际职能要求信息的内容和载体必须是双方都能同样理解的，这就对文字提出了"明"的要求；交际职能还要求提高书面交际的效率，这就对文字提出了"简"的要求。由此可知，汉字的简化和规范化是人们对文字工具的普遍要求在汉字身上的具体体现。综观汉字发展的全过程，历代都曾进行过汉字的简化和规范化工作，区别仅在于有的微小、有的明显、有的自发、有的自觉而已。因此，繁体字与简化字是存在于汉字发展的整个历史过程之中的。

fáng 楼房、远房亲戚　☞上左包围结构。

◆ 8　画
□ 户　部
⊠ 半包围

fǎng 相仿、模仿、仿纸、仿佛

◆ 6　画
□ 亻　部
⊠ 左右

(訪) fǎng 寻访、拜访、访问
☞讠两画，第二画是乀，不分为两笔或三笔。

◆ 6　画
□ 讠　部
⊠ 左右

(紡) fǎng 纺线、纺绸
☞纟3画，上部不是幺。

spring

◆ 7　画
□ 纟　部
⊠ 左右

fàng 放任、释放、放羊、放学、怒放、放大、存放、投放
☞右部是攵不是夂。

to put

◆ 8　画
□ 方　部
⊠ 左右

(飛) fēi 飞翔、起飞、飞奔、飞来横祸

◆ 3　画
□ 飞　部
⊠ 独体

fēi 非法、为非作歹、非难、非亲非故
☞中部是两竖，左右各三横。

◆ 8　画
□ 非　部
⊠ 左

féi 肥肉、肥沃、肥田、化肥、损公肥私、肥缺、肥瘦

◆ 8　画
□ 月　部
⊠ 左右

楷书如立，行书如走，草书如飞，此就字体言之。用笔亦然。执笔落纸，如人之立地，脚跟既定，伸腰舒背，骨立自然强健，稍一转动，四面皆应。不善用笔者，非坐卧纸上，即跨伏纸上矣。（楷书像站立，行书像快走，草书像疾飞，这是就字体本来说的。用笔也是一个道理。拿笔写字，就像人站立在地上一样，脚跟立稳了，那么伸腰舒背，并不会改变巍然挺立的形态，稍稍转动一下，四面都会呼应。不善于用笔的，那姿势不是趴在纸上，就是蹲在纸上。）
——周星莲《临池管见》

古字形像张开飞翔的双翅。非（金文）

沸、费的弗，5画、第三画是ㄣ，不分为两笔。

fěi 匪徒、剿匪

☞ 上中下包围结构。非的中部是两竖，左右各三横。末笔乚不分为两笔。

✎ 10 画
□ 匚 部
☒ 半包围

匪匪匪匪匪匪匪匪匪匪

---

fèi 肺病、肺叶

☞ 右边部件4画，竖笔贯穿上下，不是市。

✎ 8 画
□ 月 部
☒ 左 右

肺肺肺肺肺肺肺肺

（廢）**fèi** 废除、废纸、变废为宝、残废、废墟、颓废

☞ 上左包围结构。左上是广，不是扩。右下是发，不是友或戊。

✎ 8 画
□ 广 部
☒ 半包围

废废废废废废废废

---

fèi 沸腾、沸水

✎ 8 画
□ 氵 部
☒ 左 右

沸沸沸沸沸沸沸沸

（費）**fèi** 浪费、经费、费鞋 ☞ 贝的第二画㇆不带钩。

✎ 9 画
□ 贝 部
☒ 上 下

费费费费费
费费费费

一弓双箭头上戴，
佛不带人自己来；
压住宝贝不让用，
叫它白白地下埋。

---

component

fēn 分离、分配、分册、分辨、分母 /**fèn** 水分、缘分、过分

☞ 上左右包围结构。

✎ 4 画
□ 八 部
☒ 半包围

分分分分分

古字形像用刀把某物分切为二。
少（金文）)((甲文)

---

fēn 芬芳

☞ 艹3画，第三画楷体是撇，宋体是竖。

✎ 7 画
□ 艹 部
☒ 上 下

芬芬芬芬芬芬芬

---

fēn 吩咐

✎ 7 画
□ 口 部
☒ 左 右

吩吩吩吩吩吩吩

（紛）**fēn** 纷乱、纠纷

☞ 纟 3 画，上部不是幺。

✎ 7 画
□ 纟部
☒ 左右

纷 纷纷 纷纷 纷纷 纷

（墳）**fén** 上坟、坟墓

☞ 土的末笔改提。

✎ 7 画
□ 土部
☒ 左右

坟 坟坟 坟坟 坟坟 坟

---

fěn 香粉、粉末、粉身碎骨、粉条、粉色

☞ 米，中间一竖不带钩，末笔改点。

✎ 10 画
□ 米部
☒ 左右

粉 粉粉 粉粉 粉粉 粉粉 粉

---

fèn 股份、一份报纸、省份、年份

Shares portion stock

✎ 6 画
□ 亻部
☒ 左右

份 份份 份份 份份

（奮）**fèn** 奋勇、勤奋

☞ 左上右包围结构。

✎ 8 画
□ 大部
☒ 半包围

奋 奋奋 奋奋 奋奋 奋奋

（糞）**fèn** 粪便、马粪 ☞ 米，中间一竖不带钩。

✎ 12 画
□ 米部
☒ 上下

粪 粪粪 粪粪 粪粪 粪
粪粪 粪粪

（憤）**fèn** 愤怒、愤愤不平 ☞ 贝的第二画 ﬁ 不带钩。

✎ 12 画
□ 忄部
☒ 左右

愤 愤愤 愤愤 愤愤 愤
愤愤 愤愤

（豐）**fēng** 丰富、丰功伟绩

plentiful great

☞ 起笔是横不是撇。

✎ 4 画
□ 一部
☒ 独体

丰 丰丰 丰丰 丰

"望部生义"
靠不住。"松柏
柳桃"从木，都是
树木，对；"笨苯
笃等"从竹，都
是竹子 ✗ 错了。

"结体"是指
每个字的笔
画、部件、偏旁
间的搭配关系、
组织规则和形
式，也叫"结构"
"结字"或"间
架"。一个字有
一个字的形态。
构成不同形态的
主要原因是笔画
的长、短、粗、
细、俯、仰、伸、
缩和偏旁部件的
宽、窄、高、低、
斜、正的不同，
就如同用不同的
木材和砖瓦可以
搭造出样样各异
的房屋一样。如
果房屋的梁、
柱、砖、瓦配搭
得不好，房屋就
显得难看，甚至
会倾斜、倒塌；
字的笔画、部
件、偏旁搭配得
不合规范，不仅
不美观，还会造
成对万认读的困
难，影响交际效
率。

峰、锋、蜂、逢、缝的夆，上部是夂不是夂，下部是丰。

(風) fēng 刮风、风俗、学风、通风报信、风传、风景、风干

wind; draft

☞ 左上右包围结构。框中是乂不是又。

✎ 4 画
国 风部
囗 半包围

 风 风 风 风

封 fēng 分封、密封、封锁、信封

seal (a letter) confer

☞ 左下土的末笔改提。

✎ 9 画
国 寸部
囗 左 右

 封 封 封 封 封 封 封 封 封

古字形像手拿树苗在土堆上种树。🔲（金文）

(瘋) fēng 疯狂、疯话、疯长

mad; insane; crazy

☞ 上左包围结构。左上是广不是广。风的框中是乂不是又。

✎ 9 画
国 广部
囗 半包围

 疯 疯 疯 疯 疯 疯 疯 疯 疯

峰 fēng 山峰、洪峰

☞ 山3画，第二画乚改竖提，不分为两笔。

✎ 10 画
国 山部
囗 左 右

 峰 峰 峰 峰 峰 峰 峰 峰 峰 峰

(鋒) fēng 刀锋、先锋

☞ 钅5画，第二画是横，不是点；第五画是乚，不分为两笔。

✎ 12 画
国 钅部
囗 左 右

 锋 锋 锋 锋 锋 锋 锋 锋 锋 锋 锋 锋

蜂 fēng 蜜蜂、蜂拥

✎ 13 画
国 虫部
囗 左 右

 蜂 蜂 蜂 蜂 蜂 蜂 蜂 蜂 蜂 蜂 蜂 蜂

逢 féng 相逢、千载难逢

come across; meet; chance; upon

☞ 左下包围结构。辶3画，第二画楷体是𠃓，宋体是𠃌。

✎ 10 画
国 辶部
囗 半包围

 逢 逢 逢 逢 逢 逢 逢 逢 逢

(縫) féng 缝补、缝纫 / fèng 无缝钢管、缝隙

☞ 纟3画，上部是纟。辶3画，第二画楷体是𠃓，宋体是𠃌。

✎ 13 画
国 纟部
囗 左 右

 缝 缝 缝 缝 缝 缝 缝 缝 缝 缝 缝 缝

（諷）**fěng** 借古讽今、嘲讽 ~~mock, satirize~~

☞ 讠两画，第二画是乀，不分为两笔或三笔。风框中是乂不是又。

✎ 6 画　讠部
☐ 左右

| 讽 | 讽讽讽讽讽讽 |

（鳳）**fěng** 凤凰、百鸟朝凤 ~~phoenix~~

☞ 左上右包围结构。框中是又不是乂，又的末笔改点。

✎ 4 画　几部
☐ 半包围

| 凤 | 凤凤凤凤 |

古字形像凤凰。
🐦（甲文）

---

fèng 奉命、信奉、奉献、奉陪 ~~present or recieve w/ Respect~~

☞ 左上右包围结构。下部是キ不是丰。

✎ 8 画　一部
☐ 半包围

| 奉 | 奉奉奉奉奉奉奉奉 |

---

fó 立地成佛、佛教 /**fú** 仿佛 ~~Buddha~~

☞ 弗5画，第三画是乚，不分为两笔。

✎ 7 画　亻部
☐ 左右

| 佛 | 佛佛佛佛佛佛佛 |

---

fǒu 否认、否定 ~~deny negate no~~

☞ 不的中间一竖不带钩，末笔是点。

✎ 7 画　口部
☐ 上下

| 否 | 否否否否否否否 |

---

fū 夫妻、渔夫 ~~husband man~~

✎ 4 画　一部
☐ 独体

| 夫 | 夫夫夫夫 |

（膚）**fū** 皮肤、肤浅 ~~skin~~

✎ 8 画　月部
☐ 左右

| 肤 | 肤肤肤肤肤肤肤肤 |

---

fú 伏案、埋伏、伏天、起伏、伏罪

~~Bendover, lie w/ ones face down, subside~~

✎ 6 画　亻部
☐ 左右

| 伏 | 伏伏伏伏伏伏 |

俘、浮的子，3画，第一画乛、第二画乚不连成一笔。

fú 搀扶、扶着栏杆、扶贫

🖊 7　画
⼿ 扌部
凶 左　右

笔画与笔画在右上角相接时，连作一笔，如：司、刁、句、月。

扶 扶扶扶扶扶扶扶

---

fú 服役、心服口服、水土不服、服毒、衣服 / fù 一服汤药

☞ 右部是⺆不是及。

🖊 8　画
月 部
凶 左　右

服 服服服服服服服服

(margin note: clothes/uniform　西服 "suit" or western clothes)

---

fú 被俘、俘虏

🖊 9　画
亻 部
凶 左　右

俘 俘俘俘俘俘俘俘俘

---

fú 漂浮、浮水、浮云、浮夸、轻浮、浮土、人浮于事

🖊 10　画
氵 部
凶 左　右

浮 浮浮浮浮浮浮浮浮浮

---

fú 音符、符合

🖊 11　画
竹 上部
凶 上　下

符 符符符符符符符符符符

---

fú 单幅、篇幅、一幅画

🖊 12　画
巾 部
凶 左

幅 幅幅幅幅幅幅幅幅幅幅幅

---

fú 享福、口福

☞ 左部是礻不是衤。

🖊 13　画
礻 部
凶 左

古字形像捧酒尊献于神主前。
福（金文）福（甲文）

福 福福福福福福福福福福福

（撫）fǔ 抚摸、安抚、抚养

☞ 右部是无不是尤。

🖊 7　画
扌 部
凶 左　右

抚 抚抚抚抚抚抚抚

斧 fǔ 斧子、板斧
　☞ 左上右包围结构。
　✎ 8 画
　⊟ 父部
　⊠ 半包围
斧 | 斧斧斧斧斧斧斧斧

府 fǔ 政府、总统府
　☞ 上左包围结构。
　✎ 8 画
　⊟ 广部
　⊠ 半包围
俯 | 府府府府府府府府

俯 fǔ 俯首帖耳、俯视
　✎ 10 画
　⊟ 亻部
　⊠ 左 右
俯 | 俯俯俯俯俯俯俯俯俯

(輔) fǔ 辅导、辅助
　☞ 车的下部一横改提，笔顺改先竖后提。
　✎ 11 画
　⊟ 车部
　⊠ 左 右
辅 | 辅辅辅辅辅辅辅辅辅辅辅

腐 fǔ 腐烂、陈腐、腐乳　☞ 上左包围结构。
　✎ 14 画
　⊟ 广部
　⊠ 半包围
腐 | 腐腐腐腐腐腐腐
腐腐腐腐腐腐腐

父 fù 父女、祖父　*father*
　✎ 4 画
　⊟ 父部
　⊠ 独 体
父 | 父父父父

古字形像手持棍棒。
𠨍(金文) 𠂇(甲文)

付 fù 付款、支付　*pay*
　✎ 5 画
　⊟ 亻部
　⊠ 左 右
付 | 付付付付付

carry on the back or shoulder
(負) fù 负重、肩负、负伤、负债、负约、胜负
负数　☞ 贝的第二画丁不带钩。
　✎ 6 画
　⊟ 刀部
　⊠ 上 下
负 | 负负负负负负

刀子头，人字脚，空
心月亮来当腰；背上
有它方知重，心上留
它受煎熬。
字谜

(婦) fù 妇科、媳妇、夫妇

☞ 女的横笔右端不出头。右部是彐,中间横笔右端不出头。

✎ 6 画
部 女 部
☑ 左 右

妇 妇 妇 妇 妇 妇 妇

fù 附属、附耳、附设

☞ 阝两画,第一画是了,不分为两笔。

✎ 7 画
部 左 阝 部
☑ 左 右

附 附 附 附 附 附 附 附

fù 吩咐、嘱咐

✎ 8 画
部 口 部
☑ 左 右

咐 咐 咐 咐 咐 咐 咐 咐

fù 赴宴、赴美

☞ 左下包围结构。

✎ 9 画
部 走 部
☑ 半包围

赴 赴 赴 赴 赴 赴 赴 赴

(復*複) fù 反复、复信、复工、复发、*复制

☞ 下边是夂不是夂。

✎ 9 画
部 夂 部
☑ 上 下

复 复 复 复 复 复 复 复 复

fù 副手、队副、副业、名副其实、一副手套

✎ 11 画
部 刂 部
☑ 左 右

副 副 副 副 副 副 副 副 副 副

fù 师傅

☞ 右上甫的第三画改丁,去钩。

✎ 12 画
部 亻 部
☑ 左 右

傅 傅 傅 傅 傅 傅 傅 傅 傅 傅 傅

fù 丰富、富强、财富

✎ 12 画
部 宀 部
☑ 上 下

富 富 富 富 富 富 富 富 富 富 富

fù 空腹、腹稿

✎ 13 画
部 月 部
四 左 右

腹 腹腹腹腹腹腹腹腹腹腹腹腹

fù 天翻地覆、覆灭、覆盖　☞上部扁框中都是竖，不写成西。

z

✎ 18 画
部 西 部
四 上 下

覆 覆覆覆覆覆覆覆覆覆覆覆覆覆覆覆覆覆

(該) gāi 应该、该人钱、该地

☞讠两画，第二画是乀，不分为两笔或三笔。

✎ 8 画
部 讠 部
四 左 右

该 该该该该该该该该

gǎi 改革、改正、修改

☞左部是己，不是已或巳，第三画乚改乀。右部是攵不是夂。

✎ 7 画
部 己 部
四 左 右

改 改改改改改改改

(蓋) gài 锅盖、膝盖、掩盖、盖章、盖世、盖房

☞上部的羊，竖笔下端不出头。

✎ 11 画
部 羊 部
四 上 下

盖 盖盖盖盖盖盖盖盖盖盖盖

gài 灌溉

☞中部艮的末两画改一画、(点)。

✎ 12 画
部 氵 部
四 左 右

溉 溉溉溉溉溉溉溉溉溉溉溉溉

gài 气概、概况、概不退换

☞木的中间一竖不带钩，末笔改点。中部艮的末两画改一画、(点)。

✎ 13 画
部 木 部
四 左 右

概 概概概概概概概概概概概概概

(*乾 **幹) gān 干戈、干涉、天干地支、*干粮、*干妈/gàn **树干、**实干、**才干、**干将

✎ 3 画
部 干 部
四 独 体

干 干干干

古字形像带权的兵器或旗杆。Ψ (甲文)

gān 苦尽甘来、甘心情愿

☞ 第二画是竖，第五画是横，不连成一笔。

✎ 5 画
囗 甘 部
☐ 独 体

甘 甘 甘 甘 甘 甘

gǎn 杆子、旗杆/gǎn 笔杆、一杆枪

☞ 木的中间一竖不带钩，末笔改点。

✎ 7 画
囗 木 部
☐ 左 右

杆 杆 杆 杆 杆 杆 杆

gān 肝脏、猪肝

✎ 7 画
囗 月 部
☐ 左 右

肝 肝 肝 肝 肝 肝 肝

gān 立竿见影、钓鱼竿

✎ 9 画
囗 竹 部
☐ 上 下

竿 竿 竿 竿 竿 竿 竿 竿 竿

gǎn 秸秆、高粱秆儿

☞ 禾的中间一竖不带钩，末笔改点。

✎ 8 画
囗 禾 部
☐ 左 右

秆 秆 秆 秆 秆 秆 秆 秆

(趕) gǎn 追赶、赶路、赶苍蝇、驱赶、赶集、赶巧

☞ 左下包围结构。

✎ 10 画
囗 走 部
☐ 半包围

赶 赶 赶 赶 赶 赶 赶 赶 赶

gǎn 勇敢、敢想敢干

☞ 左上是丷两画，不是工。右边是攵不是夂。

✎ 11 画
囗 攵 部
☐ 左 右

敢 敢 敢 敢 敢 敢 敢 敢 敢 敢

gǎn 感动、手感、感到、感谢

☞ 上下结构。心的第二画楷体是乀(卧钩)，宋体是L(竖弯钩)。

✎ 13 画
囗 心 部
☐ 上 下

感 感 感 感 感 感 感 感 感 感 感

读音完全相同，而形体和意义都不同的一组字，被称为同音字。普通话有1200多个音节，现代汉语通用字有7000个，平均每个音节有5.8个汉字。在《现代汉语通用字表》中，没有同音字的有：āng 肮、bāi 掰、bèi 北、cān 惨、dà 大、néng 能；有少量同音字的，如āo 熬凹、bǎng 绑榜膀、cāo 操糙、cūn 村皴、diǎn 点典碘踮；有大量同音字的，如bì 币必闭毕庇泌畀哔愊贲陛铋狴毖敝庳婢筚弼愎痹裨跸蓖彃荜碧滗蔽篦壁避濞癖臂躄襞。

字谜
边走边干为哪般？
只因担心误时间。
人生苦短向它学，
争分夺秒莫等闲。

（岡） gāng 山冈

☞ 左上右包围结构。

✎ 4 画
□ 门 部
囚 半包围

冈 冈 冈 冈

（剛） gāng 刚强、刚才、刚刚、刚好

✎ 6 画
□ 刂 部
囚 左 右

刚 刚 刚 刚 刚 刚

（綱） gāng 纲领、大纲

☞ 纟3画，上部不是幺。

✎ 7 画
□ 纟 部
囚 左 右

纲 纲 纲 纲 纲 纲 纲

（鋼） gāng 钢铁／gàng 把菜刀钢一钢

☞ 钅5画，第二画是横，不是点；第五画是乚，不分为两笔。

✎ 9 画
□ 钅 部
囚 左 右

钢 钢 钢 钢 钢 钢 钢 钢 钢

gāng 水缸、酒缸

☞ 缶的第五画改竖提。

✎ 9 画
□ 缶 部
囚 左 右

缸 缸 缸 缸 缸 缸 缸 缸 缸

（崗） gǎng 土岗、岗楼、岗位

☞ 山3画，第二画是乚，不分为两笔。

✎ 7 画
□ 山 部
囚 上 下

岗 岗 岗 岗 岗 岗 岗

gǎng 港口、港币

☞ 右下是巳，不是已或己。

✎ 12 画
□ 氵 部
囚 左 右

港 港 港 港 港 港 港 港 港 港 港 港

gàng 铁杠、双杠、打红杠

☞ 木的中间一竖不带钩，末笔改点。

✎ 7 画
□ 木 部
囚 左 右

杠 杠 杠 杠 杠 杠 杠

gāo 高楼、身高、登高、高档、高龄、高手

古字形像高耸的建筑物。髙（金文）
髙（甲文）

✎ 10 画
部首 高
上下
部 高
下

高 高 高 高 高 高 高 高 高 高

gāo 民脂民膏、牙膏/gào 膏车、膏笔　⤳ 月的起笔改竖。

✎ 14 画
部首 高
上下
部 膏
下

膏 膏 膏 膏 膏 膏 膏 膏 膏 膏 膏
膏 膏 膏

gāo 蛋糕、年糕　⤳ 米的中间一竖不带钩，末笔改点。右上羊的竖笔下端不出头。

✎ 16 画
部首 米
左右
部 糕

糕 糕 糕 糕 糕 糕 糕 糕 糕 糕 糕 糕
糕 糕 糕 糕

搞

gǎo 搞好生产、搞球票、搞垮

✎ 13 画
部首 扌
左右
部 搞

搞 搞 搞 搞 搞 搞 搞 搞 搞 搞 搞 搞 搞

稿

gǎo 初稿、稿件　⤳ 禾的中间一竖不带钩，末笔改点。

✎ 15 画
部首 禾
左右
部 稿

稿 稿 稿 稿 稿 稿 稿 稿 稿 稿 稿
稿 稿 稿 稿

告

gào 转告、告假、告一段落、告辞、控告　⤳ 上部牛的中间一竖下端不出头。

✎ 7 画
部首 口
上下
部 告

告 告 告 告 告 告 告

gē 堂哥、老大哥　⤳ 上部可的末笔去钩改竖。

✎ 10 画
部首 一
上下
部 哥
下

哥 哥 哥 哥 哥
哥 哥 哥 哥 哥

gē 胳膊　⤳ 右上是夂不是夊。

✎ 10 画
部首 月
左右
部 胳

胳 胳 胳 胳 胳
胳 胳 胳 胳 胳

国家机关以普通话和规范汉字为公务用语用字。

学校及其他教育机构以普通话和规范汉字为基本的教育教学用语用字。

公共服务行业以规范汉字为基本的服务用字。提倡公共服务行业以普通话为服务用语。

信息处理和信息技术产品中使用的国家通用语言文字应当符合国家的规范和标准。

——《中华人民共和国国家通用语言文字法》

搁、阁的门，起笔丶嵌在第二笔丨和第三笔丁之间。各的上边是夂不是夊。

（鴿） gē 信鸽、鸽子

☞ 合的第二笔改点。鸟5画，第一画丿、第二画乛不连成一笔；第四画乙不分为两笔。

✎ 11 画
部首 鸟部
结构 左 右

鸽 鸽鸽鸽鸽鸽鸽鸽鸽鸽鸽鸽

（擱） gē 搁放、搁置／gé 搁得住

✎ 12 画
部首 扌部
结构 左 右

搁 搁搁搁搁搁搁搁搁搁搁搁

gē 切割、分割、割爱 ☞ 害的中间是丰，竖笔上下两端出头。

✎ 12 画
部首 刂部
结构 左 右

割 割割割割割割割割割割割割

立刀来除害，毒瘤靠它开；
杀猪又宰羊，把肉分成块；
夏秋丰收图，全靠它劐裁。
字谜

gē 歌唱、歌曲、民歌 ☞ 左上的可，末笔去钩改竖。

✎ 14 画
部首 欠部
结构 左 右

歌 歌歌歌歌歌歌歌歌歌歌歌歌歌

gé 皮革、改革、革职

☞ 廿4画，第二画竖、第四画横不连成一笔。

✎ 9 画
部首 革部
结构 上 下

革 革革革革革革革革革

古字形像整治、展示兽皮。
革（金文）

（閣） gé 闺阁、楼阁、内阁

☞ 左上右包围结构。

✎ 9 画
部首 门部
结构 半包围

阁 阁阁阁阁阁阁阁阁阁

gé 方格、格式、品格、格斗

☞ 木的中间一竖不带钩，末笔改点。右上是夂不是夊。

✎ 10 画
部首 木部
结构 左 右

格 格格格格格格格格格格

葛

gé 葛麻、毛葛／gě 姓

☞ 艹3画，第三画楷体是撇，宋体是竖。下边的部件5画，不是匈。

✎ 12 画
部首 艹部
结构 上 下

葛 葛葛葛葛葛葛葛葛葛葛葛葛

gé 隔开、相隔

☞ 阝两画，第一画是了，不分为两笔。右下框内是丷，不是半或羊。

✎ 12 画
🔲 左阝部
🔳 左右

隔 隔隔隔隔隔隔隔隔隔隔隔隔

（個）**gè** 三个苹果、个性、小个子/**gě** 自个儿 ~measure word most extensively used~

☞ 竖笔不带钩。

✎ 3 画
🔲 人部
🔳 独体

个 个个个

gè 各位、各执一词 ~each, every~

☞ 左上右包围结构。上部是夂不是夊。

✎ 6 画
🔲 夂部
🔳 半包围

各 各各各各各各

（給）**gěi** 给人欺负了、给奶奶鞠躬/**jǐ** 给予、供给、家给人足

☞ 纟3画，上部是幺。 ~give~

✎ 9 画
🔲 纟部
🔳 左右

给 给给给给给给给给给

gēn 草根、舌根、根源、根据、根治 ~ROOT~

☞ 木的中间一竖不带钩，末笔改点。

✎ 10 画
🔲 木部
🔳 左右

根 根根根根根根根根根根

gēn 脚后跟、跟进、跟天斗、咱俩是谁跟谁 ~follow~

☞ 左下止的末笔改提。

✎ 13 画
🔲 足部
🔳 左右

跟 跟跟跟跟跟跟跟跟跟跟跟跟

gēng 更新、三更半夜/**gèng** 更上一层楼、更难了

~change, replace~

✎ 7 画
🔲 一部
🔳 独体

更 更更更更更更更

gēng 春耕、耕地

☞ 耒，起笔是横不是撇，中间一竖不带钩，末笔改点。

✎ 10 画
🔲 耒部
🔳 左右

耕 耕耕耕耕耕耕耕耕耕耕

更换一种造字法，另造笔画简易的会意字，是汉字简化的一种方法，如"體"（形声字）简化作"体"（会意字）。

功、攻的工，末笔改提。

gōng 矿工、工期、工商局、工整

worker, workman

✎ 3 画
囗 工部
囗 独体

圭 工工工

---

gōng 弓箭、琴弓子、弓腰 *bow (and arrow)*

☞ 第三画是㇡，不分为两笔。

✎ 3 画
囗 弓部
囗 独体

书 弓弓弓

---

gōng 公款、办公、公道、公理、公海、公演、公公、公鸡

official business, fair, just

✎ 4 画
囗 八部
囗 上 下

厽 公公公公

---

gōng 功劳、功效、基本功

✎ 5 画
囗 工部
囗 左 右

功 功功功功功

---

gōng 攻打、攻读

☞ 右部是攵不是夂。

✎ 7 画
囗 工部
囗 左 右

攻 攻攻攻攻攻攻攻

---

gōng 供养、供参考／gòng 供佛、上供、口供

lay, confess, own up

✎ 8 画
囗 亻部
囗 左 右

供 供供供供供供供供

---

gōng 宫殿、龙宫、少年宫 *Palace*

☞ 两口分离。

✎ 9 画
囗 宀部
囗 上 下

宫 宫宫宫宫宫宫宫宫宫

---

gōng 恭喜、恭贺

☞ 左上右包围结构。下部是小4画，不是小或氺。

✎ 10 画
囗 心部
囗 半包围

恭 恭恭恭恭恭恭恭恭恭恭

gōng 鞠躬、躬身
☞ 身的末笔上端不出头。弓3画，第三画勾不分为两笔。

✎ 10 画　□ 身部　⊠ 左　右

躬 躬躬躬躬躬躬躬躬躬躬

(鞏) gǒng 巩固
☞ 工的末笔改提。

✎ 6 画　□ 工部　⊠ 左　右

巩 巩巩巩巩巩

gòng 共事、共性、共管、共计　一共 -altogether

✎ 6 画　□ 八部　⊠ 上　下

共 共共共共共共

古字形像两手同持
木棍。(金文)

(貢) gòng 贡献、进贡
☞ 贝的第二画㇆不带钩。

✎ 7 画　□ 工部　⊠ 上　下

贡 贡贡贡贡贡贡贡

gōu 勾销、勾画、勾结／gòu 勾当
☞ 上右包围结构。

✎ 4 画　□ 勹部　⊠ 半包围

勾 勾勾勾勾

包围结构的字，如果是
左上右包围的，被包围
部件要稍向上靠，避免
空荡荡地吊在下边。包
围的外框，上两肩要
"开"，下两脚要"合"，
传统术语叫"开两肩"，
如"罔、同、网"
等。

(溝) gōu 排水沟、壕沟

✎ 7 画　□ 氵部　⊠ 左　右

沟 沟沟沟沟沟沟沟

(鉤) gōu 衣钩、钩取、竖弯钩、打钩
☞ 共5画，第二画是横，不是点；第五画是乚，不分为两笔。

✎ 9 画　□ 钅部　⊠ 左　右

钩 钩钩钩钩钩钩钩钩钩

gǒu 狼狗、狮子狗

✎ 8 画　□ 犭部　⊠ 左　右

狗 狗狗狗狗狗狗狗

（構） gòu 构图、构思

☞ 木的中间一竖不带钩，末笔改点。

✎ 8 画
▣ 木 部
◿ 左 右

构 构构构构构构构构

（購） gòu 购买、采购

☞ 贝的第二画﹁不带钩。

✎ 8 画
▣ 贝 部
◿ 左 右

购 购购购购购购购购

gòu 够吃了、天够冷的 ☞ 多的两夕写在一条中轴线上。

✎ 11 画
▣ 夕 部
◿ 左 右

够够够够够够
够够够够够

gū 估计、估价／gù 估衣

✎ 7 画
▣ 亻 部
◿ 左 右

估 估估估估估估估

gū 孤儿、孤单

☞ 子3画，第一画是一、第二画是亅，不连成一笔；末笔改提。右部是瓜不是爪。

✎ 8 画
▣ 子 部
◿ 左 右

孤 孤孤孤孤孤孤孤孤

gū 姑妈、小姑子、姑娘、尼姑

☞ 女的横笔右端不出头。

✎ 8 画
▣ 女 部
◿ 左 右

姑 姑姑姑姑姑姑姑姑

gū 无辜、辜负

☞ 下部是辛不是幸。

✎ 12 画
▣ 辛 部
◿ 上 下

辜 辜辜辜辜辜辜辜辜辜辜辜

gǔ 古代、考古、古书

✎ 5 画
▣ 十 部
◿ 上 下

古 古古古古古

具有两个或两个以上的读音，而不同的读音记录的是同一个字义，这样的字是异读字。其来源主要有三：一是文白异读，如"跃"文读是yuè，白读是yào；二是方音影响，如"质"本读zhì，又读为zhǐ；三是误读，如"档"应读dàng，误读为dǎng。主管部门对异读词进行审音。1985年发布的《普通话异读词审音表》共审定847个异读字的读音。定为"统读"的583字，有31字保留了文白异读。

(*穀) gǔ 山谷、*五谷丰登、*稻谷　☞ 左上右包围结构。

valley. gorge; cereal, grain

谷谷谷

✎ 7 画
☐ 谷 部
☒ 半包围

谷 谷谷谷谷

一个字内有几个笔画都是捺的，书法上讲究要"减捺"或叫"避重(chóng)捺"，如"黍"是上捺避下捺，"食"是下捺避上捺，"餐"是上下两捺避中间的捺。

gǔ 股骨、两股绳子、炒股
　☞ 右上不是几，末笔不带钩。

✎ 8 画
☐ 月 部
☒ 左右

股股股股股股股股

gǔ 骨肉相连、骨气、伞骨/gū 骨朵儿、骨碌
　☞ 第三画是乛，不分为两笔。月的起笔改竖。

✎ 9 画
☐ 骨 部
☒ 上下

骨骨骨骨骨骨骨骨骨

gǔ 小鼓、鼓掌、鼓动、鼓腮帮子
　☞ 左上是士不是土。左下末笔改捺。

✎ 13 画
☐ 鼓 部
☒ 左右

鼓鼓鼓鼓鼓鼓鼓鼓鼓鼓鼓鼓鼓

古字形像手拿槌击鼓。
（金文）（甲文）

gù 坚固、固体、顽固、固守、固然
　☞ 全包围结构。

✎ 8 画
☐ 囗 部
☒ 包围

固固固固固固固固

gù 缘故、事故、故意、故乡、病故
　☞ 右部是攵不是夂。

✎ 9 画
☐ 攵 部
☒ 左右

故故故故故故故故

(顧) gù 左顾右盼、顾客、顾此失彼
　☞ 左下是巳，不是已、巳或己，它的末笔改竖提。

✎ 10 画
☐ 页 部
☒ 左右

顾顾顾顾顾顾顾顾顾顾

guā 瓜果、西瓜、南瓜
　☞ 中部两画：竖提、点，不分为三笔。

✎ 5 画
☐ 瓜 部
☒ 独体

瓜瓜瓜瓜瓜

(*颳) guā 刮胡子、搜刮、*刮风
☞ 舌的起笔是撇不是横。
8画 舌 左右
刮 刮刮刮刮刮刮刮刮

guà 悬挂、挂念、挂着笑容、挂号
9画 扌 左右
挂 挂挂挂挂挂挂挂挂

guāi 乖巧、乖孩子
☞ 对称结构。北的第三画是提，第四画是撇，都不是横。
8画 丿 对称
乖 乖乖乖乖乖乖乖

guǎi 拐杖、一瘸一拐、拐弯、拐骗
8画 扌 左右
拐 拐拐拐拐拐拐拐

龙字家族成员多，读音相近义不同。两人挨近叫靠拢，不闻声响叫耳聋。月光不明叫朦胧，田间小路叫垄。草木繁茂叫蓊茏，竹编笼子叫竹笼。精巧细致叫玲珑，甘肃简称叫陇。

guài 怪物、鬼怪、大惊小怪、责怪
8画 忄 左右
怪 怪怪怪怪怪怪怪怪

(關) guān 关闭、关门、关口、海关、难关、关键、关心
6画 丷 上下
关 关关关关关关

用简单的记号代替原来比较复杂的部件，是汉字简化的一种方法，如用记号"又"代替原先的音符"巠"，把"鷄"简化作"鸡"；用记号"×"代替原先的意符"品"，把"區"简化作"区"。

(觀) guān 观察、外观、乐观 /guàn 道观
☞ 又的末笔改点。
6画 又 左右
观 观观观观观观

guān 官价、官员、器官
8画 宀 上下
官 官官官官官官官官

灌、罐的艹3画，第三画楷体是撇，宋体是竖，只覆盖右半。右下是隹不是住。

guān 衣冠、花冠/guàn 冠军、夺冠
上部是冖不是宀。

✎ 9 画
⿰ 一 上 部 下
⺍ 冠 冠 冠 冠 冠 冠 冠 冠 冠

(館) guǎn 宾馆、大使馆、博物馆、饭馆
饣3画，第二画是㇇，不是点；第三画是㇈，不分为两笔。

✎ 11 画
⿰ 饣 部
⺍ 左 右
馆 馆 馆 馆 馆 馆 馆 馆 馆 馆 馆

guǎn 双簧管、钢管、电子管、管理、管吃管住、管保

✎ 14 画
⿱ 竹 部
⺍ 上 下
管 管 管 管 管 管 管
管 管 管 管 管 管 管

《康熙字典》
附有"辨似"一
栏，分"二字相似、
三字相似、四字相似、
五字相似"，说明"笔画
近似，音义显别，毫厘
之间，最易混淆"。
总计收900来
个形近字。

(貫) guàn 贯通、籍贯
上部是毌不是母。贝的第二画㇆不带钩。

✎ 8 画
⿱ 贝 部
⺍ 上 下
贯 贯 贯 贯 贯 贯 贯 贯 贯

(慣) guàn 习惯、娇惯
贯，上部是毌不是母。贝的第二画㇆不带钩。

✎ 11 画
⿰ 忄 部
⺍ 左 右
惯 惯 惯 惯 惯 惯 惯 惯 惯 惯 惯

灌

guàn 灌溉、灌暖壶

灌 灌 灌 灌 灌 灌 灌 灌 灌 灌
灌 灌 灌 灌 灌 灌 灌 灌 灌

✎ 20 画
⿰ 氵 部
⺍ 左 右

罐

guàn 罐子、盆盆罐罐
缶的第五画改竖提。

✎ 23 画
⿰ 缶 部
⺍ 左 右
罐 罐 罐 罐 罐 罐 罐 罐 罐 罐
罐 罐 罐 罐 罐 罐 罐 罐 罐 罐 罐 罐

guāng 光线、光明、光荣、光临、光阴、
溜光、吃光、光头、光说不做

✎ 6 画
⿱ 小 部
⺍ 上 下
光 光 光 光 光 光 光

古字形像人的头顶有火
光照耀。（金文）
（甲文）

light moonlight   ray, sunshine

广

(廣) guǎng 宽广、广泛、两广

broad, vast, extensive

✎ 3　画独
部件
四　广独　体
 广 广 广

中国国家标准《信息交换用汉字编码字符集·基本集》(GB2312-80)收6763个汉字，分为两级：第一级常用汉字3755个，第二级次常用汉字3008个。

归

(歸) guī 归国、归还、归并、归属

☞ 左部是一竖一撇，不是两竖。右部是彐，中间一横右端不出头。

✎ 5　画　部件
彐　左　右
 归 归 归 归 归 归

go back to, return

龟

(龜) guī 乌龟、龟龄、龟缩

☞ 下边电的乚上端不出头。

✎ 7　画　部件
龟　上　下
 龟 龟 龟 龟 龟 龟 龟

古字形像乌龟。✿（金文）⚓（甲文）

规

(規) guī 圆规、法规、规划、规劝

☞ 夫的末笔改点。

✎ 8　画　部件
见　左　右
 规 规 规 规 规 规 规 规

轨

(軌) guī 轨道、铁轨、越轨

rail, track, order

☞ 车的下边一横改提，笔顺改先竖后提。右部是九不是丸。

✎ 6　画　部件
车　左　右
 轨 轨 轨 轨 轨 轨

鬼

guī 鬼神、吸血鬼、捣鬼、鬼鬼祟祟、机灵鬼

☞ 第六画从白中直接撇下，不分为两笔。右下有厶。

✎ 9　画　部件
鬼　独　体
 鬼 鬼 鬼 鬼 鬼 鬼 鬼 鬼 鬼

柜

(櫃) guì 书柜、保险柜

cupboard, cabinet

☞ 木的中间一竖不带钩，末笔改点。巨的末笔是乚，不分为两笔。

✎ 8　画　部件
木　左　右
 柜 柜 柜 柜 柜 柜 柜 柜

贵

(貴) guì 昂贵、贵宾、珍贵、贵姓

expensive, costly, valuable

☞ 贝的第二画冂不带钩。

✎ 9　画　部件
贝　上　下
 贵 贵 贵 贵 贵 贵 贵 贵 贵

guì 桂花、肉桂

☞ 木的中间一竖不带钩，末笔改点。

✎ 10 画
⊞ 木 部
◁ 左右

桂 桂桂桂桂桂桂桂桂桂桂

---

guì 下跪、跪拜

☞ 左下止的末笔改提。右下是巳，不是已、已或己。

✎ 13 画
⊞ 足 部
◁ 左右

跪 跪跪跪跪跪跪跪跪跪跪跪跪

---

gǔn 翻滚、滚开、滚热

☞ 中间是厶不是口。

✎ 13 画
⊞ 氵 部
◁ 左右

滚 滚滚滚滚滚滚滚滚滚滚滚滚

---

gùn 棍子、木棍、赌棍

☞ 木的中间一竖不带钩，末笔改点。比，第二画是乚，不分为两笔；右边是比不是匕。

✎ 12 画
⊞ 木 部
◁ 左右

棍 棍棍棍棍棍棍棍棍棍棍棍

（鍋） guō 高压锅、烟袋锅

☞ 钅5画，第二画是横，不是点；第五画是竖提，不分为两笔。

✎ 12 画
⊞ 钅 部
◁ 左右

锅 锅锅锅锅锅锅锅锅锅锅锅

（國） guó 祖国、国歌、国画

☞ 全包围结构。

✎ 8 画
⊞ 口 部
◁ 包围

国 国国国国国国国国

古字形像用武器保卫邑外四界。⫶ (金文)

---

guǒ 水果、前因后果、果真、果断

second part appui

✎ 8 画
⊞ 丨 部
◁ 独体

果 果果果杲杲果果果

---

guǒ 包裹、裹挟   ☞ 果嵌在衣中。果的末笔改点。

✎ 14 画
⊞ 亠 部
◁ 上下

裹 裹裹裹裹裹裹裹
裹裹裹裹裹裹裹

（過） guò 过河、过节、过门、过秤、过期、过错／guō 姓过
　左下包围结构。辶3画，第二画楷体是乀，宋体是乀。

✎ 6 画
辶 部
半包围

过 过过过过过过

pass, cross, go through a process

hā 哈气、哈哈大笑、点头哈腰／hǎ 哈巴狗、哈达

breath out, laugh heartily

✎ 9 画
口 部
左 右

哈 哈哈哈哈哈哈哈哈

hái 孩子、男孩儿、女孩儿　*child*
　子3画，第二画→，第三画丿不连成一笔，末笔改提。

✎ 9 画
子 部
左 右

孩 孩孩孩孩孩孩孩孩

hǎi 海浪、海带、林海、夸海口

Sea or big lake
extra large or of great capacity
　母5画，第一画乚、第二画乛都不分为两笔。

✎ 10 画
氵部
左 右

海 海海海海海海海海海

hài 害人、有益无害、病虫害、害鸟、杀害、害病、害怕　*evil, harm,*
calamity, disaster
　中间是丯，竖笔上下两端出头。 *— due harm to*

✎ 10 画
宀 部
上 下

害 害害害害害害害害害 *— impair*

hán 含块糖、包含、含笑
keep in the mouth, contain (nurse)
　上部是今不是令。

✎ 7 画
人 部
上 下

含 含含含含含含含

"临帖"的
"帖"，这里做
样本、范本的代称。
临学范本，不是为和
它完全一样，不是要
写成为自己手边帖
上字的复印本，而是
以范本为镜子，练熟
自己手下的技巧。
　—— 启功《论书
随笔》

hán 寒风、寒假、胆寒、贫寒

✎ 12 画
宀 部
上 下

寒
寒寒寒寒寒寒
寒寒寒寒寒寒

hǎn 叫喊、我喊她

✎ 12 画
口 部
左 右

喊 喊喊喊喊喊喊喊喊喊喊喊

(漢) hàn 汉族、汉字、男子汉

The Han nationality

✎ 5 画
☐ 又 部
△ 左 右

汉 汉汉汉汉汉

hàn 汗水、出汗 /hán 可(kè)汗(古代鲜卑等族君主的称号)

sweat, perspiration

✎ 6 画
☐ 氵 部
△ 左 右

汗 汗汗汗汗汗汗

hàn 干旱、抗旱、旱烟、旱路

dry spell draught

✎ 7 画
☐ 日 部
△ 上 下

旱 旱旱旱旱旱旱旱

háng 航行、航空、航海

boat ship

☞ 舟的横笔改提，右端不出头。

✎ 10 画
☐ 舟 部
△ 左 右

航 航航航航航航航航航航

háo 毫毛、挥毫作画、毫米、毫无办法

fine long hair, milli?
(used in negative...in the least)

✎ 11 画
☐ 毛 部
△ 上 下

毫 毫毫毫毫毫毫毫毫毫毫毫

a person of outstanding talent

háo 豪杰、豪放、巧取豪夺、自豪

豪豪豪豪豪豪豪豪豪豪豪

✎ 14 画
☐ 豕 部
△ 上 下

豪 豪豪豪

hǎo 美好、病好了、好多人、好办、好看 /hào 好客、好哭

☞ 女的横笔右端不出头。子的第一笔是 乛，第二笔是 ），不连成一笔。

good

✎ 6 画
☐ 女 部
△ 左 右

好 好好好好好好

(號) hào 吹号、口号、称号、号码、型号 /háo 呼号、哀号

☞ 下部是 丂，丂上端不出头。

wail, cry

✎ 5 画
☐ 口 部
△ 上 下

号 号号号号号

行书是草书向楷书演变过程中的一种中介书体。行书的最大特点是用连笔和省笔，却不用或少用草化符号，较多地保留正体字的可识性结构，从而达到既能简易快速书写又能通俗易识的实用目的。通俗易识是行书的文化个性，雅俗共赏是行书的艺术个性。这两性决定了行书的盛行不衰。行书始终是世俗、实用和艺术相交融的一种书体，这是它始终盛行于篆、隶、楷、草诸体消长之间的根本原因。

hào 消耗、噩耗、耗时间 *Consume cost*

☞ 耒的起笔是横不是撇，末笔改点。

✎ 10 画
部 耒
部 左 右

耗 耗耗耗耗耗耗耗耗耗耗耗

---

hào 浩荡、浩大 *great vast grand*

☞ 右上牛的竖笔下端不出头。

✎ 10 画
部 氵
左 右

浩 浩浩浩浩浩浩浩浩浩

---

hē 喝茶、喝醉 /hè 喝彩 *to DRink*

☞ 右下部件5画，不是匂。

✎ 12 画
部 口
左 右

喝 喝喝喝喝喝喝喝喝喝喝喝

---

hé 禾苗、禾穗 *standing grain*

☞ 中间一竖不带钩。

✎ 5 画
部 禾
独 体

禾 禾禾禾禾禾

古字形像庄稼。
𥝍（金文）𥝌（甲文）

(*閤) hé 合眼、合并、合唱、*合家 /gě 10合等于1升

Close, shut, close, combine

✎ 6 画
部 人
上 下

合 合合合合合合

---

denoting interrogation - who, what time, when what place, where?

hé 为何、从何说起、何不试试

✎ 7 画
部 亻
左 右

何 何何何何何何何

---

denote

hé 和谐、和棋、你和她 /hè 应和 /huó 和面 /huò 搅和 /hú 和牌

☞ 禾，中间一竖不带钩，末笔改点。

and, with

✎ 8 画
部 禾
左 右

和 和和和和和和和和

---

hé 黄河、运河

✎ 8 画
部 氵
左 右

河 河河河河
河河河河

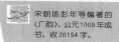

宋朝陈彭年等编著的《广韵》，公元1008年成书，收26194字。

hé 荷花／hè 荷枪实弹、荷重

☞ 共3画，第三画楷体是撇，宋体是竖。

✎ 10 画
⊟ 艹 部
⊠ 上 下

荷　荷荷荷荷荷荷荷荷荷荷荷

hé 枣核、细胞核、核武器、考核／hú 杏核儿

☞ 木的中间一竖不带钩，末笔改点。

✎ 10 画
⊟ 木 部
⊠ 左 右

核　核核核核核核核核核核核

hé 饭盒、火柴盒

✎ 11 画
⊟ 人 部
⊠ 上 下

盒　盒盒盒盒盒盒
盒　盒盒盒盒盒

汉字的符号有三类：(1) 图形体，如金文、甲骨文、大篆、小篆；(2) 笔画体，如隶书、楷书；(3) 流线体，如草书、行书。

(贺) hè 庆贺、贺信　congratulate

☞ 贝的第二画乛不带钩。

✎ 9 画
⊟ 贝 部
⊠ 上 下

贺　贺贺贺贺贺贺贺贺贺

hēi 黑斑、黑夜、起早贪黑、手黑心毒、黑市　black, dark　secret, shady

☞ 上边部件8画，不是里。

✎ 12 画
⊟ 黑 部
⊠ 上 下

黑　黑黑黑黑黑黑黑黑黑黑黑黑

hén 伤痕、泪痕　mark, trace

☞ 上左包围结构。右下是艮不是良。

✎ 11 画
⊟ 疒 部
⊠ 半包围

痕　痕痕痕痕痕痕痕痕痕痕

hěn 很快、好得很　very, quite　awfully

✎ 9 画
⊟ 彳 部
⊠ 左 右

很　很很很很很很很很

hěn 凶狠、狠狠打击　ruthless, relentless

✎ 9 画
⊟ 犭 部
⊠ 左 右

狠狠狠狠狠
狠　狠狠狠狠

宋朝丁度等编著的《集韵》，公元1039年成书，收53525字。

恨 hèn 仇恨、悔恨　*hate, be unusually stick w/*

恨恨恨恨恨
恨恨恨恨

✎ 9 画
⿰ 忄 部
⿰ 左 右

殷商金文，其规范美、装饰美、象形美远远超过甲骨文，加上字大、笔画厚重，大大增加了欣赏性。

恒 héng 恒温、持之以恒　*permanent, lasting eternal*

恒恒恒恒
恒恒恒恒恒

✎ 9 画
⿰ 忄 部
⿰ 左 右

横 héng 横排、横跨、血肉横飞、横行霸道／hèng 蛮横、横财　*harsh & unreasonable*

☞ 木的中间一竖不带钩，末笔改点。

横横横横
横横横横横横横横横横横

✎ 15 画
⿰ 木 部
⿰ 左 右

衡 héng 衡器、衡量、平衡　☞ 中间下部的大，末笔改点。

衡衡衡衡衡衡衡衡衡衡
衡衡衡衡衡

✎ 16 画
⿰ 彳 部
⿰ 左 右

（轟）轰 hōng 轰炸、轰走、轰的一声　*bang, boom, rumble*
☞ 左下的又末笔改点。

轰轰轰轰轰轰轰轰

✎ 8 画
⿱ 车 部
⿱ 上 下

哄 hōng 哄堂大笑／hǒng 哄骗、哄孩子／hòng 起哄　*fool, coax, humor*

哄哄哄哄哄
哄哄哄哄

✎ 9 画
⿰ 口 部
⿰ 左

汉字有几千年的历史，发展到后来，字数越来越多，笔画也越来越繁复，给认读、书写和印刷带来不便，需要对汉字进行整理、简化。事实上，早在政府统一地有组织地进行简化以前，群众在应用中已在自行简化，不过印刷体和手写体同时并存，而手写体又有各地区和各行业的简化方式的不同，形成不少的混乱罢了。
——胡乔木《乔木文丛》

烘 hōng 烘干、烘托　☞ 火的末笔改点。

烘烘烘烘烘
烘烘烘烘烘

✎ 10 画
⿰ 火 部
⿰ 左 右

（紅）红 hóng 红色、红白喜事、红人、又红又专　*red, popular, revolution*
☞ 纟3画，上部不是幺。　*successful*

红红红红红红　*RED*

✎ 6 画
⿰ 纟 部
⿰ 左 右

喉、猴的右边是侯不是候。右上的部件是ㄱ两画，不是工。

great grand, magnificent

hóng 宏大、宽宏

7 画
宀部
上下

宏宏宏宏
宏宏宏

专家列出的典型的顽固性别字有下面36个：狠（很）、材（才）、块（快）、钉（丁）、睛（晴）、圆（园）、气（气）、理（里）、幸（辛）、极（级）、傍（旁）、稼（家）、倒（到）、喝（渴）、那（哪）、座（坐）、漫（慢）、买（卖）、己（已）、棵（颗）、篮（蓝）、支（只）、做（作）、常（长）、得（地）、已（以）、意（义）、象（向）、戴（带）、查（察）、再（在）、相（象）、拔（拨）、坏（环）、没（设）、些（此）。

hóng 彩虹 / jiàng 天边出虹了

9 画
虫部
左右

虹虹虹虹虹
虹虹虹虹

hóng 山洪、洪福齐天 *big, vast*

9 画
氵部
左右

洪洪洪洪洪
洪洪洪洪

hóu 喉头、喉咙

12 画
口部
左右

喉喉喉喉喉喉喉喉喉喉喉

hóu 猴子、猿猴

12 画
犭部
左右

猴猴猴猴猴猴猴猴猴猴

hǒu 怒吼、狮吼龙啸

子3画，第一画一、第二画乚不连成一笔，末笔横改提。

7 画
口部
左右

吼吼吼吼吼吼吼

（*後）hòu 皇后、*先来后到、*后背 *empress, queen afterwards*

上左包围结构。

6 画
厂部
半包围

后后后后后后

字义为皇后，转换为繁体时仍写成后；字义表时间、空间先后时，繁体为後。

hòu 厚嘴唇、厚礼、厚此薄彼、深情厚谊、宽厚

上左包围结构。右下为上曰(不是白)下子。子的第一画一、第二画乚不连成一笔。

厂部
半包围

厚厚厚厚厚厚厚厚厚

hòu 问候、候车、气候、候鸟、火候

☞ 左右部件之间有短竖。右上的部件两画，不是工。

✎ 10 画
部 亻 左　右

候　候候候候候候候候候候

---

hū 出乎意料、合乎常情 *(expressing doubt or conjecture)*

✎ 5 画
部 丿 独体

乎　乎乎乎乎乎

---

hū 呼吸、高呼、呼唤

breathout, exhale, shout, cry out

✎ 8 画
部 口 左　右

呼　呼呼呼呼呼呼呼呼

---

hū 忽视、忽然、忽高忽低

neglect, overlook, ignore

☞ 心的第二画楷体是㇃(卧钩)，宋体是乚(竖弯钩)。

✎ 8 画
部 心 上　下

忽　忽忽忽忽忽忽忽忽

---

hú 狐狸、狐皮

☞ 右部是瓜不是爪。

✎ 8 画
部 犭 左　右

狐　狐狐狐狐狐狐狐

反犬最馋瓜，长条长尾巴；
给鸡去拜年，把鸡当傻瓜。

字谜

(*鬍) hú 胡人、胡萝卜、胡闹、*胡须、胡同

non-Han nationalists living in North & West in ancient times

húluábo - cucumber

✎ 9 画
部 十 左　右

胡　胡胡胡胡胡胡胡胡

(壺) hú 茶壶、酒壶 *Kettle, pot*

☞ 上部是士不是土，下部是业不是亚。

古字形像一把壶。
(金文)壺 (小篆)壺

✎ 10 画
部 士 上　下

壶　壶壶壶壶壶壶壶壶壶壶

---

hú 湖泊、湖水 *lake*

✎ 12 画
部 氵 左　右

湖　湖湖湖湖湖湖湖湖湖湖

hú 蝴蝶

蝴蝴蝴蝴蝴蝴蝴蝴蝴蝴蝴
蝴蝴蝴蝴

🖊 15 画
🔲 虫部
◩ 左 右

hú 糊信封、浆糊／hù 芝麻糊／hū 糊墙缝　☞ 米的中间一竖不带钩，末笔改点。

糊糊糊糊糊糊糊糊糊糊
糊糊糊糊

🖊 15 画
🔲 米部
◩ 左 右

hǔ 老虎、虎将　☞ 上左包围结构。右下是几不是儿。

虎虎虎虎
虎虎虎虎

🖊 8 画
🔲 虍部
◩ 半包围

上下结构的字，如果上半部的笔画少、下半部的笔画多，应该使上半部收得紧一些，所占的空间小一些，以免使全字显得空旷、发虚，如"孟、癸"等。

hù 互相、互助　mutual

☞ 第二画是L，第三画是7，都不分为两笔。

互互互互

🖊 4 画
🔲 一部
◩ 独体

hù 夜不闭户、户口、个体户　door, household, family

户户户户

🖊 4 画
🔲 户部
◩ 独体

古字形像单扇门。
月（甲文）

（護）hù 护航、拥护、祖护　protect, guard, shield, speak in defens

护护护护护护护

🖊 7 画
🔲 扌部
◩ 左 右

huā 采花、火花、纺花、花白、花镜、花招、挂花、花钱　flower, blossoming flower, anything resembly a flower

☞ 丬3画，第三画楷体是撇，宋体是竖。

花花花花花花花

🖊 7 画
🔲 艹部
◩ 上 下

古代钱币上有简体字。汉代的"五铢"钱，有的写成"五朱"。南宋"建炎通宝"，把繁体宝简成上宀下贝。太平天国的钱币把繁体国简成外口内王。

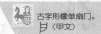

（嘩）huā 水哗哗地流／huá 喧哗

哗哗哗哗哗
哗哗哗哗

🖊 9 画
🔲 口部
◩ 左 右

（華）huá 繁华、华灯、年华、精华、华人 /huà 华山

brilliant, magnificent, splendid, prosperous
flashy, extravagant

6 画
十 上 下
华 华华华化华华

huá 狡猾

12 画
犭 左 右
猾猾猾猾猾猾猾猾猾猾猾

huá 光滑、滑冰、耍滑　*slippery, smooth*

12 画
氵 左 右
滑滑滑滑滑滑滑滑滑滑滑

huà 转化、感化、化缘、化铁炉、化痰、火化、化肥、绿化

change, turn, transfor

4 画
亻 左 右
化化化化

（劃）huà 划分、策划、划拨 /huá 划船、划算、划玻璃

differentiate

6 画
戈 左 右
划划划划划划

（畫）huà 画圈、油画、描画、笔画

draw, paint, make a sketch

☞ 左下右包围结构。凵两画，第一画凵不分为两笔。

8 画
凵 部
半包围
画画画画画画画画

（話）huà 说话、对话　*word, remark*

☞ 讠两画，第二画乛，不分为两笔或三笔。

8 画
讠 部
左 右
话话话话话话话话

（懷）huái 敞胸露怀、怀旧、怀恨、情怀、怀胎

bosom, keep in mind, cherish

☞ 不的竖笔不带钩。末笔是点不是捺。

7 画
忄 左
怀怀怀怀怀怀怀

上中下结构的字，三个部件的笔画数、形态各有特点，就不要故意把三个部件写得同样大小，避免刻板。如"霄"，其"雨""小""月"三个部件的笔画数有多有少、宽窄大小不同，就应该使它们的形态有所变化，像"霄""素"等字，结体较长，要特别注意间架的端正。

坏、还、环的不，竖笔不带钩，末笔是点不是捺。

huái 槐树、槐花

☞ 木的竖笔不带钩，末笔改点。鬼的第六画从自中直接撇下，不分为两笔，右下有厶。

✎ 13 画
部 木部
囗 左右

槐 槐槐槐槐槐槐槐槐槐槐槐槐

（壞）huài 破坏、坏人、使坏、累坏了

☞ 土的末笔改提。

✎ 7 画
部 土部
囗 左右

坏 坏坏坏坏坏坏坏

（歡）huān 欢庆、越学越欢

☞ 又的末笔改点。

（xǐhuān）
（to like）

✎ 6 画
部 又部
囗 左右

欢 欢欢欢欢欢欢

（還）huán 还原、归还、还礼／hái 还在医院、还问了什么、比想象的还好

☞ 左下包围结构。辶3画，第二画楷体是乛，宋体是乁。

✎ 7 画
部 辶部
囗 半包围

还 还还还还还还还

（環）huán 花环、环行、环节

☞ 王的末笔改提。

✎ 8 画
部 王部
囗 左右

环 环环环环环环环环

（緩）huān 缓解、缓慢、缓刑、缓过气来

☞ 纟3画，上部不是幺。

✎ 12 画
部 纟部
囗 左右

缓 缓缓缓缓缓缓缓缓缓缓缓缓

huàn 幻觉、幻术

☞ 右部是乛不是力。

✎ 4 画
部 幺部
囗 左

幻 幻幻幻幻

上下结构的字，如果上下两部分的笔画数相近，应该使上面部分写得稍窄小、下面略微宽大，收到下面托住上面的效果，如"皇"等字。

huàn 交换、换衣服

☞ 右下像央，但撇笔的上端不出头。

✎ 10 画
部 扌部
囗 左右

换 换换换换换换换换换

huàn 呼唤、唤醒

☞ 右like央，但撇笔的上端不出头。

✎ 10　画
口部
左　右

唤唤唤唤唤唤唤唤唤唤

huàn 忧患、后患、患病

☞ 心的第二画楷体是乀(卧钩)，宋体是乚(竖弯钩)。

✎ 11　画
心部
上　下

患患患患患患患患患患

huāng 荒芜、开荒、荒年、荒地、荒废、荒诞

✎ 9　画
⺾部
上　下

荒荒荒荒荒荒荒荒荒

> 草下亡，川上葬：不像川，弯儿长。
> 乱草狂，不长粮：无人烟，太凄凉。
> **字谜**

huāng 慌乱、闲得慌

✎ 12　画
忄部
左　右

慌慌慌慌慌慌慌慌慌慌慌

huáng 女皇、皇宫

✎ 9　画
白部
上　下

皇皇皇皇皇皇皇皇皇

huáng 黄色、黄河、蛋黄、买卖黄了

☞ 中部是由不是田。

✎ 11　画
黄部
上　下

黄黄黄黄黄黄黄黄黄黄黄

huáng 辉煌、明星煌煌

☞ 火的末笔改点。

✎ 13　画
火部
左　右

煌煌煌煌煌煌煌煌煌煌煌

晃

huǎng 晃眼、虚晃一枪 /**huàng** 摇头晃脑、晃悠

✎ 10　画
日部
上　下

晃晃晃晃晃晃晃晃晃晃

挥、辉的车，第二画是乚，不分为两笔。谎的荒，中部是亡不是云。

（謊） huǎng 撒谎、谎言

☞ 讠两画，第二画乚不分为两笔或三笔。艹3画，第三画楷体是撇，宋体是竖。

◈ 11 画
▯ 讠 部
◹ 左 右

谎 谎谎谎谎谎谎谎谎谎谎谎

---

huī 烟灰、灰尘、抹灰、银灰、心灰意冷

☞ 上左包围结构。

◈ 6 画
▯ 火 部
◹ 半 包围

灰 灰灰灰灰灰灰

（揮） huī 挥鞭、挥泪、挥发

◈ 9 画
▯ 扌 部
◹ 左 右

挥 挥挥挥挥挥 挥挥挥挥

右边结构的字，如果两边都比较长，笔画也相近，要上下齐平、左右并立、右边稍宽，如"被、纲、貌"等。

---

huī 恢复原状、气度恢弘、天网恢恢

◈ 9 画
▯ 忄 部
◹ 左 右

恢 恢恢恢恢 恢恢恢恢恢

（輝） huī 余辉、灯火辉煌、交相辉映

☞ 光的末笔改竖提。

◈ 12 画
▯ 小 部
◹ 左 右

辉 辉辉辉辉辉辉辉辉辉辉辉辉

（*迴） huí *回旋、回头、回家、回赠、那是两回事

☞ 全包围结构。

◈ 6 画
▯ 口 部
◹ 包围

回 回回回回回回

---

huǐ 后悔、悔过

☞ 母的第一画乚、第二画冂都不分为两笔。

◈ 10 画
▯ 忄 部
◹ 左 右

悔 悔悔悔悔悔悔悔悔悔

---

huǐ 毁坏、销毁、毁谤

☞ 左上白，左下工。工的末笔改提。右上不是几，末笔不带钩。

◈ 13 画
▯ 殳 部
◹ 左 右

毁 毁毁毁毁毁毁毁毁毁毁毁毁毁

汇　(匯*彙)　huì 汇合、*汇编、*字汇、汇款
　⎯ 末笔是乚，不分为两笔。
　5　画
　氵　部
　左　右　 汇汇汇汇汇

会　(會)　huì 会餐、会客、会议、省会、机会、领会、会开车 /kuài 会计
　⎯ 上左右包围结构。
　6　画
　人　部
　半包围　 会会会会会会

古字形像蒸饭的炊具上有盖扣着，用盖和器相合表示会合。(金文)

绘　(繪)　huì 绘图、描绘
　⎯ 纟3画，上部不是幺。
　9　画
　纟　部
　左　右　 绘绘绘绘绘绘绘绘绘

贿　(賄)　huì 行贿、受贿
　⎯ 贝的第二画┐不带钩。
　10　画
　贝　部
　左　右　 贿贿贿贿贿贿贿贿贿

惠　huì 小恩小惠、互惠、惠顾、贤惠
　12　画
　心　部
　上　下　 惠惠惠惠惠惠惠惠惠惠惠

慧　huì 智慧、聪慧　⎯ 中部是彐，中间一横右端不出头。
　15　画
　心　部
　上　下　 慧慧慧慧慧慧慧慧慧慧慧
慧慧慧

昏　hūn 黄昏、昏花、昏头昏脑、昏迷
　8　画
　氏　部
　上　下　 昏昏昏昏昏昏昏昏

婚　hūn 婚礼、结婚
　⎯ 女的横笔右端不出头。
　11　画
　女　部
　左　右　婚婚婚婚婚婚婚婚婚婚

(渾) hún 浑水、浑身
☞ 车的第二画是乚，不分为两笔。
✎ 9 画
部 氵部
冈 左 右
浑 浑浑浑浑浑浑浑浑浑

hún 灵魂、神魂颠倒、民族魂
☞ 鬼的第六画从白中直接撇下，不分写为两笔。右下有厶。
✎ 13 画
部 鬼部
冈 左 右
魂 魂魂魂魂魂魂魂魂魂魂魂魂

hùn 混杂、蒙混、厮混、混饭吃
☞ 比的第二画是乚，不分为两笔；右边是匕不是匕。
✎ 11 画
部 氵部
冈 左 右
混 混混混混混混混混混混

huó 死去活来、农活儿、活期、活跃、活受罪
☞ 舌的第一画是撇不是横。
✎ 9 画
部 氵部
冈 左 右
活 活活活活活活活活活

huǒ 篝火、火速、发火、恼火、军火、开火、火鸡
✎ 4 画
部 火部
冈 独 体
火 火火火火

古字形像火苗。（甲文）

(*夥) huǒ *伙伴、*散伙、*合伙、伙食
✎ 6 画
部 亻部
冈 左 右
伙 伙伙伙伙伙伙

简体转繁体时，字义是"伙食"的词语，仍写作伙。

huò 或者、或多或少
☞ 上右包围结构。
✎ 8 画
部 戈部
冈 半包围
或 或或或或或或或或

(貨) huò 进货、蠢货、货币
☞ 贝的第二画冂（横折）不带钩。
✎ 8 画
部 贝部
冈 上 下
货 货货货货货货货货

（獲＊穫）huò 捕获、获利、＊收获

☞ 艹 3画，覆盖全字，第三画楷体是撇，宋体是竖。

✎ 10 画　部 艹
▣ 上 下　获　获获获获获获获获获获

（禍）huò 车祸、祸国殃民

☞ 左边是礻不是衤。

✎ 11 画　部 礻
▣ 右　祸　祸祸祸祸祸祸祸祸祸祸

huò 迷惑、惑众

☞ 上下结构。心的第二画楷体是⺄（卧钩），宋体是L（竖弯钩）。

✎ 12 画　部 心
▣ 上 下　惑　惑惑惑惑惑惑惑惑惑惑惑

（撃）jī 击鼓、击剑、攻击、撞击

☞ 凵两画，第一画凵不分为两笔。

✎ 5 画　部 凵
▣ 独　体　击　击击击击击

（飢＊饑）jī 饥寒交迫、＊饥荒

☞ 饣 3画，第二画是乛（横钩），不是点；第三画是㇙（竖提），不分为两笔。

✎ 5 画　部 饣
▣ 左 右　饥　饥饥饥饥饥

jī 垃圾

☞ 土的末笔改提。及的第二画是㇉，不分为两笔。

✎ 6 画　部 土
▣ 左 右　圾　圾圾圾圾圾圾

（機）jī 电视机、机智、机场、危机、机会、机密、心机

☞ 木的中间一竖不带钩，末笔改点。

✎ 6 画　部 木
▣ 左 右　机　机机机机机机

肌 jī 肌肉、三角肌

☞

✎ 6 画　部 月
▣ 左 右　肌　肌肌肌肌肌肌

有的哲学家说，线条比色彩更具有审美性质。汉民族的先民用线条创造了书法艺术，难怪汉字书法艺术具有永恒的魅力。

及、级、极的及，第二画是 ㇇，不分为两笔。

(鷄) jī 火鸡、母鸡、鸡肉　chicken

☞ 又的末笔改点。鸟5画，第一画丿和第二画㇆不连成一笔；第四画㇖不分为两笔。

✎ 7　画
部 又　部
□ 左　右

鸡 | 鸡鸡鸡鸡鸡鸡鸡

(積) jī 积累、积怨

☞ 禾，中间一竖不带钩，末笔改点。

✎ 10　画
部 禾　部
□ 左　右

积 | 积积积积积积积积积积

---

jī 路基、基调

☞ 左上右包围结构。

✎ 11　画
部 土　部
□ 半包围

基 | 基基基基基基基基基基

---

jī 激起、激战、激动、激怒　☞ 右部是攵不是夂。

✎ 16　画
部 氵　部
□ 左　右

激激激激激激激激
激 | 激激激激激激激激

---

jí 望尘莫及、及格、家长及老师

✎ 3　画
部 丿　部
□ 独　体

及 | 及及及

古字形像一只手触到前面的人。

🐎

🀄 (金文)　🀄 (甲文)　🀄 (小篆)

---

jí 逢凶化吉、吉祥

☞ 上部是士不是土。

✎ 6　画
部 土　部
□ 上　下

吉 | 吉吉吉吉吉吉

(級) jí 等级、石级、升级、八级技工

☞ 纟3画，上部不是幺。

✎ 6　画
部 纟　部
□ 左　右

级 | 级级级级级级

古人讲述写字"结体"理论，后人比较熟悉的有唐代欧阳询的《三十六法》和明代李淳(chún)的《大字结构八十四法》。其中有很多传统的书法术语，如上面的笔画盖尽下面的笔画叫"天覆"，下面的笔画载托起上面的笔画叫"地载"，等等。

(極) jí 登峰造极、物极必反、极限、极其、电极

☞ 木的中间一竖不带钩，末笔改点。

✎ 7　画
部 木　部
□ 左

极 | 极极极极极极极

jí 可望不可即、即日、一触即发、非此即彼、即使

☞ 左部艮的末两画改一画、丶(点)。右部是卩不是阝。

✎ 7 画
▣ 卩 部
△ 左 右

即即即即即即即即

---

jí 急转弯、急件、救急、操之过急

☞ 中部是彐,中间一横右端不出头。心的第二画,楷体是丶(卧钩),宋体是乚(竖弯钩)。

✎ 9 画
▣ 心 部
△ 上 下

急急急急急急急急急

字谜
头戴刀形帽,心情如山倒;
看那慌张样,似火烧眉毛。

---

jí 疾驰、疾病、疾苦、疾恶如仇

☞ 上左包围结构。

✎ 10 画
▣ 疒 部
△ 半包围

疾疾疾疾疾疾疾疾疾疾

古字形像腋下中箭。
大(金文) 疾(甲文)

---

jí 集中、文集、上下两集、集市

☞ 上部是隹不是住。木的中间一竖不带钩。

✎ 12 画
▣ 隹 部
△ 上 下

集集集集集集集集集集集

---

jí 书籍、祖籍、学籍

☞ 上部是⺮不是艹。耒的末笔改点。

✎ 20 画
▣ 竹 部
△ 上 下

籍籍籍籍籍籍籍
籍籍籍籍籍籍籍籍籍籍籍籍籍

(*幾) jǐ *几点钟? *十几岁 /jī 茶几、几乎

✎ 2 画
▣ 几 部
△ 独 体

几几

楷体是印刷体中常用的一种字体。它的特点是形体跟手写体基本一致,笔迹挺秀、美观,便于初学文化的读者认读,因而多用来排印识字课本、儿童读物和通俗书刊。如:新华写字字典。

---

jǐ 戊己庚辛、知己知彼

☞ 末笔乚(竖弯钩)跟第二画横相接,不出头。

✎ 3 画
▣ 己 部
△ 独 体

己己己

(擠) jǐ 拥挤、排挤、挤奶

☞ 齐的下部是一撇一竖,不是两竖。

✎ 9 画
▣ 扌 部
△ 左 右

挤挤挤挤挤挤挤挤挤

记、纪、忌的己，末笔乚(竖弯钩)跟第二画横相接，不出头，不是巳或己。

jǐ 脊梁、山脊

☞ 在上右包围结构。月的起笔改竖。

✎ 10 画
☐ 月 部
凵 半包围

脊 脊脊脊脊脊脊脊脊脊脊

(計) jì 统计、设计、妙计、不计报酬、温度计

☞ 讠两画，第二画是乚，不分为两笔或三笔。

✎ 4 画
☐ 讠 部
凵 左右

计 计计计计

(記) jì 记账、惦记、标记、日记

☞ 讠两画，第二画是乚，不分为两笔或三笔。

✎ 5 画
☐ 讠 部
凵 左右

记 记记记记记

有些简化字采用的是同音代替的方法，这样，这些字形对应于繁体字而言，它们是简化字，但它们另一个基本的身分是没有经过简化的传承字形。如"里"，它的基本身分是记录长度单位的"里"和"故里""邻里"的"里"，同时它又是繁体字"裏"（"裏面"）的简化字形。这些简化字还原成繁体字的时候，要根据字义词义准确对应，千万不可张冠李戴，弄出类似"鄰裏"（应为"鄰里"）、"皇後"（应为"皇后"）、"肝髒"（应为"肝臟"）、"復印"（应为"複印"）的笑话。

(紀) jì 军纪、世纪、纪念 / jǐ 姓纪

☞ 纟3画，上部不是幺。

✎ 6 画
☐ 纟 部
凵 左右

纪 纪纪纪纪纪纪

---

jì 演技、技艺

☞ 左部是扌不是木。

Skilled ability; trick

✎ 7 画
☐ 扌 部
凵 左右

技 技技技技技技技

---

jì 猜忌、顾忌、忌口、忌酒

☞ 心的第二画楷体是㇃(卧钩)，宋体是乚(竖弯钩)。

✎ 7 画
☐ 己 部
凵 上下

忌 忌忌忌忌忌忌忌

(際) jì 天际、交际、国际

☞ 阝两画，第一画是乛，不分为两笔。

✎ 7 画
☐ 阝 部
凵 左右

际 际际际际际际际

---

jì 四季、雨季

☞ 禾，中间一竖不带钩。子3画，第一画乛、第二画亅不连成一笔。

✎ 8 画
☐ 禾 部
凵 上下

季 季季季季季季季季

剂 (劑) jì 调剂、防腐剂

左上文的末笔改点。左下是一撇一竖，不是两竖。

8 画　齐 部　左 右

剂　剂剂剂剂剂剂剂剂

迹 jì 足迹、劣迹、古迹

左下包围结构。辶3画，第二画楷体是㇋，宋体是㇇。

9 画　辶 部　半包围

迹　迹迹迹迹迹迹迹迹迹

济 (濟) jì 同舟共济、救济、得济 /jǐ 济济一堂

齐的下部是一撇一竖，不是两竖。

9 画　氵 部　左 右

济　济济济济济济济济济

既 jì 既成事实、既深且急、既然

左部艮的后两画改为一画、(点)。右部不是无。

9 画　无 部　左 右

既　既既既既既既既既既

古字形像吃完扭头的样子，表示完成。(金文) (甲文)

继 (繼) jì 夜以继日、继续

纟3画，上部不是幺。米的末笔改点；左下框是㇗，不分为两笔。

10 画　纟 部　左 右

继　继继继继继继继继继继

寄 jì 寄养、寄居、寄信

大的末笔改点。

11 画　宀 部　上 下

寄　寄寄寄寄寄寄寄寄寄寄寄

绩 (績) jì 绩麻、业绩　纟3画，上部不是幺。贝的第二画㇆不带钩。

11 画　纟 部　左 右

绩　绩绩绩绩绩绩
绩绩绩绩绩

加 jiā 添加、加大、施加、加法

5 画　力 部　左 右

加　加加加加加

"每天要写多少字？"这和每天要吃多少饭的问题一样，每人的食量不同，不能规定一致。总在食欲旺盛时吃，消化吸收也很容易。
——启功《论书随笔》

(夾) jiā 夹击、皮夹、夹缝、夹生 /jiá 夹袄 /gā 夹肢窝

✎ 6 画 部 体
口 一 独

夹 夹 夹 夹 夹 夹 夹

古字形像腋下夹着两人。
杰（金文）**夼**（甲文）

---

jiā 佳节、佳话

佳 佳 佳 佳 佳
佳 佳 佳

字谜
别看此人土又土，
美人堆里把它数。

(*傢) jiā 搬家、成家、东家、科学家、仇家、家兔、百家争鸣、*家具

house,home

家 家 家 家 家 家 家 家 家 家

---

jiā 嘉宾、嘉奖　☞ 上部是士不是土。吉和加之间是丷，不是艹。

嘉 嘉 嘉 嘉 嘉 嘉 嘉
嘉 嘉 嘉 嘉 嘉 嘉 嘉

---

jiǎ 甲等、甲天下、龟甲、指甲、盔甲

甲 甲 甲 甲 甲

写字者，写志也。（写字就是写自己的心意志向）——刘熙载《艺概》

---

jiǎ 假公济私、假定、假使、假牙、打假 /jià 暑假

☞ 右部是叚不是段，右上是口不是几。

假 假 假 假 假 假 假 假 假 假

(價) jià 价格、减价

价 价 价 价 价 价

(駕) jià 驾辕、驾驶、劳驾

☞ 马的第一画是乛，第二画是乚，都不分为两笔；左上角开口。

驾 驾 驾 驾 驾 驾 驾 驾

jià 房架、架桥、架不住、打架、一架钢琴

☞ 木的中间一竖不带钩。

✎ 9 画
口 木 部
囗 上下

架 架架架架架架架架架

jià 嫁闺女、转嫁

☞ 女的横笔右端不出头。

✎ 13 画
口 女 部
囗 左右

嫁 嫁嫁嫁嫁嫁嫁嫁嫁嫁嫁嫁

jià 庄稼

☞ 禾，中间一竖不带钩，末笔改点。

✎ 15 画
口 禾 部
囗 左右

稼稼稼稼稼稼稼
稼稼稼稼稼稼稼稼

jiān 尖刀、笔尖、冒尖、尖叫、耳朵尖

☞ 小的第一画竖钩去钩改丨。

✎ 6 画
口 小 部
囗 上下

尖 尖尖尖尖尖尖

jiān 奸笑、奸细、汉奸、奸污

☞ 女的横笔右端不出头。

✎ 6 画
口 女 部
囗 左右

奸 奸奸奸奸奸奸

（殲）jiān 围歼、歼灭

✎ 7 画
口 歹 部
囗 左右

歼 歼歼歼歼歼歼歼

（堅）jiān 坚固、攻坚战、坚定

☞ 左上是两竖，不是一竖一撇。

✎ 7 画
口 土 部
囗 上下

坚 坚坚坚坚坚坚坚

（間）jiān 席间、期间、卫生间／jiàn 间隙、间接、间断、离间、间苗

☞ 左上右包围结构。起笔、嵌在第二笔丨和第三笔冂之间。

✎ 7 画
口 门 部
囗 半包围

间 间间间间间间间

jiān 肩膀、肩负

☞ 上左包围结构。月的起笔改竖。

✎ 8 画
⊟ 户 部
⊠ 半包围

肩 肩肩肩肩肩肩肩肩

(艱) jiān 艰苦、艰难

☞ 又的末笔改点。

✎ 8 画
⊟ 又 部
⊠ 左右

艰 艰艰艰艰艰艰艰艰

(監) jiān 监视、监牢 /jiàn 国子监

☞ 左上是两竖，不是一竖一撇。

✎ 10 画
⊟ 皿 部
⊠ 上下

监 监监监监监监监监监

古字形像对着一盆水照看容颜。
（金文）（甲文）

jiān 兼课、兼容、兼程

☞ 中部不是彐，第二画横的右端出头。中间两竖都不带钩。

✎ 10 画
⊟ 八 部
⊠ 上下

兼 兼兼兼兼兼兼兼兼兼

jiān 煎鸡蛋、煎中药

☞ 月的起笔改竖。

✎ 13 画
⊟ 灬 部
⊠ 上下

煎 煎煎煎煎煎煎煎煎煎煎煎煎

(揀) jiǎn 挑拣

☞ 右部不是东，第三画是乛(横折钩)。末两笔楷体都是点，宋体是一撇一点。

✎ 8 画
⊟ 扌 部
⊠ 左右

拣 拣拣拣拣拣拣拣拣

(繭) jiǎn 蚕茧

☞ 艹 3 画，第三画楷体是撇，宋体是竖。

✎ 9 画
⊟ 廿 部
⊠ 上下

茧 茧茧茧茧茧茧茧茧

(儉) jiǎn 节俭、俭朴

☞ 人下有一短横。

✎ 9 画
⊟ 亻 部
⊠ 左右

俭 俭俭俭俭俭俭俭俭俭

（撿）jiǎn 把地上的书捡起来

✎ 10 画
⊞ 扌部
⊠ 左右

捡 捡捡捡捡捡捡捡捡捡捡

（檢）jiǎn 检点、检查

☞ 木的中间一竖不带钩，末笔改点。

✎ 11 画
⊞ 木部
⊠ 左右

检 检检检检检检检检检检检

jiǎn 减少、减速、减法

✎ 11 画
⊞ 冫部
⊠ 左右

减 减减减减减减
减减减减减

jiǎn 剪除、剪纸、剪刀、火剪

☞ 月的起笔改竖。

✎ 11 画
⊞ 刀部
⊠ 上下

剪 剪剪剪剪剪剪剪剪剪剪剪

（簡）jiǎn 竹简、简单、精简

☞ 门的起笔、嵌在第二画丨和第三画乛之间。

✎ 13 画
⊞ 竹部
⊠ 上下

简 简简简简简简简简简简简简简

（見）jiàn 罕见、高见、见效、参见、看见

☞ 第二画乛不带钩。

✎ 4 画
⊞ 见部
⊠ 独体

见 见见见见

古字形突出人体上方的眼睛，
表示张目注视。 （金文）
（甲文）

jiàn 零件、急件　　*indicating Things that can be counted*

✎ 6 画
⊞ 亻部
⊠ 左右

件 件件件件件件件

jiàn 建造、建国、建议

☞ 左下包围结构。右上不是彐，中间一横右端出头。廴两画，第一画是乛，不分为两笔。

✎ 8 画
⊞ 廴部
⊠ 半包围

建 建建建建建建建建

(薦) jiàn 推荐、举荐

☞ 艹 3画，第三画楷体是撇，宋体是竖。

✎ 9 画
部 艹 部
画 上 下

荐 荐荐荐荐荐荐荐荐荐

(賤) jiàn 贱买贵卖、贫贱、下贱

☞ 贝的第二画乛不带钩。戋的斜钩上是两横一撇，不是三横一撇。

✎ 9 画
部 贝 部
画 左 右

贱 贱贱贱贱贱贱贱贱贱

(劍) jiàn 舞剑、宝剑

☞ 人的第二画改点。人下有一短横。左边部件的末笔改提。

✎ 9 画
部 刂 部
画 左 右

剑 剑剑剑剑剑剑剑剑剑

jiàn 强健、健身、健谈

☞ 右上不是彐，中间一横右端出头。又两画，第一画乛，不分为两笔。

✎ 10 画
部 亻 部
画 左 右

健 健健健健健健健健健

(艦) jiàn 军舰、舰队

☞ 舟的横笔改提，右端不出头。见的第二画乛不带钩。

✎ 10 画
部 舟 部
画 左 右

舰 舰舰舰舰舰舰舰舰舰

(漸) jiàn 渐渐、逐渐

☞ 车下部的横笔改提，笔顺改先竖后提。

✎ 11 画
部 氵 部
画 左 右

渐 渐渐渐渐渐渐渐渐渐渐

(踐) jiàn 践踏、实践

☞ 左下止的末笔改提。戋的斜钩上是两横一撇，不是三横一撇。

✎ 12 画
部 足 部
画 左 右

践 践践践践践践践践践践

(鑒) jiàn 借鉴、鉴定

☞ 左上是两竖，不是一竖一撇。

✎ 13 画
部 金 部
画 上 下

鉴 鉴鉴鉴鉴鉴鉴鉴鉴鉴鉴鉴鉴

将、浆的右上是夕，不是夕或爫。

(键) jiàn 关键、琴键

⌐ ㇐5画，第二画横，不是点；第五画竖提，不分为两笔。右上不是彐，横笔右端出头。

✎ 13 画
⬚ 钅 部
◁ 左 右

键键键键键键键键键键键键键

jiàn 射箭、箭袋

⌐ 月的起笔改竖。

✎ 15 画
⬚ 竹 部
◁ 上 下

箭箭箭箭箭箭箭箭箭箭箭箭箭箭箭

jiāng 长江、江河湖海

✎ 6 画
⬚ 氵 部
◁ 左 右

江江江江江江

(将) jiāng 恩将仇报、将他一军、即将/jiàng 将士、上将

✎ 9 画
⬚ 丬 部
◁ 左 右

将将将将将
将将将将

(*薑) jiāng *生姜、*姜粉、姓姜

ginger

⌐ 上部羊的竖笔下端不出头。

✎ 9 画
⬚ 羊 部
◁ 上 下

姜姜姜姜姜姜姜姜

(漿) jiāng 豆浆、浆被单

⌐ 上部不是将。水4画，第二画㇖不分为两笔，第三画丿、第四画㇏不连成一笔。

✎ 10 画
⬚ 水 部
◁ 上 下

浆浆浆浆浆浆浆浆浆浆

jiāng 僵硬、僵持

✎ 15 画
⬚ 亻 部
◁ 左 右

僵僵僵僵僵僵僵僵僵僵
僵僵僵僵

jiāng 疆界、边疆、万寿无疆

⌐ 弓3画，第三画㇆不分为两笔。弓内的土末笔改提。

✎ 19 画
⬚ 弓 部
◁ 左 右

疆疆疆疆疆疆疆疆疆疆疆疆
疆疆疆疆疆疆疆

"小篆"是古代汉字一种字体的名称。又称"秦篆"，是秦代通行的规范汉字。小篆是由春秋战国时代的秦国汉字逐渐演变而成的。它在结束战国时代"文字异形"进而实现汉字"书同文"（统一规范）中起了重要作用。小篆的象形程度进一步降低，字形进一步趋于规整匀称，是汉字形体发展史上一种重要的字体。如"八"（人）"彖"（象）。

奖、桨、酱的上部不是将。右上是夕，不是夕或爫。

 (講) jiǎng 讲话、讲条件、讲课、讲卫生

☞ 讠两画，第二画𠃌不分为两笔或三笔。

✎ 6　画
◎ 讠　部
四 左　左右

讲 讲讲讲讲讲讲

 (奬) jiǎng 夸奖、奖励、颁奖

✎ 9　画
◎ 大　部
四 上　下

奖 奖奖奖奖奖奖奖奖奖

 (槳) jiǎng 船桨、荡起双桨

☞ 木的中间一竖不带钩。

✎ 10　画
◎ 木　部
四 上　下

桨 桨桨桨桨桨桨桨桨桨桨

 jiàng 木匠、能工巧匠、巨匠、匠心

☞ 上左下包围结构。末笔乚，不分为两笔。

✎ 6　画
◎ 匚　部
四 半包围

匠 匠匠匠匠匠匠

 jiàng 降落、降旗/xiáng 投降、降伏

☞ 阝两画，第一画了不分为两笔。右上是夂不是夂。

右下3画，第二画一不分为两笔。

✎ 8　画
◎ 阝　部
四 左　左右

降 降降降降降降降降

古字形像两足沿山而下。
（金文）　（甲文）

 (醬) jiàng 黄酱、酱牛肉、芝麻酱

☞ 酉的框内有一短横。

✎ 13　画
◎ 酉　部
四 上　下

酱 酱酱酱酱酱酱酱酱酱酱酱酱

 jiāo 交界、交际、邦交、杂交、交流、交加、转交

✎ 6　画
◎ 亠　部
四 上　下

交 交交交交交交

 jiāo 远郊、郊游

☞ 交的末笔改点。阝两画，第一画了不分为两笔。

✎ 8　画
◎ 阝　部
四 右上　左

郊 郊郊郊郊郊郊郊郊

（澆） jiāo 浇花、浇筑、浇铸　　☞ 右上不是戈或弋。右下是兀不是元。

✎ 9 画
▢ 氵部
✗ 左右

浇浇浇浇浇
浇浇浇浇

西周甲骨文，在书法上，细如粟米，近似微雕。有人说，西周甲骨是微雕艺术之祖，也是蝇头小楷之祖。
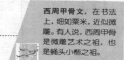

（嬌） jiāo 娇艳、娇气、娇生惯养
☞ 女的横笔右端不出头。

✎ 9 画
▢ 女部
✗ 左右

娇娇娇娇娇娇娇娇娇

（驕） jiāo 骄阳、骄傲
☞ 马的第一画乛、第二画㇆，都不分为两笔；左上角开口；末笔改提。

✎ 9 画
▢ 马部
✗ 左右

骄骄骄骄骄骄骄骄骄

（膠） jiāo 胶水、胶合板、胶泥、胶皮

✎ 10 画
▢ 月部
✗ 左右

胶胶胶胶胶胶胶胶胶胶

jiāo 花椒、辣椒
☞ 木的中间一竖不带钩，末笔改点。小的左侧楷体是点，宋体是撇。

Second part of pepper

✎ 12 画
▢ 木部
✗ 左右

椒椒椒椒椒椒椒椒椒椒椒

jiāo 烧焦、焦急、焦炭
☞ 上部是隹不是住。

✎ 12 画
▢ 隹部
✗ 上下

焦焦焦焦焦焦焦焦焦焦焦

jiāo 芭蕉、香蕉、美人蕉　　☞ 灬3画，第三画楷体是撇，宋体是竖。中部是隹不是住。

✎ 15 画
▢ 艹部
✗ 上下

蕉蕉蕉蕉蕉蕉蕉蕉蕉蕉蕉
蕉蕉蕉蕉

jiáo 细嚼慢咽/jué 咀(jǔ)嚼/jiào 倒嚼　　☞ 爵的中部是横"目"，下部不是即或则。

艮的末两画改一画丶(点)。

嚼嚼嚼嚼嚼嚼嚼

✎ 20 画
▢ 口部
✗ 左右

嚼嚼嚼嚼嚼嚼嚼嚼嚼嚼嚼

jiǎo 牛角、号角、豆角、眼角／jué 主角、丑角、角逐

☞ 下部是用，框中不写作土。

7 画 角部 上 下

角 | 角角角角角角角

古字形像兽角。🦌（金文）🦴（甲文）

---

jiǎo 狡猾、狡辩

9 画 犭部 左 右

狡 | 狡狡狡狡狡狡狡狡狡

（餃）jiǎo 饺子、水饺

first part of dumpling 子

☞ 饣3画，第二画是一，不是丶（点）；第三画是乚，不分为两笔。

9 画 饣部 左 右

饺 | 饺饺饺饺饺饺饺饺饺

绞

（絞）jiǎo 绞干、绞刑　☞ 纟3画，上部不是幺。

9 画 纟部 左 右

绞 | 绞绞绞绞绞
绞绞绞绞

中国书法艺术起始于汉字的创始阶段。甚至可以这样说，中华民族第一位用线条记录汉语的先民，就是中国书法史上第一位书法家。他创作的第一个汉字图形就是第一件书法作品。

脚

jiǎo 小脚女人、墙脚

☞ 右部是卩不是阝。

11 画 月部 左 右

脚 | 脚脚脚脚脚脚脚脚脚脚脚

搅

（攪）jiǎo 打搅、搅拌

☞ 右上是⺍不是⺌，右下见的第二画是𠃌，不带钩。

12 画 扌部 左 右

搅 | 搅搅搅搅搅搅搅搅搅搅搅

缴

（繳）jiǎo 缴纳、缴费、缴枪　☞ 纟3画，上部不是幺。右部是攵不是夂。

16 画 纟部 左 右

缴 | 缴缴缴缴缴缴缴缴缴缴缴
缴缴缴缴

叫

jiào 叫喊、喳喳叫、叫两个菜、大夫叫病人休息、叫人笑话

to be called

5 画 口部 左 右

叫 | 叫叫叫叫叫

轿、较的车,下部横笔改提,笔顺也改为先竖后提。

(轎) jiào 轿子、花轿、轿车

✎ 10 画
车 部
🔲 左 右

轿 轿轿轿轿轿轿轿轿轿轿

(較) jiào 比较、较大成绩、较前有进步

✎ 10 画
车 部
🔲 左 右

较 较较较较较较较较较

jiào 教育、宗教/jiāo 教书、教游泳

☞ 子3画,第一画乛、第二画亅不连成一笔,横笔改提。右部是攵不是攵。

✎ 11 画
攵 部
🔲 左 右

教 教教教教教教教教教教

(階) jiē 台阶、军阶

☞ 阝两画,第一画乛不分为两笔。

✎ 6 画
阝 部
🔲 左 右

阶 阶阶阶阶阶阶

jiē 皆大欢喜、尽人皆知

☞ 比,左部第二画是乚,不分为两笔;右部是匕不是匕。

✎ 9 画
比 部
🔲 上 下

皆 皆皆皆皆皆皆皆皆皆

jiē 接近、衔接、青黄不接、接班、接球、接人

✎ 11 画
扌 部
🔲 左 右

接接接接接接
接接接接接

jiē 揭竿而起、揭开、揭露、揭邮票

☞ 右下不是匐。框中人的末笔改点。

✎ 12 画
扌 部
🔲 左 右

揭 揭揭揭揭揭揭揭揭揭揭

jiē 大街小巷、街道

☞ 中部两土,第二个土的末笔改提。

✎ 12 画
彳 部
🔲 左 右

街 街街街街街街街街街街街街

原始汉字有了一定数量的积累以后,在它形成相对成熟的文字符号体系的阶段,一定会由经常跟汉字打交道的人,如传说中的黄帝史官"仓颉"们,凭着成天跟文字接触而获得的经验和知识,对汉字进行整理。没有"仓颉"们的整理,汉字不可能由原始走向成熟,从散落的符号组合成完整的体系。

(節) jié 枝节、节令、节省、礼节、晚节、节拍／jiē 节骨眼儿

艹 3画，第三画楷体是撇，宋体是竖。

5画　艹部　上下

 节 节节节节节

jié 抢劫、劫持、浩劫

7画　力部　左右

 劫 劫劫劫劫劫劫劫

jié 杰出、豪杰

木的中间一竖不带钩。

8画　木部　上下

 杰 杰杰杰杰杰杰杰杰

郭沫若认为培养学生写好字还有助于培育学生良好的思想和道德素养。他说："培养中小学生写好字，不一定要人人都成为书法家，总要把字写得合乎规格，比较端正、干净、容易认。这样养成习惯有好处，能够使人细心，容易集中意志，善于体贴人。草草了事，粗枝大叶，独行专断，是最容易误事的。练习写字可以逐渐免除这些毛病。"（《人民教育》1962.9）

(潔) jié 清洁、廉洁

9画　氵部　左右

洁 洁洁洁洁洁洁洁洁洁

1st part: to pay bill: 结账 jiézhàng

(結) jié 结网、领结、结冰、结交、结业／jiē 开花结果、结巴、结实

纟 3画，上部不是幺。

9画　纟部　左右

结 结结结结结结结结结

jié 大捷、敏捷、便捷

右边中部不是ヨ，中间横笔右端出头。

11画　扌部　左右

捷 捷捷捷捷捷捷捷捷捷捷捷

jié 截断、堵截、截至　　上右包围结构。左下是隹不是住。

14画　隹部　半包围

截截截截截截截截截截
截截截截

jié 衰竭、竭尽全力、枯竭　　立的末笔改提。右下不是匋，框中人的末笔改点。

14画　立部　左右

竭竭竭竭竭竭竭竭
竭竭竭竭

jiě 姐姐、表姐

elder sister, sister, general term for young woman

☞ 女的横笔右端不出头。

✎ 8 画
□ 女部
☒ 左右

姐 姐姐姐姐姐姐姐姐

古字形像
两手解剖
牛角。

(金文) (甲文)

jiě 解剖、解散、解渴、小解、理解／jiè 解送／xiè 姓解、解州

☞ 角，下部是用，框中不写成土。右部上刀下牛。

✎ 13 画
□ 角部
☒ 左右

解 解解解解解解解解解解解解

jiè 介入、介绍、中介、介意

be situated between — to take seriously

☞ 左上右包围结构。

✎ 4 画
□ 人部
☒ 半包围

介 介介介介

对日常书写的要求：用
硬笔写字，写得正确、
端正、整洁，行款整齐，
有一定速度。用毛笔临
帖，字写得匀称，纸面
干净。——《九年义务
教育全日制小学·语文
教学大纲》

jiè 戒备、戒烟、杀戒

☞ 上右包围结构。左下是廾不是 ナ。

✎ 7 画
□ 戈部
☒ 半包围

戒 戒戒戒戒戒戒戒

jiè 届时、应届毕业生

☞ 上左包围结构。

✎ 8 画
□ 尸部
☒ 半包围

届 届届届届届届届届

在世界文字之林中，汉
字是一种历史悠久的
自源文字，是汉族人民
独立创造、逐步发展起
来的文字符号体系。公
元前1300年以前，中国
人已经拥有相当成熟
的金文和甲骨文。汉字
经历了几千年的发展
演变，仍然作为记录汉
语的主要文字工具被
广泛应用着。汉字是人
类文字的活化石，是一
种自源文字的完整标
本。它在世界文字史上
的地位没有哪一种文
字可以代替。

jiè 国界、外界、科学界

✎ 9 画
□ 田部
☒ 上下

界 界界界界界
界界界界

（*藉）jiè 借钱、*借口、*借故

✎ 10 画
□ 亻部
☒ 左右

借 借借借借借
借借借借借

jīn 手巾、围巾

a piece of cloth

✎ 3 画
□ 巾部
☒ 独体

巾 巾巾巾

middle part of napkin 餐 巾 纸
can jīn zhǐ

jīn 斤斤计较、500 克等于 1 市斤

chinese unit of weight

✎ 4 画
部 独体

斤　斤斤斤斤

1939 年在河南安阳出土的"司母戊鼎"，是殷商前期器物。鼎重 875 公斤，为出土青铜器之最。鼎身四周铸有精巧的盘龙纹和饕餮(tāotiè)纹，增加了器物威武凝重之感。大鼎腹内壁铸有"司母戊"三字。这是商王为祭祀他的母亲戊而铸造的鼎。

jīn 今天、古为今用

modern, now present day today

✎ 4 画
人 部
四 上 下

今　今今今今

jīn 冶金、奖金、黄金、金灿灿

money. ancient money. gold

✎ 8 画
金 部
四 上 下

金　金金金金金金金金

古字形像熔金的铸器。点像熔化的金属溅液。注（金文）

jīn 问津、津液、天津

☞ 聿的上部不是ヨ，中间横笔右端出头。

✎ 9 画
氵 部
四 左 右

津　津津津津津津津津津

jīn 伤筋动骨、筋骨、青筋

✎ 12 画
竹 部
四 上

筋　筋筋筋筋筋筋筋筋筋筋筋筋

（僅）jǐn 仅供参考、侦破这个案件仅用了一天时间

✎ 4 画
亻 部
四 左 右

仅　仅仅仅仅

（緊）jǐn 前紧后松、紧握、紧张、日子过得紧、时间紧

☞ 左上是两竖，不是一竖一撇。下部小的左侧楷体是点，宋体是撇。

✎ 10 画
糸 部
四 上 下

紧　紧紧紧紧紧紧紧紧紧

（錦）jǐn 壮锦、锦旗、锦上添花

☞ ⺙ 5 画，第二画是横，不是、(点)；第五画是乚，不分为两笔。

✎ 13 画
钅 部
四 左 右

锦　锦锦锦锦锦锦锦锦锦锦锦锦

(謹) jǐn 谨慎、谨赠

☞ 讠两画，第二画是乛，不分为两笔或三笔。廿4画，第二画竖和第四画横不连成一笔。

✎ 13 画
辶 讠部
左 右

谨 谨谨谨谨谨谨谨谨谨谨谨谨

within the limits of, give priority to

(盡*儘) jǐn 用尽力气、尽心/jìn *尽快、*先尽老人坐、*尽前头

☞ 左上右包围结构。 *to the greatest extent*

✎ 6 画
尸部
半包围

尽 尽尽尽尽尽尽

(進) jìn 前进、进言、进门、进款、引进

☞ 左下包围结构。

✎ 7 画
辶部
半包围

进 进进进进进进进

jìn 近代、亲近、近似、平易近人

☞ 左下包围结构。

✎ 7 画
辶部
半包围

近 近近近近近近近

(勁) jìn 劲儿、药劲儿、劲头、高兴劲儿、带劲/jìng 劲敌、劲旅

☞ 左上是ス不是又。左下工的末笔改提。

✎ 7 画
力部
左 右

劲 劲劲劲劲劲劲劲

jìn 晋升、晋见、晋剧

✎ 10 画
日部
上 下

晋 晋晋晋晋晋晋晋晋晋晋

jìn 浸泡、浸润、浸透、浸种

☞ 右上是彐，中间横笔右端不出头。

✎ 10 画
氵部
左 右

浸 浸浸浸浸浸浸浸浸浸

jìn 禁止、犯禁、监禁、禁忌/jīn 禁受、情不自禁、皮鞋禁穿

☞ 在上木的末笔改点。小的左侧楷体是点，宋体是撇。

✎ 13 画
示部
上 下

禁 禁禁禁禁禁禁禁禁禁禁禁禁

京、惊的小，左侧楷体是点，宋体是撇。睛、精的月，起笔改竖。

(莖) jing 球茎、块茎

☞ 艹 3画，第三画楷体是撇，宋体是竖。

✎ 8 画
□ 艹 部
☒ 上 下

茎 茎茎茎茎茎茎茎茎茎

---

jing 京城、京剧

✎ 8 画
□ 亠 部
☒ 上 下

京 京京京京京京京京

古字形像高大的建筑物。 �（金文）
𠮷（甲文） 京（小篆）

(經) jing 经线、经典、经常、经商、身经百战、经不起

☞ 纟 3画，上部不是幺。右上是又不是又。

✎ 8 画
□ 纟 部
☒ 左 右

经 经经经经经经经经

(驚) jing 马惊了、惊慌、惊扰

✎ 11 画
□ 忄 部
☒ 左 右

惊 惊惊惊惊惊惊
惊惊惊惊惊

从夏商周，经过春秋战国，再到秦汉王朝，共计二千五百年历史。这个时期，甲骨文、金文、石刻文、简帛朱墨手迹相继出现，篆体、隶体、草体、楷体等书体在数百种杂体的筛选海汰过程中逐渐定型完备。中国的书法艺术开始了有序的发展。

---

jing 亮晶晶、墨晶、结晶

✎ 12 画
□ 日 部
☒ 上 下

晶 晶晶晶晶晶晶晶晶晶晶晶晶晶

---

second part MSG！味米青

jing 目不转睛、画龙点睛

✎ 13 画
□ 目 部
☒ 左 右

睛 睛睛睛睛睛睛睛睛睛睛睛睛睛

---

jing 精华、精神、妖精、精兵、精良、精通、精密、精明   ☞ 米，中间一竖不带钩，末笔改点。

second MSG part

✎ 14 画
□ 米 部
☒ 左 右

精 精精精精精精精
精精精精精精精

---

jing 水井、油井、背井离乡、井井有条

✎ 4 画
□ 一 部
☒ 独 体

井 井井井井

点，在字的上面或左上角，先写（丶 亠 广）；在字的右上角或里面，后写（一弋戈戋，一亡瓦瓦）。

(頸) jing 颈椎、长颈鹿/gěng 脖颈子

☞ 工的末笔改提。

✎ 11 画
▥ 页部
△ 左 右

 颈颈颈颈颈颈颈颈颈颈颈

---

jing 景象、景色、布景、景仰

☞ 小的左侧楷体是点，宋体是撇。

✎ 12 画
▥ 部
△ 上 下

 景景景景景景景景景景景

---

jing 警告、警备、警惕、民警、报警　☞ 艹3画，第三画楷体是撇，宋体是竖。右

警警警警警警　　　上是攵不是夂。

✎ 19 画
▥ 言部
△ 上 下

 警警警警警警警警警警警警警

(徑) jing 小径、半径、捷径、径直

✎ 8 画
▥ 彳部
△ 左 右

 径径径径径径径径

---

jing 纯净、净手、净重、净是垃圾、净写错字

☞ 争的中部不是彐，中间横笔右端出头。

✎ 8 画
▥ 丷部
△ 左 右

 净净净净净净净净

(競) jing 竞争、竞赛

☞ 中部是口不是日。

古字形像两人竞争。𥫡（金文）𥫡（甲文）

✎ 10 画
▥ 立部
△ 上 下

竞竞竞竞竞竞竞竞竞竞

---

jing 未竟事业、有志者事竟成、竟敢

☞ 中部是日不是口。

✎ 11 画
▥ 音部
△ 上 下

 竟竟竟竟竟竟竟竟竟竟竟

---

jing 敬意、敬重、敬酒

☞ 艹三画，第三画楷体是撇，宋体是竖。右边是攵不是夂。

✎ 12 画
▥ 攵部
△ 左 右

敬敬敬敬敬敬敬敬敬敬敬敬

jìng 静坐、镇静、寂静　☞ 右下月的起笔改竖。争的中部不是彐，中间横笔右端出头。

静静静静静静静
静静静静静静静

14 画
⻘ 部
左 右

---

jìng 国境、环境、境遇　☞ 土的末笔改提。

境境境境境境境境境
境境境

14 画
土 部
左 右

（鏡）jìng 镜子　☞ 钅5画，第二画是横，不是点；第五画是竖提，不分为两笔。

镜镜镜镜镜镜镜镜镜镜镜
镜镜镜镜

16 画
钅 部
左 右

（糾）jiū 纠集、纠缠、纠正　☞ 纟3画，上部不是幺。

纠纠纠纠纠

5 画
纟 部
左 右

---

jiū 研究、追究

究究究究究究究

7 画
穴 部
上 下

---

jiū 揪住不放　☞ 禾的中间一竖不带钩，末笔改点。

揪揪揪揪揪揪
揪揪揪揪揪揪

12 画
扌 部
左 右

---

jiǔ 九死一生、三九天　NINE

九九

2 画
丿 独

---

jiǔ 持久、久远

久久久

3 画
丿 独

部件是现代汉字字形中具有独立组字能力的构字单位，它大于或等于笔画，小于或等于整字。绝大多数部件都大于笔画，如："冖""扌""氵""灬"等。也有少数部件是等于笔画的，如："一"是笔画（横），又是部件（如"旦"由"日"和"一"两个部件构成）；"丨"是笔画（竖），又是部件（如"引"由"弓"和"丨"两个部件构成）。不少部件都小于整字，如："彡""冫""忄""宀"等。但也有不少部件是等于整字的，如：构成"扣"的两个部件，"扌"小于整字，"口"等于整字；构成"泳"的两个部件，"氵"小于整字，"永"等于整字；构成"好"字的两个部件，"女""子"都是整字；构成"碧"字的三个部件，"王""白""石"都是整字；构成"器"字的五个部件，"口""口""犬""口""口"都是整字。

jiǔ 酒菜、葡萄酒　☞ 酉的框中有一短横。

✎ 10 画
□ 酉 画部
△ 左 右

酒酒酒酒
酒酒酒酒酒酒

(舊) jiù 旧房子、旧思想、旧居、访旧
　☞ 第一、二画都是竖，不是一竖一撇，跟归不同。

✎ 5 画
□ 日 画部
△ 左 右

旧旧旧旧旧

jiù 救火、挽救
　☞ 求的末笔改点。右部是攵不是夂。

✎ 11 画
□ 攵 画部
△ 左 右

救救救救救救救救救救救

jiù 就近入学、就座、就业、马上就走、就剩一人、功成名就
　☞ 小的左侧楷体是点，宋体是撇。右部是尤不是犬。

✎ 12 画
□ 丶 画部
△ 左 右

就就就就就就就就就就就就

jiù 舅父、妻舅　☞ 臼6画，末笔横不分为两短横。

✎ 13 画
□ 臼 画部
△ 上 下

舅舅舅舅舅舅舅舅舅
舅舅舅舅

jū 拘留、拘束、拘泥

✎ 8 画
□ 扌 画部
△ 左 右

拘拘拘拘
拘拘拘拘

jū 居民、新居、后来居上、居多
　☞ 上左包围结构。

✎ 8 画
□ 尸 画部
△ 半包围

居居居居居居居居

jū 鞠躬　☞ 廿4画，第二画竖、第四画横不连成一笔。米的末笔改点。

✎ 17 画
□ 革 画部
△ 左 右

鞠鞠鞠鞠鞠鞠鞠鞠鞠鞠鞠鞠
鞠鞠鞠鞠鞠

绝大多数汉字都是由古代汉字一脉相承演变来的，都可以沿用传统的"六书"分析它们的造字法。用"六书"分析现代汉字的造字法必须追溯到古代字形，因而我们称之为动态溯源。"六书"即指事、象形、会意、形声、转注、假借。前四书是造字的方法，后二书是用字的方法。

jú 局限、税务局、时局、局势
　　☞ 上左包围结构。
　✎ 7　画
　▢ 尸　部
　▢ 半包围
 局局局局局局局

jú 赏菊、菊展
　　☞ 卄 3 画，第三画楷体是撇，宋体是竖。米的末笔改点。
　✎ 11　画
　▢ 卄　部
　▢ 上　下
 菊菊菊菊菊菊菊菊菊菊菊

jú 橘子、蜜橘　　☞ 木的中间一竖不带钩，末笔改点。右下框中是上八下口。规范简化
　　　　　　　　　　　　　　　　　　　　　字不作桔。
橘橘橘橘橘橘
　✎ 16　画
　▢ 木　部
　▢ 左　右
 橘橘橘橘橘橘橘橘橘橘

jǔ 规矩、矩形、矩尺
　　☞ 矢的末笔改点。
　✎ 9　画
　▢ 矢　部
　▢ 左　右
 矩矩矩矩矩矩矩矩矩

(舉) jǔ 举重、举止、举行、举荐、举例、举国
　　☞ 左上右包围结构。下部是十不是丰。
　✎ 9　画
　▢ 、　部
　▢ 半包围
 举举举举举举举举举

jù 巨人、巨款、巨大
　　☞ 上左下包围结构。
　✎ 4　画
　▢ 匚　部
　▢ 半包围
 巨巨巨巨

字谜

大框口朝右，小框口朝左；
两框套一起，大得没法说。

jù 句子、造句
　　☞ 上右包围结构。
　✎ 5　画
　▢ 勹　部
　▢ 半包围
 句句句句句

 在中国，书画向来是并称的。象形是汉字字形最本质的基础。所以，传统书法有"取形用势，写生揣意"的原则。于是，有人"见蛇斗而草书长"，仔细观察两条蛇相斗的形态，从而使自己的草书有了进步；唐代著名书法家张旭，看了公孙大娘舞剑器而领悟到草书的奥妙。

jù 拒敌、拒不执行
　✎ 7　画
　▢ 扌　部
　▢ 左
 拒拒拒拒拒拒拒

具

jù 文具、炊具、具有、独具特色

✎ 8 画
⿱ 八 上 下

 具具具具具具具具

隶书的笔画形态比小篆丰富多变，因为隶书更多地保留了毛笔书写的自然形态。毛笔带来的隶书笔画的粗细、方圆和藏锋露锋等形态，是毛笔特性和指腕运动节奏综合的结果，既丰富了笔画线条的视觉形态，又明显提高了书写的节奏感。隶书的书写艺术高峰有两座，一是汉隶，一是清隶。至今，汉隶仍是隶书艺术没能逾越的高峰。

俱

jù 一应俱全、万事俱备、俱乐部

✎ 10 画
⿰ 亻 左 部 右

 俱俱俱俱俱
俱俱俱俱俱

剧 （劇）

jù 剧变、戏剧

✎ 10 画
⿰ 刂 左 部 右

剧剧剧剧剧
剧剧剧剧剧

据 （據）

jù 据点、据理力争、证据、窃据／jū 拮据

✎ 11 画
⿰ 扌 左 部 右

据据据据据据据据据据

距

jù 差距、距离

☞ 左下止的末笔改提。巨的末笔是乚，不分为两笔。

✎ 11 画
⿰ 足 部 右

距距距距距距距距距距距

惧 （懼）

jù 畏惧、临危不惧

✎ 11 画
⿰ 忄 部 右

惧惧惧惧惧惧惧惧惧惧

锯 （鋸）

jù 电锯、锯钢管

☞ 45画，第二画是横，不是点；第五画是竖提，不分为两笔。

✎ 13 画
⿰ 钅 部 右

锯锯锯锯锯锯锯锯锯锯锯锯锯

聚

jù 聚会、聚餐　　☞ 耳的末笔改提，又的末笔改点。下部是乑不是㐱。

✎ 14 画
⿱ 耳 上 下

 聚聚聚聚聚聚聚
聚聚聚聚聚聚聚

古字形上边是声旁取，下边像三人相聚。（小篆）

卷的下部、倦的右下是巳，不是巳、已或己。

juān 捐款、税捐

☞ 月的起笔改竖。

✎ 10 画 扌部 左右

捐 捐捐捐捐捐捐捐捐捐捐

(*捲) **juàn** 手卷、第二卷、试卷、卷宗/**juǎn** *卷铺盖、*卷入旋涡、*烟卷儿 ☞ 左上右包围结构。

✎ 8 画 卩部 半包围

卷 卷卷卷卷卷卷卷卷卷

juàn 疲倦、厌倦

✎ 10 画 亻部 左右

倦倦倦倦倦
倦倦倦倦倦

(絹) **juàn** 绢花、手绢

☞ 纟3画，上部不是幺。月的起笔改竖。

✎ 10 画 纟部 左右

绢 绢绢绢绢绢绢绢绢绢绢

> 意符、音符、记号这三类部件分别组合，构成现代汉字的七种类型：独体表意字（凹）、会意字（从）、形声字（枫）、半意符半记号字（刻）、半音符半记号字（球）、独体记号字（我）、合体记号字（杂）。

jué 决口、决裂、判决、处决、决战、坚决

☞ 左部是冫不是氵。

✎ 6 画 冫部 左右

决 决决决决决决

(覺) **jué** 觉醒、不知不觉、视觉/**jiào** 睡懒觉

☞ 上部是⺍不是⺌。见的第二画乛不带钩。

✎ 9 画 见部 上下

觉 觉觉觉觉觉觉觉觉觉

(絕) **jué** 绝交、弹尽粮绝、绝招、绝密、绝路、绝不答应、绝命

☞ 纟3画，上部不是幺。

✎ 9 画 纟部 左右

绝 绝绝绝绝绝绝绝绝绝

jué 掘土、发掘

☞ 右下出的第一画、第四画是乚，都不分为两笔。

✎ 11 画 扌部 左右

掘 掘掘掘掘掘掘掘掘掘掘

(軍) jūn 军队、参军

⟳ 车的第二画是乚，不分为两笔。

✎ 6 画
▢ 一 部
◿ 上 下

军 军军军军军军

jūn 平均、均已达标

⟳ 土的末笔改提。

✎ 7 画
▢ 土 部
◿ 左 右

均 均均均均均均均

jūn 君主、诸君

⟳ 上左包围结构。上部不是彐，中间横笔右端出头。

✎ 7 画
▢ 口 部
◿ 半包围

君 君君君君君君

jūn 灭菌、真菌

⟳ 艹3画，第三画楷体是撇，宋体是竖。禾的末笔改点。

✎ 11 画
▢ 艹 部
◿ 上 下

菌 菌菌菌菌菌菌菌菌菌菌

jùn 俊杰、英俊、俊美

⟳ 右下是夂不是夕。

✎ 9 画
▢ 亻 部
◿ 左 右

俊 俊俊俊俊俊俊俊俊

(開) kāi 开门、开戒、开锅、开荒、开会、开炮、开胶、开价、开销

✎ 4 画
▢ 一 部
◿ 独 体

开 开开开开

(凱) kǎi 凯旋、凯歌

⟳ 山3画，第二画是乚，不分为两笔。左下是己，不是已或巳，己的末笔改竖提。

✎ 8 画
▢ 几 部
◿ 左 右

凯 凯凯凯凯凯凯凯凯

kǎi 愤慨、感慨

⟳ 艮的末两画撇、捺改一画乀(点)。右部是旡不是无。

✎ 12 画
▢ 忄 部
◿ 左 右

慨 慨慨慨慨慨慨慨慨慨慨慨

"草书"是汉字一种字体的名称。作为一种特定的字体，草书到汉代才形成。古隶的正体演变成为"八分书"，古隶的俗体则演变成为草书。草书把汉字的复杂结构简易化，运笔连续化，字与字之间也往往呼应乃至相连，后来发展成为一种艺术性高于实用性的字体。如"人象"。

康、糠的康，右下的隶，上部是⇒不是∃；下部是水，不写成水。

kān 刊正、创刊、月刊
☞ 左部是干不是千，它的末笔是竖不是撇。

✎ 5 画
□ 干 部
⊠ 左 右

刊 刊刊刊刊刊

---

kān 狼狈不堪、堪当重任
☞ 土的末笔改提。甚的末笔是乚，不分为两笔。

✎ 12 画
□ 土 部
⊠ 左 右

堪 堪堪堪堪堪堪堪堪堪堪堪

---

kǎn 砍木材、砍掉

✎ 9 画
□ 石 部
⊠ 左 右

砍 砍砍砍砍砍砍砍砍砍

---

to have a look, read, watch

kàn 看书、照看、试试看、看病、看朋友 /kān 看家、看押
☞ 上左包围结构。

✎ 9 画
□ 目 部
⊠ 半包围

看 看看看看看看看看看

古字形像用手挡光看远物。看（小篆）

---

kāng 康乐、小康、健康
☞ 上左包围结构。

✎ 11 画
□ 广 部
⊠ 半包围

康 康康康康康康康康康康

---

kāng 吃糠咽菜、萝卜糠了 ☞ 米，中间一竖不带钩，末笔改点。

✎ 17 画
□ 米 部
⊠ 左 右

糠糠糠糠糠糠糠糠糠糠糠
糠糠糠糠糠

---

káng 扛枪、扛活儿

✎ 6 画
□ 扌 部
⊠ 左 右

扛 扛扛扛扛扛扛

写字时要养成正确的姿势。对坐姿的基本要求是：头正、身直、臂平、足安（两脚平放在地）。如果歪着头、斜着肩、曲着背，甚至翘着二郎腿，就容易使整个字失去重心，并可能使一行字一路斜下去，使一篇字东倒西歪。不正确的写字姿势还会使你感到心胸不舒、四肢容易疲劳，久而久之，会有损健康。

---

kàng 抗洪、违抗

✎ 7 画
□ 扌 部
⊠ 左 右

抗 抗抗抗抗抗抗抗

kàng 火炕、炕席

8 画　火部　左右

炕 炕炕炕炕炕炕炕炕

"指事" 是汉字的一种造字方法。汉代许慎的定义是："视而可识，察而见意。"前半句说，一眼看去就可以大致认识；后半句说，仔细观察才能发现它的字义。如"上""下""本""刃"等。

kǎo 考核、考试、高考、思考

☞ 上左包围结构。

6 画　耂部　半包围

考 考考考考考考

kǎo 烤馒头、烤火

10 画　火部　左右

烤 烤烤烤烤烤烤烤烤烤烤

kào 背靠大树、靠拢、投靠、可靠　☞ 非，中间是两竖，左右各三横。

15 画　非部　上下

靠 靠靠靠靠靠靠靠
靠靠靠靠靠靠靠靠

kē 科目、文科、科室

☞ 禾，中间一竖不带钩，末笔改点。

9 画　禾部　左右

科 科科科科科科科科科

a branch of academic study, family / species division

kē 两棵树、一棵草

☞ 木的中间一竖不带钩，末笔改点。

12 画　木部　左右

棵 棵棵棵棵棵棵棵棵棵棵棵

(顆) kē 颗粒、几颗子弹、一颗红心　☞ 木的中间一竖不带钩，末笔改点。

14 画　页部　左右

颗 颗颗颗颗颗颗
颗颗颗颗颗颗颗颗

(殼) ké 鸡蛋壳儿/qiào 地壳

☞ 上部是士不是土，几上没有一横。

7 画　士部　上下

壳 壳壳壳壳壳壳壳

南朝梁顾野王编著的《玉篇》，公元543年成书，收16917字。

ké 咳嗽、百日咳 /hāi 咳声叹气、咳，吃饭了吗

✎ 9 画
口 口 部
⊠ 左 右

咳 咳咳咳咳咳咳咳咳咳

---

kě 认可、可吃可不吃、可怜、可是、可心 /kè 可汗（古代鲜卑等族君主的称号）

☞ 上右包围结构。

✎ 5 画
口 口 部
⊠ 半包围

可 可可可可可

古字形像斧头柄。加口，
表示可否的句。

可（甲文） 可（金文）

---

kě 饥渴难耐、渴望

☞ 右下不是匈，框内人的末笔改点。

✎ 12 画
氵 氵 部
⊠ 左 右

渴 渴渴渴渴渴渴渴渴渴渴渴

(*剋) kè *攻克、克服、*克扣、1000毫克等于1克

✎ 7 画
十 部
⊠ 上 下

克
克克克
克克克克

铅笔与钢笔的执笔方法
相同：大拇指与食指捏
在离笔尖三厘米左右的
笔杆上，食指稍前，大拇
指稍后，中指在内侧抵
住笔杆，无名指、小指依
次自然地放在中指旁，
并向手心弯曲。笔杆斜
靠在虎口上，虎口成扁
圆形，笔杆跟纸面成40
度角。食指由外向内用
力（称"压"），一内一外，
将笔杆夹住。

---

kè 雕刻、苛刻、石刻、此刻

✎ 8 画
刂 部
⊠ 左 右

刻
刻刻刻刻
刻刻刻刻

---

visitor, guest, traveler

kè 客人、客店、政客、客队、游客、客观

☞ 中部是夂不是夂。

✎ 9 画
宀 部
⊠ 上 下

客 客客客客客客客客客

(課) kè 上课、公共课、第一课

☞ 讠两画，第二画乛不分为两笔或三笔。木的中间一竖不带钩。

✎ 10 画
讠 部
⊠ 左 右

课 课课课课课课课课课课

---

kěn 首肯、肯定

☞ 月的起笔改竖。

✎ 8 画
止 部
⊠ 上 下

肯 肯肯肯肯肯肯肯肯

垦 (墾) kěn 开垦、垦荒、垦田 *cultivate, reclaim*

☞ 上部是艮不是良。

✎ 9 画
▯ 艮 部
▱ 上 下

垦垦垦垦垦垦垦垦垦

恳 (懇) kěn 诚恳、恳请 ☞ 上部是艮不是良。 *earnestly, sincerely*

✎ 10 画
▯ 艮 部
▱ 上 下

恳恳恳恳恳
恳恳恳恳恳

"会意" 是汉字的一种造字方法。汉代许慎的定义是："比类合谊，以见指挥(huī)。"意思是比合字形所画的事物，就可以看出字形所指的字义。它跟 "象形" 的区别在于 "会"。有了这个 "会" "意" 的过程，字形就能记录比较抽象的字义。以形会意的如 "从"，以义会意的如 "歪"。

坑 kēng 水坑、坑害、坑道 *hole, pit, hollow*

☞ 土的末笔改提。

✎ 7 画
▯ 土 部
▱ 左 右

坑坑坑坑坑坑坑

空 kōng 空房子、空洞、凭空、真空、空忙、空军、空间、空气、扑空/kòng 空缺、空地、抽空 *leave empty or blank* *empty hollow*

✎ 8 画
▯ 穴 部
▱ 上 下

空空空空空空空空

孔 kǒng 毛孔、一孔窑 *hole, opening, aperture*

☞ 子3画，第一画乛、第二画亅不连成一笔，末笔改提。

✎ 4 画
▯ 子 部
▱ 左 右

孔孔孔孔

恐 kǒng 恐惧、恐吓、恐怕

☞ 工的末笔改提。

✎ 10 画
▯ 心 部
▱ 上 下

恐恐恐恐恐恐恐恐恐

控 kòng 控制、控告

✎ 11 画
▯ 扌 部
▱ 左 右

控控控控控控控控控控控

口 kǒu 漱口、口气、户口、瓶口、进出口贸易、伤口、刀口 *mouth, opening*

✎ 3 画
▯ 口 部
▱ 独 体

口口口

古字形像口。 (甲文)

　　库、裤的库，上左包围结构，车的第二画是乚，不分为两笔。

 kòu 钮扣、活口儿、扣留、扣除、折扣、扣篮

✎ 6 画
国 扌部
囚 左 右

扣　扣扣扣扣扣扣

 kòu 敌寇、入寇

☞ 元的右上是攴不是寸。

✎ 11 画
国 宀部
囚 上 下

寇　寇寇寇寇寇寇寇寇寇寇寇

 kū 枯树、枯井、枯燥

☞ 木的中间一竖不带钩，末笔改点。

✎ 9 画
国 木部
囚 左 右

枯　枯枯枯枯枯枯枯枯枯

 kū 号啕大哭、哭泣

✎ 10 画
国 犬部
囚 上 下

哭　哭哭哭哭哭
　　哭哭哭哭哭

kǔ 苦胆、艰苦、苦劝、苦日子、苦恼

☞ 艹3画，第三画楷体是撇，宋体是竖。

✎ 8 画
国 艹部
囚 上 下

苦　苦苦苦苦苦苦苦苦

(庫) kù 仓库、国库

☞ 上左包围结构。

✎ 7 画
国 广部
囚 半包围

库　库库库库库库库

(褲) kù 游泳裤、棉毛裤

☞ 左部是衤不是礻。

✎ 12 画
国 衤部
囚 左 右

裤　裤裤裤裤裤裤裤裤裤裤裤

 kù 冷酷、酷热　　☞ 酉，框内有一短横。右上牛的竖笔下端不出头。

✎ 14 画
国 酉部
囚 左 右

酷　酷酷酷酷酷酷酷酷酷
　　酷酷酷酷酷

夸 (誇) kuā 夸张、夸奖
☞ 左上右包围结构。
✎ 6 画　大部　半包围
 夸夸夸夸夸夸

垮 kuǎ 冲垮、垮台、累垮　☞ 土的末笔改提。
✎ 9 画　土部　土右
 垮垮垮垮垮垮垮垮垮

"象形"是汉字的一种造字方法。汉代许慎的定义是："画成其物，随体诘诎(jiéqū)。"意思是按照物体的外形描摹出字形。它跟"指事"的区别在于它的字形记录的就是所画的那个物。如"人""牛""日""月"等。

挎 kuà 挎篮子、骑马挎刀、挎包
✎ 9 画　扌部　扌右
 挎挎挎挎挎挎挎挎挎

跨 kuà 跨越、跨上马背、跨世纪
☞ 左下的止末笔改提。
✎ 13 画　足部　左右
 跨跨跨跨跨跨跨跨跨跨跨跨

块 (塊) kuài 土块、一块金表、两块三毛钱
☞ 土的末笔改提。
✎ 7 画　土部　左右
 块块块块块块块

快 kuài 愉快、心直口快、快速、快刀、手疾眼快、快干完了
✎ 7 画　忄部　左右
 快快快快快快快

宽 (寬) kuān 宽广、长宽各1米、宽心、宽容、宽裕
☞ 艹3画，第三画楷体是撇，宋体是竖。见的右下无点。
✎ 10 画　宀部　上下
 宽宽宽宽宽宽宽宽宽宽

款 kuǎn 款待、落款、款式、公款、第四款
☞ 左部上士下示。
✎ 12 画　欠部　左右
 款款款款款款款款款款款款

筐、框的匡，末笔是乚，不分为两笔。

kuāng 编筐、两筐土豆　BASKET (of apples)

✎ 12 画
部首 竹 部
结构 上 下

筐 筐 筐 筐 筐 筐 筐 筐
筐 筐 筐 筐

---

kuáng 发狂、狂妄、狂饮、狂奔　MAD, CRAZY, LUNATIC - WILD

✎ 7 画
部首 犭 部
结构 左 右

狂 狂 狂 狂 狂 狂 狂

（曠）kuàng 旷野、心旷神怡、旷工
vast, spacious
(free of petty ideas)

✎ 7 画
部首 日 部
结构 左 右

旷 旷 旷 旷 旷 旷 旷

---

kuàng 状况、况且、何况
condition, situation

✎ 7 画
部首 冫 部
结构 左 右

况 况 况 况 况 况 况

（礦）kuàng 金矿、爱矿如家、矿工、矿井
ore deposit

✎ 8 画
部首 石 部
结构 左 右

矿 矿 矿 矿 矿 矿 矿 矿

---

frame, case, circle
kuàng 窗框、镜框、边框、框住手脚
☞ 木的中间一竖不带钩，末笔写点。

✎ 10 画
部首 木 部
结构 左 右

框 框 框 框 框 框 框 框 框 框

---

loss, lose, be deficient
（虧）kuī 盈亏、理亏、亏待、幸亏
☞ 末笔在二之下，不写成亏。

✎ 3 画
部首 一 部
结构 上 下

亏 亏 亏 亏

---

kuí 向日葵、葵花子
☞ 艹3画，第三画楷体是撇，宋体是竖。中部是癶不是夂。天的末笔改点。

✎ 12 画
部首 艹 部
结构 上 下

葵 葵 葵 葵 葵 葵 葵 葵 葵 葵 葵 葵

捆、困的木，中间一竖不带钩，末笔改点。

kuì 惭愧、愧对、问心无愧　*ashamed, conscience stricken*

☞ 鬼的第六画从白中直接撇下，不分为两笔。右下有厶。

✎ 12 画
口 部
囗 左　右

愧 愧愧愧愧愧愧愧愧愧愧愧

kūn 昆虫、昆仑　*elder brother*

☞ 比，第二画是乚，不分为两笔；第三画是撇，不是横。

✎ 8 画
日 部
囗 上　下

昆 昆昆昆昆昆昆昆昆

kǔn 捆绑、成捆儿、一捆旧书

✎ 10 画
扌 部
囗 左　右

捆 捆捆捆捆捆捆捆捆捆

be stranded, be hard pressed

(*睏) kùn 贫困、困难、困在旅途、困乏、*困得睁不开眼

☞ 全包围结构。

✎ 7 画
口 部
囗 包围

困 困困困困困困

(擴) kuò 扩大、扩张、扩展

✎ 6 画
扌 部
囗 左　右

扩 扩扩扩扩扩

写铅笔字时要做到三个"一"：胸口与桌沿保持一个拳头的距离，头梢前倾；眼睛与桌面保持一尺左右的距离；大拇指与食指捏在离笔尖约一寸（约三厘米）的笔杆上。

kuò 包括、括号

✎ 9 画
扌 部
囗 左　右

括 括括括括括括括括

(闊) kuò 辽阔、阔步、阔气、阔别

☞ 左上右包围结构。起笔，嵌在第二笔丨和第三笔冂之间。氵在框内，不写在框外。

✎ 12 画
门 部
囗 半包围

阔 阔阔阔阔阔阔阔阔阔阔

lā 垃圾

☞ 土的末笔改提。

✎ 8 画
土 部
囗 左　右

垃 垃垃垃垃垃垃垃

喇的中部、辣的右部、赖的左部是束，不是束，中间一竖不带钩。

lā 拉车、拉胡琴、拉开距离、拉关系、拉屎／lá 拉个口子

slash, slit, cut

✎ 8 画　🔲 扌部　左右

拉 拉拉拉拉拉拉拉拉

---

la 哗啦啦／la 您回来啦

✎ 11 画　🔲 口部　左右

啦啦啦啦啦啦
啦啦啦啦啦

> 小学阶段写字的总要求是：使学生会写铅笔字和钢笔字，学习写毛笔字；养成良好的书写习惯；书写工整，注意不写错别字。

---

lǎ 喇叭、喇嘛

🖉 束的末笔改点。

✎ 12 画　🔲 口部　左右

喇喇喇喇喇喇喇喇喇喇喇喇

（臘）là 腊月、腊肉

✎ 12 画　🔲 月部　左右

腊腊腊腊腊腊腊腊腊腊腊腊

（蠟）là 石蜡、蜡烛、点蜡

wax, candle (floor) polish

✎ 14 画　🔲 虫部　左右

蜡蜡蜡蜡蜡蜡蜡蜡蜡蜡
蜡蜡蜡

---

là 辣椒、辣酱、毒辣　🖉 辛的末笔改撇。

first part of pepper

✎ 14 画　🔲 辛部　左右

辣辣辣辣辣辣辣辣辣辣辣辣
辣辣

（來）lái 来往、将来、近来、六十来岁

COME, ARRIVE

🖉 中间一竖不带钩。

✎ 7 画　🔲 一部　独体

来来来来来来来

> 古字形像小麦。后借表来去的来。
> 来（金文）　米（甲文）

（賴）lài 依赖、撒赖、不分好赖、赖账、诬赖、无赖

✎ 13 画　🔲 刀部　左右

🖉 束的末笔改点。右边是负不是页。

赖赖赖赖赖赖赖赖赖赖赖赖赖

depend on, hang on in one place

（蘭）lán 兰花、吊兰　ORCHID

✎ 5　画
▭ 八　部
⚅ 上　下

兰　兰兰兰兰兰

上边倒开八朵花，下边三层把根扎；
幽香扑面纸上来，传遍千万百姓家。

字谜

（攔）lán 阻拦、拦腰截断

BAR, BLOCK, HOLD BACK

✎ 8　画
▭ 扌　部
⚅ 左　右

拦　拦拦拦拦拦拦拦拦

（欄）lán 栏杆、牛栏、栏目、布告栏、跨栏

☞ 木的中间一竖不带钩，末笔改点。

FENCE, RAILING, PEN SHED

✎ 9　画
▭ 木　部
⚅ 左　右

栏　栏栏栏栏栏栏栏栏栏

（藍）lán 青出于蓝、天蓝　BLUE

☞ 艹3画，第三画楷体是撇，宋体是竖。

✎ 13　画
▭ 艹　部
⚅ 上　下

蓝　蓝蓝蓝蓝蓝蓝蓝蓝蓝蓝蓝蓝蓝蓝

（籃）lán 竹篮、篮球、投篮、篮坛　BASKET

篮篮篮篮篮篮篮篮

✎ 16　画
▭ 竹　部
⚅ 上　下

篮　篮篮篮篮篮篮篮篮

（覽）lán 展览、阅览　MOURING ROPE, CABLE

☞ 左上两竖，不是一竖一撇。见的第二画乛不带钩。

✎ 9　画
▭ 见　部
⚅ 上　下

览　览览览览览览览览览

（懶）lán 偷懒、懒洋洋、懒得说她　☞ 中部是束不是束，末笔改点。右部是负不

是页。

懒懒懒懒懒

✎ 16　画
▭ 忄　部
⚅ 左　右

懒　懒懒懒懒懒懒懒懒懒懒

---

sodden, mashed, (clothes) worn out

（爛）làn 烂面条、烂泥、腐烂、破衣烂衫、烂账、烂熟

☞ 火的末笔改点。

✎ 9　画
▭ 火　部
⚅ 左　右

烂　烂烂烂烂烂烂烂烂

郎、廊、朗的良，末两画丿和乀改一画丶(点)；阝两画，起笔了不分为两笔。

(濫) làn 泛滥、狂轰滥炸、滥调 *overflow, flood, excessive indiscriminate*

☞ 监的左上是两竖，不是一竖一撇。

✎ 13 画
部 氵部
⿰ 左 右

 滥滥滥滥滥滥滥滥滥滥滥滥滥

láng 员外郎、郎君、女郎 *an ancient official title*

✎ 8 画
⿰ 右 阝部
左 右

 郎郎郎郎郎郎郎郎

láng 狼狗、色狼 *wolf*

✎ 10 画
部 犭部
⿰ 左 右

 狼狼狼狼狼狼狼狼狼

láng 走廊、长廊 *porch, corridor*

☞ 上左包围结构。

✎ 11 画
部 广部
⿸ 半包围

 廊廊廊廊廊廊廊廊廊廊

lǎng 晴朗、朗诵 *light, bright loud & clear*

✎ 10 画
部 月部
⿰ 左 右

朗朗朗朗朗朗朗朗朗朗

làng 波浪、气浪、浪费 *wave, billow unrestrained*

✎ 10 画
部 氵部
⿰ 左 右

 浪浪浪浪浪浪浪浪浪

(撈) lāo 捞鱼、捞外快 *drag, dredge up — fish for*

☞ 扌+3画，第三画楷体是撇，宋体是竖。

✎ 10 画
部 扌部
⿰ 左 右

捞捞捞捞捞捞捞捞捞

(勞) láo 劳累、劳神、劳驾、功劳、劳务 *work, labour*

☞ 艹+3画，第三画楷体是撇，宋体是竖。

✎ 7 画
部 艹部
⿱ 上 下

 劳劳劳劳劳劳劳

以汉字字形为材料的文学，可以称为"字形文学"，主要是"拆字对联"。如：上联：冻雨洒窗，东二点、西三点。下联：切糕分客，上七刀、下八刀。"东二点"："冻"，"西三点"："洒"；"上七刀"："切"，"下八刀"："分"。

láo 亡羊补牢、监牢、牢固、牢靠

pen, fold ~ *sacrifice, prison, gail* ~ *firm fast durable*

✎ 7 画
⿱ 宀部
上 下

牢 牢牢牢牢牢牢牢

古字形像牲口栏。
(金文)
(甲文)

---

lǎo 尊老爱幼、老手、老字号、老脑筋、肉炒老了、老鼠

old, aged

☞ 上左包围结构。

✎ 6 画
⿸ 老部
半包围

老 老老老老老老

老师
lǎo shī - teacher

---

lǎo 姥姥

☞ 女的横笔右端不出头。

✎ 9 画
⿰ 女部
左 右

姥 姥姥姥姥姥姥姥姥姥

（澇） lào 旱涝保收、排涝 *waterlogging*

☞ 艹3画，第三画楷体是撇，宋体是竖。

✎ 10 画
⿰ 氵部
左 右

涝 涝涝涝涝涝涝涝涝涝涝

（樂） lè 快乐、取乐、喜闻乐见 /yuè 音乐

happy, cheerful, joyful

☞ 第二画是乚，不分为两笔。小的左侧楷体是点，宋体是撇。

✎ 5 画
丿部
独体

乐 乐乐乐乐乐

古字形把丝附在木上，像琴瑟。
(金文)
(甲文)

---

lè 悬崖勒马、勒索 /lēi 勒紧腰带

stop, force, coerce ~ *carve*

☞ 艹4画，第二画竖、第四画横不连成一笔。

✎ 11 画
⿰ 革部
左 右

勒 勒勒勒勒勒勒勒勒勒勒勒

---

léi 春雷、地雷 *thunder, (land) mine*

☞ 雨，第二画改、(点)，第三画改一(横钩)，里边楷体是四点，宋体是四横。

✎ 13 画
⿱ 雨部
上 下

雷 雷雷雷雷雷雷雷雷雷雷雷雷雷

（壘） lěi 堡垒、垒墙

☞ 上部是三个厶，不是三个又。

✎ 9 画
⿱ 厶部
上 下

垒 垒垒垒垒垒垒垒垒垒

(*纍) lěi *累计、*连篇累牍、牵累 /léi 劳累、累了一生 /lèi *累赘、*硕果累累

pile up, accumulate,

☞ 小的左侧楷体是点，宋体是撇。

✎ 11 画
田 部
上 下

累 累累累累累累累累累累累累

lèi 流泪、热泪 *tear, teardrop*

✎ 8 画
氵 部
左 右

泪 泪泪泪泪泪泪泪泪

(類) lèi 类别、类似 *kind, type, class, resemble to.*

☞ 米，中间一竖不带钩，末笔改点。下边是大不是犬。

✎ 9 画
米 部
上 下

类 类类类类类类类类类

lěng 寒冷、冷淡、冷清、冷僻、冷枪、冷门

cold — strang, rare

✎ 7 画
冫 部
左 右

冷 冷冷冷冷冷冷冷

lí 10厘等于1分、利息降为2厘、厘米 *a unit of length*

☞ 上左包围结构。左上是厂不是广。

✎ 9 画
厂 部
半包围

厘 厘厘厘厘厘厘厘厘

lí 狸猫 /lí 狐狸

狸狸狸狸狸

✎ 10 画
犭 左 右

狸 狸狸狸狸狸

有些部件的笔顺会随着笔画形状的改变而改变，如"车"作部件出现在左侧位置时，第三笔横改为提，同时变笔顺一ナ左车车为一ナ车车车。

(離) lí 离别、离心离德、距离

☞ 下部是凵4画，不是凵5画。

✎ 10 画
亠 上 下

离 离离离离离离离离离

lí 香水梨、梨罐头 *PEAR*

☞ 禾的竖笔不带钩，末笔改点。右上是刂不是勹。木的中间一竖不带钩。

✎ 11 画
木 部
上 下

梨 梨梨梨梨梨梨梨梨梨梨梨

犁、黎的禾，竖笔不带钩，末笔改点。

---

lí 铁犁、犁田 *Plough*

✎ 11 画
部 牛 上下

犁 犁犁犁犁犁犁犁犁犁犁犁

---

lí 玻璃、琉璃 ☞ 王的末笔改提。右下是禸4画，不是禸5画。

✎ 14 画
部 王 左右

璃璃璃璃璃璃璃璃璃璃璃
璃璃璃

---

lí 黎民百姓、黎明 ☞ 黎的右上是勿不是勿；下部是氺5画，不写成水4画。

✎ 15 画
部 水 上下

黎黎黎黎黎黎黎黎黎黎黎
黎黎黎黎

(禮) *ceremony, right*

lǐ 婚礼、礼教、礼节、礼品

☞ 左边是礻不是衤 *etiquette, manners*

✎ 5 画
部 礻 左右

礼 礼礼礼礼礼

《世说新语》记载一则有关字谜的故事：曹操新修的门太大，不直说，让人在门上写了一个"活"字。众人不明白曹操的意思，问杨修。杨指着字说：这不是一个"阔"字吗。他嫌门修得大了。

---

lǐ 李子、桃李满天下 *plum*

☞ 木的中间一竖不带钩。

✎ 7 画
部 木 上下

李 李李李李李李李

(*裏) lǐ 邻里、故里，1市里等于500米、*被里/li *屋里、*这里、*哪里

in, inside (the room)

— neighborhood

✎ 7 画
部 里 独体

里 里里里里里里里

---

texture, reason, logic, truth

lǐ 理财、理睬、清理、条理、理论、理科 *manage, run*

☞ 王的末笔改提。 *put in order*

✎ 11 画
部 王 左右

理 理理理理理理理理理理理

---

lì 体力、生命力、药力、据理力争

strength

✎ 2 画
部 力 独体

力 力力

古字形像农具耒(lěi)。(金文)(甲文)

历

（歷＊曆）lì 历程、简历、历代、＊历法、＊年历

☞ 上左包围结构，右下是力。

✎ 4 画
□ 厂 部
☒ 半包围

历　历 历 历 历

厉

（厲）lì 严厉、厉行节约 *strict, rigorous.* *stern*

☞ 上左包围结构。

✎ 5 画
□ 厂 部
☒ 半包围

厉　厉 厉 厉 厉 厉

立

lì 站立、成立、立法、立柜、势不两立、立刻 *stand, stand up* *found, establish, exist, live*

✎ 5 画
□ 立 部
☒ 独体

立　立 立 立 立 立

丽

（麗）lì 美丽、富丽 *beautiful*

☞ 上部是一横，不分为两小横。

✎ 7 画
□ 一 部
☒ 上 下

丽　丽 丽 丽 丽 丽 丽 丽

励

（勵）lì 鼓励、激励 *encourage, reward, award*

✎ 7 画
□ 力 部
☒ 左 右

励　励 励 励 励 励 励 励

利

lì 锋利、顺利、有利无害、薄利、利国利民 *sharp, favourable, advantage*

☞ 禾，中间一竖不带钩，末笔改成点。

✎ 7 画
□ 禾 部
☒ 左 右

利　利 利 利 利 利 利 利

古字形像用刀收割庄稼。

（金文）（甲文）

例

lì 先例、例证、条例、例会

✎ 8 画
□ 亻 部
☒ 左 右

例　例 例 例 例 例 例 例 例

隶

（隸）lì 奴隶、隶属、隶书

☞ 上部不是彐，中间一横右端出头；下部是水5画，不写成水4画。

✎ 8 画
□ 隶 部
☒ 独体

隶　隶 隶 隶 隶 隶 隶 隶 隶

在历史上，汉字除了自身发展演变以外，它的传播路线有三条：一条向南和西南，传播到广西壮族和越南京族，稍晚又传播到四川、贵州、云南和湖南等省的苗、瑶（yáo）、布依、侗（dòng）、白、哈尼、水、傈僳（lìsù）等少数民族。一条向东，传播到朝鲜和日本。一条向西北和西北，传播到宋代的契丹（qìdān）、女真和西夏。汉字传播到非汉语的民族和国家，成为各种汉字式的文字。据专家统计，汉语的汉字和非汉语的汉字式文字一共有20种，有的现在仍是正式应用的文字，有的早已成为过去，有的正在消亡。

连、莲的车，第二画是乚，不分为两笔；辶3画，第二画楷体是ㄋ，宋体是乁。

lì 栗子、不寒而栗

☞ 上部扁框中都是竖笔，不写成西。木的中间一竖不带钩。

✎ 10 画
□ 西 部
⊠ 上 下

栗 栗 栗 栗 栗 栗 栗 栗 栗 栗

---

lì 盐粒、颗粒、几粒面包屑

☞ 米，中间一竖不带钩，末笔改点。

✎ 11 画
□ 米 部
⊠ 左 右

粒 粒 粒 粒 粒 粒 粒 粒 粒 粒 粒

（倆） liǎ 兄弟俩、挣了俩钱儿／liǎng 伎俩 ☞ 两内的二人末笔都改点。

✎ 9 画
□ 亻部
⊠ 左 右

俩 俩 俩 俩 俩
俩 俩 俩 俩

> 在长期书写实践的基础上，方块汉字经过自然的筛选，形成了若干种基本的间架结构类型。除了独体结构以外，汉字的间架结构主要有左右类型、上下类型、包围类型、对称类型四大类。具体分为左右结构（群）、左中右结构（灏）、上下结构（粪）、上中下结构（曼）、上左包围结构（疾）、上右包围结构（司）、左下包围结构（过）、左上右包围结构（闻）、上左下包围结构（匠）、左下右包围结构（凶）、全包围结构（国）和对称结构（罂）等十二小类。

（連） lián 连续、藕断丝连、连队 ☞ 左下包围结构。

✎ 7 画
□ 辶 部
⊠ 半包围

连 连 连 连
连 连 连

（憐） lián 可怜、爱怜

✎ 8 画
□ 忄部
⊠ 左 右

怜 怜 怜 怜 怜 怜 怜 怜 怜

（＊簾） lián ·窗帘、酒帘

✎ 8 画
□ 穴 部
⊠ 上 下

帘 帘 帘 帘 帘 帘 帘 帘 帘

（蓮） lián 采莲、莲子

☞ 艹3画，覆盖全字，第三画楷体是撇，宋体是竖。

✎ 10 画
□ 艹 部
⊠ 上 下

莲 莲 莲 莲 莲 莲 莲 莲 莲 莲

（聯） lián 蝉联冠军、联系、对联

☞ 耳的末笔改提。

✎ 12 画
□ 耳 部
⊠ 左 右

联 联 联 联 联 联 联 联 联 联 联

lián 清廉、物美价廉

✎ 13 画
☐ 广 部
☒ 半包围

廉 廉廉廉廉廉廉廉廉廉廉廉廉

(鐮) lián 镰刀、开镰

☞ 钅5画，第二画是横，不是点；第五画是乚，不分为两笔。

✎ 18 画
☐ 钅 部
☒ 左 右

镰 镰镰镰镰镰镰镰
镰镰镰镰镰镰镰镰镰镰

(臉) lián 洗脸、丢脸、愁眉苦脸、门脸儿

☞ 右部人下有一短横。

✎ 11 画
☐ 月 部
☒ 左 右

脸 脸脸脸脸脸脸脸脸脸脸

(練) liàn 彩练、练习、熟练

☞ 纟3画，上部不是幺。右部不是东，第三画是乛。

✎ 8 画
☐ 纟 部
☒ 左 右

练 练练练练练练练练

(煉) liàn 炼钢、锻炼、炼字

☞ 火的末笔改点。右部不是东，第三画是乛。

✎ 9 画
☐ 火 部
☒ 左 右

炼 炼炼炼炼炼炼炼炼炼

(戀) liàn 依恋、恋爱

☞ 上部不是亦，中间是两竖。心的第二画楷体是⺄(卧钩)，宋体是乚(竖弯钩)。

✎ 10 画
☐ 心 部
☒ 上 下

恋 恋恋恋恋恋恋恋恋恋恋

(鏈) liàn 链条、拉链

☞ 钅5画，第二画是横，第五画是乚(竖提)。辶的第二画楷体是乛，宋体是乛。

✎ 12 画
☐ 钅 部
☒ 左 右

链 链链链链链链链链链链链链

liáng 良田、良久

✎ 7 画
☐ 艮 部
☒ 独 体

良 良良良良良良良

凉、谅的小，左侧楷体是点，宋体是撇。

liáng 凉菜、悲凉、荒凉、凉鞋/**liàng** 粥凉一会儿再喝

✎ 10 画
冫部
左右

凉凉凉凉凉凉凉凉凉凉

liáng 桥梁、房梁、鼻梁

☞ 右上不是刃。木的中间一竖不带钩。

✎ 11 画
木部
上下

梁梁梁梁梁梁梁梁梁梁梁

字谜
三点边上瞧，两点飞上刀；
一木把它撑，千斤不弯腰。

liáng 量血压、估量/**liàng** 度量衡、产量、量力而行

✎ 12 画
日部
上下

量量量量量量量量量量量

（糧）**liáng** 粮食、公粮

☞ 米，中间一竖不带钩，末笔改点。

✎ 13 画
米部
左右

粮粮粮粮粮粮粮粮粮粮粮粮

liáng 高粱

☞ 米，中间一竖不带钩。

✎ 13 画
米部
上下

粱粱粱粱粱粱粱粱粱粱粱粱粱

（兩）**liǎng** 两只手、势不两立、多待两天

☞ 下部框内两人的末笔都改点。

✎ 7 画
一部
独体

两两两两两两两

liàng 明亮、亮着灯、响亮、心明眼亮、亮相

✎ 9 画
亠部
上下

亮亮亮亮亮亮亮亮亮

piào liang
漂亮
(second part beautiful)

（諒）**liàng** 原谅、谅你不敢　☞ 讠两画，第二画讠
不分为两笔或三笔。

✎ 10 画
讠部
左右

谅谅谅谅谅
谅谅谅谅谅

出言操京腔，教人
多忍让；都说它可
交，为人有肚量。
字谜

(輛) liàng 车辆、一辆轿车 *for vehicles a lorry*

车下部的一横改提，笔顺改先竖后提。两，框内二人的末笔都改点。

11 画
车 部
左 右

辆 辆 辆 辆 辆 辆 辆 辆 辆 辆 辆

(遼) liáo 辽远、辽阔 *distant, far away*

左下包围结构。辶 3 画，第二画楷体是乁(横折折撇)，宋体是乁(横折)。

5 画
辶 部
半包围

辽 辽 辽 辽 辽

(療) liáo 治疗、疗养 *treat, cure*

上左包围结构。

7 画
疒 部
半包围

疗 疗 疗 疗 疗 疗 疗

liáo 官僚、同僚 *official*

右下小的左侧，楷体是点，宋体是撇。

14 画
亻 部
左 右

僚 僚 僚 僚 僚 僚 僚 僚
僚 僚 僚 僚 僚 僚

"了"读 liǎo 的时候，仍是"瞭"的简化字形，但已不再作为"瞭"(liào)的简化字形。所以，"瞭望"已不能简化作"了望"。

(*瞭) liǎo 了结、*了解、了不得

/le 下雪了、刮风了 *to know or understand*

2 画
乛 部
独体

了 了

liào 预料、料理、衣料、颜料、资料 *expect, predict, anticipate*

米，中间一竖不带钩，末笔改点。

10 画
米 部
左 右
料 料 料 料 料
料 料 料 料 料

"金文"是古代汉字一种字体的名称，是商、西周、春秋、战国时期铸刻在钟、鼎、壶、爵、戈、剑等所有铜器上的汉字字体的总称。先秦称铜为金，所以把青铜器上的文字称为金文。金文的象形味道比较浓，是我国商代晚期和周代早期汉字的正体。如"亻"(人)、"象"(象)。

liè 列队、行列、列强、列入 *line up, arrange, list*

6 画
刂 部
左 右

列 列 列 列 列 列

liè 优劣、劣等 *Bad, inferior, of low quality*

少，中间一竖不带钩；左侧楷体是点，宋体是撇。

6 画
力 部
上 下
劣 劣 劣 劣 劣 劣

lìe 烈日、刚烈　*Strong, violent, intense*

烈烈烈烈烈
烈烈烈烈烈

（獵）lìe 猎人、猎取

猎猎猎猎猎猎
猎猎猎猎猎

lìe 破裂、分裂／liě 上衣没扣好，裂着怀

裂裂裂裂裂裂裂裂裂裂裂裂

（鄰）lín 左邻右舍、邻国

☞ 令的第二画改点。阝两画，第一画了不分为两笔。

邻邻邻邻邻邻邻

lín 竹林、林业、碑林　*woods, grove, forest*

林林林林林林林林

（臨）lín 居高临下、降临、临街、临终、临摹

☞ 左部是两竖，不是一竖一撇。右下是横"日"，不是两口。

临临临临临临临临

lín 淋浴、淋雨／lìn 淋盐、淋病　*pour, drench*

淋淋淋淋淋淋淋淋淋淋淋

líng 名伶、伶俐　*actor, actress*

伶伶伶伶
伶伶伶

所谓一笔和一画，指的是写字时从落笔到提笔的过程中写出的点或线。现代汉字现有的笔画是在长期书写实践过程中约定俗成的。我们今天分析现代汉字的笔画，无论是笔画数、笔画形状、笔画与相邻笔画的关系或书写时笔画出现的先后顺序，都以国家语言文字工作委员会和新闻出版署于1988年联合发布的《现代汉语通用字表》所提供的规范字形为依据。

双木非两棵，成片长满坡；春夏一片绿，护土保动物。
字谜

古字形突出眼睛，像俯视众物。（金文）

黑体是印刷体中比较常用的一种字体。它的特点是笔画粗重、横竖一致，显得醒目、有力，多用于标题和正文中需要强调的地方。如：**新华写字字典**。

（靈）líng 心灵、灵车、灵验、机灵、灵便 *quick, clever, sharp*

☞ 上部是彐，中间一横右端不出头。

✎ 7 画　部 彐 上　画部 下

灵｜灵灵灵灵灵灵灵

（鈴）líng 摇铃、杠铃

☞ 钅5画，第二画是横，不是点；第五画是乚，不分为两笔。

✎ 10 画　画 钅 左　部 右

铃｜铃铃铃铃铃铃铃铃铃铃

líng 丘陵、陵园

☞ 阝两画，第一画了不分为两笔。右下是夂不是夊。

✎ 10 画　画 阝左　部 左　右

陵｜陵陵陵陵陵陵陵陵陵陵

líng 凋零、零碎、零头 *Zero*

☞ 雨，第二画改、（点），第三画改一（横钩），里边楷体是四点，宋体是四横。

✎ 13 画　部 雨 上　画部 下

零｜零零零零零零零零零零零零零

（齡）líng 年龄、工龄

☞ 齿，人的末笔改点，第七画改竖提。

✎ 13 画　画 齿 左　部 右

龄｜龄龄龄龄龄龄龄龄龄龄龄龄龄

（嶺）líng 分水岭、兴安岭

☞ 左右结构，不作上下结构。山，第二画改竖提，不分为两笔。

✎ 8 画　画 山 左　部 右

岭｜岭岭岭岭岭岭岭岭

（領）líng 领带、领口、纲领、占领、领路、领教、领悟

☞ 令的第二画改点。

✎ 11 画　画 页 左　部 右

领｜领领领领领领领领领领

líng 另册、另立门户 *another, separately*

✎ 5 画　口 上　画部 下

另｜另另另另另

国家标准局于1987年3月公布《信息交换用汉字编码字符集·第二辅助集》（GB7589-87），收7237字，是简化汉字集。

líng 命令、时令、利令智昏、县令 /lìng 500张纸是1令

command, order, decree

✎ 5 画
□ 人 部
囚 上 下

 令令令令令

liū 溜冰、溜走、滑溜 /liù 一溜烟、一溜衣柜、溜墙缝

Slide, glide, sneak off

✎ 13 画
□ 氵部
囚 左 右

 溜溜溜溜溜溜
溜溜溜溜溜溜溜

（劉）liú 姓刘
☞ 文的末笔改点。

✎ 6 画
□ 文 部
囚 左

 刘刘刘刘刘刘

---

liú 停留、挽留、保留、残留、留心、留学

✎ 10 画
□ 田 部
囚 上 下

 留留留留留留留留留留

---

liú 流淌、流浪、流传、水流、气流、流派、流畅

✎ 10 画
□ 氵部
囚 左 右

 流流流流流流流流流流

---

liú 石榴　☞ 木的中间一竖不带钩，末笔改点。

✎ 14 画
□ 木 部
囚 左 右

 榴榴榴榴榴榴榴
榴榴榴榴榴榴榴

---

liǔ 杨柳
☞ 木的中间一竖不带钩，末笔改点。右部是卯不是卬。

✎ 9 画
□ 木 部
囚 左

 柳柳柳柳柳柳柳柳柳

---

liù 三加三得六　*six*

✎ 4 画
□ 亠 部
囚 上 下

 六六六六

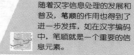

(龍) lóng 画龙点睛、龙袍、龙舟、恐龙

 龙龙龙龙龙
5 画　龙部　独体

(聾) lóng 耳聋眼花、聋子

 聋聋聋聋聋聋聋聋聋聋聋
11 画　龙部　上下

(籠) lóng 鸟笼、小笼包子／lǒng 笼罩、箱笼

 笼笼笼笼笼笼笼笼笼笼笼
11 画　竹部　上下

lóng 隆重、隆起、隆冬／lōng 轰隆一声

阝两画，第一画了不分为两笔。

 隆隆隆隆隆隆隆隆隆隆隆
11 画　阝部　左右

(攏) lǒng 拉拢、靠拢、归拢、拢头发

 拢拢拢拢拢拢拢拢
8 画　扌部　左右

(壟) lǒng 垄沟、宽垄密植

 垄垄垄垄垄垄垄垄
8 画　龙部　上下

(樓) lóu 楼房、牌楼、茶楼

木的中间一竖不带钩，末笔改点。

楼楼楼楼楼楼楼楼楼楼楼楼楼
13 画　木部　左右

(摟) lǒu 搂腰、搂抱／lōu 搂树叶、搂钱

搂搂搂搂搂搂搂搂搂搂
12 画　扌部　左右

lòu 漏水、走漏、挂一漏万

✎ 14 画
🔲 氵左 右

漏漏漏漏漏漏漏
漏漏漏漏漏漏漏

屋外滴水流，屋内雨不住。
"至"字哪里去？早被雨冲走。

字谜

（蘆）lú 芦苇 /lǔ 油葫芦

☞ 艹3画，第三画楷体是撇，宋体是竖。

✎ 7 画
🔲 艹上 下

芦芦芦芦芦芦芦

（爐）lú 炉子、火炉

☞ 火的末笔改点。右部是户不是卢。

✎ 8 画
🔲 火部左 右

炉炉炉炉炉炉炉炉

（虜）lǔ 俘虏 ☞ 上左包围结构。

✎ 8 画
🔲 虍部半包围

虏虏虏虏
虏虏虏虏

毛笔的执笔方法：(1) 拇指在内，食指在外，捏紧笔杆；(2) 中指靠在食指下边，辅助食指，使笔杆正直；(3) 无名指抵在笔杆内侧，向外抵住笔杆，以保住笔杆稳定；(4) 小指紧贴无名指之下，但不贴住笔杆，以辅助无名指；(5) 五指执笔，既不要"松"，也不要"死"，而以"紧"为度；(6) 执毛笔时要做到指实掌虚；(7) 捏笔杆的部位要看所写字的大小。写小字，执笔略低；写中字，稍高；写大字，再高些。

（魯）lǔ 粗鲁、鲁菜

✎ 12 画
🔲 鱼部上 下

鲁鲁鲁鲁鲁鲁
鲁鲁鲁鲁鲁鲁

（陸）lù 陆地、陆运 /liù "六"的大写是陆

☞ 阝两画，第一画了不分为两笔。

✎ 7 画
🔲 阝部左 右

陆陆陆陆陆陆陆

（録）lù 记录、通讯录、录用、录音

☞ 上部是彐不是⺕。下部是水5画，不写成水4画。

✎ 8 画
🔲 彐部上 下

录录录录录录录录

---

lù 梅花鹿、鹿茸 ☞ 上左包围结构。比，第二画是乚，不分为两笔；右部不是匕不是匕。

✎ 11 画
🔲 鹿部半包围

鹿鹿鹿鹿鹿鹿鹿鹿鹿鹿

古字形像鹿。（金文）（甲文）

路、露的路，左下止的末笔改提，右上是夂不是夂。

lù 庸碌、劳碌 /liù 碌碡(zhou)

☞ 右上是彐不是彑。右下是水5画，不写成水4画。

✎ 13 画
▢ 石 部
◹ 左 右

碌 *碌碌碌碌碌碌碌碌碌碌碌碌碌*

lù 道路、门路、思路、大路货

✎ 13 画
▢ 足 部
◹ 左 右

路 *路路路路路路路路路路路路路*

lù 露水、露天、暴露、果子露 /lòu 露脸、露一手

☞ 雨，第二画改点，第三画改横钩，里边楷体是四点，宋体是四横。

✎ 21 画
▢ 雨 部
◹ 上 下

露 *露露露露露露露露露露露露露露露露露露露露露*

(驢) **lǘ** 毛驴、驴肉 ☞ 马的第一画㇖、第二画㇆都不分为两笔；左上角开口；末笔改提。右边是户不是卢。

✎ 7 画
▢ 马 部
◹ 左 右

驴 *驴驴驴驴驴驴驴*

lǚ 军旅、旅客

☞ 右下是氏不是氏。

✎ 10 画
▢ 方 部
◹ 左 右

旅 *旅旅旅旅旅旅旅旅旅旅*

古字形用多人集中在军旗下表示军旅的意思。
(甲文) (金文)

(屢) **lǚ** 屡战屡胜、屡败屡战

☞ 上左包围结构。米的中间一竖不带钩。

✎ 12 画
▢ 尸 部
◹ 半包围

屡 *屡屡屡屡屡屡屡屡屡屡屡屡*

lǜ 音律、法律、严于律己

☞ 右部的上边不是彐，中间一横右端出头。

✎ 9 画
▢ 彳 部
◹ 左 右

律 *律律律律律律律律*

(慮) **lǜ** 考虑、顾虑 consider punder think

☞ 上左包围结构。心的第二画楷体是㇃(卧钩)，宋体是乚(竖弯钩)。

✎ 10 画
▢ 虍 部
◹ 半包围

虑 *虑虑虑虑虑虑虑虑虑*

（绿）lǜ 花红柳绿 /lù 绿林　　*green*

☞ 纟3画，上部不是纟。右上是彐不是彑，右下是水5画，不写成水4画。

✎ 11　画
☐ 纟　部
☑ 左　右

绿　绿绿绿绿绿绿绿绿绿绿绿绿

（滤）lǜ 过滤、滤纸

☞ 心的第二画楷体是㇃(卧钩)，宋体是L(竖弯钩)。

✎ 13　画
☐ 氵　部
☑ 左　右

滤　滤滤滤滤滤滤滤滤滤滤滤滤

luǎn 产卵、鸟卵、卵生、杀鸡取卵

✎ 7　画
☐ 丿　部
☑ 左　右

卵　卵卵卵卵卵卵卵

> 杭州孤山的西泠印社有一镇社之宝，就是山颠的东汉《三老讳字忌日碑》藏石。这块碑1852年出土于馀姚。1921年，有人把这块石碑运到上海，想卖给洋人。西泠印社在上海的社员听到这一消息，立即募捐八千，将碑赎回，运回杭州，藏于孤山。他们这一义举功垂青史。

（亂）luàn 杂乱、兵荒马乱、慌乱、乱花钱

☞ 舌的起笔是撇不是横。

✎ 7　画
☐ 舌　部
☑ 左　右

乱　乱乱乱乱乱乱乱

lüè 掠夺、海燕掠过海面

☞ 小的左侧楷体是点，宋体是撇。

✎ 11　画
☐ 扌　部
☑ 左　右

掠　掠掠掠掠掠掠掠掠掠掠掠

lüè 侵略、策略、传略、粗略、省略

☞ 右上是夂不是夂。

✎ 11　画
☐ 田　部
☑ 左　右

略　略略略略略略略略略略略

（輪）lún 车轮、轮流、年轮、海轮、一轮明月、首轮影院

☞ 车的下部一横改提，笔顺改先竖后提。

✎ 8　画
☐ 车　部
☑ 左　右

轮　轮轮轮轮轮轮轮轮

（論）lùn 讨论、论罪、论小时收费、一概而论、自有公论

☞ 讠两画，第二画㇊不分为两笔或三笔。

✎ 6　画
☐ 讠　部
☑ 左　右

论　论论论论论论论

罗、萝、锣、箩的罗，上部是横"目"，不写成四。骆、络的右上是夂不是夂。

(羅) luó 罗网、搜罗、绫罗绸缎、绢罗、罗面、星罗棋布

8画　皿部　上下

罗 罗 罗 罗 罗 罗 罗 罗 罗

húluóbo -carrot

(蘿) luó 藤萝、萝卜

艹3画，第三画楷体是撇，宋体是竖。

11画　艹部　上下

萝 萝 萝 萝 萝 萝 萝 萝 萝 萝 萝

(鑼) luó 敲锣打鼓

钅5画，第二画是横，不是点；第五画是乚，不分为两笔。

13画　钅部　左右

锣 锣 锣 锣 锣 锣 锣 锣 锣 锣 锣 锣

(籮) luó 箩筐

箩 箩 箩 箩 箩 箩 箩

14画　竹部　上下

箩 箩 箩 箩 箩 箩 箩

(騾) luó 骡子　马的第一画𠃌、第二画𠃌都不分为两笔，左上角开口，末笔改提。小的左侧楷体是点，宋体是撇。

14画　马部　左右

骡 骡 骡 骡 骡

骡 骡 骡 骡 骡 骡 骡 骡 骡

luó 螺丝、螺纹　右下小的左侧楷体是点，宋体是撇。

17画　虫部　左右

螺 螺 螺 螺 螺 螺 螺 螺 螺 螺 螺

螺 螺 螺 螺 螺

(駱) luò 骆驼　马的第一画𠃌、第二画𠃌都不分为两笔，左上角开口，末笔改提。

9画　马部　左右

骆 骆 骆 骆 骆 骆 骆 骆 骆

(絡) luò 网络、笼络 /lào 络子　纟3画，上部不是幺。

9画　纟部　左右

络 络 络 络 络 络 络 络 络

luò 落泪、衰落、旁落、落款、村落 /lào 落枕 /là 丢三落四
⚘ 艹+3画，第三画楷体是撇，宋体是竖。各的上部是夂不是夂。
✎ 12 画　艹部
☐ 上 下

落 落落落落落落落落落落落落

（媽）mā 妈妈、姑妈、李大妈 *mummy, ma*
⚘ 女的横笔右端不出头。
✎ 6 画　女部
☐ 左 右

妈 妈妈妈妈妈妈

heme, flax, jute
má 亚麻、麻油、麻子、麻木、麻辣烫
⚘ 上左包围结构。木的中间一竖不带钩，左边木的末笔改点。
✎ 11 画　麻部
☐ 半包围

麻 麻麻麻麻麻麻麻麻麻麻麻

（馬）mǎ 骏马、马蜂
horse
✎ 3 画　马部
☐ 独体

马 马马马

古字形像马。🐎（金文）（甲文）

（碼）mǎ 号码、筹码、码放、两码事
yard, indicates matter
✎ 8 画　石部
☐ 左 右

码 码码码码码码码码

（螞）mǎ 蚂蟥、蚂蚁
✎ 9 画　虫部
☐ 左 右

蚂 蚂蚂蚂蚂蚂蚂蚂蚂

（罵）mà 骂人、责骂
scold, curse
⚘ 上部是两个口，不是横"目"。
✎ 9 画　口部
☐ 上 下

骂 骂骂骂骂骂骂骂骂骂

（嗎）ma 去过四川吗 /mǎ 吗啡
question - what?
✎ 6 画　口部
☐ 左 右

吗 吗吗吗吗吗吗

草书是社会要求快速书写的产物。草化的方法主要有两种：一是省笔，一是连笔。草化的省笔和连笔，强化并丰富了汉字点画线条化的表现能力。草书一旦草到不能辨识的地步就成了天书，也就无所谓艺术性。任何书体都应该以识读为基础。无识读性的书体几乎都无生命力。这应该是中国书法的基本规律之一。

mái 埋葬、埋没 /mán 埋怨　BURY
☞ 土的末笔改提。
✎ 10　画
土部
左　右　埋　埋 埋 埋 埋 埋 埋 埋 埋 埋

（買）　mǎi 买房、买通　BUY, Purchase
☞ 上部是一(横钩)不是一。
✎ 6　画
一部
独体　买　买 买 买 买 买 买

（邁）　mài 迈步、年迈　step, stride
☞ 左下包围结构。辶3画，第二画楷体是㇋，宋体是乛。
✎ 6　画
辶部
半包围　迈　迈 迈 迈 迈 迈 迈

（麥）　mài 麦子、燕麦　wheat
☞ 下部是夂不是夊。
✎ 7　画
麦部
上　下　麦　麦 麦 麦 麦 麦 麦

字谜　青山藏明月，友人不露头；
　　　到了夏收时，场上堆如丘。

（賣）　mài 卖菜、卖艺、卖力、卖弄　sell, betray, exert one's self
☞ 上部是十，不是士或土。十下是一不是亠。
✎ 8　画
十部
上　下　卖　卖 卖 卖 卖 卖 卖 卖 卖

---

mài 动脉、诊脉、山脉 /mò 脉脉含情　arteries veins
☞ 永的第二画是丁(横折钩)，不分为两笔。
✎ 9　画
月部
左　右　脉　脉 脉 脉 脉 脉 脉 脉 脉 脉

（蠻）　mán 蛮横、蛮干　rough, unreasoning
☞ 上边不是亦，中间是两竖。
✎ 12　画
虫部
上　下　蛮　蛮 蛮 蛮 蛮 蛮 蛮 蛮 蛮 蛮 蛮 蛮

（饅）　mán 馒头　☞ 饣3画，第二画是一，不是丶；第三画是㇟，不分为两笔。
✎ 14　画
饣部
左　右　馒　馒 馒 馒 馒 馒 馒 馒 馒 馒 馒 馒
馒 馒

(瞒) mán 隐瞒、欺上瞒下　☞ 艹3画，第三画楷体是撇，宋体是竖。右下两，框内二人的末笔都改点。

✎ 15 画
目 部
左 右

瞒瞒瞒瞒瞒瞒瞒瞒
瞒瞒瞒瞒瞒瞒瞒瞒

(满) mǎn 客满、满足、自满、满口答应　☞ 艹3画，只覆盖两。艹第三画楷体是撇，宋体是竖。右下两，框内二人的末笔都改点。

✎ 13 画
氵 部
左 右

满满满满满满满满满满满满满

overflow, all over the place

---

màn 弥漫、散漫、漫长

✎ 14 画
氵 部
左 右

漫漫漫漫漫漫漫
漫漫漫漫漫漫漫

slow, slow down, postpone defer

---

màn 怠慢、不急不慢

✎ 14 画
忄 部
左 右

慢慢慢慢慢慢慢
慢慢慢慢慢慢慢

---

máng 麦芒、锋芒、光芒

✎ 6 画
艹 部
上 下

芒芒芒
芒芒芒

> 偏旁是汉字的一种结构单位。用传统的汉字字形分析法，习惯把左方称为"偏"，把右方称为"旁"。后来则把字形结构中的上下左右的构件统称为偏旁，比如"伟"左边的"亻"和右边的"韦"，"警"上边的"折"和下边的"言"，"闻"外边的"门"和里边的"耳"，"逞"左下的"辶"和右上的"皇"。其中，表示字义所属类别和范围的叫"形旁"或"义旁"或"意符"，如上列"亻""言""耳""辶"等；标志字音的叫"声旁"或"音旁"或"音符"，如上列"韦""折""门""皇"等。

---

máng 繁忙、匆忙　　*busy, fully occupied, hasty-hurry*

✎ 6 画
忄 部
左 右

忙忙忙
忙忙忙

---

máng 盲人、色盲、盲从、盲点、盲文、盲动、盲干、盲流、盲棋、盲肠

☞ 上部是亡不是亾。　*Blind*

✎ 8 画
目 部
上 下

盲盲盲盲盲盲盲盲

---

máng 茫无边际、茫然、茫无头绪

☞ 艹3画，覆盖氵和亡。艹的第三画楷体是撇，宋体是竖。

✎ 9 画
艹 部
上 下

茫茫茫茫茫茫茫茫茫

māo 波斯猫 /máo 猫腰　*cat, kitten, purring*

⺾ 只覆盖右下的田。

✎ 11　画
部　犭　左　右

猫 猫猫猫猫猫猫猫猫猫猫

---

máo 汗毛、毛毛雨、毛重、毛坯、毛糙、心里发毛

hair, feather, small

毛 毛毛毛毛

古字形像羽毛。屮（金文）

---

máo 长矛、矛头　*spear*

✎ 5　画
矛　上　下

矛 矛矛矛矛矛

"行书"是汉字一种字体的名称。它产生在东汉晚期。行书近于楷书而不像楷书那样拘谨端庄，近于草书而又没有草书那样恣放潦草。它的笔画连绵适度而又清晰易认，成为适应性最强、应用范围最广、延续时间最长的一种字体。如"人"。

---

máo 茅草、白茅

✎ 8　画
⺾　上　下

茅 茅茅茅茅
茅茅茅茅

---

mào 茂密、声情并茂、根深叶茂

⺾ 下部是戊，不是戍或戌。

✎ 8　画
⺾　上　下

茂 茂茂茂茂茂茂茂茂

---

emit, give off, risk, brave

mào 冒险、冒犯、冒失、假冒、冒烟

⺾ 冂内两横跟左右都不相接。

✎ 9　画
日　上　下

冒 冒冒冒冒冒冒冒冒冒

（貿）mào 贸易、贸然　*foreign trade*

⺾ 贝的第二画乛不带钩。

✎ 9　画
贝　上　下

贸 贸贸贸贸贸贸贸贸贸

---

mào 礼帽、笔帽

⺾ 右上冂内两横跟左右都不相接。

✎ 12　画
巾　左　右

帽 帽帽帽帽帽帽帽帽帽帽帽

looks, appearance, good looks

mào 容貌、外貌、全貌 ☞ 左部是豸不是犭。右部7画，上白下儿。

貌

✎ 14 画
▣ 豸部 左右

貌貌貌貌貌貌貌貌貌貌貌
貌貌貌

what, how, why?

（麼）**me** 这么、那么、怎么、多么

☞ 第一画是丿（撇），不是乚（撇折）。

么

✎ 3 画
▣ 厶部 独体

么么么

2nd part How 怎么 zen me

学书者，始由不工求工，继由工求不工。不工者，工之极也。（学习书法的人，开始阶段应从写得不工整去追求工整，到后来就由刻板的工整再去追求个性的变化。个性变化表现出来的不工整，是工整的更高层次。）——刘熙载《艺概》

1st part not have 没有

méi 没有 /**mò** 沉没、隐没、没收、没顶之灾

☞ 右上不是几，末笔不带钩。

没

✎ 7 画
▣ 氵部 左右

没没没没没没没

méi 描眉、书眉

☞ 上左包围结构。

眉

✎ 9 画
▣ 目部 半包围

古字形像眼睛眉。

眉眉眉眉眉眉眉眉眉

méi 梅花、梅子

☞ 木的中间一竖不带钩，末笔改点。

梅

✎ 11 画
▣ 木部 左右

梅梅梅梅梅梅梅梅梅梅

méi 煤炭、煤矿 *coal*

☞ 火的末笔改点。木的中间一竖不带钩。

煤

✎ 13 画
▣ 火部 左右

煤煤煤煤煤煤煤煤煤煤煤煤

mould, mildew

（*黴）**méi** 发霉、*霉菌 ☞ 雨，第二画改点，第三画改横钩，里边楷体是四点，宋体是四横。

霉

✎ 15 画
▣ 雨部 上下

霉霉霉霉霉霉霉
霉霉霉霉霉霉霉霉

every, each, everytime

měi 每天、每队10人、每到过年都回家

每

✎ 7 画
▣ 母部 上下

每每每每每每每

门、闷、们的门，它的起笔，嵌在第二画丨和第三画乛之间。

美 měi 美丽、美容、物美价廉、美元　*pretty, beautiful, good satisfactory*
☞ 上部的羊，竖笔下端不出头。
✎ 9 画　部 羊　区 上下
美 美美美美美美美美美

妹 mèi 三妹、表妹　*younger sister*
☞ 女的横笔右端不出头。右部是未不是末。
✎ 8 画　部 女　区 左右
妹 妹妹妹妹妹妹妹妹

门（門）mén 铁门、球门、门类、窍门　*door, gate, entrance*
✎ 3 画　部 门　区 独体
门 门门门

> 古字形像门。𭹹（金文）𭹹（甲文）

闷（悶）mèn 烦闷、闷罐子车／mēn 闷热、闷在小屋里、闷声闷气、闷头儿干　*bored, depressed, low spirits*
☞ 左上右包围结构。心的第二画楷体是㇃（卧钩），宋体是乚（竖弯钩）。
✎ 7 画　部 门　区 半包围
闷 闷闷闷闷闷闷闷

们（們）men 我们、同胞们　*used after pronoun to make plural*
✎ 5 画　部 亻　区 左右
们 们们们们们　我们

萌 méng 萌芽、萌生　*sprout, bud, germinate*
☞ ⺿ 3画，第三画楷体是撇，宋体是竖。
✎ 11 画　部 ⺿　区 上下
萌 萌萌萌萌萌萌萌萌萌萌萌

蒙（*濛 **矇 ***懞）méng 蒙眼、启蒙、*蒙蒙细雨、**蒙眬、***蒙懂／mēng **蒙骗、蒙头转向／měng 蒙古　*cheat, deceive, senseless*
☞ ⺿ 3画，第三画楷体是撇，宋体是竖。
✎ 13 画　部 ⺿　区 上下
蒙 蒙蒙蒙蒙蒙蒙蒙蒙蒙蒙蒙蒙

盟 méng 盟国、盟誓、同盟　*alliance*
✎ 13 画　部 皿　区 上下
盟 盟盟盟盟盟盟盟盟盟盟盟盟盟

měng 猛兽、猛烈、猛醒 *fierce, violent, vigorous*

☞ 子3画，第一画是ㄱ，第二画是丿，不连成一笔。

✎ 11 画
□ 犭 左 右
△ 猛 猛猛猛猛猛猛猛猛猛猛

---

mèng 孟春

☞ 子3画，第一画是ㄱ，第二画是丿，不连成一笔。

✎ 8 画
□ 子 部
△ 上 下 孟 孟孟孟孟孟孟孟孟

（夢）**mèng** 恶梦、梦想 *dream, daydream*

☞ 木的中间一竖不带钩。左上木的末笔改点。

✎ 11 画
□ 夕 部
△ 上 下 梦 梦梦梦梦梦梦梦梦梦梦梦

---

mí 迷惑、迷恋、球迷、鬼迷心窍 *be confused, lost*

☞ 左下包围结构。米的中间一竖不带钩。末笔改点。 *be fascinated by*

✎ 9 画
□ 辶 部
△ 半包围 迷 迷迷迷迷迷迷迷迷迷

---

mí 灰沙眯眼／**mī** 眯着眼笑、眯了一刻钟 *get in one's eye*

☞ 米的中间一竖不带钩。

✎ 11 画
□ 目 部
△ 左 右 眯 眯眯眯眯眯眯眯眯眯眯

（謎）**mí** 猜谜、谜团 *riddle, mystery, puzzle*

☞ 讠两画，第二画乛不分为两笔或三笔。米的中间一竖不带钩。末笔改点。

✎ 11 画
□ 讠 部
△ 左 右 谜 谜谜谜谜谜谜谜谜谜谜

---

mǐ 大米、虾米、1米等于100厘米 *rice,*

☞ 中间一竖不带钩。 *shelled or husked seed*

✎ 6 画
□ 米 部
△ 独 体 米 米米米米米米

---

mì 秘密、秘方／**bì** 秘鲁（国名）

☞ 禾，中间一竖不带钩，末笔改点。必的第二画楷体是丶，宋体是乚。

✎ 10 画
□ 禾 部
△ 左 右 秘 秘秘秘秘秘秘秘秘秘秘

mì 密谈、保密、稠密、密友、精密

☞ 山3画，第二画是乚，不分为两笔。

✎ 11 画
部首 宀部
四 上下

密 密密密密密密密密密密

mì 采蜜、蜜桃、甜言蜜语

✎ 14 画
部首 宀部
四 上

蜜 蜜蜜蜜蜜蜜蜜蜜
蜜蜜蜜蜜蜜蜜蜜

"形声"是汉字的一种造字方法。汉代许慎的定义是："以事为名，取譬(pì)相成。"意思是以事物的类型作为形旁的名称，用读音相同或相近的字比拟字音，组合而成形声字。如"疤""桐""沪""狮"等。

mián 睡眠、冬眠

✎ 10 画
部首 目部
四 左右

眠 眠眠眠眠眠
眠眠眠眠眠

(綿) mián 连绵、绵里藏针、绵软　　soft, continuous

☞ 纟3画，上部不是幺。

✎ 11 画
部首 纟部
四 左右

绵 绵绵绵绵绵绵绵绵绵绵绵

mián 棉衣、木棉　　cloth-cotton

☞ 木的中间一竖不带钩，末笔改点。

✎ 12 画
部首 木部
四 左右

棉 棉棉棉棉棉棉棉棉棉棉棉棉

miǎn 免税、避免、闲人免进

☞ 第六画直接从扁框中撇下，不分为两笔。

✎ 7 画
部首 刀部
四 上下

免 免免免免免免免

miǎn 勤勉、共勉、勉强

☞ 左下包围结构。免的第六画直接从扁框中撇下，不分为两笔。

✎ 9 画
部首 力部
四 半包围

勉 勉勉勉勉勉勉勉勉勉

(*麵) miàn 泪流满面、面谈、面面俱到、*面粉、*药面、*方便面

(first part of noodle)

✎ 9 画
部首 面部
四 上下

面 面面面面面面面面面

miáo 育苗、鱼苗、火苗、疫苗

🖊 8 画
部 艹 部
结 上 下

苗

苗苗苗苗
苗苗苗苗

miáo 描绘、描眉

🖊 11 画
部 扌 部
结 左 右

描

描描描描描
描描描描描描

miǎo 1分钟等于60秒、争分夺秒

☞ 禾，中间一竖不带钩，末笔改点。

🖊 9 画
部 禾 部
结 左 右

秒

秒秒秒秒秒秒秒秒秒

miào 妙龄、奥妙

☞ 女的横笔右端不出头。

🖊 7 画
部 女 部
结 左 右

妙

妙妙妙妙妙妙妙

（廟）miào 寺庙、庙会

☞ 上左包围结构。

🖊 8 画
部 广 部
结 半包围

庙

庙庙庙庙庙庙庙庙

（滅）miè 熄灭、灭火、自生自灭

🖊 5 画
部 火 部
结 上 下

灭

灭灭灭灭灭

（*蔑）miè 蔑视、*诬蔑　☞ 艹3画，第三画楷体是撇，宋体是竖。下部是戍，不是戌、戉或戎。

🖊 14 画
部 艹 部
结 上 下

蔑

蔑蔑蔑蔑蔑蔑蔑
蔑蔑蔑蔑蔑蔑蔑

mín 国民、民歌、回民、农民、民用

🖊 5 画
部 一 部
结 独体

民

民民民民民

摸、模、膜的艹，第三画楷体是撇，宋体是竖。

mǐn 敏感、聪敏

☞ 母的第一画是乚，第二画是𠃌，都不分为两笔。右部是攵不是夂。

✎ 11 画
📖 攵部
⊿ 左右

敏　敏敏敏敏敏敏敏敏敏敏

---

name, famous, celebrated

míng 名单、名正言顺、著名、名牌

☞ 上左包围结构。

✎ 6 画
📖 夕部
⊿ 半包围

名　名名名名名名

---

míng 鲜明、明年、简明、不明真相、明码标价、失明、精明　*bright, brilliant, clear, distinct*

✎ 8 画
📖 日部
⊿ 左右

明　明明明明明明明明

古字形有的像月照窗棂，有的像日月交辉。◑ꓒ（金文）◉ꓳ（甲文）

(鳴) míng 鸟鸣、雷鸣、百家争鸣

ring, sound, express, voice

✎ 8 画
📖 口部
⊿ 左右

鸣　鸣鸣鸣鸣鸣鸣鸣鸣

---

life, lot, fate, destiny

mìng 命令、待命、听天由命、救命、命题

☞ 右下是卩不是阝。

✎ 8 画
📖 人部
⊿ 上下

命　命命命命命命命命

---

mō 抚摸、摸底、摸黑

feel, stroke, touch, grope for

✎ 13 画
📖 扌部
⊿ 左右

摸　摸摸摸摸摸摸摸摸摸摸摸摸

---

pattern, standard, imitate

mó 模范、模仿 / mú 铜模、模样　☞ 木的中间一竖不带钩，末笔改点。

✎ 14 画
📖 木部
⊿ 左右

模　模模模模模模模
模模模模模模模

"楷书"是汉字一种字体的名称，又称"正书"或"真书"。楷书与隶书的区别主要在行笔风格的不同，而在结构方面变化不大。"楷书"的原意应该是有法度的、可以作为楷模的字体。如"人"象。

---

mó 耳膜、薄膜　*membrane all membrane*

✎ 14 画
📖 月部
⊿ 左右

膜　膜膜膜膜膜膜膜
膜膜膜膜膜膜膜

mó 摩擦、按摩、观摩　〆上左包围结构。

touch, rub, scratch, mull over

摩摩摩摩摩摩摩摩摩摩

✎ 15 画
⽥ 麻 部
⊠ 半包围

 摩摩摩摩

mó 琢磨、磨刀、磨灭、磨洋工、软磨硬泡 /mò 磨盘、磨豆腐　〆上左包围结构。

RUB

磨磨磨磨磨磨磨　*MUSHROOM*

✎ 16 画
⽥ 麻 部
⊠ 半包围

 磨磨磨磨磨磨磨磨磨　*mill, millstone, grind*

mó 魔鬼、魔王、魔力　〆上左包围结构。鬼的第六画直接从白中撇下，不分为两笔。

魔魔魔魔魔魔魔魔

✎ 20 画
⽥ 麻 部
⊠ 半包围

 魔魔魔魔魔魔魔魔

mǒ 抹护肤霜、涂抹、抹眼泪 /mò 抹墙、拐弯抹角 /mā 抹布
〆右部是末不是未。　*daub, plaster*

✎ 8 画
⽥ 扌部
⊠ 左右

 抹抹抹抹抹抹抹抹

mò 末梢、周末、末日、本末倒置、药末

tip, end, last stage

✎ 5 画
⽥ 木 部
⊠ 独体

 末末末末末

古字形用横或点指明木梢处。木（金文）末（小篆）

mò 泡沫、唾沫　*foam, froth*
〆右部是末不是未。

✎ 8 画
⽥ 氵部
⊠ 左右

 沫沫沫沫沫沫沫沫

mò 望尘莫及、闲人莫入
〆艹3画，第三画楷体是撇，宋体是竖。

✎ 10 画
⽥ 艹部
⊠ 上下

 莫莫莫莫莫莫莫莫莫莫

mò 沙漠、冷漠
〆艹3画，第三画楷体是撇，宋体是竖。

✎ 13 画
⽥ 氵部
⊠ 左右

漠漠漠漠漠漠漠漠漠漠漠漠漠

mò　墨汁、墨镜、油墨　　☞ 上部8画，不是里。

✎ 15 画
▣ 黑 部
◹ 上 下

墨墨墨墨墨墨墨墨墨墨墨墨
墨墨墨

mò　默许、默写　　☞ 左右结构，黑的四点不托住犬。黑的上部8画，不是里。

✎ 16 画
▣ 黑 部
◹ 左 右

默默默默默默默默默默默默
默默默默

(谋)　móu　*plan, scheme, consult*　密谋、阴谋、谋求、不谋而合

☞ 讠两画，第二画丁不分为两笔或三笔。

✎ 11 画
▣ 讠 部
◹ 左 右

谋谋谋谋谋谋谋谋谋谋谋

mǒu　某人、某年某月某日

certain, some

✎ 9 画
▣ 甘 部
◹ 上 下

某某某某某某某某某

mother, one's female elders

mǔ　慈母、岳母、母牛、螺母、字母

☞ 第一画乚、第二画丁都不分为两笔。

✎ 5 画
▣ 母 部
◹ 独体

母母母母母

古字形像妇女，两点是双乳。

李(金文)　电(甲文)

(畝)　mǔ　10分等于1亩

a unit of area

✎ 7 画
▣ 亠 部
◹ 上 下

亩亩亩亩亩亩亩

mù　树木、红木、木器、麻木　TREE

☞ 木的中间一竖不带钩。

✎ 4 画
▣ 木 部
◹ 独体

木木木木

mù　耳闻目睹、项目、书目、题目

EYE

✎ 5 画
▣ 目 部
◹ 独体

目目目目目

旁的可假，字不可假。一个人有一个人的笔迹，旁人无论如何模仿不来。不必要毛笔才可以认笔迹，就是钢笔铅笔，亦可以认笔迹。是谁写的，一看就知道，因为各人个性不同，所以写出来的字也就不同了。美术一种要素是在发挥个性，而发挥个性最真确的，莫如写字。——康有为《书法指导》

mù 牧羊、畜牧

　☞ 牛的第二横改提，笔顺改先竖后提。右部是攵不是夂。

　✎ 8 画
　□ 牛 部
　☒ 左 右

牧 牧牧牧牧牧牧牧牧

mù 墓碑、坟墓、墓地、墓祭、墓室、墓葬、墓志

grave tomb, mausoleum

　✎ 13 画
　□ 艹 部
　☒ 上 下

墓 墓墓墓墓墓墓墓墓墓墓墓墓墓

mù 帐幕、开幕、第四幕、银幕、夜幕、幕僚

curtain, screen

　✎ 13 画
　□ 艹 部
　☒ 上 下

幕 幕幕幕幕幕幕幕幕幕幕幕幕幕

mù 慕名、思慕　　*admire, yearn, admire, adore worship*

　☞ 下部是小不是小或水。

　✎ 14 画
　□ 艹 部
　☒ 上 下

慕 慕慕慕慕慕慕慕
慕 慕慕慕慕慕慕

mù 暮色苍茫、朝三暮四、岁暮

　✎ 14 画
　□ 艹 部
　☒ 上 下

暮 暮暮暮暮暮暮暮
暮 暮暮暮暮暮暮暮

古人认为，书法还能表现写字人的性格、修养和风度。有人说，唐代著名书法家颜真卿"虽犯难不可屈，刚正之气，发于诚心，与其字体无异"，认为颜真卿为人处世刚正严毅，正像他写的字一样刚健笃实。宋朝朱熹在评论欧阳修的字的时候说："欧公作字，如其为人。外若优游，中实刚劲。"认为欧阳修的字跟他的为人一样，外表虽然恬淡平和，骨子里却有一股刚劲之气。

ná 拿笔、捉拿、拿架子、拿名次

hold, sieze, capture

　✎ 10 画
　□ 人 部
　☒ 上 下

拿 拿拿拿拿拿拿拿拿拿拿

nǎ 哪儿、哪怕、哪儿凉快去哪儿/na 谢谢您哪　　*which, what*

　☞ 阝两画，第一画了不分为两笔。

　✎ 9 画
　□ 口 部
　☒ 左 右

+ 在儿
is where

哪 哪哪哪哪哪哪哪哪哪哪

nà 那天、问这问那　　*That, Then*

　☞ 阝两画，第一画了不分为两笔。

　✎ 6 画
　□ 阝 部
　☒ 左 右

文字是文化的产物，又服务于文化，促进文化的发展，它自身又是文化的一个部分。

那 那那那那那那

乃、奶的乃，第一画是 ㇕，不分为两笔。

(納) nà 采纳、纳税、纳鞋底

recieve, accept, pay, offer, adopt

☞ 纟3画，上部不是纟。

✎ 7 画
部 纟部
左右

纳 纳纳 纳纳 纳纳 纳

nǎi 失败乃成功之母   *BE*

✎ 2 画
部 一部
独体

乃 乃乃

nǎi 奶头、喂奶、奶孩子、奶牙   *Breast, milk, baby*

☞ 女的横笔右端不出头。

✎ 5 画
部 女部
左右

奶 奶奶 奶奶 奶

nài 耐用、忍耐、耐心

be able to bear, endure

✎ 9 画
部 而部
左右

耐 耐耐 耐耐 耐耐 耐耐

nán 男女老少、生男生女都一样   *man, male*

✎ 7 画
部 田部
上下

男 男男 男男 男男

古字形用田地和犁杖表示农业劳动中充当主力的男子。

 （金文） 田（甲文）

nán 南方、南味   *SOUTH*

✎ 9 画
部 十部
上下

南 南南 南南 南南 南南

(難) nán 难题、难倒英雄汉、难吃 /nàn 难民、非难

hard, difficult, unpleasant, unforgettable

☞ 又的末笔改点。右部是隹不是住。

✎ 10 画
部 又部
左右

难 难难 难难 难难 难难

náng 皮囊、囊括、胆囊   *Bag, sack, pocket*

✎ 22 画
部 一部
上下

囊囊 囊囊 囊囊 囊囊 囊囊 囊
囊囊 囊囊 囊囊 囊囊 囊囊

恼、脑的右半是6画，第五画是乚，不分为两笔。

（撓） náo 阻挠、挠痒痒、不屈不挠 ~scratch, scratch an itch~

☞ 右上不是戈或弋。右下是尢不是元。

✎ 9 画
☐ 扌部
☒ 左 右

 挠挠挠挠挠挠挠挠挠

（惱） náo 恼火、恼羞成怒、烦恼、苦恼 ~to be angry, annoyed, vexed~

✎ 9 画
☐ 忄部
☒ 左 右

 恼恼恼恼恼恼恼恼恼

（腦） nǎo 脑子、脑海、摇头晃脑、动脑、脑力劳动者、脑满肠肥、豆腐脑儿 ~Brain~

✎ 10 画
☐ 月部
☒ 左 右

 脑脑脑脑脑脑脑脑脑脑

（鬧） nào 喧闹、连哭带闹、闹事、闹病、打闹、闹不明白 ~noisy~

☞ 左上右包围结构。起笔、嵌在第二笔丨和第三笔乛之间。

✎ 8 画
☐ 门部
☒ 半包围

 闹闹闹闹闹闹闹闹

nèi 内外、内疚、内行、内侄 ~within, inside, interior~

☞ 框内人的末笔改点。

✎ 4 画
☐ 门部
☒ 独体

 内内内内内

> 保留特征是汉字简化的一种方法，如"聲"简化作"声"、"醫"简化作"医"。

nèn 嫩黄瓜、嫩绿 ~tender, delicate, tender shoot~

☞ 女的横笔右端不出头。中部是束不是束，束末笔改点。右部是攵不是夂。

~light - inexperienced, unskilled~

✎ 14 画
☐ 女部
☒ 左

嫩嫩嫩嫩嫩嫩嫩
嫩嫩嫩嫩嫩嫩嫩

néng 无能、能人、能歌善舞 ~can, be able to, capable, skill~

☞ 右部是上下两个匕，不是匕。

古字形像熊一类的野兽。

（金文）

✎ 10 画
☐ 厶部
☒ 左 右

能能能能能能能能能能

ní 尼姑、尼龙 ~Buddhist, nun~

☞ 上左包围结构。右下是匕不是匕。

✎ 5 画
☐ 尸部
☒ 半包围

尼尼尼尼尼

呢、泥的尼，下部是匕，不是匕。

 ní 呢绒 /ne 怎么跟孩子讲呢

— woolen cloth
— at the end of question

✎ 8 画
部 口部
⚄ 左 左右

呢 呢呢呢呢呢呢呢呢

汉人造字之初就同时造了笔。文字胚胎是刻画符号和文字画，所以最初的笔多是简陋的木棍、竹片、骨片、刻刀等，它们是第一代硬笔。用第一代硬笔写出来的作品就是甲骨文、铭文、刻石等。春秋战国时代，书法工具革新，出现成型的毛笔。长沙出土的战国墓中，发现一支顶端缠裹着兔剪毛的圆竹条，这应该是最早的"楚笔"，距今已有二千四百多年的历史，比欧洲人发明羽毛笔早了九百多年。

 ní 泥泞、枣泥 /nì 泥缝、拘泥

c river, or dab w/ putty

✎ 8 画
部 氵部
⚄ 左 左右

泥 泥泥泥泥泥泥泥泥

 ní 你我之间、你方

you

✎ 7 画
部 亻部
⚄ 左 左右

你 你你你你你你你

逆 nì 逆行、逆境、叛逆

go against, conquer

☞ 左下包围结构。辶3画，第二画楷体是了，宋体是⻌。

✎ 9 画
部 辶部
⚄ 半包围

逆 逆逆逆逆逆逆逆逆逆

年 nián 年产、年龄、老年、过年

year

✎ 6 画
部 丿部
⚄ 独

年 年年年年年年

古字形像人背负成熟的庄稼。

㑥(金文) （甲文）

念 niàn 念旧、杂念、念书

think of, miss

☞ 心的第二画楷体是㇃(卧钩)，宋体是乚(竖弯钩)。上部是今不是令。

study, be a pupil

✎ 8 画
部 心部
⚄ 上下

念 念念念念念念念念

mother, ma, mum

 niáng 爹娘、大娘、姑娘

☞ 女的横笔右端不出头。

✎ 10 画
部 女部
⚄ 左 左右

娘 娘娘娘娘娘娘娘娘娘

（釀）niàng 酿造、酝酿 ☞ 酉的框内有一短横。

✎ 14 画
部 酉部
⚄ 左 左右

酿 酿酿酿酿酿酿酿酿酿酿
酿酿酿

make by fermentation, lead to, resulting

（鳥）niǎo 飞鸟、花鸟　*BIRD*

☞ 第一画丿、第二画丁不连成一笔。第四画勹不分为两笔。

〄 5 画
⺌ 鸟部
△ 独体

鸟 鸟 鸟 鸟 鸟

上海辟为商埠的时候，钢笔随欧美人士一起进来。著名古文字学家吴大澂（chéng）于光绪己丑年（1889 年）就用钢笔写了一幅篆体对联，因此有人称之为中国硬笔书法第一人。

niào 撒尿、尿床／suī 尿(niào)了一泡尿　*urine urinate*

☞ 上左包围结构。

〄 7 画
⺌ 尸部
△ 半包围

尿 尿 尿 尿 尿 尿 尿

niē 捏橡皮泥、捏造、捏紧拳头　*hold between the fingers, pinch*

☞ 右部上日下土，不是上白下工。

〄 10 画
⺌ 扌部
△ 左右

捏 捏 捏 捏 捏 捏 捏 捏 捏

您 nín 老师，您好　*formal you*

☞ 心的第二画楷体是⺄(卧钩)，宋体是L(竖弯钩)。

〄 11 画
⺌ 心部
△ 上下

您 您 您 您 您 您 您 您 您 您 您

（寧）níng 心绪不宁、沪宁公路／nìng 宁死不屈、宁缺毋滥　*Rather or peaceful tranquil*

〄 5 画
⺌ 宀部
△ 上下

宁 宁 宁 宁 宁

níng 凝固、凝视　☞ 中部上匕下矢，矢的末笔改点。

〄 16 画
⺌ 冫部
△ 左右

凝 凝 凝 凝 凝 凝 凝 凝 凝 凝 凝 凝 凝 凝 凝

niú 水牛、牛脾气　*beef*

〄 4 画
⺌ 牛部
△ 独体

牛 牛 牛 牛

古字形像牛头。

牜（金文）
牜（甲文）

niǔ 扭伤、扭转、扭秧歌、扭送　*turn around, twist wrench*

☞ 丑的中间一横右端不出头。

〄 7 画
⺌ 扌部
△ 左右

扭 扭 扭 扭 扭 扭 扭

农、浓的农，第三画从一中撇下。奴、努、怒的女，横笔右端不出头。

（紐）niǔ 秤纽、纽扣、纽带、枢纽

☞ 纟3画，上部不是幺。丑的中间一横右端不出头。

✎ 7 画
纟 画部：左右
四：左右

纽纽纽纽纽纽纽

（農）nóng 农林牧副渔、农民、菜农

farming. agriculture

✎ 6 画
丶 独体
四：独体

农农农农农农

古字形像手拿蛤蜊（古农具）在田间薅草。🧧（金文）🧧（甲文）

（濃）nóng 浓度、浓艳、浓厚

✎ 9 画
氵 左右
四：左右

浓浓浓浓浓
浓浓浓浓

"隶书"是汉字一种字体的名称，由篆书简化演变而成。早期的隶书是人们为了适应繁忙的书面交际的需要，用毛笔快速书写篆书时自然而然形成的。从篆书演变为隶书的过程称为"隶变"。隶变彻底消除了篆书中遗存的图画意味，使汉字从书写风格到文字结构都发生了较大的变化，成为汉字演进史上的一个大转折。隶变是汉字史上古今汉字的分水岭。如"人""象"。

---

nòng 摆弄、弄假成真 /lòng 弄堂

✎ 7 画
廾 上下
四：上下

弄弄弄弄
弄弄弄

---

nú 农奴、奴役、洋奴

✎ 5 画
女 左右
四：左右

奴奴奴
奴奴

---

nǔ 努力、努嘴

✎ 7 画
力 上下
四：上下

努努努努努努努

---

nù 发怒、怒放

☞ 心的第二画楷体是㇃（卧钩），宋体是乚（竖弯钩）。

✎ 9 画
心 上下
四：上下

怒怒怒怒怒怒怒怒怒

---

nǚ 男女老幼、子女

✎ 3 画
女 独体
四：独体

女女女

印刷体指汉字在书籍、报纸、杂志等印刷品上出现的字体形式。目前经常用到的印刷字体有宋体、仿宋体、楷体和黑体四种。

nuǎn 暖和、暖酒、暖融融、暖房、暖流、暖气

☞ 右下是横下一个友。

✎ 13 画
日 部
左 右

暖暖暖暖暖暖暖暖暖暖暖暖暖

nuó 挪开、挪用

☞ 阝两画，第一画了不分为两笔。

✎ 9 画
扌 部
左 右

挪挪挪挪挪挪挪挪挪

(歐) ōu 北欧、欧盟

☞ 区4画，第四画是乚，不分为两笔。

✎ 8 画
欠 部
左 右

欧欧欧欧欧欧欧欧

ǒu 木偶、偶数、丧偶、偶然

☞ 右下是禸5画，不是内4画。

✎ 11 画
亻 部
左 右

偶偶偶偶偶偶偶偶偶偶

pā 趴下、趴在桌子上睡觉

☞ 左下止的末笔改提。

✎ 9 画
足 部
左 右

趴趴趴趴趴趴趴趴

pá 爬行、爬树　　 左下包围结构。左下是爪不是瓜。

✎ 8 画
爪 部
半包围

爬爬爬爬
爬爬爬爬

pà 害怕、怕苦怕累

✎ 8 画
忄 部
左 右

怕怕怕怕
怕怕怕怕

pāi 拍蚊子、球拍、合拍、拍照

✎ 8 画
扌 部
左 右

拍拍拍拍拍拍拍拍

笔画是构成现代汉字字形的最小单位。现代汉字中只有极少数字的字形结构单位是笔画、部件和整字三者合一的，如"一""乙"。大多数汉字都不是由一个笔画构成的。7000个通用字中9画～12画的字最多。3500个常用字中笔画最多的是"矗"24画，通用字中笔画最多的是"齉"36画。

判、叛的左部是半，末笔改撇。

pái 排水、排列、前排、木排、排球 /pǎi 排子车

　☞ 非，中间是两竖，左右各三横。

11画 扌部 左右

排 排 排 排 排 排 排 排 排 排 排

---

pái 招牌、打牌、名牌

　☞ 片4画，末笔是⼅。右上第六画直接从白中撇下，不分为两笔。

12画 片部 左右

牌 牌 牌 牌 牌 牌 牌 牌 牌 牌 牌

---

pài 流派、气派、摊派　☞ 右部不是瓜，厂下不是氏或民。

9画 氵部 左右

派 派 派 派 派 派 派 派 派

---

pān 攀登、攀亲　☞ 木的中间一竖不带钩。两木的末笔都改点。

19画 手部 上下

攀 攀 攀 攀 攀 攀 攀 攀 攀 攀 攀 攀
攀 攀 攀 攀 攀 攀 攀

（盤）**pán** 盘子、盘绕、盘点、棋盘

11画 舟部 上下

盘 盘 盘 盘 盘 盘 盘 盘 盘 盘 盘

---

pàn 判断、裁判、判案

7画 刂部 左右

判 判 判
判 判 判 判

---

pàn 左顾右盼、盼望

9画 目部 左右

盼 盼 盼 盼
盼 盼 盼 盼 盼

---

pàn 叛国、背叛

9画 又部 左右

叛 叛 叛 叛 叛
叛 叛 叛 叛

有人问练写字、临碑帖，其中都是繁体字，与今天贯彻规范字的标准岂不背道而驰。我的理解，可作个粗浅的比喻来说，碑帖好比乐谱。练钢琴，弹贝多芬的乐谱，是练指法、练基本技术等等。肯定贝多芬的乐谱中找不出现代的某些调子。但能创作新乐曲的人，他必定是通过练习弹名家乐谱而学会了基本技术的。由此触类旁通，推陈出新，才具备音乐家的多面修养。在书法方面，点画形式和写法上，简体和繁体并没有两样；在结字上，聚散疏密的道理，简体和繁体也没有两样，只如穿衣，各有单、夹之分，盖楼房略有十层、三层之分而已。
——启功《论书随笔》

乓

pāng 乒乓球、乓的一声

6 画
丿 部
独 体

乓乓乓乓乓乓

旁

páng 旁门、旁证、竖心旁

10 画
亠 部
上 下

旁旁旁旁旁
旁旁旁旁旁

胖

pàng 胖小子/pán 心广体胖

9 画
月 部
左 右

胖胖胖胖胖
胖胖胖胖

抛

pāo 抛锚、抛弃 ☞右部是左下包围结构。

7 画
扌 部
左 右

抛抛抛抛
抛抛抛

炮

páo 炮制/bāo 炮羊肉/pào 大炮、鞭炮

☞火的末笔改点。

9 画
火 部
左 右

炮炮炮炮炮炮炮炮炮

袍

páo 棉袍、皮袍

☞左部是衤不是礻。

10 画
衤 部
左 右

袍袍袍袍袍袍袍袍袍袍

跑

pǎo 跑步、跑买卖、逃跑、跑气

☞左下止的末笔改提。

12 画
足 部
左 右

跑跑跑跑跑跑跑跑跑跑跑跑

泡

pào 气泡、灯泡、泡茶、泡病号/pāo 豆腐泡、这块木料发泡

8 画
氵 部
左 右

泡泡泡泡泡泡泡泡

从众多的汉字形体结构中，分析归纳出某些相同的笔画构件，分别部类，列在它所统属的若干汉字之首，在汉字学中称之为“部首”。建立部首的主要作用是为了便于排列和查检汉字。比如，从“江、河、湖、海、深、浅、浇、灌”等字形结构中归纳出相同的笔画构件“氵”，在汉字工具书中列为“氵”部；从“矾、矽、矿、码、砖、砌、砚、硬”等字形结构中归纳出相同的笔画构件“石”，在汉字工具书中列为“石”部。部首有的能独立成字，如“木”“工”“口”“见”等；有的不能独立成字，如“冫”“忄”“辶”“纟”等。(东汉)许慎在《说文解字》中首创部首。他以小篆为字形根据，建立540部，每部立一部首，共定540个部首。他所列的部首主要是作为义旁来统属字的意义范畴的。后世的字书辞书改从检字法原则按字形偏旁来建立部首。

péi 陪伴、陪读

☞ 阝两画，第一画㇌不分为两笔。

✎ 10 画
阝部
左 左阝 右

陪 陪陪陪陪陪陪陪陪陪陪

---

péi 培土、培养

☞ 土的末笔改提。

✎ 11 画
土部
左 右

培 培培培培培培培培培培

---

péi 赔款、赔了老本、赔礼

✎ 12 画
贝部
左 右

赔 赔赔赔赔赔赔赔赔赔赔赔

---

pèi 佩戴、敬佩

☞ 右下的巾上有一短横。

✎ 8 画
亻部
左 右

佩 佩佩佩佩佩佩佩佩

---

pèi 元配、交配、调配、分配、配角、般配

☞ 酉，框内有一短横。右部是己，不是已或巳。

✎ 10 画
酉部
左 右

配 配配配配配配配配配配

(噴) pēn 喷射、喷泉/pèn 喷香的桂花

☞ 右上部分是上十下艹。

✎ 12 画
口部
左 右

喷 喷喷喷喷喷喷喷喷喷喷喷

---

pén 脸盆、花盆、瓦盆、搪瓷盆

✎ 9 画
皿部
上 下

盆 盆盆盆盆盆盆盆盆

古字形像并排挂着的两串贝。
拜（金文）拜（甲文）

---

péng 朋友、亲朋好友

✎ 8 画
月部
左 右

朋 朋朋朋朋朋朋朋朋

棚 péng 草棚、工棚

☞ 木的中间一竖不带钩，末笔改点。

✎ 12 画
部 木
⽥ 左 右

棚 棚棚棚棚棚棚棚棚棚棚棚棚

蓬 péng 飞蓬、蓬松

☞ ⺾3画，第三画楷体是撇，宋体是竖。

✎ 13 画
部 ⺾
⽥ 上 下

蓬 蓬蓬蓬蓬蓬蓬蓬蓬蓬蓬蓬蓬蓬

膨 péng 膨胀、膨体纱 ☞ 彡写在一条中轴线上。

✎ 16 画
部 月
⽥ 左 右

膨膨膨膨膨膨膨膨
膨 膨膨膨膨膨膨膨膨

捧 pěng 捧腹大笑、捧场 ☞ 右下是丰不是丰。

✎ 11 画
部 扌
⽥ 左 右

捧捧捧捧捧
捧 捧捧捧捧捧捧

碰 pèng 碰杯、碰机会

✎ 13 画
部 石
⽥ 左 右

碰碰碰碰碰碰
碰 碰碰碰碰碰碰碰

批 pī 批示、眉批、批评、批发

☞ 比4画，第二画是乚，不分为两笔；右部是匕不是匕。

✎ 7 画
部 扌
⽥ 左

批 批批批批批批批

披 pī 披荆斩棘、披头散发、披肩发

✎ 8 画
部 扌
⽥ 左 右

披披披披
披 披披披披

劈 pī 劈柴、劈头盖脸 / pǐ 劈叉、劈高粱叶

✎ 15 画
部 刀
⽥ 上 下

劈劈劈劈劈劈劈劈劈劈劈劈
劈 劈劈劈

常有人问："我已二三十岁了，还能学书法吗？" 我个人的回答是：书法不同于杂技，腰腿灵活，须要自幼锻炼，学习书法艺术，甚至恰恰相反。……我有一次遇到一个家长，勒令他的几岁小孩，每天必须写若干篇字，缺了一篇，不许吃饭。我当面告诉他，"你已把小孩对书法的感情、兴趣杀死，更无望他将来有所成就了。" 正是由于人的年龄大了，理解力、欣赏力强了，才更易有见解、有判别、有选择，以至写出自己的风格。所以我个人的答案是：练写字与练杂技不同，是不拘年龄的。但练写字要有合理的方法、熟练的工夫，也是各类年龄人同样需要的。

——启功《论书随笔》

pí 树皮、皮革、皮糖、皮筋、地皮、顽皮

✎ 5 画
⊞ 皮部
⊠ 独体

皮 皮 皮 皮 皮

古字形像手剥兽皮。

（金文）

pí 精疲力竭、疲倦

⊤ 上左包围结构。

✎ 10 画
⊞ 疒部
⊠ 半包围

疲 疲 疲 疲 疲 疲 疲 疲 疲 疲

pí 脾脏、脾胃、脾气

⊤ 右上6画，第六画从白中直接撇下，不分为两笔。

✎ 12 画
⊞ 月部
⊠ 左右

脾 脾 脾 脾 脾 脾 脾 脾 脾 脾 脾

pǐ 匹配、单枪匹马、一匹布

⊤ 上左下包围结构。末笔是乚，不分为两笔。

✎ 4 画
⊞ 匚部
⊠ 半包围

匹 匹 匹 匹 匹

pì 偏僻、冷僻、孤僻

✎ 15 画
⊞ 亻部
⊠ 左右

僻 僻 僻 僻 僻 僻 僻
僻 僻 僻 僻 僻 僻 僻

piān 射偏、偏心、偏离、偏要

✎ 11 画
⊞ 亻部
⊠ 左右

偏 偏 偏 偏 偏 偏
偏 偏 偏 偏 偏

piān 篇章、歌篇儿、一篇论文

✎ 15 画
⊞ 竹部
⊠ 上下

篇 篇 篇 篇 篇 篇 篇
篇 篇 篇 篇 篇 篇 篇 篇

piàn 片刻、照片、片段 / **piān** 唱片

⊤ 末笔是乛，不分为两笔。

✎ 4 画
⊞ 片部
⊠ 独体

片 片 片 片 片

有人曾问我：有些"书法家"不爱写"简化字"，你却肯用简化字去题书签、写牌匾，原因何在？我的回答很简单：文字是语言的符号，是人与人交际的工具。简化字是国务院颁布的法令，我来应用它、遵守它而已。它的点画笔法，都是现成的，不待新创造，它的偏旁拼配，只要找和它相类的字，研究它们近似部分的安排办法，也就行了。我自己给人写字时有个原则是，凡作装饰用的书法作品，不但可以写繁体字，即使写甲骨、金文，等于画个图案，并不见得便算"有违功令"；若属正式的文件、教材，或广泛的宣传品，不但应该用规范字，也不宜应简的不简。
——启功《论书随笔》

漂、飘、票的票，上部扁框中是两竖，不写成西。

（騙）pián 骗子、骗钱

🖊 12 画 马部
⊠ 左右

骗骗骗骗骗骗骗骗骗骗骗骗

马的第一画𠃌、第二画𡿨都不分为两笔；左上角开口；末笔改提。

---

piāo 漂流 / piǎo 漂洗、漂白 / piào 漂亮

🖊 14 画 氵部
⊠ 左右

漂漂漂漂漂漂漂漂漂
漂漂漂漂

first part beautiful

漂亮
liang

（飄）piāo 飘扬、飘移、飘来阵阵清香

🖊 15 画 风部
⊠ 左右

飘飘飘飘飘飘飘飘飘飘
飘飘飘飘飘

float, flutter
(think snowflakes!)

---

piào 车票、邮票、电影票、钞票

🖊 11 画 西部
⊠ 上下

票

票票票票票票票票票票票

---

piě 撇开、撇沫子 / piē 撇瓦片、撇嘴、一撇一捺

🖊 14 画 扌部
⊠ 左右

撇撇撇撇撇撇撇撇
撇撇撇撇撇撇

中部的竖笔贯通上下，不分为两笔。右部是攵不是夂。

---

pīn 拼凑、拼音、拼版、拼命、拼搏

右上是丷不是厶。

🖊 9 画 扌部
⊠ 左右

拼

拼拼拼拼拼拼拼拼拼

（貧）pín 贫困、贫血、贫嘴

贝的第二画𠃌不带钩。

🖊 8 画 贝部
⊠ 上下

贫

贫贫贫贫
贫贫贫贫

《百寿图》中"寿"字有100种不同写法。近来有人辑录"千寿集锦"，觅得"寿"字有1056种不同写法。作为娱乐品，写法越多越招人喜欢；作为实用品，汉字写法应该规范化：只用一种写法。

---

pǐn 商品、品级、品德、品位、品味

🖊 9 画 口部
⊠ 上下

品

品品品品品
品品品品品

píng 乒乓球、乒乓地响

✎ 6 画
部体
独 丿

乒乒乒
乒乒乒

写字讲究笔顺，才能把字写得好看。每个字，不管它有多少笔画、多少部件，都要均匀地分布在一个个方方正正的框架里。要把每一个字写得方正平稳、布局得当，重要的一条也是要注意笔画的走向和顺序。为了把"山"字均匀地分布在一个方块平面里，应先写中间一竖，为全字的布局确定一条基准线，然后再写左边的竖折和右边的竖，使它们跟基准线对应。这样才能使全字显得端庄匀称、紧凑内聚。

píng 平坦、平局、平均、平稳、平叛、平常

✎ 5 画
部体
一独

平平平
平平

(評) píng 评论、批评、好评

讠两画，第二画乁不分为两笔或三笔。

✎ 7 画
部右
讠左

评 评评评评评评评

西安碑林始建于北宋元祐二年(1087年)，收集散落于长安城外的唐代石经与重要碑刻。以后陆续增立。1948年，民国政府将一批新出土的唐代名碑移立碑林。1961年，国务院将西安碑林列为全国第一批重点文物保护单位，并移入《熹平石经·周易残石》《曹全碑》《仓颉庙碑》《广武将军碑》《晖福寺碑》《同州圣教序碑》等珍品。碑林藏品增至2000余块。

(蘋) píng 苹果 *first part apple!*

艹3画，第三画楷体是撇，宋体是竖。

✎ 8 画
部下
艹上

苹 苹苹苹苹苹苹苹苹

(憑) píng 凭本事、凭票、凭据、凭你怎么说，他也不信

✎ 8 画
部下
几上

凭凭凭凭
凭凭凭凭

píng 花瓶

瓦4画，第二画是乚，第三画是乁，都不分为两笔。

✎ 10 画
部右
瓦左

瓶 瓶瓶瓶瓶瓶瓶瓶瓶瓶

píng 浮萍、萍水相逢

艹3画，第三画楷体是撇，宋体是竖。艹覆盖氵、平。

✎ 11 画
部下
艹上

萍 萍萍萍萍萍萍萍萍萍萍

坡

pō 高坡、坡度

土的末笔改提。

✎ 8 画
部右
土左

坡 坡坡坡坡坡坡坡坡

（潑）pō 泼水、不要把污水泼到大街上 、泼妇

☞ 右部是发，不是友或友。

✎ 8 画
氵部
⊠ 左右

泼泼泼泼泼泼泼泼

pó 外婆、婆媳

✎ 11 画
女部
⊠ 上下

婆婆婆婆婆
婆婆婆婆婆婆

具有两个或两个以上的读音、而不同读音又跟不同的字义相联系的字，被称为多音多义字。如："脏"读zāng时，指不干净；读zàng时，指动物体内的器官、脏器。

pò 迫近、强迫、迫切 / pǎi 迫击炮

☞ 左下包围结构。辶 3画，第二画楷体是乛，宋体是乛。

✎ 8 画
辶部
⊠ 半包围

迫迫迫迫迫迫迫迫

破

pò 破坏、破例、破费、破零钱、侦破

✎ 10 画
石部
⊠ 左右

破破破破破破破破破破

pò 魂魄、魄力 ☞ 鬼9画，第六画从白中直接撇下，不分为两笔。

✎ 14 画
白部
⊠ 左右

魄魄魄魄魄魄魄
魄魄魄魄魄魄魄

pōu 剖腹、剖析

✎ 10 画
刂部
⊠ 左右

剖剖剖剖剖
剖剖剖剖剖

"甲骨文"是古代汉字一种字体的名称，是商周时期刻在龟甲、兽骨上的汉字字体的总称。记录的内容主要是日常的占卜（一种预测吉凶祸福的迷信活动），使用的书写工具又是坚硬的划刀和龟甲兽骨，所以，它的字迹比同时期的另一种字体金文显得潦草。甲骨文是我国商代晚期和周代早期汉字的俗体，离开现今已经有三千四五百年。如 （人）（象）。

（*僕）pū 前仆后继 /pú *女仆、*风尘仆仆

✎ 4 画
亻部
⊠ 左右

仆仆仆仆仆

（撲）pū 扑灭、饿虎扑食、扑鼻

✎ 5 画
扌部
⊠ 左右

扑扑扑扑扑

铺 (鋪) pū 铺被、铺展 / pù 药铺、上下铺

☞ 钅5画，第二画是横，不是点；第五画是竖提，不分为两笔。

✎ 12 画
部 钅 部
左右

铺 铺铺铺铺铺铺铺铺铺铺铺铺

葡 pú 葡萄

☞ 艹3画，第三画楷体是撇，宋体是竖。

✎ 12 画
部 艹 上下

葡 葡葡葡葡葡葡葡葡葡葡葡葡

朴 (樸) pǔ 朴素 / piáo 姓朴

☞ 木的中间一竖不带钩，末笔改点。

✎ 6 画
部 木 部
左右

朴 朴朴朴朴朴朴

普 pǔ 普遍、普及、普通

✎ 12 画
部 日 上下

普 普普普普普普普普普普普普

谱 (譜) pǔ 菜谱、乐谱、谱曲、离谱、摆谱

☞ 讠两画，第二画是乁，不分为两笔或三笔。

✎ 14 画
部 讠 左右

谱 谱谱谱谱谱谱谱
谱谱谱谱谱谱谱

七 qī 七上八下

seven

✎ 2 画
部 一 独体

七 七七

在几千年的漫长过程中，汉字记录了汉族人民乃至全人类的文明历史，记录了汉族人民乃至全人类在政治、经济、文化、艺术、生产、生活中的历史经验和发明创造。汉字自身也积累了丰富的文化内容，成为一部形象生动的文化百科全书。汉字在世界文化史上的地位是怎么估计也不为过的。

妻 qī 妻子、夫妻

☞ 上部不是彐，中间一横右端出头。

✎ 8 画
部 女 上下

妻 妻妻妻妻妻妻妻妻

戚 qī 悲戚、亲戚

☞ 左上右包围结构。小的左侧楷体是点，宋体是撇。

✎ 11 画
部 戈 半包围

戚 戚戚戚戚戚戚戚戚戚戚

字谜

写成没写全，成字里面空；
上字来探望，带着一小童。
问它是哪个？原是亲家公。

（手写：xīng（星）qī 1st T. last part of week）

期 qī 按期、过期作废、学期、两个月为一期、期待

✎ 12 画
月 部
左 右

期 期期期期期期期期期期期

欺 qī 欺骗、欺软怕硬、仗势欺人、欺负

✎ 12 画
欠 部
左 右

欺 欺欺欺欺欺欺欺欺欺欺欺

漆 qī 油漆、漆家具　☞ 右上不是夹或夹；右下是水5画，不写成水4画。

漆漆漆漆漆漆漆

✎ 14 画
氵 部
左 右

漆 漆漆漆漆漆漆漆

（齊）qí 齐整、齐腰深、齐心、齐唱、齐备

☞ 左上右包围结构。下部是一撇一竖。

✎ 6 画
齐 部
半包围

齐 齐齐齐齐齐齐

古字形像谷物的穗长得齐整。

卝（金文）

其 qí 其他、有其父必有其子、名副其实

✎ 8 画
八 部
上 下

其 其其其其其其其其

奇 qí 奇迹、奇兵、惊奇 / jī 奇数

☞ 大的末笔改点。

✎ 8 画
大 部
上 下

奇 奇奇奇奇奇奇奇奇

骑 （騎）qí 骑马、坐骑、铁骑

☞ 马的第一画乛、第二画乛都不分为两笔；左上角开口；末笔改提。

✎ 11 画
马 部
左 右

骑 骑骑骑骑骑骑骑骑骑骑骑

棋 qí 象棋、举棋不定

☞ 木的中间一竖不带钩，末笔改点。

✎ 12 画
木 部
左 右

棋 棋棋棋棋棋棋棋棋棋棋棋

qí 国旗、旗开得胜、旗鼓相当　☞ 其的上边有部件ノ。

🖊 14 画
部 方 部
四 左 右

旗旗旗旗旗旗旗旗旗旗旗旗旗

---

qǐ 乞讨、乞丐

🖊 3 画
丿 部
四 上 下

乞 乞乞乞

（豈）qǐ 岂有此理、岂敢
☞ 山，第二画是凵，不分为两笔。
下边是己，不是已或巳。

🖊 6 画
山 部
四 上 下

岂 岂岂岂岂岂岂

---

qǐ 企盼、企图、企业
☞ 左上右包围结构。

🖊 6 画
人 部
四 半包围

企 企企企企企企

（啓）qǐ 启封、启发、启程、启事
☞ 上左包围结构。

🖊 7 画
户 部
四 半包围

启 启启启启启启启

---

qǐ 起伏、起痱子、起风、起草、经得起
☞ 左下包围结构。右上是己，不是已或巳。

🖊 10 画
走 部
四 半包围

起 起起起起起起起起起

（氣）qì 煤气、天气、气人、怄气、香气、志气、娇气
☞ 跟乞不同，中部有一短横。

🖊 4 画
气 部
四 独体

气 气气气气

---

qì 弃权、抛弃
☞ 最后两画是一撇、一竖，不是两竖。

🖊 7 画
廾 部
四 上 下

弃 弃弃弃弃弃弃弃

---

qì 汽笛、汽船
☞ 右部不是乞。
✎ 7 画
部 氵部
⚕ 左右
汽汽汽汽汽汽汽

qì 砌墙、堆砌
☞ 中部是七不是土，七的末笔改为竖提。
✎ 9 画
部 石部
⚕ 左右
砌砌砌砌砌砌砌砌砌

qì 器皿、器量、器重、器官 ☞ 中部是犬不是大。
器器器器器器
✎ 16 画
部 口部
⚕ 上下
器器器器器器器器器

古字形像用犬守护器皿内的
食物。（金文）

qiǎ 卡壳、发卡、哨卡、卡脖子 / kǎ 卡车、卡片、卡通
✎ 5 画
部 卜部
⚕ 上下
卡卡卡卡卡

字谜
五画写上下，六画就出差；
要上上不去，想下不能下。

qià 融洽、洽谈
✎ 9 画
部 氵部
⚕ 左右
洽洽洽洽洽洽洽洽洽洽

qià 恰当、恰巧、恰恰、恰如其分
✎ 9 画
部 忄部
⚕ 左右
恰恰恰恰恰恰恰恰恰

（*韆）qiān 成千上万、千锤百炼、一落千丈、*秋千
✎ 3 画
部 十部
⚕ 独体
千千千

（遷）qiān 迁居、变迁
☞ 左下包围结构。辶3画，第二画楷体是⻌（横折折撇），宋体是⻌（横折）。
✎ 6 画
部 辶部
⚕ 半包围
迁迁迁迁迁迁

（牵） qiān 牵牛、牵涉、牵挂

大的末笔改点。

画 9 大 部 上 下

牵 牵牵牵牵牵牵牵牵牵

（鉛） qiān 铅字、铅笔

右上第二画是乚，不带钩。

画 10 钅 部 左 右

铅 铅铅铅铅铅铅铅铅铅铅

（謙） qiān 谦虚、谦让

讠两画，第二画是乚。兼的两竖不带钩；中部不是彐，中间横笔右端出头。

画 12 讠 部 左 右

谦 谦谦谦谦谦谦谦谦谦谦谦谦

（簽 *籤） qiān 签名、*抽签、*书签

中部人下有一短横。

画 13 竹 部 上 下

签 签签签签签签签签签签签签签

qián 勇往直前、房前、前人、前程

左下月的第一画改竖。

画 9 八 部 上 下

前 前前前前前前前前前

（錢） qián 铜钱、零钱、房钱   money

戋的斜钩上是两横一撇，不是三横一撇。

画 10 钅 部 左 右

钱 钱钱钱钱钱钱钱钱钱钱

（鉗） qián 铁钳、钳制

甘5画，第二画竖和第五画横不连成一笔。

画 10 钅 部 左 右

钳 钳钳钳钳钳钳钳钳钳

潜 qián 潜水、潜伏、潜逃   右上两夫，左边夫的末笔改点。

潜潜潜潜潜潜潜潜潜潜潜

画 15 氵 部 左 右

潜 潜潜潜潜

（淺） qiǎn 深浅、肤浅、浅显、浅绿、资历浅、交情浅

☞ 戋的斜钩上是两横一撇，不是三横一撇。

✎ 8 画
氵部
□ 氵 左右

浅 浅浅浅浅浅浅浅浅

qiǎn 派遣、消遣

☞ 左下包围结构。右上不是贵。辶3画，第二画楷体是㇋，宋体是㇂。

✎ 13 画
辶部
□ 半包围

遣 遣遣遣遣遣遣遣遣遣遣遣遣

qiàn 打哈欠、欠妥、欠钱、欠欠身子

欠 欠欠欠欠

古字形像掉过脸去打哈欠。
（甲文）

✎ 4 画
欠部
□ 欠 上下

（縴 *纖） qiàn 拉纤、纤夫/xiān *纤维、*化纤

☞ 纟3画，上部不是幺。

读 qiàn的繁体是縴，读 xiān的繁体是纖。

✎ 6 画
纟部
□ 纟 左右

纤 纤纤纤纤纤纤

qiàn 歉收、抱歉

☞ 兼，两竖不带钩，中部不是彐，它的中间一横右端出头。

歉 歉歉歉歉歉歉歉歉歉歉歉
歉歉

✎ 14 画
欠部
□ 左右

（槍） qiāng 步枪、焊枪

☞ 木的中间一竖不带钩，末笔改点。仓的下边是巳不是匕。

✎ 8 画
木部
□ 木 左右

枪 枪枪枪枪枪枪枪枪

qiāng 胸腔、腔调、打官腔

✎ 12 画
月部
□ 月 左右

腔 腔腔腔腔腔腔腔腔腔腔腔腔

强 qiáng 富强、强身、强盗、强攻、求知欲强/qiǎng 强词夺理/jiàng 倔强

☞ 弓3画，第三画是㇉，不分为两笔。右上是口，不是厶。

✎ 12 画
弓部
□ 弓 左右

强 强强强强强强强强强强强

乔、侨、桥的乔，上部是夭，不是天；下部是一撇一竖，不是两竖。

（墙）qiáng 土墙、围墙 ☞ 土的末笔改提。

墙墙墙墙墙墙墙墙墙墙墙
墙墙墙

✎ 14 画
土 部首
☒ 左 左右

（搶）qiǎng 抢夺、抢购、抢救 / qiāng 呼天抢地

☞ 仓的下部是巳，不是匕、已或己。

✎ 7 画
扌 部首
☒ 右 左右

抢抢抢抢抢抢抢

（鍫）qiāo 铁锹 ☞ 钅5画，第二画是横，不是点；第五画是竖提，不分为两笔。

锹锹锹锹锹锹锹锹锹锹锹
锹锹锹

✎ 14 画
钅 部首
☒ 右 左右

qiāo 敲门、敲诈 ☞ 右部是攴不是支。

敲敲敲敲敲敲敲敲敲敲
敲敲敲

✎ 14 画
高 部首
☒ 左 左右

（喬）qiáo 乔木、乔装

☞ 左上右包围结构。乔乔

乔乔乔乔

✎ 6 画
丿 部首
☒ 半包围

（僑）qiáo 侨民、华侨

侨侨侨侨
侨侨侨侨

✎ 8 画
亻 部首
☒ 左 左右

1963年，有一名青年拿着一捆字画来到荣宝斋，内有一幅宋米芾出书法家米芾的《苕溪诗卷》。慧眼识珠的店主立即用高价买下。米芾传世瑰宝有二，一是《蜀素帖》，现藏中国台北故宫博物馆；一是《苕溪诗卷》，长期遍访未得，现在重新发现。这一墨宝原来保存在清宫内。1932年，日本帝国主义扶植清废帝，立伪满洲国。不少珍贵字画被溥仪携往长春，后又从伪皇宫流散出去，其中就有《苕溪诗卷》。这一国宝失而复得，荣宝斋功不可没。

（橋）qiáo 桥梁、立交桥

☞ 木的中间一竖不带钩，末笔改点。

✎ 10 画
木 部首
☒ 左 左右

桥桥桥桥桥桥桥桥桥桥

瞧 qiáo 瞧病、瞧朋友 ☞ 灬只托住隹，不托目。右上是隹不是住。

瞧瞧瞧瞧瞧瞧瞧瞧
瞧瞧瞧瞧瞧瞧瞧瞧瞧

✎ 17 画
目 部首
☒ 左 左右

切、窃的切，右部七的第二画竖弯钩(乚)改竖提(乚)。

qiǎo 心灵手巧、巧妙、花言巧语、巧遇
☞ 左部工的末笔改提。
✎ 5 画
口 工 部
△ 左 右
巧 巧巧巧巧巧

qiǎo 悄然无声 / qiāo 静悄悄
☞ 右下月的起笔改竖。
✎ 10 画
口 忄 部
△ 左 右
悄 悄悄悄悄悄悄悄悄悄悄

qiē 切瓜、切断 / qiè 切齿、亲切、迫切、切题、切记
✎ 4 画
口 刀 部
△ 左 右
切 切切切切

qié 茄子 / jiā 雪茄
☞ 艹3画，第三画楷体是撇，宋体是竖。
✎ 8 画
口 艹 部
△ 上 下
茄 茄茄茄茄茄茄茄茄

qiě 暂且、既饿且困
✎ 5 画
口 丨 部
△ 独 体
且 且且且且且

古字形像神主的牌位或男性生殖器，应是祖的本字。
（金文）

（竊） qiè 偷窃、窃听
✎ 9 画
口 穴 部
△ 上 下
窃 窃窃窃窃窃窃窃窃窃

qīn 侵占、侵害
☞ 右上是彐，中间一横右端不出头。
✎ 9 画
口 亻 部
△ 左 右
侵 侵侵侵侵侵侵侵侵侵

（親） qīn 亲密、亲属、定亲、亲爹、亲吻、亲历 / qìng 亲家
☞ 立的下边是木，不写成木。
✎ 9 画
口 立 部
△ 上 下
亲 亲亲亲亲亲亲亲亲亲

青、清的青，下部月的起笔改竖。

qín 芹菜

☞ 艹 3 画，第三画楷体是撇，宋体是竖。

✎ 7 画
▣ 艹 部
⊠ 上 下

芹 芹芹芹芹芹芹芹

qín 胡琴、钢琴

☞ 左上王的末笔，楷体是提，宋体是横。下部是今不是令。

✎ 12 画
▣ 王 部
⊠ 上 下

琴 琴琴琴琴琴琴琴琴琴琴琴

qín 禽兽、家禽

☞ 下部是内4画，不是内5画。

✎ 12 画
▣ 人 部
⊠ 上

禽 禽禽禽禽禽禽禽禽禽禽禽

古字形像捕兽用的网，应是擒的本字。𫝀（金文）𰀀（甲文）

qín 勤劳、后勤、出勤

☞ 廿 4 画，第二画竖和第四画横不连成一笔。左下末笔改提。

✎ 13 画
▣ 力 部
⊠ 左 右

勤 勤勤勤勤勤勤勤勤勤勤勤勤

qīng 青天、青菜、老中青结合

✎ 8 画
▣ 青 部
⊠ 上 下

青 青青青青青青青青

(輕) qīng 分量轻、轻音乐、礼轻情重、轻敌、轻薄、轻伤

☞ 车下部的一横改提，笔顺改先竖后提。右部是上又下工，不是上又下土。

✎ 9 画
▣ 车 部
⊠ 左 右

轻 轻轻轻轻轻轻轻轻轻

(傾) qīng 倾斜、倾向、倾覆、倾诉、倾盆大雨

✎ 10 画
▣ 亻 部
⊠ 左 右

倾 倾倾倾倾倾倾倾倾倾倾

qīng 清泉、清唱、清洗、清点、清廉、冷清

✎ 11 画
▣ 氵 部
⊠ 左 右

清 清清清清清清清清清清

qīng 蜻蜓点水

✎ 14 画
虫 部
⚄ 左 中 右

蜻 | 蜻蜻蜻蜻蜻蜻蜻蜻蜻蜻蜻
蜻蜻蜻

---

qíng 情绪、情理、情况、爱情、求情

✎ 11 画
忄 部
⚄ 左 右

情 | 情情情情情情情情情情

---

qíng 雨过天晴、阴转晴、晴朗

✎ 12 画
日 部
⚄ 左 右

晴 | 晴晴晴晴晴晴晴晴晴晴晴

(頃) qǐng 100亩等于1顷、顷刻

☞ 右部是两画：横、竖提，不写成匕。

✎ 8 画
页 部
⚄ 左 右

顷 | 顷顷顷顷顷顷顷顷

(請) qǐng 请求、请客、请讲 *please*

☞ 讠两画，第二画乚不分为两笔或三笔。

✎ 10 画
讠 部
⚄ 左 右

请 | 请请请请请请请请请

(慶) qìng 庆祝、国庆、喜庆

☞ 上左包围结构。右下是大不是犬。

✎ 6 画
广 部
⚄ 半包围

庆 | 庆庆庆庆庆庆

(窮) qióng 穷尽、穷凶极恶、穷追猛打、贫穷、穷乡僻壤

✎ 7 画
穴 部
⚄ 上 下

穷 | 穷穷穷穷穷穷穷

---

qiū 山丘、丘陵

✎ 5 画
丿 部
⚄ 独体

丘 | 丘丘丘丘丘

求、球的求，中部不写成水。区、驱的区，末笔是乚(竖折)，不分为两笔。

(*鞦) qiū 秋季、千秋万代、收秋、*秋千
　　禾，中间一竖不带钩，末笔改点。
　9　画
　禾　部
　左　右
秋秋秋秋秋秋秋秋秋

qiú 求学、求情、要求、供大于求
　7　画
　一　部
　独　体
求求求求求求求

古字形像带毛的兽皮，是裘的本字。（金文）

qiú 球体、眼球、全球、足球
　　王的末笔改提。
　11　画
　王　部
　左　右
球球球球球球球球球球球

(區) qū 禁区、区别、特区 / ōu 姓区
　　上左下包围结构。框内是メ不是又。
　4　画
　匚　部
　半包围
区区区区

(*麯麴) qū 曲线、歪曲、*酒曲 / qǔ 歌曲、谱曲
　6　画
　丨　部
　独　体
曲曲曲曲曲曲

源远流长的汉字，像横贯中国历史的大江大河一样，千百年来，用它宽广的胸膛承托着、传送着中华民族悠久而灿烂的文化。这条文字长河之所以能够满载古老而又新鲜的中华文化不知疲倦地破浪前行，这条古老的文字长河之所以能够经历千年百年而不遭淤塞，没有干涸，除了它自身的应变能力以外，一个重要的原因就是千百年来中国人民对它的维护、疏浚，为它清淤，替它开拓。这项"清淤开拓工程"的总名称就是"汉字整理"。

(驅) qū 驱赶、驱散、长驱直入
　　马，第一画𠃌、第二画𠃌，都不分为两笔；
　　左上角开口；末笔改提。区的框内是メ。
　7　画
　马　部
　左　右
驱驱驱驱驱驱驱

qū 屈膝、屈服、冤屈、理屈词穷
　　上左包围结构。出的两个乚(竖折)，都不分为两笔。
　8　画
　尸　部
　半包围
屈屈屈屈屈屈屈屈

(趨) qū 趋名逐利、趋势
　　左下包围结构。刍的下部是彐，中间一横右端不出头。
　12　画
　走　部
　半包围
趋趋趋趋趋趋趋趋趋趋趋趋

qú 沟渠、渠道

☞ 巨4画，末笔是∟，不分为两笔。木的中间一竖不带钩。

✎ 11 画
□ 木 上下

渠 渠渠渠渠渠渠渠渠渠渠

qǔ 领取、取暖、取材

☞ 耳的末笔改提。

✎ 8 画
□ 耳部
□ 左右

取 取取取取取取取取

古字形像手执一耳。

（金文）

qù 去世、去粗取精、去年、去向

✎ 5 画
□ 土部
□ 上下

去 去去去去去

qù 志趣、趣味、趣闻 ☞ 左下包围结构。耳的末笔改提。又的末笔改点。

✎ 15 画
□ 走部
□ 半包围

趣趣趣趣趣趣趣趣趣趣趣
趣趣趣

quān 圆圈、救生圈、艺术圈、圈地 / juàn 猪圈 / juān 把鸡圈起来

☞ 全包围结构。卷的下部是己，不是已、已或己。

✎ 11 画
□ 口部
□ 全包围

圈 圈圈圈圈圈圈圈圈圈圈圈

（權）quán 权衡、权力、选举权

☞ 木的中间一竖不带钩，末笔改点。

✎ 6 画
□ 木部
□ 左右

权 权权权权权权

云峰山现代碑林建于
1987年。云峰山为书法
圣地，其北朝摩崖刻石
久负盛名，特别是清代
碑派书风兴起，前来观
瞻者更多。20世纪80年
代后，国内外著名书法
家、书法理论家纷纷前
来。他们登云峰、谒摩
崖，即兴挥毫，留下墨
宝。莱州市博物馆遂将
这些书家的作品刻上碑
石，并特辟云峰山现代
碑林馆。

quán 齐全、成全、全新 ☞ 左上右包围结构。

✎ 6 画
□ 人部
□ 半包围

全全全
全全全

quán 山泉、温泉

✎ 9 画
□ 白部
□ 上下

泉泉泉泉泉
泉泉泉泉

quán 握拳、拳曲、打拳

☞ 左上右包围结构。

✎ 10 画
📖 手 部
⊠ 半包围

拳 拳拳拳拳拳拳拳拳拳拳

quǎn 警犬、猎犬

✎ 4 画
📖 犬 部
⊠ 独体

犬 犬犬犬犬

古字形像犬。（金文）（甲文）

（勸）**quàn** 劝勉、劝说

☞ 又的末笔改点。

✎ 4 画
📖 又 部
⊠ 左 右

劝 劝劝劝劝

古代书法
家常写简体字。
王羲之的《兰亭序》
中有三分之一是简体字。
欧阳询的《九成宫》
中有六分之一
是简体字。

quàn 入场券 / **xuàn** 发券、打券

☞ 左上右包围结构。下部是刀不是力。

✎ 8 画
📖 刀 部
⊠ 半包围

券 券券券券券券券券

quē 残缺、缺医少药、缺点、缺席

☞ 缶的第五画改竖提，不分为两笔。

✎ 10 画
📖 缶 部
⊠ 左 右

缺 缺缺缺缺缺缺缺缺缺缺

què 退却、推却、忘却

☞ 右部是卩不是阝。

✎ 7 画
📖 卩 部
⊠ 左 右

却 却却却却却却却

què 麻雀 / **qiāo** 脸上长雀子

☞ 上小下佳。小的一竖去钩；左侧楷体是点，宋体是撇。佳的起笔丿拉长。

✎ 11 画
📖 小 部
⊠ 上 下

雀 雀雀雀雀雀雀雀雀雀雀雀

（確）**què** 确信、千真万确

☞ 右下用内是用，不是丰。

✎ 12 画
📖 石 部
⊠ 左 右

确 确确确确确确确确确确确

（鹊）què 喜鹊
⌇ 鸟5画，第一画丿、第二画乛不连成一笔；第四画乚，不分为两笔。
13 画
鸟部 左右
鹊 鹊鹊鹊鹊鹊鹊鹊鹊鹊鹊鹊鹊鹊

qún 裙子、墙裙
⌇ 左边是衤不是礻。
12 画
衤部 左右
裙 裙裙裙裙裙裙裙裙裙裙裙裙

qún 人群、群山、群情激奋
13 画
羊部 左右
群 群群群群群群群群群群群群

rán 当然、显然、不以为然、然而
12 画
灬部 上下
然 然然然然然然然然然然然

rán 燃烧、燃放 ⌇ 火的末笔改点。灬只托住右半部，不托住左部。
16 画
火部 左右
燃 燃燃燃燃燃燃燃燃燃燃燃燃燃燃燃燃

rǎn 染布、染病、污染
⌇ 右上是九不是丸。木的中间一竖不带钩。
9 画
木部 上下
染 染染染染染染染染

rǎng 土壤、天壤之别、穷乡僻壤 ⌇ 土的末笔改提。
20 画
土部 左右
壤 壤壤壤壤壤壤壤壤壤壤壤壤壤壤壤壤

rǎng 大叫大嚷 / rāng 乱嚷嚷
20 画
口部 左右
嚷 嚷嚷嚷嚷嚷嚷嚷嚷嚷嚷嚷嚷嚷嚷嚷嚷嚷嚷

(讓) ràng 让道、让位、让茶、让人骂了

☞ 讠两画，第二画是乚，不分为两笔或三笔。

✎ 5 画
讠 部
☐ 左 右

让 让让让让让

(饒) ráo 富饶、饶恕、饶舌

☞ 饣三画，第二画是乛，不是点；第三画是乚，不分为两笔。

✎ 9 画
饣 部
☐ 左 右

饶 饶饶饶饶饶饶饶饶饶

(擾) rǎo 打扰、扰民

☞ 扌三画，第二画是乚，不分为两笔。

✎ 7 画
扌 部
☐ 左 右

扰 扰扰扰扰扰扰扰

(繞) rào 缠绕、环绕、绕道

☞ 纟3画，上部不是幺。右上不是戈或弋。

✎ 9 画
纟 部
☐ 左

绕 绕绕绕绕绕绕绕绕绕

rě 惹祸、惹不起

☞ 艹三画，第三画楷体是撇，宋体是竖。心的第二画楷体是乚，宋体是乚。

✎ 12 画
心 部
☐ 上 下

惹 惹惹惹惹惹惹惹惹惹惹惹

(熱) rè 不冷不热、热爱、热点、旅游热、热闹

☞ 灬托住上边të、丸两个部件。

✎ 10 画
灬 部
☐ 上 下

热 热热热热热热热热热热

rén 人类、成年人、助人为乐、人手一册、丢人现眼

☞ 两画的交接点在撇笔上。

✎ 2 画
人 部
☐ 独 体

人 人人

古字形像侧立的人形。 (金文) (甲文)

rén 仁慈、核桃仁

✎ 4 画
亻 部
☐ 左 右

仁 仁仁仁仁

rěn 忍耐、忍心、残忍

☞ 心的第二画楷体是㇃（卧钩），宋体是乚（竖弯钩）。

✎ 7 画
⊞ 心部
⊠ 上下

忍 忍忍忍忍忍忍忍

 rèn 刀刃、白刃战

✎ 3 画
⊞ 刀部
⊠ 独体

刃 刃刃刃

（認）rèn 辨认、认罪

☞ i 两画，第二画是乚，不分为两笔或三笔。

✎ 4 画
⊞ 讠部
⊠ 左右

认 认认认认

在中国内地日常的书面交际中，不规范的字形，主要指：1.《简化字总表》中已被简化的繁体字字形，如：後漢書；2.1986年国务院废止的《第二次汉字简化方案（草案）》收录的简化字字形，如：亠夛；3.经调整后的《第一批异体字整理表》淘汰的异体字字形，如：怸槑；4. 1977年由中国文字改革委员会、国家标准计量局联合发布的（部分计量单位名称统一用字表）中淘汰的译名用字字形，如：瓩糎；5.社会上出现的自造简化字字形，如砼(建)、彡(影)；6.1965年因中华人民共和国文化部、中国文字改革委员会联合发布《印刷通用汉字字形表》而淘汰的相应的旧字形，如：迅吳。

 rèn 任教、任重道远、委任、任凭/rén 姓任

☞ 右部壬是撇下士。

✎ 6 画
⊞ 亻部
⊠ 左右

任 任任任任任任

 rēng 扔沙袋、扔垃圾

✎ 5 画
⊞ 扌部
⊠ 左右

扔 扔扔扔扔扔

 réng 仍旧、仍然

✎ 4 画
⊞ 亻部
⊠ 左右

仍 仍仍仍仍

 rì 烈日、日场、今日、日积月累、生日

✎ 4 画
⊞ 日部
⊠ 独体

日 日日日日

 （榮）róng 欣欣向荣、荣耀、繁荣

☞ 艹3画，第三画楷体是撇，宋体是竖。木的中间一竖不带钩。

✎ 9 画
⊞ 艹部
⊠ 上下

 荣荣荣荣荣荣荣荣荣

柔、揉的木，中间一竖不带钩。

(絨) róng 鸭绒、呢绒

☞ 纟3画，上部不是幺。右部是戎不是戍、戌或戍。

✎ 9 画
▭ 纟 部
☒ 左 右

绒 绒绒绒绒绒绒绒绒绒

---

róng 容器、宽容、容许、面容

✎ 10 画
▭ 宀 部
☒ 上 下

容 容容容容容容容容容容

---

róng 熔化、熔炉 ☞ 火的末笔改点。

✎ 14 画
▭ 火 部
☒ 左 右

熔 熔熔熔熔熔熔熔熔熔熔
熔熔熔

---

róng 融合、融化 ☞ 左下框内是虫四画，不是羊或羊。

✎ 16 画
▭ 鬲 部
☒ 左 右

融 融融融融融融融融融融融融
融融融融

---

róu 柔软、温柔

☞ 木的中间一竖不带钩。

✎ 9 画
▭ 矛 部
☒ 上 下

柔 柔柔柔柔柔柔柔柔柔

---

róu 揉眼睛、揉面

☞ 木的中间一竖不带钩。

✎ 12 画
▭ 扌 部
☒ 左 右

揉 揉揉揉揉揉揉揉揉揉揉揉

---

ròu 猪肉、果肉

meat, flesh

✎ 6 画
▭ 肉 部
☒ 独 体

肉 肉肉肉肉肉肉

古字形像被截割的大
块兽肉。🜚（小篆）

---

rú 如实、犹如、如果、不如

☞ 女的横笔右端不出头。

✎ 6 画
▭ 女 部
☒ 左 右

如 如如如如如如

rǔ 乳房、哺乳、乳胶、乳牙

☞ 子3画，第一画乛、第二画乚，都不分为两笔。

✎ 8 画
◨ 丿 一 画部
☒ 左 右

乳 乳乳乳乳乳乳乳乳

---

rǔ 耻辱、侮辱

☞ 上下结构，辰的第二画撇不包孕寸。

✎ 10 画
◨ 辰 画部
☒ 上 下

辱 辱辱辱辱辱辱辱辱辱辱

---

rù 入口、纳入、入学、入时 enter

☞ 两画的交接点在捺笔上。

✎ 2 画
◨ 人 部
☒ 独 体

入 入入

汉字学可以分为三部分：历史汉字学、现代汉字学和外族汉字学。外族汉字学研究汉字流传到汉族以外的各民族中以后的发展。

（軟） ruǎn 软糖、腿软、心软、领导太软

☞ 车的下边一横改提，笔顺改先撇后提。

✎ 8 画
◨ 车 画部
☒ 左 右

软 软软软软软软软软

（銳） ruì 锐利、锐气、锐减

☞ 钅5画，第二画是横，不是点；第五画是竖提，不分为两笔。

✎ 12 画
◨ 钅 画部
☒ 左 右

锐 锐锐锐锐锐锐锐锐锐锐锐锐

---

ruì 祥瑞、瑞雪兆丰年

☞ 王的末笔改提。山3画，第二画是乚，不分为两笔。

✎ 13 画
◨ 王 画部
☒ 左 右

瑞 瑞瑞瑞瑞瑞瑞瑞瑞瑞瑞瑞瑞瑞

（潤） rùn 湿润、浸润、光润、利润

☞ 门的第一画、（点）嵌在第二画丨和第三画冂之间。

✎ 10 画
◨ 氵 画部
☒ 左 右

润 润润润润润润润润润润

---

ruò 大智若愚、旁若无人

☞ 艹3画，第三画楷体是撇，宋体是竖。

✎ 8 画
◨ 艹 画部
☒ 上 下

若 若若若若若若若若

ruò 弱者、衰弱、老弱病残、怯弱

week feeble, inferior

☞ 弓 3 画，第三画是乚，不分为两笔。

✎ 10 画
□ 弓 部首
☒ 左 右

弱 弱弱弱弱弱弱弱弱弱弱弱

---

sā 撒网、撒泼 /sǎ 撒种、撒了一地　☞ 月的起笔改竖。右部是 攵 不是 夂。

✎ 15 画
□ 扌 部首
☒ 左 右

撒撒撒撒撒撒撒撒撒撒撒撒撒撒撒撒

(灑) sǎ 洒水　*sprinkle, spray, spill*

☞ 西的第五画是竖弯，不带钩。

✎ 9 画
□ 氵 部首
☒ 左 右

洒洒洒洒洒洒洒洒洒

---

sāi 塞耗子洞、耳塞 / sè 闭塞 / sài 边塞

strategic stronghold

✎ 13 画
□ 宀 部首
☒ 上 下

塞塞塞塞塞塞塞塞塞塞塞塞塞

(賽) sài 赛跑、一个赛一个、田径赛　☞ 贝的第二画 ㇕ 不带钩。

match, game, competition

✎ 14 画
□ 宀 部首
☒ 上 下

赛赛赛赛赛赛赛赛赛赛赛赛赛

赛：规范简化字不作"寋"。

---

sān 三番五次、三五成群　*three*

✎ 3 画
□ 一 部首
☒ 独 体

三三三

(傘) sǎn 雨伞、降落伞

umbrella

✎ 6 画
□ 人 部首
☒ 上 下

伞伞伞伞伞伞

"像"在原来的《简化字总表》(1964年)中被简化为"象"。"像"在日常的印刷物中被停止使用。1986年重新发表的《简化字总表》恢复了"像"的规范字身分，不再作为"象"的繁体字。

---

sàn 散摊、散布、散心 /sǎn 散装、丸散膏丹、松散

☞ 月的起笔改竖。右边是 攵 不是 夂。

✎ 12 画
□ 攵 部首
☒ 左

散散散散散散散散散散散散

桑、嗓的桑，上部三个又的末笔都改点。

（喪） sāng 治丧 / sàng 丧失、懊丧

☞ 下部4画：横、竖提、撇、捺，不是衣去点。

✎ 8 画
田部 十
区 上下

丧 丧 丧 丧 丧 丧 丧 丧

sāng 桑叶、蚕桑

✎ 10 画
田部 木
区 上下

古字形像桑树。
Ψ（甲文）**桑**（小篆）

桑 桑 桑 桑 桑 桑 桑 桑 桑 桑

sǎng 嗓音、嗓门儿

✎ 13 画
田部 口
区 左右

嗓 嗓 嗓 嗓 嗓 嗓 嗓 嗓 嗓 嗓 嗓

（掃） sǎo 扫地、扫雷、扫视 / sào 扫帚

☞ 右部是彐，中间一横右端不出头。

✎ 6 画
田部 扌
区 左右

扫 扫 扫 扫 扫 扫

sǎo 大嫂、他张嫂

☞ 女的横笔右端不出头。白中一竖穿过底部。

✎ 12 画
田部 女
区 左右

嫂 嫂 嫂 嫂 嫂 嫂 嫂 嫂 嫂 嫂

sè 面不改色、景色、货色、色彩、姿色 / shǎi 上色

COLOR

✎ 6 画
田部 色
区 上下

色 色 色 色 色 色

sēn 森林、阴森 ☞ 木的中间一竖不带钩，左下木的末笔改点

✎ 12 画
田部 木
区 上下

森 森 森 森 森 森
森 森 森 森 森 森

（殺） Kill, slaughter shā 杀猪、杀进杀出、杀价

☞ 下部是木，不写成术。

✎ 6 画
田部 木
区 上下

杀 杀 杀 杀 杀 杀

一变二，二变三，大字加横变成天。十字加横成干字，早字加横变成旦。火字加横就要灭，日字加横变成旦。止字加横变方正，问字加横变成间。帅字加横成一师，坏字加横变成环。

shā 沙漠、豆沙、沙哑

☞ 少的中间一竖不带钩。

✎ 7 画
▢ 氵 部
▨ 左 右

沙 沙沙沙沙沙沙沙

古字形像水中散落的沙粒。
（金文）

（纱）shā 棉纱、纱巾

☞ 纟3画，上部不是幺。少的中间一竖不带钩。

✎ 7 画
▢ 纟 部
▨ 左 右

纱 纱纱纱纱纱纱纱

shǎ 傻子、傻干

☞ 右下是夂不是夊。

✎ 13 画
▢ 亻 部
▨ 左 右

傻 傻傻傻傻傻傻傻傻傻傻傻

shà 高楼大厦 / xià 厦门

☞ 上左包围结构。左上不是广。右下是夂不是夊。

✎ 12 画
▢ 厂 部
▨ 半包围

厦 厦厦厦厦厦厦厦厦厦厦厦

（篩）shāi 筛子、筛米

☞ 左下一竖一撇，不是两竖。

✎ 12 画
▢ 竹 部
▨ 上 下

筛 筛筛筛筛筛筛筛筛筛筛筛

（曬）shài 晒得脱层皮、晒太阳

Shine upon, dry in mesun

☞ 西第五画是乚（竖弯），不带钩。

✎ 10 画
▢ 日 部
▨ 左 右

晒 晒晒晒晒晒晒晒晒晒

shān 高山、冰山

hill, mountain

☞ 第二画是乚，不分为两笔。

✎ 3 画
▢ 山 部
▨ 独 体

山 山山山

古字形像山峰层叠。（金文）

shān 删繁就简、删节

✎ 7 画
▢ 刂 部
▨ 左 右

删 删删删删删删删

on lined upper garment

shān 衬衫、夹克衫

☞ 左边是 衤 不是 礻。彡写在一条中轴线上。

✎ 8 画　衤部
田 左　右

衫衫衫衫衫衫衫衫

（閃）*lodge. duck*

shǎn 闪开、闪念、打闪、闪了腰

☞ 左上右包围结构。门的起笔、嵌在第二笔丨和第三笔𠃌之间。人的末笔改点。

✎ 5 画　门部
田 半包围

闪闪闪闪闪

（陝）shǎn 陕西、陕南

☞ 阝两画，第一画是𠃌，不分为两笔。

✎ 8 画　阝部
田 左　右

陕陕陕陕陕陕陕陕

shàn 电扇、隔扇 / shān 扇炉子

☞ 上左包围结构。

✎ 10 画　户部
田 半包围

扇扇扇扇扇扇扇扇扇扇

shàn 改善、和善、行善、能歌善舞、善变

☞ 羊、口之间是丷不是艹。

✎ 12 画　羊部
田 上　下

善善善善善善善善善善善

（傷）shāng 受伤、伤天害理、忧伤、伤寒

☞ 右部是𠂆不是𠂢。

✎ 6 画　亻部
田 左

伤伤伤伤伤伤

伤：规范简
化字不作
"傷"。

shāng 商业、商务、磋商

☞ 下边框内是上八下口，不是古。

✎ 11 画　亠部
田 上　下

商商商商商商商商商商商

shǎng 晌午、后半晌

☞ 左边是日，不是口。

✎ 10 画　日部
田 左　右

晌晌晌晌晌晌晌晌晌

掮、梢、稍右下的月，起笔改竖。

（赏） **shǎng** 赏赐、重赏、赞赏、赏花

☞ 上部是⺌不是⺍（学字头）。贝的第二画丁不带钩。不简化为尝。

✎ 12 画
□ 小　部
凶 上　下

赏 赏赏赏赏赏赏赏赏赏赏赏赏

shàng 上游、上午、上等、上山、上账、上课 / **shǎng** 上声

upper

古字形用短横在长横之上来表示。
二（金文）

✎ 3 画
□ 卜　部
凶 独　体

土 上上上

first put to serve: 上菜 shàng cài

still, yet

shàng 高尚、尚武、尚未结婚

☞ 左上右包围结构。

✎ 8 画
□ 小　部
凶 半包围

尚 尚尚尚尚尚尚尚尚

shang 衣裳　☞ 上部是尚，下部是衣。

✎ 14 画
□ 小　部
凶 上　下

裳 裳裳裳裳裳
裳裳裳裳裳裳裳裳裳

字谜

和尚头，衣字底，偏偏不是和尚衣；
男女老少都穿它，请问这是啥东西？

shāo 捎脚、捎信 / **shào** 往后捎、捎色

✎ 10 画
□ 扌　部
凶 左　右

捎 捎捎捎捎捎捎捎捎捎

（烧） **shāo** 燃烧、烧水、高烧

☞ 火的末笔改点。右上不是戈或弋。

✎ 10 画
□ 火　部
凶 左　右

烧 烧烧烧烧烧烧烧烧烧烧

shāo 树梢、眉梢

☞ 木的中间一竖不带钩，末笔改点。

✎ 11 画
□ 木　部
凶 左　右

梢 梢梢梢梢梢梢梢梢梢梢

shāo 稍微、稍不留意就被骗

☞ 禾的中间一竖不带钩，末笔改点。

✎ 12 画
□ 禾　部
凶 左　右

稍 稍稍稍稍稍稍稍稍稍稍稍

sháo 汤勺、马勺、用勺舀汤

⌐ 上右包围结构。

✎ 3 画
▢ 勹 部
▢ 半包围

勺 勺勺勺

shǎo 少数、必不可少、缺少/shào 少年、少校

⌐ 上部小的竖笔不带钩。

✎ 4 画
▢ 小 部
▢ 独体

少 少少少少

many/much duō shǎo 多

统计原则是选取常用字的一条重要原则。确定一个字是否常用，主要的依据是该字在书面语中出现的频率。为了提高统计的科学性，要保证统计语料足够的数量。在字量适度的基础上尽量扩大语料的覆盖面。

(紹) shào 介绍

⌐ 纟3画，上部不是纟。

✎ 8 画
▢ 纟部
▢ 左 右

绍 绍绍绍绍绍绍绍绍

shào 哨卡、吹哨

⌐ 月的起笔改竖。

✎ 10 画
▢ 口 部
▢ 左 右

哨 哨哨哨哨哨哨哨哨哨哨

shé 舌头、火舌 *tongue*

⌐ 起笔是撇不是横。

✎ 6 画
▢ 舌 部
▢ 上 下

舌 舌舌舌舌舌舌

古字形像张口伸舌。
舌 (小篆)

shé 毒蛇、蟒蛇

⌐ 它的下部是匕，不是匕。

✎ 11 画
▢ 虫 部
▢ 左 右

蛇 蛇蛇蛇蛇蛇蛇蛇蛇蛇蛇

(設) shè 摆设、开设、设计、设想

⌐ 讠两画，第二画是乁，不分为两笔或三笔。右上不是几，第二画不带钩。

✎ 6 画
▢ 讠部
▢ 左 右

设 设设设设设设

shè 社会、出版社、旅社 *organized body, agency*

⌐ 左部是礻不是衤。

✎ 7 画
▢ 礻部
▢ 左 右

社 社社社社社社社

(*捨) shè 宿舍、舍弟、鸡舍 / shě *舍近求远 ~~give up, abandon~~

☞ 左上右包围结构。下部不是舌，下部的起笔是横。

✎ 8 画
▣ 人 部
☒ 半包围

舍 舍舍舍舍舍舍舍舍

---

shè 射箭、喷射、影射、反射

☞ 身的末笔上端不出头。

✎ 10 画
▣ 身 部
☒ 左 右

射 射射射射射射射射射射

---

shè 跋山涉水、涉嫌、涉险

☞ 止下不是少，右上无点，竖笔无钩。

古字形像徒步从水里走过去。
（金文） （甲文）

✎ 10 画
▣ 氵 部
☒ 左 右

涉 涉涉涉涉涉涉涉涉涉涉

(攝) shè 摄影、拍摄

☞ 聂的左下又末笔改点。

✎ 13 画
▣ 扌 部
☒ 左 右

摄 摄摄摄摄摄摄摄摄摄摄摄摄

(誰) shéi 外面是谁、谁都可以

☞ 讠两画，第二画是乁，不分为两笔或三笔。右部是隹不是住。

✎ 10 画
▣ 讠 部
☒ 左 右

谁 谁谁谁谁谁谁谁谁谁谁

---

shēn 申请、申酉戌亥 ~~state, express, explain~~

✎ 5 画
▣ 丨 部
☒ 独 体

申 申申申申申

---

shēn 伸缩、伸展、一条小路伸向远方 ~~stretch, extend~~

✎ 7 画
▣ 亻 部
☒ 左 右

伸 伸伸伸伸伸伸伸

汉字本身有两面性，一方面是技术性，另一方面是艺术性。重视技术性的人们成为汉字的"改革派"。重视艺术性的人们成为汉字的"国粹派"。
——周有光《汉字的技术性和艺术性》

---

shēn 身体、船身、以身作则、终身、身分

☞ 末笔撇的上端出头。~~BODY~~

✎ 7 画
▣ 身 部
☒ 独 体

身 身身身身身身身

shēn 深坑、进深、深入浅出、深交、深秋、深知

☞ 木的中间一竖不带钩。

✎ 11 画
□ 氵 部
囚 左 右

深 深深深深深深深深深深深

 shén 神仙、神医、出神、神态　god, deity, spirit

☞ 左部是 礻 不是 衤。

✎ 9 画
□ 礻 部
囚 左 右

神 神神神神神神神神神

 （*瀋） shěn *沈阳、姓沈

✎ 7 画
□ 氵 部
囚 左 右

沈 沈沈沈沈沈沈沈

> 包围结构的字，如果
> 是上右包围的，被包
> 围部件要向右上靠近，
> 以求字框的胸中填满。
> 如字框"横折钩"要略
> 向左斜，给人包得很
> 紧的视觉形象，如
> "司、勾、句"等。

 （審） shěn 审稿、精审、审判

careful, examine, interrogate, try

✎ 8 画
□ 宀 部
囚 上 下

审 审审审审审审审

 （嬸） shěn 婶子、他张婶　wife of father's younger brother

☞ 女的横笔右端不出头。

✎ 11 画
□ 女 部
囚 左 右

婶 婶婶婶婶婶婶婶婶婶

 （腎） shèn 肾脏　kidney

☞ 左上是两竖。月的起笔改竖。

✎ 8 画
□ 月 部
囚 上 下

肾 肾肾肾肾肾肾肾肾

 shèn 甚好、甚佳　very, extremely

✎ 9 画
□ 一 部
囚 独 体

甚 甚甚甚甚甚甚甚甚

 （滲） shèn 渗出、渗透　ginseng

ooze, seep

☞ 彡写在一条中轴线上。

✎ 11 画
□ 氵 部
囚 左 右

渗 渗渗渗渗渗渗渗渗渗渗

shèn 慎重、谨慎

☞ 真的框内是三横。

✎ 13 画
囗 忄部
⊠ 左 右

慎 慎慎慎慎慎慎慎慎慎慎慎

shēng 升旗、升级、10升等于1斗

move upward, promote

✎ 4 画
囗 丿部
⊠ 独 体

升 升升升升

shēng 生长、诞生、学生、生病、永生、生物、生米、生僻

give birth to, grow

✎ 5 画
囗 生部
⊠ 独 体

生 生生生生生

古字形像草木出土。
丫(金文) 丫(甲文)

(聲) shēng 笑声、名声、声调

☞ 上部是士不是土。

✎ 7 画
囗 士部
⊠ 上 下

声 声声声声声声声

shēng 牲口、牲畜

☞ 牛的第二横改提，笔顺改先竖后提。

✎ 9 画
囗 牛部
⊠ 左 右

牲 牲牲牲牲牲牲牲牲

(繩) shéng 麻绳、准绳、绳之以法

☞ 纟3画，上部不是幺。右部上口下电。

✎ 11 画
囗 纟部
⊠ 左 右

绳 绳绳绳绳绳绳绳绳绳绳

economize, save

shěng 省略、节省、省会 /xǐng 反省、不省人事

☞ 左上右包围结构。少的中间一竖不带钩。

✎ 9 画
囗 目部
⊠ 半包围

省省省省省
省 省省省省

sage, saint

(聖) shèng 圣人、棋圣、神圣、圣旨、圣经

☞ 上部是又，下部是土。

✎ 5 画
囗 又部
⊠ 上 下

圣 圣圣圣圣圣

国家标准局于1987年3月发布《信息交换用汉字编码字符集·第四辅助集》(GB7590-87)，收7039字，是简化汉字集。

师、狮的师，左部是一竖一撇，不是两竖。

（勝） shèng 胜任、胜负、胜于、名胜

✎ 9 画
月 部
左 右
胜 胜胜胜胜胜胜胜胜胜

shèng 兴盛、盛况、盛行、盛情/chéng　盛饭、盛不下
☞ 上下结构。成的第二画撇不包孕皿。

✎ 11 画
皿 部
上 下
盛 盛盛盛盛盛盛盛盛盛盛盛

shèng 剩余、过剩
☞ 乘的中间一竖不带钩，末笔改点，上部的北，第三画是提，第四画是撇。

✎ 12 画
刂 部
左 右
剩 剩剩剩剩剩剩剩剩剩剩剩

shī 死尸、尸首

✎ 3 画
尸 部
独 体
尸 尸尸尸

lose, deviate from normal

shī 丢失、失踪、失手、失常、失望、失信、失约
fail to get a grip of

✎ 5 画
丿 部
独 体
失 失失失失失

☞《史记·万石张叔列传》记载：有一次，郎中令石建给皇帝上奏折。奏折批下来以后，石建又读了一遍，发现自己写了一个错字，"馬（马）"字少写了一笔。石建顿时吓得汗流满面，连连跺脚："糟了！糟了！奏折上写了错字了。上面一定要治我死罪了！"

（師） shī 雄师百万、师傅、医师、法师
teacher, master

✎ 6 画
巾 部
左 右
师 师师师师师师

（詩） shī 古诗、叙事诗　*poetry, verse, poem*
☞ 讠两画，第二画是乁，不分为两笔或三笔。右上是土，不是士。

✎ 8 画
讠 部
左 右
诗 诗诗诗诗诗诗诗诗

（獅） shī 狮子、雄狮

✎ 9 画
犭 部
左 右
狮 狮狮狮狮狮狮狮狮

shī 施礼、施舍、施肥、施工

✎ 9 画
⿰ 方 部右
⿰ 独

施施施施施施施施施施

（濕）shī 潮湿、湿透

✎ 12 画
⿰ 氵 部左
⿰ 左

湿湿湿湿湿湿湿湿湿湿湿湿

shí 十分、十全十美 ten

✎ 2 画
⿰ 十 部独
⿱ 独 体

十 十十

shí 什锦糖 / shén 什么 assorted, varied

✎ 4 画
⿰ 亻 部左
⿰ 左

什 什什什什

shí 石头、矿石 / dàn 10斗等于1石 stone, rock

✎ 5 画
⿰ 石 部独
⿱ 独 体

石 石石石石石

（時）shí 时令、时间、时局、时机、时紧时松 time, opportunity, chance

✎ 7 画
⿰ 日 部左
⿰ 左

时 时时时时时时时

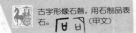

（識）shí 识字、学识 / zhì 博闻强识、款识

☞ 讠两画，第二画是乛，不分为两笔或三笔。

✎ 7 画
⿰ 讠 部右
⿰ 左

识 识识识识识识识识

（實）shí 充实、实效、老实、事实、果实 solid, real, true, honest fact

☞ 宀头的末笔是点。

✎ 8 画
⿱ 宀 部下
⿱ 上

实 实实实实实实实实

shí 拾取、拾圆整

✎ 9 画
部 扌 部
结构 左 右

拾 拾拾拾拾拾拾拾拾拾

---

shí 副食、蚕食、月食、食品

☞ 良的末笔变点。

✎ 9 画
部 食 部
结构 上 下

食 食食食食食食食食食

古字形像用嘴凑近食器吃东西。

合 (金文) 仓 (甲文)

(蝕) shí 腐蚀、蚀本

☞ 饣 3画，第二画是 ㇆，不是点；第三画是 乚，不分为两笔。

✎ 9 画
部 饣 部
结构 左 右

蚀 蚀蚀蚀蚀蚀蚀蚀蚀

---

shǐ 史实、史料   history

BLEGRAM(SOMC)

✎ 5 画
部 丨 部
结构 独 体

史 史史史史史

---

shǐ 支使、使人吃惊、学使筷子、使馆

send, tell, use, employ, apply

✎ 8 画
部 亻 部
结构 左 右

使 使使使使使使使

---

shǐ 始终、开始   beginning, start

☞ 女的横笔右端不出头。

✎ 8 画
部 女 部
结构 左 右

始 始始始始始始始

(駛) shǐ 疾驶、驾驶   drive, sail, speed past

☞ 马的第一画是 ㇆，第二画是 乚，都不分为两笔；左上角开口；末笔改提。

✎ 8 画
部 马 部
结构 左 右

驶 驶驶驶驶驶驶驶

---

shì 绅士、烈士、护士、士兵、下士

scholar

✎ 3 画
部 土 部
结构 独 体

士 士士士

国际旅行家中偏爱古代的一派认为，中国最宝贵的旅游资源是长城、兵马俑和汉字，埃及最宝贵的旅游资源是金字塔和圣书字。

shì 姓氏、摄氏

✎ 4　画
⊟ 氏　部
△ 独　体

氏 氏氏氏氏

shì 出示、启示、示范

✎ 5　画
⊟ 示　部
△ 上　下

示 示示示示示

古字形像神主。
（甲文）

shì 世世代代、人生一世、世界、逝世

☞ 第二画是竖，第四画是短横，不连成一笔。第五画是乚，不分为两笔。

✎ 5　画
⊟ 一　部
△ 独　体

世 世世世世世

shì 菜市、都市、市尺

(super)MARKET

✎ 5　画
⊟ 巾　部
△ 上　下

市 市市市市市

构词构字原则是选取常用字的一条重要原则。各个汉字的构词能力是不一样的。一般说来，构词能力强的字，在书面语中出现的机会就多，它的使用频率就高。许多汉字除了构词能力以外，还有构字能力，常常作为构字部件锒别的部件组合成新字。如"非"，既能独立出现，还能构成"匪、啡、菲、翡、诽、蜚、棑、纰、榧、腓、扉、斐、琲、蜚、霏、靠、鲱"等字，这二者就保证了它的常用字的地位。

shì 格式、样式、阅兵式、公式

☞ 上右包围结构。右上是弋，不是戈。

✎ 6　画
⊟ 弋　部
△ 半包围

式 式式式式式式

（势） shì 权势、气势、地势、姿势、局势

✎ 8　画
⊟ 力　部
△ 上　下

势 势势势势势势势势

shì 事情、平安无事、不事生产

matter, affair, thing, business —
job, work, affair,
responsibility —
involvement

☞ 下部不是彐，中间一横右端出头。

✎ 8　画
⊟ 一　部
△ 独　体

事 事事事事事事事

shì 服侍、侍从

☞ 右上是土不是士。

✎ 8　画
⊟ 亻　部
△ 左　右

侍 侍侍侍侍侍侍侍侍

(飾) shì 修饰、首饰、掩饰、饰演

　ℱ 饣 3 画，第二画是→，不是点；第三画是乀，不分为两笔。

🖊 8　画
🔲 饣　部
🔳 左　右

饰 饰饰饰饰饰饰饰饰

(試) shì 尝试、考试　　*to try*

　ℱ 讠 两画，第二画是乀，不分为两笔或三笔。

🖊 8　画
🔲 讠　部
🔳 左　右

试 试试试试试试试试

(視) shì 注视、巡视、重视

　ℱ 左部是 礻 不是 衤。

🖊 8　画
🔲 礻　部
🔳 左　右

视 视视视视视视视视

---

shì 柿子、柿饼

　ℱ 木的中间一竖不带钩，末笔改点。

老师 *lǎo shī : Teacher*

🖊 9　画
🔲 木　部
🔳 左　右

柿 柿柿柿柿柿柿柿柿柿

---

shì 我是学生、似是而非、实事求是　　*to be*

🖊 9　画
🔲 日　部
🔳 上　下

是 是是是是是是是是是

(適) shì 适龄、适得其反、不适

　ℱ 左下包围结构。

🖊 9　画
🔲 辶　部
🔳 半包围

适 适适适适适适适适适

---

shì 卧室、家室、收发室

🖊 9　画
🔲 宀　部
🔳 上　下

室室室室室
室室室室

在日常语体的现代汉语书面语中使用频率高的字被称为现代汉语常用字。

---

shì 消逝、病逝

　ℱ 左下包围结构。

🖊 10　画
🔲 辶　部
🔳 半包围

逝 逝逝逝逝逝逝逝逝逝逝

（釋） shi 释放、释疑、解释、爱不释手

☞ 左部7画，丿下米，不是采。

✎ 12　画
部 禾　左
四 左　右

释 释释释释释释释释释释释释

---

shì 发誓、宣誓

☞ 誓誓誓誓誓誓誓誓誓誓誓

✎ 14　画
部 言　上
四 上　下

誓 誓誓誓

---

receive accept, put away, take in

shōu 收集、收入、收割、收税、收容、收敛、收场

☞ 右部是攵不是夂。

✎ 6　画
部 攵　左
四 左　右

收 收收收收收收

---

shǒu 握手、手表、手稿、毒手、水手

hand

✎ 4　画
部 手　独
四 独　体

手 手手手手手

古字形像两手交接东西，中间的舟也是声旁。

曲阜孔庙碑林共有碑刻 2000 余块，上自两汉，下迄民国。其中汉代碑刻为全国第一，有《史晨碑》《乙瑛碑》《孔庙碑》《礼器碑》等稀世珍品。

---

shǒu 保守、守法、守卫、守护、守着大海

guard, defend

✎ 6　画
部 宀　上
四 上　下

守 守守守守守守

---

shǒu 斩首、祸首、首创、首届、自首

head (leader chief)

✎ 9　画
部 丷　上
四 上　下

首 首首首首首首首首首

（壽） shòu 寿星、寿命、祝寿、寿材

☞ 上左包围结构。

✎ 7　画
部 寸　半包围
四 半包围

寿 寿寿寿寿寿寿寿

---

shòu 享受、受苦、受不了

古字形像两手交接东西，中间的舟也是声旁。𠬏（金文）（甲文）

✎ 8　画
部 爪　上
四 上　下

受 受受受受受受受受

shòu 授奖、授课

11 画 扌部
左 右 授 授 授 授 授 授 授 授 授 授

 shòu 售货、零售

☞ 上部是隹不是住。

11 画 隹部
上 下 售 售 售 售 售 售 售 售 售 售 售

 （獸）shòu 走兽、兽行 *beast, animal*

11 画 丷部
八 上 兽 兽 兽 兽 兽 兽 兽 兽 兽 兽 兽

 shòu 瘦弱、瘦肉、衣服太瘦 ☞ 上左包围结构。白的中间一竖穿过底部。

14 画 疒部
广 半包围 瘦 瘦 瘦 瘦 瘦 瘦 瘦 瘦 瘦 瘦 瘦
瘦 瘦 瘦

 （書）shū 书法、隶书、读书、文书、家书

4 画 一部
独体 书 书 书 书

 shū 叔父、小叔子、表叔

☞ 小的左侧楷体是点，宋体是撇。

8 画 又部
又 左 右 叔 叔 叔 叔 叔 叔 叔 叔

殊 shū 悬殊、特殊

10 画 歹部
歹 左 右 殊 殊 殊 殊 殊 殊 殊 殊 殊 殊

 shū 梳子、梳头发

☞ 木的中间一竖不带钩，末笔改点。

11 画 木部
木 左 右 梳 梳 梳 梳 梳 梳 梳 梳 梳 梳 梳

疏、蔬的疏，左下止的末笔改提，右上是㐬不是亡。

shū 舒心、舒缓、舒畅

☞ 舍的第二画改点。右部是予不是矛。

✎ 12 画
⽥ 人 画部
四 左 右

舒 舒舒舒舒舒舒舒舒舒舒舒

---

shū 疏通、疏散、稀疏、疏远、荒疏

✎ 12 画
⽥ 疋 画部
四 左 右

疏 疏疏疏疏疏疏疏疏疏疏疏疏

（輸）shū 输送、输球

☞ 车的下部一横改提，笔顺改先竖后提。月的起笔改竖。

✎ 13 画
⽥ 车 画部
四 左 右

输 输输输输输输输输输输输输

---

shū 蔬菜 ☞ 艹 3 画，第三画楷体是撇，宋体是竖。

shūcài
艹柔
regulaih

✎ 15 画
⽥ 艹 画部
四 上 下

蔬 蔬蔬蔬蔬蔬蔬蔬蔬蔬蔬蔬蔬
蔬蔬蔬

---

shú 熟食、成熟、熟人、熟练、深思熟虑 / shóu 煮熟了 ☞ 孑 3 画，第一画⁊，第二画丿，不连成一笔。灬托住上边两个部件。

✎ 15 画
⽥ 灬 画部
四 上 下

熟 熟熟
熟熟熟熟熟熟熟熟熟熟熟熟

---

shǔ 暑天、暑假、寒暑

✎ 12 画
⽥ 日 画部
四 上 下

暑 暑暑暑暑暑暑暑暑暑暑暑暑

（屬）shǔ 直属、属实、属相、金属、军属

☞ 上左包围结构。右下是禸5画，不是禸4画。

✎ 12 画
⽥ 尸 画部
四 半包围

属 属属属属属属属属属属属

---

shǔ 老鼠、鼠疫

☞ 上部是臼不是白。下部7画：两个竖钩、四个点和一个斜钩。

✎ 13 画
⽥ 鼠 画部
四 上 下

鼠 鼠鼠鼠鼠鼠鼠鼠鼠鼠鼠鼠鼠

术、述的术，中间一竖不带钩，右上有点。

shǔ 红薯、马铃薯　☞艹 3 画，第三画楷体是撇，宋体是竖。

✎ 16 画
部 艹
结 上 下

薯薯薯薯薯薯薯薯薯薯薯
薯薯薯薯薯

(*術) shù *手术、*学术 / zhú 苍术

✎ 5 画
部 木
结 独 体

术术术术术术

---

shù 约束、光束、花束　*bind*
tie *control,*
restrain
☞中部是扁口，中间一竖不带钩。

古字形像一束捆扎的柴火。
（金文）（甲文）

✎ 7 画
部 一
结 独 体

束束束束束束束

---

shù 述说、论述
☞左下包围结构。辶 3 画，第二画楷体是㇈，宋体是㇇。

✎ 8 画
部 辶
结 半包围

述述述述述述述述

(樹) shù 十年树人、树碑、植树
☞木的中间一竖不带钩，末笔改点。又的末笔改点。

✎ 9 画
部 木
结 左 右

树树树树树树树树树

(竪) shù 竖立、竖井、竖排、竖琴
☞左上是两竖，不是一竖一撇。

✎ 9 画
部 立
结 上 下

竖竖竖竖竖竖竖竖竖

(數) shù 岁数、数人 / shǔ 数人数(shù)、数他显老、数落
☞米的末笔改点。女的横笔右端不出头。右边是攵不是夂。

✎ 13 画
部 攵
结 左 右

数数数数数数数数数数数数数

---

shuā 牙刷、刷墙、刷洗、刷新、刷刷响

✎ 8 画
部 刂
结 左 右

刷刷刷刷刷刷刷刷

shuǎ 玩耍、耍弄、耍龙灯、耍手腕

☞ 上部是而不是西。

✎ 9 画　画部首 而　结构 上下

耍 耍耍耍耍耍耍耍耍耍

shuāi 衰弱、衰败

☞ 中部是口中一横，两端出头，嵌在衣中。

✎ 10 画　画部首 亠　结构 上下

衰 衰衰衰衰衰衰衰衰衰衰

shuāi 摔玻璃杯、从楼顶摔下来、摔跤

摔摔摔摔摔摔摔摔摔摔

✎ 14 画　画部首 扌　结构 左右

摔 摔摔摔

shuǎi 甩鞭子、远远甩掉

☞ 左上右包围结构。

✎ 5 画　画部首 丿　结构 半包围

甩 甩甩甩甩甩

(帥) shuài 元帅、帅气 *handsome*

☞ 左部是一竖一撇，不是两竖。

✎ 5 画　画部首 巾　结构 左右

帅 帅帅帅帅帅

> 左右结构的字，如果两部分是相背的，如"兆、北"等，要注意组织好笔画，不要令全字结构显得松散。如"北"的第三笔向右上挑，跟第四笔呼应，使全字"背"中有"向"。

shuài 率领、表率、轻率、直率／lǜ 利率

✎ 11 画　画部首 亠　结构 上下

率 率率率率率率率率率率

shuān 拴马

✎ 9 画　画部首 扌　结构 左右

拴 拴拴拴拴拴拴拴拴拴

(雙) shuāng 双手、双份、一双大眼

☞ 左边又的末笔改点。

✎ 4 画　画部首 又　结构 左右

双 双双双双

古字形像一手抓两只鸟。

雙 (小篆)

shuāng 霜冻、柿霜　◁ 雨，第二画改点，第三画改横钩，里边楷体是四点，宋体是四横。木的末笔改点。

◇ 17 画
□ 雨部
▣ 上中下

霜霜霜霜霜霜
霜霜霜霜霜霜霜霜霜霜

shuǎng 清爽、直爽、身体不爽　*bright, clear, crisp*

◁ 对称结构。

◇ 11 画
□ 大部
▣ 对称

爽爽爽爽爽爽爽爽爽爽

shuǐ 流水、跋山涉水、药水　*water*

◁ 第二画是 ㇆，不分为两笔。第三画 丿，第四画 ㇏ 不连成一笔。

◇ 4 画
□ 水部
▣ 独体

水水水水

古字形像流水。(金文) (甲文)

shuì 税收、所得税、纳税　*tax, duty*

◁ 禾，中间一竖不带钩，末笔改点。

◇ 12 画
□ 禾部
▣ 左右

税税税税税税税税税税税

shuì 入睡、酣睡、睡眼　*sleep*

◁ 右中部的 ㇛ 3 画，第三画楷体是撇，宋体是竖。

◇ 13 画
□ 目部
▣ 左右

睡睡　睡睡睡睡睡睡睡睡睡睡睡

（顺）shùn 顺从、顺序、通顺、顺畅、顺手牵羊

◁ 页部

◇ 9 画
□ 页部
▣ 左右

顺顺顺顺顺顺顺顺顺

（说）shuō 说明、学说、劝说 / shuì 游说

◁ 讠两画，第二画是 ㇋，不分为两笔或三笔。

◇ 9 画
□ 讠部
▣ 左右

说说说说说说说说说

言字旁，八字头，一位老兄在下头。
字谜

sī 司炉、人事司　*take charge of, attend to, manage*

◁ 上右包围结构。

◇ 5 画
□ 一部
▣ 半包围

司司司司司

司马迁的《史记》，全书 518284 字，只用了 4987 个不同的汉字。

丝

(絲) sī 蚕丝、粉丝、一丝不苟 SILK

☞ 上部两个纟，不是两个幺。下部是一横，不是两短横。

5 画
一 部
上 下

丝 丝丝丝丝丝

古字形像缠扎的两束蚕丝。（金文）（甲文）

私

personal, private, secret

sī 私事、私有、自私、私货、私吞

☞ 禾，中间一竖不带钩，末笔改点。

7 画
禾 部
左 右

私 私私私私私私私

思

sī 思考、思念、哀思 think, consider -long for

☞ 心，第二画楷体是㇃(卧钩)，宋体是乚(竖弯钩)。

9 画
田 部
上 下

思 思思思思思思思思思

斯

sī 生于斯，长于斯、斯文扫地

12 画
斤 部
左 右

斯 斯斯斯斯斯斯斯斯斯斯斯斯

撕

sī 撕开、撕毁

15 画
扌 部
左 右

撕 撕撕撕撕撕撕撕撕撕撕撕撕撕撕撕

死

die, fixed, rigid

sǐ 病死、死守、死心塌地、钉死、死敌、死水、高兴死了

☞ 上左包围结构。右下是匕不是七。

6 画
歹 部
半包围

死 死死死死死死

四

sì 四面出击、三从四德 FOUR

☞ 全包围结构。第四画是竖弯，不带钩。

5 画
口 部
包 围

四 四四四四四

遵循笔顺规则的目的是为了书写汉字时能顺应手腕的生理机能和汉字的构形原理，使书写顺手快速，使写出的字形平衡稳定、匀称内聚、笔断意不断。

寺

sì 寺庙、清真寺 temple, mosque

☞ 上部是土不是士。

6 画
土 部
上 下

寺 寺寺寺寺寺寺

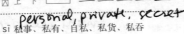

similar, like

似 sì 相似、似懂非懂 / shì 被大雨淋得落汤鸡似的
　　☞ 以4画，第一画是丶，不分为两笔。
　6　画
　亻左　部右
似 似似似似似似

饲 (飼) sì 饲养、饲料 _raise, rear_
　　☞ 亻3画，第二画是㇇，不是点；第三画是乚，
　　　不分为两笔。
　8　画
　饣左　部右
饲 饲饲饲饲饲饲饲

肆 sì 放肆、肆无忌惮 ☞ 右上不是彐，中间横笔右端出头。
　13　画
　镸长　部左
肆肆肆肆肆肆
肆肆肆肆肆肆肆

松 (*鬆) _loose, slack_ sōng 迎客松、*松散、*松手、*鱼松
　　☞ 木的中间一竖不带钩，末笔改点。
　8　画
　木左　部右
松 松松松松松松松松

宋 sòng 南宋、姓宋
　　☞ 木的中间一竖不带钩。
　7　画
　宀上　部下
宋 宋宋宋宋宋宋宋

送 _deliver, carry, give as a present_ sòng 送行、送礼、送信、送死
　　☞ 左下包围结构。辶的末笔改点。辶3画，第二画楷体是㇍，宋体是㇋。
　9　画
　辶左　部半包围
送 送送送送送送送送送

诵 (誦) sòng 背诵、传诵
　　☞ 讠两画，第二画是㇗，不分为两笔或三笔。
　9　画
　讠左　部右
诵 诵诵诵诵诵诵诵诵

颂 (頌) sòng 歌颂、《黄河颂》 _praise, extol_
　　☞ 公的第二画改点。
　10　画
　页左　部右
颂 颂颂颂颂颂颂颂颂颂

历代积累的汉字总数数以万计。近年出版的汉字字典收字总数从五万多逼近八万多。但历代日常书面语常用的汉字一般都控制在三四千字。这是字数繁多的汉字千百年来能为人们接受、成为汉族人民记录汉语的主要文字工具的一个重要原因。也正因为这样，选取当代的常用字作为学习和使用汉字的重点，是历代历朝整理和教学汉字的一个重点内容。历史上的《三字经》《千字文》都是用当时的常用字编写的识字课本。

sōu 搜身、搜寻

✎ 12 画
部 扌
四 左右

搜搜搜搜搜搜搜搜搜搜搜搜

sōu 一艘驱逐舰

☞ 舟的横笔改提，右端不出头。

✎ 15 画
部 舟
四 左右

艘艘艘艘艘艘艘艘艘艘艘
艘艘艘

sòu 咳嗽

☞ 中部是束，它的末笔改点。右部是欠不是攵

✎ 14 画
部 口
四 左右

嗽嗽嗽嗽嗽嗽嗽嗽嗽嗽嗽
嗽嗽嗽

(蘇*囌) sū 苏醒、苏绣、*噜苏

☞ 艹 3画，第三画楷体是撇，宋体是竖。

✎ 7 画
部 艹
四 上下

苏苏苏苏苏苏苏

人类的特点
是能不断延长
手和脑。筷子和笔是手
的延长。书本是脑的延长和扩
大，有人称为体外的"纸
脑"。计算机也是脑的延
长、扩大和优化，是
体外的"电脑"。"人
脑""纸脑""电脑"，
一人多脑。

sú 民俗、粗俗、通俗、还俗

✎ 9 画
部 亻
四 左右

俗俗俗俗俗俗俗俗俗

(訴) sù 告诉、起诉 *tell, relate, infirm*

☞ 讠 两画，第二画是𠃌，不分为两笔或三笔。右部是斥不是斤。

✎ 7 画
部 讠
四 左右

诉诉诉诉诉诉诉

(肅) sù 肃立、严肃、肃清

☞ 对称结构。上部不是彐，中间横笔右端出头。下部不从米。

✎ 8 画
部 聿
四 对称

肃肃肃肃肃肃肃肃

white, vegetables, be a vegetarian

sù 素服、素雅、朴素、元素、平素、素来、吃素

☞ 小的左侧楷体是点，宋体是撇。

✎ 10 画
部 糸
四 上下

素素素素素素素素素

sù 迅速、风速　　*fast, rapid, quick*

　⁛ 左下包围结构。

✎ 10 画
□ 辶 部
⊠ 半包围

速 速速速速速速速速速速

---

sù 住宿、宿愿 / xiǔ 一宿没睡 / xiù 星宿

put up for the night, long standing, old

✎ 11 画
□ 宀 部
⊠ 上 下

宿 宿宿宿宿宿宿宿宿宿宿宿

古字形像人卧在室内席上。
𡩠（金文）　𡩃（甲文）

---

sù 塑料、塑像、塑造、塑封　　*model, mod. mould*

✎ 13 画
□ 土 部
⊠ 上 下

塑 塑塑塑塑塑塑塑塑塑塑塑

---

acid, sour, tart (distressed …)

suān 酸辣汤、心酸、酸痛、盐酸　　⁛ 酉，框内有一横。右下是夂不是夂。

✎ 14 画
□ 酉 部
⊠ 左 右

酸 酸酸酸酸酸酸酸酸酸酸
酸酸酸

---

suàn 大蒜　　*garlic*

　⁛ 艹 3画，第三画楷体是撇，宋体是竖。

✎ 13 画
□ 艹 部
⊠ 上 下

蒜 蒜蒜蒜蒜蒜蒜蒜蒜蒜蒜蒜蒜蒜

---

calculate, include, count, plan, consider

suàn 算账、打算、说话算话

✎ 14 画
□ 竹 部
⊠ 上 下

算 算算算算算算算
算算算算算算算

（雖）suī 虽然、虽死犹生　　*though, although*

✎ 9 画
□ 口 部
⊠ 上 下

虽 虽虽虽虽虽虽虽虽虽

（隨）suí 随从、随手、随便、随意、随地　　*follow, comply w/ let*

　⁛ 阝 两画，第一画是了，不分为两笔。右上是有不是肎。

✎ 11 画
□ 左阝部
⊠ 左 右

随 随随随随随随随随随随随

(歲) suì 岁月、岁数　*year*

☞ 山，第二画是乚，不分为两笔。

✎ 6 画
部首 山 部
结 上 下

岁 岁岁岁岁岁岁

suì 打碎、粉身碎骨、零碎、嘴碎

☞ 辛的中部两人，末笔都改点。

✎ 13 画
部首 石 部
结 左 右

碎 碎碎碎碎碎碎碎碎碎碎碎碎

ear of grain, tassel, fringe

suì 麦穗、灯笼穗儿　☞ 禾，中间一竖不带钩，末笔改点。心的第二画楷体是乀(卧钩)，宋体是乚(竖弯钩)。

✎ 17 画
部首 禾 部
结 左 右

穗 穗穗穗穗穗穗穗穗穗穗
穗穗穗穗穗穗

(孫) sūn 子孙、外孙、曾孙　*grandson*

☞ 子3画，第一画是乛，第二画是亅，不连成一笔，末笔改提。小的左侧楷体是点，宋体是撇。

✎ 6 画
部首 子 部
结 左 右

孙 孙孙孙孙孙孙

(損) *decrease, lose, harm, damage*

sǔn 损失、损公肥私、话太损、破损

☞ 贝的第二画丁不带钩。

✎ 10 画
部首 扌 部
结 左 右

损 损损损损损损损损损损

sǔn 竹笋、笋鸡　*bamboo shoot*

☞ 尹的上部不是彐，中间横笔右端出头。

✎ 10 画
部首 竹 部
结 上 下

笋 笋笋笋笋笋笋笋笋笋

(縮) *contract, shrink, drawback, flinch*

suō 收缩、缩脖子、退缩、缩编　☞ 纟3画，上部不是幺。

✎ 14 画
部首 纟 部
结 左 右

缩 缩缩缩缩缩缩缩缩缩缩
缩缩缩

suǒ 住所、所见所闻、研究所　*place, dwelling place office*

✎ 8 画
部首 斤 部
结 左 右

所 所所所所所所所所

索 suǒ 绳索、思索、索要 *large rope / demand, ask*

☞ 小的左侧楷体是点，宋体是撇。

✎ 10 画
⽥ 十 部
⼞ 上 下

 索索索索索索索索索

锁 (鎖) suǒ 拉锁、门锁、锁车、封锁、锁边 *lock*

☞ ⻐ 5画，第二画是横，不是点；第五画是竖提，不分为两笔。贝的第二画⼝不带钩。

✎ 12 画
⽥ ⻐ 部
⼞ 左 右

 锁锁锁锁锁锁锁锁锁锁锁

他 tā 他人、你我他 *he, another, other*

✎ 5 画
⽥ 亻 部
⼞ 左 右

他他他他他

它 tā 它是电影里的恐龙 *it*

☞ 下部是匕不是七。

✎ 5 画
⽥ 宀 部
⼞ 上 下

它它它它它

她 tā 她是我妹妹 *she*

☞ 女的横笔右端不出头。

✎ 6 画
⽥ 女 部
⼞ 左 右

她她她她她她

塌 tā 倒塌、塌鼻梁 *collapse, fall down, cave in*

✎ 13 画
⽥ 土 部
⼞ 左 右

塌塌塌塌塌塌塌塌塌塌塌

塔 tǎ 宝塔、电视塔 *Buddhist Pagoda*

☞ 艹三画，第三画楷体是撇，宋体是竖。

✎ 12 画
⽥ 土 部
⼞ 左 右

塔塔塔塔塔塔塔塔塔塔塔塔

踏 tà 践踏、踏看 / tā 踏实 *step on, tread, stamp* ☞ 左下止的末笔改提。

✎ 15 画
⽥ 足 部
⼞ 左 右

踏踏踏踏踏踏踏
踏踏踏踏踏踏踏踏

摹帖，就是用透明纸蒙在范本上，然后仿照帖上的字迹写字。这种方法通常叫做"写仿影"。为了保护字帖，人们习惯先把帖上的字迹描下来，双钩成空心，作为范本，然后再把仿纸蒙在上面填墨书写。摹帖时，既要求结构稳，还要求用笔准。切忌不动脑子，只是一遍一遍地描。这样，一旦离开字帖，就不知道如何下笔了。

（臺*檯**颱）tái 亭台楼阁、*灯台、*讲台、*写字台、台胞、**台风

platform, stage, support

- 5 画
- 厶 部
- 上 下

台 台台台台台

tái 抬举、抬担架

lift raise, drive up prices

- 8 画
- 扌 部
- 左 右

抬 抬抬抬抬抬抬抬抬

tài 太爷爷、太妙了、不太满意

highest, greatest, too much

- 4 画
- 大 部
- 独 体

太 太太太太

（態）form appearance, condition

tài 姿态、动态

☞ 心的第二画楷体是乀（卧钩），宋体是乚（竖弯钩）。

- 8 画
- 心 部
- 上 下

态 态态态态态态态态

泰 safe, peaceful, tranquil

tài 康泰、国泰民安

☞ 左上右包围结构。下部是氺5画，不写成水4画。

- 10 画
- 水 部
- 半包围

泰 泰泰泰泰泰泰泰泰泰泰

（貪）corrupt

tān 贪睡、贪污 covet, hanker after

☞ 上部是今不是令。贝的第二画丁不带钩。

- 8 画
- 贝 部
- 上 下

贪 贪贪贪贪贪贪贪贪

（攤）spread out, take a share in

tān 摊开、分摊、倒霉事让她摊上了、摊位

☞ 中部是又，末笔改点。右部是隹，不是住。

- 13 画
- 扌 部
- 左 右

摊 摊摊摊摊摊摊摊摊摊摊摊

（灘）tān 险滩、沙滩 beach, sand

☞ 中部是又，末笔改点。右部是隹，不是住。

- 13 画
- 氵 部
- 左

滩 滩滩滩滩滩滩滩滩滩滩滩滩

(壇 *罎) tán 天坛、花坛、体坛、讲坛、*坛坛罐罐

☞ 土的末笔改提。 *earthen jar*

✎ 7 画
部 土
左 左右

坛 坛坛坛坛坛坛坛

(談) tán 交谈、美谈

☞ 讠两画，第二画是乁，不分为两笔或三笔。

✎ 10 画
部 讠
左 左右

谈 谈谈谈谈谈谈谈谈谈谈

---

tán 黏痰、痰盂 *PHLEGM*

☞ 上为包围结构。上边火的末笔改点。

✎ 13 画
部 疒
半包围

痰 痰痰痰痰痰痰痰痰痰痰痰痰

---

tǎn 坦途、舒坦、坦白 *level, smooth*
—calm and fearless

☞ 土的末笔改提。

✎ 8 画
部 土
左 左右

坦 坦坦坦坦坦坦坦

---

tǎn 地毯、线毯 *blanket, rug, carpet*

☞ 左下包围结构。两火的末笔都改点。

✎ 12 画
部 毛
半包围

毯 毯毯毯毯毯毯毯毯毯毯毯

(嘆) tàn 叹气、赞叹 *sigh*

✎ 5 画
部 口
左 左右

叹 叹叹叹叹叹

> "七、己、光、毛" 等部件作左旁时，它们的末笔竖弯钩要改作竖提，如：切沏、改凯、辉耀、橇撬。

---

tàn 焦炭、木炭 *charcoal*

☞ 山，第二画是乚，不分为两笔。

✎ 9 画
部 山
上 上下

炭 炭炭炭炭炭炭炭炭炭

---

tàn 探囊取物、探险、窥探、侦探、探望、探头

☞ 木的中间一竖不带钩。 *try to find out, explore, visit*

✎ 11 画
部 扌
左 左右

探 探探探探探探探探探探探

唐、塘、糖的唐，口上不是彐，中间一横右端出头。

（湯）tāng 汤锅、汤药、绿豆汤　*Soup*

☞ 右部是𢎡不是易。𢎡不分作两画。

✎ 6 画
部 氵
结构 左右

汤　汤汤汤汤汤汤汤

—hot water
—boiling wator

---

tāng 蹚水、蹚地 / tàng 一天走两趟　☞ 左下包围结构。

✎ 15 画
部 走部
结构 半包围

趟　趟趟趟趟趟趟趟趟趟趟趟趟趟趟

---

táng 荒唐、唐突　☞ 上左包围结构。　*disrespect*

✎ 10 画
部 广部
结构 半包围

唐　唐唐唐唐唐唐唐唐唐唐

The main room if a house or HALL

táng 济济一堂、公堂、食堂、堂兄弟

☞ 上部是𫩏不是⺍。

✎ 11 画
部 小部
结构 上下

堂　堂堂堂堂堂堂堂堂堂堂堂

---

táng 荷塘月色、海塘、澡塘

☞ 土的末笔改提。

ward off, keep out, evade

✎ 13 画
部 土部
结构 左右

塘　塘塘塘塘塘塘塘塘塘塘塘塘

---

táng 胸膛、炉膛　☞ 右上是𫩏不是⺍。

✎ 15 画
部 月部
结构 左右

膛　膛膛膛膛膛膛膛膛膛膛膛膛膛膛膛

---

táng 冰糖、水果糖　☞ 米，中间一竖不带钩，末笔改点。

✎ 16 画
部 米部
结构 左右

糖　糖糖糖糖糖糖糖糖糖糖糖糖糖糖糖

---

tǎng 倘若、倘使

✎ 10 画
部 亻部
结构 左右

倘　倘倘倘倘倘倘倘倘倘倘

躺 tǎng 平躺 ☞ 身的末笔上端不出头。

✎ 15 画
□ 身 部
△ 左右

躺躺躺躺躺躺躺躺躺躺躺躺
躺躺躺

(燙) tàng 烫伤、滚烫、烫酒 ☞ 汤的右部是𢎞不是易，弓不分作两画。

✎ 10 画
□ 火 部
△ 上下

烫烫烫烫烫烫
烫烫烫烫

> "复"在原来的《简化字总表》中，既是"復、複"的简化字，还是"覆"的简化字形。1986年重新发表的《简化字总表》规定，"复"不再作"覆"的简化字。"覆"字恢复规范字的身分。

叨 tāo 叨扰 / dāo 叨叨、叨唠 / dáo 叨咕 ☞ 右边是刀不是刁。

✎ 5 画
□ 口 部
△ 左右

叨叨叨叨叨

(濤) tāo 波涛、林涛 ☞ 寿，上左包围结构。

✎ 10 画
□ 氵 部
△ 左右

涛涛涛涛涛
涛涛涛涛涛

> "零"用现代汉字表达还可以写作圆圈的0，比阿拉伯数字的0圆多了。《新华字典》《现代汉语词典》都收了，但国家主管部门发布的《常用字表》《通用字表》都没收。于光远呼吁应该收，陈原认为"恰当之至"。当然，还需规定它的笔顺和部首。

掏 tāo 掏洞、掏耳朵、掏心窝子话

✎ 11 画
□ 扌 部
△ 左右

掏掏掏掏掏掏
掏掏掏掏掏

滔 tāo 白浪滔天、滔滔不绝 ☞ 右部是舀不是臽。

✎ 13 画
□ 氵 部
△ 左

滔滔滔滔滔滔滔滔滔滔滔滔滔

逃 táo 逃跑、逃学 ☞ 辶下包围结构。辶3画，第二画楷体是乛，宋体是𠃑。

✎ 9 画
□ 辶 部
△ 半包围

逃逃逃逃逃逃逃逃逃

桃 táo 桃花、棉桃 ☞ 木的中间一竖不带钩，末笔改点。

✎ 10 画
□ 木 部
△ 左右

桃桃桃桃桃桃桃桃桃桃

陶、萄、淘的缶6画，第五画是乚，不分为两笔。

táo 陶器、陶冶、陶醉

☞ 阝两画，第一画是了，不分为两笔。

✎ 10 画
▨ 左阝 部
◰ 左 右

陶 陶陶陶陶陶陶陶陶陶陶

táo 葡萄

☞ 艹3画，第三画楷体是撇，宋体是竖。

✎ 11 画
▨ 艹 部
◰ 上 下

萄萄萄萄萄萄
萄萄萄萄萄

东汉初年，不少人根据当时通行的、已经不再象形的隶书字形随意演绎汉字字义，曲解经书，什么"马头人为'长'""人持十为'斗'""虫'者屈'中'也"，不一而足，甚至引用这些错误的说解歪曲法律条文的内容。为了阐明字义、消除乱释字义的不良影响，许慎用了22年的时间编著了中国文字学的宝典《说文解字》，对汉字的规范、字义的说解、字序的排列和字典的编纂都起到了重要的示范作用。

táo 大浪淘沙、淘井、淘气

✎ 11 画
▨ 氵 部
◰ 左 右

淘淘淘淘淘
淘淘淘淘淘淘

（討）**tǎo** 讨伐、声讨、讨论、讨债、讨厌

☞ 讠两画，第二画是乛，不分为两笔或三笔。

✎ 5 画
▨ 讠 部
◰ 左 右

讨 讨讨讨讨讨

tào 手套、套色、配套、老一套、套车、圈套、套汇

☞ 左上右包围结构。不简化为套。

✎ 10 画
▨ 大 部
◰ 左半包围

套套套套套套套套套套

tè 特殊、特派、敌特

☞ 牛的第二横改提，笔顺改先竖后提。

✎ 10 画
▨ 牛 部
◰ 左 右

特特特特特特特特特特

téng 疼痛、疼爱

☞ 上左包围结构。冬的上部是夂不是夊。

✎ 10 画
▨ 广 部
◰ 左半包围

疼疼疼疼疼疼疼疼疼疼

（騰）**téng** 飞腾、腾越、沸腾、折腾、腾地方

☞ 马3画，第一画是乛，第二画是乚，都不分为两笔；左上角开口。

✎ 13 画
▨ 月 部
◰ 左 右

腾腾腾腾腾腾腾腾腾腾腾腾腾

tī 电梯、梯队

☞ 木的中间一竖不带钩，末笔改点。弟的第六画是竖，不带钩。

✎ 11 画
□ 木 部首
△ 左 左右

梯 梯梯梯梯梯梯梯梯梯梯梯

tī 踢门、踢球　☞ 右部是易，不是昜或易。

✎ 15 画
□ 足 部首
△ 左 左右

踢 踢踢踢踢踢踢踢踢踢踢踢
踢踢踢踢

tí 提箱子、提早、提名、酒提、提货 / dī 提防、提溜

✎ 12 画
□ 扌 部首
△ 左 左右

提 提提提提提提提提提提提

(題) tí 题目、习题、题诗　☞ 左下包围结构。

✎ 15 画
□ 页 部首
△ 半包围

题 题题题题题题题题题题题
题题题题

tí 马蹄、铁蹄

✎ 16 画
□ 足 部首
△ 左 左右

蹄 蹄蹄蹄蹄蹄蹄蹄蹄蹄蹄蹄
蹄蹄蹄蹄蹄

(體) tǐ 肢体、物体、液体、体例、字体、体会、体谅

☞ 本不写成上大下十。

✎ 7 画
□ 亻 部首
△ 左 左右

体 体体体体体体体

tì 剃刀、剃头　☞ 弟的第六画是竖，不带钩。

✎ 9 画
□ 刂 部首
△ 左 左右

剃 剃剃剃剃剃
剃剃剃剃

老舍的《骆驼祥子》，全书
总字数107360字，其中，
光是"的"就出现了4423
次，"他"就出现了2573次，
"不"就出现了2417次。
"的、他、不"三个字加起
来的出现次数竟高达9413
次，几乎占了全书总字数
的9%。也就是说几乎每10
个字里就有1个"的"或
"他"或"不"。可见，汉字
字数繁多的缺点被常用字
高频化这一规律缓解了。

tì 警惕

☞ 右部是易，不是昜或易。

✎ 11 画
□ 忄 部首
△ 左 左右

惕 惕惕惕惕惕惕惕惕惕惕惕

tì 代替、接替

☞ 左上的夫末笔改点。

✎ 12 画
▯ 日 部
◰ 上 下

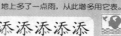

替替替替替替替替替替替替

---

tiān 天空、天灾、天资、阴天、天线

✎ 4 画
▯ 大 独
◰ 体

天天天天

---

tiān 添加、添设

☞ 右上是天，不是夭。右下是小，不是氺或水。

✎ 11 画
▯ 氵 部
◰ 左 右

字谜

天上水分有些小，借了一点往下飘；
地上多了一点雨，从此增多用它表。

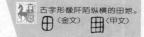

添添添添添添添添添添添

---

tián 稻田、油田、田径赛

✎ 5 画
▯ 田 部
◰ 独 体

古字形像阡陌纵横的田地。

田（金文）　田（甲文）

田田田田田

---

tián 甜蜜、睡得很甜

☞ 舌的起笔是撇不是横。甘5画，第二画是竖，第五画是横，不连成一笔。

✎ 11 画
▯ 舌 部
◰ 左 右

甜甜甜甜甜甜甜甜甜甜甜

---

tián 填井、填补、填表

☞ 土的末笔改提。真的框内是三横。

✎ 13 画
▯ 土 部
◰ 左 右

填填填填填填填填填填填

---

tiāo 挑担、挑错 / tiǎo 挑刺儿、挑逗、挑大拇指

✎ 9 画
▯ 扌 部
◰ 左 右

挑挑挑挑挑挑挑挑挑

---

measure word (for clothes)

（條）tiáo 枝条、面条、条纹、井井有条、条约

☞ 左上右包围结构。上部是夂不是攵。下部是木，不写成木。

✎ 7 画
▯ 夂 部
◰ 半包围

条条条条条条条

Second part noodle

调(調) tiáo 调配、调味、调解、调戏 / diào 调动、调查、曲调

讠 两画，第二画是乁，不分为两笔或三笔。

✎ 10 画
讠 部
左 右

 调调调调调调调调调调调

跳 tiào 跳跃、跳级

左下止的末笔改提。

✎ 13 画
足 部
左 右

 跳跳跳跳跳跳跳跳跳跳跳跳跳

贴(貼) tiē 张贴、贴近、贴补

贝的第二画乁不带钩。

✎ 9 画
贝 部
左 右

 贴贴贴贴贴贴贴贴贴

铁(鐵) tiě 炼铁、手无寸铁、铁证、铁腕、铁石心肠

钅5画，第二画是横，不是点；第五画是竖提，不分为两笔。

✎ 10 画
钅 部
左 右

 铁铁铁铁铁铁铁铁铁铁

帖 tiè 字帖 / tiě 请帖、一帖药 / tiē 妥帖、俯首帖耳

✎ 8 画
巾 部
左 右

 帖帖帖帖帖帖帖帖

厅(廳) tīng 办公厅、歌舞厅

上左包围结构。左上是厂不是广。

✎ 4 画
厂 部
半包围

 厅厅厅厅

听(*聽) tīng *听音乐、*听话、*听凭、一听啤酒

✎ 7 画
口 部
左 右

 听听听听听听听

亭 tíng 亭子、售货亭

古字形像亭子。下边是声旁丁。

（战国文字）（小篆）

✎ 9 画
亠 部
上 下

 亭亭亭亭亭亭亭亭亭

庭、蜓、挺、艇的爻两画，起笔是乛，不分为两笔。壬是撇下土。

---

tíng 大庭广众、庭院、法庭

☞ 上左包围结构。

✎ 9 画
🔲 广 部
⼌ 半包围

庭 庭庭庭庭庭庭庭庭

〈现代汉语通用字表〉规定"廷、庭、蜓、挺、艇"等字所从部件为壬，撇下土。〈现代汉语通用字笔顺规范〉"廷"组字形改为从壬，撇下土，但没有见到有关修订〈现代汉语通用字表〉字形的正式文件，所以仍从撇下土。

停

tíng 停止、停靠、停当

✎ 11 画
🔲 亻 部
⼌ 左 右

停停停停停
停停停停停停

作为社会重要交际工具的文字，总是具有两面性：一方面是个人书写时为了追求快速方便而出现的难以避免的随意性，另一方面是社会交际为了提高效率而反复要求的字形的统一性。这是一对方向不同的分力。文字字形就是在这样两种矛盾力量的交替作用下向前演进的。就社会而言，为了提高交际效率，就要在社会公共交际活动中遏制文字字形的个人变异、地区变异和行业变异，提倡字形的规范化、标准化。

---

tíng 蜻蜓

✎ 12 画
🔲 虫 部
⼌ 左 右

蜓蜓蜓蜓蜓蜓
蜓蜓蜓蜓蜓蜓

挺

tíng 挺身、硬挺、挺干净

✎ 9 画
🔲 扌 部
⼌ 左 右

挺 挺挺挺挺挺挺挺挺挺

艇

tíng 汽艇

☞ 舟的横笔，楷体改提，右端不出头。

✎ 12 画
🔲 舟 部
⼌ 左 右

艇 艇艇艇艇艇艇艇艇艇艇艇

通

tōng 畅通、精通、通顺、共通、沟通、通告 / tòng 一通乱打、吵了一通

☞ 左下包围结构。辶3画，第二画楷体是乛，宋体是乛。

✎ 10 画
🔲 辶 部
⼌ 半包围

通 通通通通通通通通通

同

tóng 同样、同学 / tòng 胡同

☞ 左上右包围结构。

✎ 6 画
🔲 冂 部
⼌ 半包围

同 同同同同同同

桐

tóng 梧桐、油桐

☞ 木的中间一竖不带钩，末笔改点。

✎ 10 画
🔲 木 部
⼌ 左 右

桐 桐桐桐桐桐桐桐桐桐桐

(銅) tóng 紫铜

☞ 钅5画，第二画是横，不是点；第五画是竖提，不分为两笔。

✎ 11 画
钅 部
囚 左 右　铜　铜铜铜铜铜铜铜铜铜铜铜

tóng 儿童、童话

✎ 12 画
立 部
囚 上 下　童　童童童童童童童童童童童童

(統) tǒng 统辖、统治、传统

☞ 纟3画，上部不是幺。右部是充不是亢。

✎ 9 画
纟 部
囚 左 右　统　统统统统统统统统统

tǒng 水桶、木桶　☞ 木的中间一竖不带钩，末笔改点。

✎ 11 画
木 部
囚 左 右　桶　桶桶桶桶桶桶桶桶桶桶桶

以前，现代常用字的研究和选取工作，较有影响的有：1928年陈鹤琴编制的《语体文应用字汇》，收4261字；1952年中央人民政府教育部公布的《常用字表》，收2000字。

tǒng 竹筒、电筒、长筒袜

✎ 12 画
竹 部
囚 上 下　筒　筒筒筒筒筒筒筒筒筒筒筒筒

tòng 疼痛、悲痛、痛打落水狗

☞ 上左包围结构。右下用的起笔改竖。

✎ 12 画
疒 部
囚 半包围　痛　痛痛痛痛痛痛痛痛痛痛痛

tōu 偷窃、小偷儿、偷听、偷空

☞ 月的起笔改竖。右上人下有一横。

✎ 11 画
亻 部
囚 左 右　偷　偷偷偷偷偷偷偷偷偷偷

(頭) tóu 头脑、头发、工头、头奖、烟头、桥头 / tou 石头、苦头

☞ 末笔是点不是捺。

✎ 5 画
丶 部
囚 独 体　头　头头头头头

tóu 投掷、投井、投资、投合、投寄、投亲、用水投衣服

　　☞ 右上不是几，末笔不带钩。

✎ 7 画
□ 扌部
◹ 左 右

投 投投投投投投投

---

tòu 透气、透彻、透雨、透露　　☞ 左下包围结构。乃两画，第一画是𠃌，不分为两笔。辶3画，第二画楷体是㇉，宋体是乀。

✎ 10 画
□ 辶部
◹ 半包围

透 透透透透透透透透透透

---

tū 秃顶、秃山、秃笔

　　☞ 禾，中间一竖不带钩。下部是几不是儿。

✎ 7 画
□ 禾部
◹ 上 下

秃 秃秃秃秃秃秃秃

---

tū 突然、突围、突出、心突突地跳

　　☞ 下部是犬不是大。

✎ 9 画
□ 穴部
◹ 上 下

突 突突突突突突突突突

(圖) tú 图画、企图、宏图

　　☞ 全包围结构。冬的上部是夂，不是夂。

✎ 8 画
□ 囗部
◹ 包围

图 图图图图图图图图

---

tú 徒步、徒弟、赌徒、徒手、徒然

✎ 10 画
□ 彳部
◹ 左 右

徒 徒徒徒徒徒
徒徒徒徒徒

> 汉字中有不少用三个相同的部件组成的汉字：众、品、森、淼、焱、鑫、晶……

---

tú 长途、路途

　　☞ 左下包围结构。辶3画，第二画楷体是㇉，宋体是乀。

✎ 10 画
□ 辶部
◹ 半包围

途 途途途途途途途途途途

(塗) tú 涂颜色、涂改、围涂造田

✎ 10 画
□ 氵部
◹ 左 右

涂 涂涂涂涂涂涂涂涂涂涂

腿、退的艮，末笔改点；辶3画，第二画楷体是乛，宋体是㇋。

tú 屠宰、屠杀

⌐ 上左包围结构。

◆ 11 画
☐ 尸部
☒ 半包围

屠 屠屠屠屠屠屠屠屠屠屠屠

---

tǔ 土壤、领土、故土、土产、土包子、土专家

◆ 3 画
☐ 土
☒ 独体

土 土土土

古字形像地上的土块或土堆。
(金文) (甲文)

---

tǔ 吐痰、谈吐、吐穗 / tù 呕吐

◆ 6 画
☐ 口部
☒ 左 右

吐 吐吐吐吐吐吐

---

tù 兔子、家兔

⌐ 第六画从扁框中直接撇下，不分为两笔。右下有、(点)。

◆ 8 画
☐ 刀部
☒ 上 下

兔 兔兔兔兔兔兔兔兔

(團 *糰) tuán 团扇、团圆、团队、疑团、剧团、*汤团

⌐ 全包围结构。

◆ 6 画
☐ 口部
☒ 包围

团 团团团团团团

---

tuī 推倒、推平、推销、推迟、推举、推测、推辞、推敲

⌐ 右部是隹不是住。

◆ 11 画
☐ 扌部
☒ 左右

推 推推推推推推推推推推

---

tuǐ 大腿、桌子腿儿

◆ 13 画
☐ 月部
☒ 左 右

腿 腿腿腿腿腿腿腿腿腿腿腿腿

---

tuì 撤退、退学、衰退、退票

⌐ 左下包围结构。

◆ 9 画
☐ 辶部
☒ 半包围

退 退退退退退退退退

tūn 狼吞虎咽、吞并　　左上右包围结构。上部是天不是夭。

✎ 7 画
部 口
⼝ 半包围

吞吞吞
吞吞吞吞

tún 屯粮、屯兵、屯子　　第二画是乚, 不分为两笔。

✎ 4 画
一 部
⼝ 独体

屯屯屯屯屯

tuō 托盘、枪托、烘托、托儿所、推托、托人

✎ 6 画
部
⼝ 扌 左右

托托托托托托

tuō 拖车、拖拉、拖累

✎ 8 画
部
⼝ 扌 左右

拖拖拖拖拖拖拖拖

tuō 脱帽、脱毛、逃脱、脱漏

✎ 11 画
月 部
⼝ 左右

脱脱脱脱脱脱脱脱脱脱脱

(駝) tuó 骆驼、驼背　　马的第一画是𠃌, 第二画是乚, 都不分为两笔; 左上角开口; 末笔改提。

✎ 8 画
马 部
⼝ 左右

驼驼驼驼驼驼驼驼

妥 tuǒ 妥善、谈妥

✎ 7 画
爪 部
⼝ 上下

妥妥妥妥妥妥妥

wā 挖坑、挖潜力　　右下是乙不是九。

✎ 9 画
部
⼝ 扌 左右

挖挖挖挖挖挖挖挖挖

18世纪,欧洲有一位化学家卡特帕·费伯将石墨粉、硫磺、锑和树脂混在一起熔铸,外面加一外壳,造出了最早的铅笔。19世纪初(1809年),美国人沃特曼发明钢笔,不久传入中国。19世纪后期(1883年),法国人威迪文研制出第一支自来水笔。1888年,美国人派克,据说因为厌倦不断地为学生修笔,遂发明了质量上乘、经久耐用的派克笔。这些硬笔的出现,为硬笔书法的崛起创造了良好的物质条件。

老舍的《骆驼祥子》,全书107360字,只用了2413个不同的汉字。

wā 青蛙、蛙声一片

画 12 画
部 虫部
四 左右

蛙蛙蛙蛙蛙蛙
蛙蛙蛙蛙蛙蛙

台湾作家柏杨曾写过一篇杂文《珍惜中国文化》，副标题是"中文横写，天经地义的应从左向右"。他说，不但横写，就是直写也应该从左向右，理由是汉字的横向结构全都是从左向右。比如"汉"，都先写"氵"后写"又"，繁体也这样。

wá 女娃、洋娃娃 ☞ 女的横笔右端不出头。

画 9 画
部 女部
四 左右

娃娃娃娃娃
娃娃娃娃

wǎ 瓦罐、瓦房、瓦特 / wà 瓦刀 ☞ 第二画是乚，第三画是乙，都不分成两笔。

画 4 画
部 瓦部
四 独体

瓦瓦瓦瓦瓦

(襪) wà 袜子、球袜 ☞ 左部是衤不是礻。右部是末不是未。

画 10 画
部 衤部
四 左右

袜袜袜袜袜袜袜袜袜

wāi 歪斜、歪风邪气 ☞ 不的中间一竖不带钩，末笔是点。

画 9 画
部 一部
四 上下

歪歪歪歪歪歪歪歪歪

wài 户外、外宾、外地、外号、外甥、见外

画 5 画
部 夕部
四 左右

外外外外外外

"工、土、马、王"等部件作左偏旁时，它们的末笔横要改作提，如：巧功顶劲、地坏坦塔、驭驮骏骗、玩球瑞璜。

(彎) wān 弯曲、弯腰、拐弯抹角 ☞ 弯的上部不是亦，中间是两竖。弓3画，第三画是乛，不分为两笔。

画 9 画
部 弓部
四 上下

弯弯弯弯弯弯弯弯弯

(灣) wān 水湾、港湾 ☞ 弯的上部不是亦，中间是两竖。弓3画，第三画是乛，不分为两笔。

画 12 画
部 氵部
四 左右

湾湾湾湾湾湾湾湾湾湾湾湾

wán 鱼丸、丸散膏丹

✎ 3画
⽥ 丿
⼞ 独体

丸 九九丸

wán 完善、完稿、完毕

✎ 7画
⽥ 宀
⼞ 上下

完 完完完完完完完

wán 游玩、玩耍、古玩、玩忽职守、玩游戏、玩花招

☞ 王的末笔改提。

✎ 8画
⽥ 王
⼞ 左右

玩 玩玩玩玩玩玩玩玩

(頑) wán 顽固、顽皮、顽强

☞ 元的末笔改竖提。

✎ 10画
⽥ 页
⼞ 左右

顽 顽顽顽顽顽顽顽顽顽

wǎn 挽弓、挽联、挽救

☞ 免的第六画从扁框中直接撇下，不分为两笔。

✎ 10画
⽥ 扌
⼞ 左右

挽 挽挽挽挽挽挽挽挽挽

wǎn 晚上、晚会、飞机晚点、晚辈

☞ 免的第六画从扁框中直接撇下，不分为两笔。

✎ 11画
⽥ 日
⼞ 左右

晚 晚晚晚晚晚晚晚晚晚晚

wǎn 饭碗、轴碗

☞ 宛，右下是㔾，不是巳、已或己。

✎ 13画
⽥ 石
⼞ 左右

碗 碗碗碗碗碗碗碗碗碗碗碗

(萬) wàn 千家万户、万幸

✎ 3画
⽥ 一
⼞ 独体

万 万万万

现代书法家林散之，在诗、书、画三方面的造诣都很高。他早年曾自名"三痴"，即痴诗，痴书，痴画。林散之的"散之"就是"三痴"的谐音。有一次，著名学者郭沫若到了南京。许多人请他写字，郭沫若说："有林散之在南京，我岂敢在南京写字。"还有一次，两个小学生登门求字，带来的礼品是两块"宝宝乐"饼干。林散之哈哈大笑，十分高兴地为他们写了字。

古字形像蝎子。后借作计数用。

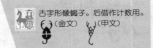

(金文)　(甲文)

wāng 汪洋大海、一汪泪水、汪汪乱叫

✎ 7 画
部
⊠ 氵左右

汪　汪汪汪汪汪汪汪

东汉许慎编著的《说文解字》，公元 121 年成书，收 9353 字，另有重文 1163 字，共收 10516 字。

---

wáng 逃亡、亡羊补牢、亡国、阵亡

✎ 3 画
亠部
⊠ 独体

亡　亡亡亡

---

wáng 国王、山大王、蜂王精

✎ 4 画
王部
⊠ 独体

王　王王王王

古字形像斧钺。
王（金文）　王（甲文）

(網)wǎng 渔网、电网、关系网、网罗

☞ 左上右包围结构。

✎ 6 画
冂部
⊠ 半包围

网　网网网网网网

古字形像一张网。
（金文）　（甲文）

---

wǎng 往返、往前看、往事

✎ 8 画
彳部
⊠ 左右

往　往往往往往往往往

---

wàng 狂妄、轻举妄动

✎ 6 画
女部
⊠ 上下

妄　妄妄妄妄妄妄

现代汉字的笔画组合形式有三类：相离，如"二八川小"；相接，如"七工乍刀厂口凹己"；相交，如"十丈九车"。

---

wàng 忘记、遗忘

☞ 心的第二画楷体是㇃(卧钩)，宋体是乚(竖弯钩)。

✎ 7 画
心部
⊠ 上下

忘　忘忘忘忘忘忘忘

旺

wàng 兴旺

✎ 8 画
日部
⊠ 左右

旺　旺旺旺旺旺旺旺旺

wàng 望尘莫及、观望、威望、失望、拜望

☞ 亡的末笔改竖提。

✎ 11 画
王 部
上 下

望 望望望望望望望望望望望

wēi 危险、危害、病危

☞ 上左包围结构。右下是㔾，不是巳、已或己。

✎ 6 画
刀 部
半包围

危 危危危危危危

wēi 威风、威胁

☞ 左上右包围结构。女的横笔右端不出头。

✎ 9 画
戈 部
半包围

威 威威威威威威威威威

wēi 微小、微妙、微笑

☞ 中部依次是山、一、几；山的第二画是乚，不分为两笔；几的末笔改竖提。右部是攵。

✎ 13 画
彳 部
左 右

微 微微微微微微微微微微微微微

（爲）**wéi** 事在人为、为首、反败为胜、为实践所证明 / **wèi** 为你高兴、为理想奋斗、为何

✎ 4 画
丶 部
独 体

为 为为为为

古字形像人牵象服劳役。
（金文）（甲文）

（違）**wéi** 久违、违法

☞ 左下包围结构。辶 3 画，第二画楷体是㇋，宋体是乛。韦的右侧没有、(点)。

✎ 7 画
辶 部
半包围

违 违违违违违违违

（圍）**wéi** 围绕、周围、腰围 *enclose, surround*

☞ 全包围结构。韦的右侧没有、(点)。

✎ 7 画
口 部
包

围 围围围围围围围

wéi 唯独、唯恐

☞ 右部是佳不是住。

✎ 11 画
口 部
左 右

唯 唯唯唯唯唯唯唯唯唯唯唯

维 (維) wéi 维系、维持

☞ 纟3画，上部不是幺。右部是隹不是住。

✎ 11画
☐ 纟部 左右

维 维维维维维维维维维维维

伟 (偉) wěi 魁伟、伟大

☞ 韦的右侧没有、(点)。

✎ 6画
☐ 亻部 左右

伟 伟伟伟伟伟伟

伪 (僞) wěi 伪装、伪军

✎ 6画
☐ 亻部 左右

伪 伪伪伪伪伪伪

尾 wěi 尾巴、末尾、扫尾 / yǐ 马尾儿

☞ 上左包围结构。

✎ 7画
☐ 尸部 半包围

尾 尾尾尾尾尾尾尾

委 wěi 委任、政委、委靡不振、委婉

☞ 禾的中间一竖不带钩。

✎ 8画
☐ 禾部 上下

委 委委委委委委委

卫 (衛) wèi 卫兵、门卫

✎ 3画
☐ 卩部 独体

卫 卫卫卫

have not, did not

未 wèi 未定、辰巳午未

☞ 上横短，下横长，中间一竖不带钩。

✎ 5画
☐ 木部 独体

未 未未未未未

位 wèi 座位、岗位、退位、个位数

✎ 7画
☐ 亻部 左右

位 位位位位位位位

1899年，国子监察酒（相当于现今的教育部部长）王懿（yì）荣因病从北京达仁堂购买中药。药材里有一味"龙骨"，上有刀刻符号。王懿荣平时喜欢收藏古董，对古代汉字有很深的研究。经仔细辨识，他认为，这些"龙骨"片上的符号不是随意刻画的道道，很可能是中国古代汉字的真迹。他让人把药店里的龙骨全部买来，又打听出"龙骨"的产地是河南安阳小屯。那儿曾是古代殷王朝的国都。"龙骨"上的符号正是三千四百多年前的汉字。甲骨文的发现是中国也是世界文化史上一件值得大书特书的盛事。

把简体字跟普及教育明确联系起来，自觉、积极地加以倡导的，首推陆费逵。1909年（宣统元年），他在《教育杂志》创刊号上发表题为《普及教育应当采用俗体字》的文章，论述教学中采用简体字的好处。把汉字简化运动具体化并推向高潮的则是钱玄同。1922年，他在国语统一筹备委会上提出"简省现行汉字的笔画案"。

firstpart MSG
口未米青

wèi 滋味、品味、海味、韵味

☞ 未，上横短，下横长，中间一竖不带钩。

🖊 8　画
□ 口部
△ 左右

wèi 畏惧、敬畏　fear, respect

畏畏畏畏
畏畏畏畏畏

🖊 9　画
□ 田部
△ 上下

要写好字，只凭自己苦思苦练是不够的，还要善于学习、借鉴前人的经验，其中一个行之有效的方法就是临摹古人的碑帖，从中学习一些规矩，领会若干规律。

wèi 肠胃　stomach

☞ 月的起笔改竖。

胃胃胃胃胃胃胃胃胃

🖊 9　画
□ 田部
△ 上下

wèi 喂猪、喂奶　hello! hey!
(breastfeed, suckle)

喂喂喂喂喂喂喂喂喂喂喂喂

🖊 12　画
□ 口部
△ 左右

console, comfort, be relieved

wèi 安慰、欣慰　☞ 小的左侧楷体是点，宋体是撇。心的第二画楷体是乀(卧钩)，宋体是乚(竖弯钩)。

慰慰慰慰慰慰慰
慰慰慰慰慰慰慰慰

🖊 15　画
□ 心部
△ 上下

wēn 温暖、温习、气温、温和
warm, lukewarm, warm up

温温温温温温温温温温温温

🖊 12　画
□ 氵部
△ 左右

wén 文身、文官、文雅、天文、文字、作文、文科、文言
character, script, writing,
language, culture?

文文文文

🖊 4　画
□ 文部
△ 独体

古字形像人身上刺着花纹。

（金文）　（甲文）

（紋）wén 指纹、皱纹　lines, wrinkles,
veins

☞ 纟3画，上部不是幺。

纹纹纹纹纹纹纹

🖊 7　画
□ 纟部
△ 左右

（聞）wén 耳闻、新闻、闻味儿

☞ 左上右包围结构。门的起笔、，嵌在第二笔丨和第三笔冖之间。

✎ 9 画
口 门 部
凶 半包围

闻 闻闻闻闻闻闻闻闻闻

小耳朵，
在门里，
它想听听收音机。
字谜

---

wén 蚊子

✎ 10 画
口 虫 部
凶 左 右

蚊 蚊蚊蚊蚊蚊蚊蚊蚊蚊蚊

（穩）wěn 稳定、稳住阵脚、稳妥、稳重

稳稳稳 ☞ 禾，中间一竖不带钩，末笔改
点。心的第二画楷体是㇃（卧钩），宋体是乚（竖弯钩）。

✎ 14 画
口 禾 部
凶 左 右

稳 稳稳稳稳稳稳稳稳稳稳

（問）wèn 询问、慰问、审问、问罪、过问

☞ 左上右包围结构。起笔、，嵌在第二笔丨和第三笔冖之间。

✎ 6 画
口 门 部
凶 半包围

问 问问问问问问

---

wēng 老翁、翁婿

✎ 10 画
口 羽 部
凶 上 下

翁 翁翁翁翁翁翁翁翁翁翁

（窩）wō 蚂蚁窝、安乐窝、挪窝、被窝、窝赃、窝工

☞ 下部是上口下内。

✎ 12 画
口 穴 部
凶 上 下

窝 窝窝窝窝窝窝窝窝窝窝窝窝

---

wǒ 我你他、我校、忘我

✎ 7 画
口 戈 部
凶 独 体

我 我我我我我我我

古字形像一种长柄、带锯齿的武器。后借表代词。我（金文）我（甲文）

---

wò 肥沃、沃土

☞ 右部是夭不是天。

✎ 7 画
口 氵 部
凶 左 右

沃 沃沃沃沃沃沃沃

赵树理的《三里湾》，全书124000字，只用了2069个不同的汉字。

乌、鸣的乌，第一画 丿、第二画 ㇆，不连成一笔；第三画 ㄣ，不分为两笔。

wò 卧倒、卧室、硬卧

lie (on back)

☞ 臣的末笔是 L，不分为两笔。

卧卧卧卧
卧卧卧卧

✎ 8 画
部 臣 部
结 左 右

---

wò 握手、握拳

握握握握握握
握握握握握握

✎ 12 画
部 扌 部
结 左 右

（烏）wū 乌云、乌鸦

crow（乌云）
black clouds

☞ 不是鸟，框内没有丶(点)。

乌乌乌乌

✎ 4 画
部 丿 部
结 独体

---

dirt, filth, corrupt

wū 去污粉、污点、贪污、污染

☞ 右部是亏不是亐。

污污污污污污

✎ 6 画
部 氵 部
结 左 右

（鳴）wū 北风呜呜地刮

toot hoot whistle

☞ 右部是乌不是鸟，框内没有丶(点)。

呜呜呜呜呜呜呜

✎ 7 画
部 口 部
结 左 右

---

wū 房屋、里屋

house, room

☞ 上左包围结构。

屋屋屋屋屋屋屋屋屋

✎ 9 画
部 尸 部
结 半包围

（無）wú 无能、无论、事无巨细

nothing - nil

☞ 上部是两横，不是冖。

无无无无

✎ 4 画
部 无 部
结 独体

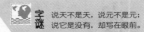
字谜 说天不是天，说元不是元；说它是没有，却写在眼前。

---

wú 姓吴

☞ 上口下天。

吴吴吴吴吴吴吴

✎ 7 画
部 口 部
结 上 下

1986 年 10 月 10 日由国家语言文字工作委员会重新发表的《简化字总表》收录的简化字，是规范的简化字。《简化字总表》共分三个表：第一表收"不作简化偏旁用的简化字" 350 个；第二表收"可作简化偏旁用的简化字" 132 个和"简化偏旁" 14 个（"讠""饣""纟"等）；第三表收"应用第二表所列简化字和简化偏旁得出来的简化字" 1753 个，全表共收录简化字 2235 个。其中，"签""须"在第一表和第三表中重复出现，所以，《简化字总表》收录的不同的简化字形实为 2233 个。

wǔ 三下五除二 *five*

✎ 4 画
🔼 一 部
☐ 独 体

五 五 五 五 五

汉字字体指不同时代、不同用途（爵彝、碑版、书册、信札等）、不同书写工具（笔、刀等）、不同书写方法（笔写、刀刻、范铸等）、不同地区所形成的汉字书写的大类别和总风格。研究汉字字体风格特征和演变规律是汉字字体学的任务。

wǔ 辰巳午未、中午 *noon, midday*

✎ 4 画
🔼 十 部
☐ 独 体

午 午 午 午 午

wǔ 队伍、为伍 *five, army, ranks, company*

✎ 6 画
🔼 亻 部
☐ 左 右

伍 伍 伍 伍 伍 伍 伍

wǔ 动武、威武、武功

☞ 上右包围结构。止的末笔改提。斜钩右下没有撇。

✎ 8 画
🔼 弋 部
☐ 半包围

武 武 武 武 武 武 武 武 武

古字形用戈代表武器，用足趾表示行进，表达征战、威武的意思。

戔（金文） 戔（甲文）

wǔ 侮辱、欺侮 *insult, bully* （外侮） *foreign aggression*

☞ 母，第一画是乚，第二画是乛，都不分为两笔。

✎ 9 画
🔼 亻 部
☐ 左 右

侮 侮 侮 侮 侮 侮 侮 侮 侮

wǔ 翩翩起舞、芭蕾舞、挥舞、舞文弄墨 *dance, perform*

☞ 左下是夕。右下的牛，3画，第二画是乚，不分为两笔。

✎ 14 画
🔼 夕 部
☐ 上 下

舞 舞 舞 舞 舞 舞 舞
舞 舞 舞 舞 舞 舞 舞

wù 闲人勿入 *indicating No-admittance, smoking*

☞ 上右包围结构。

✎ 4 画
🔼 勹 部
☐ 半包围

勿 勿 勿 勿 勿

（務）wù 务农、务实、任务、务必 *affair, business*

☞ 左上右包围结构。上部是夂不是夂。

✎ 5 画
🔼 夂 部
☐ 半包围

务 务 务 务 务 务

距今两千来年的汉魏六朝，在碑刻上就有很多简体字。罗振玉等编的《增订碑别字》中就有"來"简作"来"，"號"简作"号"，"亂"简作"乱"，"質"简作"质"等。

wù 物品、言之有物、物质、物色

☞ 牛的第二横改提，笔顺改先竖后提。

🖊 8 画　牛 部　左 右

物 物物物物物物物物

---

mistake, error

（誤）**wù** 误会、笔误、误事、误人子弟、误入歧途

☞ 讠两画，第二画乛不分为两笔或三笔。

🖊 9 画　讠 部　左 右

误 误误误误误误误误误

---

wù 领悟、觉悟、恍然大悟

🖊 10 画　忄 部　左 右

悟 悟悟悟悟悟悟悟悟悟

（霧）**wù** 云雾、喷雾器

☞ 雨，第二画改点，第三画改横钩，里边楷体是四点，宋体是四横。

🖊 13 画　雨 部　上 下

雾 雾雾雾雾雾雾雾雾雾雾雾雾雾

---

xī 夕阳、除夕　*sunset, evening*

🖊 3 画　夕 部　独 体

夕 夕夕夕

---

west

xī 西方、西装

☞ 第五画是竖弯，不带钩。

🖊 6 画　西 部　独 体

西 西西西西西西

古字形像鸟巢。后借表方向。

（金文）（甲文）

---

xī 吸气、吸收、吸引

☞ 及3画，第二画乛不分为两笔。

🖊 6 画　口 部　左 右

吸 吸吸吸吸吸吸

---

xī 希望、希图

🖊 7 画　巾 部　上 下

希 希希希希希希希

到了初唐，学术界出现了整理异体、辨别俗讹、统一字体、刊正经籍的强烈呼声，产生了一系列类似于今天正字法字典一类的"字样"之书。如:《开元文字音义》、颜师古的《字样》、颜元孙的《干禄字书》等。

息、悉的心，第二画楷体是㇃(卧钩)，宋体是乚(竖弯钩)。

析

xī 分崩离析、辨析

木的中间一竖不带钩，末笔改点。

8 画
木 部
左 右

析

析析析析析析析析

牺

(犧) xī 牺牲

牛的第二横改提，笔顺改先竖后提。西6画，第五画是竖弯，不带钩。

10 画
牛 部
左 右

牺

牺牺牺牺牺牺牺牺牺牺

息

BREATH, news, interest

xī 气息、休息、息怒、利息、信息

10 画
自 部
上 下

息

息息息息息
息息息息息

表意文字和拼音文字是世界文字中并存的、代表着两种发展趋势的文字系统，它们各有其特点，又各有其发展规律，而汉字又是表意文字的代表；所以，研究汉字的构形特点和使用规律，不仅是中国文字学的课题，而且是世界文字学的课题。

悉

xī 熟悉、悉心 上部7画，丿下米，不是采。

11 画
采 部
上 下

悉

悉悉悉悉悉
悉悉悉悉悉悉

惜

xī 可惜、爱惜、惜力

11 画
忄 部
左 右

惜

惜惜惜惜惜惜惜惜惜惜惜

稀

xī 稀疏、稀客、稀粥、糖稀

禾，中间一竖不带钩，末笔改点。

12 画
禾 部
左 右

稀

稀稀稀稀稀稀稀稀稀稀稀稀

锡

(錫) xī 焊锡

钅5画，第二画是横，不是、；第五画是乚，不分为两笔。右部是易，不是昜或易。

13 画
钅 部
左 右

锡

锡锡锡锡锡锡锡锡锡锡锡锡锡

溪

xī 小溪、溪水

13 画
氵 部
左 右

溪

溪溪溪溪溪溪溪溪溪溪溪溪溪

xī 熄火、熄灯 　☞ 火的末笔改点。心的第二画楷体是乀(卧钩)，宋体是乚(竖弯钩)。

✎ 14 画
田 火 部首
四 左 右

熄熄熄熄熄熄熄
熄熄熄熄熄熄熄

xī 膝盖、膝关节 　☞ 右上不是夹或夹，右下是氺，不写成水。

✎ 15 画
田 月 部首
四 左 右

膝膝膝膝膝
膝膝膝膝膝膝膝膝膝膝

(習) xī 练习、习惯、积习

☞ 上右包围结构。

✎ 3 画
田 一 部首
四 半包围

习习习习

xī 草席、硬席、酒席

☞ 上左包围结构。廿4画，第二画是竖、第四画是横，不连成一笔。

✎ 10 画
田 广 部首
四 半包围

席席席席席席席席席席

(襲) xí 沿袭、世袭、偷袭

☞ 龙的右下乚上只有一撇，不是两撇或三撇。

✎ 11 画
田 龙 部首
四 上 下

袭袭袭袭袭袭袭袭袭袭袭

xǐ 洗脸、洗礼、清洗、洗劫、冲洗、洗胶卷、洗牌

☞

✎ 9 画
田 氵 部首
四 左 右

洗洗洗洗洗洗洗洗洗

xǐ 欢喜、喜讯、报喜、好(hào)大喜功

☞ 上部是士。两口之间是䒑不是廿。

✎ 12 画
田 土 部首
四 上 下

喜喜喜喜喜喜喜喜喜喜喜

(戲) xì 游戏、戏弄、京戏

☞ 又的末笔改点。

✎ 6 画
田 又 部首
四 左 右

戏戏戏戏戏戏

系

(*係 **繫) xì 派系、中文系、*关系、**系念 / jì **系领带

☞ 小的左侧楷体是点，宋体是撇。

7 画
糸 部
独 体

系

系系系系系系系

古字形像手拿丝束。

(金文) (甲文)

细

(細) xì 细小、细菌、精细、精打细算、奸细

☞ 纟3画，上部不是幺。

8 画
纟 部
左 右

细

细细细细细细细细

隙

xì 缝隙、间隙、寻隙闹事、嫌隙

☞ 阝两画，起笔是了，不分为两笔。

12 画
左阝 部
左 右

隙

隙隙隙隙隙隙隙隙隙隙隙隙

虾

(蝦) xiā 龙虾、对虾

9 画
虫 部
左 右

虾

虾虾虾虾虾虾虾虾虾

瞎

xiā 盲人瞎马、瞎指挥 ☞ 害的中部是丰，竖笔上下两端出头。

15 画
目 部
左 右

瞎

瞎瞎瞎瞎瞎瞎瞎
瞎瞎瞎瞎瞎瞎瞎瞎

峡

(峽) xiá 峡谷

☞ 山3画，第二画改竖提，不分为两笔。

9 画
山 部
左 右

峡

峡峡峡峡峡峡峡峡峡

狭

(狹) xiá 狭窄、狭隘

9 画
犭 部
左 右

狭

狭狭狭狭狭狭狭狭狭

霞

xiá 霞光、晚霞 ☞ 雨，第二画改点，第三画改横钩，里边楷体是四点，宋体是四横。下部是叚不是段。

17 画
雨 部
上 下

霞

霞霞霞霞霞霞霞霞
霞霞霞霞霞霞霞霞霞

xià 地下、下次、下级、下楼、下岗、下雪 / xia 跳下、留下

down, under, below

✎ 3 卜 画部
⊟ 独 体
☒ 下 下 下 下

古字形用短横在长横之下来表示。二（金文）（甲文）

（嚇）

frighten; scare into ms data

xià 吓得直哭、吓唬 / hè 恐吓

✎ 6 口 画部
⊟ 左 右
☒ 吓 吓吓吓吓吓吓

summer

xià 夏季、华夏 ☞ 下部是夂不是夂。

夏夏夏夏夏
夏夏夏夏夏

古代的字书，
包括识字课本，
主要是按义用韵
语编排的。以现存的
《急就篇》为例。它的开头
五句是：“急就奇觚与众异：罗列
诸物名姓字，分别部居不杂厕，用
日约少诚快意，勉力务之必有
喜。”全书正文分为三部
分：一是姓氏名字，
二是器用百物，三
是政治职官。

celestial being; immortal

xiān 神仙、仙女

☞ 山3画，第二画是乚，不分为两笔。

✎ 5 画部
⊟ 亻 左 右
☒ 仙 仙仙仙仙仙

earlier, before, first

xiān 先锋、先人、先烈、原先

✎ 6 儿 画部
⊟ 上 下
☒ 先 先先先先先先

古字形像止（人足）在人前。

 （金文）（甲文）

掀

xiān 掀起大浪、掀锅盖

✎ 11 扌 画部
⊟ 左 右
☒ 掀 掀掀掀掀掀掀掀掀掀掀

（鮮）

fresh! (bright-tasty)

xiān 海鲜、时鲜、鲜货、鲜美、鲜花、鲜艳 / xiǎn 鲜见 ☞ 鱼的末笔改提。

鲜鲜鲜鲜鲜鲜鲜
鲜鲜鲜鲜鲜鲜鲜

✎ 14 鱼 画部
⊟ 左 右

 字谜

我有一物生得巧，
半边鳞片半边毛；
半边水中去玩耍，
半边山上去吃草。

（閑）

idle, unoccupied

xián 闲散、闲置、闲谈、农闲

☞ 左上右包围结构。起笔、嵌在第二笔丨和第三笔丁之间。木的中间一竖不带钩，末笔是点。

✎ 7 画部
⊟ 门 半包围
☒ 闲 闲闲闲闲闲闲闲

(賢) xián 贤人、圣贤、贤惠、贤弟

☞ 左上是两竖，不是一竖一撇。贝的第二画丁不带钩。

✎ 8 画　贝部
⊞ 上下

贤 贤 贤 贤 贤 贤 贤 贤 贤

---

xián 弓弦、琴弦、上弦

☞ 弓3画，第三画是乛，不分为两笔。

✎ 8 画　弓部
⊞ 左右

弦 弦 弦 弦 弦 弦 弦 弦 弦

(*鹹) xián 老少咸宜、*咸淡正好

☞ 左上右包围结构。

✎ 9 画　戈部
⊞ 半包围

咸 咸 咸 咸 咸 咸 咸 咸 咸

(銜) xián 燕子衔泥、衔接、学衔

☞ 中部是⺈，5画，第二画是横，不是点；第五画是竖提，不分为两笔。

✎ 11 画　彳部
⊞ 左右

衔 衔 衔 衔 衔 衔 衔 衔 衔 衔 衔

---

xián 嫌隙、嫌弃、嫌疑

☞ 女的横笔右端不出头。兼的两竖不带钩，中部不是彐，中间横笔右端出头。

✎ 13 画　女部
⊞ 左右

嫌 嫌 嫌 嫌 嫌 嫌 嫌 嫌 嫌 嫌 嫌

(顯) xiǎn 显著、显露、显赫

✎ 9 画　日部
⊞ 上下

显 显 显 显 显
显 显 显 显

(險) xiǎn 险峻、天险、阴险、惊险、脱险

☞ 阝两画，起笔是了，不分为两笔。

✎ 9 画　阝部
⊞ 左右

险 险 险 险 险 险 险 险 险

(縣) xiàn 县城、县令 *county*

☞ 上部是且，下部是厶。

✎ 7 画　厶部
⊞ 上下

县 县 县 县 县 县 县

中华人民共和国成立以后，要在旧中国的破烂摊子上建设一个崭新的国家，经济建设和文化建设的任务都异常繁重。年轻的共和国想用最快的速度扫除文盲、普及教育、提高全民的文化素质，于是在语言文字领域提出了文字改革的任务，一方面积极探索用拼音文字代替汉字的可能性和具体途径，另一方面大刀阔斧地整理汉字，"以利目前的应用"。

限、陷的阝两画，起笔是了，不分为两笔。

（現）xiàn 现象、现状、现烤现吃、现金、兑现

　🖊 王的末笔改提。

✎ 8 画
部 王 部
四 左　右

现 现现现现现现现现

---

xiàn 限额、限量

✎ 8 画
部 阝 部
四 左　右

限 限限限限限限限限

（綫）xiàn 毛线、光线、路线、线索、前线、死亡线

　🖊 纟3画，上部不是幺。戋的斜钩上是两横一撇，不是三横一撇。

✎ 8 画
部 纟 部
四 左　右

线 线线线线线线线线

（憲）xiàn 宪法、立宪

✎ 9 画
部 宀 上部下

宪 宪宪宪宪宪宪宪宪宪

---

xiàn 陷入、沦陷、陷害、凹陷、缺陷

✎ 10 画
部 阝 部
四 左　右

陷 陷陷陷陷陷陷陷陷陷

（餡）xiàn 肉馅儿、菜馅儿

　🖊 饣3画，第二画是𠃌，第三画是𠄌，都不分为两笔。右部是臽不是舀。

✎ 11 画
部 饣 部
四 左　右

馅 馅馅馅馅馅馅馅馅馅馅

---

xiàn 羡慕、羡余

　🖊 羊的竖笔下端不出头。

✎ 12 画
部 羊 部
四 上部下

羡 羡羡羡羡羡羡羡羡羡羡羡

（獻）xiàn 献花、献艺

　🖊 左南右犬。

✎ 13 画
部 犬 部
四 左　右

献 献献献献献献献献献献献

（鄉）xiāng 乡村、故乡

✎ 3 画
一 独体
| 乡 | 乡 乡 乡

xiāng 相见、相信、相亲 /
xiàng 相面、相貌、坐相、首相

✎ 9 画
木 左右

相 相相相相相相相相相

（1）下列词语用相，字义为容貌：相貌、纷相、亮相、面相、破相、色相、上相、洋相、站相、长相、照相、装相。

（2）古字形像用眼睛看树木。

（金文）　（甲文）

xiāng 芳香、香甜、睡得香、蚊香

☞ 禾的中间一竖不带钩。

✎ 9 画
香 上下

香 香香香香香香香香香

xiāng 箱子、信箱

✎ 15 画
竹 上下

箱 箱箱箱箱箱箱箱箱箱箱箱
箱 箱箱

（詳）xiáng 详细、不详

☞ 讠两画，第二画是乛，不分为两笔或三笔。

✎ 8 画
讠 左右

详 详详详详详详详详

xiáng 吉祥、祥和、不祥

☞ 左部是礻不是衤。

✎ 10 画
礻 左右

祥 祥祥祥祥祥祥祥祥祥祥

xiǎng 享受、享乐

☞ 子3画，第一画是乛，第二画是亅，不连成一笔。

✎ 8 画
亠 上下

享 享享享享享享享享

（響）xiǎng 响应、声响、响亮

✎ 9 画
口 左右

响 响响响响响响响响响

象、像、橡的象，11画，第六画从扁框中直接撇下，不分为两笔。

xiǎng 想办法、猜想、想念

☞ 木的竖笔不带钩，末笔改点。心的第二画楷体是 ㇏(卧钩)，宋体是 乚(竖弯钩)。

✎ 13 画
⊞ 心部
⊠ 上下

想 想想想想想想想想想想想想

(*嚮) **xiàng** *向前、*风向、*志向、向来

direction

☞ 左上右包围结构。

✎ 6 画
⊞ 丿部
⊠ 半包围

向 向向向向向向

> 两名轿夫抬着一顶轿子，里面坐着一位贵夫人。轿夫问：夫人的"夫"和轿夫的"夫"有什么分别？夫人扬起高傲的头回答：夫人的"夫"是"一大"，轿夫的"夫"是"二人"。轿夫听后，使劲让轿子颠了几下以示不满。

(項) **xiàng** 项链、项目、进项

nape of the neck

☞ 工的末笔改提。

✎ 9 画
⊞ 工部
⊠ 左右

项 项项项项项项项项项

---

xiàng 街头巷尾 / **hàng** 巷道 *lane, alley*

☞ 左上右包围结构。下部是巳，不是已或己。

✎ 9 画
⊞ 己部
⊠ 半包围

巷 巷巷巷巷巷巷巷巷巷

---

xiàng 印度象、印象、象形

elephant

✎ 11 画
⊞ 刀部
⊠ 上下

象 象象象象象象象象象象

> (1) 下列词语用象，字义为形状、样子：象征、表象、抽象、旱象、幻象、迹象、景象、气象、万象、现象、形象、意象、印象 (2) 古字形像大象。(金文)(甲文)

---

xiàng 相像、画像、像他那样活着

portrait, picture

✎ 13 画
⊞ 亻部
⊠ 左右

像 像像像像像像像像像像像

> 下列词语用像，字义为比照人或物做成的图形：像章、雕像、佛像、画像、蜡像、录像、偶像、群像、人像、摄像、神像、塑像、铜像、头像、图像、肖像、胸像、绣像、遗像、音像。字义为相似：好像、相像。

---

oak, rubber tree

xiàng 橡树、橡胶、橡皮 ☞ 木的竖笔不带钩，末笔改点。

✎ 15 画
⊞ 木部
⊠ 左右

橡 橡橡橡橡橡橡
橡橡橡橡橡橡橡

---

peel w/ knife, cut, chop

xiāo 削铅笔 / **xuē** 削足适履、削价、削职、剥削

☞ 月的起笔改竖。

✎ 9 画
⊞ 刂部
⊠ 左右

削 削削削削削削削削削

xiāo 消失、取消、消遣、消费
disappear, vanish; pass time in leisure
✎ 10 画
笔 氵 部
区 左 右
 消消消消消消消消消消

xiāo 通宵、夜宵、宵禁 night
✎ 10 画
笔 宀 部
区 上 下
宵宵宵宵宵宵宵宵宵宵

（銷）xiāo 销毁、注销、开销、滞销、插销 cancel, annul
☞ 钅5画，第二画是横，不是点；第五画是竖提，不分为两笔。
✎ 12 画
笔 钅 部
区 左
 销销销销销销销销销销销

small, little, petty
xiāo 小事、小住、小儿子、全家大小
☞ 左侧楷体是点，宋体是撇。
✎ 3 画
笔 小 部
区 独 体
小小小

古字形像细碎的东西。
 八（金文） 八（甲文）

（曉）xiǎo 拂晓、晓得、晓以利害 dawn, break of day
(know, tell)
☞ 右上不是戈或弋，右下是兀不是元。
✎ 10 画
笔 日 部
区 左 右
晓晓晓晓晓晓晓晓晓晓

xiào 孝顺、披麻带孝
☞ 上左包围结构。子3画，第一画是乛，第二画是丨，不连为一笔。
✎ 7 画
笔 耂 部
区 半包围
孝孝孝孝孝孝孝

xiào 学校、少校 / jiào 校对
学校
xué xiào : School
☞ 木的中间一竖不带钩，末笔改点。
✎ 10 画
笔 木 部
区 左 右
校校校校校校校校校校

xiào 笑声、耻笑、笑料
☞ 下部是夭不是天。
✎ 10 画
笔 竹 部
区 上 下
笑笑笑笑笑笑笑笑笑笑

xiào 仿效、效忠、效果

☞ 交的末笔改点。右部是攵不是夂。

✎ 10 画
囗 攵部
凵 左 右

效 效效效效效效效效效效

xiē 有些、一些

☞ 左上止的末笔改提。右上是匕不是匕。

✎ 8 画
囗 止部
凵 上 下

此 此此此此此此此此

xiē 歇脚、歇业

☞ 左下不是匈，框内人的末笔改点。

✎ 13 画
囗 欠部
凵 左 右

歇 歇歇歇歇歇歇歇歇歇歇歇歇

(協) **xié** 协作、协调、协助

☞ 左部是十不是忄。

✎ 6 画
囗 十部
凵 左 右

协 协协协协协协

xié 邪说、避邪、邪火

☞ 牙4画，第二画是乚，不分为两笔。阝两画，第一画是了，不分为两笔。

✎ 6 画
囗 牙部
凵 左 右

邪 邪邪邪邪邪邪

(脅) **xié** 胁骨、胁迫

✎ 8 画
囗 月部
凵 左 右

胁 胁胁胁胁
　 胁胁胁胁

xié 斜坡、太阳西斜 ☞ 余的第二画改点。

✎ 11 画
囗 斗部
凵 左 右

斜 斜斜斜斜斜
　 斜斜斜斜斜斜

两个或两个
以上的汉字列在
一起，就有一个排序
问题。汉字字数的众多使
汉字的科学排序显得分外重
要。编制工具书索引、编排图书档
案资料、排列姓名次序，以及
研制电脑输入汉字的编码方
案等，都需要有一个好的
排序方法，以方
便查找。

xié 携手、携带

☞ 右上是隹不是住。右下乃两画，第一画是乃，不分为两笔。

✎ 13 画
囗 扌部
凵 左

携 携携携携携携携携携携

xié 鞋底、草鞋

☞ 廿 4画，第二画是竖，第四画是横，不连成一笔。

✎ 15 画
☐ 革 部
◪ 左 右

鞋鞋鞋鞋鞋鞋鞋鞋鞋鞋鞋
鞋鞋鞋鞋

（寫）xiě 写生、写字、写作

☞ 上部是一不是宀。

✎ 5 画
☐ 一 部
◪ 上 下

写写写写写

xiè 排泄、泄愤、泄密、泄气

☞ 世 5画，第二画竖、第四画横，不连成一笔；第五画是乚，不分为两笔。

✎ 8 画
☐ 氵部
◪ 左 右

泄泄泄泄泄泄泄泄

（瀉）xiè 倾泻、泻肚

☞ 右上是一不是宀。与 3画，第二画是勹，不分为两笔。

✎ 8 画
☐ 氵部
◪ 左 右

泻泻泻泻泻泻泻泻

xiè 卸鞋口、卸妆、推卸

☞ 左部7画，上午下止。右部是卩不是阝。

✎ 9 画
☐ 卩 部
◪ 左 右

卸卸卸卸卸卸卸卸

xiè 纸屑、琐屑、不屑

☞ 上左包围结构。月的起笔改竖。

✎ 10 画
☐ 尸 部
◪ 半包围

屑屑屑屑屑屑屑屑屑屑

xiè 机械、枪械

☞ 木的中间一竖不带钩，末笔改点。右部是戒不是戉、戌、戊或戎。

✎ 11 画
☐ 木 部
◪ 左 右

械械械械械械械械械械

（謝）xiè 谢绝、凋谢、谢幕

☞ 讠两画，第二画是乛，不分为两笔或三笔。身的末笔上端不出头。

✎ 12 画
☐ 讠 部
◪ 左 右

谢谢谢谢谢谢谢谢谢谢

如果把"死字"去掉，把重复多余的异体字去掉，那么同时在社会上通行的汉字大约只有五六千到六七千个左右。据文字学家考证，中国历朝历代通行的汉字，虽然在具体的字种上略有差别，有新的字在不断产生，有旧的字在陆续隐退，但在总体上维持着通行字总量的相对稳定。这里显然有汉字记录汉语的规律和人们认知汉字的能力在起作用。

新、薪的左下是木，不写成木。

xīn 心脏、心得、谈心、手心

☞ 第二画楷体是乚(卧钩)，宋体是乚(竖弯钩)。

✎ 4 画
心 部
⊠ 独体

心 心心心心

现代书法家林散之，72岁的时候，有一次洗澡，一不小心跌入烫水池中，浑身烫伤。右手无名指、小指都被烫坏。经抢救苏醒后，他问的第一句话是："我的右手还能写字吗？"伤愈后，右手无名指和小指弯曲，他就用三个手指执笔，继续从事他痴迷的书法事业。

xīn 辛辣、辛劳、心酸、辛酉戌亥

✎ 7 画
辛 部
⊠ 上 下

辛 辛辛辛辛辛辛辛辛

xīn 欣喜、欣慰

✎ 8 画
斤 部
⊠ 左 右

欣 欣欣欣欣欣欣欣欣

xīn 新居、耳目一新、新鞋新袜、新人、迎新、新近

✎ 13 画
斤 部
⊠ 左 右

新 新新新新新新新新新新新新新

xīn 卧薪尝胆、工薪 ☞ 艹3画，第三画楷体是撇，宋体是竖。

✎ 16 画
艹 部
⊠ 上 下

薪薪薪薪薪薪薪薪薪薪薪
薪薪薪薪

xìn 信用、印信、信息、证明信、信任、信徒、信步

✎ 9 画
亻 部
⊠ 左 右

信 信信信信信信信信信

(興) xīng 兴师动众、兴建、时兴 / xìng 兴趣

✎ 6 画
八 部
⊠ 上 下

兴 兴兴兴兴兴兴

xīng 星空、唾沫星儿、秤星、歌星

✎ 9 画
日 部
⊠ 上 下

星 星星星星星星星星

古字形像闪烁的群星。另加声旁生。 🌟(金文) 🌟(甲文)

xīng 荸腥、腥臊

✎ 13 画
月 部
左 右

腥 腥腥腥腥腥腥腥
腥腥腥腥腥腥

一幅漫画：身穿西服的胖胖君子端坐在"八大件"（汽车、洋房等）之间。画题：《先天下之优而优》。仅仅换了一个汉字："忧"换"优"，语义全变，挖苦之情溢于纸上。

刑
xíng 徒刑、受刑

✎ 6 画
刂 部
左 右

刑 刑刑刑刑刑刑

行
xíng 航行、发行、行医、言行 / háng 行列、商行、同行、内行

OK

行 行行行行行行

✎ 6 画
彳 部
左 右

古字形像四通八达的街道。

（金文）　（甲文）

形
xíng 形体、地形、喜形于色、相形见绌

☞ 彡写在一条中轴线上。

✎ 7 画
彡 部
左 右

形 形形形形形形形

型
xíng 模型、血型

✎ 9 画
土 部
上 下

型 型型型型型型型型型

醒
xǐng 苏醒、觉醒、醒目 ☞ 酉的框内有一横。

✎ 16 画
酉 部
左 右

醒 醒醒醒醒醒醒醒醒醒醒醒
醒醒醒醒

杏
xìng 杏树、杏仁

☞ 木的中间一竖不带钩。

✎ 7 画
木 部
上 下

杏 杏杏杏杏杏杏杏

明朝梅膺祚编《字汇》时就有意识地收入许多简体字。他说："近世事繁，字趋便捷，徒拘乎古，恐戾于今，以今时所尚者酌而用之。"

幸
xìng 幸存、荣幸、庆幸

☞ 下部是幸不是辛。

✎ 8 画
土 部
上 下

幸 幸幸幸幸幸幸幸幸

凶、胸的凶4画，第三画是乚，不分为两笔。

xìng 个性、共性、科学性、性别

✎ 8 画
□ 忄 部
△ 左 右

性 性性性性性性性性

xìng 姓名 *proper name*

☞ 女的横笔右端不出头。

✎ 8 画
□ 女 部
△ 左 右

姓 姓姓姓姓姓姓姓姓

xiōng 凶兆、凶狠、凶手

☞ 左下右包围结构。

✎ 4 画
□ 凵 部
△ 半包围

凶 凶凶凶凶

xiōng 兄妹、表兄、仁兄

✎ 5 画
□ 口 部
△ 上 下

兄 兄兄兄兄兄

xiōng 胸腔、胸襟

✎ 10 画
□ 月 部
△ 左 右

胸 胸胸胸胸胸
胸胸胸胸胸

xióng 雄蜂、英雄、雄心

☞ 右部是隹不是住。

✎ 12 画
□ 隹 部
△ 左 右

雄 雄雄雄雄雄雄雄雄雄雄雄雄

xióng 白熊、熊掌 ☞ 月的起笔改竖。右上是两匕，不是两匕。灬托住全字。

✎ 14 画
□ 灬 部
△ 上 下

熊 熊熊熊熊熊熊
熊熊熊熊熊熊熊

xiū 休假、休战、休想

☞ 木的中间一竖不带钩。

✎ 6 画
□ 亻 部
△ 左 右

休 休休休休休休

原先在印刷物中有若干用作计量单位的字，从字形来看，跟一般汉字一样，也只占一个方格，但读出来，却是两个音节，不同于一般汉字的一字一音节，如"瓩"，读作qiānwǎ；"哩"，读作yīnglǐ。1977年原中国文字改革委员会和国家标准计量局联合发布《部分计量单位名称统一用字表》，淘汰了这些一字二音节的字形，改用"千瓦""英里"等一字一音节的字形。

有人提倡诉之视觉的诗。如一首题目为《车祸》的视觉诗，用了这样的形式：车·车·车，"表现了车子迎面冲来的那有速度、有远近、有行动的紧张的感觉"。

古字形像人靠着大树，在树阴下休息。㭭（金文）休（甲文）

xiū 修饰、修理、兴修、自修

⊓ 中部有一竖。右上是夂不是攵。彡写在一条中轴线上。

✎ 9 画
◰ 亻 部
◰ 左右

修 修修修修修修修修

xiū 羞愧、怕羞　　⊓ 上左包围结构。羊的末笔改撇。丑的中间一横右端不出头。

✎ 10 画
◰ 羊 部
◰ 半包围

羞 羞羞羞羞羞羞羞羞

一只山羊实在丑，尾巴偏要往左扭；扭来扭去怕见人，装模作样为遮丑。

 字谜

xiǔ 腐朽、不朽、老朽

⊓ 木的中间一竖不带钩，末笔改点。

✎ 6 画
◰ 木 部
◰ 左右

朽 朽朽朽朽朽朽

战国时代，各国"文字异形"，给书面交际带来了极大的不便，社会出现了统一文字的强烈要求。秦始皇统一中国，由李斯等成功地进行了著名的"同文字"的工作，"罢其不与秦文合者"，废除了六国文字中跟秦文不同的异体。李斯、赵高、胡母敬分别编写了《仓颉篇》《爰历篇》和《博学篇》，作为推行规范文字的范本。政府还用规范字形书写大量诏版，随同权、量等器物颁发各地，在日常生活中扩大规范文字的影响。秦始皇二十八年（公元前219年）琅邪刻石上"同书文字"四个大字宣告了这次汉字整理工作的成功。

xiù 秀穗、优秀、新秀、俊秀

✎ 7 画
◰ 禾 部
◰ 上下

秀 秀秀秀秀秀秀秀

xiù 短袖、袖手旁观　⊓ 左部是衤不是礻。

✎ 10 画
◰ 衤 部
◰ 左右

袖 袖袖袖袖袖
袖袖袖袖袖

（綉）xiù 刺绣、苏绣　✎ 彡3画，上部不是幺。

✎ 10 画
◰ 纟 部
◰ 左右

绣 绣绣绣绣绣
绣绣绣绣绣

（銹）xiù 铁锈、不锈钢、茶锈

⊓ 钅5画，第二画是横，不是点；第五画是竖提，不分为两笔。

✎ 12 画
◰ 钅 部
◰ 左右

锈 锈锈锈锈锈锈锈锈锈锈锈

（須*鬚）xū 必须、*胡须、*须根

⊓ 彡写在一条中轴线上。

✎ 9 画
◰ 彡 部
◰ 左右

须 须须须须须须须须

古字形像脸上长满长须。

（金文）

must, have to

xū 空虚、谦虚、乘虚而入、虚弱、虚名、虚度、心虚

☞ 上左包围结构。

✎ 11 画
虍部
半包围

虚 虚虚虚虚虚虚虚虚虚虚

xū 需要、军需　☞ 雨，第二画改点，第三画改横钩，里边楷体是四点，宋体是四横。

✎ 14 画
雨部
上下

需 需需需需需需需
需需需需需需需

xú 清风徐来、徐缓

✎ 10 画
彳部
左右

徐 徐徐徐徐徐徐徐徐徐徐

（許）**xǔ** 允许、许配、称许、也许、许久

☞ 讠两画，第二画是丁，不分为两笔或三笔。

✎ 6 画
讠部
左右

许 许许许许许许许

xù 程序、序言、序曲

☞ 上左包围结构。

✎ 7 画
广部
半包围

序 序序序序序序序

要能准确计算一个字的笔画数，必须具备两个条件，一是统计的对象必须是规范字形（如"鬼"，规范字形是9笔，旧字形是10笔；"象"，规范字形是11笔，旧字形是12笔），二是要遵守汉字书写的基本规则（至少有两条：在同一笔画上，笔尖只能走一次，不能走回路；横笔的笔向只能从左到右，竖笔、撇笔、捺笔的笔向只能从上到下）。做到了这两点，一般字的笔画数都能准确地数出来。

xù 叙谈、叙述、叙事诗

☞ 余的第二画改点。

✎ 9 画
又部
左右

叙 叙叙叙叙叙叙叙叙叙

xù 畜牧／**chù** 牲畜

✎ 10 画
田部
上下

畜 畜畜畜畜畜畜畜畜畜畜

（緒）**xù** 头绪、心绪

☞ 纟3画，上部不是幺。

✎ 11 画
纟部
左右

绪 绪绪绪绪绪绪绪绪绪绪

（續） xù 连续、继续

☞ 纟3画，上部不是幺。卖的上部是十不是士。

✎ 11 画
部 纟 部
四 左 右

续 续续续续续续续续续续续

xù 柳絮、棉絮、絮棉被、絮叨

☞ 女的横笔右端不出头。小的左侧楷体是点，宋体是撇。

✎ 12 画
部 糸 部
上 下

絮 絮絮絮絮絮絮絮絮絮絮絮絮

xù 储蓄、蓄谋、蓄须明志

☞ 艹3画，第三画楷体是撇，宋体是竖。

✎ 13 画
部 艹 部
上 下

蓄 蓄蓄蓄蓄蓄蓄蓄蓄蓄蓄蓄蓄

xuān 宣传、宣泄

✎ 9 画
部 宀 部
上 下

宣 宣宣宣宣宣宣宣宣宣

（懸） xuán 悬挂、悬殊、悬案、悬念、悬空、真悬

☞ 心的第二画楷体是乚(卧钩)，宋体是乚(竖弯钩)。

✎ 11 画
部 心 部
上 下

悬 悬悬悬悬悬悬悬悬悬悬悬

xuán 盘旋、凯旋、旋涡 / xuàn 旋风、旋水果皮、旋做旋卖

✎ 11 画
部 方 部
左 右

旋 旋旋旋旋旋旋旋旋旋旋

（選） xuǎn 选择、入选、人选、诗选

☞ 左下包围结构。辶3画，第二画楷体是㇋，宋体是㇆。

✎ 9 画
部 辶 部
半包围

选 选选选选选选选选选

xué 洞穴、巢穴、穴位

✎ 5 画
部 穴 部
上 下

穴 穴穴穴穴穴

台湾作家柏杨曾经因为提倡简体字坐牢。

雪、寻的彐，中间一横右端不出头。

(學) xué 学习、大学、真才实学、经济学

☞ 上部是⺍不是⺌。子3画，第一画乛、第二画亅，不连成一笔。

✎ 8　画
部 子部
囚 上下

学 学学学学学学学学

学校
xué xiào
school

---

xuě 雪花、雪白、雪耻

☞ 雨，第二画改点，第三画改横钩，里边楷体是四点，宋体是四横。

✎ 11　画
部 雨部
囚 上下

雪 雪雪雪雪雪雪雪雪雪雪雪

---

xuè 鲜血、血统、血性男儿 / xiě 吐血

✎ 6　画
部 血部
囚 独体

血 血血血血血血血

---

xún 上旬、六旬大寿

☞ 上右包围结构。

✎ 6　画
部 勹部
囚 半包围

旬 旬旬旬旬旬旬

据对香港教育学院一年级学生错别字的调查，除了跟内地学生相同的类型外（笔画增删、结构颠倒、音同音近别字、形近别字等），还有一种把汉字部件西文化的毛病，如把"口"写成英文字母"O"，把"日"写成英文字母"B"，把"⺌"写成两个英文字母"k"等。这可能跟香港学生接触拉丁字母较多有关。

(尋) xún 寻人、寻找

✎ 6　画
部 彐部
囚 上下

寻 寻寻寻寻寻寻

---

xún 巡视、巡行、酒过三巡

☞ 左下包围结构。辶3画，第二画楷体是𠃊，宋体是乀。

✎ 6　画
部 辶部
囚 半包围

巡 巡巡巡巡巡巡

(詢) xún 咨询、询问

☞ 讠两画，第二画是乛，不分为两笔或三笔。

✎ 8　画
部 讠部
囚 左右

询 询询询询询询询询

---

xún 遵循、循规蹈矩、循循善诱

✎ 12　画
部 彳部
囚 左右

循 循循循循循循循循循循循循

（訓）xùn 训诫、校训、集训、训释

　　讠两画，第二画是㇆，不分为两笔或三笔。

✎ 5 画　讠部
口 左右

训 训训训训训

（訊）xùn 问讯、审讯、通讯

　　讠两画，第二画是㇆，不分为两笔或三笔。右部是卂，上㇆下十，不是凡。

✎ 5 画　讠部
口 左右

讯 讯讯讯讯讯

---

xùn 迅速、迅猛

　　左下包围结构。右上是卂，上㇆下十，不是凡。辶3画，第二画楷体是㇇，宋体是㇆。

✎ 6 画　辶部
凶 半包围

迅 迅迅迅迅迅迅

（壓）yā 压制、技压群芳、大军压境、积压、高压

　　上左包围结构。右下是土加丶（点）。

✎ 6 画　厂部
凶 半包围

压 压压压压压压

---

yā 呀，下雪了、呀的一声 / ya 快请坐呀

　　牙4画，第二画是㇄，不分为两笔。

✎ 7 画　口部
口 左右

呀 呀呀呀呀呀呀呀

根据统计，在现代汉字中，左右结构类型的字约占64.93%；其次是上下结构类型的字，约占21.11%。这两种类型的字就占了统计总字数的86.04%。

---

yā 抵押、扣押、押送、押韵

✎ 8 画　扌部
凶 左

押 押押押押押押押押

（鴉）yā 乌鸦、鸦雀无声、鸦片

　　牙4画，第二画是㇄，不分为两笔。

✎ 9 画　牙部
凶 左

鸦 鸦鸦鸦鸦鸦鸦鸦鸦鸦

（鴨）yā 烤鸭、鸭舌帽

✎ 10 画　鸟部
凶 左右

鸭 鸭鸭鸭鸭鸭鸭鸭鸭鸭鸭

牙、芽、雅的牙4画，第二画是乚(竖折)，不分为两笔。

 yá 刷牙、牙雕

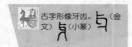
古字形像牙齿。(金文) (小篆)

　4 画
　牙 部
　独 体

牙 牙牙牙牙

 yá 发芽、肉芽

⌐ 艹3画，第三画楷体是撇，宋体是竖。

　7 画
　艹 部
　上 下

芽 芽芽芽芽芽芽芽

 yá 山崖、悬崖

⌐ 山，第二画是乚，不分为两笔。

　11 画
　山 部
　上 下

崖 崖崖崖崖崖崖崖崖崖崖崖

 (啞) yǎ 哑巴、哑剧、沙哑 / yā 哑哑学语

　9 画
　口 部
　左 右

哑 哑哑哑哑哑哑哑哑哑

 yǎ 高雅、雅观

⌐ 右部是隹不是住。

　12 画
　牙 部
　左 右

雅 雅雅雅雅雅雅雅雅雅雅雅

 (軋) yà 轧路机、倾轧 / zhá 轧钢

⌐ 车的下边一横改提，笔顺改先竖后提。

　5 画
　车 部
　左 右

轧 轧轧轧轧轧

 (亞) yà 亚军、亚洲

因鸦片战争时抗击英国侵略军而闻名的广东虎门，有一副被人津津乐道的对联："烟锁池塘柳 炮镇海城楼。"妙就妙在上联和下联的五个汉字中都整齐地含有"金木水火土"这"五行"的部件。

　6 画
　业 部
　独 体

亚 亚亚亚亚亚亚

 yān 咽喉 / yàn 狼吞虎咽 / yè 哽咽

⌐ 因内的大，末笔改点。

　9 画
　口 部
　左 右

咽 咽咽咽咽咽咽咽咽咽

yān 炊烟、烟雾、松烟、吸烟、烟土

☞ 火的末笔改点。囚内的大,末笔改点。

✎ 10 画
囗 火 部
囚 左 右

烟 烟烟烟烟烟烟烟烟烟烟

yān 淹没、淹留

✎ 11 画
囗 氵 部
囚 左 右

淹 淹淹淹淹淹淹淹淹淹淹淹

yán 延伸、延期

☞ 左下包围结构。正 4 画,起笔是丿,末笔是㇏。
廴两画,起笔㇋不分为两笔。

✎ 6 画
囗 廴 部
囚 半包围

延 延延延延延延

电子计算机
是人类 20 世纪
40 年代的伟大创造。
先只用于计数,后又
用于语言文字处理。七八
十年代微型计算机大发展,
进入各行各业、千家万
户。电子计算机推
动社会跨人信
息时代。

(嚴) yán 严肃、严格、严冬、严密

✎ 7 画
囗 一 部
囚 独 体

严 严严严严严严

yán 不言而喻、留言、五言诗

✎ 7 画
囗 言 部
囚 上 下

言 言言言言言言言

yán 岩石、岩层

☞ 山 3 画,第二画㇄,不分为两笔。

✎ 8 画
囗 山 部
囚 上 下

岩 岩岩岩岩岩岩岩岩

yán 炎热、炎黄子孙、发炎

☞ 上部火的末笔改点。

✎ 8 画
囗 火 部
囚 上 下

古字形用两火表示火势猛烈。

(金文)   (甲文)

炎 炎炎炎炎炎炎炎炎

沿 yán 沿袭、前沿

☞ 右上不是几,第二画不带钩。

✎ 8 画
囗 氵 部
囚 左 右

沿 沿沿沿沿沿沿沿沿

yán 研碎、研究

✎ 9 画
□ 石 部
☒ 左 右

研 研 研 研 研 研 研 研 研

(鹽) yán 食盐、精盐

☞ 土的末笔改提。不简化为盐。

✎ 10 画
□ 皿 部
☒ 上 下

盐 盐 盐 盐 盐 盐 盐 盐 盐 盐

(顔) yán 鹤发童颜、颜色、颜面   ☞ 彡写在一条中轴线上。

✎ 15 画
□ 页 部
☒ 左 右

颜 颜 颜 颜 颜 颜 颜 颜 颜 颜 颜
颜 颜 颜

yǎn 掩盖、掩门

✎ 11 画
□ 扌 部
☒ 左 右

掩 掩 掩 掩 掩 掩
掩 掩 掩 掩 掩

两晋有一位著名的女书法家卫铄(shuò)，人称"卫夫人"。她是两晋卫氏书法世家中杰出的一员。她秉承家风，擅长隶、正、行三体。在东西晋交替时期，名声大振。王羲之拜在她门下。她的《笔阵图》受到后代书法家的推崇。这是我们见到的最早一篇论执笔、笔法和结体艺术的论述。

yǎn 眼睛、泉眼、节骨眼儿、有板有眼

✎ 11 画
□ 目 部
☒ 左 右

眼 眼 眼 眼 眼 眼 眼 眼 眼 眼 眼

yǎn 演变、扮演、演算

✎ 14 画
□ 氵 部
☒ 左 右

演 演 演 演 演 演 演
演 演 演 演 演 演

(厭) yàn 贪得无厌、厌战

☞ 上左包围结构。右下是犬不是大。

✎ 6 画
□ 厂 部
☒ 半 包围

厌 厌 厌 厌 厌 厌

统计汉字使用的频率，得出最常用的 10 个字是"的、一、是、在、不、了、有、和、人、这"。有趣的是，如果将测试英文10个最高频词对照一下，可以发现大致也是这类语义的词：the, of, and, a, to, in, is, you, that, it。可见，越是最常用的字(词)，它们的笔画往往越少。

(艷) yàn 艳丽、鲜艳

✎ 10 画
□ 色 部
☒ 左 右

艳 艳 艳 艳 艳 艳 艳 艳 艳 艳

yàn 宴请、便宴

✎ 10 画
部 宀 部
结 上 下

宴 宴宴宴宴宴宴宴宴宴宴

（驗） yàn 验证、验收

☞ 马的第一画乛、第二画乚，都不分为两笔；左上角开口；末笔改提。右部人下有横。

✎ 10 画
部 马 部
结 左 右

验 验验验验验验验验验验

yàn 大雁、雁过拔毛

☞ 上是包围结构。右下是：左亻右隹。

✎ 12 画
部 厂 部
结 半包围

雁 雁雁雁雁雁雁雁雁雁雁雁

yàn 火焰、气焰

☞ 火的末笔改点。右部是臽不是舀。

✎ 12 画
部 火 部
结 左 右

焰 焰焰焰焰焰焰焰焰焰焰焰焰

yàn 燕子 / yān 燕赵

廿4画，第二画竖、第四画横不连成一笔。北5画，第三画是提，第四画是撇。

✎ 16 画
部 灬 部
结 上 下

燕 燕燕燕燕燕燕燕燕
燕燕燕燕燕燕燕燕

yāng 中央、央求

✎ 5 画
部 丨 部
结 独 体

央 央央央央央

yāng 遭殃、祸国殃民

✎ 9 画
部 歹 部
结 左 右

殃 殃殃殃殃殃殃殃殃

yāng 秧苗、育秧

☞ 禾，中间一竖不带钩，末笔改点。

✎ 10 画
部 禾 部
结 左 右

秧 秧秧秧秧秧秧秧秧秧秧

扬、杨的右部是 *raise, spread, make known* 易。

(揚) yáng 扬帆、飘扬、张扬、表扬

☞ 刃3画，第一画刁，不分成两笔。

✎ 6 画　扌 部
□ 左　右

扬 扬 扬 扬 扬 扬

---

yáng 山羊、羊羔
sheep

✎ 6 画　羊 部
□ 独体

羊 羊 羊 羊 羊 羊

古字形像羊头。（金文）（甲文）

(陽) yáng 太阳、阳沟、阳文、阳世、阳极

☞ 阝 两画，第一画是了，不分为两笔。

✎ 6 画　阝 部
□ 左　右

阳 阳 阳 阳 阳 阳

(楊) yáng 杨树、杨柳 *poplar*

☞ 木的中间一竖不带钩，末笔改点。

✎ 7 画　木 部
□ 左　右

杨 杨 杨 杨 杨 杨 杨

---

vast, foreign
yáng 洋溢、海洋、留洋、洋为中用

✎ 9 画　氵 部
□ 左　右

洋 洋 洋 洋
洋 洋 洋 洋 洋

唐朝著名书法家怀素，练字的时候非常刻苦。他种了很多芭蕉，用芭蕉叶当作练字的纸张。因而以"绿天庵"作为居所的名称。又用漆盘、漆板来练字，写过以后抹掉再写，直到盘板皆穿。他把写秃的笔头堆在一起，埋起来，起名叫"笔冢"（冢 zhǒng，坟墓）。

---

yǎng 仰望、信仰、仰仗 *face upward, admire, respect*

☞ 中部是⺋不是匕。

✎ 6 画　亻 部
□ 左　右

仰 仰 仰 仰 仰 仰

(養) *support, provide for*
yǎng 养猪、抚养、休养、教养、养子

☞ 左上右包围结构。上部羊的竖笔改撇。

✎ 9 画　八 部
□ 半包围

养 养 养 养 养 养 养 养

---

yǎng 氧气、缺氧 *oxygen*

☞ 上右包围结构。右上是气不是乞。

✎ 10 画　气 部
□ 半包围

氧 氧 氧 氧 氧 氧 氧 氧 氧 氧

窑、谣、摇的缶6画，第五画是L，不分为两笔。

（癢）yǎng 不痛不痒、刺痒 *itch*

☞ 上左包围结构。

✎ 11 画
▢ 疒部
⊠ 半包围

（樣）yàng 样子、榜样、各样商品 *appearance shape sample, pattern*

☞ 木的中间一竖不带钩，末笔改点。

✎ 10 画
▢ 木 左
⊠ 左 右

yāo 妖怪、妖言、妖娆、妖艳 *goblin demon spirit*

☞ 女的横笔右端不出头。右部是夭不是天。

✎ 7 画
▢ 女部
⊠ 左 右

yāo 扭腰、腰子、裤腰、半山腰

☞ 右上扁框内是两竖，不写成西。

✎ 13 画
▢ 月部
⊠ 左 右

yāo 应邀、邀请 ☞ 左下包围结构。右上是夂不是夂。辶3画，第二画楷体是乁，宋体是乀。

✎ 16 画
▢ 辶部
⊠ 半包围

yáo 砖窑、窑洞

✎ 11 画
▢ 穴上
⊠ 上下

（謠）yáo 民谣、谣言

☞ 讠两画，第二画是乁，不分为两笔或三笔。

✎ 12 画
▢ 讠部
⊠ 左 右

yáo 摇摆、摇手

✎ 13 画
▢ 扌部
⊠ 左 右

yáo 遥控、遥遥无期　☞ 左下包围结构。辶3画，第二画楷体是乁，宋体是㇋。缶6画，第五画是㇄，不分为两笔。

✎ 13 画
部 辶 部
结构 半包围

遥 遥遥遥遥遥遥遥遥遥遥遥遥

yǎo 咬人、咬牙、反咬一口、咬字清楚、咬文嚼字

✎ 9 画
部 口 部
结构 左 右

咬 咬咬咬咬咬咬咬咬咬

(藥) yào 中药、药蟑螂、火药　☞ 艹3画，第三画楷体是撇，宋体是竖。纟3画，上部不是幺。

✎ 9 画
部 艹 部
结构 上 下

药 药药药药药药药药药药

yào 要闻、需要、要账、要是 / yāo 要求、要挟　☞ 上部扁框中都是竖，不写成西。

✎ 9 画
部 覀 部
结构 上 下

要 要要要要要要要要要

(鑰) yào 钥匙　☞ 钅5画，第二画是横，不是点；第五画是竖提，不分为两笔。

✎ 9 画
部 钅 部
结构 左 右

钥 钥钥钥钥钥钥钥钥钥

yào 耀眼、炫耀、荣耀　☞ 光的末笔改竖提。右上两个习的第一画都去钩。右下是隹不是住。

耀耀耀耀耀耀耀耀耀耀

✎ 20 画
部 小 部
结构 左 右

耀 耀耀耀耀耀耀耀耀耀

(爺) yé 老爷爷、老大爷、县太爷、佛爷　☞ 左上右包围结构。下部是卩不是阝。

✎ 6 画
部 父 部
结构 半包围

爷 爷爷爷爷爷爷

yě 这也行、也想参军、眼皮也不眨一下

✎ 3 画
部 一 部
结构 独体

也 也也也 also! too!

包围结构的字，凡是四面包围的，被包围部件要写得匀称、圆满，如"园、圈、固"等。

yě 冶金、陶冶　smelt

⺀ 左部是⺀不是氵。

✎ 7 画部　⼏左右　冶　冶冶冶冶冶冶冶

yě 野外、下野、野蛮、野狗、视野　⺀里的末笔改提。右部是予不是矛。

✎ 11 画部　里左右　野　野野野野野野野野野野野

（業）yě 学业、就业、行业、开业、创业　trade, industry, profession, occupation

✎ 5 画部　业独体　业　业业业业业

（葉）yè 树叶、清代中叶、肺叶　leaf

✎ 5 画部　口左右　叶　叶叶叶叶叶

笔性墨情，
皆以其人之性情
为本。是则理性情者，书
之首务也。（笔墨表现的情趣都
是取决于书写者本人的性情，
所以调理性情是从事书
法艺术的首要任务。）
——刘熙载《艺概》

（頁）yè 插页、活页　leaf, page

✎ 6 画部　页独体　页　页页页页页页

古字形像人头，并用人身作衬托。 𦣻（金文） 𩑋（甲文）

night, evening

yè 夜以继日、夜班

✎ 8 画部　亠上　夜　夜夜夜夜夜夜夜夜

yè 液体、唾液

✎ 11 画部　氵左右　液　液液液液液液液液液液液

1935年，国语统一筹备委员会的一个工作组在钱玄同的主持下编成《简体字谱》草稿。同年春天，上海陈望道等发起组织"手头字推行会"，选定第一批手头字300个，并用来排印杂志。1935年8月，国民政府教育部从《简体字谱》草稿中选取324个简体字编成《第一批简体字表》公布。1936年2月又被废止。抗日战争期间，简体字在解放区广泛流行，油印书报采用和创造了许多简体字。

yī 一五一十、一样、一心一意、一人一盒、试一试

✎ 1 画部　一独体　一　一

yī 衣服、糖衣
clothing, clothes

✎ 6 画
部 衣部
☒ 上下

衣 衣 衣 衣 衣 衣 衣

（醫） yī 医生、医疗、医学 *doctor*

☞ 上左下包围结构。矢的末笔改点。医的末笔是乚，不分为两笔。

✎ 7 画
部 匚部
☒ 半包围

医 医 医 医 医 医 医

yī 依傍、依靠、依顺、依据
depend on

✎ 8 画
部 亻部
☒ 左右

依 依 依 依 依 依 依 依

（儀） yí 仪式、仪表、仪器

✎ 5 画
部 亻部
☒ 左右

仪 仪 仪 仪 仪

suitable, appropriate
yí 适宜、适合、不宜

✎ 8 画
部 宀部
☒ 上下

宜 宜 宜 宜 宜 宜 宜 宜

one's mother's sister
yí 小姨子、姨妈、阿姨

☞ 女的横笔右端不出头。夷6画，第四画是乛，不分为两笔。

✎ 9 画
部 女部
☒ 左右

姨 姨 姨 姨 姨 姨 姨 姨

yí 移动、移风易俗

☞ 禾，中间一竖不带钩，末笔改点。两个夕写在一条中轴线上。

✎ 11 画
部 禾部
☒ 左右

移 移 移 移 移 移 移 移 移 移

（遺） yí 遗失、遗留、遗嘱
lose, omit, forget
leave behind

☞ 左下包围结构。贝的第二画𠃌不带钩。辶3画，第二画楷体是𠃋，宋体是𠃌。

✎ 12 画
部 辶部
☒ 半包围

遗 遗 遗 遗 遗 遗 遗 遗 遗 遗

yí 疑惑、猜疑、疑问 　☞ 左上是匕不是比。左下矢的末笔改点。

疑疑疑疑疑疑疑疑疑疑疑
✎ 14 画
⊞ 匕 部
◁ 左 右
疑疑疑

---

yǐ 甲乙丙丁、乙型肝炎　second

✎ 1 画
⊞ 一 部
◁ 独 体
乙

左中右结构的字，容易显得扁宽。写的时候，要力求三部分紧凑、内聚。

---

yǐ 大笑不已、已经　stop, cease, end

☞ 末笔竖弯钩跟第二画横相接，稍出头，注意跟己、巳的区别。

✎ 3 画
⊞ 己 部
◁ 独 体
已已已

---

yǐ 以理服人、以成绩分班、以利再战、以前

☞ 起笔是丨，不分为两笔。　use, take

✎ 4 画
⊞ 人 部
◁ 左 右
以以以以

西汉建平年间的《郫县碑》上就有简体字"万"，距今约有1900年了。

（蟻）yǐ 蚂蚁、蚁穴

✎ 9 画
⊞ 虫 部
◁ 左 右
蚁蚁蚁蚁蚁蚁蚁蚁蚁

---

yǐ 倚靠、倚仗、不偏不倚　lean on, rely, depend o

✎ 10 画
⊞ 亻 部
◁ 左 右
倚倚倚倚倚倚倚倚倚

---

yǐ 椅子、藤椅

☞ 木的中间一竖不带钩，末笔改点。

✎ 12 画
⊞ 木 部
◁ 左 右
椅椅椅椅椅椅椅椅椅椅椅

（億）yì 亿万人关注

✎ 3 画
⊞ 亻 部
◁ 左 右
亿亿亿

义 (義) justice, righteousness
yì 正义、情义、义诊、义子、义肢、含义
meaning, significance

✎ 3 画 部
☒ 独 体

 义 义 义

艺 (藝) skill
yì 技艺、艺坛

☞ 艹 3画，第三画楷体是撇，宋体是竖。

✎ 4 画 部
☒ 艹 上 下

 艺 艺 艺 艺

忆 (憶)
yì 回忆、忆旧

✎ 4 画 部
☒ 忄 左 右

 忆 忆 忆 忆

议 (議) opinion, view
yì 商议、评议、建议

☞ 讠 两画，第二画是乁，不分为两笔或三笔。

✎ 5 画 部
☒ 讠 左 右

 议 议 议 议 议

亦 also, too
yì 人云亦云
vice versa

✎ 6 画 部
☒ 亠 上 下

 亦 亦 亦 亦 亦 亦

异 different, unusual, strange
yì 异国、异议、异香、惊异

☞ 上部是巳，不是已或己。

✎ 6 画 部
☒ 巳 上 下

 异 异 异 异 异 异

役
yì 奴役、服役、杂役、战役

☞ 右上不是几，第二画不带钩。

✎ 7 画 部
☒ 彳 左 右

 役 役 役 役 役 役 役

译 (譯)
yì 翻译、破译、译文

☞ 讠 两画，第二画是乁，不分为两笔或三笔。右下是十不是丰。

✎ 7 画 部
☒ 讠 左 右

 译 译 译 译 译 译 译

yì 变易、交易、轻易、平易

上下之间没有横，注意跟昜的区别。不简化为昜。

8 画
日 部
上 下

易 易易易易易易易易

yì 疫病、防疫

上左包围结构。又上不是几，第二画不带钩。

9 画
疒 部
半包围

疫 疫疫疫疫疫疫疫疫疫

benefit, profit, advantage

yì 延年益寿、多多益善、利益、益虫

（1）两个八字背对背，中间一横分南北；端端坐在器皿上，能得好处不吃亏。
（2）古字形像水溢出容器，应是溢的本字。

字谜

10 画
皿 部
上 下

益 益益益益益益益益益

(誼) yì 情长谊深、联谊

讠两画，第二画是乚，不分为两笔或三笔。

10 画
讠 左 右 部

谊 谊谊谊谊谊谊谊谊谊

yì 民意、来意、意外 *meaning, idea have different views wish, desire*

心的第二画楷体是乀（卧钩），宋体是乚（竖弯钩）。

13 画
音 部
上 下

意 意意意意意意意意意意意

yì 毅力、刚毅 右上不是几，第二画不带钩。

15 画
殳 部
左 右

毅 毅毅毅毅毅毅毅毅毅毅 毅毅毅毅

yì 机翼、右翼 上部两个习的第一画都去钩。

17 画
羽 部
上 下

翼 翼翼翼翼翼翼翼翼翼翼翼翼 翼翼翼翼翼

yīn 因袭、因地制宜、因果、因故 *on the basis of, in light of, because of, a result of...*

全包围结构。框内大的末笔改点。

6 画
囗 部
包 围

因 因因因因因因

隐的右下是心，它的第二画楷体是 ㇃（卧钩），宋体是 ㇄（竖弯钩）。

(陰) yīn 阴天、背阴、阴沟、阴谋、阴文、阴魂、阴极

☞ 阝 两画，第一画是了，不分为两笔。

✎ 6 画
📖 阝 部
🔲 左 右

阴｜阴 阴 阴 阴 阴 阴

yīn 声音、双音节、音信

✎ 9 画
📖 音 部
🔲 上 下

音｜音 音 音 音 音 音 音 音 音

yīn 婚姻、姻亲

☞ 女的横笔右端不出头。因内的大末笔改点。

✎ 9 画
📖 女 部
🔲 左 右

姻｜姻 姻 姻 姻 姻 姻 姻 姻 姻

(銀) yín 银子、银行、银幕

☞ 钅5画，第二画是横，不是点；第五画是竖提，不分为两笔。

✎ 11 画
📖 钅部
🔲 左 右

银｜银 银 银 银 银 银 银 银 银 银 银

yǐn 引申、牵引、引航、引经据典

☞ 弓3画，第三画是㇉，不分为两笔。

✎ 4 画
📖 弓 部
🔲 左 右

引｜引 引 引 引

(飲) yǐn 饮水、独饮、饮恨、冷饮 / yìn 饮马

☞ 饣3画，第二画是㇆，不是点；第三画是㇟，不分为两笔。

✎ 7 画
📖 饣部
🔲 左 右

饮｜饮 饮 饮 饮 饮 饮 饮

(隱) yǐn 隐藏、隐瞒、隐私、难言之隐

☞ 阝 两画，第一画是了，不分为两笔。右部的中间是彐，第二画横的右端不出头。

✎ 11 画
📖 左阝 部
🔲 左 右

隐｜隐 隐 隐 隐 隐 隐 隐 隐 隐 隐

yìn 印章、印证、烙印、复印

☞ 左部是 𠂒 不是 𠃜。

✎ 5 画
📖 卩 部
🔲 左 右

印｜印 印 印 印 印

古字形像用手压人跪下，应是抑的本字。𐤇（金文）𐤄（甲文）

(應) yīng 应该、应允 / yìng 响应、应邀、得心应手、应付、应验

☞ 上左包围结构。

✎ 7 画　🀫 广部　◇ 半包围

应 应应应应应应应

---

yīng 英明、英杰、英镑

(first part...Brit(ain))

☞ 艹3画，第三画楷体是撇，宋体是竖。

✎ 8 画　🀫 艹部　◇ 上 下

英 英英英英英英英英

(櫻) yīng 樱花、樱桃　☞ 木的中间一竖不带钩，末笔改点。右上两个贝，它们的第二画乛都不带钩。

✎ 15 画　🀫 木部　◇ 左 右

樱樱樱樱樱樱樱
樱樱樱樱樱樱樱樱

(鷹) yīng 苍鹰　☞ 上左包围结构。框内上部是亻右隹，下部是鸟。

✎ 18 画　🀫 广部　◇ 半包围

鹰鹰鹰鹰鹰鹰鹰鹰鹰鹰鹰鹰
鹰鹰鹰鹰鹰鹰

---

yíng 迎接、迎头赶上

☞ 左下包围结构。右上是卬不是卯。辶 3画，第二画楷体是𠃌，宋体是乛。

✎ 7 画　🀫 辶部　◇ 半包围

迎 迎迎迎迎迎迎迎

---

yíng 喜盈门、盈余

☞ 乃两画，第一画乃不分为两笔。又的末笔改点。

✎ 9 画　🀫 皿部　◇ 上 下

盈 盈盈盈盈盈盈盈盈盈

(營) yíng 营地、营长、营建、营救

☞ 艹3画，第三画楷体是撇，宋体是竖。中部是一不是冖。

✎ 11 画　🀫 艹部　◇ 上 下

营 营营营营营营营营营营营

(蠅) yíng 苍蝇、蝇头小楷　☞ 右部上口下电。

✎ 14 画　🀫 虫部　◇ 左 右

蝇蝇蝇蝇蝇蝇蝇蝇蝇蝇
蝇蝇蝇

（赢） yíng 输赢、官司赢了　☞ 亡3画，第三画L不分为两笔。贝的第二画丁不带钩。

赢赢赢赢赢赢赢赢赢
赢赢赢赢赢赢赢赢

✎ 17 画
部 月 贝 凡
⿱ 上 下

影 yǐng 树影、倒影、摄影、电影　☞ 小的左侧楷体是点，宋体是撇。彡写在一条中轴线上。

影影影影影影影影影影影
影影影影

✎ 15 画
部 彡
⿰ 左 右

shadow, reflection, impressi...
photograph, picture.

汉字是"表意兼标音的文字"，
造字者可以从不同的角度去表
达字义。喝水的"bēizi"，"仓颉甲"
着眼于它是一种器皿，于是用
"皿"作形旁；"仓颉乙"着眼于它
当时使用的材料，于是用"木"作
形旁。汉字中充当标音符号的又
是现成的汉字，造字者也可以挑
选同音或近音的汉字来出任声旁。
　于是记录同一个语素"kù"（下
衣）的形声字，"仓颉甲"选用
了声旁"库"，"仓颉乙"选用了
声旁"夸"；再加上多数汉字是多
部件字，造字者又可以根据自己
的爱憎确定该字的结构方式。记
录家禽"é"的形声字，"仓颉甲"
组合成左"我"右"鸟"，"仓颉乙"
倒了个个儿，组合成左"鸟"右
"我"，"仓颉丙"又把"我"放到
"鸟"的上头，组成了上下结构。异
体纷呈是汉字字数众多的另一个
原因。

映 yìng 映入眼帘、上映

映映映映映
映映映映

✎ 9 画
部 日
⿰ 左 右

硬 yìng 坚硬、强硬、硬挺、过硬、僵硬

硬硬硬硬硬硬
硬硬硬硬硬硬

✎ 12 画
部 石
⿰ 左 右

（傭） yōng 雇佣、佣人 / yòng 佣金

佣佣佣佣
佣佣佣

✎ 7 画
部 亻
⿰ 左 右

（擁） yōng 拥抱、簇拥、拥挤、拥护

拥拥拥拥
拥拥拥拥

✎ 8 画
部 扌
⿰ 左 右

庸 yōng 平庸、庸医
☞ 上左包围结构。框内的上部不是彐，中间一横右端出头；下部用的起笔改竖。

庸庸庸庸庸庸庸庸庸庸

✎ 11 画
部 广
⿸ 半包围

永 yǒng 永久、永远
☞ 第二画是丁，第三画是㇇，都不分为两笔；第四画撇和第五画捺不连成一笔。

永永永永永

✎ 5 画
部 、
⿻ 独体

yǒng 歌咏、咏史

✎ 8 画
口部
左右

咏

咏咏咏咏
咏咏咏咏

yǒng 游泳、蝶泳

✎ 8 画
氵部
左右

泳

泳泳泳泳
泳泳泳泳

yǒng 勇敢、散兵游勇

☞ 用的起笔改竖，第二画丁不带钩。

✎ 9 画
力部
上下

勇

勇勇勇勇勇勇勇勇勇

yǒng 泪如泉涌、风起云涌

☞ 右下用的起笔改竖。

✎ 10 画
氵部
左右

涌

涌涌涌涌涌涌涌涌涌涌

yòng 用品、功用、费用

☞ 左上右包围结构。

✎ 5 画
门部
半包围

用

用用用用用

（優）yōu 优厚、拥军优属、优良

✎ 6 画
亻部
左右

优

优优优优优优

（憂）yōu 忧愁、为国分忧

✎ 7 画
忄部
左右

忧

忧忧忧忧忧忧忧

yōu 悠久、悠然、悠荡

☞ 右上是攵不是夂。丿、攵间有竖。心的第二画楷体是乀（卧钩），宋体是乚（竖弯钩）。

✎ 11 画
心部
上下

悠

悠悠悠悠悠悠悠悠悠悠

在废除的第二批简化字中，被批评得最尖锐的是"尸"（"展"）。批评者说，一看见这个字就恶心。上面陈列一具尸体（"尸"），下面还放了一块木板。难道"展览"就是"暴尸于市"吗？这种批评当然有点偏颇，他忘了"屋"也从"尸"，我们进屋难道是"尸体入室"吗？但由此可知，汉字字形有"表意"的传统，我们中国人有"见形"猜义"的习惯。在汉字字形上是万万大意不得的。

笔画数和笔画形状都相同，只因为笔画的组合形式不同就可以构成不同的字形，比如"八人入""刀力""田由甲申""工土干"。可见，笔画组合的形式在现代汉字中也是构成不同字形的重要手段。

yóu 尤其、怨天尤人

✎ 4　画
部 尤　部
六 独　体

尤　尤尤尤尤

yóu 由衷、由南到北、由此可见、理由、身不由己

✎ 5　画
部 丨　部
六 独　体

由　由由由由由

(郵) yóu 邮寄、邮局、集邮

☞ 阝 两画，第一画是了，不分为两笔。

✎ 7　画
部 阝　部
六 左　右

邮　邮邮邮邮邮邮邮

(猶) yóu 犹如、记忆犹新

✎ 7　画
部 犭　部
六 左　右

犹　犹犹犹犹犹犹犹

yóu 花生油、油漆家具、油腔滑调

✎ 8　画
部 氵　部
六 左　右

油　油油油油油油油油

yóu 游动、游逛、游戏、游泳、上游

☞ 子 3画，第一画㇇、第二画亅不连成一笔。

Suim, wonder about, tour travel

✎ 12　画
部 氵　部
六 左　右

游　游游游游游游游游游游

yǒu 朋友、友好、友邻

☞ 上左包围结构。

✎ 4　画
部 又　部
六 半包围

友　友友友友

yǒu 家里有人、有功、有人喜欢有人愁

☞ 上左包围结构。 *to have*

✎ 6　画
部 月　部
六 半包围

有　有有有有有有

yòu 一遍又一遍、纯而又纯、又黑又亮

✎ 2 画
📖 又 部
📐 独体

又 又

yòu 右边、右翼

👉 上左包围结构。

✎ 5 画
📖 口 部
📐 半包围

右 右 右 右 右

yòu 幼虫、老弱病残幼

✎ 5 画
📖 幺 部
📐 左右

幼 幼 幼 幼 幼

（誘）**yòu** 诱导、诱惑、诱因

👉 讠两画，第二画是乛，不分为两笔或三笔。

✎ 9 画
📖 讠 部
📐 左右

诱 诱 诱 诱 诱 诱 诱 诱 诱

yú 游离于两大集团之间、嫁祸于人、勇于助人、高于一切

✎ 3 画
📖 一 部
📐 独体

于 于 于

（餘）**yú** 余粮、业余、一百余人

👉 左上右包围结构。

✎ 7 画
📖 人 部
📐 半包围

余 余 余 余 余 余 余

（魚）**yú** 鲤鱼、金鱼、鱼尾

✎ 8 画
📖 鱼 部
📐 独体

鱼 鱼 鱼 鱼 鱼 鱼 鱼 鱼

古字形像鱼。 （金文）（甲文）

yú 娱乐、自娱

👉 女的横笔右端不出头。

✎ 10 画
📖 女 部
📐 左右

娱 娱 娱 娱 娱 娱 娱 娱 娱 娱

东汉著名书法家张芝刻苦练字。他把家里刚织好的白布，先用来练字，一直写到分不清黑白了，才拿去染颜色，做衣服。他就着池塘学习书法，一直练到池水变黑，所以后人把学习书法称为"临池"。张芝的草书尤其得到书法界的推崇，他被尊称为"草圣"。

愉、榆的月，起笔改竖。与、屿的与3画，第二画是乛，不分为两笔。

古字形像用手在水中抓鱼。
（金文）

（漁） yú 渔民、渔利

✎ 11 画
氵部
左右

渔 渔 渔 渔 渔 渔 渔 渔 渔 渔

yú 愉快、欢愉
☞ 右上人下有一横。

✎ 12 画
忄部
左右

愉 愉 愉 愉 愉 愉 愉 愉 愉 愉 愉

yú 榆树、榆钱
☞ 木的中间一竖不带钩，末笔改点。右上人下有一横。

✎ 13 画
木部
左右

榆 榆 榆 榆 榆 榆 榆 榆 榆 榆 榆

yú 愚蠢、愚民、愚见　☞ 禺的下部是内5画，不是内4画。心的第二画楷体是乀（卧钩），宋体是乚（竖弯钩）。

✎ 13 画
心部
上下

愚 愚 愚 愚 愚 愚 愚 愚 愚 愚 愚 愚

（與） yǔ 授与、老师与学生 / yù 参与

✎ 3 画
一部
独体

与 与 与

yǔ 免予处分、予以赞助
☞ 注意跟矛的区别。

✎ 4 画
一部
独体

予 予 予 予

（嶼） yǔ 岛屿
☞ 山，第二画是乚，不分为两笔，改为竖提。

✎ 6 画
山部
左右

屿 屿 屿 屿 屿 屿

yǔ 庙宇、宇宙、气宇轩昂

✎ 6 画
宀部
上下

宇 宇 宇 宇 宇 宇

唐代著名书法家张旭嗜好喝酒。每当喝得酩酊大醉的时候，他就一路狂走呼喊，然后拿笔就写。有的时候，干脆用长长的头发蘸饱墨水，用头疾书。酒醒以后，他看到自己的书法作品也连连称"神！"人称"张颠"。张旭的草书、李白的诗歌和裴旻（mín）的剑舞，被当时人并称为"三绝"。

yǔ 羽毛、羽扇

6 画
羽 部
左 右

古字形像羽毛。

（甲文）

羽 羽 羽 羽 羽 羽 羽

yǔ 倾盆大雨、雨季

8 画
雨 部
独 体

雨 雨 雨 雨 雨 雨 雨 雨

（語）yǔ 自言自语、外语、旗语

讠 两画，第二画是乛，不分为两笔或三笔。

9 画
讠 部
左 右

语 语 语 语 语 语 语 语

yù 玉雕、亭亭玉立、玉照

5 画
王 部
独 体

1988 年由国家语言文字工作委员会和中华人民共和国新闻出版署联合发布的《现代汉语通用字表》共收录7000字，其中包括了《现代汉语常用字表》收录的3500字。

玉 玉 玉 玉 玉

yù 生育、养儿育女、封山育林、体育

月的起笔改竖。

8 画
月 部
上 下

育 育 育 育 育 育 育 育

（獄）yù 冤狱、监狱

讠 两画，第二画是乛，不分为两笔。

9 画
犭 部
左 右

狱 狱 狱 狱 狱 狱 狱 狱

yù 洗浴、浴血奋战

10 画
氵 部
左 右

浴 浴 浴 浴 浴 浴 浴 浴 浴 浴

（預）yù 预料、干预

左部是予不是矛。

10 画
页 部
左 右

预 预 预 预 预 预 预 预 预 预

yù 地域、流域

☞ 土的末笔改提。

✎ 11 画
部 土
四 左 右

域 域 域 域 域 域 域 域 域 域 域 域

yù 畅所欲言、食欲、摇摇欲坠

☞ 谷的第四画改点。

✎ 11 画
部 谷
四 左 右

欲 欲 欲 欲 欲 欲 欲 欲 欲 欲 欲 欲

yù 遭遇、待遇、机遇　☞ 左下包围结构。禺的下部是冂5画，不是冂4画。辶3画，第二画楷体是ㄟ，宋体是ㄟ。

✎ 12 画
部 辶
四 半包围

遇 遇 遇 遇 遇 遇 遇 遇 遇 遇 遇 遇

(＊禦) yù 驾御、＊抵御、御医

☞ 中部上午下止，止的末笔改提。右部是卩不是阝。

✎ 12 画
部 彳
四 左 右

古字形像人执鞭驾御车马。

御（金文）　㣲（甲文）

御 御 御 御 御 御 御 御 御 御 御 御

yù 富裕、宽裕

☞ 左部是衤不是礻。

✎ 12 画
部 衤
四 左 右

裕 裕 裕 裕 裕 裕 裕 裕 裕 裕 裕 裕

yù 痊愈、愈合、愈益

☞ 月的起笔改竖。心的第二画楷体是ㄥ(卧钩)，宋体是乚(竖弯钩)。

✎ 13 画
部 心
四 上 下

愈 愈 愈 愈 愈 愈 愈 愈 愈 愈 愈 愈

(譽) yù 赞誉、信誉

☞ 左上右包围结构。上部是龸不是龷。

✎ 13 画
部 言
四 半包围

誉 誉 誉 誉 誉 誉 誉 誉 誉 誉 誉 誉 誉

冤

yuān 冤枉、冤家、冤大头

☞ 上部是冖不是宀。下部是兔不是免，它的第六画从扁框中直接撇下，不分为两笔。

✎ 10 画
部 冖
四 上 下

冤 冤 冤 冤 冤 冤 冤 冤 冤 冤

yuán 元帅、元旦、元素

✎ 4 画
⬚ 元部
⊠ 独体

元 元元元元

古字形像人形，突出头部，表示人头的本义。

（金文）　（甲文）

（園）yuán 果园、公园

⬚ 全包围结构。

✎ 7 画
⬚ 囗部围
⊠ 包

园 园园园园园园园

（員）yuán 职员、会员

⬚ 贝的第二画丁不带钩。

✎ 7 画
⬚ 口部下
⊠ 上

员 员员员员员员员

---

yuán 原始、原料、原意、原谅、平原

⬚ 上左包围结构。

✎ 10 画
⬚ 厂部围
⊠ 半包

原 原原原原原原原原原

（圆）yuán 圆周、圆桌、圆满、圆场、银圆

⬚ 全包围结构。贝的第二画丁不带钩。

round, circular, spherical, tactful satisfactory

✎ 10 画
⬚ 囗部围
⊠ 包

圆 圆圆圆圆圆圆圆圆圆圆

---

yuán 攀援、援用、救援

⬚ 右下是横下方。

✎ 12 画
⬚ 扌部右
⊠ 左

援 援援援援援援援援援援

（緣）yuán 缘故、缘分

⬚ 纟3画，上部不是幺。左上是彑不是彐。

✎ 12 画
⬚ 纟部右
⊠ 左

缘 缘缘缘缘缘缘缘缘缘缘

---

yuán 源头、财源

✎ 13 画
⬚ 氵部右
⊠ 左

源 源源源源源源源源源源源

怨、愿的心，第二画楷体是 ∖(卧钩)，宋体是 乚(竖弯钩)。

(遠) yuǎn 遥远、疏远

左下包围结构。辶 3画，第二画楷体是 乁，宋体是 乁。

7 画
辶 部
半包围

远 远远远远远远远

---

yuàn 怨恨、任劳任怨

右上是巳，不是已、已或己。心的第二画楷体是 ∖(卧钩)，宋体是 乚(竖弯钩)。

9 画
心 部
上 下

怨 怨怨怨怨怨怨怨怨

---

yuàn 四合院、庭院、法院、医院

9 画
阝 部
左 右

院 院院院院院院院院院

(願) yuàn 愿望、情愿、许愿 上左包围结构。

14 画
厂 部
半包围

愿 愿愿愿愿愿愿
愿愿愿愿愿愿愿

(約) yuē 约束、预约、条约、节约 / yāo 约约有多少斤

纟 3画，上部不是幺。

6 画
纟 部
左 右

约 约约约约约约

---

yuè 月亮、月份、月刊、月饼

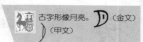

古字形像月亮。(金文) (甲文)

4 画
月 部
独 体

月 月月月月

(閱) yuè 阅兵、阅览、阅历

左上右包围结构。起笔，嵌在第二笔 丨和第三笔 ㇆ 之间。

10 画
门 部
半包围

阅 阅阅阅阅阅阅阅阅阅

---

yuè 喜悦、悦耳

10 画
忄 部
左 右

悦 悦悦悦悦悦悦悦悦悦悦

(躍) yuè 跃进、跳跃
☞ 左上止的末笔改捺。右部是夭不是天。
11画 足部 左右
跃 跃跃跃跃跃跃跃跃跃跃跃

yuè 跨越、越级、优越、越游越快
☞ 左下包围结构。戉的起笔是横。
12画 走部 半包围
越 越越越越越越越越越越

(*雲) yún *白云、人云亦云
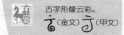
古字形像云彩。
4画 厶部 上下
云 云云云云

yún 均匀、匀出半天时间
☞ 上右包围结构。
4画 勹部 半包围
匀 匀匀匀匀

广泛使用电脑写字以后，错字少了，别字多了。用拼音输入，应特别注意误用同音字；用形码输入，要注意区分有一个或两三个部件相同的字。电脑要靠人脑指挥。不学会规范写字、正确用字，用电脑写出来的文章也容易别字连篇。电脑写出来的字再整齐，也不是富有个性的书法作品。无论日常书写还是书法艺术，都要求使用者先学会写字。电脑的广泛使用并不意味着人们可以不学习写字。

yǔn 允许、公允
4画 厶部 上下
允 允允允允

yùn 孕育、怀孕
☞ 乃两画，起笔是𠃌，不分为两笔。
5画 子部 上下
孕 孕孕孕孕孕

(運) yùn 运动、运输、运用、命运
☞ 左下包围结构。辶3画，第二画楷体是𠃌，宋体是乛。
7画 辶部 半包围
运 运运运运运运运

(暈) yùn 月晕、晕车 / yūn 头晕、晕倒
☞ 车4画，第二画是乚，不分为两笔。
10画 日部 上下
晕 晕晕晕晕晕晕晕晕晕晕

yùn 韵母、押韵、韵味

✎ 13 画
音 部
左 右

韵 韵韵韵韵韵韵韵韵韵韵韵韵

（雜） **zá** 杂乱、混杂、学杂费

☞ 下部是木，不写成朩。

✎ 6 画
木 部
上 下

杂 杂杂杂杂杂杂

笔画形状有时要受到左右邻笔笔形的制约。为了保持全字的紧凑匀称，有的笔画在特定场合要改变形状，如"车"作左偏旁时，末笔横要改为提。

---

zāi 灾难、招灾惹祸

✎ 7 画
宀 部
上 下

灾 灾灾灾灾灾灾灾

---

zāi 栽培、栽赃、栽跟斗

☞ 上右包围结构。木的中间一竖不带钩，末笔改点。

✎ 10 画
木 部
半包围

栽 栽栽栽栽栽栽栽栽栽栽

---

zǎi 屠宰、宰相、主宰

☞ 下部是辛不是幸。

✎ 10 画
宀 部
上 下

宰 宰宰宰宰宰宰宰宰宰宰

---

zài 一改再改、再见

☞ 第三个横笔左右都出头。

✎ 6 画
一 部
独 体

再 再再再再再再

孔尚任的《桃花扇》，全书80121字，只用了3315个不同的汉字。

---

zài 存在、在岗、事在人为、他在加班

☞ 上左包围结构。

✎ 6 画
土 部
半包围

在 在在在在在在

to exist.
to be at, in or on a place

（載） **zài** 装载、怨声载道、载歌载舞 / **zǎi** 千载难逢、转载

☞ 上右包围结构。车的下边一横改提，笔顺改先竖后提。

✎ 10 画
车 部
半包围

载 载载载载载载载载载载

zán 咱俩、咱懂

✎ 9 画
▣ 口 部
△ 左 右

咱 咱咱咱咱咱咱咱咱咱

（暫）zàn 暂时、暂缓

☞ 车的下边一横改提，笔顺改先竖后提。

✎ 12 画
▣ 日 部
△ 上 下

暂 暂暂暂暂暂暂暂暂暂暂暂暂

（贊）zàn 赞成、称赞　　☞ 左上先的末笔改竖提。贝的第二画㇉不带钩。

✎ 16 画
▣ 贝 部
△ 上 下

赞 赞赞赞赞赞赞赞
赞赞赞赞赞赞赞赞

（臟*髒）zàng 五脏六腑、肾脏／zāng*小脸脏了

☞ 右部是庄不是压。

✎ 10 画
▣ 月 部
△ 左 右

脏 脏脏脏脏脏脏脏脏脏脏

---

zàng 埋葬、火葬、葬送

☞ 艹 3画，第三画楷体是撇，宋体是竖。死的右下是匕，不是匕。

✎ 12 画
▣ 艹 部
△ 上 下

葬 葬葬葬葬葬葬葬葬葬葬葬

---

zāo 遭遇、一遭生两遭熟　　☞ 左下包围结构。辶 3画，第二画楷体是㇍，宋体是㇄。

✎ 14 画
▣ 辶 部
△ 半包围

遭 遭遭遭遭遭遭遭遭遭
遭遭遭

---

zāo 酒糟、糟蛋、梁木糟了、一团糟　　☞ 米，中间一竖不带钩，末笔改点。

✎ 17 画
▣ 米 部
△ 左 右

糟 糟糟糟糟糟糟糟糟糟糟糟
糟糟糟糟糟

---

zǎo 早市、早春、三年早知道、您早

✎ 6 画
▣ 日 部
△ 上 下

早 早早早早早早

澡、燥、躁右下的木，中间一竖不带钩。

（棗） zǎo 甜枣

☞ 左上右包围结构。上部是朿不是束，中间一竖不带钩。

❂ 8 画
囗 一 部
囚 半 包围

枣 枣 枣 枣 枣 枣 枣 枣 枣

zǎo 洗澡、搓澡

澡 澡 澡 澡 澡 澡 澡 澡
澡 澡 澡 澡 澡 澡 澡 澡

❂ 16 画
囗 氵部
囚 左 右

zào 青红皂白、香皂

皂 皂 皂 皂
皂 皂 皂

❂ 7 画
囗 白 部
囚 上 下

（竈） zào 炉灶、亲自下灶

☞ 火的末笔改点。

❂ 7 画
囗 火部
囚 左 右

灶 灶 灶 灶 灶 灶 灶

zào 制造、捏造、造访、深造　☞ 左下包围结构。右上的牛竖笔下端不出头。辶 3 画，第二画楷体是乛，宋体是乁。

❂ 10 画
囗 辶 部
囚 半包围

造 造 造 造 造 造 造 造 造 造

zào 干燥、燥热　☞ 火的末笔改点。

燥 燥 燥 燥 燥 燥 燥 燥 燥 燥
燥 燥 燥 燥 燥 燥 燥

❂ 17 画
囗 火 部
囚 左 右

zào 急躁、戒骄戒躁　☞ 左下足的末笔改提。

躁 躁 躁 躁 躁 躁 躁 躁 躁 躁 躁 躁
躁 躁 躁 躁 躁 躁 躁 躁

❂ 20 画
囗 足部
囚 左 右

（則） zé 规则、以身作则、穷则思变

☞ 贝的第二画乛不带钩。

❂ 6 画
囗 贝 部
囚 左 右

则 则 则 则 则 则

魏晋著名书法家钟繇，被称为"楷书之祖"。他"精思学书三十年"，"若与人居，画地广数步"，晚上在被窝里练指法，常常把被子的衬里划破了。上厕所时也念念不忘练写字，以致长时间蹲在茅坑忘了回家。看见万事万物，他都要描摹事物的形象。

古字形像用刀在鼎上刻写。𩇓（金文）

（責） zé 责成、斥责、负责

☞ 贝的第二画 ㄱ 不带钩。

✎ 8 画　部 贝　框 上下

责 责责责责责责责责

（擇） zé 选择、不择手段 / zhái 择菜

✎ 8 画　部 扌　框 左右

择 择择择择择择择择

> 包围结构的字，如果是上左下包围的，被包围部件要居于字框当中，但字框的末横要略长，托得稳重，如"匡、匠、匮"等。

（澤） zé 沼泽、润泽、光泽

✎ 8 画　部 氵　框 左右

泽 泽泽泽泽泽泽泽泽

（賊） zéi 盗贼、奸贼、贼头贼脑

☞ 贝的第二画 ㄱ 不带钩。右部是戎不是戒。

✎ 10 画　部 贝　框 左右

贼 贼贼贼贼贼贼贼贼贼贼

---

zěn 怎么、怎样

☞ 心的第二画楷体是㇃（卧钩），宋体是㇁（竖弯钩）。

1st pt.　zěn me
怎么

✎ 9 画　部 心　框 上下

怎 怎怎怎怎怎怎怎怎怎

---

zēng 曾祖父 / céng 曾经

> 字谜
> （1）两个日字真梯奇，一个横躺一个立；横日偏爱倒八字，上下两个紧相依。
> （2）古字形像蒸饭用的炊具，应是甑的本字。

✎ 12 画　部 八　框 上下

曾 曾曾曾曾曾曾曾曾曾曾曾曾

---

zēng 增加、增产　☞ 土的末笔改提。

增增增增增增增
增增增增增增增增

✎ 15 画　部 土　框 左右

增

（贈） zèng 赠送、捐赠　☞ 贝的第二画 ㄱ 不带钩。

赠赠赠赠赠赠赠赠赠赠赠赠
赠赠赠赠

✎ 16 画　部 贝　框 左右

赠

zhā 扎针、扎猛子、驻扎 / zhá 挣扎 / zā 捆扎

✎ 4　画
部首 扌部
结构 左　右

扎　扎扎扎扎

---

zhā 豆腐渣、馒头渣儿

☞ 木的中间一竖不带钩。

✎ 12　画
部首 氵部
结构 左　右

渣　渣渣渣渣渣渣渣渣渣渣渣渣

（閘）zhá 水闸、闸住洪水、刹闸

☞ 左上右包围结构。起笔丶嵌在第二笔丨和第三笔 ㇆ 之间。

✎ 8　画
部首 门部
结构 半包围

闸　闸闸闸闸闸闸闸闸

---

zhǎ 一眨眼的工夫、眨眼皮

☞ 乏 3 画，第二画 ㇇ 不分为两笔。

✎ 9　画
部首 目部
结构 左　右

眨　眨眨眨眨眨眨眨眨眨

---

zhà 爆炸、轰炸 / zhá 炸鱼

☞ 火的末笔改点。

✎ 9　画
部首 火部
结构 左　右

炸　炸炸炸炸炸炸炸炸炸

---

zhà 榨油、榨甘蔗、油榨　☞ 木的中间一竖不带钩，末笔改点。

✎ 14　画
部首 木部
结构 左　右

榨榨榨榨榨榨榨榨榨榨榨
榨榨榨

---

zhāi 采摘、摘要、指摘　☞ 右部是商不是商，框内是古。

✎ 14　画
部首 扌部
结构 左　右

摘摘摘摘
摘摘摘摘摘摘摘摘摘摘

---

zhái 住宅、宅院

✎ 6　画
部首 宀部
结构 上　下

宅　宅宅宅宅宅宅

zhǎi 狭窄、心胸窄

✎ 10 画
⌨ 穴 部
⊠ 上 下

窄 窄窄窄窄窄窄窄窄窄窄

(債) zhài 欠债、还债、血债

☞ 贝的第二画㇆不带钩。

✎ 10 画
⌨ 亻 部
⊠ 左 右

债 债债债债债债债债债债

---

zhài 安营扎寨、村寨   ☞ 下部是木，不写成水。

✎ 14 画
⌨ 宀 部
⊠ 上 下

寨寨寨寨寨寨寨
寨寨寨寨寨寨寨

其实有史以来中国字是一直总在简化着呐，只是有时快有时慢就是了。碰巧现在这时候有很多的大批的简化提议就是了。——赵元任《通字方案》

---

zhān 占卜 / zhàn 占领、占地、占上风

✎ 5 画
⌨ 卜 部
⊠ 上 下

占 占占占占占

---

zhān 沾湿、沾光、沾染

✎ 8 画
⌨ 氵 部
⊠ 左 右

沾 沾沾沾沾沾沾沾沾

---

zhān 粘连、粘贴

☞ 米，中间一竖不带钩，末笔改点。

✎ 11 画
⌨ 米 部
⊠ 左 右

粘 粘粘粘粘粘粘粘粘粘粘

(斬) zhǎn 斩首、快刀斩乱麻

☞ 车的下边一横改提，笔顺改先竖后提。

✎ 8 画
⌨ 车 部
⊠ 左 右

斩 斩斩斩斩斩斩斩斩

(盞) zhǎn 酒盏、一盏灯

☞ 戋 5 画，斜钩上是两横一撇，不是三横一撇。

✎ 10 画
⌨ 皿 部
⊠ 上 下

盏 盏盏盏盏盏盏盏盏盏盏

张、涨的弓 3 画，第三画 ㇖不分为两笔。

zhǎn 展开、扩展、文物展、大展宏图

☞ 上左包围结构。右下是㐄不是㐆。

✎ 10 画
部 尸部
囗 半包围

展 展展展展展展展展展展

（嶄）zhǎn 崭露头角、崭新

☞ 山 3 画，第二画㇄不分为两笔。车的下边一横改提，笔顺改为先竖后提。

✎ 11 画
部 山部
囗 上下

崭 崭崭崭崭崭崭崭崭崭崭崭

（戰）zhàn 战争、论战、战栗

✎ 9 画
部 戈部
囗 左右

战 战战战战战战战战战

zhàn 站立、站住、汽车站、保健站

☞ 立的末笔改提。

✎ 10 画
部 立部
囗 左右

站 站站站站站站站站站

（張）zhāng 张口、扩张、张灯结彩、张望

☞ 长 4 画，第三画㇄贯穿上下，不分为两笔；末笔捺上无撇。

measure word for paper, pnap, bed etc

✎ 7 画
部 弓部
囗 左右

张 张张张张张张张

zhāng 规章、章节、杂乱无章、肩章、印章

✎ 11 画
部 音部
囗 上下

章 章章章章章章章章章章

（漲）zhǎng 河水暴涨、物价飞涨

☞ 长 4 画，第三画㇄贯穿上下，不分为两笔；末笔捺上无撇。

✎ 10 画
部 氵部
囗 左右

涨 涨涨涨涨涨涨涨涨涨

zhǎng 鼓掌、掌旗、掌权、脚掌、马掌

☞ 上部是⺌不是⺍。

✎ 12 画
部 小部
囗 上下

掌 掌掌掌掌掌掌掌掌掌掌掌

zhàng　10 尺等于 1 丈、丈量、丈夫、老丈

✎ 3 画
□ 一 独体
⼋
丈丈丈

zhàng　明火执仗、依仗、败仗

✎ 5 画
□ 亻 部
⼋ 左 右
仗仗仗仗仗

（帐）zhàng　蚊帐、帐篷

✎ 7 画
□ 巾 部
⼋ 左 右
帐帐帐帐
帐帐帐

（胀）zhàng　膨胀、头昏脑胀

✎ 8 画
□ 月 部
⼋ 左 右
胀胀胀胀胀胀胀胀

障

zhàng　障碍、屏障

☞ 阝 两画，第一画 了 不分为两笔。

✎ 13 画
□ 左 阝 部
⼋ 左 右
障障障障障障障障障障障障

招

zhāo　招手、招生、招惹、招供、花招

✎ 8 画
□ 扌 部
⼋ 左
招招招招招招招招

爪

zhǎo 张牙舞爪 / zhuǎ 鸡爪子

✎ 4 画
□ 爪 部
⼋ 独体
爪爪爪爪

找

zhǎo　找材料、找零钱

☞ 左部是 扌 不是禾，右部是戈。

✎ 7 画
□ 扌 部
⼋ 左 右
找找找找找找找

1980 年 5 月 20 日，中国文字改革委员会原则通过了王力、叶籁士、倪海曙、周有光四位委员提出的《关于研究和制订标准现代汉字表的建议》和《制订标准现代汉字表的科研计划（草案）》。这份《建议》和《计划》的目标是，对于“五四”以来的现代汉语用字进行全面的、系统的、科学的整理，做到“字有定量、字有定形、字有定音、字有定序”，为今后我国的语文教学、出版印刷、新闻通讯、各种文字机器和电子计算机中文信息处理等，提供用字的规范。

古字形像指爪。 ✍(甲文) 爪(小篆)

zhào 号召、召唤、召开

✎ 5 画
部 刀 上 下

召 召召召召召

zhào 征兆、瑞雪兆丰年

✎ 6 画
部 丿 左 右

兆 兆兆兆兆兆兆兆

1956年，国务院全体会议讨论简化字。会议由周恩来总理亲自主持。讨论到"葉"简作"叶"时，赞成和反对的意见相持不下。周恩来问对面的外贸部长叶季壮："你姓叶的有什么意见？"叶说："我赞成以'叶'代'葉'，写起来省事。"周总理环顾一下四周，说："哦，你们看姓叶的都同意了，我看就通过吧。"

（趙）zhào 姓赵

☞ 左下包围结构。

✎ 9 画
部 走 半包围

赵 赵赵赵赵赵赵赵赵赵

zhào 照射、照镜子、对照、照顾、照相、护照、照章办事

☞ 灬托住全字。

✎ 13 画
部 灬 上 下

照 照照照照照照照照照照照照照

zhào 口罩、笼罩

☞ 上部是横"目"，不写成四。

✎ 13 画
部 罒 上 下

罩 罩罩罩罩罩罩罩罩罩罩罩罩

zhē 云遮月、遮掩　☞ 左下包围结构。辶3画，第二画楷体是乛，宋体是乚。

✎ 14 画
部 辶 半包围

遮 遮遮遮遮遮遮遮遮
遮遮遮遮遮遮遮

古字形像用斧子割草。

𣂟（金文）　𣂆（甲文）

zhé 骨折、挫折、转折、*存折、折价/shé 棍折了、折本/zhē 折跟斗

✎ 7 画
部 扌 左 右

折 折折折折折折折

zhé 哲学、哲人

✎ 10 画
部 口 上 下

哲 哲哲哲哲哲哲哲哲哲

贞、侦的贝，第二画是 ７，不带钩。

者 zhě 读者、作者、参与者
　　上左包围结构。
　8 画　部 耂
　半包围
 者 者 者 者 者 者 者 者

（這）这 zhè 这个、这些、我这就出发　　This
　　左下包围结构。文的末笔改点。辶 3画，第二画楷体是 ㇋，宋体是 ㇇。
　7 画　部 辶
　半包围
 这 这 这 这 这 这 这 这

浙 zhè 江浙是富庶之区
　10 画　部 氵
　左 右
 浙 浙 浙 浙 浙 浙 浙 浙 浙

（貞）贞 zhēn 坚贞不屈
　6 画　部 卜
　上 下
 贞 贞 贞 贞 贞 贞

1988年由中华人民共和国教育委员会和国家语言文字工作委员会联合发布的《现代汉语常用字表》选收了2500个常用字、1000个次常用字，共3500字。

（針）针 zhēn 银针、扎针、时针、针筒
　　钅5画，第二画是横，不是点；第五画是竖提，不分为两笔。
　7 画　部 钅
　左 右
 针 针 针 针 针 针 针

（偵）侦 zhēn 侦察、侦破
　8 画　部 亻
　左 右
 侦 侦 侦 侦 侦 侦 侦 侦

珍 zhēn 珍宝、珍贵、珍惜
　　王的末笔改提。彡写在一条中轴线上。
　9 画　部 王
　左 右
 珍 珍 珍 珍 珍 珍 珍 珍 珍

真 zhēn 真人真事、真切、真美、传真
　　框内是三横，不是两横。
　10 画　部 十
　上 下
真 真 真 真 真 真 真 真 真

(診) zhěn 诊断、诊所

讠 两画，第二画是乀，不分为两笔或三笔。

7 画
讠部
左右

诊 诊诊诊诊诊诊诊

分布原则是选取常用字的一条重要原则。"分布"就是一个字在各组语言材料中出现的次数。甲字只在一组语言材料中出现，而乙字在多组语言材料中出现，乙字的分布率就大于甲字。

zhěn 枕头、枕着胳膊睡

木的中间一竖不带钩，末笔改点。

8 画
木部
左右

枕 枕枕枕枕枕枕枕枕

(陣) zhèn 阵容、上阵、一阵子

阝 两画，第一画乛不分为两笔。

6 画
左阝部
右

阵 阵阵阵阵阵阵

zhèn 振翅、振奋

10 画
扌部
左右

振 振振振振振振振振

zhèn 地震、抗震、震惊 雨，第二画改点，第三画改横钩，里边楷体是四点，宋体是四横。

15 画
雨部
上下

震 震震震震震震震
震震震震震震震震

(鎮) zhèn 镇压、镇静、镇守、乡镇、冰镇 钅5画，第二画是横，不是点；第五画是竖提，不分为两笔。

15 画
钅部
左右

镇 镇镇镇镇镇镇镇
镇镇镇镇镇镇镇镇

zhēng 争夺、战争、争吵

中部不是彐，中间一横右端出头。

6 画
刀部
上下

争 争争争争争争

天津："张力""张英""张健"各有2000多个。广州："梁妹""陈妹"各有2400多个。沈阳："王玉兰""刘淑珍"各有4000多个。邮递、储蓄、档案、医疗、寻访，都发生混乱。人称"信息污染"。

(*徵) zhēng 远征、征发、*征兵、*征文、*象征

8 画
彳部
左右

征 征征征征征征征征

睁、筝的争，中部不是彐，中间一横右端出头。

zhēng 睁一眼闭一眼

✎ 11 画
⌗ 目部
⼌ 左　右

睁 睁睁睁睁睁睁睁睁睁睁

zhēng 古筝、风筝

✎ 12 画
⌗ 竹部
⼌ 上　下

筝 筝筝筝筝筝筝筝筝筝筝

zhēng 蒸气、蒸饭

✎ 13 画
⌗ 艹部
⼌ 上　下

☞ 艹+3画，第三画楷体是撇，宋体是竖。

蒸 蒸蒸蒸蒸蒸蒸蒸蒸蒸蒸蒸蒸

zhēng 整齐、整队、整修、整人、完整

☞ 左上是束，中间一竖不带钩，末笔改点。右上是攵不是夊。

✎ 16 画
⌗ 攵部
⼌ 上　下

整 整整整整整整整整整整整整整整整整

zhèng 正中间、正规、正直、正音 / zhēng 正月

✎ 5 画
⌗ 止部
⼌ 独体

正 正正正正正

（證）zhèng 证明、工作证

☞ 讠两画，第二画乛不分为两笔或三笔。

✎ 7 画
⌗ 讠部
⼌ 左　右

证 证证证证证证证

（鄭）zhèng 郑重、姓郑

☞ 关的末笔改点。阝两画，第一画是了，不分为两笔。

✎ 8 画
⌗ 右阝部
⼌ 左　右

郑 郑郑郑郑郑郑郑郑

zhèng 政府、财政

☞ 正的末笔改提。右边是攵不是夊。

✎ 9 画
⌗ 攵部
⼌ 左　右

政 政政政政政政政政

zhèng 挣脱、挣钱 / zhēng 挣扎

☞ 争的中部不是ヨ，中间一横右端出头。

✎ 9 画
部 扌部
⊠ 左 右

挣　挣挣挣挣挣挣挣挣

(*癥) zhèng 炎症 / zhēng *症结

☞ 上左包围结构。

✎ 10 画
部 疒部
⊠ 半包围

症　症症症症症症症症症

---

a welcome opportunity

zhī 置之不理、光荣之家、总之、十分之一

之后 zhīhòu afterwards

✎ 3 画
部 丶部
⊠ 独体

之　之之之

---

prop up; support

zhī 支架、支持、支农、支流、支配、开支、地支

✎ 4 画
部 支
⊠ 上 下

支　支支支支

古字形像手拿一根小草。（金文）

---

zhī 果汁、汁液 *juice*

✎ 5 画
部 氵部
⊠ 左 右

汁　汁汁汁汁汁

学书必须模仿。不得古人形质，无自得性情也。（学写字、学书法，开始阶段必须模仿前人的字。如果连前人写的字的形态都没学到，就不可能学到前人字中表达出来的精气神。）——康有为《广艺舟双楫》

---

zhī 芝麻、灵芝

☞ 艹 3画，第三画楷体是撇，宋体是竖。

✎ 6 画
部 艹部
⊠ 上 下

芝　芝芝芝芝芝芝

---

zhī 树枝、枝繁叶茂

☞ 木的中间一竖不带钩，末笔改点。

✎ 8 画
部 木部
⊠ 左 右

枝　枝枝枝枝枝枝枝枝

---

zhī 求知、熟知、通知

☞ 矢的末笔改点。

to know, be aware of

✎ 8 画
部 矢部
⊠ 左 右

知　知知知知知知知知

zhī 四肢、下肢

✎ 8 画
部 月 部
⊠ 左 右

肢 肢肢肢肢肢肢肢肢

（織）zhī 男耕女织、编织

☞ 纟3画，上边不是幺。

✎ 8 画
部 纟 部
⊠ 左 右

织 织织织织织织织织

weave, knit, spin

---

zhī 脂肪、脂粉 *fat, grease*

☞ 右上是匕不是匕。

✎ 10 画
部 月 部
⊠ 左 右

脂 脂脂脂脂脂脂脂脂脂

---

zhī 蜘蛛 ☞ 矢的末笔改点。

✎ 14 画
部 虫 部
⊠ 左 右

蜘 蜘蜘蜘蜘蜘蜘蜘
蜘蜘蜘蜘蜘蜘蜘

（執）zhí 执笔、执政、执法、固执

✎ 6 画
部 扌 部
⊠ 左

执 执执执执执执

古字形像人的双手被戴上木制
手铐。（金文）（甲文）

---

zhí 直线、伸直、耿直、直爽、直达

straight, straight line

✎ 8 画
部 十
⊠ 十 上 部 下

直 直直直直直直直直

---

zhí 侄子

✎ 8 画
部 亻 部
⊠ 左 右

侄 侄侄侄侄侄侄侄侄

---

zhí 正值、轮值、价值、值得、比值 *value, cost*

✎ 10 画
部 亻 部
⊠ 左 右

值 值值值值值值值值值

植、殖的直，框内是三横，不是两横。

(職) zhí 职务、职位、职责

☞ 耳的末笔改提。

✎ 11 画
▣ 耳部
◹ 左右

职职职职职职职职职职职

---

zhí 植树、培植、植皮、植株

☞ 木的中间一竖不带钩，末笔改点。

✎ 12 画
▣ 木部
◹ 左右

植植植植植植植植植植植

---

zhí 繁殖 / shi 骨殖

✎ 12 画
▣ 歹部
◹ 左右

殖殖殖殖殖殖殖殖殖殖殖

---

zhǐ 终止、止痛

✎ 4 画
▣ 止部
◹ 独体

止止止止

古字形像足趾所止。
（金文） （甲文）

(祇*隻) zhī 只有、只能 / zhǐ *只身、*只言片语

only, merely

✎ 5 画
▣ 口部
◹ 上下

只只只只只

常识原则也是**选取常用字**的一条重要原则。这一原则是为了弥补统计原则的不足而确定的。有些字虽然在现代汉语书面语中出现的机会不多，但它记录的语词确实是日常生活中不可或缺的，如"厕"，如果单纯根据统计数字把它排除在常用字之外，实在是违背常理。有了常识原则，就可以保证把这类字列入常用字的行列。

---

zhǐ 旨意、圣旨

☞ 上部是匕不是七。

✎ 6 画
▣ 匕部
◹ 上下

旨旨旨旨旨旨

---

zhǐ 地址、遗址

☞ 土的末笔改提。

✎ 7 画
▣ 土部
◹ 左右

址址址址址址址

(紙) zhǐ 纸张、报纸

☞ 纟3画，上边不是幺。右部是氏不是氐。

✎ 7 画
▣ 纟部
◹ 左右

纸纸纸纸纸纸纸

lastpart of napkin: 餐 巾 纸 cān-jīn-zhǐ

zhǐ 手指、指南针、指示、指控、指望

☞ 右上是匕不是匕。

✎ 9 画
🈶 扌部
𝄂 左 右

指 指指指指指指指指指

zhì 无微不至、至宝、至少

古字形用箭矢和一横表示
箭射到地面或目标。

⚓（金文） ⚓（甲文）

✎ 6 画
🈶 至部
𝄂 上 下

至 至至至至至至

zhì 志愿、永志不忘、杂志、标志

☞ 上部是士不是土。心的第二画楷体是㇃(卧钩)，宋体是㇂(竖弯钩)。

✎ 7 画
🈶 土部
𝄂 上 下

志 志志志志志志志

（幟）zhì 旗帜

✎ 8 画
🈶 巾部
𝄂 左 右

帜 帜帜帜帜帜帜帜帜

（*製）zhì *制造、制订、制度、限制

✎ 8 画
🈶 刂部
𝄂 左 右

制 制制制制制制制制

德国的名牌
汽车Benz，我国
通行的翻译用字是
"奔驰"。海外有华人
戏用"笨死"，幽默之至！
可见，用汉字翻译外
来词，用了褒义字，
可以上天；用了
贬义字，也
能入地。

（質）zhì 物质、品质、优质、质朴无华、质问、人质

☞ 上左包围结构。贝的第二画㇖不带钩。

✎ 8 画
🈶 厂部
𝄂 半包围

质 质质质质质质质质

zhì 治理、长治久安、处治、诊治、治学

✎ 8 画
🈶 氵部
𝄂 左 右

治 治治治治治治治治

（*緻）zhì 致谢、致死、专心致志、兴致、*细致

☞ 至的末笔改捷。右边是攵不是夂。

✎ 10 画
🈶 至部
𝄂 左 右

致 致致致致致致致致致

zhì 秩序

☞ 禾，中间一竖不带钩。末笔改点。

✎ 10 画
部 禾
四 左 右

秩 秩秩秩秩秩秩秩秩秩秩

---

zhì 智勇双全、机智

☞ 矢的末笔改点。

✎ 12 画
部 日
四 上 下

智 智智智智智智智智智智智

---

zhì 设置、购置、安置

☞ 上边是横"目"，不写作四。直的框内是三横，不是两横。

✎ 13 画
部 罒
四 上 下

置 置置置置置置置置置置置置

---

zhōng 居中、家中、中等、中外、中用 / **zhòng** 击中、中暑

middle

✎ 4 画
部 丨
四 独 体

中 中中中中

古字形像古代一种测风的工具。

髙（金文） 髙（甲文）

---

zhōng 忠心、忠告

☞ 心的第二画楷体是 ㇃ (卧钩)，宋体是 ㇄ (竖弯钩)。

✎ 8 画
部 心
四 上 下

忠 忠忠忠忠忠忠忠忠

(终) **zhōng** 始终、剧终、临终、终身、终会成功

☞ 纟3画，上边不是幺。右上是夂不是夂。

✎ 8 画
纟 左
四 左 右

终 终终终终终终终终

(鐘 *鍾) **zhōng** 铜钟、钟表、钟点、*钟情

☞ 钅5画，第二画是横，不是点；第五画是竖提，不分为两笔。

✎ 9 画
部 钅
四 左 右

钟 钟钟钟钟钟钟钟钟钟

(腫) **zhǒng** 浮肿、红肿

✎ 8 画
部 月
四 左 右

肿 肿肿肿肿肿肿肿肿

（種）zhǒng 麦种、配种、人种、品种／zhòng 种树、播种

☞ 禾，中间一竖不带钩，末笔改点。

✎ 9 画
〔〕禾 画部左右
种 种种种种种种种种种

（衆）zhòng 群众、众人

☞ 左下的人，第二画改点。

古字形像三人相聚在太阳下劳作。 （金文） （甲文）

✎ 6 画
〔〕人 画部上下
众 众众众众众众

zhòng 毛重、重要、尊重、病重、慎重／chóng 重合、重建

☞ ノ 画部独体
✎ 9 画
重 重重重重重重重重重

zhōu 漓江泛舟

✎ 6 画
〔〕丿 画部独体
舟 舟舟舟舟舟舟

临帖，就是把字帖放在面前，看着帖练习写字。帖帖时，切忌看一笔写一笔，至少要看一字写一字，进一步要看一行写一行，看一句写一句。既要学笔法，也要学结体，还要学布局。平时要多读、多记、多写、多用，最好能把帖上的字形背下来，做到不看帖。这种临帖的方法古人称为"背临"。

zhōu 州县、自治州

✎ 6 画
〔〕丶 画部独体
州 州州州州州州

zhōu 周而复始、周全、周到、周围、周期、周济

☞ 左上右包围结构。框内上土下口。

✎ 8 画
〔〕冂 画部半包围
周 周周周周周周周周

zhōu 绿洲、亚洲

✎ 9 画
〔〕氵 画部左右
洲 洲洲洲洲洲洲洲洲洲

粥
zhōu 八宝粥、绿豆粥

☞ 弓 3画，第三画是㇆，不分为两笔。米的末笔改点。

✎ 12 画
〔〕弓 画部左
粥 粥粥粥粥粥粥粥粥粥粥粥粥

左上是𦰩，耳的末笔改提，又的末笔改点；右下是釆不是豕。

---

zhòu 宇宙

✎ 8 画
上 下 部 下
宀

宙 宙宙宙宙宙宙宙宙

(晝) zhòu 昼夜 DAYTIME ☀

☞ 左上右包围结构。

✎ 9 画
尸 半包围 部
昼 昼昼昼昼昼昼昼昼昼

(皺) zhòu 皱纹、皱皱巴巴

☞ 左下是彐，中间一横右端不出头。

✎ 10 画
皮 左右 部
皱 皱皱皱皱皱皱皱皱皱

(驟) zhòu 暴风骤雨、骤然 ☞ 马 3 画，第一画乛、第二画乛都不分为两笔；左上角开口，末笔改提。

sudden, abrupt

✎ 17 画
马 左右 部
骤 骤骤骤骤骤骤骤骤
骤 骤骤骤骤骤骤骤骤

(*硃) zhū 朱红、·朱砂 vermillion - bright red

☞ 中间一竖不带钩。

✎ 6 画
丿 独体 部
朱 朱朱朱朱朱朱

---

zhū 珍珠、泪珠 bead, pearl

☞ 王的末笔改提。朱的中间一竖不带钩。

✎ 10 画
王 左右 部
珠 珠珠珠珠珠珠珠珠珠

---

zhū 守株待兔、株距 for plants, trees?

☞ 木的中间一竖不带钩，末笔改点。朱的中间一竖不带钩。

✎ 10 画
木 左右 部
株 株株株株株株株株株

(諸) zhū 诸侯、诸位 all various

☞ 讠两画，第二画是乚，不分为两笔或三笔。

✎ 10 画
讠 左右 部
诸 诸诸诸诸诸诸诸诸诸

zhū 肥猪、猪鬃   *Pig*

✎ 11 画
冫犭 部首
囗 左右

猪 猪猪猪猪猪猪猪猪猪猪猪

zhū 蜘蛛、蛛网   *Spider*

☞ 朱，中间一竖不带钩。

✎ 12 画
虫 部首
左右

蛛 蛛蛛蛛蛛蛛蛛蛛蛛蛛蛛蛛

zhú 毛竹、丝竹乐   *Bamboo*

☞ 第三画是竖，第六画是竖钩。

✎ 6 画
竹 部首
左右

竹 竹竹竹竹竹竹

persue, drive out, expel

zhú 心潮逐浪高、驱逐、逐个

☞ 左下包围结构。豕的末笔改点。辶 3画，
第二画楷体是⻌，宋体是⻎。

✎ 10 画
辶 部首
半包围

逐 逐逐逐逐逐逐逐逐逐逐

古字形像追逐野兽。下边的止代表追逐者。

⻌（金文） 𧀠（甲文）

（燭） zhú 蜡烛、烛光   *Candle*

☞ 火的末笔改点。

✎ 10 画
火 部首
左右

烛 烛烛烛烛烛烛烛烛烛

zhǔ 店主、客随主便、主编、主和、主角

owner, master, head of family

✎ 5 画
王 部首
独体

主 主主主主主

zhǔ 煮玉米   *boil, cook*

✎ 12 画
灬 部首
上下

煮 煮煮煮煮煮煮煮煮煮煮煮

enjoin, advise, urge

（囑） zhǔ 叮嘱、遗嘱   ☞ 右部禹的下部是禸5画，不是禸4画。

嘱嘱嘱嘱

✎ 15 画
口 部首
左右

嘱 嘱嘱嘱嘱嘱嘱嘱嘱嘱嘱

zhù 帮助、互助

且的末笔改提。

✎ 7 画 | 部 力 | 左 右

助 助助助助助助助

《国家通用语言文字法》规定，有下列情形的，可以保留或使用繁体字、异体字：1. 文物古迹；2. 姓氏中的异体字；3. 书法、篆刻等艺术作品；4. 题词和招牌的手写书；5. 出版、教学、研究中需要使用的；6. 经国务院有关部门批准的特殊情况。

zhù 住址、住手、抓住、记住

live, stay, reside

✎ 7 画 | 部 亻 | 左 右

住 住住住住住住住

zhù 注射、注意、赌注、注释、注册

pour, concentrate

✎ 8 画 | 部 氵 | 左 右

注 注注注注注注注

(駐) zhù 驻足观看、驻扎　*stay, be stationed*

马的第一画乛、第二画㇟，都不分为两笔；左上角开口；末笔改提。

✎ 8 画 | 部 马 | 左 右

驻 驻驻驻驻驻驻驻

zhù 木柱、水银柱　*post, pillar, column*

木的中间一竖不带钩，末笔改点。

✎ 9 画 | 部 木 | 左 右

柱 柱柱柱柱柱柱柱柱

offer good wishes

zhù 祝酒、祝贺

左边是礻不是衤。

✎ 9 画 | 部 礻 | 左 右

祝 祝祝祝祝祝祝祝祝

古字形像一人跪拜在神主前祷告。（金文）（甲文）

zhù 显著、著名、编著、新著

艹3画，第三画楷体是撇，宋体是竖。

✎ 11 画 | 部 艹 | 上 下

著 著著著著著著著著著著

(鑄) zhù 浇铸、铸造　钅5画，第二画是横，不是点；第五画是竖提，不分为两笔。

古字形像手持坩埚浇铸器皿。（金文）

✎ 12 画 | 部 钅 | 左 右

铸 铸铸铸铸铸铸铸铸铸铸铸

（築）zhù 建筑、筑路　　**Build**

✎ 工的末笔改提。

✎ 12 画　竹部　下
☐ 竹 上　⊠

筑 筑筑筑筑筑筑筑筑筑筑筑

zhuā 猫抓老鼠、抓小偷、抓耳挠腮、抓科技

seize, catch, grab, arrest

✎ 7 画　手部　右
☐ 扌 左　⊠

抓 抓抓抓抓抓抓

（專）zhuān 专门、专心、专权　**special**

✎ 4 画　一部　体
☐ 独　⊠

专 专专专专

（磚）zhuān 瓷砖、城砖、冰砖

✎ 9 画　石部　右
☐ 石 左　⊠

砖 砖砖砖砖砖砖砖砖砖

（轉）zhuǎn 转向、转交 / zhuàn 转动 / zhuǎi 转文

✎ 车的下边一横改提，笔顺改先竖后提。

✎ 8 画　车部　右
☐ 车 左　⊠

转 转转转转转转转转

（賺）zhuàn 赚钱、有赚头　✎ 贝的第二画乛不带钩；兼的两竖不带钩；中部不是⺕，中间一横右端出头。

✎ 14 画　贝部　右
☐ 贝 左　⊠

赚 赚赚赚赚赚赚
赚赚赚赚赚赚赚赚

（莊）zhuāng 庄严、村庄、饭庄

✎ 上左包围结构。右下是土，不加丶(点)。

✎ 6 画　广部　围
☐ 广 半包围　⊠

庄 庄庄庄庄庄庄

（裝）zhuāng 服装、装扮、装订、装糊涂、装电话

✎ 12 画　衣部　下
☐ 衣 上　⊠

装 装装装装装装装装装装装装

包围结构的字，如果左下右包围的，被包围部件要稍向下靠，不要空荡荡地悬空在上边，以使全字显得安稳，如"凶、幽、函"等。

（壯）zhuàng 强壮、壮志凌云、壮胆

strong, stout, healthy

✎ 6 画 士部
⊟ 扌 左 右
⊠ 左右　壮　壮壮壮壮壮壮

（狀）zhuàng 形状、状况、状纸、奖状

✎ 7 画 犬部
⊟ 扌 左 右
⊠ 左右　状　状状状
　　　　　状状状状

刘夏、李家瑞合编的《宋元以来俗字谱》收集了宋元明清12种民间刻本中出现的6240个俗字，其中绝大多数是简体字。

zhuàng 撞击、撞见

✎ 15 画 扌部
⊟ 扌 左 右
⊠ 左右　撞　撞撞撞撞撞撞撞
　　　　　撞撞撞撞撞撞撞

zhuī 追赶、追忆、追认、追求、追查

☞ 左下包围结构。辶 3画，第二画楷体是 ㇅，宋体是 ㇆。

✎ 9 画 辶部
⊟ 辶 半包围
⊠ 半包围　追　追追追追追追追追追

（準）zhǔn *准则、*准确、*准赢、准许

✎ 10 画 冫部
⊟ 冫 左 右
⊠ 左右　准　准准准准准
　　　　　准准准准准

现代汉字的字形多数由三个或三个以上的部件组合而成。《汉字信息字典》（科学出版社，1988年）对组成7785个现代汉字的部件数进行了统计。结果表明，现代汉字中由三个部件组成的字占40.321％，由四个部件组成的字，占16.39％。

zhuō 代人捉笔、捉贼

✎ 10 画 扌部
⊟ 扌 左 右
⊠ 左右　捉　捉捉捉捉捉
　　　　　捉捉捉捉捉

zhuō 书桌、电脑桌

✎ 10 画 木部
⊟ 木 上 下
⊠ 上下　桌　桌桌桌桌桌桌桌桌桌桌

（濁）zhuó 浑浊、嗓音粗浊

✎ 9 画 氵部
⊟ 氵 左 右
⊠ 左右　浊　浊浊浊浊浊浊浊浊浊

zhuó 啄木鸟、啄虫子

☞ 右部是豕中加丶（点）。

✎ 11 画
口 口部
左 左 右

啄 啄啄啄啄啄啄啄啄啄啄啄

---

zhuó 着陆、着装 / zháo 着凉、找着了 / zhāo 看棋别支着儿、
一着一式 / zhe 吃着

☞ 上左包围结构。左上的羊末笔改撇，直接从三横撇下。

✎ 11 画
羊 羊部
半包围 半包围

着 着着着着着着着着着着着

---

zī 姿态、姿色

✎ 9 画
女 女部
上 上下

姿 姿姿姿姿姿姿姿姿姿

（资）zī 物资、资金、资助、天资、资历

☞ 贝的第二画乛不带钩。

✎ 10 画
贝 贝部
上 上下

资 资资资资资资资资资资

---

zī 滋长、滋味、滋事

☞ 右上是䒑不是艹。

✎ 12 画
氵 氵部
左 左右

滋 滋滋滋滋滋滋滋滋滋滋滋滋

---

zǐ 母子、男子、子鸡、瓜子、棋子 / zi 刀子、瘦子

☞ 第一画乛、第二画亅不连成一笔。

✎ 3 画
子 子部
独体 独体

子 子子子

---

zǐ 仔鸡、仔细 / zǎi 打工仔

✎ 5 画
亻 亻部
左 左右

仔 仔仔仔仔仔仔

---

zǐ 万紫千红、赤橙黄绿青蓝紫

☞ 左上止的末笔改提。右上是匕不是七。小的左侧楷体是点，宋体是撇。

✎ 12 画
糸 糸部
上 上下

紫 紫紫紫紫紫紫紫紫紫紫紫紫

宗、棕、踪的小，左侧楷体是点，宋体是撇。

zì 自理、自有道理、自古以来

✎ 6　画
部首 自 部
结构 独　体

自 自自自自自自自

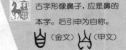
古字形像鼻子，应是鼻的本字。后引申为自称。
自（金文）　山（甲文）

zì 汉字、草字

☞ 子3画，第一画乛、第二画亅不连成一笔。

✎ 6　画
部首 宀 部
结构 上　下

字 字字字字字字

zōng 祖宗、宗派、宗旨

✎ 8　画
部首 宀 部
结构 上　下

宗 宗宗宗宗宗宗宗宗

zōng 棕榈、棕刷

☞ 木的中间一竖不带钩，末笔改点。

✎ 12　画
部首 木 部
结构 左　右

棕 棕棕棕棕棕棕棕棕棕棕棕

zōng 踪迹、行踪　　☞ 左下止的末笔改提。

✎ 15　画
部首 足 部
结构 左　右

踪踪踪踪踪踪踪踪踪踪踪踪
踪踪踪

（總）zǒng 总结、总复习、总经理、总爱出神

☞ 心的第二画楷体是乚（卧钩），宋体是乚（竖弯钩）。

✎ 9　画
部首 八 部
结构 上　下

总 总总总总总总总总总

（縱）zòng 纵队、放纵、纵使、纵身一跳

☞ 纟3画，上边不是幺。左边的人末笔改点。

✎ 7　画
部首 纟 部
结构 左　右

纵 纵纵纵纵纵纵纵

zǒu 逃走、行走、离家出走、走漏、走样、走亲戚

✎ 7　画
部首 走 部
结构 上　下

走 走走走走走走走

奏 zòu 启奏、奏效、奏国歌

☞ 左上右包围结构。天的末笔改点。

✎ 9 画
部 一 半包围

 奏奏奏奏奏奏奏奏奏奏

租 zū 租用、出租、房租

☞ 禾，中间一竖不带钩，末笔改点。

✎ 10 画
部 禾 左右

 租租租租租租租租租

足 zú 足迹、富足、微不足道

☞

✎ 7 画
部 足 上下

 足足足足足足足

族 zú 家族、藏族、贵族

✎ 11 画
部 方 左右

 族族族族族族族族族族族

历代积累的汉字总数数以万计。近年出版的汉字字典收字总数从五万多逼近八万多。但历代日常书面语常用的汉字一般都控制在三四千字。这是字数繁多的汉字千百年来能为人们接受、成为汉族人民记录汉语的主要文字工具的一个重要原因。

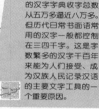

阻 zǔ 阻挡、拦阻

☞ 阝 两画，第一画了不分为两笔。

✎ 7 画
部 左阝 左右

 阻阻阻阻阻阻阻

(組) zǔ 组合、编辑组、组诗

☞ 纟3画，上边不是幺。

✎ 8 画
部 纟 左右

 组组组组组组组组

祖 zǔ 祖宗、祖母、祖师爷

☞ 左边是礻 不是衤。

✎ 9 画
部 礻 左右

 祖祖祖祖祖祖祖祖

(鑽) zuān 钻孔、钻研、钻地道 / zuàn 电钻、钻石

☞ 钅5画，第二画是横，不是点；第五画是竖提，不分为两笔。

✎ 10 画
部 钅 左右

 钻钻钻钻钻钻钻钻钻

醉、尊、遵的酉，框内有一短横。

zuǐ 嘴巴、烟嘴、零嘴、顶嘴　　☞ 此的左部止，末笔改提；右部是匕不是匕。

嘴 □嘴 □嘴 □嘴 □嘴 □嘴 □嘴 □嘴 □嘴 □嘴 □嘴 嘴
嘴 嘴 嘴 嘴

✎ 16 画
🔲 口部
⊠ 左右

zuì 最长、最大

☞ 取的第一画横向右延长，覆盖又。

✎ 12 画
🔲 日部
⊠ 上下

最 最 最 最 最 最 最 最 最 最 最 最

zuì 犯罪、死罪、罪过

☞ 上边是横"目"，不写成四。

✎ 13 画
🔲 罒部
⊠ 上下

罪 罪 罪 罪 罪 罪 罪 罪 罪 罪 罪 罪 罪

zuì 醉汉、陶醉、醉虾　　☞ 卒，中部两人的末笔都改点。

✎ 15 画
🔲 酉部
⊠ 左右

醉 醉 醉 醉 醉 醉 醉 醉 醉 醉 醉 醉
醉 醉 醉

zūn 尊贵、尊老爱幼、尊姓

✎ 12 画
🔲 八部
⊠ 上下

尊 尊 尊 尊 尊 尊 尊 尊 尊 尊 尊 尊

古字形像双手捧着酒器。

尊（金文）　尊（甲文）

zūn 遵照、遵守　　☞ 左下包围结构。辶 3画，第二画楷体是㇄，宋体是㇙。

✎ 15 画
🔲 辶部
⊠ 半包围

遵 遵 遵 遵 遵 遵 遵
遵 遵 遵 遵 遵 遵 遵

zuó 昨天、昨夜

✎ 9 画
🔲 日部
⊠ 左右

昨 昨 昨 昨 昨
昨 昨 昨 昨

适应信息技术发展的需要，1981年至1987年，国家有关部门先后发布了《信息交换用汉字编码字符集》的基本集、第二和第四辅助集。这三个字符集都是国家标准，共收规范汉字21039个。

zuǒ 左边、旁门左道、意见相左、左派

☞ 上左包围结构。

✎ 5 画
🔲 工部
⊠ 半包围

左 左 左 左 左

zuò 操作、兴风作浪、作文、大作、弄虚作假 / zuō 作坊

✎ 7 画
囗 亻 部
囚 左 右

作　作作作作作作作

工作 gong zòu
to work
work, job

zuò 坐冷板凳、坐飞机、坐北朝南、坐标
　　☞ 对称结构。

✎ 7 画
囗 土 部
囚 对 称

坐　坐坐坐坐坐坐坐

两个小人堆土堆，堆起土堆人已累；
一边一个立不住，用它当椅歇一会。

字谜

zuò 座位、底座、花瓶座子
　　☞ 上左包围结构。

✎ 10 画
囗 广 部
囚 半包围

座　座座座座座座座座座

zuò 做工、做饭、做作业、做鬼脸、做作
　　☞ 右部是攵不是夂。

✎ 11 画
囗 亻 部
囚 左 右

做　做做做做做做做做做做

to do

附　　录

汉字笔画名称表

类别	序号	笔形	名称	例字
基本笔形	1	一	横	十
	2	丨	竖	中
	3	丿	撇	八
	4	丶	点	主
	5	㇏	捺	人
	6	㇀	提	地
派生笔形	7	𠃍	横折	口
	8	𠃌	横撇	又
	9	㇇	横钩	写
	10	𠃌	横折钩	月
	11	㇌	横折提	记
	12	㇈	横折弯	朵
	13	㇎	横折折	凹
	14	㇂	横折斜钩	飞

续 表

类别	序 号	笔 形	名 称	例 字
	15	乙	横折弯钩	九
	16	孑	横撇弯钩	队
派	17	孓	横折折撇	及
	18	㇆	横折折折钩	乃
	19	㇅	横折折折	凸
生	20	㇄	竖提	民
	21	凵	竖折	山
	22	亅	竖钩	小
	23	㇟	竖弯	四
笔	24	乚	竖弯钩	儿
	25	㇡	竖折撇	专
	26	㇉	竖折折	鼎
形	27	㇅	竖折折钩	马
	28	乀	撇点	女
	29	乁	撇折	么
	30	乀	斜钩	我
	31	乁	弯钩	家

汉字笔顺规则表

类别	序号	规 则	例 字
基本规则	1	先横后竖	十 十
	2	先撇后捺	人 人
	3	从上到下	三 三 三
	4	从左到右	仁 仁 仁 仁
	5	先外后里	问 问 问 问 问 问
	6	先外后里再封口	国 国 国 国 国 国 国 国
	7	先中间后两边	小 小 小
补充规则	1	点在上部或左上，先写	衣 衣 衣 衣 衣 衣 / 为 为 为 为
	2	点在右上或字里，后写	发 发 发 发 发 / 瓦 瓦 瓦 瓦
	3	上右和上左包围结构，先外后里	司 司 司 司 司 / 厅 厅 厅 厅
	4	左下包围结构，先里后外	远 远 远 远 远 远 远
	5	左下右包围结构，先里后外	凶 凶 凶 凶
	6	左上右包围结构，先外后里	同 同 同 同 同 同
	7	上左下包围结构，先上后里再左下	区 区 区 区

笔顺易错字表

1.本表从《现代汉语通用字表》(7000字)中挑选出最容易写错笔顺的72个字，按照《现代汉语通用字笔顺规范》提供的标准，逐笔标出笔顺。

2.本表按字的笔画数从少到多排列，同笔画数的字按第一笔笔形横、竖、撇、点、折的顺序排列。

3.以表内字作为构字部件的字，不再重复列出。

2笔

九（九九）

匕（匕匕）

乃（乃乃）

3笔

与（与与与）

山（山山山）

义（义义义）

及（及及及）

叉（叉叉叉）

4笔

五（五五五五）

巨（巨巨巨巨）

比（比比比比）

瓦（瓦瓦瓦瓦）

长（长长长长）

丹（丹丹丹丹）

方（方方方方）

火（火火火火）

丑（丑丑丑丑）

办（办办办办）

5笔

甘（甘甘甘甘甘）

世（世世世世世）

北（北北北北北）

凸（凸凸凸凸凸）

由（由由由由由）

凹（凹凹凹凹凹）

鸟（鸟鸟鸟鸟鸟）

必（必必必必必）

出（出出出出出）

母（母母母母母）

6 笔

考（考考考考考考）

耳（耳耳耳耳耳耳）

再（再再再再再再）

舟（舟舟舟舟舟舟）

兆（兆兆兆兆兆兆）

壮（壮壮壮壮壮壮）

州（州州州州州州）

那（那那那那那那）

迅（迅迅迅迅迅迅）

7 笔

戒（戒戒戒戒戒戒戒）

报（报报报报报报报）

巫（巫巫巫巫巫巫巫）

里（里里里里里里里）

坐（坐坐坐坐坐坐坐）

免（免免免免免免免）

卯（卯卯卯卯卯卯卯）

8 笔

非（非非非非非非非非）

齿（齿齿齿齿齿齿齿齿）

垂（垂垂垂垂垂垂垂）

夜（夜夜夜夜夜夜夜）

肃（肃肃肃肃肃肃肃）

贯（贯贯贯贯贯贯贯贯）

9 笔

革（革革革革革革革革革）

幽（幽幽幽幽幽幽幽幽幽）

重（重重重重重重重重重）

鬼（鬼鬼鬼鬼鬼鬼鬼鬼鬼）

差（差差差差差差差差差）

10 笔

爸（爸爸爸爸爸爸
　　爸爸爸爸）

套（套套套套套套
　　套套套套）

脊（脊脊脊脊脊脊
　　脊脊脊脊）

11 笔

兜（兜兜兜兜兜兜兜
　　兜兜兜兜）

象（象象象象象象

象象象象）

祭（祭祭祭祭祭祭祭
祭祭祭祭）

傲（傲傲傲傲傲傲傲
傲傲傲傲傲）

焰（焰焰焰焰焰焰焰
焰焰焰焰焰）

12笔

插（插插插插插插插
插插插插插）

搜（搜搜搜搜搜搜搜
搜搜搜搜搜）

葵（葵葵葵葵葵葵葵
葵葵葵葵葵）

鼎（鼎鼎鼎鼎鼎鼎鼎
鼎鼎鼎鼎鼎）

黑（黑黑黑黑黑黑黑
黑黑黑黑黑）

缘（缘缘缘缘缘缘缘
缘缘缘缘缘）

14笔

弊（弊弊弊弊弊弊弊
弊弊弊弊弊弊）

16笔

燕（燕燕燕燕燕燕燕燕燕燕
燕燕燕燕燕燕）

矗（矗矗矗矗矗矗矗矗矗
矗矗矗矗矗矗）

汉字形体结构类型表

现代汉字的间架结构，可以分为五大类型、十三种。五大类型是：独体、左右、上下、包围和对称。十三种结构形式是：独体、左右、左中右、上下、上中下、上左包围、上右包围、左下包围、左上右包围、上左下包围、左下右包围、全包围、对称。现略加归并，图示如下：

1. 独体字结构

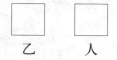

乙   人

2. 左右结构(含左中右结构)

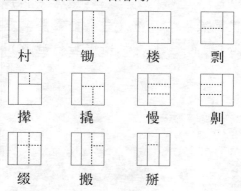

村   锄   楼   剽

撵   撬   慢   剐

缀   搬   掰

3. 上下结构(含上中下结构)

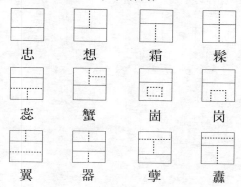

忠　　　想　　　霜　　　鬃

蕊　　　蟹　　　崮　　　岗

翼　　　器　　　挈　　　纛

4. 上左包围结构

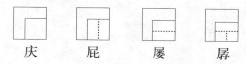

庆　　　屁　　　屡　　　屏

5. 上右包围结构

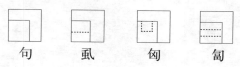

句　　　虱　　　匈　　　匐

6. 左下包围结构

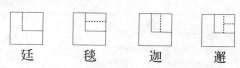

廷　　　毯　　　迦　　　邂

7. 左上右包围结构

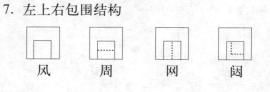

风   周   网   囹

8. 上左下包围结构

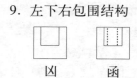

区   匼   甌

9. 左下右包围结构

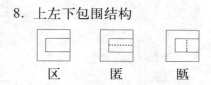

凶   函

10. 全包围结构

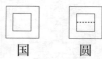

国   圆

11. 对称结构

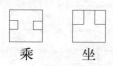

乘   坐

新旧字形对照表

字　形	笔画数	例字	主　要　特　点
新　阝	2	陈都	第一笔横撇弯钩。
旧　阝	3		新字形的第一笔旧字形为横撇、弯钩两笔。
新　艹	3	花草	一横两竖(楷体为一横一竖一撇)。
旧　艹	4		新字形的一横旧字形为两短横。
新　及	3	极吸	第二笔是横折折撇。
旧　及	4		新字形的第二笔横折折撇旧字形为横折、横撇两笔。
新　辶	3	远连	左上角一点。
旧　辶	4		左上角两点。
新　丰	4	艳洋	起笔是横。
旧　丰	4		起笔是撇。
新　开	4	形研	第一、二笔都是横。
旧　开	6		新字形的第一笔横旧字形为撇、横两笔,新字形的第二笔横旧字形为两短横。
新　巨	4	苣渠	第四笔是竖折。
旧　巨	5		新字形的第四笔竖折旧字形为竖、横两笔。
新　屯	4	顿纯	起笔是横。
旧　屯	4		起笔是撇。
新　瓦	4	瓶瓷	第二笔是竖折。
旧　瓦	5		新字形的第二笔竖折旧字形为竖、提两笔。

续表

字　形		笔画数	例字	主　要　特　点
新	反	4	板 版	起笔是撇。
旧	反	4		起笔是横。
新	户	4	沪 扁	起笔是点。
旧	戶	4		起笔是撇。
新	礻	4	社 神	起笔是点，第二笔是横撇。
旧	示	5		起笔是横。新字形的第二笔横撇旧字形为横、撇两笔。新字形的第四笔点旧字形为竖。
新	丑	4	扭 纽	第三笔横右端不出头。
旧	丑	4		第三笔横右端出头。
新	发	5	拔 跋	第三笔是横撇。
旧	发	5		第三笔是撇。
新	令	5	冷 零	第三、五笔都是点。第四笔是横撇。
旧	令	5		第三笔是横。第四笔是横折钩。第五笔是竖。
新	印	5	茚	第二笔是竖提。
旧	印	6		新字形的第二笔竖提旧字形为竖、横两笔。
新	耒	6	耕 耘	起笔是横。
旧	耒	6		起笔是撇。
新	吕	6	侣 宫	两口相离。
旧	呂	7		两口相连。
新	修	6	修 條	第五笔是横撇。
旧	修	7		新字形的第五笔横撇旧字形为横、撇两笔。

续 表

字 形		笔画数	例字	主 要 特 点
新	争	6	挣 筝	上部是撇、横撇两笔。
旧	爭	8		上部是撇、撇、点、点四笔。
新	产	6	铲 彦	第三笔是点，第四笔是撇。
旧	产	6		第三笔是撇，第四笔是点，两笔相交。
新	羊	6	差 羞	第六笔从三横中直接撇下。
旧	羊	7		新字形的第六笔撇旧字形为竖、撇两笔。
新	并	6	拼 屏	第三、四笔都是横。
旧	幷	8		起笔是撇。新字形的第三笔横旧字形为两短横。新字形的第四笔横旧字形为提、横两笔。
新	羽	6	翔 翁	第二、五笔都是点。第三、六笔都是提。
旧	羽	6		第二、三、五、六笔都是撇。
新	吴	7	娱 虞	第四笔是横。
旧	吳	7		第四笔是竖折折。
新	肖	7	消 霄	第二笔是点，第三笔是撇。
旧	肖	7		第二笔是撇，第三笔是点。
新	肖	7	敝 蔽	第一笔是点，第二笔是撇。
旧	肖	7		新字形的第一笔点旧字形为撇。新字形的第二笔撇旧字形为点。
新	兑	7	悦 说	第一笔是点，第二笔是撇。
旧	兌	7		第一笔是撇，第二笔是横捺。
新	角	7	解 确	末笔竖下端出头。
旧	角	7		第六笔竖下端不出头。

续　表

字　形		笔画数	例　字	主　要　特　点
新	奂	7	换痪	下部像央，仅撇笔上端不出头。
旧	奂	9		框中有撇、竖弯钩两笔。
新	耳	7	敢瞰	第一笔是横折。
旧	耳	8		新字形的第一笔横折旧字形为横、竖两笔。
新	青	8	清静	冂中是两横。
旧	青	8		冂中是一竖一横。
新	者	8	都著	日上无点。
旧	者	9		日上有点。
新	直	8	值植	末笔是横。
旧	直	8		末笔是竖折。
新	隶	8	捷	中间一竖贯串上下。
旧	隶	9		新字形的中间原为一竖，旧字形分为两短竖。
新	非	8	排绯	起笔是竖，第四笔是横。
旧	非	8		起笔是撇，第四笔是提。
新	垂	8	睡睡	中部是一横两竖。
旧	垂	9		中部是两个十。
新	郎	8	螂廊	左部良的末两笔改一笔点。
旧	郎	10		左部良的末笔捺改点。右耳旁三笔：横撇、弯钩、竖。
新	录	8	禄绿	上部三笔：横折、横、横。
旧	录	8		上部三笔：竖折、横折、横。

字　形		笔画数	例字	主　要　特　点
新	昷	9	温 瘟	上部是日。
旧	昷	10		上部是囚。
新	骨	9	滑 骼	上部框中一笔：横折。
旧	骨	10		上部框中两笔：横、竖。横笔跟右边竖笔相接。
新	卸	9	御	左部七笔。
旧	卸	8		左部六笔，新字形的第六、七笔旧字形为一笔：竖折。
新	鬼	9	槐 嵬	第六笔从白中直接撇下。
旧	鬼	10		新字形的第六笔撇旧字形为竖、撇两笔。
新	俞	9	愉 愈	右下是立刀旁。
旧	俞	9		右下是巛。
新	既	9	溉 厩	左部是艮的变体，末两笔改为一笔：点。
旧	旣	11		左部是上白下匕。
新	蚤	9	搔 骚	上部仅又中一点。
旧	蚤	10		上部又的中间和左侧各有一点。
新	敖	10	傲 遨	左上四笔：横、横、竖、横。左下两笔：横折钩、撇。
旧	敖	11		左上士，左下方。
新	莽	10	蟒	下部三笔：横、撇、竖。
旧	莽	12		新字形下边的横旧字形为提、横两笔。
新	真	10	滇 填	上部二笔：横、竖。第八笔是横。
旧	眞	10		上部是匕。第八笔是竖折。

续 表

字 形		笔画数	例 字	主 要 特 点
新	䍃	10	摇遥	上部四笔：撇、点、点、撇。
旧	䍃	10		上部四笔：撇、横撇、点、点。
新	隺	10	鹤榷	上部是秃宝盖加一撇。
旧	寉	11		上部是宝盖头。
新	黄	11	横璜	上部四笔：横、竖、竖、横。
旧	黃	12		上部五笔：廿下边加一横。
新	虚	11	墟歔	下部是业。
旧	虛	12		新字形第九笔点旧字形为竖折。新字形第十笔撇旧字形为竖、横两笔。
新	象	11	像橡	第六笔从扁框中直接撇出。
旧	象	12		新字形的第六笔撇旧字形为竖、撇两笔。
新	奥	12	澳懊	上部框中是米。
旧	奧	13		上部框中是米上加一撇。
新	普	12	谱镨	第六笔是点，第七笔是撇。
旧	普	13		新字形第六笔点旧字形为竖折。新字形第七笔撇旧字形为竖、横两笔。
新	虏	13	摅	下部"男"：上"田"下"力"。
旧	虜	13		新字形的中间原为"田"，旧字形"田"中一横两端出头。

汉字统一部首表(草案)[修订稿]

说　　明

　　1. 本部首表为1983年中国文字改革委员会和国家出版局联合发布的《汉字统一部首表(草案)》的修订稿。这次修订，依据1997年4月国家语委、国家新闻出版署联合发布的《现代汉语通用字笔顺规范》，对部分部首笔形的归类和排序作了调整，并增加了部分变形部首。

　　2. 部首共201个，按笔画数和起笔笔形顺序排列。其繁体和变形加括号列出，以便按不同画数检索。右侧为例字。

　　3. 部首以简化字或繁体字为主，以原字形或变形为主，各种类型的辞书可以变通处理。

一　画		
[1] 一	二 东	
[2] 丨〔丿〕	中 临	
〔亅〕		
[3] 丿	九 垂	
[4] 、	为 州	
[5] 一〔乚乛乛乙〕		
乚乙乛	了 书	
〔乚〕	乡	
〔乚〕		
〔乛〕	习 司	
〔乚〕	乱 虬	

〔乚〕	乱 乳	
〔乙〕	乙	
〔乛〕	乃	

二　画		
[6] 十	古 华	
[7] 厂〔厂〕	历 雁	
[8] 匚	区 匪	
〔十〕	上 占	
〔刂〕	刑 刻	
[9] 卜〔⺊〕	卜 卦	
[10] 冂〔冂〕	同 网	
〔亻〕	仅 修	

〔厂〕	反 后	
[11] 八〔丷〕	分 兴	
[12] 人〔亻人〕	令 禽	
〔入〕	佘 籴	
〔⺈〕	危 兔	
〔冂〕	用 周	
[13] 勹	勿 旬	
〔几〕	凤 凰	
[14] 儿	元 先	
[15] 匕	北 旨	
[16] 几〔几〕	朵 凭	
[17] 亠	亡 京	

[18] 冫	冰 减	[40] 彳	行 得	[61] 韦〔韋〕	韧 韪
〔丷〕	兰 酋	[41] 彡	形 影	〔耂〕	孝 考
[19] 冖	冗 冠	〔犭〕	狗 猫	[62] 木	村 查
〔讠〕	论 话	[42] 夕	外 多	[63] 支	翅 鼓
[20] 凵	凶 出	[43] 夂	务 夏	[64] 犬〔犭〕	哭 献
[21] 卩〔㔾〕	卫 却	〔饣〕	饥 馍	[65] 歹〔歺〕	殃 殖
〔阝左〕	队 险	[44] 丬〔爿〕	状 妆	[66] 车〔車〕	转 轰
〔阝右〕	邦 邻	[45] 广	庙 唐	[67] 牙	邪 雅
[22] 刀〔𠂉刂〕	切 券	[46] 门〔門〕	间 闻	[68] 戈	戍 戒
[23] 力	动 势	〔氵〕	泳 湖	〔旡〕	既 悉
[24] 又	友 对	〔忄〕	性 情	[69] 比	毕 皆
[25] 厶	允 能	[47] 宀	宫 富	[70] 瓦	瓷 瓶
[26] 辶	廷 建	〔辶〕	还 送	[71] 止	此 肯
〔巳〕	卷 卺	〔彐〕	寻 灵	[72] 攴〔攵〕	敲 斅
三　画		[48] 彐〔彑彑〕	录	〔小〕	尕 恭
[27] 干	刊 邗	[49] 尸	尾 屋	〔囘〕	冒 冕
[28] 工	贡 攻	[50] 己〔巳巳〕 改 忌		〔日〕	曹 显
[29] 土〔士〕	坚 培	〔已〕	已	[73] 日〔曰日〕	明 旧
〔士〕	吉 声	〔巳〕	导 异	〔月〕	脊 臂
〔扌〕	打 拍	[51] 弓	张 弧	[74] 贝〔貝〕	则 资
〔艹〕	荣 菜	[52] 子	孙 孟	[75] 水〔氵水〕	沓 浆
[30] 寸	寿 封	[53] 屮〔㞢〕		[76] 见〔見〕	览 规
[31] 廾	弊	〔㞢〕		[77] 牛	牲 犁
[32] 大	夺 奖	[54] 女	奴 婴	[78] 手〔扌龵〕	拳 擎
〔兀〕	尧 尴	[55] 飞〔飛〕	飞	〔龵〕	看 拜
[33] 尢〔兀尣〕 尤 尬		[56] 马〔馬〕	驰 驾	[79] 气	氢 氧
[34] 弋	式 忒	〔幺〕	象 豫	[80] 毛	毡 毪
[35] 小〔⺌〕	尕 尘	〔纟〕	纱 综	〔攵〕	政 救
〔⺌〕	光 堂	[57] 幺	幻 幼	[81] 长〔長镸〕	长
[36] 口	可 哪	[58] 巛	邕 巢	[82] 片	版 牌
[37] 囗	因 圆	**四　画**		[83] 斤	欣 斯
[38] 山	岩 峰	[59] 王〔玉〕	主 珠	[84] 爪〔爫〕	爪
[39] 巾	帅 帽	[60] 无〔旡〕	无	[85] 父	爷 爸

〔允〕

〔冖〕　　　采 爱

[86] 月〔月〕　肢 脱

[87] 氏　　　氏 昏

[88] 欠　　　欧 歉

[89] 风〔風〕　飓 飘

[90] 殳　　　段 殷

[91] 文　　　刘 斋

[92] 方　　　放 旗

[93] 火〔灬〕　灭 炉

〔灬〕　　　热 照

[94] 斗　　　斜 斟

[95] 户　　　启 房

〔衤〕　　　视 福

[96] 心〔忄忄〕态 想

〔聿〕　　　　肃

〔爿〕　　　牁 牂

[97] 毋〔母〕　　毌

五　画

〔玉〕　　　玺 璧

[98] 示〔礻〕　祘 禁

[99] 甘　　　邯 某

[100] 石　　　砍 确

[101] 龙〔龍〕　垄 聋

〔歹〕

[102] 业　　　邺 凿

〔氺〕　　　泰 黎

[103] 目　　　眼 眉

[104] 田　　　界 畦

[105] 罒　　　罗 署

[106] 皿　　　盛 盟

〔钅〕　　　钱 铁

[107] 生　　　甥 甦

[108] 矢　　　知 短

[109] 禾　　　和 科

[110] 白　　　皂 的

[111] 瓜　　　瓞 瓢

[112] 鸟〔鳥〕　鸪 鸳

[113] 疒　　　病 疹

[114] 立　　　站 竞

[115] 穴　　　穷 窗

〔礻〕　　　补 衬

〔聿〕

〔疋〕　　　　　疏

[116] 疋〔𤴓〕　蛋 楚

[117] 皮　　　皱 颇

[118] 癶　　　癸 登

[119] 矛　　　柔 矜

〔母〕　　　每 毒

六　画

[120] 耒　　　耕 耢

[121] 老〔耂〕　耆 耄

[122] 耳　　　耻 职

[123] 臣　　　　卧

〔覀〕

[124] 西〔覀西〕要 票

〔西〕　　　　　西

[125] 而　　　耐 耍

[126] 页〔頁〕　顺 颗

[127] 至　　　到 致

[128] 虍〔虎〕　虏 虑

[129] 虫　　　虹 蚕

[130] 肉　　　胬 胔

[131] 缶　　　缸 缺

[132] 舌　　　刮 辞

[133] 竹〔⺮〕　　竹

〔⺮〕　　　竿 笆

[134] 臼〔臼〕　舁 舅

[135] 自　　　臭 息

[136] 血　　　　衅

[137] 舟　　　舢 舷

[138] 色　　　艳 艴

[139] 齐〔齊〕　剂 斋

[140] 衣〔衤〕　袋 裂

[141] 羊〔羊羋〕　　群

〔羊〕　　　差 翔

〔羋〕　　　美 羔

[142] 米　　　类 精

[143] 聿〔肀聿〕　肆 肇

[144] 艮　　　良 垦

[145] 艸〔艹〕

[146] 羽　　　翎 翠

[147] 糸〔丝纟〕系 素

〔糹〕

七　画

[148] 麦〔麥〕　麸 麨

〔镸〕　　　　　肆

[149] 走　　　赴 超

[150] 赤　　　郝 赦

〔車〕

[151] 豆　　　豇 豉

[152] 酉　　　酝 醉

[153] 辰　　　辱 唇

[154] 豕　　　豢 豯

[155] 卤〔鹵〕　虓 鹾

〔貝〕

〔見〕

[156] 里　　　里 野

〔𧾷〕　　　距 跟

[157] 足〔⻊〕 趸 蹙

[158] 邑〔阝右〕 邑

〔臼〕

[159] 身　　　　射 躺

[160] 疌〔辶〕

[161] 采　　　　悉 释

[162] 谷　　　　欲 豁

[163] 豸　　　　豹 貂

[164] 龟〔龜〕　　　龟

[165] 角　　　　斛 解

[166] 言〔讠〕　誓 誉

[167] 辛　　　　辟 辜

八　画

[168] 青　　　　静 靛

〔長〕

[169] 卓　　　　韩 朝

[170] 雨　　　　雪 雷

[171] 非　　　　辈 靠

[172] 齿〔齒〕　龄 龈

〔虎〕　　　虓 彪

〔門〕

[173] 黾〔黽〕　黾 鼋

[174] 隹　　　　隽 雏

[175] 阜〔阝左〕　阜

[176] 金〔钅〕　鉴 鎏

〔食〕

[177] 鱼〔魚〕　鲁 鲜

[178] 隶　　　　隶

九　画

[179] 革　　　　勒 鞋

〔頁〕

[180] 面　　　　勔 靦

[181] 韭　　　　韭

[182] 骨　　　　骷 骼

[183] 香　　　　馥 馨

[184] 鬼　　　　魂 魁

[185] 食〔饣 食〕餐 飨

〔風〕

[186] 音　　　　歆 韵

[187] 首　　　　馗 馘

〔韋〕

〔飛〕

十　画

[188] 髟　　　　髡 髦

〔馬〕

[189] 鬲　　　　融 翮

[190] 鬥

[191] 高　　　　敲 膏

十一画

[192] 黄　　　　斟 黇

〔麥〕

〔鹵〕

〔鳥〕

〔魚〕

[193] 麻　　　　磨 麾

[194] 鹿　　　　麒 麋

十二画

[195] 鼎　　　　鼐 鼏

[196] 黑　　　　墨 默

[197] 黍　　　　黍 黏

十三画

[198] 鼓　　　　瞽 鼖

〔黽〕

[199] 鼠　　　　鼢 鼬

十四画

[200] 鼻　　　　劓 鼾

〔齊〕

十五画

〔齒〕

十六画

〔龍〕

十七画

〔龜〕

[201] 龠　　　　龢

后　记

　　为了配合《中华人民共和国国家通用语言文字法》的制订和施行，商务印书馆辞书研究中心决定编写一本写字字典，以促进规范汉字的推行。因为我编过《汉字写法规范字典》(上海辞书出版社，1992年)，承蒙他们信任，邀我出任写字字典的主编。编写的目的是这样明确、纯正，我当然不便推辞，但我深知自己的能力有限。

　　说实话，在充分肯定这些年制订和推行汉字规范标准成绩的同时，我对规范标准的某些具体内容是有看法的，但这属于学术讨论的范畴。在确定写字字典的编写方案时，我们一致同意，应该严格遵循国家有关部门制订的一系列有关的法规和标准。

　　退休以后，感到自己的精力还可以，总希望能再编几本让读者比较满意、自己也比较满意的图书奉献给社会，所以，这本写字字典，从创意到编写到印制，大家都是十分认真的。但到了后期，留给我们的时间紧了点儿，大家不得不连续高速运作，这就必然会更多地留下这样那样的疏漏。这是我们深感遗憾并一直担心的。我们恳请方家和读者给予指正。

　　编写工作始终得到商务印书馆领导的关心和该馆汉语编辑室的全力支持。北京大学出版社胡双宝编审，在百忙中认真通读了字典正文，提出了宝贵的意见。国家语委黄佑源、亓艳萍，北京语言文化大学赵永丰、郝恩美、宋永波等先生也给予许多帮助。本书的责编、美编和校对自始至终尽心尽力地配合。这一切都是这本字典能在短时间内顺利出版的重要条件。在此谨向他们表示谢意。

编写时参考了许多专家的著述，限于本字典的性质，不能一一注明出处，敬请谅解，并在此一并致谢。

费锦昌

2000 年 12 月 5 日于北京前门寓所

图书在版编目（CIP）数据

新华写字字典／商务印书馆辞书研究中心编写－北京：
商务印书馆，2001

ISBN 978-7-100-03247-6

I. 新…　II. 商…　III. 汉语－字典　IV. H163

中国版本图书馆 CIP 数据核字（2000）第 74796 号

XĪNHUÁ　XIĔZÌ　ZÌDIĂN
新 华 写 字 字 典

商务印书馆辞书研究中心编写

商 务 印 书 馆 出 版
（北京王府井大街 36 号　邮政编码 100710）
商 务 印 书 馆 发 行
北京中科印刷有限公司印刷
ISBN 978-7-100-03247-6

2001 年 1 月第 1 版　　　　开本 787×1092 1/32
2010 年 3 月北京第 8 次印刷　印张 12　插页 1
定价：21.00 元

Russell
HOWARD

GOOD NEWS, BAD NEWS

ABI SMITH

JOHN BLAKE

Published by John Blake Publishing,
3 Bramber Court, 2 Bramber Road,
London W14 9PB, England

www.johnblakebooks.com

www.facebook.com/johnblakebooks 🆕
twitter.com/jblakebooks 🆕

First published in paperback in 2017

ISBN 978-1-78606-446-2

British Library Cataloguing-in-Publication Data:

A catalogue record for this book is available from the British Library.

Design by www.envydesign.co.uk

Printed in Great Britain by CPI Group (UK) Ltd

1 3 5 7 9 10 8 6 4 2

Papers used by John Blake Publishing are natural, recyclable products
made from wood grown in sustainable forests. The manufacturing processes
conform to the environmental regulations of the country of origin.

Every attempt has been made to contact the relevant copyright-holders,
but some were unobtainable. We would be grateful if the appropriate people
could contact us.

John Blake Publishing is an imprint of Bonnier Publishing
www.bonnierpublishing.com

To Lily, Henry and Tommy

CONTENTS

PROLOGUE

'If I wasn't a stand-up, what would I be? A teacher, maybe?
I quite like the idea of being a teacher. I'd be one of those,
"Hey, call me Russ", kind of teachers.'
RUSSELL HOWARD

There is genuinely not much that can faze Russell Howard. This is a man who, when faced with an overwhelming sense of stage fright or angst, or when feeling in a particularly 'life-is-meaningless-mood', likes to put things in perspective: 'We have one life, we are all going to die, we might as well go for it. My take on it is, you could be a slug...'

It is this sense of joy that makes him a man of the people. Better still, a 'boy wonder', because although he is slowly edging his way to forty, you might still expect him to be asked for ID in any off-licence, club or bar. Not that he would mind, as long as you don't expect him to be funny when he's out shopping. He can't do comedy when he's not on stage, on the contrary, he can do thoughtful, shy, quiet, pensive, troubled. On stage, he's battier than a box of frogs, excitable, hyperactive in a had-too-much-sugar kind of way.

But this is normal, isn't it? You can't be that funny on stage and off it too – it would be exhausting. And Russ likes to be the best performer he can be. There is no harder-working comedian out there than the West Country perfectionist who grew up writing jokes in his bedroom and has now become a record-breaking comic with a worldwide audience of several millions. This is more than just 'garden-centre famous' that his mum now enjoys, it's fame and fortune on a global scale.

'I'll tell you what's good, Google. It's brilliant,' says his 'twinkly-eyed smasher of a mum', Ninette. We would argue that Russ is equally brilliant and good. And equally searched for on the Internet. But how has the eldest child of a dinner lady and call-centre designer become such a global comedy icon? Perhaps the answer lies in that question: there aren't too many families who would be happy to be relentlessly mocked, lampooned, ridiculed and teased on stage as much as the Howard clan, who, without question, love every minute of their indirect fame.

Russell has always been close with his family. 'I'm quite lucky that my family are insane. It made sense to talk about because almost everyone can relate to having a crazy family. When I go back home at Christmas it's like being in the middle of a Pogues' music video – red-faced, toothless relatives swirling around you, kids skidding on their knees. I was always quite shy around my family and I would just sit and observe the anarchy. My parents were, and still are, hilarious. A lot of my material is about my family, my brother and my mum especially. We're a very open family so we all just take the mickey out of each other,' Russell told *Mail Online*.

Regularly on stage he talks about masturbation, having sex with his dad, shoving marbles up his brother's arse and how drunken girls on a hen do scare him. Then he talks about helping a stranger from killing himself, goes up in arms about how wonderful the NHS is and how pitiful the BNP are; there is seriousness mixed with smutty, sensitive combined with shameful

He has never worn a suit on stage, even at the Royal Albert Hall, and quite happily admits to being 'pretty skanky' because he likes to scrap between his toes with his socks. But there are some good points too. The best thing about being Russell Howard, he says, is that his girlfriend is nice, his family are nice, and he does a job that he loves. Which sort of sums it up, doesn't it?

There is a pulse that beats loudest in both his stand-up and his BBC Two Good News shows; taking on the nation's ingrained tendency towards sarcasm and contempt, while insisting on making the most of life. Mining the fleeting moment, the incidental encounter or the casual domestic detail in his stand up to finding the fun and heart-warming in the news and making the stories seem poetic. It's why we love him, and why we will continue to love him as he continues to entertain us on stage and screen. But how did a young, wonky-toothed, wonky-eyed fella from the West Country become one of the world's finest comedians?

Well, let's start at the beginning of this gert lush tale...

ACKNOWLEDGEMENTS

Thanks, ta and *muchas gracias* to my favourite Granny Sue and Grandman for . . . well, everything.

To Bells, Toodle and Mrs P., my favourite trio of ladies who love, help and shower me with chocolate and support (both equally welcomed). And Grampy, I not only love your constant appreciation of my housework, but how much you love my children.

For my number one, live-in comic, Mr Smith. Shit the bed, you are funny. And not bad at fixing boilers, either.

And for Lily and Henry, my favourite joke will always be: 'What do you call two robbers?' You know the punchline, guys. Tommy Bear, Mummy will explain it to you when you are older.

Chapter 1

TIME AT THE BAR, PLEASE...

'I love Russell Howard yet I have never met him.'
BELINDA, YEAR 6 PUPIL, TRANQUIL PARK
PRIMARY SCHOOL

Picture the scene... Russell Howard is in hospital. He's hurt his thumb and has had to undergo two operations. He's been a patient for nearly a week now and is spending his time wandering the wards, holding his thumb up in the air, passing the time. He sits down to idly thumb, er, flick, his way through the waiting room magazines and is staring into space when a exhausted-looking man walks past and sits down next to him. Russ asks if he is OK.

'I've just seen my wife give birth,' says the man.

'Wow, what was that like? Was it great?' asks Russ.

The man turns to him. 'No... It's like watching your favourite pub burn down to the ground.'

It was one of the funniest things Russ had ever heard. And

1

one that sums up his joy at meeting new people – you can't make this stuff up.

Thankfully, the birth of Mr Russell Joseph Howard wasn't quite like the labour just described. Born on 23 March 1980 to David and Ninette Howard, it is unlikely that Russ's father described the birth of his firstborn as being akin to watching his local go down in flames.

If you were a cosmic sort who charted the births and deaths of entertainers and superstars, you might set some credence behind the idea that the year Russell Howard was born was also the year that an array of famous stars died. Former Beatle John Lennon was assassinated in the archway of the Dakota, his New York City apartment building. Director and producer Sir Alfred Hitchcock, actors Peter Sellers and Hattie Jacques and celebrated photographer Sir Cecil Beaton all passed away in 1980. 'Some in, some out,' as they say. Time for a new generation of entertainers and stars and who would ever have guessed that that the firstborn Howard would, some thirty-plus years later, be entertaining the world by making us giggle.

Laugh-out-loud, belly-ache from chuckles – piss ourselves with laughter, basically.

Russell might well have been born with some of that comic genius. His parents weren't in the entertainment business: his mum was a housewife and an occasional dinner lady (at school Russ used to pretend to his mates that it was Ninette who had made all the tastiest things on the menu to try and impress them) and his dad had his own design business, designing call centres. But it was at home where his fun-loving personality and quick-witted humour grew and was nurtured.

'Both my parents are funny, I guess,' he admits. 'My dad sends me ideas a lot for jokes and quite often they are quite mental but I love that. And my mum is inadvertently hilarious. She has this incredible skill where she can turn a conversation back to some kind of suffering she's had. Even if she met Nelson Mandela she'd be like, "Yeah, I spent a lot of time on my own too, Nelson, so I know what you're talking about." Hilarious.'

Russell wasn't an only child for long and two years later, on 24 March 1982, he found himself sharing his parents' attention with a brother and sister when his mum gave birth to twins, Kerry and Daniel. Although according to Kerry, it was actually Russell and Daniel who were closest growing up.

'Russell is two years older than me and Daniel but they were really the twins when we were growing up. They loved playing football together. I was reluctantly in goal and they called me Bruce Grobbelaar. For years I thought I was a great goalie because I always stopped the ball but it was only recently that they revealed they were actually aiming for my head!'

Growing up in a sprawling old vicarage in a tiny village in Hampshire, much of Russell's childhood was spent playing outside and having fun with his siblings.

'Daniel and I were a constant disappointment to our parents, partly because our clothes were always covered in mud,' he confessed. 'We looked like street urchins, despite being quite well-off. We just spent all our time outdoors, rolling around in the dirt.'

As a youngster he was definitely the most timid of the three and when his younger brother and sister wanted to play dressing up and perform plays for the family, it was Russell who would insist on taking a more low-key role: 'I was always behind the camera. They were natural show-offs, I wasn't.' There were several occasions when the Howard family indulged in some amateur dramatics, though, and the whole clan would get involved – his mum even made most of the costumes – 'I have a really great photo of my nan in a crocodile costume when we were doing Captain Hook.'

The closeness he shared with his brother Daniel meant that Kerry was quite often the target of their pranks – as well as taking pot shots at her head after tricking her into becoming goalie, her toys were also fair game.

'We were pretty mean to her, we used to dunk her doll's head in the toilet and made its hair fall out,' he later confessed.

But being a girl also had its advantages and Kerry made sure she got the biggest bedroom – 'She made the dubious claim that she needed the extra space to practise her ballet,' remembers Russ.

As with most brothers, there was a spot of healthy competitiveness between Russell and Daniel as they were growing up. But there was no competition when it came to who was the biggest show-off – that was Daniel without a doubt. Confident and funny, he would often leave the quite nervous Russell on the periphery of big family gatherings while he entertained relatives. But years later this sort of experience would provide the perfect fodder for some of Russell's sketches.

'It became something I spoke about in my comedy,' he later told revealed in an interview with *Metro*. 'My family have never censored what I say. The only thing that has been censored was a routine about my mum in a hot tub, but I censored that. What she says is far too horrific.'

In fact, he does censor some of the sketches about his family life, putting his own spin on an event he has attended and then retelling it in his boyishly rude fashion – 'My mum will just see it as, "Ah, I remember that barbecue, we had a lovely time, didn't we?"'

His mum, Ninette, it's fair to point out, is a bit of a comedy legend herself. With three children to bring up, including two cheeky boys, her sense of humour was, and still is, to be brutally honest: dirty and completely insane, but completely hilarious too. Russell has no qualms about admitting that his mum should be the one on stage, as she is a far better comic.

'She could do stand-up herself but then I wouldn't have a career,' he told the *Daily Mirror* in 2016. 'She'd be far better at it than me. She is unwittingly funny and I take quite a lot of stuff from her because she just has no idea of how funny she is.'

You only have to look at Ninette's reaction when she watched Russell perform for the very first time at Wembley, a proud moment for any parent, to see her wicked sense of humour. She has always adored watching him perform and on that momentous occasion pointed out her nether regions to other members of the public and informed them in a completely deadpan tone of voice: 'That's where the magic comes from.' Russell was mortified, but amused: 'No one knew she was my mum so they all just thought she was some mad lady claiming to have a magic vagina.'

And what about the time when Russell was driving his mum on the motorway a few years ago and there was a horrific crash? The traffic had slowed down and there was a huge traffic jam as the incident was only a few hundred yards away from them. People started to get out of their cars and some of them then recognised Russell and wanted to take photos. It was a little awkward to say the least, not least because there was a major road traffic accident, but then to Russ's humiliation, his mum then started screaming out of the window, 'He's kidnapped me!' and people started to look worried.

'I had to start shouting, "She's my mum, it's just my mum!" to these strangers,' he recalls. And her response when a mortified Russell asked why she did such an embarrassing thing? She simply replied that she was fifty-seven years old and she didn't care. 'How could I not grow up to be a comedian?' he mused.

Although that's not to say he always wanted to be a comic. The self-confessed shy boy was only eight years old when he discovered his true calling in life: to be a Jedi knight. Bless. And then that ambition briefly changed to wanting to be Indiana Jones. 'But I realised that wouldn't work either,' he recalls. Somewhat amusingly, his Jedi ambition still holds strong, especially when it was rumoured he would be performing for a Scientology convention a few years ago. There was a baseless rumour that the Church of Scientology had advertised that Russell Howard would be performing for their followers and were selling tickets for an extortionate amount. Russ had to clarify the situation immediately. 'Of course it's not true,' he tweeted, 'I'm not a Scientologist; I'm a Jedi.'

Growing up in a house full of fun and games and excitement was the norm. 'There was always lots of people and dogs and screaming,' Russell explained to *The Independent*. 'Me and my brother and sister were very excited all the time. We used to lose our minds on the rare occasion when my dad would say, "Let's get a Chinese takeaway." I get pissed off when I see an eight-year-old looking really bored in Wagamama.'

Growing up in the eighties and early nineties, it was the simple things like listening to the Top 40 songs every Sunday that would stick in Russell's memory, or maybe the fact that his dad was trying to teach them all how to dance.

'Every week Daniel, Kerry and I would dance to *The Chart Show* and Dad would try and teach us how to move. He wasn't a good teacher and would just say, "Find the rhythm, kids, move to the beat." I think my best move was the lunge. Every time we heard music we had this Pavlovian response to "find the rhythm".'

The closeness he enjoyed with his brother also fell into friendly rivalry on occasion, and one of Russell's favourite childhood memories is when he and Daniel were both desperate to outdo each other in a childhood game of 'Waking Up Early'.

'One time we thought, "Let's see if we can get up as early as possible". So we'd get up at 6am and be down in the kitchen, on our own, feeling bloody incredible that no one else was awake. Then it got to 5am, then 4am, and it ended with me and Daniel fully dressed in our school uniform at, like, 2am. My dad came down, stark bollock naked, going; "What's wrong with you two?" He was really angry and shaking but at the same time, any ability to tell us off had gone because we were watching his willy swing about. It was a really weird moment.'

Dan remembers Russell constantly using him as a 'toy' by making him do crazy things when they were out as a family. Once on a family holiday in Spain at Christmas time, Russ dared his brother to take off all his clothes and run into the sea.

'That doesn't sound difficult, does it?' recalls Dan. 'But I had to strip without our parents noticing and it was Christmas Eve and freezing! Russell thought it was hilarious but Mum and Dad were mortified. 'They bundled us into the car and drove us all straight home.'

As well as the weird nakedness and brother-goading, there were also the embarrassing moments of growing up that any youngster will sympathise with. The first record ten-year-old Russ bought was SL2, *'On A Ragga Tip'* on cassette tape, which he only bought to impress a girl. And at eleven years old he had the soul-destroying experience of puking in front of all of his mates. Unfortunately for Russell, it didn't just happen in front of a few friends, he was trying to show off to his pals at a theme park and went on a ride as a joke, pretending he was too old and too cool:

'It was the tea-cup ride at a theme park and to my horror a few older lads decided to jump on and spin the cups really fast and I was sick all over my new LA Raiders jacket. For the next six months I was known as the Tea Cup Sick Boy,' he told *The Student Pocket Guide* website.

Of course, amusing moments such as this were all part and parcel of growing up. Russell recently admitted he'd struggle to be a kid in this day and age: 'I spent a lot of my childhood sat on a wall, thinking, waiting for my mum to pick me up. It's that time your brain can just freely associate and obviously that's really good for you because your brain kind of drifts from hither and dither, but then, if I'd have had an iPhone I would have been all over that. I think it's quite hard to have an imagination because an eight-year-old brain cannot possibly compete with the Internet.'

During a recent appearance on the hit BBC One TV show, *Would I Lie to You?*, Russ admitted that he suffered terrible acne as a youngster and when he was twelve years old, with greasy hair and spots on his face, he used to sleep with pants on his head to cure his skin condition.

'I only did it at night. I was into Nirvana and I didn't want to ask Mum for a hairnet so I took the pants and put them round my head, nice and tight.'

It seems that wasn't the only embarrassing ailment either. At the same time one of Russ's nipples started to grow larger and so he went to the doctor for advice, concerned he was about to become a woman or something: 'My mum chose that moment to tell the doctor that I also put pants on my head at night and the doctor told me in no way would it get rid of my acne so I stopped doing it. It was a brutal summer – spots and one boob.'

As well as the amusing and embarrassing experiences that Russell had as a youngster, there was also the serious incident that occurred when he was twelve years old, which affected his and Daniel's life forever. I'm sure you must know what I am talking about. For years, fans of the comedian have been laughing themselves silly over tales of Daniel's epilepsy as Russ often shares embarrassing moments of his brother's seizures in his routines. But back then it was quite a scary experience...

Chapter 2

BIKES, BULLIES AND EXPLODING BALLS...

*'It was a totally surreal situation dealing with someone you thought
might be dying while trying to ignore his rock-hard cock. Every time we
tried to put him in the recovery position his penis acted as a pivot.
It was just an inherently funny moment.'*
RH

Boys and their bikes... No youngster these days would cycle without a helmet but back in the childhood days of Russ and Daniel Howard, things like bike helmets weren't quite such a strict safety rule. Boys and girls didn't worry about helmets; they just got on their bikes and rode off at great speed. And one sunny day, twelve-year-old Russell and ten-year-old Daniel did just that. Sadly, it all went horribly wrong and there was a terrible accident. Riding down a steep hill near their home, the battery in the light on Russell's handlebars fell out and it was sheer bad luck that it became stuck in the spokes of Daniel's front wheel as he rode behind him. Daniel flew over the handlebars, over Russell, and landed on his head. He was knocked unconscious and a frightened Russ ran for help. It was his quick reaction that saved his brother's life and Daniel was taken to hospital, where, to the relief of everyone, the family were told he was going to be OK. But it was a short-lived emotion and just a few weeks later, Daniel suffered his first epileptic fit.

For Russell, the experience of seeing his brother fit can now be made fun of (with Daniel's permission, of course), but it was utterly horrifying at the time.

'I got angry because I thought he was messing around [during his fit], but it was terrifying,' Russell admits. 'Our family just descended into mad panic. I understand why people used to believe that epileptics were possessed by the devil. Daniel went into this weird trance and started hallucinating, saying he could see monsters. By the time they took him away in an ambulance we were all in tears.'

It was the first time that Russell had seen his dad cry and combined with the upset over Daniel he felt an enormous sense of guilt over what had happened. His sister Kerry remembers the incident well and admits that the whole family thought Daniel was going to die, having no idea what epilepsy was. They later discovered it is a condition which affects the brain and it was diagnosed in Daniel due to his repeating seizures. During a seizure, there are abnormal bursts of neurons (specialised cells in the brain) firing off electrical impulses that can cause the brain and the body to behave strangely. The severity of those seizures can differ from person to person and Daniel suffered varying levels of fits over the years.

He continued to have piercing headaches for a year after the crash and following the initial seizure, he had another one two months later and continued to have one every month for about twelve months until they were brought under control by medication.

At twelve years old, Russell blamed himself completely for what happened. 'The lights came off my bike, I have always felt guilty,' he admits. 'I blamed myself for the accident for a long time but I know it wasn't my fault.'

At this point the dynamic among the siblings changed and Kerry became the one in charge of her brothers, ensuring the physically exuberant Russell didn't do anything to inadvertently harm Daniel – 'I would fret every time Russ and Dan had playfights. I was always shouting at Russ, "Don't hit his head!"'

If the three siblings learnt anything from the experience it was how brave Daniel was, and how resilient he was at coping with his newfound condition. Had it been Russell or Kerry who had had the accident, the latter is convinced they would not have coped so seamlessly: 'We were a couple of softies, Daniel was just so brave.'

As if to confirm his 'softy' status, Russell, it seems, is still scared of the dark. It is something that he is constantly teased about by his brother – well, who wouldn't?

'Can you believe that my big brother is still scared of the dark?' mocks Daniel. 'Still! Even now I get calls from him late at night, saying, "Dan, I'm at the Tube station, will you come and walk back with me?"'

Mocking his older brother aside, Daniel gets very

concerned when he sees young kids on their bikes without helmets – 'I always shout at them to put one on,' he insists.

Growing up and living with a brother who has been diagnosed with epilepsy didn't affect how close Russell and Daniel were. If anything, Russ was impressed that Dan never dwelt on his condition or seemed to feel sorry for himself.

'Daniel never came crying to me if people mocked him about his epilepsy. It must have been traumatic for him,' he revealed in an interview with the *Sunday Times in 2013*. 'Once, he was 13, he had a fit in front of his entire school year during a trip to Reading Museum. The reaction of one female teacher, who had quite a large bottom, was to sit on him to try and stop him fitting. It was a weirdly comic scenario, but he was mortified, and the fact he wet himself didn't help to lessen his embarrassment.'

Shocking though the situation was, Russell wasn't ever going to pity his brother and to this day, they share a unique, close bond.

Daniel didn't let his epilepsy define him but when he was put on strong medication that controlled his fits, this in turn had some quite serious side effects.

'It slowed him down on the football pitch, which meant he couldn't play for our local team any more,' explains Russ. 'That upset him. And he also got the shakes all the time, which made doing school work difficult, but we've all dealt with his epilepsy by making light of it and trying to see the humour. I've talked openly in my stand-up, especially the fit he had on Christmas morning when he was fifteen. My parents and I found him naked in his bed with a massive erection. It was a totally surreal situation dealing with someone you thought might be dying while trying to ignore his rock-hard cock. Every time we tried to put him in the recovery position, his penis acted as a pivot. It was just an inherently funny moment.'

And it was a moment Russell shared with audiences over the years, but never without the go-ahead from Dan. You might say that incorporating jokes about his brother and his condition has helped Russ process the accident. It is also a good way of raising awareness about the condition too, of course – with Daniel's help.

'Dan has managed to turn something that was really bad in his life into something that is good and out there. He's a funny guy and I always consult him before using any material about his epilepsy in my gigs,' he confirms. 'Dan has always been my toughest audience, he is brutally honest and I really appreciate it. If he gives one of my jokes the seal of approval then I definitely know it's good enough to perform.'

Daniel is equally supportive: 'Of course my condition has since become a talking point in his act, but I'm not offended when he makes jokes about it. He has turned something deeply unpleasant into humour and at the same time is raising awareness about it. He knows he doesn't need to ask my permission, if it's a good gag he should just do it.'

Unfortunately, there are gags that maybe shouldn't get a mention. The things he did to Dan while growing up, for example – the marbles-up-his-bum gag, anyone? It's all true, of course, although Russ claims the exact amount might have been exaggerated for his act. 'It was seven [times] at the most,' he confirms.

When not making his brother get naked at Christmas or dancing with his dad to the Top 40 on the radio, Russell attended the Bedford Modern School, an independent day school, for a year when he was eight years old before starting at Perins School in Alresford, Hampshire, where all he really remembers is fancying one of the teachers, Mrs Storey, when he was about nine years old. Well, that, and being told off a lot for disrupting lessons – 'I remember getting a bollocking off my German teacher for making people laugh in class and I was just like, "Honestly, I can't help it." It's just out before I think about it. I was nerdy and I wrote a lot of jokes.'

At the end of one lesson his German teacher took him to one side to try and establish why he always had to muck about in class and Russ decided to be blunt: '"I can't help it," I said, "it's an illness. I wish I could stop but I can't and I don't know what to do." And she kind of almost admired my honesty. She said, "Well, let's just deal with it the best we can." She would laugh at me, and then tell me off, and when I knew I was in trouble was when I said something and she didn't laugh, I'd be like, "Oh shit... I'm going to be sent out here." So I guess I have always been a bit of a show-off. But everyone's funny at school, I think. It's all being silly together and mucking around.'

Was this behaviour one of the first indications of Russell's future career? You could say that. He was happy at school, although his sister Kerry recalls that he wasn't always full of good humour: 'I remember one Christmas when he was fourteen he really wanted a pair of Nike Air Jordans. Unfortunately, my parents weren't that flush so he got a pair of High-Tecs. He was so upset, he cried all day. I felt sorry for him. Your trainers define you at that age,' she revealed to *Radio Times* in 2015

Of course another defining thing for any young boy is his appearance. Until that point Russell's mum, Ninette, had always cut his hair (his auntie then took over), but at fourteen years old, on the cusp of manhood, naturally you want to stand out and look good. Russell, who was at the time obsessed with teen actor Sean Maguire from the BBC children's drama *Grange Hill*, decided to take matters into his own hands.

'I got a bus from Ropley where I used to live to Alton and I had a picture from Sean Maguire in my pocket. He played Tegs in *Grange Hill*. I went into Chaps in Alton and I said, "Can I have a Sean Maguire, please?" I was really into him for a while, I had a really big thing for him. He had flowing hair, I didn't. I don't think I ended up looking anything like him. It was the worst haircut I ever had.'

The antics of growing up, particularly his early teens, feature a lot in Russell's stand-up shows and there are a couple of sketches that define those years. His story of masturbating at fourteen years old was a sketch he performed on his *Right Here, Right Now* Tour but does give you an idea: he was a normal bloke and he was happy to share a very personal experience with a wider audience for laughs. Of course, as everything with Russell, the parts that were exaggerated and the parts that are true have a tendency to blur, but suffice to say, it's still hilarious. He tells the story of when he was fourteen years old and was masturbating in front of the TV one evening. Then a strange bloke knocks on the window and grins at him and Russell describes it as absolutely 'terrifying'. But worse news was to come when his mum gets home and tells a petrified Russ that a neighbouring house has been burgled meaning that the creepy bloke looking through the window at Russ with a boner was the burglar.

If that story has been heavily embellished for the purposes of comedy then it worked. But there are things that happened to Russell when he was fourteen that he remembers vividly with no jokes attached. He was in the car with his dad, who, out of the blue, turned to Russ and said, 'The trouble with you, son, you'll never be happy. And that's the way it is.' It was so matter-of-fact, but completely true, according to Russ, so true that he agrees with this sentiment without question: 'I am so much like my dad, I am my dad's son,' he admitted years later in a podcast interview for *ComediansComedian*. 'I am driven completely by fear and I am so loath to fix that because then I think, I won't be me, I won't be funny. I do get moments of joy and I get to do loads and loads of cool things but they are all driven by fear. You don't come offstage after a gig at the O2 and think, "Nailed it". You come offstage going, "Was that OK? It felt good, was it good?" You take half an hour to come down after that but the fear is always there. Rugby player Jonny Wilkinson is a fantastic person and I remember reading, when he did that drop-goal kick and won the World Cup in 2003, there was a thing in his brain that said, "You nearly missed that". And the next day he was out practising his kicking again. I really recognise that – that sentiment spoke to me. I will always have something in my brain going, "Yeah, that was good but..." Nothing is ever perfect, you are always struggling to get something right.'

Russell was happy to accept his dad's blunt yet honest truth, because he recognised that he was a lot like him. And while it is mostly his mum that is mentioned and he has a lot of pleasure in quoting, his dad has always had a heavy influence on his life too: 'My dad is a really great and driven man. My mum gets a lot of praise and rightly so because she is an incredible woman and raised us with a lot of zest and silliness, but my dad has an iron will like nobody. If he sets out to achieve something he will do it. He has passed that down to me and my little sister so I am really grateful for the way he taught us to be – and that is to always try really, really hard. My dad's work ethic is insane.'

Like any teen growing up, life had its highs and lows. At school Russell wasn't in the 'cool' gang, but he did have mates he could goof around with – like when they pretended they were werewolves...

'Me and my mates thought, because of the film *Teen Wolf*, we could turn into wolves too. And I can remember being really annoyed with someone in the playground because she scratched me and I just started twisting and turning and moving, and thinking I was going to change... but nothing happened. I was called spastic.'

The nineties film *Teen Wolf*, starring Michael J. Fox, was a favourite among youngsters, as was the Australian TV soap series *Neighbours*, which starred Kylie Minogue, who was fresh out of high school.

'I loved *Neighbours*,' recalls Russ. 'One of the best things that happened in the show was when Granny Helen died. God, that was funny. One of her granddaughters, who looked a bit like a rabbit, was just sat there chatting away to her and she had died on the sofa. It was hilarious.'

And of course wearing the right clothes was important for a young lad too – you didn't want to look stupid, did you, Russ? Perhaps wearing his trousers backwards at a school disco might not have been the best idea therefore. Although in his defence he was trying to copy the hip hop duo Kriss Kross, whose signature look was back-to-front baggy jeans.

'It led to some bullying,' he revealed some years later to *The Independent*. Ah yes, the bullies. Being bullied isn't great for any kid, let alone a small, shy boy with a lazy eye. His eye was the source of much name-calling, and general playground nastiness – a fact he has since shared with fans. Like many bullied children, however, he is, quite literally, having the last laugh over those who taunted him.

'I used to get bullied really bad when I was younger, cos I had a lazy eye. I've had an operation but you can still see it,' he told audiences over the years on stage. 'Kids used to say as I walked past, "Look at him, he's obsessed with his nose!"'

Russell decided to ask his parents for advice and his sensible dad decided, luckily for his son's future career, that the best way to beat the bullies wasn't to beat them up, it was to retort with words.

'I used to cry a lot, I looked like a Picasso in the rain,' he recalled to a laughing audience. So I went to my parents and said, "Dad, I need advice." So he told me that if I say this to the bullies, I will be OK: "Bullies, how can my eye be lazy when it wanders around so freely? I think you'll find I have an imaginative eye." I think I got the kick shitted out of me day that day.'

He has since come to terms with the lazy eye, which of course marks him out as a comic and now features heavily in his stand-up routines. It would, however, still be the one thing he would change about himself.

'I would love to have eyes that face in the right direction. That would be pleasant. People often think I'm arrogant or pissed because of my lazy eye,' he told the *Independent in* 2012.

Making light of the situation now, although pretty horrific at the time, Russ can empathise with the environment that kids these days are growing up in. For him, being bullied was at school and stopped the minute he got home. Nowadays, thanks to social media, it's relentless – 'It must be awful if you're a kid and you're getting bullied at school as now you can still get bullied at home. If that's happening, that must be pretty shit,' he muses.

That's not to say that Russell was squeaky clean either and at his school he witnessed some highly amusing antics by some of the tougher, meaner kids. There was one school camping trip he went on where kids from a rival school were setting up their tents not too far away. One of the bigger boys from Russ's school decided to defecate on his hand and then lob it over to the kids from the other school.

'He actually shit in his hand, we couldn't believe it. His own shit! And then this kid said, "Look at this, I'm going to throw it at them." And because he was so hard, no one wanted to say, "Er, that's a bit weird!"'

And of course Russell was happy to join in with class jokes at the expense of others too, sniggering at a boy in the year below when rumours started that his balls had exploded – yes, really. Although Russ admits he can't remember how they started. Then there was the time when the gossip started up about a girl in his class who had allegedly slept with someone who worked at the local fairground. Russell and his mates took it upon themselves to start singing the circus theme tune every time her name was called out in the register, which of course they thought was hilarious.

But it wasn't all silliness and pranks. At the same time Russell was a very bright, studious young chap and he remembers vividly one teacher who helped him cultivate an interest in literature and poetry – 'Mrs Whale taught English and was always getting pregnant. We were a bunch of reprobates and she was brilliant and really funny,' he recalls. 'She turned me on to war poetry – it was easy to get if you were 15, it's not a million miles away from Radiohead lyrics.'

Sounds like something from E4's *The Inbetweeners*, doesn't it? Funnily enough, looking back, Russell readily admits life was a bit like the teen comedy series more than he might have realised at the time: 'Together you are funny and in a group you gee each other along, but it is such a different thing to suddenly declare yourself as funny.'

So when did this declaration of 'funny' come about?

Well, at fifteen years old Russell had only one interest and it wasn't being a comedian...

Chapter 3

KNOCK, KNOCK. WHO'S THERE? RUSSELL. RUSSELL WHO?

'Sometimes the sky is blue. It's just blue, it doesn't mean a bloody thing.
It really annoys me sometimes; when people try to find deeper meanings.'

RH

Football... It's a pretty natural thing for boys to be into footie and Russell was, big time. Having played constantly as a youngster with his brother, Daniel, it became his ambition to be a professional footballer. In fact he played for Basingstoke Town FC when he was younger and was picked to play in the first round of the FA Youth Cup. It wasn't a brilliant result, they were beaten 18–0, but for Russ the experience was exhilarating. Sadly, he wasn't quite good enough to make the cut from semi-serious league to the super-serious. And that realisation was heartbreaking.

'He was desperate to be a footballer when he was younger,' recalls Daniel. 'He was devastated when he realised he wasn't good enough.'

An incident at school when he was fifteen years old also,

also thanks to football, changed his outlook on friendships. Russell found himself going from the 'jocks' of the school, thanks to his footie skills, to the 'freaks and geeks' circle. He won't reveal what the incident was but afterwards he found a new direction. Nevertheless. what was a loss to the football world – though he is still quite nifty with a football and plays for his local pub team (left midfield) – was a huge gain for the comedy world.. And the love affair with comedy all started with one comedian called Lee.

In the nineties Lee Evans was a multi-award winning British comedian, writer, actor and musician. He has since become one of Britain's highest-selling stand-ups and his performances on stage often leave him dripping in sweat and in need of an outfit change during the interval. But for the teenage Russell Howard, he was a hero. Glued to the VHS of his *Live At Her Majesty's Theatre* show, his *Live From The West End* and *Live – Different Planet* Tour, both of which were filmed at the Lyric Theatre in London, Lee Evans was without doubt a huge influence. It was his *Live In Norwich* video that Russell watched over and over with his mate, Craig – to a point where he could repeat the routine word for word. And that became the start of an interest in performing. Lee wasn't particularly macho and he would take the mickey out of himself and act like the fool on stage, something that struck a chord with Russell.

'Up until that point there was an assumption that all stand-up was alpha male. Lee clearly wasn't. I'd argue he was one of the first mainstream, low-status comics of my era. He was interesting to a whole bunch of blokes who weren't the most popular boys in school. Watching that, I thought, "I could do that." I'd never be the most powerfully funny man or the bloke that slammed everybody around him but I could take the mickey out of myself,' Russell told *Radio Times* in 2014.

Lee Evans became a family favourite, thanks to Russell's obsession, and every Christmas the family would sit watching the latest video. He was a hit with everyone that is apart from Russell's granddad, who thought the comic was 'too fast, too sweaty'.

And so at fifteen years old, Russell began putting pen to paper, having being influenced 'solely based on that video'. He has since met Lee Evans and admits that he was totally in awe – 'My inner fan boy is just in utter thrall to him,' he recalled.

The idea of watching a VHS or DVD over and over, becoming lost in the repetitiveness of the jokes, focusing on the small details of holding the microphone, or how the performer walks around on stage are all lost on this generation, believes Russell. Today, the need for quick clips, videos uploaded to YouTube and the constant streaming of shows and performances all mean that sitting down to watch a full stand-up show on DVD is lost – and it does upset him – 'I was excited, watching Lee Evans, rewinding it, pausing it, rewinding it on VHS. Before YouTube, me and my mates used to pass round videos of the cool stuff. The Internet is great but I do get nostalgic for the days where you'd unearth a dusty VHS and discover someone like Billy Connolly for the first time.'

Lee Evans, Billy Connolly and Frank Skinner changed his world and after watching these three iconic comics, Russell knew what he wanted to do with the rest of his life. For the next few years, while studying at Alton College in Hampshire, he began writing jokes. He wasn't ready to show the world just yet what he had to offer but at sixteen years old, he was starting to work on material that he would later use in performances.

Alton College, a sixth-form college, was built in 1978 and was one of the first institutions in the UK to be a purpose-built sixth-form college. Studying Business Studies, English Language, Media Studies and Computing, Russell enjoyed all his subjects bar Media Studies. He didn't enjoy trying to meta–analyse every little thing: 'I did it for three weeks at college and it killed me,' he remembers. 'It was the only time that I walked out. They made us analyse an advert, saying, the sky is blue, which means calming, and there's a table, which is very earthy and means this is an organic product... I said, "Sometimes the sky is blue. It's just blue, it doesn't mean a bloody thing." It really annoys me sometimes when people try to find deeper meanings. If you like stuff, why try and make it into something bigger? It's just an advert, it's just a person, or a song or a joke. That's all they are.'

Quitting Media Studies allowed Russ some spare time to start jotting down jokes and writing sketches in the privacy of his bedroom. And it was also a very poignant gift from his dad (although Russ might have preferred a Nintendo Game Boy) that spurred him on to believe that penning jokes wasn't a waste of time. It was a plaque with a T.E. Lawrence

quote written on it and it had a powerful effect on Russell.
The quote read:

> Those who dream by night in the dusty recesses of their
> minds wake in the day to find that it was vanity: but the
> dreamers of the day are dangerous men, for they act their
> dreams with open eyes, to make it happen.

'It was an incredible gift to give a 16-year-old,' admits
Russell. 'It was like he was saying, "You can do anything,
so go for it".'

There was also an element of tragedy which shaped Russ's
ambition. While all of his mates, including Russ himself, were
talking about the future and what universities they would be
going to, one 'really talented bloke' who was only eighteen
years old died in a car crash. 'It had a profound effect on
me,' Russell told the *Telegraph* in an interview years later.
'He wasn't a great mate of mine but I knew him and I'd
chat to him and he just died in a car crash. It was so sad. He
was clearly going to be an extraordinary person. I remember
getting the call and being really shaken and thinking, "That's
it – it could all end tomorrow".'

'Eventually I saw it as this thing I had to do; just once and
then that's it, I've done it.'

But while the ambition was there, the reality wasn't always
so glamorous and Russell decided to take on a part-time job
picking weeds out of watercress during sixth form to earn
himself some extra cash. He later went on to describe it as
one of the worst jobs he's ever had – 'I was working in a

watercress factory, I had to pick out the weeds. But it was 1996 and £5 an hour, which was really good back then.' Russ didn't last long, though – the 5am starts were too brutal for the teen and he wasn't that good at the job either: 'Most weeds look like watercress anyway.'

Romance-wise, eighteen-year-old Russell wasn't exactly a big dater but found that girls would enjoy his sense of humour and company and, for now , that was enough for him. However, he also found himself at the end of a disgruntled husband's fist when he thought Russ was having an affair with his wife. It wasn't funny at the time, of course, but Russ took it all in his stride, maintaining to this day that he had 'never met her'. In years to come he would be voted a 'pan-generational sex symbol' by the readers of *Radio Times* and in 2013, voted top of *Heat* magazine's Weird Crush poll – 'I have been called a lazy-eyed twat and dickhead a lot at school,' he recalled, 'never sex symbol.'

While studying, writing and, er, weeding, Russell was one of the key pupils involved in setting up the Alton College Radio Station, which broadcasts to students in the refectory and student common room. He used this platform as a very early way of seeing how audiences reacted to some of his jokes. It wasn't a one-man show, but Russ presented a range of topical sketches on all aspects of college life for the entertainment of others and it was a good way to see if what he was saying was actually liked.

After finishing his A-levels in 1998, he left Alton College and gained a place at UWE Bristol, studying Economics. Fans have since commented on student chatroom threads that he is one of the celebrities they are most shocked by when they realise what degree he has – apparently most comics don't seem to be experts in Economics.

Russell needed a part-time job to help him through his studies and so he became a trolley boy for Tesco, which he readily admits wasn't particularly sexy: 'When you try and create an impression for a girl you fancy and then she sees you in the supermarket car park arranging trolleys, I learned there is no sexy way to push a trolley.'

During his studies he began to gain more momentum with his comedy and at eighteen, he and his mates visited a comedy club in Bath. Every Tuesday they would be enthralled by the performances of Ross Noble, Ed Byrne and Daniel Kitson. But watching a routine performed by the legendary Johnny Vegas was mind-blowing for Russ and a specific piece of interaction with an audience member has remained with him from all those years ago and he remembers it vividly:

'Johnny is talking to this girl in the audience and asks, "What do you do?" She was really nervous and said, "It's too embarrassing to say." "I'll tell you embarrassing," Vegas replied and started telling this story: "When I was a boy I wasn't allowed bath toys so I'd get a flannel and wrap it around my genitals and he was my friend. Then my dad lost his job and we all had to have a bath together, me and my two brothers, and I started playing with the flannel and my brother said, 'Johnny, you're a pervert, you're going to jail.' That's embarrassing. What do you do?" And then the girl told him what she did. The whole point of Johnny's story was to put her at ease.'

A year later, at nineteen years old, Russell decided that the time was right to put his writing to the test. He chickened out several times, booking some club slots and then cancelling them before biting the bullet. There was a small gig called Virgin Merk, which was run by some older Bristolian men who were, admits Russell, really eccentric. They had an open comedy spot and he decided to go down there and perform, not telling a soul about it.

The night was compered by circuit comic James Dowdeswell and all Russ can remember was that he puked – a lot. 'That first gig was a bit of a blur,' he recalls. 'I threw up before I went on and threw up after I'd been on. It was quite a high-tempo show. Most comics' first gig is either brilliant or horrific. I still get nervous before the bigger ones but I do more pacing nowadays than throwing up.'

Russell had crept out of his halls of residence and performed at the now-defunct Le Chateau bar on Park Street, in the centre of Bristol, without any of his mates knowing. And for him, performing in complete anonymity was key: 'If I'd gone to those gigs with my mates in the crowd they would have absolutely slaughtered me! It was just a nervous thing, really. If you had your mates there and you made them laugh, you still wouldn't learn anything. I needed to put myself in a room full of people I didn't know and gauge their reaction.'

And the reaction was...? There were about twenty punters watching this debut and the resounding conclusion was that they loved him. Russell loved them too. And more importantly, he loved the experience of being on stage: 'It was great, everyone on stage was nuts,' he recalls. 'I had to follow a man who would eat a banana with a spoon and sing the theme tune to *The Sweeney* [seventies police TV drama]. I just thought to myself, I'll give it a go, I can't be that bad.'

It was after this first gig that Russ had that epiphany moment: he knew what he wanted to do with his life and he knew he could make it work. It was the moment he first realised he was funny. 'Everyone thinks they're funny when they're little but I properly thought after that first gig. It was the first time I thought, "Yeah, I can do this,"' he revealed in an interview with *Dave TV* website in 2008. It was also the moment when he saw a future on stage and suddenly had a hunger for being the best comedian he could be -- he wanted to be a circuit comic and perform at the Edinburgh Festival Fringe, he wanted to compere Late'n'Live (an Edinburgh institution) and he wanted to win the Perrier Comedy Awards.

'Genuinely, after that first gig it felt like the world had shifted. I realised that I had stumbled upon a mechanism through which you could view life. Everything could be pushed through this thing, it made life fun. Gigs changed my life. When I found comedy and this is the corniest thing you'll hear me say... you have probably heard me say this before but in the film, *Interview With The Vampire*, Brad Pitt gets bitten by a vampire and he wakes up, and he's now a vampire and his eyes are different and he sees the world in a different way and that is genuinely how I felt the day after I did my first gig. I have found something that makes everything worthwhile. This is going to be wonderful. That is genuinely how I felt. I was so happy to get laughs and be different and be the guy who wasn't ignored in nightclubs by girls – I was a comedian! It changed everything.'

And what fun he had. After this first gig, he took part in more shows to work out what worked, what didn't, how to interact with the audience and worked within his performance style. Gig number five was at a club called Club Fandango in Plymouth and this time acting as his chauffeur was his little brother Daniel, an experience they both loved. Russell performed for five minutes at the club and was well received. It felt like the brothers were at the start of a huge adventure together – 'It gave you a reason to get out of the house and go for it. I loved it, I still love it.'

It was a six-hour round trip for just a five-minute open-mic slot but it was worth it. It made Russell realise that his new life could take him anywhere – there were pubs all around the country that would host comedy nights. This was a revelation. And of course he treated his brother to a McDonald's on the way home. With five gigs now under his belt, the sixth gig was memorable for all the wrong reasons. It was at Jesters Comedy Club in Bristol. The venue was a big hitter when it came to comedy – past acts included Peter Kay, Russell Brand and Catherine Tate. Russell's confidence was high when he climbed up on stage, having had nothing but praise so far, but his opening joke about Captain Kirk flicking Spock's ears didn't go down well – in fact it bombed. But Russell thought the audience hadn't heard him properly and so he repeated the joke. Silence. The experience knocked him and for the next five minutes he struggled his way through his routine before finishing early, visibly shaken.

It was an experience he didn't ever want to repeat. 'They thought I was a prat,' he recalls. 'There was complete and utter silence, it was like nothing I'd ever experienced. It was the worst feeling in the world. You come off and go, "What happened? I've lost my powers." I was properly awful and it was a real moment of flight or flight.'

That night he walked back home broken, thinking his chosen path now gone – 'I was on with Scott Capurro and Paul B. Edwards and I said to Scott, "I'm broken, what do you do after a bad gig?", and Scott's like, "I like to get a cock in my mouth as soon as possible," and there's me going, "I'm not sure I want to do that, but is that what you have to do?!"'

But Russell knew he had to get back out there, put the failure behind him and claim his rightful 'powers' – 'I remember thinking, "I'm going to have to work a lot harder because that can't happen again and rather than running away, I thought, "Right, I need to rebuild the machine." It was a weird conversation with myself, but I knew I had to work harder otherwise I would just get a rubbish job and be unhappy.'

Years later, he would impart similar advice to Stuart Goldsmith, a comic he met who was struggling and didn't think his routines were going well. Russell told him to remember one thing: 'You are only six months away from being great again. We all get stuck in ruts, we all get times when it's not going right, but if you work at it, you can't be stopped.'

Helping him rebuild was his brother Daniel, who once

again took on the role of chauffeur. Daniel drove him to the Komedia in Brighton, a premier live entertainment venue, to perform in five-minute open-mic slots and then on most weekends he would drive him around the UK to more gigs. Although he was younger and it was a time when most of his mates had started drinking and going out to pubs, for Dan, alcohol wasn't an option. Due to the nature of his epilepsy medication, he was therefore happy to shepherd his big brother around, strengthening their bond even more. Having witnessed to his early gigs and then performing at the O2 years later, Daniel has been there for the highs and lows – 'It is the best thing about my brother, he was there for the first moments and there is genuinely no hint of jealousy or bitterness that he's not doing those things,' admits Russ.

It wasn't always easy being eighteen years old and trying to perform to a crowd who were sometimes unenthusiastic, especially as Russell admitted to looking about twelve years old, even though he was in his late teens. Some of his jokes about pop music didn't go down too well with big, old, burly blokes either: 'They weren't interested in Craig David or what sort of week he had had, I don't even think they knew who he was,' Russ recalls.

Little did he know that it was all part of the process of being a brilliant comic – simple trial and error. He was making notes all the time and jotting down ideas wherever he went to then work on them later. The master was perfecting his craft...

Chapter 4

THE FUCKIN' BFG

'It was astonishing. Who brings a noose to a gig? Go with hope.'
RH

At nineteen years old, Russell Howard was officially ready to make his mark on the comedy world. He decided to enter the competition, *So You Think You're Funny?*, an annual contest which sees novice comedians performing in a series of heats. Open only to those who have been performing for less than eighteen months and who are identified as 'emerging' rather than 'established' talent, the competition has kickstarted the careers of some of the most identifiable comedians in the UK. Comedy legend and sitcom star Lee Mack cited winning the coveted title in 1995 as the 'pinnacle of my career' – 'From the bottom of my heart, nothing has been as exciting as that moment when they said, "The winner is Lee Mack."'

So, in 1999, it was a competition that Russ Howard too

felt ready to enter. Several heats, which last one and a half hours, take place across the UK and each stand-up is allowed just eight minutes to win over both the audience and judges. The judges then select the best acts they have seen over the entire run to take part in one of seven heats at the hugely popular Edinburgh Festival Fringe. The lucky few then make it to the final performance at The Gilded Balloon during the Edinburgh Festival Fringe, one of the most popular nights at the Fringe, with tickets sold out within a couple of hours.

And guess what? Russell was one of those finalists, having impressed the judges with his unique style and anecdotes. Although it's a bit of a mystery to him as to how he quite did it – 'I totally fluked my way in with absolutely no material,' he recalls. 'The semi-final was like an out-of-body experience. I just went for it and bantered with the audience, which I'd never done before, and got to the final. Suddenly there's loads of people there and all the other comics appeared to have jokes.'

The competition was fierce and Russ found himself alongside the likes of David O'Doherty, Jimmy Carr, Josie Long and Andy Zaltzman. The day before the final, he met Jimmy Carr, who looked him up and down and told him that he looked like he'd been on a lot of caravanning holidays. The pair have been friends ever since.

Russell had tweaked his comedy routines slightly so that everything wasn't quite so rehearsed. Having started off with pages and pages of material that he now admits was a little wishy-washy, if he got laughs from particular jokes he would then pick up on the laughter in the audience and found that naturally, his style of performance was changing. He had seen Justin Lee Collins perform, who did lots of improv (which meant he made everything up on the spot as he went along) and Russell followed suit and ditched the material. His whole set was based on an observation of something he had seen the day before the final: a man painted blue, dragging a toilet down the Royal Mile.

Peter Kay was the host for the evening and somehow he knew that he had a selection of explosive, untapped talent to introduce to the eager audience. The third act to perform (and they were only five-minute slots), Russell performed his complete act as an improv, going on and kissing a baby in the front row. Of course, this is something that would be a bit risky now. Only politicians would do such a thing. He is the first to admit that being only a teenager might have worked in his favour and that the audience laughed because he was super-excited to be there and they thought he looked so young and so sweet: 'It was probably the madness of youth. I had two minutes of material probably and then the rest, I was winging it. I think Thierry Henry once said that you aren't scared of taking a penalty when you're eighteen because you've never missed. It was a bit like that for me, I wasn't nervous at all. But I would never dream of doing that now.'

He found the experience liberating and enjoyable but in the end it was the Irish musical comic, David O'Doherty, who came out on top. O'Doherty, who went on to become a regular on the stand-up circuit, knew full well the importance of such a win: 'The final was the biggest gig I had ever done. Winning it definitely gave me the confidence to keep writing the stupid crappy jokes and songs I still do today.'

For Russ, being a finalist and experiencing the competition of such heavyweight comedians was a huge confidence boost and he continued to play all the regular comedy club haunts in Bristol. That same year he went on tour with Phil Kay as his support act, which proved to be an invaluable experience for the nineteen-year-old. He took a week off university to perform with Kay, taking part in ten gigs and getting £50 a show. It was like an apprenticeship and as he watched Phil do fearless stuff, it had a profound effect on him: 'I realised then that you could be anyone. You could leap into the room and be mad, be wild. I had a real fixation with that. I dyed my hair blue, I was a kid, I wanted to be different. I didn't want to do material, I wanted to walk on tables and drink peoples' drinks. I was a poor rip-off but I was relentlessly trying to be mad and weird.'

With comedy now his focus, Russell didn't want to throw away the previous two years of university life and so he decided that he would work extra-hard in his third and final year to make it all worthwhile. This newfound work ethic paid off; he graduated with a 2:1 and his family were immensely proud. Russ himself was still a little peeved though as he found out he was just a fraction off receiving a first-class degree.

'I was really fucked off,' he told *Student Pocket Guide* website in 2011. 'I tried really hard in my last year because I'd always drifted through school and I thought if I topped off my studies with a first it would be great, but I missed out. I was 1 per cent off a first. Gutted!'

But if he was disappointed in his degree ('I got away from

numbers as soon as I could') then his comedy performances were proving rather more successful. Success was made easier by the fact that after he finished his degree his parents agreed to support him for a year to allow him to concentrate on his comedy. He didn't ask for their help, he had started working part-time at the Royal Shakespeare Company when he turned twenty-one, but his dad told him to quit, urging him to realise his dreams: 'He told me to give up the job and "just do comedy or you never will". He told me to give myself a year and see where I was.'

For his parents to see the potential in their eldest son with a career in comedy was a huge confidence boost to Russ. It's just a shame that he can't return the favour when it comes to supporting his dad when he comes up with new ideas.

'My dad will occasionally give me ideas and I have to politely turn them down. Unfortunately, some of his ideas need to be more forcibly shot down. He told me he was working on an idea for a children's TV character and it's terrible. Me and my sister go, "It's the BFG it is the BFG!" It's about this old guy who gives dreams to children. And we're like, "Dad, it's the fuckin' BFG!"'

With comedy now his focus, Russ decided to continue to continue plying his trade in the comedy clubs of Bristol. Young but determined, he would rock up at gigs with a blank page and go for it. It gave him a real platform to build his comedy status and try out his material, he remembers.

'I look back on those days in Bristol with such fondness. Doing comedy in Bristol gave birth to the life I now have. We didn't know it at the time but there was a whole bunch of us on the Bristol scene who would go on to forge successful careers in comedy,' he told *The Exeter Express & Echo*.

The 'whole bunch of us' he refers to include Mark Olver, who is now an in-demand warm-up act on TV shows such as *8 Out of 10 Cats*, *Countdown*, *Pointless*, *The Last Leg*, Jonathan Ross's and Alan Carr's shows. Olver still describes himself as a 'comic' after performing in the comedy clubs with Russ but soon moved into the 'warm-up man' market because the pay was significantly better.

'The thing about stand-up is that the money hasn't improved over the years,' he explains. His latest venture is a weekly new-material night called A Bunch Of Japes at the Smoke & Mirrors club (formerly The Bunch of Grapes) in Bristol's theatre district. 'I started doing stand-up in late 1998 and began running a few little gigs the following year. Mainly as places where me and Russell and Richardson and many others could have hometown gigs. Then we started booking our friends plus other comics who started at the same time like Jimmy Carr. Good comics like doing good gigs and most people who do well have snuck through Bristol and slept on my sofa bed or in my mum and dad's spare room.'

Another of the gang that was working the comedy circuit in Bristol in the early 00s was Jon Richardson. In fact, it was Jon, Russell and another comic, John Robins, and Mark Olver who all decided to flat share. Robins, who has since moved to London to host his own XFM Radio show, cites those days as a sitcom waiting to happen. 'What wisdom did I pick up from my future superstar flatmates?

From Richardson, hygiene and slow roasts,' he told *Time Out* magazine in 2013. 'From Russell, swagger and bench-pressing. Living with them taught me to always "be on", which is infuriating for some people to be around, but when you're all there, exchanging top-level banter, with rolling jokes and callbacks – man, I felt so alive!'

Living with lads who all shared a similar dream and worked the same Bristol comedy circuit was a dream come true for Russ, who readily admits there must have been 'something in the water as Bristol has produced some great comedy talent'.

Can you imagine the sort of antics the lads got up to living together? When quizzed years later on *8 Out of 10 Cats Does Countdown*, Russell and Jon admitted they probably got on each other's nerves a fair bit too: 'Probably the worse thing I did to Russell and the others was when they had all gone out one time,' remembers Jon. 'I was so tired of cleaning the flat that I left them an itemised bill for my time at minimum wage. I didn't want to overcharge the guys but it was important that they learnt this shit doesn't happen for free.' And what of Russell as a flatmate? Well, it turns out his most annoying habit were to do with teaspoons and foot flossing.

'Russell's most annoying habit? Undoubtly teaspoons, he likes to burrow them away like there's gonna be some sort of apocalypse and teaspoons will be the only currency – he will be King of the World!' moans Jon. 'His other most annoying habit is that he flosses the skin in between the toes of his feet with his socks in the front room. It's disgusting.'

Nice. Besides winding each other up, the trio were good mates at home and doing the circuits, also becoming friendly with Wil Hodgson, who is also a professional stand-up. So you can imagine the evenings spent performing at the clubs in Bristol for these guys: fun, laughs, experience and hard graft.

'There used to be a loyal group of comedy fans who would traipse around to see us,' recalls Russ. 'There was a group of jugglers who would come to watch us. We used to look out and say, "Oh Christ, the jugglers are here again," and we would have to come up with new material so the jugglers wouldn't heckle. I owe it all to the jugglers – they made me work harder and be funnier.'

But when the work is so much fun, those years performing in intimate gigs gave Russell and the gang some of the best experiences of their lives. Some of the venues they played, Ashton Court Festival, Bristol's Comedy Box, The Bunch of Grapes and the Richmond Spring, were keen to re-book the comedians and Russell in particular created quite a buzz among the local comedy fans.

The Comedy Box advertised his gigs on their website, remarking that Russell, 'is one of the most exciting newer acts on the comedy circuit. Currently still based around Bristol, he is not afraid to take risks with his particular stream-of-consciousness style of comedy. Russell creates a world of high jinx, casual slapstick and surreal flights of fancy. He is a truly inventive comic and his passion for the art form shows through his every performance. And for all his tender years, Russell demonstrates a consummate command of the stage and takes control whatever the nature of the comedy night. This is your rare opportunity to support a Bristol act who is really going places'.

And 'going places' he was. One of the regular gigs he did for about three years was at the pub called The Bunch of Grapes (now Smoke & Mirrors), a great comedy bar situated on Denmark Street, beside the Bristol Hippodrome. Years later he would return to his home city on a worldwide tour and took much delight in remembering how these intimate gigs gave birth to his sell-out arena tours: 'There's something really cool about me walking down that same alley, past Bunch of Grapes and turning left into the Hippodrome instead of right into The Bunch of Grapes. The Hippodrome to me is what New York was to Bob Dylan.'

And it was at the Ashton Court Festival that Russell witnessed his worst-ever heckle: 'An old woman handed my friend Andy a noose that she'd made. She pulled out of her bag – that takes some beating, to actually prepare a noose. She said, "End your misery and mine." You can't really say anything back to that, you know. It was astonishing. Who brings a noose to a gig? Go with hope.'

That's not to say it was all work and no play for Russ. He was twenty-one after all and after finishing his degree was definitely up for a lads' holiday, the only location of course for a group of red-blooded blokes being Magaluf in Mallorca, and Russell still had his blue hair... As you do. He later admitted that while some blokes are happy to get pissed and try and pull girls all day and all night, he didn't. Therefore, he can't class himself as a 'proper lad' – 'We played football, drank manky cocktails and laughed till it hurt, but when we were greeted by people dressed as peanut M&M's I was thinking, "Kill me now".'

Not that he didn't have fun, playing pranks on his mates. When one of the gang had fallen asleep, Russ and his other mates covered half of his face with a T-shirt so one side was beautifully brown and the other side was white. Apparently that didn't help his pulling techniques either: 'He would only approach them side on, like a randy crab,' recalls Russ. And did his mate get his own back? Naturally. 'My friends threw me off a pedalo and I had to swim back with them shouting, "There are sharks here!" I'm pathetic and I go to bits, imagining that a bit of seaweed is the tentacle of the biggest squid ever.'

There was another memorable incident when the gang managed to get into a nightclub. Before that, they had failed magnificently when it came to getting into clubs – they had been 'getting drunk too early and ended up not going out'. Which was lucky as the one time they did make it inside they nearly got into a fight: 'The DJ kept taking the micky out of my friend Liam's hair. Liam said he would start a fight with him but then we saw the DJ came out of the booth and bottled someone and Liam said, "I think he has learnt his lesson" and we all left fairly quickly. We all very nearly got into a fight. As a holiday it was spectacularly unsuccessful.'

Fortunately, Russ survived his stay amid the warm waters of Mallorca and made it back to the comedy scene. His popularity on the circuit was growing and he and the likes of Richardson, Olver and Will Hodgson performed in clubs in Bristol on a weekly cycle. They would write new material on Saturday and perform it in The Bunch of Grapes on the Sunday. On the Tuesday of that week they would all perform at the Richmond Spring and hone the stuff they had performed on Sunday. On Wednesday it was Student Night at Jesters and they all took part in the open spot, now completely smashing the gig out of the water. The Bristol comedy circuit taught them all discipline and confidence they needed, which was perfect for Russell, who had a new challenge just around the corner.

Still only twenty-one years old, he took part in the BBC's New Comedy Award in 2001. The awards, since replaced by the BBC Radio New Comedy Award, first appeared in 1995 on BBC One, where Lee Mack was the finalist, eventually losing out to Julian Barratt. In 2001, Russell Howard was one of the finalists of the much-acclaimed show, alongside Rob Deering, Justin Moorhouse, Markus Birdman and Alan Carr. Judging the performances were Graeme Garden, Ralf Little, Sean Lock and Nina Wadia. More than eight hundred aspiring stand-ups entered the competition and these were whittled down over a number of regional heats before the final. TV presenter, chat-show host and comedy legend Alan Carr went on to win but for Russ, the experience of performing at the final in the Pleasance Dome in Edinburgh was incredible.

Russell was now inching his way to more mainstream recognition. He was putting in the hours and working on his gigs and now it was time to hit the Edinburgh Festival Fringe properly, not just on the back of a competition. In 2002 that is exactly what he did, performing in a show entitled *Ebony & Irony* with another upcoming comic, Matt Blaize.

Matt had trained as an actor at the Drama Centre London in King's Cross before deciding to turn his hand to stand-up and he had won the Laughing Horse New Act of the Year competition the previous year. Still relatively unknown but enthusiastic too, this was his first series of performances at the much-acclaimed Edinburgh Festival and he was the perfect partner for Russ to share a show with.

TheatreguideLondon.co.uk reviewed the show, which was performed at Underbelly, a popular venue at the Fringe. It's a three-storey building probably best described as post-apocalyptic – lots of concrete walls, damp bits and dust, but very atmospheric and plenty of ambiance. Compromising of half-hour sets from both performers, the comics were described as 'two new hard-edged faces on the scene who look as if they could kick things into the next generation'. Russell was then described as someone whose 'boyband persona lasts only up to the point he opens his mouth'. The conclusion of the review was that both were natural comics and two guys with 'personalities to match their potential'. However, *Chortle* website, the guide to comedy news, tours, comedians and reviews of the Edinburgh Fringe shows, wasn't quite so excited – they decided the title was the funniest bit of the show:

'Howard launches into a dialogue with the minuscule but attentive "crowd", although nothing of any humour emanated from this as his initial gambit received merely a muted response. Howard's confidence then appeared to ebb away as he alighted on the surreal subjects of Siamese twins and midgets riding on dogs to universal bewilderment. Realising that all is not well, he reassures himself – if not the paying punters – by reminding himself he has had a great day and nothing can spoil it. Unfortunately, it's too late for the audience, who will remember this day only for this awful experience that is unfolding.' Ouch!

The review then goes on to suggest that Russ 'becomes increasingly defensive and implies that those who did make the effort to attend are somehow at fault'.

Not a particularly flattering review for the comic but then it was Russell's first proper taste of performing in one of the biggest stand-up events of the year. *The Scotsman* was slightly more positive, deciding that although Russ didn't fulfil the 'Irony' partnership particularly well, he was 'like a charming blond, baby Ross Noble. He has the same ability to riff joyfully on anything and everything around him'.

And *Venue Magazine* were also impressed with the twenty-two-year-old's first foray at Edinburgh: 'He has a tiggerish restlessness, bounding around the stage perpetually in search of new angles for his seemingly limitless imagination'.

If nothing else, the Edinburgh Festival had provided Russell with an experience of performing to tough crowds – the punters at the Fringe want good comedy and will pay to be entertained night and day by the comedians hoping to impress. Plus, the show was a sell-out for the duration of the event, which spoke volumes. Now it was time to get gigging again and this time he was asked to be the support act for the 2002 Perrier Comedy Award winner (later renamed the Edinburgh Comedy Awards), Daniel Kitson.

Chapter 5

ON THE FRINGE OF SUCCESS

'You can't please all the people all the time or there'd be spunk everywhere.'
RUSSELL'S MATE, MARIO

After finishing the Edinburgh Fringe in August 2002, Russell spent the next few months – from October to December – touring the length and breadth of the UK and Ireland with Daniel Kitson and the Comedy Network, who organised gigs in universities.

Kitson had a reputation within the comedy industry for shunning TV work due to the lack of control he had over the final edit. He used to make regular appearances as recurring barman 'Spencer' in Peter Kay's *Phoenix Nights* but became quite outspoken in his dislike for Kay and his experiences on the show. Russell, however, was very excited to be alongside Dan as his support act. It was a role that gave him plenty of experience in venues other than dimly lit comedy clubs, performing to eclectic audiences rather than the regular comedy club patrons. He learnt some important lessons throughout that tour, including how to make his material fresh each time. 'You had to have new stuff when you went back the following year, you couldn't perform the same half an hour of comedy,' he recalled in a podcast with The *ComediansComedian* in 2016. 'Every year when I went back, I would have a new set because that is what Olver did, that was what Kitson did. I had to be as good as them, I had to try.'

Learning under Kitson also taught him a style of comedy that he uses to this day – to take everyday situations, the experiences of life, and use them in his stand-up. He would see stuff happen to Dan during the day – fairly inconsequential stuff – and then he would watch him turn this event into a brilliant anecdotal story in his stand-up. 'I would think to myself, holy shit, I was there, what happened to him wasn't that good, how has he made it that good?' recalls Russ. 'It was incredible, watching him. Once he went on stage and just started pulling stuff out of his pockets and talking about it. He was getting comfortable with the audience and it was incredible. I am very lucky to have worked and be mates with geniuses who have a very insane work ethic that has rubbed off on me. Not being a genius, I figured I will have to work a million times harder than them to be any good!'

In December 2002, he and Kitson performed at the University of East Anglia and proved a big hit with the three hundred-strong crowd of students.

'It's like being part of a teenage gang rather than an audience when Daniel Kitson and Russell Howard let you in on their private jokes in a UEA lecture theatre,' said BBC reviewer Chris Goreham. 'If there's a happier tour bus on the road at the moment I'd like to see it. It can't be down to a rock 'n' roll lifestyle because Daniel and his support act Russell both claim to be teetotal.'

The following year, 2003, Russell was back at the Edinburgh Festival Fringe after spending his time performing in club after club: 'It was a conveyor belt of gigs and open mic nights,' he confirmed.

It was also a time when he was also developing a new style to his comedy. The previous 'winging it' phase had always worked and he found that he always managed to get laughs, but he was getting a little bored with it. So he changed tactics and decided to give the phase of just 'badgering people' a rest and start writing and performing some pre-planned material. The first piece he wrote and performed was about two blokes in South Africa who are thrown off a plane for kissing. It got a lot of big laughs and he realised that he could write a sketch and perform to great success. But while the actual performing was never a problem, writing was a lot harder for him – 'I sound like such a tit but performance wise, I had been used to performing in front of 50-odd people in Bristol, every week to the same people, so they forced a discipline in me to entertain them. I couldn't tell the same crowd the same jokes, it didn't work. I had an A4 spiral notebook, where I had a list of joke after joke.'

So, in August at the Fringe, he took part in The Comedy Zone, one of Edinburgh's favourite late-night cabaret shows. 'The Fringe's leading stand-up showcase,' declared by *The Times*.

Compiled by comedy agency Avalon, of which Russell was now part, the show is split into quarters, with four performers each given a slot and a chance to showcase themselves as the best new acts around. It boasts popular performers such as Frankie Boyle, Harry Hill, Al Murray and Chris Addison, who were all introduced to the comedy world after performing in The Comedy Zone. The line-up that year consisted of Russell, Al Pitcher, Matthew Osbourn and Stan Stanley. Russ was second on stage and unfortunately, it wasn't his best show. *Chortle. co.uk* were none too impressed: 'Howard relies heavily on rapport with punters for his confidence and his performance can suffer disproportionately if he cannot win us over with his zany and spontaneous repartee. On this occasion we remained largely unmoved by his antics and we briefly travel from the comedy zone to the entertainment free zone.'

But Russell remained undeterred. Being on stage performing was where he wanted to be, and he carried on – 'When you are doing stand-up, it is the most glorious house when you are an *X-Men* version of yourself, with lasers coming out of your eyes.' And so he carried on gigging and working on his show. There were a few memorable moments encountered along the way too. One specifically at a gig in East Kilbride, South Lanarkshire, where he found his audience interspersed with pensioners. For someone who likes to talk about masturbation, cocks and boyish silliness, he found himself on the end of much disapproval – 'There were about 18 pensioners in the audience and I've never heard so many tuts in my life. One tut isn't loud, but 18 is like The Frog Chorus. It was weirdly funny.'

On tour with John Oliver and Andy Zaltzman the following July, he found himself performing at the A1 Comedy Festival at Jacksons Lane Theatre in Highgate, north London. Still referred to as a 'newcomer in the shape of Russell Howard', he was fast making a name for himself with his relentless work ethic. A few months earlier he had flown to New Zealand to take part in the New Zealand Comedy Festival, joining Andy Parsons, Ross Noble and Lee Mack as a 'Brits abroad' contingent. He was supporting Lee Mack at the festival, which ran from 20 April to 22 May.

He then returned to the Edinburgh Festival Fringe in August 2004 and this time he had his very own show. It was a major breakthrough for the twenty-four-year-old and time to show the world what he could do solo. He told the *Independent* at the start of the Fringe that his first show would be a 'stripped-down' approach, which promised, 'no slides, no costume changes... just a mic and a man'.

The aim of his self-titled show was simple: 'It's not groundbreaking. It's not slides of me travelling to Peru – I struggle getting from London to Bristol. It's just about the little things that have ever happened to me.'

He was also reacting against the Ben Elton-style ranters who used to rule the circuit: 'I wasn't schooled in political comedy – I'm not aware of much that happens outside my bedroom. My style is not to tell you how to think. I don't hide behind telling you that George Bush is stupid and Tony Blair is rubbish – that's just whingeing and not offering the audience anything. I like it when a gig is like kids staying up late around a camp-fire. That doesn't work if someone runs into the middle of it, shouting, "What do you think about bin Laden, eh?" And I thought we were just toasting marshmallows...'

So what was it like for the comic, his first solo show and a full hour of just him entertaining the crowds? The thought of this show catapulting him into the big league added to his nerves, but he was ready: it was time to perform.

'Like a fat child on a treadmill, the ragged young clown of comedy embarks upon his first full-length show,' said *Chortle* magazine. 'Big things are predicted for 24-year-old Russell Howard and with his first show, it's easy to see why. If there's one word to describe this mild-mannered Bristolian it would have to be jaunty. He's a perky, playful character, full of almost childlike delight at the world and its workings, and with a pesky mischievous streak to boot. But while he has a juvenile outlook, he has a grown-up vocabulary and loves nothing more than constructing elaborately florid sentences with such delightfully semi-archaic words as "kerfuffle", "poppycock", or even, well, "jaunty". It's a verbal trait he shares with his friend Daniel Kitson.'

The reference to Kitson was not unusual. Having toured with him for the past few years, Russ readily admits to having been influenced by his style. But *Chortle* were impressed and continued: 'With Howard, the emphasis is firmly on fun. Whether it's bidding for a world record for the world's campest frog, "bumming a mongoose", or prick-teasing horses in a genuine, if worrying, Equus moment from his childhood, there's a winning mix of the inquisitive, eager and carefree in many of his other anecdotes. Not every anecdote is laugh-out-loud hilarious, for sure, but they are all well-told by a quirkily, charming comic, who's equally, if not more, comfortable chatting spontaneously as he is with his prepared material, with the off-the-cuff comments delivered with the same wonderfully ornate language that colours the set piece so vividly.'

It was an incredibly positive review from a website who hadn't enjoyed Russell's previous shows and they finished with an amazing homage: 'When Howard does make his name, and that probably won't be too long now, you'll be glad you saw the show where it all started.'

'I loved him,' said one punter. 'I love his banter with us.'

'He's manic, you have to keep pace with him but he's very cute,' agreed another. 'He jumps from one story to another and they seem unconnected but then he comes back and completes his stories, which is clever.'

It wasn't Russell's only engagement at the Fringe, he was also asked to compere the press launch in the Pleasance Grand in 2004, where he picked out a female audience member and then challenged her to an arm wrestle. He lost, but the crowd loved him.

'Talented and fun,' I thought, said one member of the crowd. 'His giggles are so infectious, his essence should be bottled up and given out free on the NHS to cheer people up.'

There was also the chance for Russell to impress with his physical as well as his verbal skills when he took part in the annual Comics versus Critics football match. It was meant to be a friendly tie but the comics decided to heat things up when the score was drawn 1–1 at half-time by goading the opposition. 'Write for a pamphlet, you only write for a pamphlet' was the war cry and it did the trick: the comedians won 3–2 in the end and Russell was by far the most impressive player on the pitch, having lost none of his love or skills for the Beautiful Game.

The reviews were good and he was buoyed by the experience; he found performing in Edinburgh a bit life-affirming too – he knew that if he had performed as well as he possibly could, if he'd given it his all, he couldn't ask any more of himself. And having worked so hard on the material, at this stage in his career he maintained that the reviews didn't matter to him – 'If you truly believe you have given everything, what does it matter that someone only gave you 2 out of 5. It's still better than 1.' It was an attitude that was not to last, however.

The BBC were equally impressed with his Edinburgh set and commissioned him to write, sing and perform on the late night comedy series, *The Milk Run*, on BBC Radio 1. He was also asked to take part in the BBC Radio 4 show, *Banter*, which was broadcast during the Fringe to November the following year. Hosted by Andrew Collins, Russ was a guest for twelve of the total eighteen half-hour shows which saw the invited guests having to name their 'top threes' in a given category. There was also a category called 'either, or' in which the comics had to pick an answer from Andrew's two. Russ had to choose either Joe 90 or WD40 – 'Joe 90 is a comic book superhero so if you need someone fighting a villain that is the choice, but come across a wench with a chastity belt you want the WD40. Could I have Joe 90 with a can of WD40 in his pocket?'

It was typical Russell – blokeish, yet fun – and earned him the regular guest slot after that first episode. While the radio stints were fun, he was back gigging as soon as he could and travelled around the UK performing stand-up. It was important to him to work on new ideas and as a comic, it was essential to try out new jokes and sequences to see if they worked. He did the Comedy Network gigs at the universities again and used those performances as a guide to see if a joke worked or needed tidying up. The audience reaction was essential and performing was a two-way process. He would give jokes about five goes in front of different audiences to see if they worked or not. That was his rule and if the audience wasn't enjoying it, he'd lose or adapt it. The acts he saw and performed with became friends, especially the likes of Josie Long, David O'Doherty, John Oliver and Wil Hodgson. While in Bournemouth after one gig, he found himself sharing a hot tub with Hodgson, smoking cigars (as you do). Former communist Wil asked Russ what he thought of war poetry to which Russ replied that he wasn't really a fan of Rupert Brooke because essentially he was tricking young people into going off to die. That didn't go down well with the mohicaned Wil, who 'went mental' according to Russ. 'That's traitorous!' he shouted at Russ. 'You can't say that about him, he was a genius!' The situation was quite bizarre if not quite amusing and for Russ, being told off by a mate while wearing just his swimming shorts was 'a bit tense but very funny' – 'I told him I preferred Wilfred Owen, but he replied that Owen was an "arsehole".'

The comic he did become good friends with was John Oliver, and when Russell was gigging properly, it was Oliver who became a confidant and mentor to him and someone whose performances he watched in awe.. Still only twenty-four but gaining experience by the year, Russell was working hard and appreciated having him as an influence. When they toured universities and colleges together, Russ was his support act for several years. He and Russell's previous touring partner, Daniel Kitson, were later described in his podcast with *ComediansComedian* as his 'elders'. Russell still can't speak more highly of Oliver, saying, 'Whatever "it" is, he's got it.' Oliver, who was doing well on the comedy scene in England, made the move to America and now hosts *Last Week Tonight with John Oliver*.

Russ told *Radio Times* in 2014: 'I'd stay over and play Xbox with him when we were appearing together – which was my apprenticeship really, just hanging out with him, performing, watching him perform. He was a pretty amazing teacher. His career is soaring after *The Daily Show*. I went to see him perform live in America and they love him. I think the reason he works so well is that he's really funny but he looks English, he's got that Mr Bean look going on. He is funny but so obviously awkward too, being so English. He loved being loved, which wasn't always the case. John was always incredible but sometimes just couldn't take the audiences finding him funny. They'd laugh and he'd go, "Yeah, whatever..."'

Chapter 6
SIZE MATTERS

'My mate and I were at a train station and we were watching this bloke absolutely legging it for a train. He was proper gunning it and he made it — he got on the train. And we both felt great, it really cheered me up. I suppose there are a lot of comics who would have been delighted if he hadn't made the train but I like it when people make the train.'
RH

The crowd were laughing; it was going well so far. It was Christmas time and the atmosphere at the Cross Keys pub in Corsham, Wiltshire, was lively but not uncontrollable as the punters gathered, full of festive booze and banter. Russ felt completely at home. Then came the heckle, or the sex toy in his face, to be more precise, lobbed at him from a disgruntled woman in the audience. Up to that particular point in his comedy career, the worst heckle he had received was from a twelve-year-old telling him he was a 'fucking cunt' at a corporate gig. Russell got his own back by 'summoning his powers of wit and wisdom and asking him if he could hire an 18-certificate film'. But this wasn't just verbal, this was a dildo sailing through the air and hitting him slap-bang right in the face.

Momentarily stunned, Russ recovered his composure to finish the set and took great delight in what had just happened: 'I got a strange bruise that was quite difficult to explain,' he revealed in The *Mirror* in 2016. 'She clearly had very little faith in the evening's entertainment, she must have been like, "I'd better bring along my Rabbit in case he's rubbish." And she hated me that much that she was willing to throw it away.' But the funniest thing was that while other comics might have walked off stage after such abuse, Russell finished his set – 'I was getting £125. I had to stay on stage, I needed the money!'

If the end of 2004 was to be remembered for having a dildo thrown at him, the start of 2005 was the beginning of a new era of fame. Russell was one of several top-named comics who were lined up to take part in a comedy fundraiser to raise money for the victims of the Boxing Day Tsunami at the end of 2004. Lee Mack, Lucy Porter, Jo Caulfield and Ricky Grover joined him to take part in the One Night Only fundraiser at London's Bloomsbury Theatre on 23 January 2005. The proceeds were going to the Buddhist Village Trust who were working to rebuild orphanages in Sri Lanka. It was the latest in a string of benefits to have been announced by the comedy world, and Russell was quick to agree to take part in the £25-per-head show.

He was back on tour with John Oliver and Scott Capurro in May at a Chambers Comedy Courtroom night in Jersey.

Russ was the compere for the evening and presiding over opening act, John Oliver, and headline act, Scott Capurro. The night was a hit and gave more experience to Russ, who was off to Edinburgh again that summer to perform in the second of his own shows, this time entitled Skylarking. His debut own-show the previous year had been a sell-out and he was hoping for the same response that year as he performed at the Pleasance Courtyard, which for many is considered to be the heart of the Fringe. The name of his show was devised because he thought it conjured up images of tomfoolery, but he was properly miffed when he discovered that it was also Jamaican gang-slang for cruising around, looking for gay people to kill. Er... However, it was too late: the posters had been printed and he couldn't do anything about it. Still, the title aside, this was a show that people were flocking to see.

His main material was about an epiphany he had after the death of the family dog. At twenty-five years old, he was questioning where his life was going, why he was scared of things – like teenagers fighting – and why he still got so excited about things like pirates and monkeys. *Chortle* website, describing Russ as an 'infectious young stand-up', were full of praise: 'He's a joyful person, almost childlike in his enthusiasm for innocent, uncomplicated fun – yet always kyboshed by the harsh realities of the rest of the world of which he is petrified. In many ways, he is the boy comic who never grew up, still getting excited by football in the park and reading all the Harry Potter books. He's so untouched by cynicism that it is instinctively endearing: you wish you could share in that unfettered, playful glee. He extends the same attitude towards his audience, happy to chat away, genuinely inquisitive about the people he meets. It's almost his undoing when he gets caught in a digressionary conversation that knocks ten minutes off his show. He is nothing if not a banterer. For an Edinburgh show, Skylarking lacks big themes and ideas as it is just a series of routines: unfailingly jolly and upbeat, occasionally genuinely funny but overall, just a bit of extended light-hearted tomfoolery'.

The *London Evening Standard* were equally impressed, stating that, 'The West Country comic shows his ability to be incredibly funny off the cuff after spotting an east target in the front row in his opening bit of banter. The beauty of Howard's material is that it blends the observational with the ludicrous,' while *The Times* were equally positive: 'Like his friend and influence Daniel Kitson, Howard combines vulnerability with defiance; a suspicion of children with a love of childish things. I'm not sure he has yet found the best way to bind his very personal material, much of it about his adolescence with his rather flat political observations. But his fluency is something. One to watch'.

Russ was just one of four comics picked to take part in Edinburgh & Beyond, a programme that showcases the best of the stand-up on the bill that year. Filmed at the Bloomsbury Theatre, it aired on the Paramount Comedy Channel the following year, 2006, and alongside Russ, it starred Ian Boldsworth, Reginald D. Hunter and Russell Kane. There was also a tour for the foursome – Ray Peacock replaced Ian Boldsworth – and 'Pub Landlord' Al Murray was asked to present the shows.

Russell was becoming increasingly aware of critics and reviews and what people were saying about him as 'the future of comedy': 'Reviews are quite weird,' he said. 'I've had most nice ones but I'm fully aware that I'm not a genius, very few people are.'

It didn't weigh heavily on his mind, however – he was having too much fun, living in Bristol with his comedy mates, entertaining crowds for a living and basically enjoying life. Although he did come second in *Zoo* magazine's Britain's Funniest Comics – a point he made sure his flatmates were well aware of. It was hard work performing, but the cheery comic was enjoying himself with his flatmates: 'We all get in really late, play pro evo [Pro Evolution Soccer] on the Xbox and shoot the breeze till we go to bed. The only time it's tricky is when I travel with my flat-mate Jon. I sleep on trains and planes pretty easily and he doesn't so he covers my face in make-up. Then I wake up totally oblivious to the fact that I look like some weird slaggy clown.'

He and his fellow comics were affectionately known as 'The Chocolate Milk Gang' during the Edinburgh Festival runs, mainly because they weren't getting drunk like many other comics on the circuit, preferring to drink milkshakes before they took to the stage. 'Those were wild days,' Russ deadpans. 'The thing is, I never really got into booze. I have a bit of red wine from time to time but generally I'm more of a milkshake man,' he told *The National Student* website. He also feels an air of responsibility to his audience and the perfectionist in him doesn't want to let anyone down. 'You can't have your blade dulled by booze,' he explained in an interview with the *Telegraph* in 2013. 'If you're doing 70 gigs in a tour, there's a lot of responsibility. People need a big night out and you're providing it. Have a drink in your own time, that's their time.'

The style of his show – and the likes of Kitson, Oliver, Hodgson and Josie Long – was also different to the previous generation of stand-ups. Their comedy wasn't about mocking people; it was celebrating the everyday. There isn't a victim, it's about sharing quirky tales of upbeat moments involving friends and family or loved ones. Russell was known for his cheerful demeanour and upbeat stance and whether he knew it yet or not, that positivity, glass is half-full mantra was to become his signature style over the next ten years. *The Times* described it in this way: 'Russell has a wide-eyed, upbeat comedy style which is an anecdote to the cynicism that has been the mainstay of comedy for so long'.

Russ himself is well aware that his style sets him apart from other comics but his style, his MO as it were, is set in stone: 'Things can be so wonderful, so glorious about existence. I quite like celebrating those things in comedy. That sounds so wanky, doesn't it? I genuinely find it easier as certain things do cheer me up. I am so happy when I am doing stand-up. There is nothing like performing to people, making them laugh and have them laughing back at you. If you can't be happy in that moment, when can you? I suppose you could put on an act but I am genuinely delighted that people come to see me and laugh at me. Especially at the beginning, I was so excited.'

His excitement was matched by the buzz surrounding him

now. He had a dedicated following among fans and critics, and 2006 was going to be the year he got even bigger. Not physically, it's worth pointing out, as he decided that his physique needed some work as the gigging lifestyle wasn't exactly keeping him in shape – 'I was 13st and I wanted to look better than I did. Doing gigs isn't great for your health – you spend a lot of time eating late-night service-station dinners of pasties, coke and crisps. You are gigging five nights a week for years then all of a sudden you're 26 and you think, Jesus, I haven't eaten a vegetable in four years.'

Not that there was much time for eating a vegetable that year either. On 20 March 2006, Russell made his TV debut on the BBC Two panel show, *Never Mind the Buzzcocks* (*NMTB*). *NMTB* was a satirical based music-panel show that saw two teams go head-to-head to answer music-based questions. It was sarcastic and scathing and the guests were quite often victim to host Simon Amstell's dry-but-brutal verbal attacks. The two team captains, Phill Jupitus and Bill Bailey, also joined in the mockery and Russ joined Phill alongside rapper Kenzie from Blazin' Squad and Friday Hill. He soon realised that the musician stars who appear on the show aren't so quick and witty as the comics and are therefore easy fodder for jokes: 'I'm on with pop stars who have to have their jokes written for them,' he revealed to *Dave* website. 'So you can just take the piss out of them if you want.'

He returned to the show the following year, 2007, for another one-off episode but it wasn't the last he would see of the TV studio that year. On 15 April he made his debut on the mainstream airways when he presented a new series on BBC Radio 2 for Saturday lunchtimes. Entitled *Out To Lunch*, Russell and Rob Deering co-hosted this comedy-packed segment, which included stand-up sketches, character monologues and chats with some of the hottest comedy talent from around the UK. It was a chance for Russ to perform to both the nation and a studio audience and new stand-up performers were desperate to get on the show to showcase their work as its popularity grew. Russell remained as host until the beginning of Series 4, which aired in 2007, when another Russell – Russell Kane – took over. But that wasn't to be his last radio stint either.

In June 2007 he took part in a charity fundraiser organised by former *Blue Peter* presenter Janet Ellis. She had assembled the best stand-ups on the circuit that year to perform and raise money for the Lyric Theatre Hammersmith's work with underprivileged youngsters. Al Murray, in 'Pub Landlord' guise, played host and Russell was the fifth act to try and impress the crowd in the 550-seater theatre – and he did. 'Russell's boyish gusto proved as contagious as always,' fawned *Chortle* website. 'He's open, cheeky and friendly but it's the fluency of his comedy that stands out: the fact that he appears to be making no effort as he recounts his anecdotes with unparalleled glee gives his set an authentic air of good humour. It's a warm and winning attitude that always triumphs.'

Chortle were undoubtedly impressed, and that wasn't to be for the first time that year. The Chortle Awards, which were first set up in 2002 by the comedy website, were organised to honour established stand-ups currently working in the

UK. A panel of reviewers draw up a shortlist of nominees in each category, which are then put up for public vote on the website. Russell was shortlisted in the Best Compere category, alongside Alfie Joey and Andrew Maxwell. The public voted for Russell and he won. His first award win for his comedy, it wasn't to be his last...

Russell flew across the Pond to Montreal, Quebec, in July 2006, where he took part in the annual comedy festival, Just For Laughs. He was performing in Britcom Night, one of several 'theme' nights at the festival and performed along with Jimmy Carr, Stewart Lee and Gina Yashere. 'It was pure showbiz,' he recalls of his time in Canada. 'We did those gigs in Montreal and I only had 20 minutes so I could just do joke after joke: Bang! Bang! Bang! My mate Kitson described my performance then and he said, "The thing about you, you go on stage and you start fucking them and straight away and after a while they just think, 'OK we're getting fucked'." Apparently I don't have comedic foreplay. I am just hello, right, let's get going...'

While there, Russell got the chance to hang out with another fellow comedian, presenter and Man of Knowledge, Stephen Fry himself, and later described the experience to the *Montreal Gazette* as 'hanging out with Google'. He also competed in the Comedy Showdown segment alongside Andy Parsons on the Brit team, Ireland's Ian Coppinger and America's Mike Britt, Big Jay Oakerson and James Cunningham. The judges included Jimmy Car, Andy Kindler and Dom Irrera. Hosting the show was Steve Patterson, who described the evening as having been inspired by hip-hop's rap-—off – think *8 Mile* – in which two comedians would face each other until there was just one man standing. In Round One they had to perform three minutes of material and then if they survived and made it back on stage for Round Two, they had to perform on a random, obscure subject chosen by the audience. This was to stop them using their own pre-prepared material and showing the audience and judges how funny they could be on the subject of, say, 'cloud animals'.

Russell did make it to the next round and was given the topic of 'flapjacks', which he cunningly answered with, 'My dog's name is Flapjack...' and then went on to perform the canine segment he had prepared earlier. He made it to the final but lost out to Andy Kindler in the final showdown. But there was no rest for the loser, er, wicked, as he was due to perform at the Latitude Festival later that month and would then be back in Edinburgh for another solo Fringe show in August 2006. The Latitude Festival in Henham Park, Suffolk, was in its debut year and was billed as 'more than just a music festival', offering art and comedy showcases too. Sean Lock, Marcus Brigstocke and Jason Manford all performed and Russ's debut performance was something special as he drew an impressive crowd and showed his easy-going rapport with an audience – 'It was clear then that while he wasn't a heavyweight just yet, he was already well on his way,' reported *The Latitude* website.

Let's just hope Russ didn't take the 'heavyweight' reference too literally – it was, after all, his year of hitting the gym...

Chapter 7

MOCK STAR IN THE MAKING

'Hello. Come and listen to me tell you some funny things. What heartache,
lunacy, monks and robots floats your boat?'

RH

On 26 June 2006, Russell had the chance to perform his Edinburgh set two months early by taking part in the Edinburgh and Beyond stand-up show. The sets are recorded for the Paramount Comedy Channel and shown later in the year, with 'Pub Landlord', Al Murray, overseeing the events once more. Recorded in London's Bloomsbury Theatre, it gives the audience a chance to be part of the recordings and watch the shows for free too.

Weeks later, Russ flew up to Scotland and was attracting such large crowds at the Edinburgh Festival Fringe that all of his shows that year were sell-outs throughout their run. Performing from 3–28 August, he made himself at home in the Pleasance Courtyard for the duration and was extremely excited when *Harry Potter* actor Rupert Grint (who played Ron Weasley) was in the audience one night – a fact he liked to share in all his subsequent performances. This was Russell's third solo show and this one, entitled Wandering, was to be the one that would earn him an if.commeddie nomination (more on that accolade later).

The reviews from websites and magazines were gushing. *Broadwaybaby* revealed that Russell had universal appeal, with a show that 'almost everyone will enjoy'. They praised his 'fresh' ideas and easy-going style when interacting with the audience, neither insulting nor brash: 'His performance is fresh and bouncy and he is clearly enjoying the show nearly as much as the audience is. This is not in-depth satire but a look at the smaller things in life. It is his ability to find humour and joy in these small things, his wanderings, that give him his comedy. A good bet for those looking for an hour of solid stand-up comedy'.

Chortle concurred: 'He is the sort of sweet-natured, uncynical person who gets a genuine kick out of seeing a monk with a skateboard, or assuming a false identity when travelling simply because of the world of possibilities it has to offer. It's the crux of his message: That while life can sometimes deal you a bad hand, there's so much more to enjoy if you escape wallowing in misery. Howard is skilful enough not to labour the point, leaving it implicit among the fast-paced japery. Added to this is a premier-league audience rapport, which allows him to flit effortlessly between punters, conjuring good-natured jokes and witty, playful asides. In short, he is the full comedy package who's come of age with this unfailingly entertaining show'.

And *One4review* website declared that they loved Russell just as much as he loves Jaffa Cakes – 'That might not mean much to you unless like me you have seen his show but it might just scare him a little. His show is entitled "Wandering" because that's what his mind does, jumping from story to story. As for the show content, it changes from day to day. For a show full of the unexpected and mentions of Jaffa Cakes, see Russell Howard'.

In a four-star review *The Guardian* described the show as follows: 'If you're in the mood for some freewheeling stories, anecdotes and a young comic with enough energy to power a small country, *Wandering* is the show you're after. A superbly funny ride'.

The reviews were amazing, the shows were a sell-out and now the best was to come – Russell had been nominated for the much-coveted Edinburgh Comedy Award. 'The Eddie', as it is more colloquially known, was also formerly called the Perrier Comedy Awards (sponsored by Perrier mineral water from 1981–2005) then the if.comedy awards or if.comeddie from 2006 onwards due to the sponsorship change to Scottish-based bank Intelligent Finance. Whatever the name, the awards are deemed to be the most prestigious comedy prize in the UK and fall into three categories: Best Comedy Show (the main prize), Best Newcomer and Panel Prize. Russell was nominated in the Best Comedy Show category for Wandering, alongside David O'Doherty, Phil Nichol, Paul Sinha and We Are Klang. To even have a nomination to his name was mind-blowing for the twenty-six-year-old and he knew he was among only a select group of comics who have been recognised on this platform for their talent. Awards producer Nica Burns described the line-up that year as 'a brilliant shortlist that reflected a huge breadth of comedy talent.' The judging panel was made up of nine critics, including *Sunday Times* reviewer Stephen Armstrong, BBC Radio Entertainment producer Victoria Lloyd and *Times* critic Dominic Maxwell.

The *Independent* were not convinced that 'this is Howard at his best' and therefore might not win, but were happy to concede that it was about time he was recognised with a nomination: 'It is good he [Russell] is being recognised for flashes of brilliance that include, in this show, the assertion that "people who say they don't swear haven't had the right sex or food," and his quandary about what emoticon is suitable to use in a reply to a text or email that contains bad news'. They also listed his best gag of the Wandering show as the one he told about a story he had read of two guys kissing on a plane in South Africa. Passengers had complained and one of men was put in prison for three days because he had refused to stop kissing his boyfriend. Russ thought that the passengers who called such an act 'unnatural' were surely being ironic... 'You're flying!' he responded, pretending to be the gay man on the plane.

Remember, this was the first piece Russ had written specifically to perform. It was a segment that he would use for several of his stand-up shows, including his debut on BBC Two's *Live at the Apollo* the following year, 2007. But it was worth noting that this was also the first bit of 'news' that he brought to his act and it was well received: 'It got such a big laugh and it was that thing when he realised, "OK, I can do this."'

Eventually Russell lost out to Phil Nichol but his disappointment was short-lived. In fact, he might not have felt any disappointment at all as he had something else on his mind, namely a TV show called *Mock the Week*.

Mock the Week is a popular BBC Two show that sees two teams of comedians answer questions/provide comical answers on news stories from that week in a satirical way. It is one of the only panel shows that books stand-up comics, meaning there are seven comedians vying to make their voices heard, with all of them professionally obliged to do their own jokes. They also get to perform small stand-up gags on random subjects and take turns in providing one-liners on topics that usually require an answer. For example, 'Unlikely letters to an agony aunt...' Popular Irish comedian and TV presenter Dara O'Briain is the host and back in 2006, Hugh Dennis, Andy Parsons and Frankie Boyle were the regular guests. Watching Russell's Wandering show in Edinburgh that year was the show's creator and producer, Dan Pattinson. He was impressed and asked Russ to attend an audition. Then he had to go and audition in the *Mock the Week* offices with other comics. When that went well, he was asked to join the team. 'It kind of snowballed from there, really,' admitted Russ to the Dave Channel in an interview in 2008. 'Yes, it was a huge amount of luck when *Mock the Week* came along, it was massive for me.' You could argue that it was lucky for him to be picked for the show but his years of working on his stand-up and appealing to the audience in turn appealed to the producers.

Russell made his *MTW* debut on the show that was aired on 14 September 2006 joining Andy Parsons' team alongside Clive Anderson. By this time the show was in its third series and viewers had come to expect outrageous comments from Frankie Boyle, deadpan impressions from Hugh Dennis and well-thought-out-but-well-paced answers from Parsons. So, what did Russell bring to the show? 'I was the young guy on the show. I didn't wear a suit, I looked a lot younger than the others, I had a different perspective,' he recalls. 'I was desperate to get my lines in because I don't want to look an idiot, like a timid young foal on telly.'

Getting 'air time', he soon discovered, wasn't as easy as he thought and what he said on the show during filming and what was used in the final edit were two very different things: 'When you first start doing it, you watch it back on TV and it's awful! You're all over the shop – you're gabbling and you need to learn how to write for TV! It's even worse when you don't know about editing a show and you're waiting for that really funny thing you remember doing in the studio and then in the show it's not there – son of a bitch! When I watched the first series back, I can remember specifics... I think I learnt to be more efficient and more economical with language. Because it is a 28-minute show, you have to be concise. I had to train myself to do, one punch, two punch, three! I had to teach myself to condense myself. I think it worked for that show, it doesn't work with live stand-up.

'It taught me a different approach to writing because when I first started doing *Mock*, it was the first time I would properly write on my own. For 3 days a week I would write and that was brilliant for me, I trained myself. You suddenly had a show that you would write for every week and it was incredible. I realised as well that certain jokes on the show wouldn't work in a comedy club, like President Bush being thick or whatever, it is just bland. But in this context, it's satire. And the more you get into it, the more fun it becomes.'

Performing alongside comedians who were constantly in the public eye was something that Russell wasn't fazed by. He might have felt like a fish out of water for those first few early episodes but it didn't take him long to get into the swing of things and to work out the mechanics of performing in such a tight show in the company of some heavyweight comics who all wanted to be heard.

'When I joined the show, Frankie [Boyle] was the nation's darling,' confessed Russ. 'My uncle loved him, he would say to me, "That Frankie, he says some awful things but he's bloody incredible." And it was true, the audience adored him. But it was really good and if at first I felt like I was playing at the adults table, playing catch-up, I got there in the end. I've learnt so much from Frankie and Dara [O'Briain] because you realise you need more strings to your bow and have to be better informed. My stand-ups are more anecdotal but it certainly benefits from having an opinionated take on the world.'

And what about the segment at the end when each comedian takes turns in providing one-liners on a particular subject? The problem is, there isn't a set sequence and if you're not quick enough, you won't get chance to speak over the likes of Hugh Dennis or Frankie Boyle, who are quick off the mark and like to hog the microphone.

'Oh, it's pretty savage!' admits Russ. 'What's interesting about it as well is that you only see it on TV about, what, four minutes? But on the night that goes on for half an hour. We just pummel the audience and each other. I really like that bit, weirdly; it's a nice spot. Someone said something piss funny, okay, I'll try and match it. I've failed! Okay! It's the ultimate dressing room, isn't it? Somebody funny says, "Here's what I've got to say that's funny", somebody else goes, "Yeah, but look what I've got." But people love it. Sometimes it can be really quite tricky, but I find it all quite funny. I'm one of the people who actually laughs at everyone else's jokes!'

Russell soon got into the swing of the show and appeared twice more that series before being officially asked to be a permanent fixture and become a co-captain with Andy Parsons. They would go head-to-head against Hugh Dennis and Frankie Boyle's team for Series 4 onwards, with just one guest comic for each side. But being on TV brought its own pitfalls too. Russ was suddenly exposed to the trappings of fame and the judgement of strangers who would comment on his appearances onscreen. It wasn't something that he was used to and it certainly didn't help with his self-esteem – even now it's the reason he will never put himself on social media sites like Twitter.

'When you first appear on TV, you go through the self-googling phase. There's such hatred. And I can't see beyond that. You get 20 people saying kind things and one person saying something horrible. It breaks you. You train yourself for a year not to do it. If I was to go on Twitter I would expose myself to people who adore me or people who absolutely hated me. Neither of those are useful to my soul,' he told *The Telegraph* in 2013.

So this step into the television world came with its downsides too but was being on TV his ultimate goal when he was just fifteen years old and trying to believe that writing jokes would be his career? For some comedians, the answer would be a resounding yes, but Russell was still young and as far as he was concerned he still had lots of ambitions to fulfil: 'You don't really have a career plan... I've been doing stand-up for nearly ten years so it's kind of that thing that I've been gigging for five nights a week at every toilet in the country,' he admitted in an interview with *The Den Of Geek* in 2008. 'There are a lot of brilliant comics who are amazing but you can see them doing the same 20 minutes that they were doing five years ago, verbatim. I think that doesn't lend itself to progressing. What's weird is that I didn't really have any ambition to do TV or such, I was perfectly happy banging around doing gigs. And then this [*Mock the Week*] came along. It just sort of helped me come into the national eye. I quite like it because they're fun and they keep you on your toes. It's all on the cuff really. You've got a vague idea of what the stories are going to be about but it's kind of responding. It's a real natural test of being funny in the moment. For me it's great, but for others it's not.'

The final show of Series 3 was aired on 19 October 2006 and, as it happened, just fourteen days before another announcement was about to come from the BBC that was to put Russ not just continually on our TV screens but on radio too...

'Award-winning comedian Russell Howard is to present a new show for BBC6 Music,' announced Lesley Douglas, Controller of BBC6 Music on 2 November 2006. 'I'm really pleased that Russell is joining 6 Music, he is one of the most exciting stand-up comics around. And yes, you have to be called Russell to present a show in this slot!'

The press statement that went out from the BBC was short and to the point and made reference to Russell's predecessor, Russell Brand, who was moving to Radio 2. Russ wanted to ask his namesake for advice so he rang him up once the news was confirmed – 'He gave me lots of ideas and then gave me a lovely send-off when he went to Radio 2. He's how I imagine Billy Connolly was: you get the impression that he isn't just reciting material.'

Russell also released a press statement that confirmed his excitement at being on his own, new three-hour radio show, a good deal longer than his previous thirty-minute airtime: 'I'm delighted and a little bit giddy to be joining 6 Music as it is a cutting-edge station with a wonderful creative approach and is undoubtedly one of the coolest places to be.'

Called *The Russell Howard Show*, Russell's slot was on Sundays from 10am–1pm. And the best thing about it? He would be hosting with his old mate, Jon Richardson. You can imagine the antics the pair of them got up to over the airways, with segments like, 'Am I Normal?', 'Time Travel' and 'Let's Play God'. 'I don't know what I'm doing with the buttons,' Russ confessed.

Listeners were encouraged to email in suggestions about where the pair could visit during the week to then report back to listeners on the Sunday, which provided much amusement. It was a chance for more family-based monologues, much mickey-taking about Jon, and general playfulness for three hours. It was an insight into their friendship, too, as among all the jibes, they also shared a brotherly relationship. For example, they would help each other in their coffee tastes by trying out different coffee drinks to see if the other would like them. If they liked a particular drink and believed the other one would too, there was a special signal code that followed: 'We would ring each other up and say, "Russell Howard speaking, we are go, we are go for the Gingerbread Latte, repeat, we are go. Over!" I did that in a crowded Starbucks and I had people looking at me like I was genuinely insane and I didn't know how to use a mobile.'

It was also a chance for Russ to work on a more 'newsy' angle. He was already doing that on *Mock the Week* and was now incorporating it more into his stand-up, and now he found bizarre, obscure stories for his listeners and dissected them. This was all good practice for a few years' time when he would take on his own show about the news...

The listeners enjoyed it and Russ was enjoying his new platform of stand-up. It was also a good chance for the two presenters to post ridiculous photos of themselves mucking about online – 'Our radio show is basically born out of the sexual tension between us. It's been described as *Brokeback Mountain* with less horses and more Xbox and that pretty much sums it up,' admitted Russ.

Now he was in the public eye, he found himself being recognised more and more, which he found could be quite amusing: 'I remember the first times I got recognised in Bath... there were these 5 lads and they had just been watching *Mock the Week* and they said to me, "Oh we really like you, we think you're great," and I said, "Thanks." Then there was an awkward beat of silence and I felt the need to say something funny so I said, "So, which one of you is going to wank me off?" and it was purely to break the silence! They looked properly horrified and left and then I tried to shout after them to explain but they just didn't get it...'

Although that particular gag backfired, it was the start of Russ realising that people would expect a comedy show whenever he was spotted – what they saw on TV was what they wanted in real life too – 'The more famous you get, the more people expect you to be funny all the time. The other day in Tesco some bloke came up and had a look in my basket, fully expecting to have some sort of comedy food in there, like a banana and two apples. I have been videoed in the supermarket too, but the bloke was very disappointed with my trolley. "That's only Weetabix," he said.'

While 2006 had brought an if.commeddie award, another sell-out show in Edinburgh, a regular radio show and a regular job as panellist on *Mock the Week*, Christmas that year was a particularly eventful time in the Howard household when Russ's brother Daniel had a horrific epileptic fit.

'In terms of a career, a big breakthrough I had was a show I did in 2006 at Edinburgh when I was nominated for a Perrier [now if.commeddie]. But it was also the year my brother nearly died after an epileptic fit. We had to put vallium up his arse on Christmas Day. He was 24, naked and having a horrific fit. But I used it in my next show, it had to have a positive outcome, I had to remind people, OK, let's look on the bright side, my brother nearly died...' but he survived.

Chapter 8
ONE BIG ADVENTURE (TOUR)

'My biggest breakthrough came after I was nominated for a Perrier when I was 26. Suddenly people started asking if I wanted to do all the sorts of things like panel shows. They're tricky: you never know what the atmosphere will be like and you don't get a say in what goes out.'
RH

His brother lived. Of course he did, Russell made sure fans up and down the country heard about the story of saving his naked brother at Christmas. A coping mechanism for dealing with a brutal truth that he could have lost his brother? Maybe, but it seemed that Russ was doing what he had always done (and continues to do to this day): he's always positive, no matter what. There is always a positive note to his gags and his shows alike. Daniel may have nearly died but for Russell, the important thing to remember was that he didn't. He focused on this thread for his new show later in the year, seeing the positive in everything and reminding his audience about the important, everyday things that we often take for granted.

With the success of Wandering at Edinburgh it was time for Russell to embark on his first solo nationwide tour. It was an immediate sell-out and was a good indication of how future tours would be received. Not that he was ever complacent about material – he was never going to sit back and perform the same routine or repeat the same material each year: 'I love my job but I never think, I'll just turn up on stage and be funny' he told the *Belfast Telegraph* in 2016. Perfecting his comedy act was very important to Russell and his lust for developing his shows made him an extremely driven, highly popular comic.

'Bob Dylan has this great mantra: Every great artist needs to be in a permanent state of becoming,' mused Russ. Or in layman's terms, no artistic creation will ever be right but there is a real beauty in striving to achieve it.

Every autumn (our spring) in Melbourne, Australia, the Melbourne International Comedy Festival (MICF) takes over the capital. The second-largest comedy festival behind Edinburgh, it was launched in 1987 by Barry Humphries and Peter Cook. There are over 525 shows to watch and the best local and international comedy acts make their way to the city for four weeks in March and April. In 2007 , in a huge nod of appreciation for the twenty-seven-year-old, Russell was nominated for a Barry Award for his show, Wandering.

The Barry Award is an honour given to the best act of the MICF and was named after the founder of the festival, Barry Humphries. It is regarded as the most prestigious award of the festival and the winner receives a trophy and cash prize. The nominees were announced on 23 April and *Chortle* website were quick to point out that only two of the seven nominated acts were from Australia – 'British acts have dominated the Barry Award shortlist for the best show at the Melbourne Comedy Festival'. Russell Howard, Daniel Kitson, We Are Klang and theatre duo Will Adamsdale and Chris Branch plus Irishman David O'Doherty were the 'Brits' dominating. In the end it was Daniel Kitson who was to take the crown but it didn't matter, the nomination was accolade enough. And Russ made sure he had fun while still in Oz, taking part in an Oxfam charity fundraiser to great acclaim. The crowd was huge, the biggest he had ever encountered in his career so far, and he persuaded Steve Hall from We Are Klang to join the encore with his penis tucked between his legs – which might sound rather odd but the alcohol was flowing freely that night and Steve wasn't self-concious! 'A drunk, naked man bogling as the Oxfam number scrolled beneath us and we sang, "We are the world".' It was a proud moment,' he later confessed.

By now Russ was receiving recognition not just from comedy critics but also big names in the comedy world too. Veteran comedy producer Michael Hurll, who has worked with everyone from Bob Hope and the Two Ronnies to Rod Hull, and was the mastermind behind the British Comedy Awards, liked him. In fact, in early 2007, he said in an interview that the act he would most like to see would be Russell Howard teamed up with Michael McIntyre – 'They are two comedians I'd put money on making it,' he said. 'They are very, very funny. If it was me, I'd put them together in a double act. It would be stunning – they're both good, clean-looking, funny guys. They would become what we're lacking. Someone able to do primetime 8pm comedy with absolutely clean, funny material.'

Hmm, perhaps he hadn't heard Russ talk about his brother's wang before now?

The point of this interview was that the producer knew the pressures a stand-up comedian faced and why not everyone is cut out for the profession: 'The loneliest job in the world is the stand-up comedian because you're master of your own destiny. And there ain't anybody going to help you when you're standing up there. I was watching Ken Dodd, who is one of the best stand-ups in the country, and I have seen him on a close-up camera, that fear come into his eyes. He was doing the Royal Variety Performance, performing new material, and wasn't getting any laughs. So he thought, "Fuck that, I'll go back to the act". And he did one of his old jokes and he didn't get any laughs. His face was like squeezing a sponge. That fear is why I have great admiration for stand-ups.'

In May 2007, ITV1 announced Russell Howard would be taking part in a new reality-type series called *Tough Gig*. Other comics, including Frank Skinner, Dara O'Briain and Patrick Kielty, were also taking part and each episode of the six-show series saw a different comedian perform out of their comfort zone. Each week, one comic would be thrown into a world they knew nothing about for seven days and then they would have to perform a stand-up gig to the people they had met with material based exclusively on their experiences.

Russ would be joining a group of Irish extreme surfers in County Clare. His episode was set to be broadcast in July but the viewing figures after Frank Skinner and Dara O'Briain's episodes were dismal and ITV pulled the plug on the rest of the series. It was eventually broadcast two years later and although Russ was a little inexperienced about the editing process of such a show, the experience itself was fantastic: 'I spent a week with these extreme surfers in Ireland and though it was a lot of fun, I was quite naïve about how they would edit it. They left out all the fun to give the gig a sense of jeopardy. Luckily, loads of great stories came out of it that ITV couldn't show. One of these surfers' initiation ceremonies is to go to a post office and try to buy pornography, which led to me being bollocked by a very angry old lady.'

There was one particular highlight for Russ: he did get to meet one of his childhood idols, Frank Skinner. But playing it cool didn't work – 'When I met Frank it was like reverting to my fifteen-year-old self. As a teenager, I was a huge fan of Frank's. I had all his videos. I'm a comedy nerd and it's fantastic getting to meet all my heroes. I wanted to ask Frank for his autograph but I felt embarrassed, so I ended up saying, "Can you please sign it for my mum? Her name is Ussell – and I added the R later!"'

In July 2007, Russ appeared in the very first series of the now cult BBC One comedy panel show, *Would I Lie to You?* Lee Mack and David Mitchell were the two team captains and each week would invite other celebrity guests to try and guess whether stories that the other team were telling them were 'truth' or a 'lie'. Angus Deayton hosted the series and

Russell (who was introduced as 'national disaster') joined Wendy Richards ('national treasure') on Mitchell's team on his debut. He was up against Lee Mack's team, with Len Goodman (*Strictly Come Dancing*) and Vic Reeves and his first truth or lie was whether he was once a contestant on *Junior MasterChef*. So, was it a lie? Vic was quick to question him and asked how he would make a hollandaise sauce. 'For me, I start with mustard,' said Russ, much to the delight of the studio audience. 'Then I put in cornflour, milk, eggs and a secret ingredient.' 'Liar!' cried Vic. Russ then told the panel what he cooked on *Junior MasterChef* to impress the judges and he said he had made tomato soup for starters, with Beef Wellington as a main. And he was eight years old when he took part on the show. 'Beef Wellington?! At 8 years old?! shrieked Lee. 'How long do you cook it for?' asked Vic. 'Ages,' replied Russ, and so his lie was rumbled.

The following year, 2008, he was back on the show alongside former BBC News reader Michael Buerk, this time on Lee Mack's team. David Mitchell's team (made up of *Strictly*'s Anton Du Beke and comedy writer and DJ Danny Baker) had to work out whether Russell was Argos' Nationwide Employee of the Year in 1997. Straight away, he was rumbled – David Mitchell didn't believe he would take part in an 'Argos Factor' and make it through the heats, and semi-finals and then final to be crowned Employee of the Year. Rumbled again. But he was back on the show in 2009, in the first episode of the third series, with Welsh comedian Rob Brydon now hosting the show. Back in Lee Mack's team, this time with presenter Carol Vorderman, it was here that he had to make the awful 'truth' known that he used to wear his underpants on his head to cure his acne. Jo Brand and David Mitchell on the opposing team had a field day with this particular gem but Russ took it all in his stride. At least he didn't try and cover up his blushes with his underwear.

But back to 2007, and Russ was back at Latitude Festival, where he found himself performing for an overflowing tent of keen listeners. The organisers of the event knew a star when they saw one and made sure that they booked him for the following year on the spot – 'His personal successes corresponded to his welcome at Latitude. He returned with fresh material and performed to an overflowing tent of keen listeners. Once again, his contribution to the Comedy line-up made a lasting impression on the weekend and it was with great enthusiasm that we invited him back the following year' reflected Latitude organisers in 2013.

It seemed there was no rest for the now in-demand star: it was time to head back up to Edinburgh in August of that year for his fourth show at the Fringe. It was his biggest yet and he received an almighty ovation. The problem the organisers had was that his show was sold out long before the event had even started and so he had to add more dates in a bigger room. 'He's a big deal,' said *The Times*. Russ's new show, Adventures, was to be the one that would make his first DVD the following year, 2008, and over the coming months he would tour with it around the UK. But for now, it was time to do what he did best and give the people of Edinburgh a mind-blowing, belly-laugh laden show. It was hard work, combining his commitments on *Mock the Week* with a month of performances in Edinburgh – 'Running back and forth nearly killed me,' he conceded. But he was determined to give a good show. And he found his fan base had grown since those early days of performing at the Fringe, now he was now 'Russell off the telly' too.

'More often than not, the people who have seen me on TV come along to my show and say, "He's actually quite good." A lot of people who see me because I'm on *Mock the Week* have never seen stand-up before and the excitement is extraordinary.'

That year for the Fringe Russ was performing at the Pleasance Courtyard and his mum probably best summed up the sell-out show: 'You're a bit like a child telling people about a day at the zoo,' she explained. And she was right. The website *Chortle* concurred: 'Like an overactive youngster, his delivery is so enthused at the various exciting things he just has to impart, he can't actually muster the patience to stick to one subject for long as the next one's already knocking on his brain. But you can't help but share his gusto for life. Howard has got some sterling set pieces of laugh-aloud brilliance. His all-purpose newspaper review especially was a wonder. Real life is experiences, adventures which Howard encourages you to encounter for yourself. Hardly a ground-breaking philosophy but one he appears to practice. The hour culminates in a comedy equivalent of Reasons To Be Cheerful, as Howard racks his brain to think of joyful experiences to tell a potential suicide victim he would miss. Howard's own show would easily earn a place in any such list.'

The Times were equally impressed: 'On stage he dances

from subject to subject with great fluidity as he celebrates the little ways in which real life is more exciting than the horrors we're fed by the media. Later he tells a story of a potential suicide and tells it beautifully.'

TheSkinny.co.uk also had great praise for Russ, who 'bounces around the stage like a frantic child on a sugar high. Though his irrepressible energy captures the attention of the audience, the breakneck speed of Russell's delivery detracts from the quality of the material as he relentlessly spews out one anecdote after another, barely pausing for breath'. There was a little advisory, however: 'Unfortunately the successful comedic pattern of Howard's act is compromised by the all-too-familiar media-bashing material which he wheels out towards the end of the show. Similarly, Howard's weak attempts at interaction with the audience threaten to disrupt an otherwise slick performance. However, these small flaws should not detract from the lashings of brilliantly funny anecdotes and quirky observations that make this show both uplifting and entertaining'.

Randomwords.wordpress.com were eager to point out that while Russell was obviously enjoying himself as a panellist on *Mock the Week*, he was a comedian who should be seen live to fully appreciate his talent: 'Russell's brief outbursts on the BBC show *Mock the Week* don't do justice to his considerable comic talent. Next to Frankie Boyle's perfectly timed, gloriously un-PC interjections, Howard is often left to look like an eager rookie playing for the easy laughs. But with an hour of our undivided attention, the self-confessed H-from-Steps-lookalike proves himself as a natural, and likeable stand-up. One criticism is that Howard tends to go for the collective, mainstream jugular when he might do better to embrace his evident eccentricity. Despite this, he's a certainly a comedian who must be enjoyed live, rather than via a tightly edited, suspiciously smooth TV gameshow'.

With an Edinburgh Festival Fringe show audience champing at the bit for more, it was time to show a wider audience what Russell had to offer. If you were a regular stand-up punter, you knew him; if you watched *Mock the Week*, then you were already familiar with his one-liners and cheeky persona. Now it was time for the nation to see him perform a well-rehearsed show courtesy of the BBC's *Live At the Apollo*. Broadcast in November, 2007, it was the first episode of Series 3 and Jack Dee introduced Russell to a 3,000-strong jeering crowd in London, his biggest audience yet. 'I've got material older than Russell,' deadpanned Dee, who asked the audience to give a warm welcome to Russell as he strode out confidently on stage. As the smoke and lights went crazy, he came out under the big Apollo sign with a timid hello. 'That's the funkiest garage of all time,' he told the audience. 'I love coming to London, it's fantastic. It's quite terrifying, though. I come from Bristol and the first thing you hear on the train as you are coming in is "do not approach unattended packages". In Bristol, I genuinely heard this, "Ere, don't feed the pigeons".'

The audience responded straight away and soon he was in his stride. It was a well-rehearsed, well-performed set, and at no point did he look out of his comfort zone. His astonishment at being asked to perform on that infamous stage – which has made household names of many a comedy star – was clear when he first came out in wide-eyed amazement but it still proves to be one of his most memorable gigs.

'It's an extraordinary feeling to hear 3000 people laughing at your jokes,' he said in an interview with the *Bolton News* the following year. 'The waves of laughter just hit you. You feel you're orchestrating the whole thing – it's an out-of-body experience. A joke explodes in front of you and rolls back across the stalls, and you stand there just thinking, wow!'

And did veteran comic Jack Dee offer the youngster any advice? Well, if he did, Russ probably didn't remember! 'I never banked on doing a gig like that, I couldn't believe it,' he confessed. 'Jack came up to me on the afternoon before the show, and asked me if I was feeling alright. I felt like I was going back to my childhood, looking at Jack's DVDs in HMV and thinking, I can't afford that – I'll have to get a paper round! I became a spluttering child once again.'

But he regained his composure to continue with his small-theatres tour with Adventures and went on to record his first ever DVD, which was filmed at London's Bloomsbury Theatre. Tickets for that show sold out within a day and he had to add three extra dates for the venue. But what was it like performing his gig, knowing that it was also being recorded for his debut DVD? A DVD? Did it thrill him that soon he would be walking into HMV and seeing his own stand-up DVD on the shelves? His comedy career began with watching comedians on VHS and now it was his turn to film his own offering.

'I felt the pressure, it could never be right,' he told *Den*

Of Geek website in 2008. 'It's a horrible feeling. Unless you have the money, which certain comics do, to go round and film ten shows and then get them all right, then it'll be fine. But it's a really difficult process, because you're thinking that got a bigger laugh three nights ago in Grimsby, and then that lady said that thing which made it a bit funnier. You just have to do it to the best of your ability and walk away.'

And not only did he feel the pressure of making a good stand-up DVD, he also felt the pressure of people – his family, his friends, his fans – seeing it in the shops. Spending money on his show, which was going to be immortalised on DVD. It was a little scary for the twenty-seven-year-old.

In 2008, Russell told independent publisher *Den of Geek*: 'Comedy isn't really meant to be watched on DVD, is it? You're meant to be there. It's an interesting process, but to be honest with you, that made me feel like a very young man in the world in which I find myself. I find myself very inexperienced in terms of making DVDs, that's the weirdest thing. To go from pissing around in comedy clubs and arsing about, to suddenly "This is shit! This is going to be in shops!" Thinking about it, you get more serious about it, which knocks the everyday fun out of it.'

He also found it funny adjusting to the 'box-ticking' requirements that came with producing a DVD. And material that he could, and could not include 'There were jokes that we couldn't put on the DVD. There was Disney's copyright of *The Lion King*. Basically, I had this story about going to the doctors and getting a testicular cancer examination and I described my penis disappearing into my stomach. And I said that my balls looked like they were dopey backing singers and the frontman had fled. I did a little dance where I had the nuts doing "wimba-whey-a-wimba-whey'. We weren't allowed to keep that in! The company that put the DVD out had to write a letter to Disney saying can we use your song and they asked in what context. Well, in the context of Russell Howard's balls. And they sent back a very firm no. It's really interesting. We did some stuff about the Bishop of Carlisle,that was libellous, so we couldn't keep that in either' he also confessed to *Den of Geek*.

But there was lots of stuff that did make it onto the DVD, including lots of extras of Russell on the road, trying to find a go-karting venue that was open, eating Minstrels with someone in the audience, getting heckled ('Nice arse!', 'How big's your cock?', 'Do you still put marbles up your brother's arse?', 'What's your favourite film ever?', etc., etc.) and having, er, fun, at Cardiff Castle. There was also lots of footage of him performing other gigs during the tour.

It was a huge commitment – he was performing more than sixty-six dates, having sold over 38,000 tickets for his Adventures show. He had an hour of material ready to perform in venues around the UK but he hadn't lost the art of improvisation. With so much of his stuff on *Mock the Week* being pre-planned one-liners and hard-hitting jokes, he relished the tour and performing to a range of live audiences: 'I will have an hour of material ready to go but I like smudging it. It kind of depends on the audience really. I was on the tour the other day, in a really great, mad little place. There were loads of heckles flying in left, right and centre. And then there was this really weird moment where this 14-year-old kid got into the gig – god knows how. He had shorts on and walked along the front of the stage halfway through my set. I asked if he was alright and he said, "Yeah, I'm just looking for the toilet." He looked properly terrified and I just couldn't bring myself to say anything other than, "They're just over there, mate." So he wandered off and I turned to the crowd and said, "I just looked into his eyes, he looked so vulnerable, I couldn't say anything else." And this bloke shouted, "Weak! You're weak, Howard!" You can't plan stuff like that, it's so funny.'

Chapter 9

THE NAME'S HOWARD...
RUSSELL HOWARD

*'I perform somewhere like Darlington and have people coming to me
and saying, "We loved the show!" Then when I get back home to my mum,
I say, "Show me some respect, Mum, they love me in Darlington!"*
RH

Russell was on the road with his Adventures Tour and
with reviews such as 'You'll find more laughs here than
many comedians manage in an entire career' [*Metro*], he was
feeling the love. The show featured an array of life-affirming
tales; from kindness to stupidity, as well as laugh-out-loud
childhood memories, not to mention stories of love for the
simple things in life – this infectious passion for everyday
pleasures had audiences up and down the UK savouring
every moment.

Not only that, each venue he visited in each town or
village or city would have a unique part in the show as Russ
was keen to 'explore' the wonders of the UK. He wanted the

punters to help and encouraged them to offer ideas on what
he could do in each place he visited to give him a real taste
of local life. 'I've put a load of messages on MySpace asking
for things to do and places to go in all the towns where I'm
playing,' he revealed in an interview with the *Bolton News* in
February 2008. 'Then, whatever happens in a particular town,
I will weave that into the show. The plan is to do lots of weird
and wonderful things all over the country. It's so much more
authentic than doing a lot of routines beginning "imagine
if..." It also means that every single gig will be unique.'

And unique they were. Russ's enthusiasm for making this
tour exciting, fresh and vibrant, and immersing himself in
local culture was also a way of being able to progress his
comedy, not resting on his laurels.

'This is a great way of generating fresh material. I collect
so many diverse experiences. It means that my show is not
all clichéd stuff about travelling on the train, being stuck in
a succession of soulless hotels and getting drunk every night.
That would bore me. I might go to a cool indie record shop or
try out a local ice cream parlour. I have never liked the idea
of standing still comedically. This way, I'm creating my own
infrastructure. With live comedy, with this Adventures tour,
you get these unforeseen moments of genuine connection
with the audience. You can wander on stage and immediately
strike up a rapport with people. I love that. I don't want to
simply hammer out the same show every night and then go
back to the hotel and get drunk. I love just going with the
flow,' he continued.

So, what sort of variety had he encountered on the road

with his Adventures Tour? Well, a gig in Telford got off to a completely unplanned but hilarious start. The moment Russ went on stage, someone in the audience shouted out, 'Russell, do you want some cheese?' Then for the next few minutes Russell and the audience explored why the man had brought cheese along to the gig and why he thought that that was the right moment to offer him some.

'Rather than sticking to a script, I ditched my pre-planned material for fifteen minutes and just responded to this guy because he was there in the room. I adore that feeling of seeing where a riff takes you. I find people fascinating so if someone shouts something out, I don't just put them down and move on. That seems rubbish to me.'

And what about other experiences in the other towns he visits? During the autumn leg of his tour, he visited the Heavy Horse Centre in Wimborne Minster, Dorset. It was a rehab centre for fat ponies and he couldn't help but stare at the obese creatures – giving him plenty of material for his local show that night: 'I expected to see horses with chocolate smeared all over their hooves, sighing, "I can't help it, I comfort eat!" I talked about it at the gig that night and it was really well received.'

Then there was the time in Sheffield when a local suggested he tried paintballing, a popular hobby. But it turns out Russell wasn't as tough as he thought and told the crowd that night at his gig what had happened. He explained that he was quite scared out in the woods, but the man in change of showing them how to use the guns was quite amusing, telling Russ that if he was good at paintballing he was 'good at women'. But Russ decided that the battlefield was no place for him and when the game started and it got quite brutal, he surmised that during a war he would be the type of soldier back safely in the barracks, writing poetry!

His enthusiastic outlook on such experiences made his gigs all the more unique and enjoyable. What other comedians would ask fans for suggestions of things to do in all the towns they visit? And Russ was well aware that the invitation to his fans to 'show him around' might sometimes backfire – 'A lot of these activities might involve me going to barbecues with strangers. It's a nice idea but it could be a horrible way to die! It would be terrible to have to cancel the tour because some bloke in Darlington has invited me to his barbecue and then tried to eat me!'

So where did this idea come from? Was it born just out of a need to keep himself entertained on the road? After all it can be an endless routine of gig, sleep, travel, gig, sleep, travel and for someone as energetic and in need of constant stimulation as Russ, there had to be some light relief – 'I remember reading how the stand-up Tommy Tiernan once hitchhiked round Ireland for an entire tour and collected stories along the way. I thought about trying that but knowing my luck, I'd never get picked up and would end up having to get the Megabus at the last minute. How humiliating!'

The actual idea for his 'twist' on tour came to him when he visited Gloucester for a show. He went along to a ceremony known as 'The Cheese Roll', where the locals roll a huge lump of cheese down a hill and then chase after it. It can be quite a dangerous pastime and ambulance crews wait at the bottom of the hill as there are plenty of accidents that happen. Russell decided to incorporate his experience of watching that 'fantastic, crazy occasion' into his show that evening and the stories went down a storm. 'It just gave the show so much more freshness,' he recalled in an interview with *The Bolton News*. 'Now, wherever the tour takes me I can think, shall I go to a car boot sale in Blackburn today because I've never done that before? Every day on this tour I'm going to try and do something I've never done.'

It was a wonderful example of his zest for life not only to broaden his horizons but also use his experiences in each show. The crowds loved it and Russ was a hit – but it was his mum who always made sure his head didn't get any bigger. 'I still find it really odd to go and perform somewhere like Darlington and have people coming to me and saying, "Thanks for coming!" or "We loved the show!" Then when I get back home to my mum, I say, "Show me some respect, Mum, they love me in Darlington!" She just tells me to stop being such an idiot.'

One of the biggest laughs from the show came from his HM The Queen playing fancy-dress impression – 'She pulls up her bedcovers to her chin and says, "Look at me, Philip, I'm a postage stamp!"'

Or his retelling of the story when he finds his brother Daniel naked after having a fit on Christmas Day: 'He's dancing with the Reaper and I develop penis envy.' Which is also part of his very serious message of 'Let's celebrate Life'.

But there's a very poignant part of the show that Russell

shares with the audience and it features an incident he witnessed, highlighting the kindness of strangers. He tells the story of seeing a man on top of the Hippodrome, Bristol's tallest building, contemplating suicide. With the group of people standing around trying to shout to the man not to jump, Russell says a young kid then rides past and tells the bloke to jump and calls him gay. But the kid, who was told off by a woman watching, had actually believed the guy was doing a bungee jump. Then Russell explains to the spellbound audience that he was then thinking about telling the young man about all the things he would miss if he jumped and what things he himself would miss if he were ever in that situation. This included seeing his mum holding his favourite dinner and that lovely feeling you get when you put on pants that have been on the radiator. Thankfully Russ's story then went on to explain that it was an old man who actually saved the day by telling the bloke to 'look around the corner and see the hope rather than jump and die.' The audience were silent. You could hear a pin drop.

'This man stunned us all and the bloke didn't jump. He leaned over and shouted, "Cheers, mate."' How incredible is that story, asked a visibably emotional Russ. 'And all I could think of was, "Radiator pants!"'

Well, the short answer is pretty incredible. And it is that warmth, that affirmation of life that punctuates his gigs and makes him such a popular performer. He summed it up nicely in an interview during his Adventures Tour: 'For me, that's what it's all about. Life isn't about *The X Factor* or

Ant and Dec. It's not about seeing the world in a cynical or ironic way, it's about those rare moments where you sit back and say, wow, that meant something.'

The end of the year saw Russ spending Christmas with his family – 'It wouldn't be Christmas if we didn't spend it together.' He made sure it was one his mum didn't forget and he took his parents to Mauritius to celebrate Ninette's fiftieth birthday. It was a memorable trip and a chance for Russell to have a bit of a break during his tour. And of course, there were some amusing tales from the trip –'There we were, at this lovely hotel, among loads of couples. A lot of the sun loungers were doubles, so you'd be on one with your mum and get some great looks from people, thinking, "She's done alright for herself".'

The holiday was a chance to unwind after his last gig from his first big tour, which made it extra-special for Russell. It was a time when the family could just 'spend time on the beach, play chess and football, read and hang out.'

Still working on dates for his Adventures Tour the following year, Russ was back on TV at the start of 2008 in a fairly unexpected place: he took on the role of backstage presenter at The Brit Awards. For someone who once said, 'I got offered lots of presenting jobs when I was younger, interviewing pop stars. If I ever have to ask Jamelia what her favourite cheese is I'd shoot myself in the mouth,' so this was quite an ironic place for him to be.

And did he enjoy it? Nope, not one smidge. The 2008 Brit Awards took place at Earl's Court in London on 20 February and The Osbournes – Ozzy, Sharon, Kelly and Jack – were hosting. Big artists like Kylie Minogue, Rihanna, Mika, Sir Paul McCartney and Amy Winehouse were all performing and winners on the night included Take That, Kanye West, Foo Fighters, Adele and Paul McCartney. Backstage, trying to get all the gossip from the stars, was Russ, who admits that he felt completely out of his depth: 'If I regret anything in my career, it would be doing backstage presenting at the Brits,' he told *TheGuardian* newspaper. 'I didn't really want to be there, I just don't care what people like Lily Allen think about stuff. But I know that some people do care so I couldn't just slouch through it. I'm not very good at presenting, I just can't get passionate about it, it's a soulless world.'

And for someone who enjoys hanging out with his 'old' mates, he found the suggestion that he should be hanging out with famous faces rather amusing.

From that point onwards, even though the TV offers were pouring in, Russ vowed not to accept anything unless he was doing what he can do and doing it well – namely stand-up and panel shows. 'I've had lots of strange offers but I haven't really fancied any of them. I was asked – as was everyone else, I presume – to a charity boxing match on television. But why would I want to go on TV and get seven bells beaten out of me? Viewers would think, "Oh look, that funny bloke is being beaten up by Les Dennis." I find real people far more interesting than celebs or, worse still, people who want to become celebs.'

With his Adventures Tour at an end, he decided to take some time out to spend with his girlfriend, Cerys. Oh yes, his girlfriend. This particular area of Russell's life hasn't been mentioned thus far, but like his family, she has featured on several occasions in his shows. Not, however, in the same great detail that is afforded to the likes of his brother,, but on his Adventures Tour, we do know that he suffered great heartache in 2006 when they briefly separated (but later got back together again). But let's go back a few years to 2001 when his comedy career was still in those 'early day' stages. He met a young woman named Cerys Morgan at a Venture Scout disco. She was seventeen years of age and Russ was twenty-one and fresh out of university. He had seen Cerys around before as she was one of his mate's little sisters and they clicked straight away – although Russ readily admits that in the early days, the relationship didn't go down too well with his mate. 'He didn't want me to date her, it caused quite a few problems at the beginning, but it's fine now.'

The couple enjoyed dating and seeing each other when they could in those early days before they went on their first holiday together to Egypt – 'Egypt is one of those places where you are shouted at a lot. I like all that, when people try to entice you into their shops. They've got really bizarre calls too: "English?", "Man United?", "Luvly Jubbly?", "118, 118?".'

They went to Sharm el Sheikh, where Russell had booked a five-star hotel: the Royal Rojana. What he didn't realise was that the place was geared up for Russian guests only – 'The food, the music, the vodka... It was for Russian people. At night some bloke was banging on our door for an hour, shouting mad Russian. We were terrified!' Not surprisingly they decided to cut their losses and move to another hotel, the Novotel on Na'ama Bay, which proved to be the best decision they ever made – 'It was so amazing that we started singing songs about it. It had a private beach.'

So what does Russ like to do on his holidays? For someone who doesn't stand very still on the stage you might imagine he likes to be continually stimulated and constantly on the go – 'I like to sunbathe, read books and swim in the shallow bit of the sea. My girlfriend liked diving in Egypt. She tells people how funny it was, watching me snorkelling along when we saw a ray. To me, it was a deadly stingray, and in a nanosecond, she heard me going, "Ahoooh!" and running back up the beach.'

The pair had a brief break-up in 2005 before getting back together again soon after. Then things got serious and they moved in together in Leamington Spa. Russ had only lived with his family and Jon Richardson before so this was a big step – but why Leamington Spa? Well, there was a very good reason for this: Cerys. She was already living there as she had joined Warwick University to study medicine. At weekends Russell would catch the train there to visit her before they decided the time was right to move their relationship on and for him to move in. Besides, the commute was beginning to get on his nerves – 'I got the train to Leamington to visit Cerys and it was packed. When I sat down it felt as though someone was glaring at me a bit; that can make you feel a bit trapped and you can't then watch people, which is where of course a lot of my comedy comes from. It's difficult if you're looking at them and they're watching you, thinking, "Why is that dickhead off the telly staring at me?"'

For Russell, the move to be with Cerys in Leamington Spa was showing his enormous admiration for her profession. 'Being a doctor is a proper job, you have to respect that,' he explains, implying her career will always be the more important one. 'I just write jokes for a living, you can't say what I do is a job.'

The pride he has in his girlfriend is clear, and for the next few years they were extremely happy in their home in the Midlands, with the comedian embracing life away from the bright lights of London or familiarity of Bristol – 'We are settled here. I really like Leamington, it's a relaxed place and I have a lot of good friends here now.'

So what is life like for Russell's girlfriend? Cerys is an intensely private person and Russ won't talk about her on stage other than to mention her existence and praise her job. But with his recognition growing in 2008, it must have been strange for her to be going out with such a well-known face. 'I don't have any groupies,' he explained to *The Scotsman* at the time. 'I get the occasional comment from a girl when I'm out with my girlfriend – it drives her mental. It's all very odd.' But he believes he may have an explanation for the sudden attention and it has nothing to do with his heart-throb status. Rather, back in 2008, the misconception that all men named Russell are rampant Lotharios – 'I've gone through my whole life never having met any Russells. I played football when I was younger and it's not a name you can cry out, it's a very feminine thing. And then all of a sudden there's a massive global superstar (Brand), me, and a brilliant young comedian (Kane). And because I have Russell Brand's people asking me if I am putting it about and I say no, I feel very inadequate. I feel this pressure on me to bang, but that's not me. But I tell you what, if there were a competition, I bet you I've played more hours of Championship Manager than Russell Brand – that's what I bring to the Russell world.'

Chapter 10

NAMING YOUR WANG

'They danced down the street like dingledodies, and I shambled
after as I've been doing all my life after people who interest me, because the
only people for me are the mad ones, the ones who are mad to live, mad to
talk, mad to be saved, desirous of everything at the same time, the ones who
never yawn or say a commonplace thing, but burn, burn, burn, like fabulous
yellow roman candles exploding like spiders across the stars.'
RH

In April 2008 Russell announced that he would be embarking on tour that autumn with a brand new show, Dingledodies. Beginning with just a run of five shows at the 630-seater Music Hall at the Assembly Rooms at the Edinburgh Festival Fringe, it would continue at fifty-eight venues across the UK. It was to be one of the biggest seasons for comedy, with the likes of Russ's childhood hero, Lee Evans, also touring, plus Steve Coogan, Rob Brydon, Paddy McGuinness and Dylan Moran.

Henham Park, Suffolk, was once again the go-to place for festival lovers, culture vultures, music and comedy fans. On Friday, 18 July, Russell, who had made the top line of billing on the Latitude poster that year, began his set to deafening crowds. 'This was a highlight of the day,' confirmed *Chortle.co.uk*. 'Every word that left his mouth led to a laugh and his warm, friendly persona had the audience hooked. He received a rousing welcome and quickly proved why he deserved it. Not only is Howard an exceptionally skilled writer, he has a real magic in his delivery that kept more than 2000 people rapt.'

The crowds had enjoyed his set so much that they shouted for more when he left the stage. The heckles and Russell's interactions with the audience (one ofhis greatest skills), resulted in some beautiful ad-libbing. 'This was a faultless set,' concluded *Chortle*.

In the month before he would make a shock announcement regarding the Edinburgh Festival Fringe, this was a good time to see the man in action. 'If you were a part of the audience that July, consider yourself one of the lucky ones,' declared Latitude's official website. 'You were a member of a crowd that saw him just as he was hitting his stride; right as he was at the cusp of becoming a worldwide star.'

That summer, Russ went to Croydon's Warehouse Theatre's Edinburgh previews and just before heading up to Scotland for the Fringe Festival itself, he announced that he would be leaving his Sunday morning BBC6 Music show with Jon Richardson. Jon would continue presenting the show for the next couple of years without his mate but the time was right for Russ to leave. 'I find radio really restrictive,' he admitted in a press release. 'Radio sketches are OK, but a show like this was completely different. We were on air on a Sunday morning. We had a whole list of words we couldn't say because families were listening. And we had to play music too. I never felt like myself, and if you find yourself too boring, which I often do, it's like you're imposing this dull person on the nation. And I realised how much I feed off the audience as a performer, but you can't gauge a reaction on the radio. The thing is, you are just in a room talking with your mates. And when you're with your mates, what do you do? You get naughtier and naughtier. Then you slowly forget what you're doing is public broadcasting. So I stopped because I didn't like the idea of being in someone's house talking in the morning.'

It was also poignant that this direction, the airwaves, wasn't somewhere that Russ envisaged would progress his comedy. He was having too much fun performing live and with no ambition to make it on radio, for him the show had now run its course – 'As a kid I used to go to HMV and look at the videos of all these geniuses like Billy Connolly but with radio the furthest you're ever going to go is to the *Radio 1 Breakfast Show* and I would never want to do that in a million years.'

But what did that mean as far as his relationship with Jon Richardson went? Well, not a lot really! 'It was a very intense relationship of staring into each other's eyes for a while but now we are taking a break. But we really want to do a TV film together – after we saw *Superbad*, we thought it was hilarious but it's not relevant to the experiences you have at parties here, growing up. We want to do a really honest reflection of crap scout hut disco parties. Someone always got shitfaced, someone always got drawn on, and there was always a girl that got naked.'

Then it was August, he was back in Edinburgh and he would normally have a month of sell-out shows to perform at the Fringe. But he decided to do things differently that year. He knew that any show he put on there would be a sell-out (after the previous year's experience it would also need extra dates in bigger venues) and he didn't think this was fair. It wasn't anything to do with him being unhappy with the Fringe, he just wanted to give new, fresh, young comedians a chance to have an audience – he didn't want any new acts to suffer from him grabbing all the punters. He told *The Scotsman* that after enjoying four successful solo shows at the Fringe the four previous years, his five-night stint at the Assembly Rooms that year would be a fitting farewell.

'I was asked to do 30 nights in a big room but I couldn't live with myself: that's just stealing from your mates. If five years ago, some Bobby Tellypants had rocked up and people were all going to see him, I know that would have killed me. I think it's just wrong, so that's me and the Fringe done. I just wanted to do five nights as a good kind of send-off almost. That's my fifth show and that'll do. I think there should be a cap on audiences of maybe 200. A lot of really good mates were playing to audiences of about eight and that's not a reflection of their talents, there is just not enough people to go round.'

It was a brave decision but with a fifty-eight-venue tour to consider, he knew it was the right one. But that wasn't to say he wasn't excited about performing at the Assembly Room with Dingledodies. He also believed the spirt of the Fringe had changed: 'Edinburgh's brilliant, but it is also a tough beast and you do whatever you can to get through it,' he told a journalist before the Festival. 'But the further you go in, you feel more like a teacher who's got Ofsted inspectors in. It's not a good way of seeing comics. Every comic up there is terrified and nervous because everything they say is at the mercy of the journalist's perception. You could rip the shit out of a gig and it could be that there's someone at the back saying, "Well, I prefer the new wave of DIY comedy." The only snag with Edinburgh is that you sometimes think it needs to be something more than funny. I don't know if it does. Touring gigs are more fun because it has that impromptu, "Waay, it's happening tonight feel". Edinburgh is just a buffet of brilliant comedians and some of the theatres are so beautiful, it's a privilege to wander around when there's no one in and look at the architecture of the place, especially old music halls.'

The press were keen to find out if he would be using any of his previous material for Dingledodies or repeating any of his *Mock the Week* jokes. It was a foolish question to ask the twenty-eight-year-old, who takes great pride in providing his audience with new material for every new show – 'I'd never do that. When you're live, it should all be brand-new for that audience – certainly for a touring show. The most enjoyable thing about stand-up is that new idea, that spark: when you are working it out on stage and it becomes really good. I remember seeing a well-known comic a few years ago and he did the exact same set that I'd seen him do on DVD and it was a horrible experience.'

This was the key to Russell's stage shows: he didn't want his audiences to feel cheated out of a fresh, new experience as he himself had been by the comedian who he refuses to name. For his new show, an hour and a half set, he revealed that probably twenty minutes of it would be improvised: 'I try to treat that 20 as the liquid funny – the things that kind of link all the set pieces. You present your ideas and you bend them around the crowd. It is a bit like *Mock the Week*, you look at what's going on over the week before the show is recorded so we will have a fair idea of the topics we're going to chat about. The best bits are always born out of knowledge – a joke will appear that wouldn't have if you hadn't done your research. So some bits are prepared but others are genuinely improvised,' he told *The Guardian* in July 2008.

His set at Edinburgh was well received and he continued to talk a lot about the things he sees that he finds funny, like 'the wonderful moments that leap out of now–where', his brilliant mate Tom, celebrity chef Gordon Ramsay, why texting has infested relationships, and a whole lot more.

'I put in stuff that I have jokes about or want to do jokes about, and with the US election coming up, I've got a lot on that now. So it's everything and anything, mixed up with improv, with, essentially, the message being a nod towards life-affirming madness.'

But the big question on everyone's lips was what the title of his show meant. For a man who likes to talk about his wang a lot on stage, the general consensus was that it must have something to do with his balls. Not so, said Russ. Well, maybe a little bit...

Russell told *The List* in August 2008: 'I've had loads of people ask, "Dingledodies? Is that what you call your balls?",' he admitted. 'Is this new show about the hilarious adventures of your knackers?'

The word is actually a reference to a cult beat-generation classic novel called *On The Road* by the American writer Jack Kerouac. Russell read the book earlier in 2008 and one passage particularly struck a chord with him. It became an extract he could repeat it word for word when asked: 'They danced down the streets like dingledodies, and I shambled after as I've been doing all my life after people who interest me, because the only people for me are the mad ones, the ones who are mad to live, mad to talk, mad to be saved, desirous of everything at the same time, the ones who never yawn or say a commonplace thing, but burn, burn, burn, like fabulous yellow roman candles exploding like spiders across the stars.'

The show allows Russ to campaign against those who are aggressive, out of touch with common sense and somewhat boorish – but he never comes across as aggressive himself when delivering his opinion on such people. He matter-of-factly just finds them dull: 'Too many people revel in their petty rage to the point where they define themselves by futile anger. People who say things like, "Britain's broken! I'm a stranger in my own country! Political correctness has gone mad, blah, blah, blah". These people bore me shitless and I much prefer the dingledodies. That's what I love to do! Plus it does sound a bit like my balls.'

'This charming rascal is an evangelist for happiness, finding glee in the strange behaviour of strangers, whether random acts of mischief or lunatic outbursts born of impotent frustration. He finds glee in everyday life, then spreads the word with a near-religious fervour. And now, thanks to *Mock the Week*, his congregation is bigger than ever, filling good-sized theatres everywhere,' declared *Chortle* in its review of the show. 'Life is for celebrating, not complaining and it would take a special kind of curmudgeon not to leave the theatre in the same elated state of mind.'

Chapter 11

'UH, HI EDDIE, CAN I HAVE A PHOTO?'

'My family is an orgy of possibilities. They actively try to get mentioned. My eight-year-old cousin sat in the dog basket for an hour Christmas Day, then looked at me and said, "If this don't get in your comedy show, nuffin' will."'

RH

At the end of August 2008, Russ headed back to the capital to take part in the Pimm's Summerfest. It was a five-day outdoor event in London's Holland Park and designed for balmy summer evenings with Pimm's on tap, burgers on the BBQ, while chilled-out folks enjoyed the entertainment on giant deckchairs. But the great British climate had other ideas and the heavens opened. Thankfully, a sturdy marquee was able to withstand the downpour and the show could go on. Which was good for those in attendance as Russ 'forcefully grabbed the laughs from the get-go and never once released them from his grip,' according to *Chortle*. For those who missed his short set at Edinburgh or weren't able to get tickets to his tour – which was due to start the following month – this was the perfect opportunity to see him.

In September it was time to start his Dingledodies Tour and he was quietly confident that the bigger venues would suit his style, telling *Metro*: 'I've done gigs from 60 and to 600 and both appear to be working. But you can really smack the crap out of big gigs – really go for it. With the little ones you have to be gently confident.'

It was just as well he was at home in larger venues as in October of that year he took part in Channel 4's *The Secret Policeman's Ball* in aid of Amnesty International. A live night event at London's Royal Albert Hall, it featured four hours of stand-up from some of the best UK comedians. Frank Skinner, Alan Carr, Graham Norton, Ed Byrne, Eddie Izzard and Shaun Williamson joined Russ on stage for a show that was then edited down to an hour and a half television special for Channel 4. The comedy marathon and sheer volume of comics performing meant that each act got roughly five minutes, give or take, to perform in a building not built for such entertainment. It's a huge venue and has the disadvantages of a stadium gig with its lack of intimacy and need for essential big-screen projectors but it doesn't have the numbers to make the laughs powerful, with only 4,000 as its maximum capacity. Russ appeared in the second act after a video link from Russell Peters in Canada. Among such a stellar line-up cast, the line describing his performance was that he merely followed Peters with 'his own winning brand of fluffy, energetic storytelling about family, Christmas and his brother's epilepsy'.

Backstage after his performance, Russ, swigging from a glass of red wine, was asked about how he thought his set went: 'I have no idea how it went, I think it went alright but you have no idea,' he confessed. 'Thousands of people are just there and you just have no idea... It is an out-of-body moment. And then you move around the stage and you see a big picture of your face moving around and it's crazy!'

As the show was in aid of Amnesty International, Russell was asked what the charity meant to him. He was extremely truthful: 'Er, it's just a gig for me, to be honest. I am sure there are people who are suffering and I feel your pain, but I'm not familiar with Amnesty. I did have an idea, it would probably be in bad taste, but I thought that after every joke I did, I could release somebody from the shackles of a radiator on stage... I thought that would be quite funny, to say to them, "You're free!" and have them scampering off stage. I thought it would be quite funny, like a bearded man shouting freedom! Then me telling a joke. The oddest thing about the night for me is wandering around before and afterwards and seeing Izzard, and he's so chatty. He'll wander up and say, "Hi, how are you?" And I just don't know what to say, you become so aware that you're talking to Eddie Izzard! You feel like you're 11 and you're at the back of the bus and all these 16-year-olds come on and go, "Alright, little 11-year-old?!" I feel just like that 11-year-old.'

But even though Russ was meeting some of the biggest names in comedy, some of his childhood heroes, he realised the importance of acknowledgment – in a sense that you are someone's idol, someone has seen you/watched you/adored you and now they're in the same room as you, you can't ever ignore that.

'I saw a famous comedian who I adore refuse to have a photo with a fan and it just broke her and I just thought, "Just have the photo, man, come on!" People want a photo, that is it, it happens all the time, but it is no problem at all. Photo, then move along. It's nice, I remember seeing David Gray... I saw him in the street and I didn't have the courage to go up to him so I have to remember that people are excited to see me and want a picture. I did it with Eddie Izzard at this gig... It was the first time I have met him and I was like, "Uh, Hi Eddie, can I have a photo?!" I just thought, fuck it!

Relaxing at the after-show party and mixing with all the big names of the comedy world appeared to be more daunting for Russ than actually performing – 'I know people like Frank Skinner, Sean Lock and Eddie Izzard first and foremost as a fan so it's a weird experience being aware of them in the same room. In that "non–asky, asky" kind of way you say, "What did you think?" It's horrible but you just want people that you love to think you're alright. Although as Eddie Izzard himself said that night, "The Green Room is the hardest room to play."'

At the fundraiser Russell also had an amusing encounter with talk-show host Jonathan 'Wossy' Ross. He was in the mens' toilets when Ross walked in and said to him, 'I know you, you're thingy-me-jig.' Russ was flustered and could only reply, 'I can be whoever you want me to be.' Wossy thought this was hilarious and the following year, when he invited Russell to come on his chat show, told the audience the story. 'And for the next half an hour he was Susan from Leicester,' guffawed Jonathan.

October was turning out to be a busy month and Russ hit the Magners Paramount Comedy Festival in Brighton as well as the Reading Comedy Festival too. Festivals were a favourite of his and backstage at Reading, he explained why he loved them: 'The beauty of them is that they huddle together so many different acts that you might turn up and look at the list and think to yourself, OK, I'll give them a watch and then you end up really liking them and it snowballs from there.'

And that is exactly what happened to one fan who saw him perform back in 2006 at a festival and homed in on him again this time around: 'I always come to the comedy festival in Brighton and we knew we wanted to see Russell this year after watching him two years ago,' confessed Laura Drane. 'It wasn't like there was a big difference in his performance style, he was confident then and he was confident now, he is so easy to watch. It's like he is just performing for his mates and you are part of the crowd. The humour is easy and I love the stuff about his family.'

You can see Russell is at home performing for an audience, as he also confessed at the Reading Festival. TV gave him a platform but his live shows are what he loves best: 'I much prefer live gigs. At the end of one of my gigs in Southend, this guys shouts out that I needed to get my support act back on stage and give him a dance. So we did.

You couldn't do that on telly. Live gigs are warts and all, and each one is different. You don't get that on TV as they edit it, censor it, cut certain things. There is more of an agenda. The live gig is a muck around.'

He was back at the Apollo in November for another recording for the series, *Live At the Apollo*, this time as guest host. His episode wasn't shown until January the following year and after his performance, he took on the role of presenter and introduced Jo Brand, a comedian he had instantly 'clicked' with after they met on *Would I Lie to You?*

It was one of three dates he was playing at the London Apollo and *Time Out* were impressed when they caught his act: 'Howard is one of the hottest young guns around and tonight he brings his excellent show, Dingledodies, to the massive Apollo. He flies around the stage like a kid high on sugar. He moves from topic to topic with effortless ease and makes the audience laugh all the way through the show with his wonderful grotesque takes on everyone and everything.'

The Evening Standard seemed to pick up on Russ's self-admission of looking like H from Steps when reviewing the show: 'With his blond hair and trim torso, Russell Howard is more boy band crooner than stand-up comedian and his growing army of devotees agree. At his biggest gig yet, they were in pure pop fan mode, waving placards and worshipping his distinctive brand of wonderful lunacy.'

It was also worth noting that Russell had now gathered a new range of fans from his *Mock the Week* appearances and for those who had just seen him appear on TV, watching him live allowed them to see just how funny he is. 'The *Mock The Week* star is definitely funnier on stage than on telly. His anecdotes have more room to breathe, even when Howard lets rip so frenetically that he barely inhales. He is scattershot but in a good way, embracing tales about everything from defiant grannies to fitting playing cards in Gordon Ramsay's face. Dazzling stuff from a comedian positively bursting with thoughts,' concluded *The Evening Standard*.

The tour continued, as well as the release of his DVD, *Russell Howard: Live*, from his tour the previous year (it had sold more than 140,000 copies so far). He was in the south of England at the end of November and got the chance to tell the *Surrey News* why he was enjoying himself: 'My show changes every night but essentially it's about the things that make me happy. That's why I've given it such a vague name, because it means I can do whatever I like with it each night. I like the idea of experiencing things and writing about them in a scattergun kind of way.' But when asked why he thought his popularity was 'snowballing' he seemed genuinely baffled – 'I have absolutely no idea. I don't dwell on things like why it works, I just go with it. I always try to come up with new jokes and move forward [so] I reckon by the time I'm 35, I'll be really good. Comedy is such an amazing job that, if you can't enjoy it, you probably can't enjoy life.'

He certainly was having the time of his life. His tour was taking him all over the UK again and he had his brother with him. Daniel was to be a permanent fixture on all of his tours and Russell loved it. Unfortunately, his younger bro didn't have much luck trying to keep him from not getting drunk after his shows, though.

'After one of the shows on my tour I stayed up all night drinking with my mate Steve,' confessed Russ. 'I only had one shoe as I'd given a girl the other one after the gig. I was like, "Yeah, have my shoe!" The next day I went shopping and I couldn't deal with it. I was just like, "Help me, help me!" The sales assistant took advantage and I left with a pair of ludicrous green trainers. I was in a terrible state.'

It was becoming increasingly clear that the interest in Dingledodies and Russell was growing at a rampant pace and the original plan of bringing the tour to an end in December 2008 wasn't going to please. So Russell decided to extend his sell-out tour into 2009 and add more dates to keep the fans happy. What else could he do? Meanwhile, the two dates that were to finish his show originally were to be performed at Wembley Arena. Yep, the big one. Who would have thought that Russell, at nineteen, taking his first steps into comedy, nearly ten years later would be playing Wembley Arena?

'You pinch yourself,' he admitted. 'It's ridiculous. The sound is incredible, you tell a joke, the audience laugh and the sound sort of rolls back and hits you, it's very orchestral.' His mum, dad and sister Kerry were all in the audience, watching him take his first steps onto that stage and it was an amazing feeling for them all. 'It's such a bizarre feeling to come out on stage and go, "Hello Wembley!"' he confessed. 'I feel like an eight-year-old girl putting a play on in front of her dolls – or so I imagine.'

The Telegraph noted that much of the arena had been cordoned off and he was playing – 'by his own estimation' – to an eighth of its capacity: 'If I pull back this curtain you can see the rest of the venue. It's massive, and at the end of it there's a big picture of Lee Evans.' He was in awe. *The Independent* declared that now he was playing Wembley, 'Russell had joined the big league.' They also likened him to the late Hollywood star, Robin Williams – 'Coyly or paradoxically for a star of a topical TV show, Howard says he doesn't know much about politics. He veers from left to right but his central plank is that we moan too much. In a way reminiscent of Robin Williams, Howard portrays his characters with exaggerated voices and an almost manic energy. Occasionally the voices border on a cacophony and he straddles the line between confidence and arrogance – but he carries it off. Much to the delight of his young audience.'

The Telegraph were similarly impressed, concluding it is Russ's warm, natural persona that is making him such a star: 'Howard's winning hand as a comic is that he has a deft way with words, a quicksilver ability to ad-lib, youthful good looks, a lithe athleticism and a quality of complicity that makes his chatter sound as if he has invited each and every one of his audience home for tea and mischievous giggles. Should he grow up? Yes, one day he'll have to or he'll become the Peter Pan of comedy, stuck in a childish groove. Not just yet though. Right now, he's flying.'

And flying high he was. Making sure he was able to commit to extra dates to fit in the tour in the New Year, he celebrated with his family at Christmas as always. This time, however, he was a big Wembley star,, and that meant the madness of his family was cranked up a gear as almost everyone wanted to be mentioned in his act.

Chapter 12

GRAND DESIGNS ON GOLLUM

'MAN GROPES ROBOT: In Japan customers are no longer allowed to touch a robot because somebody groped it. How did the robot communicate that it had been groped? I wasn't aware that they had personal space issues. Is that an initial decision – I'm going to grope a robot? I imagine he'd built his way up. He'd started touching toasters, maybe Henry the hoover, which instead of a happy face had a sad face.'

RH

Russell had great plans for 2009 and the first few months of that year were to be spent doing... Not a lot, actually. With the tour finishing – or supposed to have finished on 5 December 2008 – he had to prepare himself for extra work on the extended leg of Dingledodies later the following year, but for now all he wanted to do was spend some quality time with his girlfriend, Cerys Morgan.

'I'm not going to do anything for three months,' he told an interviewer at the end of December 2008. 'I'm just going to hang out with my girlfriend, do a bit of travelling and just get my love back. It's just been a two-year slog and I kind of feel like I need to be re-stimulated by life. I've become a bit like, trains, hotels, cars, backstage, gig, see you later, trains, hotels, cars... And you don't see enough of the world, you just see the same things about the world. I don't want to be one of those comics who says, "Hey, what's wrong with air travel?" and stuff like that. I just need to get out there really and just do different things.'

So in February 2009, in a move he later described as one of the most romantic things he has ever done, he whisked Cerys away for a month on holiday. A much-needed break for them both, they found it exciting to see the world together. It gave Russ a chance to feed his inner-traveller enthusiast as they jet-setted around the globe on a whirlwind trip which saw them stay 'Five days here, five days there'. And it suited Russ 'I'm not good at sitting around' Howard.

First stop was Hong Kong and the sights and sounds of the dazzling city amid the hustle and bustle of the skyscrapers and backdrop of beautiful harbours. 'You see so many peculiar sights,' he later revealed to *The Sunday Times* in 2009. 'Or maybe it's that your eyes are open because you're wandering around free of stress.' There are over 124 retail complexes in the city that feed the appetite of the population's insatiable desire for shopping – but it blew Russell's mind. 'I was amazed by all the shopping malls. In one shop there was a piano made out of a Porsche. Somebody had obviously gone, "Do you like music? And do you like cars?" Then we saw a man walking a dog that was wearing a waiter's costume and shades. It was bizarre!"'

The next step of their holiday was Sydney, a complete contrast. It was laid-back, it was hot, it was health-conscious, and it had a profound effect on the twenty-nine-year-old. He embraced a new way of life in this short time of visiting, much to the amusement of Cerys, who couldn't understand why he was turning into 'Australia Man' – 'It was roasting so I got up early every morning to the annoyance of my girlfriend and ran round the Opera House and the Botanic Gardens. I throw myself into things – a run, then porridge and a smoothie,' he told *The Sunday Times*. But as well as adopting an Aussie lifestyle for the holidays, he and Cerys were in agreement about the things they wanted to do together, such as visiting nice restaurants. It had become a bit of thing back in the UK, one of Russell's favourite things to do would be to spend time – when their busy schedules would allow – with friends in nice restaurants. Now they were in Sydney, they decided to keep up that tradition and Russell, who had done his research, found a couple of award-winning establishments to visit: Aria and Rockpool. Aria is a picturesque restaurant at Circular Quay, which is situated on the edge of Sydney's glistening harbour, while Rockpool Bar & Grill is one of Australia's most acclaimed restaurant groups.

But they couldn't spend all of their holiday enjoying the best grub, it was soon time to travel again and so they headed north to visit Cairns in Far North Queensland before heading to New Zealand. It was there that they discovered the Hot Water Beach on the north of the island. It's an extremely magical place to visit as you can dig your own hot pool, metres from the Pacific Ocean. Near the rocks at the southern end of the beach is the best place for digging and you have two hours either side of the low tide when it is low enough to expose the area of sand with hot water underneath. The experience of lying in a pool of hot water just metres from the refreshing sea was a big hit for the lovebirds – 'We got a little shovel from the local shop and began digging out our own bubbling hot tub. When the sun goes down, it's a real highlight.'

After their month of travelling it was time to head back to Leamington Spa and settle back to life together. Russ was feeling pleased with himself for treating Cerys to such an adventure, believing it made up for his lack of romantic gestures – 'I feel guilty about not being romantic so I lavish her with holidays. I wish I was more romantic and she does too, I'm sure, but it's hard when you're British,' he told *The Mirror* in 2009. It's worth noting that they didn't live alone either: there was a third member of the household and he came in the four-legged shape of their dog, Archie. Archie the Jack Russell was a hit with Russell himself from the word woof. He had grown up with the breed, his mum and dad once having had four in the house, and he calls them 'phenomenal dogs'. He was also rather upset when his favourite dog from his parents' house died – 'He was blind. If anyone says there's nothing funny about disability they've obviously never see a blind dog start a fight with the wind.'

Archie fitted quite nicely into their home and cemented just how settled they felt in Leamington. Russ had made lots of good friends in the area and had joined the local football team too. It was also an ideal location for his touring and as he shunned the showbiz lifestyle of London, he felt safe and happier leading a normal life, which he believed helped his comedy too. 'If you jump headlong into celebrity life it affects who you are and what you talk about. There's more comedy in Tesco than there is in London nightclub Mahiki. Actually I've never been to Mahiki. It might be hilarious but it's just not my world. You just have to stay normal. It's the same thing about people thinking I am always a super, energetic, super-happy person all the time. That is the strange thing about people considering me upbeat is that I'm really not. I just love my job. I'm not normally a bloke going round shouting "wheey" and being super-happy. If you saw me in Tesco, I'm a real let-down. People say hello and I reply, "Hey alright, just doing some fucking shopping." What a load of shit. It's very different doing a gig when people applaud you and want you to show off. It's the ultimate mental and absurd job. People don't want to talk to you, they just want you to talk and they actually want to listen to you. If you don't enjoy that job, you have to be pretty miserable.'

Cerys has a similar, private outlook on her relationship and while studying for her degree didn't want to draw attention to herself as the girlfriend of 'that bloke off the telly'. She even got rid of a photo she had of him on her laptop when she was studying in the local library in case anyone thought she was obsessed with Russell – 'She realised someone would think that she was a mad stalker rather than my girlfriend so she got rid of that. Now she has a photo of the dog.' She much preferred to keep her head down although she knew that when she was out with Russell, they were likely to get spotted and he would be stopped for photos or autographs. But at home, when it's the three of them, life couldn't be happier. And she even finds some of his jokes quite funny. 'Although she has a specific remit,' confesses Russ. 'If it's anything to do with dogs or kids then she's a big fan, we don't have kids but we do have a dog.'

Archie, it seems, keeps the pair of them on their toes and being a typical Jack Russell, likes to chew, yap and cause general mayhem – 'Archie runs the place, it's full of Frisbees and chewed socks and clothes he's been bought, he is spoilt rotten.'

Russell has been asked many times about marriage and starting a family and has never made secret to his fans of the fact he would love to get married one day and have children. But he has become a lot more guarded in interviews when it comes to his personal life after a bitter experience with a women's consumer publication:

So, apart from not reading magazines, how does Russell relax? It seems he loves watching *Grand Designs* with Kevin McCloud and playing five-a-side footie – the more normal, the better. He told *Radio Times* in 2011: 'I do the usual really, the thing about being a comic is that you have to stay as normal as possible. I go down the park with my mates, take the dog for a walk and get stalked in Tesco from time to time. And it's not fashionable but I like *Grand Designs*. Kevin McCloud is a legend in the Howard household. Watching posh people build a moat? I'm there. The flamboyance of it is just beautiful. I love it so much I sky+ it. You see these wonderful posh people saying, "The roof is going to be thatched with dragon pubes, and the tiles we've brought in from Romania." And I'm just sort of sat there eating Cheerios with my dog, thinking, "One day." Not that I have plans to build my own castle. That's the amazing thing. I don't put up shelves. I have no inclination to do anything like that. I think I just live through them vicariously for an hour.'

Entourage was also a popular choice of TV show but Cerys enjoys more practical shows. 'My girlfriend likes watching *The Dog Whisperer*. You can recognise people who've watched that show because they'll say things to you like, "Your dog thinks you're the pack leader", as if a dog makes decisions based on anything other than food.'

But there was one show that he could not stand – *Loose Women*. 'I really struggle with it. I just can't watch it. I maybe get 30 seconds in. It's the lowest common denominator and rabble-rousing. My mum loves it, she's a massive fan. I really like Sarah Millican but the rest of it...'

Not that it was all about watching TV. Russell was also a sociable creature, who was embracing life in the community – 'I like drinking in the White Horse and playing for their football team, the Cricketers Reserves. You couldn't find a finer team, although I admit we haven't been doing very well lately.'

Then there is his obsession with guitars and cookery books, which take up rather a lot of space in their home – and neither get a lot of use: 'I've got five guitars and I can't play them but they look beautiful. And I spend a lot of money on cookery books too. I love them, I've got the lot.

I have a funny relationship with them, though. If I'm eating my cereal in the morning, I'll just peruse one of my cookery books and think, "Oh, I'll cook that tonight." I get quite animated too. I came across a recipe for a peanut butter and chocolate cheesecake in a Nigella Lawson cookbook the other day and it honestly made me punch the table, it looked so good. Stop it, Nigella, I know what game you're playing!'

But back to business and things were about to step up a notch for Russell workwise now. As well as the extended dates for Dingledodies in June, 2009, news came about in May that BBC Three were planning a topical news comedy show and wanted Russ at the helm. The press release stated that he would be piloting an episode of the show – which had yet to be named– in the summer. The pilot was commissioned by Avalon Television and would be directed by Peter Orton, who had worked on Harry Hill's *TV Burp* and Al Murray's *Happy Hour*. BBC Three controller Danny Cohen was excited that Russ was on board: 'I'm thrilled Russell Howard is going to be working with BBC Three. He's a huge talent who already has a great following with young people.'

Intriguing...

It's June and a boiling hot day in Brighton. Russell is thinking about Christmas. Well, he is thinking about recording his show, Dingledodies, live at the Brighton Dome shortly as it will be released in time for Christmas that year. After the success of his debut DVD, there were high hopes for this next one too as the release date was in time for the Christmas market. Stand-up DVDs were experiencing a massive surge in popularity when it came to gifts at Christmas. According to the Official Charts Company and Worldpanel Entertainment, 77 per cent of comedy titles are sold between October and December. So *Russell Howard: Live Dingledodies*, which was set for release on 9 November 2009, would hopefully enjoy some of that success too. But why were comedy titles so big? It seemed there was a massive surge in people wanting to laugh – in particular at live comedy shows. In 2006, *Little Britain Live* topped the charts and sold 330,000 copies. Then in 2008, *Lee Evans Live at the O2* topped 1 million copies sold. It was a huge market and with millions of DVDs being sold, *beyondthejoke* website argued, there was millions to be made. 'A royalty is around 7 per cent,' they concluded. 'So if a DVD retails for £20 and sells a million copies that is £1.4 million. Production costs and an advance night might have to be covered but the star of a top-selling DVD could trouser a seven-figure sum.'

Not bad for a day's work in Brighton.

At the end of the month Russell was at the Manchester Apollo as he supposedly finished off his extended Dingledodies Tour... But the demand for his stand-up show continued and so he agreed to extend the tour once more, seeing him perform until the end of July at sell-out venues.

At the beginning of August he performed at The Big Chill Festival at Eastnor Castle Deer Park in Herefordshire. It was a collection of some of his best of Dingledodies material and he performed on the final night – with the laughs heard all the way at Castle Stage.

'The audience was massive at the Big Chill,' he told *The Mirror*. 'It's dead exciting performing to such crowds, but that was the biggest one I have done so far, there were 7000 people. I love festivals. There's always an air of lunacy about the place, as everyone casts off their normal work-day selves and suddenly decides they are Earth Children. I loved looking out to an audience of hippies.'

But while an audience of thousands of people might freak the best comics, Russ took it all in his lumbering stride – '7000 people is honestly easier than doing a gig in front of, say, 10, because the latter just feels like a pep talk for substance abuse.'

The balmy August month also brought with it some red, hot *Good News*. On 29 August it was announced that the pilot of the new BBC Three show had been a success and they wanted Russell to front a new series entitled *Russell Howard's Good News*. The press release issued by the BBC stated that there would be a seven-part series, which would be aired in the autumn, followed by a 'best of' and a Christmas special. The programmes would be recorded in front of a live studio audience and a BBC spokesperson said, 'Russell will offer his unique perspective on the big stories dominating all of our news outlets, from online and print to broadcast, as well as picking up on those sometimes overlooked things that make him smile.'

It was a huge accomplishment and a huge nod to his popularity – especially among young people who make up the BBC Three target audience. And the best thing was that he was allowed to do pretty much what he wanted with the show in terms of its content and editing. He couldn't refuse. It was a complete contrast to *Mock the Week* – where he had no say over the editing process –and when the job was offered to him, he jumped at the chance.

Russell told *Radio Times* in April, 2012: 'I was told I could do whatever I wanted, and that was the beauty of it, BBC Three let us do anything. I was on a steep learning curve with *Mock the Week* when you're suddenly with people like Dara, Frankie, Hugh and Andy, classic topical comedians who are so economical with language. As a waffly stand-up I had to learn quickly. For a younger comic, working on the circuit, I remember doing the first *Mock the Week* and thinking Frankie was incredible. His jokes are all juicy fillets of filth. And Dara is an amazing Master of Ceremonies, the way he holds things together. Hugh is one of the best comedic performers, he has an ability to make lines funny just by pulling a face, and Andy is a really great political comic. I put so much effort into the show. When you don't see the version of it you want to see... That's when I jumped at the chance to do *Good News*.'

Chapter 13

THE LIFE OF SLUGS

'I remember when I first started being famous and a little old lady came up to me in a coffee shop. She said, "I really like what you do because you brighten my day up because I live alone and it cheers me up and thanks for that." I literally went, "Thank you" to her and then went for a cry in the toilet.'

RH

In July 2009 *Mock the Week* returned for a new series and Russell was now very much at home among the studio lights, the comedy legends and the idea of being more succinct with his answers. 'What I love about *Mock the Week* is that it's big belly laughs rather than that kind of sneering laugh,' he told the *Daily Post*. 'Half the battle is compliance, what can and can't be shown. And the great thing is that it's topical so every time there's a new story we have to have a new approach to it. Dara is the most accomplished master of ceremonies you could imagine. Like a really funny version of a big top circus man, he's like the one who introduces the lion tamer.'

The seventh series of the show had guests such as Frank Skinner and David Mitchell and although filming in front of a live studio audience can take up to three hours for each half-hour episode, the experience was all good preparation for his own show.

'There are moments when our brains go blank and when we say stuff that could never, ever get on TV,' admits Russ. 'Then we have to rein it back in and remember it's a TV show.'

The long recording session wasn't good for the fidgety Russ. He didn't like sitting still for such a long time and would often kneel on his chair rather than sit at the panel properly, which resulted in excruciating pain during one particularly long recording session – 'I once got horrible pins and needles and had this terrible moment where I had all these comedic legends around me while I was screaming about having cramp. Adam Hills, the comedian who's only got one leg, came over and starting twisting my leg back. It's happened twice since then.'

The production team soon realised that the best way to stop him sitting on his knees was to get him a cushion for his chair, which they eventually did – bless!

On 22 October, Episode 1, Series 1 of *Russell Howard's Good News* was broadcast on BBC Three. Backstage at the filming of the show, the feelings of 'terror' and 'fear' went through Russell's mind as the studio filled with audience members and the time had nearly come to deliver the first montage of his show. He had twelve minutes before filming began and he was brushing his teeth: he had prepared for this, he was ready, it had been a long day but now it was time to deliver.

After filming, he was pleased – he thought it had gone well, he hoped it had gone well, but like anything else he did, he was focusing on improvement: 'I think the audience had their fill of mirth and merriment for 30 minutes... I always look back at the things that didn't work so we will work on those and make it better.'

And what did the critics make of it? The TV guides were all positive in their previews, encouraging readers to tune in for Russell's first own solo show. 'The very good news for the likeable *Mock the Week* panellist and stand-up is that he's been rewarded with his own show,' wrote the *Mirror*. 'The bad news is it sounds like a strangely similar format to *Mock the Week* (a knock-off of *Have I Got News For You*) with Russell taking the mickey out of news and topical events.'

What's On TV wrote: '*Mock the Week* star and comedian Russell Howard returns with a new show. Just look at that impish grin and cheerily goofy mug – there's no way that's a face to impart grim economic updates or news of brutal violence during major civil unrest. Therefore it makes complete sense for Russell Howard to report on stories that won't have you reaching for a tin of black paint to decorate the walls, as he does in this sparky new show.'

TheMetro were probably the most enthusiastic: 'Good to see Russell Howard, the agreeably warm foil to Frankie

Boyle's savage humour on *Mock the Week* and an excellent stand-up in his own right, has earned his own show. As with *Mock the Week*, he'll be riffing off the week's news – and since he's a Bright Young Thing they'll be accompanying blogs and tweets and whatever else.'

'If you like your comedy raw and confrontational, Russell Howard is not for you,' confirmed *The Times*. 'But while he lacks the vein-throbbing intensity of fellow *Mock the Week* panellists Frankie Boyle and Andy Parsons, he's on a roll. This week he continues his rise to top rank of Brit-comedy with his new TV show, *Good News*. It celebrates, he says, 'news stories that make you go: "ahh, how lovely".' An apt description of Howard himself. His wide-eyed, upbeat style is an antidote to the cynicism that has been the mainstay of comedy for so long. He has no time for comedy that is downbeat for the sake of it. I saw a stand-up the other day who said, "It's outrageous there are no longer any local post offices any more!" You're a 25-year-old comic, you don't care about that. I hate celebration of petty rage – it doesn't achieve anything.'

Episode 1 saw Russ dissect the big stories in the news that week, including the recent political conferences. He makes fun of BNP leader Nick Griffin and gave us a glimpse of himself when he was younger, eight years old, in fact and dancing to Michael Jackson – after pictures emerged of former PM David Cameron as a youngster at school. He also referenced a news story that 'Here in Blighty we have a company to train bees to look for bombs.' Russell was then concerned that bees actually communicate through dance and therefore surely wouldn't be able to tell where a bomb is. To illustrate this point, he had a man come on stage and dress up as a bee and perform a series of dances.

Each week he also invited a mystery guest to the studio. It would be someone from the news and for his first episode he had the most tattooed pensioner in the world. She was sixty-seven years old and had a big jacket on, and Russell had to guess what his mystery guest involved – 'She threw open her coat at the end to show me all these tattoos and wasn't wearing much and I never thought I'd be on telly with an elderly woman who had her bangers swinging around in front of me, saying, "Can you guess who I am?!" She looked like a very edgy dinner lady.'

It was a great first show, the studio audience seemed to approve and viewing figures were high. Russell was insistent that his appeal wasn't just for the young, he told one interviewer that he wanted everyone to enjoy the show: 'What is my style? Probably on *Mock the Week*, the whole family would sit around to watch and yes, maybe young people would be drawn to me. It wasn't something I deliberately planned on – to speak to the yoof. Doing *Good News* on BBC Three wasn't something I specifically thought, what are young people into, let's appeal to them.'

But what did the critics make of it? *News:Lite* wrote: 'Russell Howard's *Good News*. Is he? Good news, I mean. Stand-up comedian Russell Howard is best-known as a regular on satirical panel show *Mock the Week* and has proven himself a likable enough panellist. But he's not a particularly extraordinary talent in my eyes. His comedy sticks to exaggerated anecdotes aimed at students. Maybe that's Howard's appeal to student-kind; he's walking proof that a middle-class lad from the countryside can make a living telling forgettable jokes with enthusiasm and cheekiness. His first solo TV project revolves around the week's news, which is part stand-up and part clip-show. As such, half its success can be attributed to the team of researchers who scour the airwaves for funny moments that Howard just has to provide a feed to. Was the show any good? Well, it wasn't bad. In fact, I rather enjoyed the first 15 minutes or so but then the format started to drag its heels and it lost all momentum when a "mystery guest" was wheeled on to be ridiculed. From there, it limped to the finish. Afterwards I couldn't remember a single joke Howard had made and didn't feel informed about politics through a comedy prism. This is half an hour of that level of comedy; good for a few giggles at the time, instantly forgotten afterwards – much like Howard's stand-up.'

Unflattering as it was, that was just one review from the very first show, and as the series continued, it hit its stride and Russell found that he was being stopped by people in the street, saying they had enjoyed the programme. That mattered more than any other critique and it had a profound effect on him – 'I remember when I first started being famous and a little old lady came up to me in a coffee shop. She said, "I really like what you do because you brighten my day up because I live alone and it cheers me up and thanks for that." I literally went, "Thank you" to her and then went for a cry in the toilet. It really shook me up, that I had this sweet old lady telling me that. Although then I started to think, what would happen if next week we covered a news story about killing old ladies or something? Not that we would do that. I was crying because I was overwhelmed by the kindness of it. Someone has just opened their heart for me.'

It's clear that Russell found these moments genuinely touching rather than playing to his ego. He found the fact that someone had bothered to tell him and thank him for his show unbelievable and it cemented his point that people can be positive and life should be too.

'You can sense when people are being genuine and she meant it. I have met people down the years who have said nice things and have had the courage to come and say it to you and you can't thank them enough because it makes you feel so good. I am glad that I have taken you out of your sadness because I feel good. Of course, when it doesn't happen, you're wandering along and thinking, I haven't had someone say anything sweet to me for a while...'

The title of his show also made people realise that when they watched Russell, they wouldn't be watching an attack on life, a negative, griping show. As a stand-up he hadn't ever performed material like that and he wasn't about to start now: 'Is the show called *Russell Howard's Good News* because I am a relentlessly positive person? No, that just happens to be a catchy title for the show,' he told *MailOnline*. 'I guess I am an optimist though. I mean, I write jokes for a living so if I can't be chipper about life, who can? Corny as it sounds, life is a party you're basically flying through. You might as well go for it. There are no prizes for cynicism.'

It was also worth noting how well Russell was looking

on the show. He had been hitting the gym and trying to eat healthily for all his shows and he'd never been in better shape. Having lost a lot of weight three years ago, he was keen to keep it off, which meant he had given up biscuits, something he wasn't happy about: 'I have a lot of time for Jaffa Cakes, but technically, they are not a biscuit, are they? There's a new yogurt-coated biscuit too, I like those. And you can't beat Maryland Cookies. I used to be a lot bigger than I am so I had to cut out the biscuits. My sister reckons I'm a manorexic. I am, in some way, trying to cheat death so I don't eat biscuits and I go to the gym.'

At the end of October 2009, Frankie Boyle left *Mock the Week* after seven series and Russ publicly acknowledged that he was disappointed to be saying goodbye to the most controversial member of the panel: 'I'm gutted. It's like losing Cristiano Ronaldo. He's one of the finest joke writers I've ever worked with and I liked hanging out with him,' he told *Metro*.

But even though there was a public sense that *Mock the Week* would not be the same without the outrageous comments from Boyle, Russ was adamant that it would continue to get better and better – as long as they didn't try and get anyone to fill the 'dark' spot on the panel: 'The show won't go downhill if we all work hard. It might mutate into a slightly different show. I think it would be a mistake if we tried to fill his place with another dark comic, because Frankie isn't really a dark comic – he is just a great joke writer who happens to toil in a dark area.'

In fact Boyle had left under a bit of a cloud as he had upset viewers with his remarks about Olympic swimmer Rebecca Adlington. Not that he, in his own words, 'gave a fuck' – 'Why did I quit *Mock The Week*? I was bored, simple as that' he told *The Mirror* in 2009. 'I'd done lots of them, about 60 shows, and it certainly felt like it! I just felt I'd done it to death, then they could get someone else new in. But it was good fun and the guys are great. There was no fucking animosity about it or anything. You can stay too long in these things and I think maybe I'm leaving it a bit too early but there you go. It's a question of how boring people want TV to be now. People are going to be happy until you boil it down to just cooking and fucking property shows. Fucking hell, it's so fucking boring already!'

Russell was equally perplexed as to why there had been such a media targeting of Boyle, who had simply tried to make a joke after all. He was public enemy number one and for Russ, this showed how screwed up the media industry was for putting him as front-page news: 'If a comedian doing a joke that people think is naughty is front-page news that proves there is no real news, does it not? The other day in *The Sun*, literally in the middle of Libya on its knees, the front page was: "How did this fox climb all the way up this 1,000ft tower?" I just find it odd.'

Russell was in-demand, both with his stand-up and now as a more mainstream 'face', and found himself a target for TV chat-show hosts. Happy to plug the show and his upcoming Arena Tour in December 2009, he agreed to appear on Jonathan Ross's show at the beginning of the month. He shared the Green Room with Gordon Ramsay and Hollywood actress Reese Witherspoon, who both looked hilariously shocked when Russ told the nation of witnessing a 'yawn rape' episode at a coffee shop in Bristol. Being on a popular chat show didn't seem to daunt him at all – he looked relaxed and was certainly enjoying himself. Reese Witherspoon then confirmed that she probably wouldn't be visiting the West Country while in the UK, 'Probably just stay in London, Jonathan,' she told a giggling Russ. Ross praised his new show, saying that it was a big hit in the Wossy household and also congratulating him on the viewing figures, which were on the rise every week. A highly modest Russell merely pointed out that most stuff on BBC Three is documentaries and so 'it's a pleasure.'

Ross then asked about his plans for the rest of the year and Russ publicly announced his new tour, Big Rooms & Belly Laughs, would be starting shortly. 'So you are playing in a lot of big stadiums, I assume?' asked Jonathan. 'Arenas mostly,' replied Russ.

The festive season tour was set for December and he had a list of big venues to go out and perform. With the tickets 'selling like the proverbial hotcakes' according to *Chortle*, Russ performed at Manchester Evening News Arena on 11 December, Cardiff International Arena on the 12th, Wembley on the 13th, Newcastle Metro Radio Arena on the 14th, Trent FM Arena in Nottingham on the 15th, Liverpool Echo Arena on the 16th, The National Indoor Arena in Birmingham on the 17th and Aberdeen, Sheffield and finally, the Odyssey Arena on 20 December. Anyone else need a lie-down? His mum, Ninette, joined him for

Above left: Russell supports autism charity Mencap at the Big Comedy Special. It took place at the Hammersmith Apollo, London, on 2 October 2013.

(© Getty Images)

Above right: Cheeking a middle finger during a risky sketch for the 2016 Leeds festival audience.
(© Getty Images)

Below: Russell Howard appears on *The Graham Norton Show* alongside Charlotte Church (second left) and Maggie Gyllenhall, occupying the comedian's seat at the end of Graham's sofa (October 2010).
(© PA Images)

Above left: A proud Russell supports actress sister Kerry Howard (right) at the premiere of her latest film, the 2014 comedy *I Give It a Year*, with mum Ninette Howard. *(© Getty Images)*

Above right: Comedy VIPs John Cleese (centre), revered for *Fawlty Towers* as well as for *Monty Python's Flying Circus*, and Martin Short, of *Saturday Night Live* fame, join Russell in a perfect photo op by Sydney Harbour Bridge (2011).

(© Getty Images)

Below left: Russell experiments with his red carpet facial expressions at the premiere of *The Inbetweeners Movie* in August 2011. *(© Getty Images)*

Below right: Russell larks around with Steve Williams, one of the writers for *Russell Howard's Good News* (2011). *(© PA Images)*

Above: Russell makes waves in the States, appearing on *The Late Late Show*, hosted by fellow British comedian James Corden, in 2017. *(© Getty Images)*

Below left: Russell offers his signature smile before introducing his BFI Screen Epiphany *The Royal Tenenbaums* at BFI Southbank, London, in September 2016.

(© Getty Images)

Below right: Howard jokily embraces a BGC member of staff at the 12th BGC Annual Charity Day at Canary Wharf, London, in September 2016. The event remembers the 658 employees who lost their lives in the 9/11 attacks in New York.

(© PA Images)

Above left: Howard attends Michael McIntyre's fortieth birthday party at the Chiltern Firehouse in London, April 2016. *(© Getty Images)*

Above right: Sticking his tongue out at the Mencap Big Comedy Special in October 2013. *(© Getty Images)*

Below left: Forget the BAFTAs – Russell wins at the Loaded Lafta awards, hosted by *Loaded* magazine at the Cuckoo Club, London, in January 2010.

(© Getty Images)

Below right: Russell takes a penalty for Liverpool during a charity football match at Anfield in April 2014, celebrating the ninety-six Liverpool supporters who lost their lives in the 1989 Hillsborough disaster. *(© Liverpool FC via Getty Images)* lots of dates on that tour and loved every minute. Although hanging out with his mum did make some people wonder about their relationship... 'Loads of people thought she was my girlfriend,' Russ confessed. His plans for Christmas that year were to spend time with his family and 'eat until I feel sick, watch Uncle Buck, get drunk and hopefully see my nan wake herself up by farting'.

His experience of performing in arenas was in stark contrast to those small gigs at the local comedy club in terms of their size and content. Russ soon learnt the best way to use both venues to improve his stand-up and revealed in a podcast interview that both have their advantages and disadvantages for the performer: 'If you have a bunch of new ideas and you do a 100-seater, that is the best gig in the world. If you are a little bit further down the line and you perform in front of 10,000 people, the feeling is incredible too. You feel the reward of all the work in that one night, the noise coming back at you. You can't be big enough. In an arena you have to exaggerate yourself a bit – you can't be more of a fool, you can't be more expressive – whereas in a small venue, you can't mess around so much, you don't have to writhe around on the floor.

'I had a bit for my Dingledodies set that was a sketch on life and I would say to the audience, "OK, things might look bad but life could be worse, you could be a slug." And I would get down on my stomach and pull myself along on the floor. It was a nice little bit and in a 100-seater venue I'd just say the gag whereas in a big arena, there was something quite nice about dragging yourself around the Apollo. I was physically acting out the joke for visual effects to exaggerate the point for my exaggerated audience. I like the bigger gigs from a performing point of view, but the smaller gigs are great at getting the ideas cooking. I always sit down at those too. I force myself to sit down otherwise I will perform too big and I will look a bit weird. I like to sit on a stool and vomit out ideas and once you have those ideas cooking, it is great to then perform them in arenas.'

So what did the critics think of his Big Rooms & Belly Laughs gigs? *The Guardian* gave his performance at Wembley two out of five stars, suggesting that 'There isn't anything ambitious about it... The laughs are predictable and his observations aren't always true – they are just crippled clichés. The parcelling is neatly done,' they also suggest, 'but this Christmas hamper is a little empty.'

But that's not to say the crowd weren't loving every moment. *The Guardian* conceded that indeed, the Wembley audience loved his 'springy energy where he bounces around, gurns and brings various sexual scenarios to life with suggestive mime'. They added: 'It's skilfully done and he loves playing live, he tells us, because on stage he can tell the truth. And he is clearly a capable host, at ease with this vast crowd, and he accepts a punter's arm-wrestle challenge and makes of it a great moment of spontaneous theatre.'

And the people of Nottingham, the ladies among the audience in particular, liked it when he swapped a T-shirt with a bloke in the audience. Cue lots of girly squeals of delight. It was this impromptu audience interaction that made each gig different, made each one personal. Which is no mean feat when you are playing to thousands of fans. It made his stand-ups rigid, but there is always scope for reacting to the unexpected heckle or shout-out. And Russ was by now a professional at dealing with such impromptu moments: 'The thing about arenas is that there has to be a beginning, a middle and an end,' he admitted to *The Student Pocket Guide* in 2011. 'You can't really talk to the front row because if you do, the people at the very back can't hear. You have to make it a pulsating monologue, which can become a bit boring as a performer because you have to do the same thing. Which is why I like to mix it up a bit with the audience banter.'

But what would an entertainer like Russ be enjoying more? He had his own TV show over which he had complete control and was also playing to massive crowds in arenas with a mixture of some of his best stand-up sketches. So, was there a preference? 'I really like stand-up for the reason that it just happens and then people remember nothing from it. It's like this magical night where people can't remember a single joke but they know they had a great time. TV can be rewound and re-watched and analysed but there's a real sense of intangibility to stand-up.'

Russell Howard's Good News final show of Series 1 was broadcast on 3 December 2009, with the following week dedicated to a 'Best Bits' show and the week after was a Christmas Special on 17 December. The ratings had been phenomenal for the channel – it was the most-requested BBC Three programme on iPlayer with, on average, 220,000 weekly requests. The total viewing figures across the week, including the repeats of the show, were 2.5 million. Little wonder then that BBC Three ordered two more series to be made, the second due to air in March the following year and the third series later that same year. BBC entertainment executive Karl Warner added: 'His first series was a huge hit with BBC Three's young audience and we're delighted he's returning to the channel with not one but two more runs.' Russ was equally thrilled and in a statement he wanted to thank his fans: 'I just want to say thanks to everyone who watched the show and I can't wait to start working on the next series.'

But first, a rest: he had been working non-stop and needed time to spend with his family at Christmas – as was their tradition. And Russell made sure he spoilt his parents and siblings, something he always liked to do the more he found he was financially able – as his sister, Kerry, will testify: 'We would always go back to Mum and Dad's in Bath for Christmas. We wake up at 8am and Christmas is over at 8.30am when all the presents have been opened,' she revealed to *Radio Times* in 2015. 'Russell is quite competitive when it comes to present giving. He can obviously afford to be outrageously generous so he wins every year. I remember I bought him a nice big black iron wall clock one year for his new flat in Leamington. He bought me a Ford Fiesta. It was so embarrassing. He just laughed and said, "I've won!" He never even put it up, Mum's got it in her hallway.'

Russ was equally sweet in admitting that he likes to spoil his family now that he can and remembers getting the clock from Kerry... and what he did with it afterwards. 'The thing I genuinely love most about Christmas is that I can get people really sweet presents. I absolutely love it! Although my family think I'm terrible because I kind of go overboard. The best present I've bought Kerry was probably a car. That year she got me a clock. It was this awful, weird, rusty, fat gigantic clock that I was never going to put in my house. Mum's got it now so everyone's happy. I remember the first year I moved out of my parents' house, Mum got me eight spoons that year. They were lovely teaspoons but spoons nonetheless. That was probably the worst present I had received. It was a pretty impressive family moment when I turned to her and said, "Cheers, Mum, I was considering taking up crack!" Thinking about it, all my parents' presents are designed to improve me in some way. My dad once got me a drill to put up shelves in my house. It was his attempt to make me more of an alpha male... Sorry, Dad, it's not going to happen!'

Gifts aside, time with his family gave him the chance to sit back and relax... and, well, be entertained by the craziness: 'I still love watching my family at Christmas. It's like being in a Pogues song. They don't mind that I speak about them in my comedy – in fact, they love it. It's now got to the point where I think they go out of their way to do and say things so they can end up in my stand-up. They are just so big and so wild. I have 40 cousins and three of them once interrupted a party at my house to exorcise a ghost they'd seen walking up and down – the Lurking Corridor Ghost. They didn't slaughter a goat or anything but they were very serious and kept saying, "He's a right nasty bugger but you don't have to worry about him any more. He was going to do something terrible." I'm sure they just wanted to get into one of my routines.'

Chapter 14

ON YER BIKE

'Essentially, my brother had offered Royalty some lube...'
RH

If Christmas 2009 was all about resting and vegging out, 2010 was to be all about Lycra. Well, sort of. In February 2010 it was announced that Russ would be joining David Walliams and a host of other celebrities, including Miranda Hart, Davina McCall, Patrick Kielty and Fearne Cotton, for a Sport Relief challenge that would test the fittest of athletes. They would be embarking on the BT Sport Relief Million Pound Bike Ride, which sees the team embark on a 80 hour-long cycle ride from John O'Groats to Land's End... non-stop.

'I've roped in a team of people to help me rise to the challenge for Sport Relief. It's a phenomenal undertaking and going to be really tough but we're all training hard to make sure we get to Land's End and hopefully raise a million pounds for Sports Relief,' said Russ in the official press release.

So how did Russ get involved? David Walliams wanted an athletic team that would be able to cope with the physical and mental challenges of such an enduring task and so he rang Russell's agent at Avalon to see if he would want to do it. For Russ the deciding factor was that Walliams told his agent that he would sort out the bike and the kit, and all he had to do was turn up on that day and do it. 'That's why I'm doing it really,' confessed Russ in a YouTube chat for Sport Relief. 'Because it is a fantastic thing to do and because everyone has arranged everything for me.'

Aside from just 'turning up', was there anything about the bike ride itself he was worried about? Yes, the normal angst, of course – saddle soreness, falling off his bike, being knocked down and, er, the classic risk of being attacked by a wild animal.

'I'm a bit of a wuss so it's this fear of the imagination and that I might be cycling along at night and you know you read these stories about the wilde cats that roam? It would be just my luck that this massive panther just came out of nowhere and took a bite out of me. And I died dressed in Lycra. The cycling will be alright.'

On Monday, 1 March 2010, at 7.30am, Russell was out on his bike. Red helmet, gloves, red Sports Relief jacket and leggings on as well as a big smile, he posed with his other celebrity cycle mates as they nervously waited for the start of their mammoth ride. It was to be a tough first twenty-four hours for the crew as they had to tackle an overall hill ascent of almost 29,000 feet – the equivalent of Mount Everest. The bagpipes played as they gathered by the John O'Groats sign. Russ told the Sports Relief Video Diary he wasn't even sure what direction they were headed – 'So, it's Day 1 here, we are at the start, just about to head off... This is probably the healthiest I'll look over the entire journey. We have four days, I don't know which direction we are headed in. That way, I think...'

But Russ was taking it all in his stride. He hadn't exactly trained for this challenge, taking part in two bike rides beforehand isn't much, but he was fit, healthy and as enthusiastic as ever. Well, he was about the bike ride – the Lycra outfit, less so.

'The riding thing is not too bad, the worst thing is getting used to the Lycra jumpsuit,' he told *The Coventry Telegraph*. 'It is all right when you are on the bike but you become aware of how stupid you look in it when you walk into a shop to get a bottle of milk and people really change how they look at you.'

As for the bike ride itself? This didn't seem to worry Russell in the slightest. Or he was being overly-confident about it to hide his panic.

'I think it will be alright. Everyone thinks it is going to be hard but it is not as hard as a stand-up show where you have to think of different jokes all the time. This is just riding your bike and is a bit like being a kid. It is fun riding your bike and getting drinks and biscuits on the way. I am still very much the outsider in the team. I am just a stand-up guy and am the least famous of them all but it will be fun.'

The celebrities completed the gruelling bike ride and raised over £1 million for Sports Relief. It was a great achievement and a fantastic challenge to have undertaken and Russ in particular was keen to see how he played his part in helping charities that benefited. At the end of the month, he visited the Merton Young Carers project, which received support from money raised on the show. The south London based project offers young carers a space to relax and have fun. 'These kids are about eleven and they have all this responsibility,' revealed Russ. 'If you had a fairly idyllic childhood like I did, it's hard to comprehend.'

But there was also a bit of a sting in the tale to his charitable efforts. The following year, in 2011, respected comedian Stewart Lee, who has a reputation as an anti-populist comic, did a sketch about Russ taking part in the bike ride. It was a dig at a report that was published by *The Independent*, who had estimated that Russell had earned £4 million from touring in 2011. Stewart's 'joke' stated that if Russell were to cycle all day every day for a year he would make over £13k for African children. But Stewart then went on to say that Russell has refused to do this and instead is happy earning £4million for himself with Stewart suggesting that an African farmer now has to explain to his son that Russ has stopped raising money for charity because he is too busy earning money for himself by telling jokes on a TV show.

For someone as sensitive as Russell, that stung. Stewart had called him beforehand to warn him about the joke and to try and assure him it wasn't personal, but it was hard for Russ not to feel under attack – 'I couldn't work out why

I'd been selected. He was trying to make out that all I was interested in was making money for myself,' he told *The Telegraph* in 2013. 'I do get what he was trying to do, but when it's about you it's very difficult to be rational. I felt like I was being bullied by the cool kid at school. Because Stu is so revered, it was exactly like being in the sixth-form common room and the smartest and most popular kid is sneering at you.'

The problem rose from the original newspaper story about his earnings and Russell insists he has no idea how the *Independent* concluded he earned such a massive amount. 'It really pissed me off,' he fumed to *Newstateman* website. 'I didn't earn £4 million that year. My mates are like, "Alright, moneybags!" and I had to show them my bank balance. That slightly pissed me off because it makes me look like this greedy bastard. I mean, I don't do any corporate gigs or adverts or things like that. I don't need that. It's just money, isn't it? Turning up to host the Stamp Of The Year Awards or something like that, I'd fucking kill myself. It's just greed really. I'm lucky, I only have to do things that I enjoy.'

That wasn't to say he wasn't earning good money. We already know he likes to spoil his family with holidays and gifts at Christmas and he reckons his mum would probably love him to pay off their mortgage – 'I haven't paid it off [their mortgage], I think they'd be delighted. I'm pretty sure my mum wants me to buy her a hot-tub.'

Also, this wasn't the first time 'scourge of the mainstream' Stewart Lee had had a pop at him. In another of his routines he referred to Russell and his TV comic namesakes Russell

Brand and Russell Kane as 'The Russell Comedians'. Russell knew of the routine and admits that it 'sort of upset him' but he didn't dwell on the joke. 'I got the point of it and it wasn't as nasty as I thought,' he told *Metro*. 'I think that if you don't like something, just write jokes and be better than what you don't like.'

The second series of *Russell Howard's Good News* aired on 25 March 2010, back in its 10.30pm slot, but with the added status of being the channel's most watched programme the previousyear.

The *Good News* team went back to the Riverside Studios in London's Hammersmith to prep while the press were eager to promote this latest series: '*Mock The Week*'s excitable puppy dog returns for a second run of his own news show,' announced *Radio Times*. 'For a no-doubt ecstatic BBC Three, the Somerset stand-up is very good news; the first series gave the channel its highest figures for an entertainment programme. And such is their confidence that they've already commissioned a third outing.'

The Mirror were equally excited about the return of 'the young, blond T-shirt wearing one from *Mock The Week*'. They revealed: 'He is back for a second series of his *Good News* show. Such is the popularity of the show a third series has been commissioned and will be aired later in the year. Russell's probably stocking up on T-shirts as we speak'.

It was equally exciting for the thirty-year-old who, although he described himself and the *Good News* writers as the 'comical version of the A-Team', knew that producing a series was a long, but worthwhile process. It was hard work and he and his team of writers would spend their weeks sitting in a room together, writing together – although, as Russ admits, he is the 'frontman' of an amazing band: 'I will do anything to make it work because I feel a big sense of responsibility to them to make it work. I am just the privileged one that gets to perform.'

But the performing was just one aspect of the show. It was all about research and trawling through footage and clips and newspapers until there was a solid collection of possibilities. And there was a rigid routine in place for how it all works too. Russell would start on a Thursday, working 10am–6pm, going through clips and articles with his team of writers. They would do the same thing on Friday and on Saturday, he would work by himself and put together how he thought the show and the jokes should sound. He put it all in 'his voice'. Sunday morning was a free morning and then he and the team would get back together and work in the afternoon to see what news stuff had happened over the weekend and if there was anything else they wanted to include. Then that evening they would go to Chiswick and do a warm-up show in front of a crowd, making notes afterwards on what had worked and what hadn't. On Monday the team would then go through the notes they had made on that dry run and write new things that might have happened. On Tuesday morning they took time to film all the sketches for the show and would then do a dry run in the afternoon. Russell watched that back Tuesday night, tweaked what was needed and then it was time to perform it for the audience on the Wednesday. And if he was lucky, he would have a woman sitting in the front row offer him sweets.

It sounds like a very well-oiled machine, doesn't it? The series, which airs over eight weeks, means that a lot of time is spent in the studio watching news clips and writing jokes and not a lot else. 'I'm basically MIA for two months when I do my show and afterwards I have to repair all my friendships,' he confessed to *The Guardian* in 2012. 'But the writing room is great, there are so many times when I have said, "No, guys, that is funny! You are all wrong!" You can have an idea and you can work on it, and then someone else adds a little line. And then someone else might say, "That's a bit shit, you can't do that!" Some weeks you have about 20 percent of your stuff in, other weeks you can have 80 percent. The writers on this only work on *Good News*, they don't write for any other show, this is the main team. It's a really fun job to do. The time I spend in the writing room, it is fun.'

With so many news stories that are heavy hitting, too dark or too depressing to touch yet hugely topical, there is always a degree of decision making over what to cover on the show. It has to be relevant but it must also be entertaining and Russell is the first to point out that the news can be funny, if you get the right angle: 'I don't mean the awful stories, but the news can be funny in the way it is presented to you. The snow was bad one year, for example, so ITV News had a journalist stick a carton of milk into the ground to show how deep it was. A slapdash approach to news presenting can always be mocked.'

There is also a team of ten researchers who spend their days trawling through TV news shows. Everything from

BBC's *Look East* (this is fertile ground, says Russ. 'There are wonderful stories from Norwich') to the more serious news channel, Russia Today. It is this raw material that is then worked on by Russ and his writers in the week leading up to the live audience recording. There is never any question of being offensive for the sake of it or smutty or arrogant in the show, which is probably one of the reasons it has such a huge fan base – from youngsters to old alike. But because of being on BBC Three, the channel aimed at sixteen- to thirty-four-year-olds, it was always assumed that Russ was a big hit with just that demographic. It's not something he dismisses but he doesn't like being simply thought of as a 'yoof' hero either. And he is at pains to emphasise that he didn't go out of his way to appeal to youngsters, telling the *ComediansComedian* podcast: 'Obviously I am incredibly lucky to do *Good News*, that is the case, but I have worked hard and I haven't kept the same 20 minutes that perhaps people who quibble about me, have. That is the difference. Why do I appeal to young people? I have no idea. I just try and make jokes, I don't have an agenda. Most comics are all outsiders to a degree. Any big comedian is always an outsider in a room, they are always watching the room and seeing what is funny about the room. When you're famous, people expect you to be funny now and you have to explain that you don't really do that, you just like to watch and observe. I have always found people very interesting and I know it sounds pervy but I like watching them. I always have. I find people fascinating, what they say. There is so much comedy in places like Tesco, for example. I have always wandered around listening to people.

I think as soon as you start plotting, start analysing why you appeal to a certain demographic, I think that's the beginning of the end. I just do what I do. I just happen to do a job that I adore and fortunately a few people like to come and see me.'

It was this nonchalant view about why he appeals to the younger generation that the media seemed to be interested in. At a press Q&A, one journalist persisted in getting a definitive answer to this and yet failed miserably. 'Young people find you funny, don't they? Why? What are they like? What makes them laugh? Your brother is younger than you, isn't he? Do you think that is why? Do you think that is why you connect with younger people? Because of your brother?'

Luckily, with Russell's knowledge of the Jack Russell breed, he recognised a dog with a bone when he saw one and couldn't explain any of it to the persistent journo. But there was one thing he could explain and that was why his brother was not allowed in the studio audience when he filmed the show, he was relegated to the Green Room only. 'We can't have him in the studio because he laughs like a walrus,' confirmed Russ. 'And because he's my little brother he likes nothing better than seeing me dying on stage. That's his favourite.'

But dying on stage isn't likely to happen when you have such an upbeat view of life. Russ insists he is full of pointless trivia because of all the news stories he uses but none of them are topics that don't interest him and more crucially, none of them involve 'petty rage' either – 'It just looks horrible.' And it is his cheerful demeanour that insists on a segment at the end of each show that is full of heart-warming stuff. It is a note of optimism that was inspired by his love of the BBC comedy *Blackadder*, in particular the final scene in which Rowan Atkinson's character, Sir Edmund Blackadder, comes out of his World War I trench to go over the top – 'You make people laugh, laugh, laugh and then right at the end you show them something magnificent to melt their heart. It's not really important but I like to do it.'

There is also a great deal of thought as to the topics and comments that make the final cut. In a slightly school-boyish style, Russ won't ever be accused of being two-faced when it comes to the content of his own show.

'The test I always like to do is ask myself, would I say that in front of the person? If I wouldn't, I won't say it on the show,' he revealed to *NewStatesman*. 'Also, because it is my show and it's me, I would rather – and this sounds profoundly wanky – I'd rather it was beautiful and brilliant rather than just slagging someone off. There was a story last year about a guy who had banned gay people from coming into his bakery and we did a whole load of jokes about that. I put forward the joke that any man who makes a living by pumping cream into buns is in no position to criticise the gay community. We're sort of tucked away on BBC Three really, and they let us get on with it. I remember there was also a woman a while ago who was fined because she fed a duck white bread and ducks have brown bread in this park. It was brilliant. So you're searching for what is interesting; that's the difference. I couldn't tell you about the intricacies about WikiLeaks because it really doesn't interest me.'

So is there any topic that is completely off-limits to Russell and the team? The general rule is that they don't always talk about the topical subjects just because they think they should. There is no forced comedy from a news story that although it might be all over the news, doesn't quite work for his show. 'We look at the merits of each story,' Russ told *New Statesman*. 'Then we try and figure out whether it's funny or not and sort of go from there. It's not as if we go, "oh, we must not talk about this" or "we must not talk about that". We just try and work it out.'

It seems as the series have progressed that he and the team have found the right balance of including serious issues with more of the silly stuff. And that is why Russell insists the show works in a similar way as a 'snaking conversation with your mates down the pub' can cover all topics – 'We just decide which of the heavier stories we want to slip in. So it's: "Here's a funny one, here's a funny one, bloody hell! Did you hear about this?!" That's kind of the aim, you chat and you're being really silly and funny and then suddenly you talk about Colonel Gaddafi. It's that kind of bizarre tone.'

And that brings us nicely to the end bit of his *Good News* shows; the bit that has us viewers at home feeling all gooey inside. Well, OK, maybe that is just us. But the point is that Russ, as he has been throughout his years as a stand-up, is all about the positive, not the negative – the bright side of comedy, not the mean, bitchy side that so many others seem to enjoy performing. 'There's no malice to *Good News*, or if there is, it's directed at people who deserve it,' he told *Radio Times* in 2012. 'I want it to be a funny, daft show about the news. What's really nice is that I have a broad range of people coming up to me, anything from 14-year-olds to sweet old men and sweet old ladies.'

Aside from his non-stop involvement in the show pre-production, do you think Russell ever sits down and watches himself on telly? Maybe an old repeat now and again? Well, he says not, but it did happen once... 'I was at my brother's flat in London and I was channel hopping and the show came on. It was the show I hasn't seen for a while so I thought, "OK, I'll watch it for a little while" and it kinda made me laugh. Then my brother and his girlfriend came in and there isn't a worse moment then having people walk in on you laughing at yourself. My brother was like, "You're such a dick." It wasn't as though I'd been sitting there watching it the whole time, like I was settled in going, "Oh god, I'm funny, this guy is so fun–ny!"'

Awkward!

But if you wonder whether Russ would immerse himself in newspapers and news stories if not for the show, you would be mistaken. Would he read the tabloids if he wasn't doing the show? That would be a big no. 'When you constantly read something like *The Daily Mail* you get this baffling, misplaced version of the country where everyone is just whingeing about things that don't really matter. I think a lot of papers misrepresent us. It isn't so much *The Mail* and *The Daily Express*, it's the message boards that get me. Like when Paul and Rachel Chandler were released [the couple held hostage for over a year by Somali pirates]. On one of the message threads was a comment from a woman who wrote, "Ooh, she's got a nice haircut for someone who's 'apparently' been away for a year." You look at something like that and you're not better for having read it. It just leaves me utterly depressed,' he told an interviewer for his *ComediansComedian* podcast in 2016. And then, maybe in a slightly sarcastic side, he revealed his 'biggest bugbear' was his addiction to the *MailOnline*: 'I find myself reading about *The Only Way Is Essex* and then stop and think, "What am I doing? I've got a degree." Yet I can't stop myself. It's like someone whispering to me, "Oi, psst, come over here – I'll tell you about the Kardashians."'

As well as recording the second series of *Good News* and with the third one confirmed for later in the year, there were yet more announcements in March 2010. Yep, in the year Russ turned thirty, he agreed to join his sister and brother in taking part in the London Marathon. The trio would be raising money for the National Society for Epilepsy. The mammoth bike ride he had endured only weeks previously didn't deter Russ who, according to his sister Kerry, failed to do any training for this 26.2-mile event either: 'He is filming a second series of his *Good News* show and I will be filming the second series of *Perrin* [Kerry is an actress and is probably best known for her role in BBC Three comedy series, *His & Her*] so we will be very busy during training. Russell hates training anyway, I think on the day we will be laughing, arguing, crying – mainly crying actually,' she told the BBC.

Sunday, 25 April and the sun was shining on the thousands of runners lined up at Blackheath, south-east London. It can take up to thirty minutes to actually cross the start line and the moment the siblings did, it wasn't so much 'one for all, all for one' as Russell decided to go on ahead. Nice. Not that he didn't get overtaken en route by some dubious characters, of course: 'I had a running duel with a man dressed as a banana for twenty miles and eventually he beat me,' he admitted on his *Good News* show the following week. As he told the studio audience, the London Marathon was the biggest news for him in the past couple of days. And when he added that he had finished in four hours and fifteen minutes, there was an almighty cheer.

Running past everyone who has lined the streets to cheer you on is a feeling like no other. The mood of the crowd spurs you on to keep putting one foot in front of the other and the supporters are invaluable to everyone involved. Although Russell joked that had he been one of the children on the side-lines he would probably have put a laxative in the jelly babies they give out. Or spiked the sweets with acid. Hmmm. Russ eventually managed to reach mile twenty before needing a bit of a push to get him to through the final six miles – which the onlookers happily contributed – 'I was so tired I needed a rest but the crowd wouldn't let me. Then someone recognised me and started shouting, "You lazy bastard!" which kept me going,' he told *The Times*. 'And everyone is there doing it for a good cause,' he told the studio audience. Then he showed a clip of himself being interviewed by the BBC just moments after finishing the race in the blistering sunshine – 'My brother has spent the last two months training for this and I beat him. So that's all that matters,' he smugly told presenter Sue Barker.

So charitable! Russ then revealed that he acted 'even more of a dick' by showing more footage of the post-run interview: 'My sister is there as well. We started off together, it was quite nice, but they were just too slow!'

Needless to say he got in trouble for that remark. Although the following year, in an interview with *The List* he tried to excuse his hideous post-race interview with a bit of humility: 'I made a prat out of myself when I was interviewed by Sue Barker and rather than graciously saying, "It's been lovely doing this for charity and we raised X amount," I'm on telly, going, "I beat my bruvva!" I just came across as an odious twerp. But I took the piss out of myself on telly the following week so I felt as though I rectified the situation.'

As it turned out, it was a comment from his brother Daniel that provided the highlight of the whole day for Russell – 'My little brother went up to Princess Beatrice [who was running for the charity, Children In Crisis and was part of a 'human caterpillar' with runners connected two by two by bungee cords] and offered her some Vaseline!' he told the studio audience of *Good News* the week after the Marathon. 'And she accepted! He essentially offered Royalty some lube.'

It was an experience that he would never forget – or repeat, however – and the trio raised over £7,000 for the charity. Good work, guys.

It hadn't gone unnoticed either that around the same time as Russ announced that he would be running the London Marathon, he also announced that he would be embarking on a brand new tour the following year, Right Here, Right Now...

Chapter 14

CLEGGY WEGGY, J.LO AND ANNE DIAMOND

'I know loads of comedians in the world of showbiz, but I don't know J-Lo or anything. Although, what's to say J-Lo and I wouldn't become firm friends?'
RUSSELL-HE'S-JUST-RUSS-FROM-THE-BLOCK-HOWARD

'Russell Howard will be appearing in 11 huge venues next February and March, including a return to Glasgow's 10,000-seater SECC, Birmingham's 13,000-capacity LG Arena and London's O2 Arena. The tour, entitled, Right Here, Right Now, is promised to be the comedian's biggest and best to date.'

The press statement announcing Russ's new tour was short and concise and had been planned for almost a year in advance. It was March 2010 and the first UK date for Right Here, Right Now, was on 1 February 2011 at Cardiff International Arena.

The Daily Mirror weren't wrong when they suggested that

'Russell Howard has gone from being just another comic to one of the biggest in the country in what seems like the blink of an eye.'

But this pre-planned tour meant he could keep on working on *Good News*, commit to his sporting adventures – like running the London Marathon – and allowed him time to work on his material and plug the future tour on a series of chat shows too. Tickets went on sale on Friday, 26 March at 9am and sold out almost immediately. Eleven dates soon turned into eighteen as seven more dates were added to deal with the public demand. Two other nights were planned at the O2, plus one night at the Newcastle Metro Arena soon turned into two due to the phenomenal demand of his north-east audiences. The O2 was the big excitement for Russ, not that he would put any venue over another, but playing at that famous landmark arena was mind-blowing: 'It's going to be fantastic,' he admitted. 'It's a massive venue and I've never performed there before but every gig is special to be honest.'

But back to 2010 and after his Sports Relief bike ride and Marathon running, it was time to enjoy a little socialising. Russell had become good friends with fellow comedian David Walliams since they had endured over 800 miles together on a bicycle and on 16 May he was thrilled to have been invited to celebrate David's wedding to supermodel Lara Stone. The couple enjoyed a very traditional wedding ceremony at the five-star London Hotel, Claridge's. The ballroom, where the nuptials took place, was decorated with £10,000 of white roses and a bevvy of famous faces and stars filled the room to celebrate the happy occasion before a reception party was held at nearby Shoreditch House. The venue was brimming with celebrity friends of the couple, including Stephen Fry (Russell's dream companion if he was ever stuck in a lift. FYI, his least favourite would be any of the *Loose Women* – 'I couldn't think of anything worse'), Elton John and his partner David Furnish, Denise Van Outen, Matt Lucas, Natalie Imbruglia, Geri Halliwell, Noel Gallagher, Russell Brand and Ronnie Corbett. But Russ had declined the invitation. He admitted to feeling 'awkward' in the celebrity gatherings he invariably finds himself in and didn't want to put himself in that situation. 'I might change in a few years,' he concluded to *New Statesman* magazine. 'It was nice to be invited to David Walliams' wedding but I'd just be on my own, just stood around, eating loads of food at the buffet, going, "Hey Elton, have you tried these sausage rolls?" Because that's what happens to me at normal weddings: I always end up on my own in a corner, so it'd be exactly like that – except with famous people.'

The showbiz/celebrity lifestyle of London didn't appeal to Russ, who was still happily living away from the bright lights in Leamington Spa. But he was beginning to realise that having a London base was an advantage when filming his *Good News* show, which was based in the capital, and so he bought a flat with his brother Daniel in Maida Vale, west London. It was a sound investment and meant that he would always have a place to stay after the long hours of filming. But that's not to say he would be dipping his toe in the celebrity party circuit, however.

'The flat gives me the best of both worlds, living in the

country gives is great for a stand-up [in terms of material]. But when I'm in London I spend a lot of time with my brother and my mates and playing five-a-side football and stuff like that. I went to the Ivy once. It was brilliant, I really enjoyed it. But I think it should be wildly exciting and like, "Ah, this is pretty cool, innit?" because if you lost that, you won't be a particularly good stand-up comedian. "Y'know when your butler's really uppity in the morning? Would it kill him to chew gum? He stinks!" So I try and lead a normal life. I get papped occasionally. I can't imagine what it must be like seeing various celebrities going, "Oh, I'll go to that nightclub because there'll be lots of paps there. Hopefully there'll be an up-skirt shot of me in the papers!" Those bastards that do that, the up-skirt shots, can you imagine that? It doesn't get worse than that. God knows what it's like to get into that world when you're desperate to get into the papers. You get a few pap shots when you go into Radio One – basically, the doors open then you see flash, flash... then nothing. "Oh it's you" and the clicks stop, which is pretty funny,' Russell told *NewStatesman* in April 2011.

It was the same situation when he attended Michael McIntyre's birthday party a few years later, the red carpet was no place for shy comics who aren't used to being papped – Russell told *The Mirror* in 2016: 'I went to the party with my mate Steve Williams who is also a comedian and there were paps taking our photo on the red carpet. We're not really used to that and Steve got heckled. It was like, "Oi mate, it's comedians only." "But he is a comedian. He's a fat comedian." He's not even fat. But that summed it up;

we got heckled before we even got into the showbiz party. And then we just found all the other comedians and went in the corner and talked about comedy. I don't know J-Lo or anything but I know loads of comedians in the world of showbiz. Although, what's to say J-Lo and I wouldn't become firm friends?'

If Russell did want any high-profile friends there was a school of thought that a certain Lib Dem politician would be biting his arm off to be his bezzer. By the time his second series of *Good News* was airing, the Election campaign in Britain was well underway and Russ would regularly do stuff on Cameron and Brown and then, because he joked he was on the BBC, he had to mention all three political parties. 'No one in the general public really knew who Nick Clegg was and nobody was really interested,' recalled Russ to *The Independent* in 2010. 'We had a gag that we'd show a clip of Nick Clegg, and it was "Hi, I'm Nick Clegg," and that was it. But then there was the first televised debate where he was really great and I had to swallow my words. All of a sudden the papers were calling him the new Obama and I then called him "Cleggy Weggy" on my show.'

That somewhat derogatory title resonated. Twitter came to a standstill – well, it started trending as one of the most popular themes. There was an idea that it undermined the Lib-Dem vote and when Nick Clegg attended a public engagement soon afterwards, he was called 'Cleggy Weggy' by a student and the clip was posted on YouTube. Such was the power of social media and a comedian who knew exactly what would appeal to his audience. Not that Russ is, for want of a better phrase, 'down with the kids' when it comes to Twitter or Facebook. His Facebook page – which has more than 1.2 million fans, making him the most popular British comic on the site – isn't run by him but a member of his PR team. His dog Archie, who has been asked to pose for lots of photos, also has his own Facebook page run by a fan in Sheffield. Another Facebook page is called 'Russell Howard is a Sexy Beast' and while he does have a Twitter account, he doesn't ever tweet – he told *The Telegraph* in 2016: 'I'm such a Luddite. There is a man at my agency, Avalon, who is wonderful. I email him tweets and he puts them on Twitter. It usually takes, like, 10 gigs before a thought becomes something publishable. If I was to put my first thoughts on Twitter it would be terrible, people would unfollow me.'

Russ did try this once, on Mother's Day, a few years later, but it didn't quite go to plan: 'I put up a picture of my mum, me, my brother and my sister, because it was Mother's Day and I thought it would be a nice thing. There was a barrage of "I'd fuck your mum!" comments or people saying she looked like Anne Diamond. It was a real lesson. I just thought: Maybe I won't do that again. But she does – she does look like Anne Diamond...'

And Russ is hopeless when it comes to anything to do with technology. He can't plug in his Xbox, he can't transfer files on his Mac or his phone. He's unable to use a dishwasher either (although that might be more of an excuse). 'We have two televisions in our home, one in the front room and one in the kitchen,' he told *Radio Times* in 2011. 'But that one doesn't work, my girlfriend has promised to fix it. I don't know how to fix it. I'm hopeless. But she still hasn't got round to it. I'm awful, I can't do anything like that. My technical ability stopped at the Commodore Amiga 500. The last time I was truly comfortable with computers was when there were disks. You knew how to fix them. My technical ability doesn't go beyond "ctrl, alt, del". Or taking the batteries out and rubbing them.'

Despite this technical inability, what an online fan base he has. Women like to bake him cup cakes and come up and say hello – 'I had a sweet thing said to me by a lady: "I enjoy your shows, you've got that lovely just-got-out-of-bed look." I had to admit to her that I had just got out of bed.' And men like to hug him – 'It's an odd thing, I get 18-year-old guys going, "Can I have a hug?" and though I'm not a particularly tactile person, I'll say, "Well, yes, if you like."'

It was the big three-oh birthday for Russell in March 2010 and a day he took stock of his life. 'Turning 30 weirded me out a bit,' he told a BBC journalist. 'I wanted to be 19 forever but I can't be. I still look young so I am going to be one of these weird baby-looking grandad people. I am not a birthday sort of person. I hate my own birthday because it just reminds me how old I'm getting and that pretty soon I'll be worm food. But I like other peoples' birthdays. I like spoiling other people and showering them with gifts but I don't like dancing at parties.' Russell was pictured celebrating his thirtieth birthday on *Tribuna* with a Liverpool FC birthday cake.

The summer months were filled with performances and

promotion. There were also the 2010 FIFA World Cup matches to fit in and watch and being such a footie-mad celeb, Russ was asked to appear on James Corden's *World Cup Live* series in June. The show was broadcast after every ITV evening football match with model and presenter Abbey Clancy and other celebrity guests. It featured interviews with some of the big names in English football and provided regular updates as to what was happening in the England players' camp. On 23 June Russ joined singer Shakira, *Dragon's Den*'s Peter Jones and former England midfielder Matt Le Tissier for much hilarity.

'You guys are always glued together, aren't you?' joked James when Russ, Shakira and Peter came into the studio. James had stroked Russell's nipples when the pair met backstage, a point Russ made on the show to which James replied that he had 'good nipples'. James then invited Shakira to rub Russ's nipples to see for herself – and she did.

'I don't need to do anything today now that's happened,' sighed Russ.

His appearance on James Corden's show and his antics with Shakira were the subject of conversation when he appeared on *The Graham Norton Show* in October. He was a guest alongside singer Charlotte Church and Hollywood actress Maggie Gyllenhaal and the chat-show host wanted to find out more about his run-in with the singer. So he started to recount his tale... on a prime-time chat show, on a Friday night, next to a Hollywood star.

'Did I dance with her on the show? No, I didn't dance with Shakira. James Corden did. What happened with Shakira was... James asked Abbey Clancy, "Are you enjoying the show?" and Abbey went, "I'm bumming it." It was like one of their catchphrases. He then asked Shakira if she was enjoying it and she pointed to me and said, "I'm bumming him!" So I was like, "Excellent!" It was the bizarrest moment of my life when Shakira turned to me during the advert break and said, "What's bumming?"'

Graham Norton thought this experience was hilarious but actress Maggie Gyllenhaal also didn't know what bumming was and so she asked Russell to explain it to her... live on *The Graham Norton Show*. 'How does my life get to this?' he laughed. Graham then cut in and proudly told him, 'On the next chat show you're on, you'll be telling the story of sitting next to Maggie Gyllenhaal and how she asked you about bumming,' he giggled.

So, what did he tell Shakira and Maggie? 'It's anal sex, that's putting it bluntly,' he told a nodding Hollywood star. 'But I didn't feel I could say that to Shakira so bluntly so I started saying, "You know when a man and a woman really, really like each other..." Then I did a sound effect, a whistle. And she got it – but her people came running over, telling her it really meant "hello".'

Russell then confessed to the studio audience and Graham that he was terrified Shakira would go out on the Glastonbury stage, where she was performing later that month, and shout, 'I'm bumming you all!'

It was Russell's second main chat show and for a man who didn't really like talking about himself, he was relaxed and confident. At least that was until Graham focused on his heartthrob status and one woman in the audience wolf-whistled. This clearlyembarrassed Russ and he asked the chat-show host to move on – which to his relief, he did.

'Your big new tour starts in February, doesn't it?' Graham asked the still-blushing comic. 'You always do a huge number of dates when you tour, don't you?'

'I used to do really, really long tours but now I am concentrating on just a few in arenas. There are nineteen dates altogether,' he said. Fellow guest Charlotte Church thought he had said ninety and looked completely in shock.

Russell then told Graham and the audience about who would be accompanying him on tour – his mum, of course: 'She loves it, she'll come on tour with me again. She came with me before, just for a week or so, on the Dingledodies Tour. She went on stage at Wembley and pretended to be a stand-up to an empty stadium. It's an amazing moment to see your mum on stage with an imaginary audience.'

And then to really hit home how crazy but loveable his mum is, he told the story of when he last visited her, back in Bath: 'I went home and she actually said to me, "Come on, we're going into town, I want people to know you're my son," and she took me to the pet shop. She was literally wandering up and down the aisles, saying, "Shall we get some dog food, Russell Howard-off-the-telly?" My mum is insane. Last Christmas, she spent about forty minutes doing an improvised song on a karaoke machine about taking my nan shopping. She just kept on going. We were just sitting entranced [by] some of the lyrics... "We mustn't ever linger, we have to buy fish fingers". I sat there thinking, "She is having a breakdown, this is what it must look like." Whereas my dad, rather than deal with it, said, "Somebody get the camera phone!" He recorded about half an hour of it.

'My family are just funny. My nan recently had a pacemaker fitted and my grandad won't let her use the microwave. And I asked him why and he said it's because he doesn't want her to explode.' It was a brilliant anecdote and Russell proved a huge hit with the audience.

The summer gave him time to focus on his Right Here, Right Now Tour and how it was going to sound. He spent those months doing smaller gigs, working on the material. Back in April 2010 it was announced that he was to be the headline act for the 20th Anniversary Larmer Tree Festival in July of that year. Set in Larmer Tree Gardens on the Wiltshire/Dorset border, the Festival was a collection of musical performances, comedy, theatre and art, and catered for all ages. Russ was billed as providing a 'rare, exclusive set headlining Friday's Comedy Club' and this gave him the chance to work on material for his upcoming arena tour.

The material for his shows is a subject that he is always asked about in interviews, the most common question being, where does he get his material from? Apart from stories about his mum and other family members he admitted in a BBC interview that it is the situations he quite often finds himself in that make for the best embellished stories. That summer, in fact, he found himself at a wedding without knowing a single guest. His girlfriend Cerys had asked him to meet her there but was running late and so he ended up sitting in the church by himself, looking like a gatecrasher

– albeit a famous one. He was left standing at the back of the congregation looking like a 'tool', he said, and heard everyone whispering, 'Why is Russell Howard here?!' But he never minds being recognised or people coming up to say hello.

In September it was announced that Russell wouldn't be appearing in the rest of the series of *Mock the Week* when it was broadcast later that month after returning from its summer break for the final six episodes of Series 9. It was for no other reason than his 'extensive BBC work commitments with his own BBC Three series'. He told *Chortle* Website. 'I love being part of *Mock The Week* but I wanted to quash the persistent rumours that Dara [O'Briain] and I inappropriately share a dressing room by taking a break until they blow over.'

The third series of *Russell Howard's Good News* aired on Thursday, 21 October and he was back to being MIA while it was filmed. One of his favourite stories of that series was the Chilean Miners story, where thirty-three miners were rescued from being underground for more than two months in October 2010. But with *Good News*, it was important for Russell to put his own spin on this enduring story: 'When we did the Chilean Miners, every comedy show was doing sketches about the idea of them shagging each other. It was all quite obvious stuff, I thought. We made it about Mario Sepulveda. They were all offered wheelchairs after all those weeks and the trial they'd been through and he said: "I won't need that wheelchair – but my wife will!" The crowd was like, "Wahey!" I just like that utter bravado. So we concentrated on that and ignored the idea of them shagging each other down there, which I think people were a bit bored with.'

But as well as having good weeks when there was uplifting news to share, perfectionist Russ also struggled when there weren't interesting or exciting stories to report. And he felt the pressure. 'Two weeks ago was one of the worst shows I've ever done,' he told presenters Miquita Oliver and Rick Edwards on *T4 Christmas*. 'I was a slave to what was happening in the news and nothing really happened. It snowed, but that was about it.'

Ironically, his next show, broadcast on 4 November, pulled in over 1 million viewers. It was a record for the channel and the show was the most popular across all digital channels (1.15 million) and held 7.3 per cent of the audience at the time of 10.30pm, up more than a quarter on the previous week's showing.

And there was more good news for him when, on 15 November, Series 1 of *Russell Howard's Good News* was released on DVD. It contained all the best bits from his first series and was out in time to feature on most people's Christmas present wish lists.

There was still more good news for Russ that month when it was revealed that he had made it on to *Heat* magazine's Weird Crush of The Year list. The previous year he had pitched in at No. 8 but that year he had moved to No. 3. He was a little miffed to learn that he was on the list despite having beaten the 'Go Compare' man from the adverts. No. 1 that year was the writer and producer Karl Pilkington, Ricky Gervais' pal and star of *An Idiot Abroad*. It would be another three years before Russ hit the No. 1 spot and was able to declare himself 'King of the Mingers!' By this time he was being referred to more frequently as an unlikely sex symbol and he was baffled by this: 'Sex symbol? Me? I don't regard myself as a sex symbol, my girlfriend certainly doesn't. I think she thinks I'm alright. I know she finds it hilarious though, so do my mates. I don't know whether to be pleased or not, being on a weird crush list isn't exactly the most prestigious list you can be on, is it? I am not really fussed by it. My friend Craig has re-named it the Pig List. It's perhaps rather galling that the Go Compare man is on the list – a fat man who sings operatic songs about car insurance. What's not to fancy?'

Perhaps this 'weird crush' status is one of the reasons he gets cupcakes made for him and not underwear thrown at him, à la Tom Jones?

'It's lovely but a bit weird... although baked goods are more useful, actually.'

It wasn't the first time that year that Russ had found himself on a 'Men to Fancy' list. And it wasn't just the readers of *Heat* magazine who lusted after him. Students from over sixty universities declared him their 'secret sex symbol' opposite *Harry Potter* actress Emma Watson. And not forgetting *Radio Times* calling him a 'pan-generational sex symbol' and website pages set up by his fans called www.russell–magic–cock–howard.tumblr.com. There really was no getting away from it. The website wasn't the only one dedicated to him of course, but with entries like, 'Oh Christ I so would', it is arguably one of the raunchiest.

An early Christmas present for Russ (no, not more teaspoons from his mum) came on 7 December when BBC Three announced it was commissioning two more series of *Russell Howard's Good News*, taking it through to the end of the following year. Series 4 was due to air in the spring of 2011 once Russ had finished his Right Here, Right Now Tour and Series 5 was scheduled for the autumn of that year. *Good News* was the channel's most successful entertainment show, with an average 800,000 viewers per episode. Karl Warner, BBC's executive editor for entertainment, revealed that the TV channel were 'thrilled' to be commissioning more shows from the comic: 'Russell has proved series after series that he's one of the best stand-up comedians and performers in the country and we are thrilled to be working with him and the team throughout 2011.'

There was more excitement to come when on 16 December the recording of his Dingledodies Tour was shown on TV for the first time. It was broadcast on BBC Three (it would be shown on BBC Two in two years' time) and was another accolade to celebrate. Now that filming for the third series of *Good News* had wrapped and his much-anticipated, Right Here, Right Now Tour was due to start in the spring of 2011 Russell was popping up in all sorts of interviews to promote his work. He appeared on the *T4* Christmas show special to tell viewers all about his plans for the festive season that year. And it was the usual yuletide family get-together, though not in the usual setting: 'My Christmas plans? I am staying at my auntie's house this year. Normally, we would all be at my parents' but they have sold the family house so weirdly we will all be staying at my auntie's house. And she has a hot tub in the garden. But she's been in the hot tub with her fella so we're not going to go in it at all. Merry Christmas! I love Christmas. It's all about *Uncle Buck* – you know it's Christmas when you're watching *Uncle Buck*.'

Chapter 16

PIN-UP AND PUT-DOWNS

['Describe the moment before I go on stage at an arena? I should say I step out of a limo, down five Red Bulls and then do a couple of handstands... but it's normally me having a cup of tea, dunking a biscuit.'
RH

New Year's Day, 2011 and in exactly thirty-one days Russell would be beginning his big nationwide arena tour, Right Here, Right Now. It had been a little under a year since the announcement was made of this new tour and from the original eleven dates, seven more had been added to keep up with popular demand. So did Russ spend Christmas practising his jokes in front of his family to get feedback? Well, knowing how truthful and frank they were he would certainly have got a few comments about his act... Whether or not they would be helpful remains unseen! But this isn't how he worked. He wasn't one to tell his jokes before performing them and he had a very good reason for this: 'Comedy is like sex and religion; you can't force it on people,' he told *Beat* magazine in 2016. 'It just doesn't work to show it to people. It's like when you're in a car and you've made a mix tape and the song comes on that you want the person to hear and you're like, "you've gotta love this song," and they never, ever do.'

But that's not to say he relies solely on his intuition. As mentioned earlier he had spent the summer of 2010 doing smaller gigs, working out the material as he performed it, and in January 2011 he performed at 200-seater art centres to really perfect his act for the big stadiums. And how he works, how he performs, isn't much different at either type of venue – 'Even the big arena shows feel exactly the same: It's still me in a dressing room writing up what I'm going to do later. It's equally as dull as it's always been.'

With his mum and brother Daniel regular attendees on his tour, there was plenty of support as he came out on stage at Cardiff International Arena on 1 February. He was ready and roaring to kick off this tour and soon he was having a ball out there. 'When you are on stage, you are free of the trappings of normal life. You can behave how you like and it's liberating. But it is an artificial hour and a half. If I get anxious it is usually before the performance. As I come off the stage I feel calm. I imagine it's how people feel when they've had a good yoga session,' he told *The Times*.

Then there were the Manchester and Nottingham gigs to enjoy next and then the LG Arena at Birmingham's NEC – performing in front of a Brummie crowd was something he always enjoyed: 'I think Bristol and Birmingham people are similar in outlook. We both have accents which are ridiculed by the rest of the country but which are beautiful and interesting, bringing the most out of the language,' he told *The Birmingham Mail*. 'They always tend to be particularly up for it. I've played Birmingham a lot, venues like Glee Club, Alexandra Theatre and Symphony Hall, and always had good shows.'

Then on 19 February it was time to hit the O2. Yep, London's premier venue, the O2. For Russ it was a surreal moment, not only because of the venue itself, but in the warm-up he had, watching his mum performing the soundcheck. She sang Lady Gaga.

'Can you imagine if she was my manager?' Russell mused. 'I'd have fake tan and be doing shows like *Strictly Come Dancing*.'

Coming on to Fat Boy Slim's 'Right Here, Right Now' (what else?), Russ lumbered out to the middle of the O2 stage to loud cheers that reverberated around the massive space – 'It's weird to play huge gigs at arenas now, but it's so exciting, to hear the roar of the crowd as you wander on stage.' And roar they did, the crowds in London loved the show. Performing for two and a half hours with a twenty-minute interval, Russ gave the fans value for money and one particular fan who watched his first of three nights at the 15,000-seater venue was most impressed, telling us 'I hadn't seen him as a stand-up before, I only knew him as the cute one from *Mock the Week* and I think I saw him one *Live at the Apollo* a couple of years ago too. Any worries that I might have had about whether his humour could transfer from short TV clips to a full show were unfounded. I really enjoyed the show and couldn't stop laughing for ages afterwards. And the bits with us [the audience] at the end were brilliant!'

Yep, in true Russell style he didn't let the fact that he was in one of the biggest arenas in the UK stop him from doing his usual audience Q&A. This carryover from his smaller-venue gigs was à bit of a risk – what would happen if he couldn't pick out individual questions but just got a blur of noise instead? But it wasn't the case: he managed to pick out the questions quite successfully, although watching him try and work out the questions was equally amusing.

The Times weren't particularly gushing about his thrice-sold out performance at the venue but praised the fact that 'the boy next door is playing the big house and he had the confidence to treat this venue as just another club'.

They continued: 'His rise to the upper branches of the premier league (no comedian gets to hold court at the Greenwich mega-tent without possessing a full complement of cojones) is a triumph for ordinariness. He shops in Tesco, he watches *Take Me Out*, he likes Footie and when he sees a Nando's he has to go in and order himself a feast. But over the course of two hours or more the mundane quality of his material wears very thin. His self-deprecating observational patter can be likeable enough and when he talks about finding graffiti by Kings Of Leon on his dressing room wall you are happy to share his excitement. But the lack of variation in the pacing and Howard's habit of building tall tales out of minor domestic details soon grows monotonous.'

The sold-out tickets for the show spoke for themselves

however and Russell was enjoying every moment. He was playing arenas now, he had a dressing room that the Kings Of Leon had graffitied tags on the walls – surely he made sure he had a list of ridiculous rider demands too? Er, no. 'I ask for Diet Coke, wine, a football and a bin so I can play chip the football in the bin,' he confirmed. 'That's the big game. That's what me and my tour manager spend ages doing. It's a great way of killing time when your brain is all a bit nervous and panicky. It'd be funny in reverse. Maybe Lionel Messi pretends to do a bit of stand-up before he goes out for a big match...'

The Telegraph were more enthusiastic, however, describing how Russ 'raised the roof like it was the most natural thing in the world'.

'We've been accustomed to the sight of comics entertaining the kind of crowd numbers normally associated with rock concerts or football matches,' they wrote. 'Even so, for this blond-haired, limber-limed Bristolian to have 10,000 fans eating out of the palm of his hand suggests remarkable audacity, verve and drive. When he's in full flow during his stand-up sets, he talks very rapidly – bouncing from topic to topic, physically inhabiting the scenarios he describes at breathless speed. With his trademark slacker look of T-shirt and jeans and flashes of that cheeky grin, he is the best "boy-next-door" act on the block'.

So what was it like for Russ as he prepared to go out on stage? Aside from playing 'chip the ball in the bin' of course. Did he pace up and down backstage, or was he all calm and confident?

'I should say I step out of a limo, down five Red Bulls and then do a couple of handstands... but it's normally me having a cup of tea, dunking a biscuit,' he confessed to *The Mirror*. 'Then someone will say, "you're on" and I'll put the Hobnob down and go straight out. No, it's not nerve-wracking. I enjoy performing at arenas, it's fun. I guess it is a bit like being footballers in the tunnel before you go out on the pitch. When you know you are quite good you are nervous that you won't quite do what you expect of yourself. That is the pressure, I guess.'

So was this arena tour everything he had worked for? Was it the pinnacle of his career? Well, yes and no. 'I pine for the old days,' he mused. 'It's strange, a lot of the friends I performed alongside in shitty pubs years ago are now selling out arenas. That's more exciting than playing to a couple of hundred people at Loughborough University, obviously, but when I did play Loughborough University it was one of the most incredible moments of my life. It is glamorous doing stand-up in clubs, there was no place I would rather have been. I loved it, I really did. I have never hated any of it. Arenas are amazing but comedy clubs are exciting, vital places. I watched Chris Rock in an arena and he bombarded the audience so it felt intimate because of his performance and I think it's what you bring to it. There are pros and cons to playing in an arena but ultimately it is a big fun, booming gig.'

And what happens when he comes off stage from his gig? Is he all hyped up and ready to party, or is it a time for quiet reflection? You've probably guessed the answer to this already. Although there was quite a funny incident when he came off stage at the O2 after one show. He took off his top to change T-shirts and all of a sudden, there was talk of Russ as a pin-up.

'Yes, there was talk of a calendar one time – genuinely! I had no T-shirt on and I just went, "that is absolutely never happening!" I got asked to do the Head and Shoulders advert before Joe Hart and Jenson Button, for a lot of money. Half a million pounds money. Isn't that a ridiculous amount? But how could I have gone on stage if I had agreed to doing that? Seeing myself on telly, washing my hair?! I couldn't watch it! Then I would go to gigs and get Head and Shoulders bottles thrown at me. I could have really embraced it but I couldn't do it. It is not me and I don't think it would be fair on the audience either,' he told *The ComediansComedian* podcast.

Before his run at the O2 finished, Russ took a photo of the audience that had come to watch him. For a comic who the press liked to stereotype as a hit with the young, his fan base was incredibly broad, if the audience that night were anything to go by: 'I took a big photo of the audience and there was a real age range, it was really cool. I usually get quite a young audience but it can be anywhere from 14 years old to 60. In the bigger gigs, like the O2, you get a far greater spread.'

After the O2 he headed back up north to Newcastle to perform his original show and added dates. We know that having his mum accompanying him meant that it was not always rock and roll on the tour but his brother was a different matter. After his gig at the Geordie arena Daniel came out on stage in front of 8,000 people and introduced himself – 'Yeah, so I'm his brother,' he said, pointing to Russ. 'I'm going out later if you fancy coming!' It was a moment Russ would never forget: 'He totally got all the groupies on board and then he'd go out with my tour manager and rock up at 4am. So in a way I lived this rock 'n' roll lifestyle vicariously through my brother. He did all the hard work.'

His last gig on the tour (it had already been twice-extended which meant that he would be back touring again later that year) was in Edinburgh on 5 March 2011. But there was no time to take a break and reflect on performing to over 160,000 fans in the past two months. There was Series 4 of *Russell Howard's Good News* to prepare for and he was back in the office to start writing as soon as his tour wrapped. While most people would find it hard to get their heads around the two different types of performance, for Russell it was a very natural transition and one he needed to balance his life: 'Between my stand-up gigs and this show, I've got the best of both worlds. Stand-up is quite solitary but when I've had enough of that it's time for another series, sitting in a room, writing with my mates.'

Writing with his mates was indeed one of the highlights of his job, although he wasn't always the only one being funny. The writing team did enjoy playing the odd prank on him when they could. 'I popped out of the writing room to take a phone call and left the boys in the office,' he told *The Student Pocket Guide* website. 'When I came back in and took a sip of coffee they were all huddled round, giggling like schoolgirls, laughing for some time. They eventually sent me a video clip to my phone of what looked like my coffee cup and my friend's penis being dunked into it! My brain took so long to realise what was going on and they were recording my reaction. As the look of realisation dawned on my face they were on the floor, laughing.'

The first show of the fourth series was broadcast on 24 March, the day before Russ's thirty-first birthday and he admitted to being 'not as depressed about that as I thought I would be'. The first episode featured a sketch of him in the bath with his mate Dan and he later confessed in some extra backstage footage from the show that there was something very odd about being a thirty-something in a bath with a mate while a lady poured fake bubbles on his chest – 'I don't know if that is really succeeding in life but there you go! We've just done the first show and it was really good – touch wood! We've had a really full-on day and it is now 10.45pm and I am going to watch the dry run of the show and decide what stays in and what doesn't. There was a great crowd tonight, there was something wonderful about a crowd who turn up ready to laugh, you could almost see them with their teeth out, ready to giggle.'

So what does happen in the hours of recording? What's it like to be a member of the audience? First up, there's a queue to get into the studio. From about 6.25pm the line of potential audience members snakes from the entrance at the back of the studio through an alley and then right out onto another street. With a maximum capacity of 310 and with once 1,500 people in the queue, disappointment is high if you aren't one of the lucky ones to make it through. The tickets are free and are more than are needed, given out to allow for no-shows. Sadly for the fans though, this rarely happens. Once you are seated in the studio the warm-up man comes out at about 7.20pm and gets the crowd gee'd up. Ray Peacock is the warm-up man for *Good News* and as well as getting the audience in good spirits he makes them aware of all the boring stuff too – like Health and Safety regulations, the legal blurb about video recording, and what to do in the event of a fire. Then about ten minutes later Russell comes out on stage and the audience goes crazy. He has a little bit of a chat then the opening credits of the TV show roll, which the audience sit and watch as if they were at home on the telly. It also means that Russell has to stand and watch it too, which usually results in him doing a rude little dance in the corner, much to the amusement of the audience.

For the next forty-five minutes or so, the audience are entertained with the news topics that are rife that week before Russell finishes with his *Good News* story that leaves everyone feeling a little bit happier and a little bit lovelier. Then it's time to applaud as he waves goodbye but it isn't the end just yet. Now it's time to record the Mystery Guest and the Stand-up Guest segments.

In between those times Russ makes sure he has a little audience interaction and answers questions that are shouted out to him as well as giving out a few autographs and having a few hugs. After the two extra segments are filmed there is a re-recording of some of the show – the 'pick-ups' which are the lines Russ wants to re-do. Then the 'trail' is recorded, the little advert bit that goes out before the show – and it has to be fifteen seconds exactly.

At 10pm the audience head home on their merry way or those with a special VIP ticket head up to the bar for drinks and nibbles with the cast and crew. Not that Russell is there for long as he heads straight back into the editing suite to work on the final edit.

The format is more or less the same each week and it's a credit to Russell and his production team that it all runs as smoothly as it does. As for the content, at the start of Series 4 in 2011 there were a lot of terrible news stories around and Russ was careful to pick what to report.

'Essentially, *Good News* is a daft show about the news,' he told *The Telegraph* in March that year. 'There's no point going on just to tell glib jokes about people suffering, I absolutely wouldn't do that. But I also don't think you should start from the basis of "I mustn't talk about this or that". I don't want to have a list of things that can't be mentioned. To take the Gaddafi situation – a dictator killing his own people. Terrible. I'm not saying we are going to do this but the kind of thing that interests me is that two days after it kicked off *The Sun* had on its front page a fox cub which had got to the top of the tallest building in England [the Shard]. The way the news is presented now is extraordinary – so although stand-up gags about a given subject might not suggest themselves, the way our media tell a story might. And the earthquake in Japan? I wouldn't go near that unless I'd found something particularly wonderful. Like after the earthquake in New Zealand there was a story of how one guy pulled 13 people out of the wreckage. And there was an incredible interview where he described rescuing them.

That kind of story is uplifting – so I would put that at the end of the show. That is the way the programme works, I take the piss and then at the end share something I believe to be a bit magic. Without wanting to sound grand about it, hopefully on a tiny level you can make people appreciate just how lucky we all are.'

He continued this response on his podcast to *ComediansComedian* too, reiterating his abhorrence of getting a cheap laugh. 'I don't want to be one of those comics who talks about current affairs to get an easy laugh. That's always been the thing about *Good News*, that we don't do all the jokes everyone kind of knows. Things like, "Who's Prince Harry's real dad?" or, "Doesn't Camilla look like a horse?" Those are the gags you have heard a 1,000 times before and if you go into comedy clubs that kind of stuff gets short shrift. But in a TV studio full of people who don't watch a lot of comedy it amazes me how you can get a round of applause with something so lazy. I think you have to be confident in your own skin and I'm generally kind of an upbeat person. That is where my comedy comes from. I wouldn't want to see Frankie Boyle upbeat. Of course I fret about there not being enough "good" news to write about and perform but I always look forward to starting a new series. I've been on my own doing stand-up by myself on my *Right Here, Right Now* tour so it's a nice change. I forget about all the hardships and go for it with my three writing mates.'

There was a bit of a sour note to one of his shows that month, however, when he showed a clip of an English Defence League (EDL) march in Blackburn, Lancashire.

The news report stated that because they couldn't clash with anti-fascist opponents, they ended up fighting each other. Russell couldn't resist commenting on such a story on his show. It was everything he despised and he was keen to make sure the EDL were mocked, predicting that they might have been cross if one of them had got a black eye and now hated that eye. Almost immediately after the show was aired, a Facebook group was set up to urge members of the EDL to demonstrate outside one of Russell's gigs in Chorley, Lancashire, in May. The comments directed at Russ were hateful and scary. 'We're going to be loud and he's going to know we're there,' commented one EDL supporter. 'Hopefully next time he'll think twice before opening his middle-class mouth about things he knows nothing about, ranting about how "thick" we all are.'

The abuse was more than a little scary. Russ wasn't used to such a personal and obvious attack and it made him seriously panicked about his safety – 'It was hairy,' he told *The Birmingham Mail in* Decemeber that year. 'I am an absolute coward and I admit that for a while I imagined that everyone coming near me was going to beat me up. I had a pretty tough month. Every time we filmed the Mystery Guest section of *Good News*, where we get someone on and I have to guess who they are, I thought it would be an EDL supporter who was going to hit me.'

But there was no way he was going to back down over what he said. Having previously not incited any controversial comments in his comedy (think Frankie Boyle), this was new territory but he was adamant that his comments were justified – 'You have to stand by your jokes. They may have been cruel but they were about people I believe are idiots. Everyone likes a good cruel joke, but you have to stay true to yourself. If you are going out of your way to be vicious, it will just have diminishing returns. Light and shade is good, rather than being unremittingly nasty.'

There were some big announcements in June of that year – of departures and pastures new, if you will. First, Russ wouldn't be returning to *Mock the Week*. He could not commit to filming the show as well as *Good News* and his touring dates, and after five years on the programme, it seemed like a good time to leave. Not that he wasn't sorry about his time and experience on the series which had made him a household name.

'It was a massive show for me. People would stop me in the street and before that ever happened, I thought I'd love that. But it's weird. Everything I've done, from getting my own show to doing the tour, was absolutely fuelled by *Mock The Week*. Totally. It was a hard show to do but all you can do is write as much as you can and try not to look stupid,' he told *The Sunday Times*. 'I enjoyed doing the show but it just took up so much time. I'm a stand-up at the end of the day and it was getting to the stage where I wouldn't have been able to do any live gigs.'

The following year host Dara O'Briain told *Radio Times* how Russell leaving the show actually changed the atmosphere, saying that it didn't have that 'bear pit' feel to it any more: 'We've been through a few different versions of the show in the 100 years it feels like we've been doing it,' he noted. 'If you look back at the first series there are eight rounds! Then there were the angry young man years, when it was very bolshy. Now it's much more reflective. It may be we're all a little bit older. Or maybe it's because Frankie [Boyle] has gone. There's not the same emphasis on savage one-liners. It's much more of a messing-around kind of show, which for me is a lot more fun. It is much less gladiatorial now that Frankie and Russell Howard have left. Russell was similar. It wasn't just that Frankie's comedy was dark: he and Russell would bang it across to each other and the other four would have to find windows within that. Frankie would distil the discussion into a brilliantly punchy killer line, bang, that's the end of that. That's the last word on that topic. That was his genius but it did breed an atmosphere where everyone had to get in there as quickly as possible. We became a bit of a bear pit.'

But Russell hit back, and in an interview with *Native Monster* website, announced that the show was never as uncomfortable as it might have seemed: '*Mock* is very similar to being backstage at a comedy club, it has that atmosphere of who can wee the highest, for want of a better phrase. It's that kind of thing, you're with your mates and you are trying to outgun them. I guess it was how it was perceived but I didn't find it that bad, I just carried on doing my own thing. I am just who I am. Every comedian is different. It wouldn't work for me if I was all kind of edgy in the same way it wouldn't work for Frankie if he was all friendly.'

Leaving *Mock the Week* also didn't have any effect on the viewing figures for *Good News* either – in fact, quite the opposite. In June 2011 it was revealed that the show was the 'biggest successes of the BBC's on-demand iPlayer'. With the first airing of Russ's show being watched by around 1 million viewers, if you then take into account repeats, iPlayer views, recordings and high-definition screenings are included, the show's figures more than treble and it had 3.5 million views. The figures came from the BBC's Live +7 data, which records the number of people who watch a show in the week after it first transmits. The original show airs at 10.30pm on BBC Three on Thursday but then over the next few days, it airs a further four times: an HD simulcast, an early-hours repeat a couple of hours later and two airings on Friday night, at 9.30pm and midnight. So, taking into account all these viewings, the BBC argued, gave a more complete picture of people's viewing habits. It also concluded that *Russell Howard's Good News* was the fifth most popular TV show on iPlayer.

With one less filming commitment now he was no longer doing *MTW*, Russ was free to take part in other big comedy events, like the Montreal Just for Laughs Comedy Festival. This was an event he hadn't performed in since 2006 due to working on *Mock* so he was very excited to be returning to Canada that July. *Chortle* confirmed that he and Nina Conti had been asked to perform solo shows at the prestigious festival (The Time Is Now and Talk To The Hand respectively). Jimmy Carr, Eddie Izzard and Tim Minchin were also performing solo shows there, which was a little unusual for the Festival, which normally revolves around short sets with a number of high-profile galas. Russ and Nina were also the only Brits to taking part in Zoofest, which showcases more alternative fare than the main programme. They would be performing alongside Adam Hills, the Pajama Men, Eugene Mirman and Maria Bamford. The segment Russ appeared in, back in 2006, Britcom, had also been scrapped, but reconfigured to produce one 'World Tour' show. Adam Hills was the host for the show and Russell was in the line-up too. As this was an invitation-only festival with a reputation for helping comics break the American market, Russ was putting all his efforts into preparing for the show.

But before hitting Canada, there was a poignant task to perform later in June 2011. Russell headlined a comedy, music and art festival called Future Perfect 2. The event was organised to celebrate the memory of Lee Wyatt, a young man who had died of bowel cancer at just twenty-five years of age. Lee had seen Russell perform at the Apollo and had been a fan ever since. His mum Linda decided to contact Russ' agency to see if there was any way he might be able to visit her sick son and give him a morale boost. For Russ it was a no-brainer – there was no way he wasn't going to help Lee if he could and he ended up buying him a pint on his twenty-fifth birthday in 2009. It was his last birthday and he died several months later in 2010, but that short meeting had a profound effect on both men. Lee had been given a much-needed boost when, although extremely unwell, he had visited his local pub with some friends to celebrate his birthday. Russell came in as a surprise to buy him a pint and, according to his mum, made it 'extra special' for Lee.

'Russell was absolutely brilliant with Lee and they got

on like a house on fire,' gushed Linda to *The Manchester Evening News*. 'They had the same sense of humour and Russell said what a cracking lad he was. When Russell turned up at the pub, Lee couldn't believe it. It was his last birthday and Russell really made it extra special for him.'

When Lee lost his battle with cancer, Russ dedicated an episode of *Good News* to him and pledged to help with fundraising for the hospital that had looked after him. In 2011 he kept his promise and on 25 June he took to the stage at Castlefield Arena to perform for the crowds at Future Perfect 2. Future Perfect is a charitable project that Lee helped to set up and one which helps people with cancer use art as an effective coping mechanism. The large-scale fundraising events raise money for Christie's cancer treatment centre and Lee's mum Linda were overwhelmed when Russell immediately agreed to headline the show at the beginning of 2011, tickets were sold out almost at once.

'When Linda asked if I would be part of Future Perfect 2, I immediately said yes. I only met Lee and his mum briefly but they had a massive impact on me. He's one of the most inspirational people I've ever met so to do a gig in memory of him is an honour and a privilege,' Russ told *The Manchester Evening News*.

At the end of Russell's performance, he came back to the microphone to ask the audience to give a big round of applause to Linda and everyone else who had organised the event, reiterating what a fantastic cause this was all for.

July was an even busier month for Russ. First up, he was heading over to America to perform some gigs in New York.

This was an amazing period in his career: if it all went to plan, he would make his American TV debut the following month. So, was he nervous? 'Excited' is probably a better word.

'Definitely, it's all very exciting. I've been going through my material to see what would work in America. I'm still pinching myself about some of the things that I'm offered. It's insane and a bit surreal. Someone called me the other day asking if I wanted to do a gig in Australia with John Cleese and Louis C.K., who is massive. I was like, "Hell yeah!" I think I would be slightly worried about myself if I didn't get excited by things like that. I think if you get to the stage where you just sigh, roll your eyes and say "alright, tell them I'll do it," then it is time to stop,' he told *The ExeterExpress & Echo*.

After his gigs in the Big Apple, which went down a storm, Russ flew back to Blighty to perform on more familiar turf at the Bristol Comedy Garden Festival in July, 2011. He was appearing on the opening night and the event promised that 'the world's biggest and best comedians' would be performing and so it was that he also shared the line-up with the likes of Ardal O'Hanlon, Stephen K. Amos, Sean Hughes, Angelos Epithemiou and many more. But it was Russ who got the biggest cheer when he came out on stage and he loved the homecoming – 'I always enjoy coming back to the city and playing to a great Bristol crowd. They've got a really good line-up and I'm on with Alun Cochrane, Pete Firman and Dan Atkinson and I'll be on for about 45 minutes doing some of the show I'm currently touring plus some new material,' he told*The Bristol Post* in 2011..

Chortle loved the opening night antics from Russell – the 'prodigal son returning' as they described him – 'It was interesting to see him in his new role as comedy megastar, with an act that is full of populist references (*Come Dine With Me, Embarrassing Bodies*) and it's easy to see why the public have fallen for him so easily and willingly. The closest he got to a heckler was a drunk girl whooping at a routine about drunken girls and his impromptu Q&A session masquerading as an encore shows he still has a sharp, observational wit. But at times he runs the risk of self-parody, and he seems too aware of his comedy heartthrob status now as at one point he gets his torso out to screams of adulation from women in the audience. I think – and hope – that it's to his embarrassment.'

There wasn't a great deal of time to dwell on his time back on home turf, Russell now had to fly to Montreal for the Comedy Festival and entertain folks over the pond.

Chapter 17

NEW BALLS, PLEASE

'It's really weird flicking through the channels and it's you, you're like, "Bloody hell!" You know when you listen to the way you sound, like when somebody plays you a message? Imagine that but seeing every gurn and facial tick. You think, "Oh Christ, is that what I look like?" So I'd rather not watch myself.'

RH

Russell was worried. He predicted that there would be one person in the audience for his debut solo show, The Time Is Now, at the Montreal Comedy Festival, Just For Laughs. And his reasoning behind such a poor turn-out? Well, he figured that while he was a household name in the UK, no one there would have heard of him, much less bother to come and see one of his shows. But he could not have been more wrong.

For a man who had played at Wembley Arena and the O2 to thousands of fans, this intimate gig was very different.

The theatre Sainte-Catherine was packed on 25 July 2011 and Russell was in his element. The *Montreal Gazette* was full of praise for him: 'Howard let loose with a solid, frequently hilarious hour of stand-up of the highly personal variety. The man has energy to burn – and he'll have to, considering his schedule here, which will see him perform in a dozen shows and sometimes three times a night. The Brit wit is like a jack-in-the-box but R rated. He doesn't seem to tire but he could conceivably exhaust audiences with his non-stop spiel. Howard's girlfriend is a doctor, she returned home from work recently and announced she had delivered a baby that day. She asked what Russell had done and he told her that he had invented a game with his brother where they toss a tennis ball at each other's head. He has no illusions about his line of work and laughed at his sexual prowess: "I've never shagged anyone's brains out. The best I've done is made her forget her novel briefly." This is not a show for the entire family – as one couple with two young kids in tow soon discovered. Hell, the disarmingly fresh-faced Howard, who could pass for 15, seems almost not old enough for his own show'.

Performing in Montreal meant that Russell couldn't rely on crowd adulation – although the Canadians are famously polite. He had to work on smaller, more intimate performances and he skilfully played the room as the audience warmed to him.

'He brings his energy levels down accordingly,' stated *Chortle*. 'Starting from a relaxed perch on a barstool there's no sign of the puppy-dog enthusiasm that usually defines his delivery. His positivity shines through and he has the child-like ability to find happiness in simple pleasures. But the act goes beyond empty optimism. Despite their cuddly wrappings most tales have, if not edge, then at least substance beyond the bland. His tales are in the spirit of being playful, not hard-hitting and he's the first to admit, alpha-male behaviour isn't his forte. If his uncynical behaviour is just a façade Howard never lets it slip and the happiness spreads almost tangibly through the room. Joy is what Howard is all about – both celebrating it and spreading it.'

So there was no need for Russ to have worried about how he was going to be received; he was a hit. And in his next performance, at the One-Stop World Tour segment of the Festival, his act was said to have equally captivated his new audience: 'The Canadians and Americans seemed suitably impressed with this fresh-faced comic, who is a blast of positive energy with solid jokes and pin-sharp imagery underpinning the effusive spirit'.

Chortle announced: 'Compere Adam Hills knows what floats a Canadian's boast and he makes a point of not highlighting the various accolades of his line-up of comics. Rather than be introduced with a list of TV shows they have been on, as is the American tradition, everyone tonight says they don't care how they are brought on stage, they just want to do their jobs. It was down to Russell Howard to energise the room with a pacy, punchy routine that leapt with an irresistible sprightliness from semi-innocent childhood pranks to playful adult stories from the bedroom'.

In short, the audiences seemed to like him. Which was

good as the following month he would be appearing on one of America's biggest late-night talk shows, *Conan*. It would be hosted by Conan O'Brien, an American television presenter, comedian and writer who was one of the longest-working of all current late-night talk show hosts in the USA.

Russell flew over to Los Angeles (which was a little more tedious than first anticipated as his manager had his luggage checked at every airport because officials thought 'he looked dodgy') after finishing his successful performances at the Montreal Festival and made his TV debut on American screens on the TBS channel on 3 August. He was a guest alongside the American actress Olivia Wilde and the Serbian tennis star Novak Djokovic on an episode that was entitled 'The Gentile's Bar Mitzvah'.

Russell was introduced by Conan after the commercial break as 'the youngest comedian to sell out the London's O2 Arena'. The camera panned across the studio to a separate curtained-off stage and out walked Russ. Looking at ease and tanned and in his trademark T-shirt and jeans combo (more on that look later), he strode out to applause and gave a little wave to the audience and a cheery 'Hello!' His first gag set the tone for his set – it involved his dad and homosexuals so right from the word go the audience were getting an insight into the world of his crazy family: 'I told my dad I was coming to LA. He told me to watch out as it was full of gays. They'll get me, he said. I said, "Dad, they'll get me? They're gay, not ninjas!"' The audience loved it. He continued with an older gag about the homosexual couple kissing on a plane – remember, he used that back in his *Live at the Apollo* debut? But the American audience loved it too. And his final joke got the biggest laughs: he told the story of his friend called Sue, whose boyfriend likes to shout 'Expelliarmus' at the point of orgasm. He then informed an enthralled studio audience that her response to such a situation was to lie back and say 'Five points to Gryffindor!' and that if you hang out with people like that then the world is a happier place, he finished off before holding up his hand to thank the 'ladies and gentleman of America'.

It was a risky five-minute set if you think about it; lots of homosexual references – with Russell acting out 'bumming', having sex with *Harry Potter* references and putting marbles up his brother's bum. But Russ wasn't about to modify his set for more easily offended folks across the Pond and that attitude was the root of his success. He told *Mayhem Magazine* in 2012: 'Americans are so PC, you could find yourself walking on eggshells. But to "make it" as they say, out there, no, I wouldn't change. I wouldn't do that at all. There's no way I'm modifying what I say to adhere to a norm. It's not even a sticking-by-my-principles-attitude. I just couldn't be bothered. If they have a problem with what I say in the States then, whatever. They can write a letter of complaint.'

Conan came straight over to shake his hand, shouting, 'Fantastic!' as he did so and he thanked Russell for coming on the show. 'Wasn't that fantastic?' he asked the audience as the applause got even louder. He then turned to Russ and bent down to whisper to him, 'Please come back, that was amazing!' before the show cut to the end credits. What a debut! When asked how it went, Russ was rightly chuffed with how the audience reacted to his humour. 'It was really nice,' he told *TV Choice*. 'And what was lovely about it was that you could hear him [Conan O'Brien] laughing, which is half the battle. Afterwards he came over to me and he's about 6ft, a huge ginger giant. Apparently he doesn't go over to everybody but he shook my hand, which was great. It wasn't so much nerve-wracking, more unsettling to see how I would be received out there. I wondered whether they would get my humour but it seemed to go alright.'

There were slight grievances he had, which he didn't air at the time, but came out the following year about the restrictions of playing to an American audience. 'It wasn't for me,' he told *Digital Spy*. 'I prefer England. You can change your act and little things but you do forget how much of your act has English references. A lot of things don't work when you translate them into universal speak. You take the line "I could murder a couple of bourbons" and switch that to "I could murder a couple of cookies", it all becomes too generic. "Can I say another brand?" "No, say cookies". "OK". It all becomes comedy for a committee and that's no fun for anyone.'

But he still had a fresh appetite for performing more in America and this first performance gave him an excitement, a drive, a hunger to find out what else he could do in the US. 'I felt like an 18-year-old rookie again, which is nice,' he said. 'It feels like a clean slate where anything can happen. I'd love to do more in the states. It's fresh territory and I'm talking to a few people now so we'll see what comes of these conversations.'

There was a memorable encounter with tennis Grand Slam winner Novak Djokovic. During the filming of *Conan*, Russell engaged in a harmless bit of small talk while Djokovic wanted a full-on deep conversation. 'It wasn't long after he had won Wimbledon and I have to say, he [Djokovic] is a bit of a character, kind of reminiscent of Sacha Baron Cohen. He congratulated me on my show, saying in this big, animated voice, "Well done, you are really funny." I come back with, "Thank you, congratulations on winning Wimbledon." You know, just a few pleasantries and I thought it would end at that. But then he asks me, "Were you there?" and I reply, "Er, no. But I watched it on the TV." And he says, "It would have been awesome if you were there, I really wish you had been." So, as it turns out, the sheen from his Wimbledon win was wiped clean simply because I didn't make an appearance at the Wimbledon men's final in 2011. Otherwise I'm sure he would have carried me on to Centre Court on that big plate trophy thing they win. Which, to be fair, sounds like a fun way to spend an afternoon.'

It was one of those moments that you just couldn't make up, and Russ was momentarily lost for words. But sadly he couldn't sun himself any longer in LA as he had been invited to the world premiere of *The Inbetweeners* movie in Leicester Square, London. Now this is a man who doesn't exactly go out of his way to walk the red carpet but *The Inbetweeners* was a favourite TV show and he often compared his student days to being similar to those of *The Inbetweeners* lads. Maybe not the fish punching, however – although he admitted to one journalist on the red carpet that that was his favourite moment from the show. The world premiere also prompted the journalist to ask whether he thought the film would do well across the Pond, given the sense of humour was different. Russ, having had the experience just weeks ago, was in a good place to ask to answer such a question: 'I've just played a few gigs over there. From a stand-up point of view, I think a lot of American stand-ups are quite aggressive so something like *The Inbetweeners* will fit in beautifully because it's not about aggression, it's about celebration of hope and everyone relates to that the world over.'

So, would he become the fifth member of *The Inbetweeners* gang? 'I'm too old! I'm far too old,' he admitted. 'Unless they can CGI me, of course.' But the journalist wasn't convinced, telling him he looked ridiculously young. It is worth noting that Russ was also looking extremely dapper in his grey suit and tie. The crowds certainly thought so too. Fans who spotted him shouted out 'Legend!' as he walked the red carpet – 'I find it bizarre, because I have done absolutely nothing that would deserve being described as such,' he told the journalist. 'I basically talk bollocks on stage for a couple of hours and try to entertain people, but if that's what people want to call me I'm fine with that!'

He had taken his brother Daniel along to the premiere, which proved most amusing as he watched him converse with the stars of the film. 'I introduced Daniel to the girls from the movie and he started telling them about a goal he'd scored playing for the cub scouts in 1990. It didn't exactly get the conversation flowing. I think he honestly thought they were going to respond, "Was it against the run of play? Did you score again?"'

A suit and tie was something that Russ wasn't used to wearing and although he didn't seem particularly awkward, he did look like he had raided his dad's wardrobe. For a man whose 'uniform' consisted of T-shirts, jeans and trainers, this was well out of his comfort zone – 'When I wear a suit I just feel I hover somewhere between estate agent and boyband member. I own two suits from the tailor Thom Sweeney but I need clothes I can lunge about in when I'm on stage. I always wear jeans, T-shirts and trainers so I can bounce around a bit. I do wear make-up when I'm doing telly but not on stage. I just have a shower, dry my hair and maybe put a bit of wax in it. It's quite simple. I have been referred to the missing errant member of Westlife before in my T-shirt and jeans and spikey blond hair. I don't mind.'

Although that's not to say that T-shirts would be in his wardrobe forever: 'I think we can all agree that it would be slightly sad if I got to 40 and still dressed like I was 20! You've got to go with your age.'

There is a more underlying annoyance to the fact that the media like to stereotype him as the 'T-shirt wearing comic'. Yes, that is his look and one he is comfortable with, but after a trip up to Edinburgh Festival Fringe where he had played for a decade, he didn't like the label of 'T-shirt comic' that had been attributed to him – 'It was really cool, really nice being in Edinburgh, and I saw everybody and everyone was really cool. It is probably one of my favourite cities in Britain, after Bath as my parents live there and I particularly like going to the Roman Baths and watching American pensioners battling against the whirlpool and losing – it's quite a sight! But with Edinburgh, I tingle with excitement whenever I am there. But then I saw there was a big article in The List with 'the T-shirt comics'. There were lots of pictures of various people doing comedy in various T-shirts and the finger was laid at me as the originator of the T-shirt comic. Stuff like that really fucks me off as it's such a moronic way of listing somebody. So I kinda feel like, the uber uber cool kids are pointing a finger at me, it's like being college again.'

However it is worth pointing out that there are dozens of clothing websites that stock 'Russell Howard T-shirts' after he is seen performing on TV or at gigs in a particular slogan. There is also a Facebook page that stocks official Russell Howard merchandise, including keyrings, mugs and of course, T-shirts. Would he wear any of the stuff himself, we wonder? 'That would be massively inappropriate – imagine the ego. I don't wear the Russell Howard branded underpants you can buy on my website... I'm not a single man but that would be pretty terrible.'

As if travelling to New York, Canada and LA wasn't enough that year, at the end of August, Russell headed Down Under to take part in the Just For Laughs international comedy gala. Remember we said how excited he was when asked if he wanted to do a gig with John Cleese a few months ago? Well, this was it. He was invited along to take part in the press conference to promote one of the most talked about events of the year in Oz, the debut of the world-famous Just For Laughs Festival. Having performed at the

Montreal version just weeks earlier, Russ was the man to have promoting the Festival as it hit Sydney Opera Theatre that month, alongside *Monty Python* actor John Cleese and US comic Martin Short. The press conference was hilarious. As the trio approached the stage set up in the Concert Hall foyer overlooking the harbour, Short told Cleese, as he was handed a cup of tea, 'Well, it's all going well so far.' And that put the kiss of death on proceedings. The wheels fell off but the *Sydney Morning Herald* pointed out that if a conference was going to go down in flames, 'you couldn't ask for better passengers than these three'.

John Cleese was the gala host and MC Julia Morris addressed him first. However, the microphone feedback caused horrific screeching and it was Russ who made the first funny of the conference – 'We're being heckled by whales.' The technical problems didn't improve and a hand-held mic didn't work either, leaving Julia to have to lean over Cleese so he could speak into the microphone pinned to her chest. You can imagine the jokes that came from that situation. 'We're just trying to lower expectations,' explained John.

Forget expectations, the tone was lowered even more by Russell when Julia addressed him for his first question: 'What is it like in this threesome?' she asked, before Martin Short re-worded the question to 'Have you ever had a threesome?' Russ was about to reveal to the Australian media his sense of humour – 'I haven't, no – I feel I would be letting two women down,' he told the bemused journalists. 'I wouldn't know where to start, it would be like getting on a roundabout. I think I would just clap and keep time... Hello Australia!'

The tone continued in that vein for a while before one journalist asked about the recent London riots. Russell, having been in London at the time, was the first to speak about it – 'In Clapham High Street every single shop was smashed up... except for a bookshop. I was on Bondi Beach earlier today and I saw people jogging for fun – the only time you see people jogging in England is when they have got a telly under their arm.'

There was then a photocall for the trio outside, where they enjoyed posing for silly photos overlooking Sydney Harbour. Following this, Russell had a couple of days to prepare for his eighty-minute set at the gala, which ran from 1–4 September as he took to the stage on the final night of the festivities.

'When placed amongst the rest of the *Just For Laughs* ensemble, Russell Howard is a relatively unknown here in Australia – a fact well represented by the largely British crowd,' observed the *AUreview* website. 'The guy is massive over there, massive. Like, "I sold out Wembley Arena" massive'. And entertaining he was, wasting not a single breath to fit as much as he possibly could into his set. So what sets Russell apart from the others? Other than having his own successful TV show that is? For one, he makes the comedy deeply personal. Everything relates to his family, his experiences and his life. You're laughing with him and occasionally at him. His delivery was impeccable and he completely owned the room. He could gauge the crowd well and moved on quickly from topics that weren't working. Like a kid who just ate a shitload of candy, Howard clearly works on his feet. And fast. No small feat'.

And in typical Russ style, he did a short Q&A with the crowd afterwards, which was something they weren't expecting, but they thoroughly enjoyed this impromptu interaction – 'It was a not-so-typical encore: taking questions from the crowd which led to a few awkward moments for people and showed this is a guy who knows how to get a crowd laughing, whatever the topic. So while Russell couldn't be accused of leading a new wave of ingenious comedians, it's safe to say he knows his audience well and does a damn good job of keeping everyone entertained. And tonight I left pretty entertained, and there's not much wrong with that', the *AU Review* noted in 2011.

As well as performing, Russell managed to have bit of time off and went out to dinner with John Cleese, a man he had watched, growing up on the legendary *Monty Python* and *Fawlty Towers*, and he tried to explain to him where he had been only a few weeks earlier, at the world premiere of *The Inbetweeners*. 'It was a bizarre moment,' he later confessed. 'I was explaining the show [*The Inbetweeners*] to him. Maybe I've inspired him to do a pensioners' version of it, like *Last Of The Summer Wine*. Actually, thinking about it, let's hope not.'

That experience aside, he loved being in Sydney. He had embraced Aussie life the last time he had holidayed there with his girlfriend Cerys and things were pretty much the same this time around too – 'I love Sydney, I loved performing at the Opera House. While I was there, I used to go for a little jog around the Botanical Gardens and then go to Surry Hills, which wasn't far from where I was staying to have breakfast in a café. And I really love being on Bondi Beach. I get a real sense of calm when I'm there. The sea is so warm, the sand is so soft. Just listening to music there is very peaceful.'

But all good things had to come to an end and it wasn't long before Russell found himself back in the *Good News* studio office to prepare for his upcoming fifth series which was to be broadcast in October 2011. He was excited to be returning to the show, having worked solo on his stand-ups it was now back to being one of the team again. And everyone was excited about its continued success.

'It's ridiculously difficult to believe a show with my name on it has gotten this far,' he said at the time. 'It's rather absurd really, if you think about it. I mean, who am I? Just some random punter blathering on about whatever comes to mind. I often think, "Who wants to hear what I have to say?" though I try not to entertain those thoughts – they'd definitely keep me awake at night. But the show is a challenge, you have raw material of the news, then select the titbits, make them link and make it look effortless. I work 8am–8pm when I am working on the series. Then we record an hour of jokes and it makes it all seem worthwhile.'

The new series of *Good News* wasn't going to change with its fifth outing. Russell was adamant that the viewing figures spoke for themselves and the viewers liked it exactly as it was – 'It'll stay exactly the same format, obviously with different jokes to keep it fresh and topical. But that's true of any series, just go with what's current and happening now.

If it ain't broke, don't fix it and all that,' he told *Mayhem* magazine in 2011.

With his solo tour earlier that year and various gigs across the world, Russell was squeezing a lot into 2011, which makes you wonder, how did he fit it all in? One of the key aspects to this was that he didn't ever try and do more than one job at once – 'The trick is, I never actually combine any two things I'm working on. That would do my head in. I find if I split my stand-up and keep it separate from my TV work, I can manage much better. Saying that, I never have any time off. My own fault of course, but I like it that way.'

The first show of Series 5 kicked off at the end of October 2011 and Russell found time to do a little backstage web chat (while enjoying a sneaky glass of red) to tell viewers how the first episode had gone – 'I'm just about to go and edit the show which we've just finished and I have to say, it was good fun, really good fun. We did loads of weird peculiar news stories tonight, we seem to have a talent for finding them, so thank you for watching! We filmed several sketches a couple of weeks ago so we are all quite organised.'

One of the sketches they did was a story from a fairly typical *MailOnline* report stating that women only looked good for two hours and twenty minutes a day. According to the article, however long they spent doing their hair or make-up didn't matter: by 10.03am, it will all fade. His sketch showed him in an office with hot women at 10.02am and then at exactly 10.03am they turned into a bunch of hags. A simple but hilarious idea, it went down a treat with viewers – 950,000 tuned in for that first episode.

Not so hilarious, however, was a few weeks later when Russ broke his hand during one of his segments. Yep, on 15 November he was filming with a stuntman who was showing him and the audience how they film 'fights' on TV. Rocky the stuntman had gone through the routine with Russell, who looked a little nervous about the upcoming stunt but was enjoying limbering up as the studio audience laughed in anticipation. Unfortunately for him, he had forgotten that the bar stool they were using in the sketch was made of fake wood – it was designed to break easily for the purposes of the stunt fight.

'The stuntman had just showed me it was balsa wood but I had just learned how to do one-armed press-ups,' he admitted rather sheepishly to The Richard Herring Leicester Square Theatre Podcast. 'So to show off, I thought I would do one on the stool but forgot it was balsa wood and broke my hand.'

Ouch! It took a while for Russell, who had his back to the audience and was doubled over in pain, to stand up and reveal that he wasn't faking his injury or his pain and very soon two production crew members came on set and took him off to examine the injury. The unsuspecting audience were still laughing, completely unaware of the severity of the injury and cheered when he returned on set, white as a sheet. Having been heard singing Queen's 'The Show Must Go On', he came back and took part in the fake fight scene – albeit a little less aggressively than he would have done before. 'I carried on with the show!' he recalled defiantly. 'I came back and did it one-handed.'

Fans were worried about his injury and one website, *The Russell Howard Fan Community*, gave regular updates as to his condition. They re-tweeted posts from @bbcgoodnews to concerned fans: 'For all the people tweeting, Russ injured himself on set tonight during filming. We are just trying to arrange taking him to hospital.' An hour later, the website gave an update: 'Cheers for all your supportive tweets about Russ injuring himself on set. He is on his way to hospital in a sec #getwellsoonRuss'

One of the show's writers, Karl Minns, also confirmed on Twitter that Russ had survived the incident: 'Russell Howard is alive and well, albeit with a busted hand. Have volunteered to punch in his PIN number for him. Now in Rio...'

The fan site loved the fact that his team were all still 'having a laugh despite an injury involved'. And they especially loved the fact Russ was such a trooper. One fan wrote on the chatstream: 'I admire Russ carrying on filming the show despite being in pain. A) he must really love the show B) He really must love us fans'.

And the series producer of *Good News*, Mark Iddon, was quick to point out on Twitter that Russell wasn't likely to be taking any time off work due to this little mishap either – 'He's a machine. He'll be back in the edit today and begin writing again for next week's show immediately – the hard working SOB! And the injury... it's his left hand, so, you know... silver lining.'

However, the following day Russ had to pull out of a gig he was due to perform at the Hammersmith Apollo. It was a benefit for Friends of the Earth but now he had his hand in cast and was still in a lot of pain. He sent his apologies to 'Laugh or The Polar Bear Gets It'.

Probably the most memorable and embarrassing thing Russell had ever done on the show, he found that people enjoyed coming up to him for a long time afterwards, reminding him of his injury – 'I got so much stick around that time, I'd get people come up and go, "Oh, are you going to do some press ups?"'

Because the show had been filmed before it aired, the studio audience in attendance, as well as the fan sites, were instrumental in getting people to talk about the show and a record number tuned in to watch how Russ actually became a cropper. Which is slightly worrying, mused the comic: 'It was the highest ever viewing figures because it was leaked. What happens tonight? Russell hurts himself. The mere idea that I hurt myself and people are like, "Wow! I'm definitely tuning in". So I think the BBC are planning a thing along the lines of where randomly at some point during each show somebody comes in and kicks me between the legs!'

It seems like a lifetime ago since Russ started his Right Here, Right Now Tour and due to its popularity, it had been extended twice, with dates scattered over that year. The DVD of the tour had been released back at the beginning of November in 2011 but for fans who wanted some live action, they made their way to the O2 in the middle of December. Russell was performing the final show on his tour (this time it definitely *was* the final) and *Chortle* was impressed at his continued positivity: 'Success couldn't have happened to a nicer guy, Howard has material that's often shaper and much better written than you might expect. That he is playing such spaces as vast as the O2 stage is an inescapable fact for a photogenic boy-next-door performing who could easily be pigeonholed as "safe" material. But how many other comedians could genuinely having something as overwhelmingly upbeat as Russell's List of Joy, which he reads from a laptop while perched on a leather armchair on stage? The show ends with a Q&A which is as messy as these things usually are, with Howard trying unsuccessfully to pick out possible seeds for humour from an arena full of people baying for him to show them his arse.'

Sadly, Russell broke many hearts when he refused to show a bit of cheek. He broke his mum's heart too when he turned down an appearance on *Strictly Come Dancing*, one of her favourite shows, that year too. It wasn't the first time he had been asked but he couldn't bring himself to do it – and didn't ever see himself taking part in the hugely popular show: 'I just couldn't do it, it's not for me. But hey, give it time. I would have to be back on mortgage repayments and not be able to gig for some reason – it would have to be bad. One day, I'll be a 50-year-old washed-up twat and I'll be next to some celebrity who asks, "Didn't you bang cats? I read it on your Wikipedia."' He was referring to a segment on the reference website that told Internet searchers that he liked to, er, have sexual activities with felines – 'They seemed determined to let the world know that I liked banging cats. I don't. If I was going to bang any animal, it certainly wouldn't be a cat. Not a fan. But there

was some really determined individual who was desperate to get this rumour out there that I'm a cat banger.'
Meow!

So, 2011 had proved to be a whirlwind of international gigs, a seemingly never-ending tour and more *Good News* shows that were occasionally marked with bad news when it came to personal injury. Bring on 2012!

Chapter 18

TIME TO RESCUE A PRINCESS...

*'I wear makeup when I do telly, but not on stage. I just have a
shower, dry my hair, maybe put a bit of wax in it. I have got quite big pointy
teeth and a lazy eye, so I think you just have to crack on, really, there's not
much you can do. Photos are the worst thing – one of my eyes is always
fascinated with my nose. I've always said if eyes are the window to
the soul, my soul is fucked.'*
RH

The year 2012 kicked off with a slightly calmer air to it... After touring heavily for the majority of the previous year, that year Russell had another focus: more specifically, a four-legged focus. He told *NewStatesman* in 2011: 'My plans for the year? I am desperately trying to convince my girlfriend to get another dog. I got to do a few series of *Good News* and I would like to say that the TV show was higher than the acquisition of another hound, but I don't know.'

But it wasn't long before he was back at Riverside Studios and focusing on the latest series of *Good News*, which was now on its sixth series. The BBC Three bosses had decided to make a change to its transmission too, moving time slots so it was no longer a late-night cult show, now it was on at primetime 9pm. And did that change the audience viewing figures? At the end of the previous year Russ was outperforming two BBC Two much publicised shows – *Life's Too Short* and *Rev*. And it was pointed out that was even though *Good News* was a digital channel and a much later timeslot. So what would happen when the first show of Season 6 aired on 12 April? That's when 850,000 people tuned in. So, fairly successful, we would say. Russell was over the moon at the success of the show and after touring for much of the previous year, focusing on the news and staying in one place for a while was quite appealing – 'I never imagined the show would last this long, it's incredible. I thought we would only do one series, so it's brilliant. We've done it for three years now and we've just knocked them out. The thing about doing a topical show like this is that there's no time to dwell on things. You're just knocking out gags and moving on. You're like Octomom, just banging a series out and then moving on to the next. Coming from the world of live comedy where you have to nurture your act for months and years, it's a really different environment. We're like a topical comedy form of the A-Team. We just burst out and go, "Look what we've put together out of this load of nonsense." And most of the time, hopefully, it works,' he admitted to *Digital Spy* in 2012.

Ever the self-deprecating star, successful as *Good News*

was, Russ never regarded his job, making people laugh, as important in the grand scheme of things. His girlfriend Cerys was always his point of reference here: she is the doctor, she is the one who saves lives. He makes people laugh. But the point is, he enjoys what he does, he is good at it and he doesn't take what he does for granted.

'There is no science to comedy. There will always be a really shit gig around the corner. It's bizarre. You are saying the same words as you said the night before, but sometimes it just doesn't work. Who knows why? But it means that a comedian can never get too blasé. Riddled with diarrhoea, more like. Real life is hard, I'm sorry but shopping at Tesco is not as much fun as writing jokes for TV shows and I struggle with it. I imagine Olympic athletes feel the same. They have an amazing two weeks, then relax. But then they start twitching. Imagine Jessica Ennis: "Just going to go for a quick jog," she tells her boyfriend, "just a quick one." Nothing else compares. It is about exposing yourself. Everything I experience in life, I put through the sausage maker that is comedy. And then I try and make it funny for others. Whether that is healthy or not remains to be seen,' Russell told *The Independent* in 2012.

He celebrated his thirty-second birthday in March and it was a point in his life when he started to reflect not on what he had achieved in his career, but what was in store for his personal life: 'I've reached the age of 32 with very little wisdom, I'm afraid. It's tragic. I still have to turn to my mum and dad for every decision I make.'

He was always very vocal about what he wanted in the

future: wife, kids... But he hadn't yet managed to ask the all-important question. 'Of course I want to get married... I just haven't asked her yet,' he told *The Birmingham Mail* in 2010. The fact that his sister Kerry was getting married that year added to the family excitement, his mum especially was over the moon.

'She was fretting about getting the new house ready for my sister's wedding, it was hilarious,' he later told *Radio Times* in 2012. 'She was going round like, "I gotta get the house done. We can't have dust on the dress."

Having dated for about a year, his sister married the English actor and singer Gabriel Vick (best-known for his role as Feuilly in *Les Misérables*) at Prior Park Chapel, a stunning location set on a hill and overlooking the city of Bath. It wasn't the only wedding that year – the other big ceremony was of course the Royal Wedding between Kate Middleton and Prince William, which was also hilariously covered on *Good News*. HM The Queen looking like Jim Carrey in *The Mask*, anyone? But for the first time in Russ's career, he said something that caused a slight upset in the television world. In an interview with *The Guardian* in 2012, he was asked what he thought the greatest threat to comedy was. And he replied, 'The TV channel Dave. Everything is repeated there, they just play the same shows over and over.' Ironically, Dave regularly showed repeats of *Russell Howard's Good News* as well as old *Mock the Week* episodes too. OK, so there wasn't really a great hoo-ha, but one publication commented that Russell had in fact, 'bitten the hand that feeds him'. It was later revealed that

Russ had made the comments in jest, but he had been taught an invaluable lesson in dealing with being misquoted.

'That'll teach me for giving a joke answer to a serious question from a broadsheet newspaper! Sorry, Dave, you know I love you,' he insisted.

There was also a little naughtiness when he picked up some points on his driving licence after being caught speeding in the summer of 2012. Having owned a BMW Z4 which he loved although confessed to *The Independent* that he looked 'ridiculous in', he had to take part in a driving awareness course which proved to be quite an amusing experience – especially if you happened to be a fan of David Brent.

'People have such little self-awareness, it always surprises me. I had to do a driving course recently after getting some points on my licence for speeding. The instructor was incredible. I used the word "assume" to answer one of his questions. "Assume?" he said. "I think you will find that 'assume' just makes an ass out of you and me." Had he never seen Ricky Gervais in *The Office*?' he told *The Independent* in 2012.

Series 6 of *Good News*, as well as airing in a new time slot of 9pm, also went on for longer than usual – 9 episodes with 3 'specials' at the end of the series. With no tour commitments Russell was able to extend the run of the series with extra episodes. As *Radio Times* put it in 2012, he was now a grown-up – 'Tousled, cheeky Russell Howard bounces back onto BBC Three for a new series of his silly, funny, topical comedy show. Such is the channel's delight in their young star, for the first time he's been given a proper, grown-up prime time slot and a longer run.'

After the original run of nine episodes, there were three 'special' shows that took the series up until the end of June 2012. The first two were compilations of the best news stories that had been covered in the complete six series of the show while the third was the best bits from this series alone. The last special, airing on 28 June, was a 'stand-up' compilation and featured a selection of performances from emerging stand-up artists that appeared on Russell's show. It was a big gesture from Russ, inviting up-and-coming stand-ups to perform on his show to an audience of thousands but he was so passionate about encouraging and nurturing new talent that he didn't think twice. Some of the acts that have since been on his show and have made a name for themselves and since credit *Good News* for giving them a much-needed boost to their careers. This wasn't a new thing for Russ: even when he was starting out and performing at the Edinburgh Festival Fringe, he was careful to tell his audience to make the time to see his pals – Daniel Kitson and Mark Olver – perform too. He wanted to celebrate new talent and wasn't afraid of celebrating a new wave of comedians.

There was a break over the summer for *Good News* and it gave him the chance to 'switch off': 'As soon as the series finishes I have a good month away from the television and newspapers. You know yourself, reading the newspapers every day isn't particularly good for you. It's an endless assault of horror. There should be less news designed to make people moan. It would be quite lovely on the *ITV News at Ten*, having Alastair Stewart going, "Now look at this, isn't it absolutely wonderful?" to send you to bed with a smile. My show proves there is an appetite for positivity. There's a nice spirit to it. There aren't any jokes like... you know, Samantha Brick [who published an article on *The Daily Mail* website in 2012 entitled 'There Are Downsides to Looking This Pretty']. It was a really big media story but the majority of people don't give a shit. I had various producers saying I should do something but what's the point of going on and saying, "See this woman? She thinks she's pretty – she's not! Hahaha!" It's bullying and I hate stuff like that. There seems to be so much bullying online nowadays. Maybe because it's anonymous and you can be as angry as you want and it's never going to get back to you. It's bizarre, isn't it? Going out of your way to say horrible things?' he told *ComediansComedian*.

After the series had come to a close at the end of June, Russell took a few weeks of well-deserved rest. Well, it would have been a restful time had he not injured his hand – his right one this time – and been sent to hospital for an operation. So, was his hand going to be amputated? Would his arm survive? Would he ever leave hospital? You can imagine the theories that plagued Twitter and Facebook about this episode – 'I think the thing was people saw me in hospital and then they went on Twitter and Facebook and said they saw me in there. People were asking what was wrong with me and making up weird rumours,' he sighed.

Rumours aside, it was a fairly serious time for Russ who had in fact picked up an infection in a tendon in his thumb and had to have not just one but two operations to try and save his digit. To put all the gossip to rest, and much to the relief of his fans, after his week-long stay in hospital he made an official statement on his Facebook page on 24 August:

Hello.

I thought I'd write an official message to you because the news of my recent stay in hospital has started to emerge and, as well as receiving lots of nice messages from well-wishers, there have also been lots of interesting theories (and a fair few bizarre ones) posted on twitter, so I thought I'd let you know what actually happened.

I've been in hospital for A WEEK. I've been on morphine, I've been flushed through with antibiotics. I've had two operations and now I'm bandaged up and typing this with my left hand.

That's right. I've managed to ruin my other hand. No I didn't break it doing press ups on a collapsible chair. I had to have 2 operations on an infected thumb. When I came round from the first operation they told me that at one point they thought they'd have to amputate my thumb, which would really have hampered my hitchhiking skills.

So that's it really, you can either feel sorry for me or do what my mates did and send me a massive foam hand.

On a serious note, I'd like to thank all the nurses, doctors and various people that looked after me.

Russ

As well as receiving over 62,000 'likes' to this post, he received a variety of comments, ranging from 'y'numpty' to 'come to mine, you can use my hands anytime Russ' followed shortly by 'sod her hands use my mouth lol'.

Then there were the people on Twitter who hadn't quite read or understood, or maybe didn't care what Russ had said. 'Messages went around Twitter saying, 'Russell Howard has lost his hands!' – 'It wasn't even Chinese Whispers, it was Chinese Being Unable to Fucking Read,' he fumed. 'I wrote it really clearly but it was amazing to see things escalate. People were saying, "He's got no arm left," "He's going to get a blade fitted," "He's going in the Paralympics." It was just incredible.'

Not ideal! But one message did get across and that was his gratitude for the doctors and nurses at the hospital, which received attention from the local press. Russ had been a patient at Coventry's University Hospital and BMI The Meriden Hospital and a spokesperson for BMI The Meriden Hospital said: 'We are always delighted to get good feedback from our patients so it was great to hear Russell praising the hospital. Mr Rana Das-Gupta who carried out the operation is a well-respected plastic surgeon who we are proud to have at BMI Meriden and it is good to see him receive such recognition.'

However, it was slightly embarrassing when Russ reflected on his time under general anaesthetic and realised he might not have been particularly coherent to the assembled hospital staff, telling Jonathan Ross, when he appeared on his chatshow: 'It's so weird, you can see the words tumbling out of your mouth but can't stop them. There were two things that I said. I thought I was a knight and asked if there was a horse so I could get out. I said, "You need to get me out. If I don't leave soon I won't be able to save the princess." And then I grabbed the nurse and said, "Get me a horse!"'

While the thought of Russ as a knight in shining armour and on a mission to rescue a princess – albeit one in his head – was a charming idea there was another side to him that came out during his semi-conscious state. And it wasn't a very nice side! 'I pointed at this bloke who had just saved my thumb, so the surgeon basically, and was like, "You're not allowed to be on my football team." I don't own a football team! I was so gone I can't be 100 per cent certain I didn't make that statement based on race, that's the worst thing. But it's not me, it's the drugs. That's why I can never take proper drugs – because general anaesthetic turned me into a racist football manager! "You just won't fit in, lad!"'

Quite a startling semi-serious confession, wasn't it? The previously squeaky-clean boy-next-door type had shown that perhaps he wasn't all sweetness and light, albeit while in a semi-drugged state. It was a confession he was happy to make, however, and rather than show a 'racist' side to him – after all the jokes about the English Defence League he had previously made – this was more illustrative that his comedy was both confessional and honest. And probably why he had so many fans who saw for themselves that he could take the mickey out of himself as well as his family and friends.

The break from filming was short and sweet and he began Series 7 of *Good News* on 27 September 2012. But he was a little peeved that the team had not been allowed to bring forward the series to cover the London 2012 Summer Olympics. He felt that there was too much 'censorship' involved during the two weeks of the Olympics, where actually there was a lot of laughter to be had: 'I was quite upset really,' he told *Digital Spy*. 'There was no comedy on during the Olympics, none whatsoever. There's too much money in it. The powers that be didn't want people making jokes about the Olympics, it's too important apparently. We'd have made jokes about it in the same way we always do. It would have been a light touch and we'd have only touched on things that were genuinely funny, like Boris on the zip wire or the Queen during the Opening Ceremony, with the most bored face ever. But nobody ever commented on these things because of a weird censorship. No, no comedy allowed during the Olympics. That moment where all this incredible stuff was happening in the stadium and they just cut up and the Queen looked so bored shitless. That was a brilliant comedy moment. We'd have been all over things like that and the Mo Farah running away from things viral. There's a preconception that all comedy is mocking and piss-taking. But it can actually still be good in a light way.'

The media was excited to be welcoming the seventh series back onscreen, with *Metro* commenting, 'On a channel that's still hit and miss with its comedy output, *Good News* has stood out like a beacon of reliability as the energetic Russell Howard gives his take on the week's news, drawn from 60 international news channels, 140 worldwide newspapers and more than a thousand news clips'.

Radio Times was equally thrilled that he was returning: 'Now that the nights are drawing in, there's nothing like a bit of topical comedy delivered by a stand-up comedian with a skewed West Country charm to warm up a chilly heart'.

And the reactions after the first episode were just as positive: '*RHGN* returned to the telly box this week and is one of BBC Three's better shows. Howard is able to get laughs from the simple things in life and *Good News* is still one of the best stand-up comedies on television,' crowed *Giggle Beats*.

But Russ's hand was still causing him some pain and was still tender when he appeared on *The Jonathan Ross Show* on 27 October. He was a guest alongside the British adventurer Bear Grylls, Aussie pop princess Kylie Minogue and rock band Muse and the first indication that all was not well with his thumb was his rather cack-handed handshake with Wossy when he came out into the studio.

'So that was an usual handshake...Why did we have to go lefty?' queried the chat-show host. 'Because I hurt my thumb,' smiled a sheepish Russ. The audience 'ahhhed' so he told them the story – 'Yes, a month ago, I cut my thumb, got the tendon infected and I nearly lost my thumb.'

At this the audience 'ahhhed' again. 'I love the sympathy I am getting here,' smiled Russ. 'My family just laughed their arses off and my brother sent me a big foam hand!' But his family were there for him in his hour of need and came to visit during his week-long stay in hospital, which cheered him up. And he told Wossy and the audience about believing he was a knight too. 'How sweet,' deadpanned the presenter.

Russ then went on to confess to everyone how much he relies on his family for comedic material because they are so naturally funny, if not completely crazy: 'Take Sunday dinner the other day,' he said. 'My mum just comes out with, "I don't see the point of flavoured condoms, it's not like my fanny can taste."' Wossy looked shocked but the audience were in hysterics. Meanwhile Kylie hid her grinning face with her hand. 'So you see,' he told a mouth-wide-open Ross, 'if you're faced with stuff like that, it's a goldmine.'

Chat then turned to his *Good News* show, which was currently airing on BBC Three as Series 7 had begun on 27 September. Russ admitted that the Royal Wedding in April of that year had given them plenty of material – especially how the press around the world had reported it. Whether he knew that Kylie was a guest and he wanted to talk specifically about Australia or if he had planned to say it all along, he then regaled the audience and Wossy (and Kylie, who was listening in the filmed Green Room) with the footage they had found from an Aussie news channel.

'Australia is always very good for crazy stories... Like the way they covered the Royal Wedding, they covered it very differently to us... We had a lot of respect for everything that was happening and it was such a wonderful event but there was a lovely moment on Australian TV where on the news this woman thought it would be a good idea to interview an Aussie rules football fan. So she said to him, "What do you think they will get up to on honeymoon?" And this man said, "Am I allowed to say on telly?" And she said "Yes!" And the bloke said, "anal!"'

Kylie held both hands over her face as the cameras flicked over to the Green Room. 'Kylie, Kylie, is this a tradition you want to tell us about?' questioned Wossy. 'You wouldn't have that on the *News at Ten*, would you, Kylie?' he persisted.

'No comment,' grinned Miss Minogue.

With his extended family regularly popping up in Russ's stand-up, Jonathan Ross wanted to find out more about his rather impressive amount of cousins. 'I have forty cousins... Not sure if they are my cousins or second cousins, I am not sure. They don't treat me any differently, I am just Russell to them. And yes, they are pretty strange. Nobody believes me with all the stuff they get up to, it all sounds so ridiculous,' he told the presenter.

'*At Home with the Howards*,' mused Wossy. 'That sounds like the greatest reality show ever invented.'

Russell was equally excited, saying, 'We should definitely try and get it off the ground. We'd have to go late night though, I would love to do that.'

Then the chat turned to his looks and as usual, Russ was deeply embarrassed, although Wossy wasn't overly gushing in the first place: 'Often when we have comedians on the show they are very funny but not the best-looking people in the world...' He paused before adding, 'And you're not the best-looking person in the world.' At this the audience booed loudly but Wossy continued firmly: 'Let me finish! But you are a good-looking young man, you are better-looking than most. I know you have a big following.'

Russell looked uncomfortable but did admit that he was 'fairly presentable'. But then he conceded that his 'presentableness' often put him on strange lists: 'I am always on a list that you hate to admit you fancy,' he joked, referring to the *Heat* Weird Crush list of 2009. 'I was beaten by Simon Cowell before and The Stig [a character on the BBC motoring programme, *Top Gear*] – and he doesn't even have a face! My dad would love to be on that list, it would be his ultimate ambition. He works out quite a lot, he's quite buff. We think he might be on the "roids"! He's got to that age where he thinks, he's fifty-five years old, he thinks he can wear Lycra around the house. Mum doesn't go in for that stuff.'

Finally, came the plug. Russell admitted that he wasn't doing a tour that year 'maybe next year' but he did take the opportunity to plug the current series of *Good News*. And the fact that *Russell Howard's Good News* Series 2 was now available to buy on DVD.

'You'll find it at most petrol stations if you are really stuck for a Christmas present,' chuckled Wossy.

'Or wait until January when you'll be able to get it really, really cheap,' suggested Russ.

And so Series 7 of *Good News* was already on our screens and it was pulling in record figures again. The run for this series was the longest ever, ten episodes and two special compilation shows at the end too, including a Christmas special on 13 December 2012. As usual there was a big wrap party for everyone involved with the show, and Russ presented them all with a big cake – 'We also had a photo that panned across, showing everyone who works on the show, from cameramen to producers to runners. I always feel quite teary with things like that,' he told *Metro* in 2013.

With the series over, Russ had time to take part in Channel 4's amusing if not risqué quiz show, *The Big Fat Quiz of the Year*. There were three teams of two comedians who were given questions on news and stories from the past twelve months to answer. Of course it was right up Russ's street and he was partnered with a familiar face: Jonathan Ross. The two went up against actor and comedian Jack Whitehall and comedian and TV host James Corden while actor and comedian Richard Ayoade and sports presenter Gabby Logan made up the third team (they eventually went on to win). While Corden and Whitehall came dressed in black tie – 'We have come dressed as we should, it's a black-tie event' – and Wossy and Ayoade wore suits, Russ was in his trademark T-shirt (actually the same one he wore when he appeared on the *Conan* show).

'Look how muscular Russell has become,' beamed Jonathan. 'Look at those muscles, what a fine specimen. He is like Madonna's dream date now – although she wouldn't know whether to sleep with him or adopt him.'

James Corden also commented on Russ's look – 'Seriously, look at those guns.' And everyone was looking at those guns when early on in the show, Russ lifted up his arms to illustrate an answer and at that point, Corden was again mesmerised.

'It was amazing,' said James. 'You can't wear that T-shirt, give us a slight glimpse at what the gun-show looks like and never let us get a good look.'

'Let's get it out the way,' ordered Wossy. 'Show everybody what they want to see and then we can move on. Go on, get them out. Right arm first.' At this the audience cheered.

Richard Ayoade then pointed out that he and Gabby Logan did not partake in this goading, or 'bullying' as he said it was, of poor Russell.

'I don't think it's bullying to say can we have a look at someone's impressive biceps,' argued James.

'Let's have a consensual gun show instead,' countered Richard.

Chapter 19

KING OF THE MINGERS

['I had a dream the other day that I was looking at batteries for eight hours in Tesco, deciding whether I should buy Duracell or Tesco's own. I woke up and thought; "What was that about?" You are so annoyed. Can we not have one where I'm riding a horse, trying to get some princess or something? Do I have to look at fucking batteries?'

RH

A chilly Thursday on 24 January 2013 saw Russell, his mum Ninette and sis Kerry posing like professionals on the red carpet outside the Vue West End in London's Leicester Square. Well, Kerry was able to move her smile around at the various paps shouting out their names while Russ and their mum forced grins in completely opposite directions. He didn't want to be there – he had taken his mum as treat and had only agreed on attending as Kerry had a role in the film. Still, it looked like a cosy trio as they posed for the premiere of *I Give It A Year*, a Brit-flick about the

245

trials and tribulations of a newlywed couple (Rose Byrne and Rafe Spall) during their first year of marriage.

Although Russ could have thought of a million and one other places he wanted to be that evening, he was incredibly proud of his sister and her acting talents... and it wouldn't be long before he appreciated fully just how amazing she was on screen when they worked together on their own TV film in the not too distant future – but more on that later.

'Now it isn't just me bringing the showbiz world to my family,' he told *The Bath Chronicle*. 'My sister has exposed my mum to the world of celebrity even more and putting my whirling, dervish of a mum in the world of celebrity has, and will, create hilarious situations. And Kerry is more of a showman than me. We had a red carpet going from Mum's house to the kerb for people rocking up to watch Kerry's film when it came out. I'd never do that.'

The year 2013 also brought with it some, ahem good news for the thirty-two-year-old. At the beginning of February, *Digital Spy* announced that *Russell Howard's Good News* was voted BBC Three's best ever TV show. Over 10,000 readers had taken part in the poll and the show beat the likes of *Gavin & Stacey*, *Being Human*, *Little Britain* and *Torchwood*. Russ was impressed, telling *Digital Spy*: 'I am delighted, it's very cool. *Good News* is just something you can watch, it is disposable telly. If you don't like one joke, there is another one coming round the corner. We are second only to *Doctor Who* on the iPlayer, how cool is that?'

And then came the really big news... On 12 February *Heat* magazine released the results of their national Weird

Crush poll and Russ was the winner! Having twice before finished third, he was gracious in his acceptance: 'Thanks, I think, to the people who voted for me. Finally, I am King of the Mingers.' That year also saw his former flatmate, Jon Richardson, on the list for the first time, coming in just behind in the No. 2 spot while last year's winner, Richard Osman from *Pointless*, was now No. 3. Russ couldn't resist making a point of bragging that he was in the top spot over Jon – 'We've always had a lot of people calling us weird, but we certainly would have been described as crushes. Then again, number five was Adam Richman [host of reality TV show, *Man V Food*]. The only time you ever see him is with a face full of dead animal. I think the crucial word is "weird".'

Heat's editor Lucie Cave said, 'Although Russell Howard has been hanging around in the Weird Crush chart for several years, this year his fans decided it was his turn for the top spot. Proof that, on Valentine's Day, there's love out there for everyone.'

Wow, what a start to the year! Ahem... It was, in fact, the beginning of lots of exciting news. In April Russ revealed in an interview that he was writing a film script with his friend Steve Williams. The pair had previously attended a creative writing course at Birkbeck, University of London, and Russell was amused at the reactions of his fellow students: 'People there were like, "What are you doing here?" I felt like an adult back at school with children – it was brilliant fun.'

The idea of writing a comedy film had come from his time in America when he realised that comedy acting probably wasn't for him. While in Hollywood, he went for some auditions when he was in LA for the *Conan* talk show. He told *TV Choice*: 'The auditions were for some terrible films. I kept changing the words because they were so bad and you could see the writers in the corner getting really pissy. That's pretty difficult for me, saying words when I know nobody is laughing. I'd love to get the thrill of speaking actors making my work even funnier. So I am writing a film with a friend which hopefully will become something, but it's pretty early at the moment. I probably won't star in it, I'm not a very good actor so it's something I'm writing, and then maybe have a tiny part in it, have proper actors do it rather than have me ruin it.' And could he reveal more about the plot?

'It's about a bloke who falls in love with his family again,' he confessed.

The film's premise might have had a hint of an autobiographical stance to it. On the surface, people who know and enjoy Russell's work know how close he and his family are and how he loves talking about them and spending time with them. But it wasn't always so. There was a time in his life, maybe around the time he left university, when he wasn't actually that close to them. But he maintains that it was his comedy that brought them all together, telling *ComediansComedian*: 'There were times when I was younger, I didn't spend a lot of time with them. Since university till I was about 25 I didn't really see a lot of them, I was just gigging. I was off doing my thing, doing stand-up, and oddly they came to me and we are now super close in a way we weren't for a long time. That is natural, I think. In my teens I hated my dad and now I love him. That is just to do with getting older and seeing him more and appreciating what he has done. I didn't set out to fix my family, I think my job as a stand-up has just brought us all together. My show is quite often me telling people how great my family are, how amazing and how much fun we all have. It wasn't always perfect when I was a kid, now, weirdly, my success has brought my family together. They all come and watch me do stand-up, they all really love it.'

Comic Relief was back in 2013 and Russ provided a special compilation of *Good News*. His special was part of the 'Funny for Money' televised comedy marathon that aired a week before the big night fundraiser. OK, so it didn't air until 11.55pm that night but it was on BBC One. And it didn't involve him wearing Lycra or cycling a million miles...

On 23 April, just as fans were getting excited about the forthcoming new series of *Russell Howard's Good News*, which was to begin its eighth edition on 25 April, as well as the anticipation that there was to be a Russell Howard film soon (well, one written by him and his mate, Steve) there was another big announcement from Russ's camp. This was a 'pinch-yourself' type moment: there was to be a new tour. And Russ would not only be embarking on a seventeen-date British tour with his new show, Wonderbox, he would be setting off around the globe to bring it to a global audience too. The tour, due to start on 23 February 2014, was his first for three years and was to be his biggest yet. The excitement over the announcement was worldwide, with fans going into a frenzy when he posted on Facebook, asking for suggestions for venues to play in. He received over 17,000 messages and following the feedback, added dates in New York, Los Angeles, San Francisco, Chicago, Washington, D.C. and Denver. He also revealed that he would be taking his show Down Under to Sydney, Melbourne, Perth, Brisbane and Auckland.

Twitter went into meltdown when his Twitter account posted a teaser of his Wonderbox Tour, showing a series of random, meaningless numbers – *Lost* lovers will appreciate that. Fans worked out that there were map co-ordinates but Russ himself had no idea what was going on. But there was something the comic was certain would happen with his new tour: he wanted to play at the Royal Albert Hall. While flying back from Australia at the end of the previous year he had watched a DVD of singer-songwriter Adele performing at the hallowed hall and wanted a piece of the action, telling Jonathan Ross: 'It is the most exciting thing, I will be doing that for 4 nights. I thought it looked so cool. It was beautiful seeing her perform against that backdrop and I just thought it looked so cool. Billy Connolly did it, Victoria Wood did it. I can't wait.'

So what was Wonderbox about? That was the question on everyone's lips in April. Russ had been away from the stand-up circuit for nearly three years and the spontaneous creation of that medium and he was ready to be back on stage. Not that he could give much away about what his latest tour was going to be about – he hadn't written it yet! 'There will be loads of jokes hopefully,' he told *The Telegraph*. 'I hope I will be really funny. And I will endeavour to make it the best show I have written yet, that is my aim. Hopefully it will be.

I just try and imagine I'm chatting to my mates. I can't stress how much I enjoy it, so I think I'm just naturally delighted to see people. The thing I love most about stand-up is that it's just an extension of your personality. It's never a chore. But I have a mortgage now, this is the reality, I am a stand-up with a mortgage.' (Russell and Cerys had by this time now bought a house and the actuality of being a grown-up had hit the comedian.)

And the meaning of Wonderbox? We know that Dingledodies had a philosophical slant and the same, it seemed, applied to Wonderbox.

'I read this book, I can't remember the author, which I probably should have done,' he confessed to *Digital Spy*, 'but it's about how German families have this thing called a "boondercama", a "wonderbox", which they put various things that they've had, trinkets and mementoes, into this box and pass it down the generations. I thought there was something interesting about that. It came from there and I have made the tour pretty much about me, grabbing stories from my family and putting them into my "Wonderbox". Does that make sense?'

In essence it was to be stories about his family, which are always a hit, as well as plans to talk about those inevitable awkward moments when two worlds collide: posing with his mum and sister on the red carpet or being recognised as 'that bloke from the telly' just as he was picking up his dog Archie's poo. And now it was going worldwide, there were perks to his global new job – 'Really the tour is just a cheeky way of travelling. I did some gigs at the Sydney Opera House last year and it was brilliant. It's a fun way to have a little holiday. Oddly I feel a lot more at home on stage than this, doing an interview. I am probably the worst person in the world in this sort of situation... Like when I'm in a shop, I have all these thoughts going through my mind like, "Is the shopkeeper looking at me funnily because of my lazy eye or because I'm famous? Or have I got something on my face?" I have all this worry. But when you are on stage, it's the only place in the world you are allowed to show off and it is expected. It's terrific. Here are my stories, everyone listen. Pay me money and listen. If you can't be in a good mood while you are doing that there must be something wrong with you.'

So, with grand designs in place to make this his best tour yet, was he feeling the pressure? It would seem in one form he was, in another, he knew what the show provided... Simply a night of light relief.

'It's just a kind of sliding scale of pressure really,' he admitted to the *ComediansComedian* podcast. 'I'll spend the next six months doing nothing but stand-up in small venues, ironing out creases and just making sure everything's good. I really like stand-up for the reason that is just happens and then people remember nothing from it. It's like this magical night where people can't remember a single joke but they know they had a great time. TV can be rewound and rewatched and analysed but there's a real intangibility to stand-up.'

So that was it... For the next few months Russ was working on his Wonderbox Tour material in a bid to get arena ready.

In June it was announced that four more dates had been added to the UK leg of his tour: Cardiff, Birmingham, Dublin and Bournemouth.

And on top of all this Series 8 of *Good News* was on our screens and not only was it reaching audience figures of over 5 million a week, the show was now being broadcast in Australia, New Zealand and Denmark. And even though he had a tour to prepare for, Russ's love and dedication for the show meant that this came first – well, after attempting to justify to journalists as to why he thought the show was so popular, seeing as it had been around for eight series by now – 'Twenty years ago you couldn't do *Good News* but now you've got 24-hour news in pretty much every country in the world and people scrabbling to fill it. The scrabbling is where you find the good bits, there was a story a while ago on Sky News that said half the horses in the UK are obese. We don't really need to know that, but there's this thing of, "Fuck, we have 24 hours to fill!"'

The team of researchers Russell now employed had grown to ten core researchers watching some three hundred hours of telly, from sixty international news channels, reading more than one hundred and forty newspapers a week. Then the two hundred most popular stories were whittled down to 50 before Russ took over and culled them to a final twelve. There was a rumour going round that Oscar-winning actress Emma Thompson wanted to be in the audience for this series as she was a big fan and Russ knew, with this series being the only one set to air in 2013, he had to focus on it being the best, telling *Digital Spy*: 'It's brutal watching some news stories slip by when the show isn't on air. I remember last year when Prince Harry got naked. That was brilliant. The supposed hysteria that people were in some way offended or shocked by it. He's a young bloke who went to Vegas and got naked. My mate Tomo went to Magaluf and shat himself four times in six days. We all know far worse stories. That's what young blokes do on holiday. So yeah, stories like that I wish we could have covered. But then we found one the other day about this guy who lives in Serbia who'd had a vagina carved into his wife's tombstone. She died at, like, 70 and that was her wish!'

In May he joined Wossy again on *The Jonathan Ross Show* – no T-shirt alert! – in a smart sweater and told him why he was so excited about going out on tour again: 'It's been three years, I've been doing the telly show and I fancied doing a new tour. I'm really looking forward to it. All new material, it's going to be great. Normally when I do stand-up I don't want to do topical stuff, it's a joy not having to do that stuff, which is of course what *Good News* is. I like to do the family stuff but I have to be canny and be careful over the universality of such things.'

Jonathan Ross remarked that it might be hard for Russell to go on tour and keep up with his fitness routine now that he was looking so buff - but he wasn't about to be distracted by that topic angle and instead started talking about how his brother Daniel comes on tour with him. Whether a conscious refusal to answer or not, Russ's story about his sibling changed the focus of the interview back to his family – a safe topic for him rather than his looks. And stories like this were always good fodder. He told Jonathan and the audience about how going on holiday with his brother before a tour was always a good way of getting material for his show. Like the time they went to Thailand and his brother's appendix burst...

With the final show of *Good News* on 11 July, it was now time to work on his material for Wonderbox. Performing at smaller venues was essential for Russ to see what did and didn't work; it was his rehearsal time and a chance to iron out any jokes/stories that weren't quite working. 'I reckon I have forty minutes so far,' he told a reporter for Digital Spy, 'twenty of which are good. It's exciting because right now I am trying out loads of new material at small gigs where I'm not getting paid, so I can just rock up and throw shit against the wall.'

So, Wonderbox: Work In Progress went on the road for the months leading up to the start of the tour, which kicked off on Sunday, 23 February 2014, at the Bournemouth International Centre. From there he would visit Cardiff and Manchester before heading to Sheffield, Belfast, Glasgow, Aberdeen, Newcastle, Nottingham, Liverpool, Birmingham and Brighton in March. Extra dates were added almost immediately after the original list sold out so he also had to slot in gigs in Leeds, the O2 and Wembley that month too. Then it was London's Royal Albert Hall from Monday, 14 until Thursday, 17 April for the final performances of the UK leg of the tour.

There was a definite new look to the publicity photos that accompanied his new tour. Here, he looked rugged:his hair was tousled, his guns were on show (just for you, James Corden!), and in one shot he stared pensively into the camera lens. But he didn't get a chance to see the finalised shots that his publicity team sent out to journalists and was a little embarrassed by the reactions: 'poster pull-out from *Mizz* magazine' was one of many on that vein.

'I got into the gym... It's quite fun to be healthy, isn't it? If your day's going badly, it's nice to have a swim. I haven't seen those photos, I probably look like a twat, don't I?' as his response.

There was still such an air of shyness and timidity when the focus was on him; he couldn't cope with it. When he took part in interviews he found that talking about himself was an incredibly difficult default setting for him.

He told *ComediansComedian*: 'I feel nervous doing this [interview]. I haven't been very funny, my job is to be funny. I am finding it quite scary to be this revealing. But my brain is telling me, "You haven't been very funny".'

Luckily, his new Wonderbox show was just that...

Chapter 20

WHERE'S MR DILDO?

'If you are feeling depressed, just think of a T. Rex trying to make a bed.'
NINETTE HOWARD

It was the opening night of his tour, Russell was out in Bournemouth and there was still no extravagant rider for the comic – 'I'm missing out, aren't I? I should be demanding a small dog at each venue and a hot tub. I just ask for sandwiches and fruit.'

His mum Ninette was once more on tour with him and reminded him of the simple pleasures to be excited about in life. Seeing it through her eyes made him appreciate 'how bloody lucky I am' – '"Look at these comfy seats! Lovely! Look at this room!" she will tell me. For my mum to see her son on stage, telling jokes about her is fucking mind-blowing. I am very aware how lucky I am to be able to do that and make her feel good. No one likes my stuff more than my mum, she is a big fan,' he told *The Argos* in 2014.

The critics, on the other hand, were a little more lukewarm to his new material, although not his new physique – 'It's official: Russell Howard has the best biceps in British comedy. They are a stand-out part of the package. They give him a distinctive phwoar factor,' declared *The Telegraph*. 'The first night of Russell Howard's Wonderbox tour reveals a fighting fit show but it's time he moved out of his juvenile comfort zone. The show is already fighting-fit – no sense in it needing more gigs to gear up – and in terms of technical proficiency reveals Howard coming on in leaps and bounds (the laughs are strong and steady). But it still feels like this tour is marking time. The Scampish Bristolian's previous tours emphasised the joy to be unearthed in everyday experiences and waged admirable battle against British miserabilism. Is it too much to ask that Howard now move outside his juvenile comfort zone of relaying amusing and smutty things that his family or friends did or said? There's an unexpectedly touching finale when he discusses his encounters with an inspirationally resilient boy contending with terminal cancer. That section holds you in awe. More from where that came from wouldn't go amiss.'

The final act of his show had made an impact, and rightly so. Back in November 2013, Russell had made thirteen-year-old Deryn Blackwell's dream come true when he visited him in a specialist unit at a Bristol hospital after recovering from a bone marrow transplant. After being diagnosed with leukaemia and Langerhans cell sarcoma (LCS), the youngster drew up a bucket list of ambitions he wanted to achieve and meeting Russell topped that list so he was over the moon when Russ visited the hospital for three and a half hours with his mum, Callie, who said, 'Deryn was cheered up a lot by Russell, which was lovely. Russell is adorable and so very funny.'

It was the first of several meetings and Russ got to know the remarkable youngster extremely well, even helping him plan, which should have been have an inconceivable event for such a young lad, his funeral. By the end of 2013, doctors told Deryn that the four bone marrow transplants he had had hadn't been successful and he and the family were moved to Children's Hospice South West in Wraxall, North Somerset. His family were given the news that they would have to come to terms with losing Deryn, but eight weeks later, after being given a fatal prognosis, Deryn was still very much alive, had seen in Christmas and the New Year and now his body was making a full recovery, it seemed. For a boy who was being sick up to five times a day and was 'looking forward to dying because he was so ill,' according to his mum, it was a miracle. And Russell, who by this time had become a close family friend, knew what he wanted to do with Deryn's story, telling *ComediansComedian*: 'I met Deryn, who was a young kid dying of cancer, and his parents asked if I could go and see him. So I did and we had a chat. It was horribly sad and it was the hardest sort of gig in a way because in that situation you are something important to someone and what people don't realise is that I am crippled with low self-esteem. People don't see that on stage so when you meet them you have to be the best version of yourself because it's so sad and you're in a hospital and so I try so hard when I meet people to make them smile.

'He told me he liked a sketch I did when I wore a dildo costume [one episode of *Russell Howard's Good News* saw Russ dress up as Mr Dildo in a sketch which asked, 'Where is Mr Dildo?'] – he is 14 and watching me wear a dildo costume was his favourite! I went to see him a few times and he was planning his own funeral. He was making his dad dress as the Grim Reaper – he had a great sense of humour even though he was so ill and he was very dark but very funny about it. He said he wanted his dad with a scythe and if anyone coughed, he had to point at them. Then he asked me to go. And of course, I said, "Yeah... what do you want me to wear?" and he said, "I think you know." He genuinely said, "I think you know." Then it dawned on me, the dildo.

'So I went to see him at the children's hospice, the bleakest places full of incredible women who help children prepare to die. He wanted to get pissed with me so I snuck in some cider to drink with a 14-year-old boy! But what happened was incredible. He was in the hospice for 80 days after being given just 2 days to live and he just got better. The doctors had no idea what happened. It was amazing and I asked him if I could tell his story at the end of my Wonderbox show and he was delighted.'

It was an incredible story and one that touched the hearts of the audience when Russ told it on his tour. But then something even more exciting happened. His next stop on the tour was the Motorpoint Arena in Cardiff, where Deryn and his family were living. It wasn't advised for children under sixteen to attend Russell's stand-up shows but there were venues where they could and one of those was Cardiff. Can you guess what happened next? Deryn the Dildo came out on stage!

'He came to the show in Cardiff on that first night [another had been scheduled for December due to popular demand] and he came out on stage dressed as Mr Dildo. There were 5000 people there and it was amazing. Everyone was stood up and were applauding this incredible boy, who was being really fun and really brave. And it was a beautiful end to an amazing evening and that is a bit of stand-up that I will look back on when I'm old, or I'll point someone towards as that's a good bit of work. The emotional involvement and investment is what makes it unique and special.'

Fans who had seen the show could not fail to be moved by the slightly unusual ending – 'The ending sequence is what makes Howard really stand out as a comedian and a person,' revealed one such fan.

But there was one annoying review from that extra-special gig in Cardiff that didn't sit well with Russ. He didn't normally read such feedback, having previously realised how detrimental it was to his state of mind, but this was frustrating. And it made him realise the way the press treated its now famous stars, having helped build them up in the first place.

'So, I got one review after that gig in Cardiff, after that massively emotionally ending. It was a 3-star review. And the thing was, that final story wasn't even mentioned! There was a whole paragraph devoted to a point about me telling a joke about the TV show, *Take Me Out*. "When oh when will we see a comedian not do a joke about *Take Me Out*?" It was something like that. But the thing was, I did one joke about the show, which was only that my brother's main aim in life is to appear on *Take Me Out*, so he can look at all the girls and then go, "Nah!"

'But the lady who did the review had an agenda. She found a chink in the armour, she heard me say the words *Take Me Out* and then went, ching! I have heard lots of comedians talk about that and then devote a whole chunk of the review to that one point. It really fucked me off cos I was like, "did you leave early?" That annoyed me. That is where I feel I am at with the press. I will do stuff that I know was really good and I'm just like, "c'mon!" You would not have been able to walk away from that gig without saying, "OK, Russell might not be my cup of tea but that bit at the end... holy shit!" There wasn't a dry eye in the house. Or you could have said, "I would like to see more of that, if possible". Or "I didn't get the bit at the end, it was too emotional..." I completely get those sort of responses. But when you are literally just commenting on one line, on me basically saying, my brother likes playing pranks, here is an example of that. It wasn't a bit about *Take Me Out*. It was used to illustrate a point,' he told *ComediansComedian*.

But it was important not to stew over such reviews, as he well knew. It was one review and the audience that night, who gave him a complete standing ovation, made up for any bad press – 'I don't dwell on the bad comments. I've found something I like doing in life and people enjoy it. I've got enough personal hatred within me without finding any more. I would just sit there and agree with them – although not that particular review. That was just a load of crap.'

But playing Wembley brought with it a much better review about his performance – which also included a special guest too: 'Russell's grand finale attested to the fact that, despite being one of the country's most successful comedians, Howard has retained a surprising amount of humility,' wrote *Nouse* website. 'It seemed that comedy had taken a back seat in the show, but it soon became apparent that there was a reason Howard had saved this story for his biggest audience. In the climax of the show, the boy came out from backstage wearing the ridiculous costume. Despite the uncharacteristic serious tone which had hung over the show, it was impossible to criticise the moment and the spontaneous standing ovation he received ended the show on a high that comedy could not have achieved.'

In April 2014, it was time to head to London for the Royal Albert Hall. Russ was playing four nights from 14 April... in his T-shirt and jeans. 'If I wore a flash suit I would just sweat through it,' he told *The Bolton News*. Which is probably true as the prestigious venue was already causing a few anxieties... He was driving towards it when he had to take a detour because nerves got the better of him, but as soon as he stepped out on stage, he was on it – 'It feels naughty to swear in here,' he told the audience, following the first 'fuck' he uttered.

'Inside the BBC Three star's Wonderbox is a collection of feel-good stories and proper schoolboy filth,' said *Time Out* magazine. 'In other words, this is much like any other Russell Howard show. He knows where his strengths lie: acting like an overgrown child and gleefully retelling tales of winding up his mum, getting up to mischief and mildly rebelling (think, eating After Eight mints before 8pm). Wonderbox is basically Howard doing what he does best: sharing joyfully funny japes. And considering the show's running gag about finding filth in the most innocent of phrases, we'd be willing to bet the title is just one big in-joke'.

Playing the Royal Albert Hall was memorable enough; playing it and revealing to the audience that your sister had gone into labour was another matter. But that is exactly what happened to Russ when on 14 April he came back from the interval to reveal to the 5,000-strong crowd that Kerry had gone into labour. He got his phone out from his back pocket and read out the text before trying to stay on track and continue his set. At the end of the show he whipped it out again and to his delight, told the audience his sister had given birth to a healthy little boy. They cheered and Russ was beaming with pride about becoming an uncle, adding that his first job in his new role was to make sure his nephew supported Liverpool FC! If sharing this intimate moment with the audience wasn't enough, Russ decided to call his brother-in-law on the phone right there and then and held up the phone to the microphone so that everyone could hear him reveal the name of the new Howard family member: Wesley. It was a generous moment to share with fans and Russ made sure his sister knew how proud he was by asking the entire audience to sing 'Happy Birthday' to Wesley. And there was also a rendition of 'You'll Never Walk Alone' too, which echoed around the Albert Hall as the fans shared in Russ's celebration. It was a wonderfully unique end to his show and one the audience will certainly remember.

In April it was announced that Russ was adding a 'major autumn extension' to the UK leg of his tour. A further eight extra dates had been added for him to play in December that year, including back at The O2 in London, Manchester, Nottingham, Liverpool, Cardiff and Sheffield. These new dates were to be played after he embarked on the worldwide leg of his tour, where he was performing in sold-out gigs in America, Australia and New Zealand.

So, after flying across the Pond at the end of April, he was in Washington, D.C. on 1 May to kick off Wonderbox with his now international audience. There had been a few tweaks to his UK set but the main bulk of his material remained the same and included the Deryn Blackwell story at the end, finishing the gig with a photo of him dressed up as Mr Dildo next to Russell.

Russ took to the stage at the Highline Ballroom in New York City on a Friday night in May. It didn't get off to the best start as his microphone went dead after five minutes. The audience cheered. He picked up another mic and the audience cheered again. Then he admitted to the audience of tough New Yorkers that he was afraid of the dark. And he was cheered again – 'I love doing gigs in America, you cheer at everything,' he grinned. There was also less of a tightly scripted show and more improv. With the venues being smaller than the UK arenas, Russ was able to do a lot of crowd work, location-based jokes and topical stories. The family bits were also in there too – 'Maybe you have an idea that a lot of British people are reserved, but we're not. My family are funny.'

He then told the audience when he once changed his name in his Mum's phone to Barack Obama. So when he called, she seriously answered. 'Barack?' He also told the audience how he loves 'adding' things to her shopping list like 'crystal meth' just so she has to ask a shopkeeper for it. So childish! But he also recounted the time when he was last on tour and staying at a hotel with his mum and someone mistook them for a couple: 'My mum told the waiter I was a male prostitute that she got cheap because my eyes are lazy!' he told the laughing audience.

Acrossthepond.wordpress.com blog loved it: 'I'd heard that Wonderbox has been getting some bad reviews so I wasn't sure what to expect. Okay, so Russell Howard isn't the most innovative and brilliant comic out there, but he was darn funny in this show. Some of the humour was too low brow for my taste – a lot of talking vaginas, dangling willies and poop-jokes – but it never got uncomfortable and it didn't stop being funny'.

After that it was a whirlwind of performances in intimate venues in Chicago, Denver, San Francisco and Los Angeles before Russ flew to Australia seven days later to perform for two nights in Perth, before heading to Melbourne, Brisbane and then on to Sydney. After his gig on 24 May in Sydney, he flew to New Zealand to perform at the Auckland SKYCITY Theatre the following day.

He loved the tour, loved how he was received in America, almost comparing the response he would get here in the UK and back over the Pond, telling *ComediansComedian*: 'In reviews I feel it is easier to slam me here now... I get a lot of three-star reviews. I am at an arc in my career when it's ok to slag you but in America, it is so much fun, they love you. There is an amazing interview that Chris Martin did with Zane Lowe and he basically says how it is quite hard to be a fan of Coldplay now. You get to a certain level of fame and then you're not cool any more. I am like that here but I am shit hot in America. People love Coldplay, so what he has to do is make his stuff so good that the people who liked Coldplay originally can hold their head up high. And that was an amazing way of getting over your feelings of inadequacy. There is something very cool about that. It is a bit like my career. I was Kitson's support in the very early days, that was how I was known. I was a hip comic when I was younger and getting five-star reviews – I remember getting a five-star review in Edinburgh and Ross Noble only got a two. And I thought, that's fucking ridiculous, I am a pale imitation of Ross at this point in time. Now you have lots of people who used to like you – you are no longer their indie album, you have gone platinum and you are now mainstream. I remember being a big fan of Kings of Leon in their early days and then they released "Sex On Fire" and it was a big hit. Everyone heard it and loved them and I was like... but I loved them! And I loved their earlier stuff. You have to make your peace with that sort of thing.'

Back in the UK, there was a big upset in June when the BBC announced it was going to move BBC Three to an online channel. But fans of *Good News* wouldn't just watch the show on an Internet stream, oh no: Russ and his show were being moved to BBC Two.

'It's brilliant news that the wonderfully funny Russell Howard is coming to BBC Two and I very much look forward to welcoming his lively take on modern life to the channel,' said BBC Two controller Kim Shillinglaw.

'Five years ago, BBC Three spotted Russell's great talent, commissioned this brilliantly funny show, nurtured and cherished it and is now passing it on to BBC Two as a fully-fledged hit,' confirmed Mark Linsey, controller of entertainment commissioning.

The new series was due to air on BBC Two in the autumn of 2014 and while Russ was 'really looking forward to the new series', he was also saddened over the move of BBC Three to online status, telling *Metro* in 2016: '*Good News* definitely wouldn't have taken off had it been on-line only. It's a terrible idea, isn't it? They've basically put a TV channel online but it's still a TV channel. It's insane the way they've set it up. My sister has a show and you can only watch it when it's on at 6pm every Friday but who goes on the Internet to go "oh, what's on?" You go on the Internet to find the show you want to watch now. *The Mighty Boosh*, *Gavin & Stacey*, *Little Britain* and *Good News* – it worked because we were on five times a week

and people watched it. You'd drip feed it and catch bits of
it until it became a thing – it was brilliant for little shows
to grow. Now you have to search stuff and if there isn't
a name attached it's really hard to find something. They
could be brilliant shows but they won't get viewed because
they're online.'

But sad as he was about the way BBC Three was now going
to be viewed, he had to concentrate on Series 9 of his *Good
News (GN)* show. It had been over a year since Russ had
worked on the *GN* format but the first episode of that series,
which aired at 10pm on BBC Two on 23 October, was a hit.
Over 1.27 million tuned in to see Russ in his new home and
for the remainder of the nine-episode series, viewing figures
were over 1 million. In November, a YouTube channel was
set up so that fans around the world who couldn't see the
programme live on TV could now watch it legitimately on
the Web. It quickly picked up over 9 million views – with
even some in North Korea.

The YouTube channel was a success although Russ was
frustrated that he couldn't bring *Good News* to US audiences
on TV. After a massively successful Wonderbox Tour –
more dates across the Pond were to be added to extend it
even more the following year – he was certain that it would
prove a hit with American audiences. But he was rejected.
'I have tried so hard, but they don't want me,' he told *BBC
Newsbeat*. 'We've tried to get it to BBC America but they're
not having it. We tried so hard but after my tour of America,
I found that lots of people watch it on YouTube anyway.'

And it was being shown in other countries around the

world, of course – 'It is on in Norway and Australia and New Zealand as well.'

The YouTube channel continued to rack up viewers and by October 2015 it had amassed 11 million global views in more than 180 countries. Allowing fans to legally watch episodes of *Good News* where the show isn't officially broadcast was a huge accolade and it had also been subtitled and uploaded for Chinese viewers as well as those in North Korea and Vatican City.

As well as moving to a mainstream channel back here in Blighty, there was more 'good' TV news that Russ could share with his fans in June 2014... He had been offered two new TV shows. Comedy Central, the digital channel, wanted him to first front a stand-up style show, with Russ performing a new set as well as introducing two other stand-up acts per episode.

The other show had more of a travel/adventure feel to it, but both were still in the developmental stages. Russ had signed the deal for both shows and managing director of Comedy Central, Jill Offman, was ecstatic: 'Ever since I saw Russell Howard's live stand-up show five years ago, it has been my dream to get him on Comedy Central,' she announced in a press release. 'The whole team loves his work and he has massive appeal with our audience. We have some exciting notional views about how the new show will look and feel. Nobody wanted a point-and-shoot stand-up show.'

The new TV deal also meant that the channel had acquired the rights to show all eight series of *Russell Howard's Good News* as well as the yet-to-be-aired ninth and tenth series, making him something of a regular fixture on the TV channel. 'To be able to broadcast his work across several genres: an exclusive stand-up series from here in Camden, comedy travelogues, his popular stand-up and the library for *Russell Howard's Good News* is great news for us and our viewers plus it further demonstrates our commitment to UK content.'

And how was Russ feeling about this new TV deal? 'I'm massively looking forward to these shows. Should be a hoot,' he declared.

And of course there was still that rumour about Russ's film script... What had happened to it? Had it been written? Well, his sister Kerry let the cat out of the bag in October of that year when she revealed that yes, her big bro had put pen to paper for a little rom-com: 'He's written something... I can't really say what it is, but it's a one-off. A rom-com kind of thing. It's brilliant and I'm going to be acting with my brother for the first time, which will be really cool.'

Little sisters, eh? Can't keep anything secret.

So after previously saying he wasn't sure he was a good actor, Russ was to star in his very first film – and one that he had written himself too.

To promote the forthcoming release of his Wonderbox Tour DVD, which was out on 24 November, earlier that month he joined Alan Carr on his hilarious Channel 4 chat show, *Alan Carr: Chatty Man*. 'I don't see you very often, it's nice, isn't it?' gushed Al as he poured the drinks. 'Your show about news must be hard because the world is so grim at the moment, isn't it? The world has gone to shit!'

'Sometimes in amongst the horror there are moments of

genuine British madness and that is what I look forward to,' explained Russ.

Alan confirmed that Russ would be 'hitting the road on tour again for the second half of [his] Wonderbox tour' and wanted to know what Wonderbox meant. Russ explained it wasn't another word for magic vagina, as one heckler had asked. And then talk turned to his guns – again.

'Look at 'em!' shrieked Carr after showing a clip from the Wonderbox DVD. 'They look like they have gone down a bit now though.'

Russ shrugged before telling the chat-show host: 'I swim, I run, I go to the gym... I juice! I remember the first time I went to the gym. It's really intimating, isn't it? There was a little machine and I didn't know what it did. And I went over to this machine and started rowing on it for a bit, then stood up, and a man went over and said under his breath, "dick." And started doing bicep pull-ups with the machine. It was a low moment.'

Back on the road in December 2014 for the additional dates of his Wonderbox Tour was an extra-special moment for Russ: he would be hitting his final locations in style, Dolly Parton style – 'The coolest thing about that is my friend Kumar, who's my tour manager, used to tour manage Dolly Parton. So we've got a cheap deal on Dolly Parton's tour bus. It has a shower in it. And a bath. It's incredible,' he told *Radio1 Newsbeat*.

But there was one aspect of touring that he found irritating: audience members recording him – 'I guess some people do record bits of my gigs on their phone. I don't really check it,

I'm not that fussed, but I do think, I would never do that. I think it must be a generational thing. I'd rather be in the here and now but it's really interesting where a lot of people want to say, "I'm at this thing, wish you were here, it's great" and you think, "Well, you're not really here, just put your phone down for a bit and BE here." I would always turn my phone off when I'm at a gig or the cinema. I'd rather concentrate than try and capture a grainy image. I think it's better when it lives in the memory.'

Chapter 21

A GERT LUSH CHAPTER

*'The idea of me writing a comedy drama seemed so absurd but
me and my mate Steve thought, "oh sod it, let's try!" I wanted to write
something about family and Christmas seemed a cool theme.'*
RH

The year 2015 was going to be a busy one. At the end of
March it was officially announced that Russ and his
sister Kerry were to star in a Christmas film together. Kerry
had pretty much given the game away the previous year but
now it was official, everyone wanted to know what was
happening. *A Gert Lush Christmas* was due to start filming
soon and was set in a fictitious West Country town. It was
set to air on BBC Two in December of that year and Russ
and his mate Steve Williams, who writes for *Good News*,
had written the script together.

'My sister is going to be in it, which is good,' confirmed
Russ. Kerry was equally full of praise for her elder sibling –

'It's brilliant, I am going to be acting with my brother for the first time, which will be really cool.'

There was also a house move to add to the mix that year as Russ and his girlfriend Cerys moved from Leamington Spa to Camden, north London, which for the first time was more geared to Russ's career as the Comedy Central show was filmed round the corner from their new home. They settled into life in London quickly, Cerys had become a qualified doctor and Russ realised there were benefits to being in a capital full of crazy stars rather than being the only famous face in Warwickshire.

He told *The Standard*: 'I live in London now and am enjoying it very much. I don't get hassled as much here as I do in the West Country, where people go kerrazee. In Camden, no one gives a flying fuck. The other day I was walking Archie and I had to quickly scoop him up when I saw a rabbit being taken for a walk on a lead by a man in head-to-toe leather. When there are people like that around, nobody is going to notice me. My mum and dad live in Bath now and when I go there it's pretty full-on. I was walking past a flower shop there and the owner saw me and said, "Come in! Could we get a photo for all the girls who work here who like you?" Then she asked something like, "Do you think our flowers look nice?" And I said, "Yeah, they look lovely." Then the next day it's in the fucking paper! I was endorsing this flower shop! "Howard says flowers look lovely." Apparently that was front-page news. It was funny. But I very much doubt that would happen in Camden. A photo of me outside Argos? That wouldn't make the front page of *The London Evening Standard*.'

But he was back in Bath, albeit briefly, when he took part in the Bath Half Marathon. On 1 March, he donned his running gear and hit the streets for the thirteen-mile half marathon. Russ was running for the charity, Time Is Precious, which works with sick children and their families in Bristol, Bath and Yeovil hospitals. He was initially asked by his cousin, Lewis Cox, to join the fundraising team: 'When we managed to get some extra places in this year's Bath Half, Lewis asked if he could have a place for his cousin but we didn't know who his cousin was,' confessed Nicky Halford, who set up the charity with her husband Neil in memory of their young son, Ben. 'We welcomed Russ on board and are glad he is behind our efforts.'

And as is tradition when Russ embarks on a physical challenge, his training is thorough. 'I had some porridge this morning, so I think that's going to push me to the finish line,' he told a charity reporter before the race. 'I just want to do it and raise a bunch of money for the charity really, but Lewis is worried about taking a poo round the course so we are going to knock on a little old lady's door and I will have to ask, "Excuse me, can my cousin take a poo in your toilet?"'

Poos and porridge aside, Russ finished in a very respectable time of one hour forty-four minutes. He became a patron of the charity after that and agreed to run the Bristol Half Marathon again – even though he did get hit on the backside by a lady pensioner who jogged past him and muttered, 'That's good news!'

Experiences like that were perfect material for his new stand-up show on Comedy Central, which now had a confirmed start date of 29 April 2015. The channel also announced that it would be a ten-part series with a headline and support act each week. The show was currently being filmed at the Electric Ballroom nightclub in Camden, which gives that great comedy club intimacy feel for both audience and performer.

'I'm really looking forward to hosting the show, we've got loads of great new comics on,' gushed Russ. 'It's me and a bunch of brilliant stand-ups from the circuit telling jokes in a tiny club. There are ten episodes and I do five or six minutes of stand-up per show so it's basically like writing ten singles. Everything has to start with, "Hello! Here's the thing: Funny! Funny! Funny! First act!" It's been quite a challenge.'

The line-up for the first series was announced as including: Doc Brown, Roisin Conaty, Rob Delaney (Channel 4's *Catastrophe*), Carl Donnelly, Nick Helm, Alex Horne, Joe Wilkinson, Katherine Ryan, Andrew Maxwell and Sara Pascoe. With Russ loving audience interaction as he does, part of the show would be him answering questions from the audience. They would write down their questions to him before the show and he would pick them out of a box at random and answer. It was a risky but hilarious feature and for a performer as skilled as Russ, a highlight of his stand-up sequence.

The first episode, which also featured stand-ups Sara Pascoe and Nish Kumar, went out on 29 April at 10pm and was watched by 100,000 viewers. One of the funniest angles was Russ's audience interaction – including insulting one stegosauru-loving punter. He pulled out a question from the box and read: 'My name is Tia and I am a Stegasuarus.'

'OK,' giggled Russ. 'I will probably pull out the next one and it will say, "Hi, my name is Roger and I am Tia's carer."'

Then a voice from the front row shouted out, 'I met you before!' Russell moved over and spoke to the woman – 'I do remember you before but I don't remember you telling me you were a reptile?' he queried. 'I am disabled though!' shouted back the woman, and the man next to her then piped up, 'And I'm her carer.' At which point Russell collapsed on stage and writhed about: 'Did you see that bit on telly the other day when Russell Howard's career ended? It was amazing!' he groaned.

A much-anticipated new show for Russ, it proved a big hit. Fans loved it, as did the critics: 'Viewers will tune in for Howard but will hopefully have their comic horizons expanded by the support acts,' wrote *Chortle*. 'His name might be in the title – and his face on all those buses and posters – a safe, known factor proved to pull in the viewers. But his contribution to the show is only a few minutes of upbeat ice-breaking. That allows his guest comedians the lion's share of the timeslot. The only real twist is that rather than simply perform a typically feel-good observation routing, much of Howard's time is spent answering questions from the audience. This gives a feeling of spontaneity, even if a cynic might think that his slick responses to some of the questions mean they might not entirely be a surprise to him'.

But it was a hit and by the end of the run – the final episode of the series, which was broadcast on 8 July – another series had been commissioned for the following year due to the massive success: 'If you like Russell Howard but are a little tired of his *Good News* shtick, then it's good news (if you will excuse the repetition) for you as this series sees him return to more traditional stand-up, which is where he really shines,' observed *Radio Times*. 'Losing the fussy extras lets the comedian do what he does best – make us laugh.'

In May 2015, as if he wasn't busy enough, Russell announced that he had added more dates to his Wonderbox Tour in America and Canada. It would run from 24 June to 11 July and he would visit Toronto, New York, Boston, Chicago, Los Angeles, Philadelphia, Washington, D.C., Nashville, Denver, Portland, Seattle and Toronto. To promote the American leg of the tour, he went on *The Tonight Show with Jimmy Fallon* at the beginning of August, his second time on a late-night American chat show. He performed a tight five-minute set that basically made fun of his mum for being so hilariously mad and gullible and told the 'whooping' audience of the many pranks he liked to play on her. It was a cunning move, not that his set didn't always involve jokes about his mum, but with a travel show planned for the following year around his tour and with talks reportedly that it might involve his mum, Ninette, it was a good idea to whet the American audience's appetite for Mrs Howard.

And then of course there was the return of *Russell Howard's Good News*, now in its new home on BBC Two, having made the successful transfer from BBC Three. It was now in its tenth series and *The Guardian* wrote something interesting about its return, which, in hindsight, could not have been more wrong: 'This light, slight, topical comedy magazine may not have produced many enduring moments but it stubbornly refuses to go away. So what is Howard's secret? He is a beige presence and unlikely to ever really polarise opinion. He seems equally unlikely to ever really distinguish himself but maybe he's just emblematic of this particular cultural moment'.

On 22 October, on the first show of the tenth series of *Good News*, Russell touched on the plight of junior doctors who were protesting about pay cuts and proposed changes to their contracts, which would see them working longer hours. After showing footage of them out on a protest march, he made his feelings clear... And they weren't beige. He told the audience that he understood why junior doctors, who he described as 'amazing, selfless human beings,' are annoyed at working as hard as they do for such a low wage. He then compared that to the large 10 per cent pay rise that MPs got earlier that year. Russ continued his heartfelt monologue by listing all the things that makes the NHS wonderful – free heart-bypass surgery, free liver transplants, and so on – before concluding that he believed the NHS deserves our support and Jeremy Hunt should not be asking them to work for longer hours for less money.

It was a passionate, heartfelt speech and although Russ had dipped into more serious tones before, this was a direct, no-holds-barred opinion coming straight to the viewers and studio audience. The episode was watched by just over 1 million viewers and Russ's call to arms highlighting the plight of junior doctors struck a chord. Before too long, the clip of his passionate speech had gone viral, amassing 6.3 million views on Facebook alone and had been shared over 100,000 times on the social networking site.

The press were also quick to report his monologue backing junior doctors and calling Health Secretary Jeremy Hunt a 'bell-end'. *The Independent* reported: 'Russell Howard might be better known for his self-deprecating stand-up but the comic has used his platform to back NHS staff over the proposed government cuts to junior doctors' pay. Howard, whose girlfriend Cerys is a doctor, said he was also really pissed off with the negative portrayal of doctors in the media'.

The Huffington Post noted: 'Russell Howard has launched a scathing and hilarious attack on the government over the junior doctors' row', while Twitter went into meltdown, with comments like, '@russellhoward brilliant! You just got 53k #juniordoctor fans & several 1000s more of us who care about them & #nhs'.

If there had been a shift in his comedy, the audience were aware of it and it marked the start of Russell being regarded as more of a serious, topical star. The comedian had used his platform to highlight some very valid points in what he regarded as a grave injustice, telling *ComediansComedian*: 'I think my comedy now is better than ever, the last series [of *Good News*] is the best stuff I've ever done consistently. It was a really strong series and lots of really big topics that we dealt with in a really funny way. The junior doctor bit, for example, 12 million people have seen that clip now. It was crazy but we connected with the nation in a way we haven't before. I would like to do that more. My last stand-up show was my best too. Now I want to do stand-up with a nod to the stuff I've done on *Good News*. So fucking hell, did you hear about this? I want to figure out a way of doing that but still keeping it light-hearted.'

So the first episode of the new series certainly, and quite rightly, got people talking. And Russ was now being asked about it in the interviews he appeared in since that airing. And he was happy to continue with his rant: 'Junior doctors are upset with the Government and every story about the NHS in the right-wing press is how much doctors get paid,' he told *NME*. 'The truth is, the NHS is an amazing institution and we should never let it die. Secretary of State for Health Jeremy Hunt wrote a book [*Direct Democracy*] on how to dismantle the NHS and now he's in charge of it!'

He even got a massive round of applause from the audience when he appeared on the *Alan Carr: Chatty Man* chat show in November, to talk about the series. He'd only been on the show the previous year and Carr opened with much the same question as he had done then – how much rubbish the news was at that moment. Russ's face showed that he wasn't exactly impressed with this lazy repetitiveness but he went with it.

'The news...' shrieked Alan, 'it's just so grim right now! You've got Syria, refugees, 5p for a carrier bag... The world has gone to shit! It must be tough for you to find a) news to get comedy out of and b) good news!'

'But there are bits of wonder in the world,' explained the

ever-positive Russ. 'There was a piece of news about a bus driver from Barnsley who had put up a notice in his bus, saying, "bell not working, if you want to stop, just shout "ding ding". Wonderful, isn't it? And I think a lot of people are interested in politics these days too. We did a thing about the NHS and it went mental.'

The audience started applauding before he had even finished, knowing exactly what he was talking about.

'Young people in particular are fascinated by this and they really want to protect the NHS and are probably slightly pissed off that MPs had an 11 per cent pay rise in the same year they were trying to give junior doctors a pay cut.'

At this the audience and Alan clapped wholeheartedly.

Russ also denied rumours that he was taking *Good News* to America, stating that although he'd like to do it, he thought they had enough comedy news shows. It was a subject he'd been questioned about before in an interview with *Digital Spy* and he simply stated that his pal, John Oliver, already had that section of the market with his show on HBO: *Last Week Tonight with John Oliver*.

'I just don't see where *Good News* would fit – they already have their version of it. They've sort of got that sewn up. I'm good mates with John Oliver and I think those guys, including Stephen Colbert, are very good at that kind of thing.'

Then talk turned to Christmas and Alan shared the news that he, of course, had once been in a film – well, the voice for one character in *The SpongeBob SquarePants Movie*. But Russell could trump that: 'I am going to be acting in *A Gert Lush Christmas*. I wrote a film and it's on at Christmas. It's about my character bringing a girl home for Christmas and his family are mental and much hilarity ensues. It was good fun,' he told Carr.

Promoting the film was equally fun as most of the publicity was done with Kerry – who was very praising of her big brother and his acting skills: 'The whole experience was amazing and it turns out he is a really good actor. Because he's a stand-up and I'm an actress, our paths have never really collided. Now the roles have kind of changed around and he was asking me for guidance. His natural trick is to improvise and that's where he gets his comic flair, but I kept telling him to trust his script and commit to what he'd written, because it's amazing. I'm playing his sister, Julie, who's a hairdresser and blonde with bleached teeth and it's not me, so it's a bit weird. But when I first read it, it's just a beautiful piece – it's really a love letter to our mum and dad. The mother character is definitely a love letter to our mum.'

The sixty-minute film was due to air on Boxing Day 2015 and also starred an array of famous faces like Sophie Thompson, Neil Morrissey and Greg Davis. Kerry and Russell went on Channel 4's *Sunday Brunch* to talk about the film and being a typical brother and sister, played up to the grown-ups in the room.

'So I wrote a film and I thought Kerry could play the role of my sister as she has played it very well for thirty-five years,' smirked Russ.

'Thirty-five years?' spluttered Kerry. 'Thirty-*three*, thank you very much!'

'Greg Davis is in it, he's my uncle. Neil Morrissey is my

dad and it's about our family,' continued Russ. 'Basically, my character brings his girlfriend home to meet his family, and they ruin it and then it all comes together at the end. It's really good. It's a beautiful rom-com.'

Talk then turned to the title of the film and what the phrase 'gert lush' meant. For those outside the Bristol area, Kerry was happy to explain: 'It means really amazing really. Like there is a sandwich shop that is called Gert Lush Sandwiches. So you say "gert lush" is something wonderful – "Ooh, that Hubba Bubba is gert lush!"'

To round up the Christmas promo, Russ also announced that he had planned to go on tour again in 2017, as in 2016 he would be travelling across America with his mum, Ninette, on a new TV travel show called *Russell Howard & Mum: USA Road Trip.*

'Get ready for her big time,' explained Kerry. 'She'll be on this show soon.'

'It's a travelogue with Mum and she's far more entertaining that I could be. I'm slightly worried about what I'm going to unleash,' confirmed Russ, during the *Sunday Brunch* interview..

'She's losing her mind about it,' agreed Kerry. 'She's already working out whether she's got time to do *Loose Women*!'

And the reality of working with his sister on set sometimes brought about its own hilarity... as you can imagine: 'On the first day of filming I walked past Kerry and clicked my fingers at her to make a cup of tea, which is a joke we do in our house,' confessed Russ. 'Sophie didn't know that we were related so she spent the first two days just thinking I was really rude! Julie, the character that Kerry plays, is an amalgamation of loads of my cousins. They're all really giddy about the show. They can't wait to tell their friends the character is based on them – they're fighting over it.'

And for an extra Christmas present that year, if you couldn't get enough of a Russ fix in his rom-com, in repeats of Stand Up Central, or old re-runs of *Good News*, and you didn't get a copy of his DVD in your stocking, you could always ring up the NHS phoneline to hear his familiar tones. Russ agreed to take part in a new campaign that would see him 'talk' to callers as they waited on hold. Instead of the familiar musical jingle, callers would be treated to a message from the funny man as part of the NHS Blood and Transplant's Organ Donation Campaign, The Wait – 'Thanks for calling, your call's in a queue and it will be answered shortly,' says the message, 'But while we are waiting consider this – some people have been waiting for an organ transplant for years due to a lack of donors'.

And Russ was honoured to be involved: 'No one likes being put on hold but it is really just a short amount of time compared to the wait endured by thousands of people due to a lack of organ donors. It takes just two minutes to sign up to the NHS Organ Donor Register and one day you could save or improve up to nine lives,' he told *The Mirror*.

Chapter 22
MUM'S THE WORD

'No matter what I put in front of my mum, I love the sheer madness that tumbles out of her mouth. At the end she told me she'd learnt something about herself, it was that one of her armpits smells more than the other.'
RH

So *A Gert Lush Christmas* was aired on Boxing Day 2015 and you can imagine the whole Howard clan sitting around the TV set, watching the episode together. It was a 'properly lovely moment,' gushed the sentimental star. But the reviews weren't exactly filled with Christmas cheer: '*A Gert Lush Christmas* was one of this year's festive highlights but fell flat,' declared *Custard TV*. 'A lot of the blame for what went wrong can be attributed to Russell Howard's one-note performance as well as his poorly-paced script.'

And unfortunately, there was someone closer to home

who liked to remind Russ about the highlights of his career at the same time as his failings – his nan. He told *ComediansComedian*: 'I am the frontman for my family, I guess. The only pressure I feel is from my nan. She has a wall with every poster, every clipping, every interview that she's ever seen of me on it. She would have the calendar if I had done one! She will cut stuff/things out that she sees in the paper, including one terrible review for a film we did at Christmas, and it's up on her wall. It was from the *Bristol Evening Post* and it says, "Russell Howard's Christmas Comedy got it horribly wrong". Yes, my "comedy offering got it horribly wrong" is smack in the middle of that wall. The pressure I feel is that I had to do a good show because if the reviews aren't good enough, I'm going to be looking at it on my nan's kitchen wall!'

Sadly, it wasn't just *The Bristol Evening Post* that didn't see the funny side, as can be seen from the review from *Custard TV* quoted above. But the bad press didn't deter Russ and he admitted he wouldn't ever 'say never' to writing a follow-up to the rom-com or working with his sis again, telling *Radio Times*: 'I'd love to do stuff with Kezza but I'll be struggling to book her! That was the cool thing about working with her, I didn't realise how talented she was and I was like, "Holy god, my sister is a lot better than me! But I'm the older one, I'm meant to be the bestest..." I'd love to write a proper film, that'd be great. I'm kind of working on a few ideas for a proper cinema film but I have so much on at the moment, that it's really hard to write, but fun. It's so different from stand-up because you don't know whether it's good until you've finished. Whereas, with stand-up, you do loads of little gigs to move it along so yeah, I'd love to do a film.'

It was around Christmas and New Year that year that his mum Ninette revealed how she was worried about getting older and being forgotten. But Russ had an idea: 'Mum said she didn't want to end up in an old folks' home where they slap her, which was so bleak and such a depressing bucket list that I thought I'd give her lots of memories before the beatings start,' he admitted to *Radio Times*. 'When Comedy Central asked me to do a travel show I said I'd like to go with my mum. I told her we'd be two weeks and we were two months.' Oh yes, Russ's mum was about to be unleashed on TV... Was the world ready?

Aside from the negative stuff about *A Gert Lush Christmas*, there was a bit of light relief in January 2016 when Russ took part in a boob-ball competition. The event was similar to dodgeball but it used rubber breasts instead of the usual balls.

Hmm, I wonder why he signed up to that?

Actually, it was all in the name of charity and the charity in question – CoppaFeel! – had featured on his *Good News* show the previous year. The cancer-awareness charity had set up a 'boob-ball' event in London's Olympic Park and Russ agreed to take part: 'It all began when our founder, Kristin Hallenga, wanged Russell in the face with a flying boob on national TV. A dream was born. That dream was CoppaFeel! Celebrity Boob Ball,' the charity confirmed.

Good old Russ, always happy to make a right tit out of himself.

Boobs aside, he was back on *The Jonathan Ross Show* in March for a more memorable experience that included pretending to be a West Country Darth Vader to read a script with the late Carrie Fisher. Then there were the England rugby players that he joined in tackling with Wossy. Just another regular chat-show appearance really. But it did give him the chance to talk about the travel show he was about to embark on with his mum. Their relationship was such a heart-warming one – he had been asked so many times in interviews if she minded being the butt of his jokes and the answer every time was a big fat NO. Never has, and never will – 'For my mum to see her son on stage telling jokes about her is fucking mind-blowing. I am very aware how lucky I am to be able to do that and make her feel good. No one likes my stuff more than my mum. She is a big fan.'

Comedians travelling with their mothers isn't a new thing (Romesh Ranganathan's *Asian Provocateur* (BBC Three) was filmed with his mum, Shanthi, and on its second series and Baz Ashmawy starred with his mum, Nancy, in the Emmy award-winning third series, *50 Ways To Kill Your Mammy*, for Sky1) but Comedy Central director Jill Offman was keen to put a new spin on this show, declaring: 'The celebrity travel genre is well worn, so we'll be looking at turning that on its head and being super ambitious.'

And it was hard to tell who was more excited about the project – and knowing what we know about Ninette (who now liked to refer to the pair of them as a double-act), who would be funniest? 'I am so super careful that I don't want her to be the butt of the joke every episode. I just want her to be natural,' revealed Russ before filming. 'It's a fun way of doing a show, exploring all the different layers of America with my mum. She is so unbelievably excited about the thought of getting recognised in the streets and she actually said to me, "Do you think this will lead to chat shows?" So I said, "I don't know, maybe," and she said, "Yeah, I'd quite like to do Jonathan Ross but I don't know about Norton because he has the same stars every week. I like Alan [Carr] too," she said.'

The show began its run on 19 October 2016 and the first episode saw mum and son alien hunting in Nevada. If you thought that was wacky, the following week they met Preppers – people who are all set for Armageddon – and learnt survival skills so they were ready to face the Zombie Apocalypse. Then there was rapping with a hip-hop gang in Atlanta, ghost hunting in Savannah, where Russell was convinced something brushed past his leg when there wasn't anything there (they both spent the night at Savannah's Most Haunted House and he ended up sleeping with his mum in her bed). Then it was time to visit South Carolina, where Russ was taking part in the All-American Demolition Derby while Ninette commentated in front of the 4,000-strong crowd. And finally, in the last episode of the series, they visited the Big Apple to work at a posh pooch hotel... and end up clearing up dog shit.

'I played at the O2,' moaned Russ, after scooping up his first dog mess of the day.

The series was a hit with fans and critics alike and if nothing else, we saw for our own eyes the bond between Russ and his mum, a genuine, fun, lovely yet mad relationship. There were several times when they were mistaken for a couple, which started to frustrate Russ but there were several things he learnt about his ma too while making the series – 'She keeps a hula hoop under the sofa, and when she hoovers she makes up songs which are sometimes so sad, they make her cry.'

Ninette didn't get to appear on a chat show to talk about the series – although she was on Radio 1's *Greg James Show* and she did make a special guest appearance on *8 Out of 10 Cats Does Countdown* as Russ's lucky mascot – but she did find fame in her hometown. 'She gets recognised at the garden centre now,' confirmed Russ. 'And funnily enough, she keeps needing more plants.' Ninette also continued to appear in Russ's stand-up sketches and his trip to the States with his mum got a mention when he took part in *Michael McIntyre's Big Show* on BBC One in November 2016: 'I was in an elevator in America with my mum. There was a woman also in there, who just started laughing so I asked her why. And she said, "Sugar, has anyone ever told you, you look like Ellen?" Everyone in the elevator started laughing too. And my mum looked at me and said, "She's got a point, Russ. You do look like a powerful lesbian!" My mum lives for those moments, she lives to embarrass me.'

Even more sadly for Russ, he was actually going for the Ryan Gosling look.

While viewers could watch the Russ-and-mum combo and their travels across the Pond (and there were, according to one review, five good reasons not to miss the show including the fact that there were more innuendos than *The Great British Bake Off*, which takes some beating, surely?), earlier in the year he also welcomed back the second series of *Russell Howard's Stand Up Central* at the end of May 2016. There were some big stars wanting to take part in the latest series – including Jimmy Carr and Katherine Ryan – and Russ was hugely excited: 'There's a bunch of people that I've recommended and then there's a bunch of people that the channel want that are more often than not younger comics that I haven't been aware of, so it's the best of both worlds. Tommy Tiernan is an Irish comic who, I believe, is one of the finest in the world. The set he did was absolutely riveting. He is a spellbinding comic and it was a pleasure to share a stage with him. I spent two hours on stage, doing bits, bantering with the crowd, ramping them up, being the compere and sometimes the guests backstage are terrified. Tommy could have done an hour, he is a phenomenal performer. He was watching the whole gig at the side of the stage too, taking it in, being in the room, steadying himself leading up to the moment he went out to unleash his performance.'

Answering questions from the audience, as part of Russell's audience banter that the guest comics didn't have to deal with – 'it's just like a club gig, I introduce them and they come on and smash it' – was probably the most popular part of the show. And often caused the most hilarity, too. Russ was adamant there was no sneaky glances beforehand – he wasn't afraid to answer any of the questions that he read out even if that meant some, er, potentially embarrassing situations: 'I don't give a fuck if the question is too rude or too shocking. They're always weird and wonderful and strange and it goes where it goes. One of the weirdest questions this year was, "In space, do astronauts engage in sexual activities on their own?" Rather bizarrely, there was an astronaut and a pervert in the audience who confirmed it was a definite yes. And it turns out they do and they just get rid of it all when they're done by throwing it out of the shuttle.'

Then there was the show that saw Russ kiss another woman – yep, in front of thousands of people on TV and a jeering comedy club audience. Not that girlfriend Cerys had any cause to worry, it was the woman's birthday – 'There was a 49-year-old woman who said she'd never been kissed... by a comedian on her birthday. So I rectified that. That was a fairly awkward moment. And it was awkward for her as well because her son was watching and apparently I looked a bit like her son. So it was awkward all round. We didn't do full-on tongue, it was just a peck, but it was enough to break their family, I think.'

Amid all the fun and banter, there was a definite shift in Russ's comedy style. As well as the usual family fodder, he was aware of how much of a reaction he received from his previous serious monologues – the junior doctors' strike, for example – and wanted to include more: 'I guess the latest bunch of stuff is possibly a bit angrier than other stand-up, but then the last series of *Russell Howard's Good News* was more ranty. It got me quite fired up. Archie [his dog] has been on two NHS marches.'

There was also adult colouring in, jellyfish attacks, patriotism that made up the eclectic show, and of course, the furore over Tesco and their croissants: 'I won't twist anything too much, I won't make stuff up – I don't think like that. There was a routine I had that I did on Comedy Central which was basically, I had read in a newspaper that Tesco no longer do curved croissants, they only sell straight ones because enough people wrote to Tesco to complain they couldn't put jam on a curved croissant. You just couldn't make that stuff up!'

It was a routine he repeated on *Michael McIntyre's Big Show* too, such was the uproar in Howard's mind over the croissant shape. But the joke might not have worked on a simple stand-up routine. Or indeed, some of the improv which works so well in the intimate comedy club would not work for filming. And Russ was well aware of such limitations, telling *Comedy.co.uk* website: 'What works in the room sometimes doesn't work at home. It's about trying to connect with someone sat bored on their sofa, watching TV, and I think that's harder sometimes. Sometimes improv doesn't work on TV because the audience had heard the thing that was shouted and they're very much alive, the audience in the room – they're alive in that moment. Whereas the audience sat at home on the sofa, that feels like a part of the party they haven't been invited to. *Stand Up Central* has to be performed for the person at home through the live audience so it's kind of a weird thing. You have two very different audiences in mind when you're doing it.'

As well as 2016 being a year of stand-ups, TV shows and American adventures with his mum, there was a very important birthday Russell wanted the whole family to celebrate. His dad turning sixty was cause for a big celebration – or in the Howard clan case, a big family holiday. Russell paid for his entire family to travel to Australia to celebrate David's birthday and it was, in Russ's words, all thanks to 'comedy' – 'It is really rare to be sat around with everyone you love and think, jokes did this. But I would never say that because I would look like a tool. It was the most amount of money I have ever spent. I still like to live like a student, and the holiday was for a month, which was a big hit financially. It was worth it, though. It was my dad's 60th and it was his dream destination. We are renting a house on the beach in Byron Bay,' he told *The Telegraph*.

Seeing it was his dad who first encouraged his dreams of wanting to be a comic, it seemed like a fitting tribute to the man who isn't mentioned quite so much as his mum in his stand-up although he has a big presence in Russ's life: 'I was talking to Dad about fame before it was his birthday, and we were walking along and this guy came up to me and said, "Mate, I love you" and then walked off. And my dad said, "That's all right, isn't it?"'

'Dad nailed it. There is no self-doubt, no feelings of inadequacy – which we all get – when people come up to you and say unbelievably kind things to you. You can't thank them enough for being so kind. English people don't really talk to strangers so for someone to go out of their way and say something nice, they have no idea of how lovely that is.'

There was no denying the close relationship Russ enjoyed with his family. They were talked about, laughed about, celebrated on stage – from his mum to his grandparents to his mad cousins. He was once asked who should play him if they ever made a film about his life and without a pause, he said his grandad, as he is the funniest man he knows... which made the world a much sadder place for him when, at the beginning of November 2016, his grandad died. It was to be something that would form a part of his Round the World Tour the following year, just as it should. The serious tone reflects his more thoughtful attitude to performing: 'I've made a real effort to do things that I care about so there is Islamic State, self-harm, politics... My grandad died on the day [Donald] Trump was elected so a big part of the show is how Trump arrived just as a kind man left. I'm trying to find something good in an awful world,' he told the *Belfast Telegraph* in 2017.

Chapter 23

AND NOW, THE END IS NEAR...

'Ol' Blue Eyes beaten by young wonky eyes... it's ridiculous.
I'd rather have had a couple of nights off, to be honest.'
RH

So here's some bad news for you... *Good News* was unlikely to return to our screens for 'the foreseeable future,' announced the BBC in November 2016. So would this have anything to do with Sky1 signing Russ up for a two-year deal, perhaps? Comedy Central had one more *Russell Howard & Mum: USA Road Trip* to air when the pair went back on the road in 2017. Meanwhile, Sky were hinting the new show they had lined up for the comic might have more of a 'chat show' feel to it.

'Russell is brilliantly funny and I can't wait for his intelligent and incisive wit to be a big part of Sky1,' confirmed Adam MacDonald, director of Sky1, in November 2016. 'His new show with us will be a fantastic mix of everything we love about Russell.'

So were the rumours true? Would he be the next Wossy? Erm, not quite...

'It'll probably be a souped-up *Good News*. The idea of having Little Mix doing their single is not what I want to do, I want to focus on the things in the last series of *Good News* when I did things about the NHS. These were things people cared about, so I think it would be wrong to do a fluffy show,' said the man himself.

But the new show was still a while away. There was the small matter of a world tour to consider first – a world tour that was, quite literally, taking Russ around the world – thirty-six international cities, no less, as part of his new mammoth Round the World Tour. No funny word titles this time, no German meanings or book extracts – Round the World: Live Tour. It did exactly what it said on the tin, as it were: 10 nights at the Royal Albert Hall, 12 arenas nationwide across the UK and a further 36 international cities and then dates in the US (18 gigs across America), the United Arab Emirates, Canada, Australia and New Zealand, Europe, China, Hong Kong and Singapore and most of Scandinavia. Quite the seasoned traveller!

'It is both exciting and scary, I guess,' Russ told *Digital Spy*. 'New experiences, new cultures and new things to talk about. It's just a joy travelling with your job. You get to wander around these interesting cities and then things happen to you and it's much better than having a holiday diary because you just go on stage and chat about what's happened. That's what I love about it.'

And China? Yes, you read that right. Russ was joining a very small group of English-speaking comics in China when he performed at the Mercedes-Benz Arena in Shanghai – 'It was bizarre... I was told I was a cult hit in China and would I like to do some gigs there? What else can you say except yes! I reckon I can probably sell about 200 tickets, which isn't bad in a country of 1.37bn,' he confirmed. 'My mum asked me if I was doing it in English. I was like, "We've known each other for many years, Mum. You might have thought once I might have let slip if I knew rudimentary Cantonese."'

World domination could be looming for Russ. Thanks to his YouTube channel, which posted sketches and sometimes whole episodes of his *Good News Show* and stand-up clips, audiences across the globe were able to see him in action. In China, the clips were translated and spread around Chinese social media, making him extremely popular and in-demand.

'We had to film the set I am going to do in China so the Government can check it beforehand. But it was a gig in Swindon so I am not sure whether people in China will understand why I am talking about Wiltshire, the Wyvern Centre, the local swimming pool and the roundabout system so much! It's so odd that all these Chinese officials will be watching the show, wondering what a roundabout is. And why is it magic? I also found out that my *Good News* show has a big following in North Korea and the Vatican City! Who knew Kim-Jong-un and the Pope liked fast-paced satire?' he added.

Plugging his tour on Facebook and Twitter and making Internet footage to encourage punters to buy tickets –

'People of Dubai, I would very much like you to come to my gig on 20, 21 or 22 April. I would like you to come otherwise it's going to be really shit' – Russ didn't have to do a lot to achieve the 'sell-out' shows he had enjoyed in the past. The only difference now was that he was selling out shows all over the globe. And yet one of the places he was going to make history was back in the UK, in London, at the Royal Albert Hall. Legenary crooner Frank Sinatra had played eight consecutive nights in the 1970s, mega singer-songwriter Barry Manilow joined him in the record books for eight nights in 1993, but Russ went two better: he was on that stage for ten nights and therefore achieved the record for the most consecutive performances by an artist. 'Ol' Blue Eyes beaten by young wonky eyes... it's ridiculous. I'd rather have had a couple of nights off, to be honest,' he grinned as he was awarded a framed photo of himself performing on the famous stage.

Remember those dreams years ago of even stepping on the boards at the Royal Albert Hall? Now he was making history at one of the most prestigious venues in the country. What next? World domination? Prime Minister? Or simply, making people laugh, as was the idea behind the Round the World Tour. The aim for the show was to offer 'a giggle in the gloom' – and it certainly was. Rewriting the national anthem in homage to the NHS, examples of Health & Safety gone mad, the joy and foolishness that can be round in the everyday, that is his stock-in-trade. Then there was stuff about his family, which always got the most heartfelt reactions – even when he disclosed that he had also recently lost his nan as well as his grandad. And as fans listened to stories of nan waking herself up farting on Christmas Day it felt right for the audience to mourn a little too. But there was so much celebrate as well – like the fact that Russ was no longer King of the Mingers in the *Heat* readers' poll, now he had made it to No. 23 in the Weird Crush list – Hodor from *Game of Thrones* was 24 and Piers Morgan was 25.

'Does that mean I'm weirder than Hodor and Piers Morgan?' he quipped.

The tour kicked off right where it should, in Bristol at the Hippodrome, with a home crowd bursting with pride. After that he moved to Dublin for one of the more intimate venues on the schedule before beginning his run at the Albert Hall on 1 March 2017. Then it was the Cardiff, Birmingham, Glasgow and Aberdeen crowds who would be enjoying his material. In fact, on 23 March, Comic Relief night, he would be on stage in Aberdeen as millions of fans around the UK watched his touching report on Ebola when he visited Liberia in one of the pre-recorded video segments for the mammoth fundraiser.

He spoke about his time as part of the Comic Relief team on BBC *Breakfast* news and appeared emotionally drained after the experience: 'I was out in Liberia with a charity called Street Child Liberia, which goes to see people affected by Ebola. I went to see a village, which was decimated by Ebola, and I met a lady who had lost thirteen family members in six months. I met people who had lost brothers, sisters, dads... And this charity, which we fund in this country, helps deal with the aftermath of Ebola. So, it was so uplifting to see all the money that we had raised helping people who really needed help. But there was one image that will stay with me forever and it was of a guy who brought his daughter in, she was four months old. She was severely malnourished and had pneumonia and the doctor looked at her and gave her a drip, gave her some oxygen and milk stuff, and a lot of it was funded by us and it was just incredible to think, this is a skilled African doctor helping this little girl from our generosity. It was amazing. This doctor was incredible. It was fascinating to see the money we raised being spent on saving lives.'

Russ was honoured to be part of the fundraising event and encouraged all the fans that saw him to donate what they could for the charity. He was nearer forty now than thirty, but he had always had that gentle side to him. But there was always a nod to the dark side too, the side that focused on death, the futility of it all, the 'why bother'-ness of his everyday existence.

'I do still have a lot of bad days. Like, I'd love to be a father, but what if my kids inherit all my madness and all my problems? "Daddy has to go out now and strangers have to laugh at Daddy or Daddy feels upset..." Maybe Daddy needs to get this out of his system before he becomes a daddy?' he mused to xxxxx.

For a man who still looks like he could be twenty-one and readily admits he goes to his parents for advice on anything and everything, he was also a tortured soul to a degree. Sure, you could over-analyse some of his death quotes but essentially, he is perhaps voicing what we all think from time to time although maybe don't vocalise as much as Russ. Or worry about as much.

'Like many comedians I have crippling low self-esteem. I'm terrified of death, I self-medicate with self-help books, but one of these days I should really see someone about it. We're all going to end up as worm food, which makes everything seem pointless and trivial – it's the fear of nothingness. Although I love what I do, when you start thinking like that, being a comedian can seem like a peculiar way to get through life. I am often asked to give advice to upcoming comics or students and I have to decide if I want to be brutally honest. If so, then we are all working towards the same thing: happiness. Unfortunately we are all going to die so you are not going to gain anything by not enjoying your life. We're only here for a short time so whatever you want in life you might as well go for it. The other piece of advice I would give is don't leave your drinks unattended with your mates!' he revealed to *The Student Pocket Guide*.

So for Russell, a man who endlessly appreciates the fun, happy, positive aspects of life, it all boils down to the fact that the future means death: 'But we have one chance to be happy, we are all going to die, we might as well go for it.' And if 'going for it' means more sell-out world tours, marriage, more dogs, starting a family, more TV work, more gigs and many more years of making people laugh, then good for him.

But to make things easier, Russ has already thought about what he'd like on his gravestone when that fateful day occurs: 'Please don't dig me up and bum me' apparently, while pointing out adamantly that there is one other thing that should not be on there – 'Don't write "He's a cunt" as my family come here.'

And his last meal on earth? Now *that* didn't need much thinking about – 'My mum's chicken lasagne, it's my favourite. Gert lush!'